Current Trends in Dynamic Personality Theory:

Problems of Normal and
Disturbed Development

Edited by
Harold B. Davis
Sybil Gottlieb

The City College

MSS Information Corporation
655 Madison Avenue, New York, N. Y. 10021

This is a custom-made book of readings prepared for the courses taught by the editors, as well as for related courses and for college and university libraries. For information about our program, please write to:

MSS INFORMATION CORPORATION
655 Madison Avenue
New York, New York 10021

MSS wishes to express its appreciation to the authors of the articles in this collection for their cooperation in making their work available in this format.

Library of Congress Cataloging in Publication Data

Davis, Harold B   comp.
    Current trends in dynamic personality theory.

    1. Psychology, Pathological--Addresses, essays, lectures. 2. Personality--Addresses, essays, lectures. I. Gottlieb, Sybil, joint comp.
II. Title. [DNLM: 1. Personality development.
2. Personality disorders. WM 100 D263c 1972]
RC458.D38   616.8'9   72-8722
ISBN 0-8422-5068-9
ISBN 0-8422-0256-9 (pbk.)

CONTENTS

PREFACE

Many colleges and universities offer courses that combine child and adolescent development with the study of deviant behavior. The organization of this book of readings reflects the editors' experiences of teaching such courses as well as a felt need to integrate current issues in psychology within such a framework. All the articles will examine controversies facing psychology today.

Thus, Section I presents the professional point of view of the concept of mental illness. Is deviant behavior an illness, calling for diagnosis and treatment? Or rather is it an emotional problem for which various interventions and preventatives are required in order to alleviate human misery? If it is the former, then the issue of values may not have any relevancy. If it is the latter, then not only is the issue of values pertinent but normal and abnormal may be defined in the light of one's particular values.

Other cleavages occur on a theoretical level. What is the most economical explanatory factor in the genesis of behavioral disorders? The essays in Section II raise such questions. Do causal explanations help us understand man or do they lead to gross misunderstandings? For example: Are the Neo-Freudian schools closer to the 'truth' when they attach prime importance to environmental processes such as interactions with early caretakers and other agents of society? Is interpersonal relatedness a function of psychic determinism whereby the individual selects others who will mesh with his inner needs and conflicts? This different, and perhaps opposing, way of viewing a problem is reflected in the various constructs which have clear and sometimes subtle shades of meaning.

In their search for material the editors selected articles for Sections III and IV that highlight the problems proposed in Sections I and II. Thus, clinical and developmental readings are included, reflecting the difficulties we face in trying to understand multivariate problems in a complex society.

The concepts and questions are difficult, but this book is intended for the graduate student in psychology as well as for the professional who is looking for some new approaches to thinking about 'abnormality'. It not only stimulates questions about abnormality as an outcome of the interactions of genetic, social and developmental factors but it also stimulates the search for new models. This book encourages the student and professional to use more than one approach to describe problems, on a non-doctrinaire basis, to look at the child before he evokes the theory in an oversimplified manner. Finally, this book promotes an optimistic approach regarding the pasticity of the child and his ability to respond to new conditions that may be offered to him.

The intent, then, of this book of readings is to serve those individuals who are concerned with behavior pathology in children and adolescents and who want both theoretical and practical knowledge in order to help them deal more adequately with the emotional and intellectual distress of young people.

The editors wish to thank the authors and publishers of the professional journals for their cooperation in granting permission to reprint the materials included in this, "Current Trends in Dynamic Personality Theory: Problems of Normal and Disturbed Development."

Sybil Gottlieb
Harold B. Davis

NORMAL AND ABNORMAL: A HEURISTIC PROBLEM

With the ever-increasing questioning of basic assumptions within our culture that have heretofore been held without question, the assumptions underlying the distinction between normal and abnormal have also been challenged. The impetus for this challenge within the areas of normal and abnormal psychology has had several sources. Initially, the conflict between psychoanalytic concepts and academic psychology was a basis for the challenge. The psychoanalytic approach questions psychology's definition of adjustment and/or adaptation to a cultural norm; for psychoanalytic practices were often made up of people who had adjusted well but nevertheless were beset with inner conflicts and anxieties. Thus, normality as defined by adaptation to social standards was an insufficient criterion. The insufficiency of this definition was glaringly noticeable when Nazi Germany was existent. Were the people who led it normal or abnormal? If adjustment to a culture implies normality, then perhaps the followers were normal. It was the difficulty accepting this premise that made this criterion of normality inadequate.

The dissatisfaction with the concepts of normality and abnormality became more apparent as awareness of the implicit, if not explicit, assumptions developed. These assumptions often reflected cultural expectations and the values of the dominant group of that culture. From divergent quarters came a host of definitions of the concept. Researchers often found it extremely difficult to distinguish the mentally ill from the healthy; and we certainly know the limitations of nosological entities for research purposes. The result was to resort to such terms as 'community' and 'non-community' to distinguish those people out of hospitals from those inside.

The articles by Szasz and by Ausubel reflect the opposing positions, if not the crux of the debate. Szasz clearly repudiates the medical model of sickness and indicates that the so-called 'mentally ill' are often expressing different ways of living based upon emotional, social and value factors. The 'mentally ill' person may be one who merely does not conform to a particular social value. On the other hand, Ausubel clearly considers a person with an emotional problem as 'mentally sick' and believes he is to be defined and treated as such by the culture.

7

Whether one agrees with Szasz or with Ausubel, the role of values in personality development cannot be overlooked. Buhler clearly indicates the importance of values in human growth. Shoben's article takes the importance of values as one criterion in his definition of normality. His article is a fitting conclusion to this section, for he deals with the difficulties involved in the normal-abnormal issue yet manages to develop criteria for normality with reasonable success.

THE MYTH OF MENTAL ILLNESS

THOMAS S. SZASZ

MY aim in this essay is to raise the question "Is there such a thing as mental illness?" and to argue that there is not. Since the notion of mental illness is extremely widely used nowadays, inquiry into the ways in which this term is employed would seem to be especially indicated. Mental illness, of course, is not literally a "thing"—or physical object—and hence it can "exist" only in the same sort of way in which other theoretical concepts exist. Yet, familiar theories are in the habit of posing, sooner or later —at least to those who come to believe in them —as "objective truths" (or "facts"). During certain historical periods, explanatory conceptions such as deities, witches, and microorganisms appeared not only as theories but as self-evident *causes* of a vast number of events. I submit that today mental illness is widely regarded in a somewhat similar fashion, that is, as the cause of innumerable diverse happenings. As an antidote to the complacent use of the notion of mental illness— whether as a self-evident phenomenon, theory, or cause—let us ask this question: What is meant when it is asserted that someone is mentally ill?

In what follows I shall describe briefly the main uses to which the concept of mental illness has been put. I shall argue that this notion has outlived whatever usefulness it might have had and that it now functions merely as a convenient myth.

MENTAL ILLNESS AS A SIGN OF BRAIN DISEASE

The notion of mental illness derives it main support from such phenomena as syphilis of the brain or delirious conditions—intoxications, for instance —in which persons are known to manifest various peculiarities or disorders of thinking and behavior. Correctly speaking, however, these are diseases of the brain, not of the mind. According to one school of thought, *all* so-called mental illness is of this type. The assumption is made that some neurological defect, perhaps a very subtle one, will ultimately be found for all the disorders of thinking and behavior. Many contemporary psychia-

trists, physicians, and other scientists hold this view. This position implies that people *cannot* have troubles—expressed in what are *now called* "mental illnesses"—because of differences in personal needs, opinions, social aspirations, values, and so on. *All problems in living* are attributed to physicochemical processes which in due time will be discovered by medical research.

"Mental illnesses" are thus regarded as basically no different than all other diseases (that is, of the body). The only difference, in this view, between mental and bodily diseases is that the former, affecting the brain, manifest themselves by means of mental symptoms; whereas the latter, affecting other organ systems (for example, the skin, liver, etc.), manifest themselves by means of symptoms referable to those parts of the body. This view rests on and expresses what are, in my opinion, two fundamental errors.

In the first place, what central nervous system symptoms would correspond to a skin eruption or a fracture? It would *not* be some emotion or complex bit of behavior. Rather, it would be blindness or a paralysis of some part of the body. The crux of the matter is that a disease of the brain, analogous to a disease of the skin or bone, is a neurological defect, and not a problem in living. For example, a *defect* in a person's visual field may be satisfactorily explained by correlating it with certain definite lesions in the nervous system. On the other hand, a person's *belief*—whether this be a belief in Christianity, in Communism, or in the idea that his internal organs are "rotting" and that his body is, in fact, already "dead"—cannot be explained by a defect or disease of the nervous system. Explanations of this sort of occurrence— assuming that one is interested in the belief itself and does not regard it simply as a "symptom" or expression of something else that is *more interesting* —must be sought along different lines.

The second error in regarding complex psychosocial behavior, consisting of communications about ourselves and the world about us, as mere symptoms

AMERICAN PSYCHOLOGIST, 1960, 15, pp. 113-118.

9

of neurological functioning is *epistemological*. In other words, it is an error pertaining not to any mistakes in observation or reasoning, as such, but rather to the way in which we organize and express our knowledge. In the present case, the error lies in making a symmetrical dualism between mental and physical (or bodily) symptoms, a dualism which is merely a habit of speech and to which no known observations can be found to correspond. Let us see if this is so. In medical practice, when we speak of physical disturbances, we mean either signs (for example, a fever) or symptoms (for example, pain). We speak of mental symptoms, on the other hand, when we refer to a patient's *communications about himself, others, and the world about him.* He might state that he is Napoleon or that he is being persecuted by the Communists. These would be considered mental symptoms *only* if the observer believed that the patient was *not* Napoleon or that he was *not* being perseucted by the Communists. This makes it apparent that the statement that *"X is a mental symptom"* involves rendering a judgment. The judgment entails, moreover, a covert comparison or matching of the patient's ideas, concepts, or beliefs with those of the observer and the society in which they live. The notion of mental symptom is therefore inextricably tied to the *social* (including *ethical*) *context* in which it is made in much the same way as the notion of bodily symptom is tied to an *anatomical* and *genetic context* (Szasz, 1957a, 1957b).

To sum up what has been said thus far: I have tried to show that for those who regard mental symptoms as signs of brain disease, the concept of mental illness is unnecessary and misleading. For what they mean is that people so labeled suffer from diseases of the brain; and, if that is what they mean, it would seem better for the sake of clarity to say that and not something else.

Mental Illness as a Name for Problems in Living

The term "mental illness" is widely used to describe something which is very different than a disease of the brain. Many people today take it for granted that living is an arduous process. Its hardship for modern man, moreover, derives not so much from a struggle for biological survival as from the stresses and strains inherent in the social intercourse of complex human personalities. In this context, the notion of mental illness is used to identify or describe some feature of an individual's so-called personality. Mental illness—as a deformity of the personality, so to speak—is then regarded as the *cause* of the human disharmony. It is implicit in this view that social intercourse between people is regarded as something *inherently harmonious,* its disturbance being due solely to the presence of "mental illness" in many people. This is obviously fallacious reasoning, for it makes the abstraction "mental illness" into a *cause,* even though this abstraction was created in the first place to serve only as a shorthand expression for certain types of human behavior. It now becomes necessary to ask: "What kinds of behavior are regarded as indicative of mental illness, and by whom?"

The concept of illness, whether bodily or mental, implies *deviation from some clearly defined norm.* In the case of physical illness, the norm is the structural and functional integrity of the human body. Thus, although the desirability of physical health, as such, is an ethical value, what health *is* can be stated in anatomical and physiological terms. What is the norm deviation from which is regarded as mental illness? This question cannot be easily answered. But whatever this norm might be, we can be certain of only one thing: namely, that it is a norm that must be stated in terms of *psychosocial, ethical,* and *legal* concepts. For example, notions such as "excessive repression" or "acting out an unconscious impulse" illustrate the use of psychological concepts for judging (so-called) mental health and illness. The idea that chronic hostility, vengefulness, or divorce are indicative of mental illness would be illustrations of the use of ethical norms (that is, the desirability of love, kindness, and a stable marriage relationship). Finally, the widespread psychiatric opinion that only a mentally ill person would commit homicide illustrates the use of a legal concept as a norm of mental health. The norm from which deviation is measured whenever one speaks of a mental illness is a *psychosocial and ethical one.* Yet, the remedy is sought in terms of *medical* measures which—it is hoped and assumed—are free from wide differences of ethical value. The definition of the disorder and the terms in which its remedy are sought are therefore at serious odds with one another. The practical significance of this covert conflict between the alleged nature of the defect and the remedy can hardly be exaggerated.

Having identified the norms used to measure

deviations in cases of mental illness, we will now turn to the question: "Who defines the norms and hence the deviation?" Two basic answers may be offered: (a) It may be the person himself (that is, the patient) who decides that he deviates from a norm. For example, an artist may believe that he suffers from a work inhibition; and he may implement this conclusion by seeking help *for* himself from a psychotherapist. (b) It may be someone other than the patient who decides that the latter is deviant (for example, relatives, physicians, legal authorities, society generally, etc.). In such a case a psychiatrist may be hired by others to do something *to* the patient in order to correct the deviation.

These considerations underscore the importance of asking the question "Whose agent is the psychiatrist?" and of giving a candid answer to it (Szasz, 1956, 1958). The psychiatrist (psychologist or nonmedical psychotherapist), it now develops, may be the agent of the patient, of the relatives, of the school, of the military services, of a business organization, of a court of law, and so forth. In speaking of the psychiatrist as the agent of these persons or organizations, it is not implied that his values concerning norms, or his ideas and aims concerning the proper nature of remedial action, need to coincide exactly with those of his employer. For example, a patient in individual psychotherapy may believe that his salvation lies in a new marriage; his psychotherapist need not share this hypothesis. As the patient's agent, however, he must abstain from bringing social or legal force to bear on the patient which would prevent him from putting his beliefs into action. If his *contract* is with the patient, the psychiatrist (psychotherapist) may disagree with him or stop his treatment; but he cannot engage others to obstruct the patient's aspirations. Similarly, if a psychiatrist is engaged by a court to determine the sanity of a criminal, he need not fully share the legal authorities' values and intentions in regard to the criminal and the means available for dealing with him. But the psychiatrist is expressly barred from stating, for example, that it is not the criminal who is "insane" but the men who wrote the law on the basis of which the very actions that are being judged are regarded as "criminal." Such an opinion could be voiced, of course, but not in a courtroom, and not by a psychiatrist who makes it his practice to assist the court in performing its daily work.

To recapitulate: In actual contemporary social usage, the finding of a mental illness is made by establishing a deviance in behavior from certain psychosocial, ethical, or legal norms. The judgment may be made, as in medicine, by the patient, the physician (psychiatrist), or others. Remedial action, finally, tends to be sought in a therapeutic —or covertly medical—framework, thus creating a situation in which *psychosocial, ethical,* and/or *legal deviations* are claimed to be correctible by (so-called) *medical action.* Since medical action is designed to correct only medical deviations, it seems logically absurd to expect that it will help solve problems whose very existence had been defined and established on nonmedical grounds. I think that these considerations may be fruitfully applied to the present use of tranquilizers and, more generally, to what might be expected of drugs of whatever type in regard to the amelioration or solution of problems in human living.

THE ROLE OF ETHICS IN PSYCHIATRY

Anything that people *do*—in contrast to things that *happen* to them (Peters, 1958)—takes place in a context of value. In this broad sense, no human activity is devoid of ethical implications. When the values underlying certain activities are widely shared, those who participate in their pursuit may lose sight of them altogether. The discipline of medicine, both as a pure science (for example, research) and as a technology (for example, therapy), contains many ethical considerations and judgments. Unfortunately, these are often denied, minimized, or merely kept out of focus; for the ideal of the medical profession as well as of the people whom it serves seems to be having a system of medicine (allegedly) free of ethical value. This sentimental notion is expressed by such things as the doctor's willingness to treat and help patients irrespective of their religious or political beliefs, whether they are rich or poor, etc. While there may be some grounds for this belief—albeit it is a view that is not impressively true even in these regards—the fact remains that ethical considerations encompass a vast range of human affairs. By making the practice of medicine neutral in regard to some specific issues of value need not, and cannot, mean that it can be kept free from all such values. The practice of medicine is intimately tied to ethics; and the first thing that we must do, it seems to me, is to try to make this clear and explicit. I shall let this matter rest here, for it does not concern us specifically in this essay. Lest there be any vagueness, however, about how or where ethics and medicine meet, let me remind the reader of such issues as birth control, abortion, suicide, and euthanasia as only a few of the major areas of current ethicomedical controversy.

Psychiatry, I submit, is very much more intimately tied to problems of ethics than is medicine. I use the word "psychiatry" here to refer to that contemporary discipline which is concerned with *problems in living* (and not with diseases of the brain, which are problems for neurology). Problems in human relations can be analyzed, interpreted, and given meaning only within given social and ethical contexts. Accordingly, it *does* make a difference—arguments to the contrary notwithstanding—what the psychiatrist's socioethical orientations happen to be; for these will influence his ideas on what is wrong with the patient, what deserves comment or interpretation, in what possible directions change might be desirable, and so forth. Even in medicine proper, these factors play a role, as for instance, in the divergent orientations which physicians, depending on their religious affiliations, have toward such things as birth control and therapeutic abortion. Can anyone really believe that a psychotherapist's ideas concerning religious belief, slavery, or other similar issues play no role in his practical work? If they do make a difference, what are we to infer from it? Does it not seem reasonable that we ought to have different psychiatric therapies—each expressly recognized for the ethical positions which they embody—for, say, Catholics and Jews, religious persons and agnostics, democrats and communists, white supremacists and Negroes, and so on? Indeed, if we look at how psychiatry is actually practiced today (especially in the United States), we find that people do seek psychiatric help in accordance with their social status and ethical beliefs (Hollingshead & Redlich, 1958). This should really not surprise us more than being told that practicing Catholics rarely frequent birth control clinics.

The foregoing position which holds that contemporary psychotherapists deal with problems in living, rather than with mental illnesses and their cures, stands in opposition to a currently prevalent claim, according to which mental illness is just as "real" and "objective" as bodily illness. This is a confusing claim since it is never known exactly what is meant by such words as "real" and "objective." I suspect, however, that what is intended by the proponents of this view is to create the idea in the popular mind that mental illness is some sort of disease entity, like an infection or a malignancy. If this were true, one could *catch* or *get* a "mental illness," one might *have* or *harbor* it, one might *transmit* it to others, and finally one could get *rid* of it. In my opinion, there is not a shred of evidence to support this idea. To the contrary, all the evidence is the other way and supports the view that what people now call mental illnesses are for the most part *communications* expressing unacceptable ideas, often framed, moreover, in an unusual idiom. The scope of this essay allows me to do no more than mention this alternative theoretical approach to this problem (Szasz, 1957c).

This is not the place to consider in detail the similarities and differences between bodily and mental illnesses. It shall suffice for us here to emphasize only one important difference between them: namely, that whereas bodily disease refers to public, physicochemical occurrences, the notion of mental illness is used to codify relatively more private, sociopsychological happenings of which the observer (diagnostician) forms a part. In other words, the psychiatrist does not stand *apart* from what he observes, but is, in Harry Stack Sullivan's apt words, a "participant observer." This means that he is *committed* to some picture of what he considers reality—and to what he thinks society considers reality—and he observes and judges the patient's behavior in the light of these considerations. This touches on our earlier observation that the notion of mental symptom itself implies a comparison between observer and observed, psychiatrist and patient. This is so obvious that I may be charged with belaboring trivialities. Let me therefore say once more that my aim in presenting this argument was expressly to criticize and counter a prevailing contemporary tendency to deny the moral aspects of psychiatry (and psychotherapy) and to substitute for them allegedly value-free medical considerations. Psychotherapy, for example, is being widely practiced as though it entailed nothing other than restoring the patient from a state of mental sickness to one of mental health. While it is generally accepted that mental illness has something to do with man's social (or interpersonal) relations, it is paradoxically maintained that problems of values (that is, of ethics) do not

12

arise in this process.[1] Yet, in one sense, much of psychotherapy may revolve around nothing other than the elucidation and weighing of goals and values—many of which may be mutually contradictory—and the means whereby they might best be harmonized, realized, or relinquished.

The diversity of human values and the methods by means of which they may be realized is so vast, and many of them remain so unacknowledged, that they cannot fail but lead to conflicts in human relations. Indeed, to say that human relations at all levels—from mother to child, through husband and wife, to nation and nation—are fraught with stress, strain, and disharmony is, once again, making the obvious explicit. Yet, what may be obvious may be also poorly understood. This I think is the case here. For it seems to me that—at least in our scientific theories of behavior—we have failed to *accept* the simple fact that human relations are inherently fraught with difficulties and that to make them even relatively harmonious requires much patience and hard work. I submit that the idea of mental illness is now being put to work to obscure certain difficulties which at present may be inherent—not that they need be unmodifiable—in the social intercourse of persons. If this is true, the concept functions as a disguise; for instead of calling attention to conflicting human needs, aspirations, and values, the notion of mental illness provides an amoral and impersonal "thing" (an "illness") as an explanation for *problems in living* (Szasz, 1959). We may recall in this connection that not so long ago it was devils and witches who were held responsible for men's problems in social living. The belief in mental illness, as something other than man's trouble in getting along with his fellow man, is the proper heir to the belief in demonology and witchcraft. Mental illness exists or is "real" in exactly the same sense in which witches existed or were "real."

[1] Freud went so far as to say that: "I consider ethics to be taken for granted. Actually I have never done a mean thing" (Jones, 1957, p. 247). This surely is a strange thing to say for someone who has studied man as a social being as closely as did Freud. I mention it here to show how the notion of "illness" (in the case of psychoanalysis, "psychopathology," or "mental illness") was used by Freud—and by most of his followers—as a means for classifying certain forms of human behavior as falling within the scope of medicine, and hence (by *fiat*) outside that of ethics!

CHOICE, RESPONSIBILITY, AND PSYCHIATRY

While I have argued that mental illnesses do not exist, I obviously did not imply that the social and psychological occurrences to which this label is currently being attached also do not exist. Like the personal and social troubles which people had in the Middle Ages, they are real enough. It is the labels we give them that concerns us and, having labelled them, what we do about them. While I cannot go into the ramified implications of this problem here, it is worth noting that a demonologic conception of problems in living gave rise to therapy along theological lines. Today, a belief in mental illness implies—nay, requires—therapy along medical or psychotherapeutic lines.

What is implied in the line of thought set forth here is something quite different. I do not intend to offer a new conception of "psychiatric illness" nor a new form of "therapy." My aim is more modest and yet also more ambitious. It is to suggest that the phenomena now called mental illnesses be looked at afresh and more simply, that they be removed from the category of illnesses, and that they be regarded as the expressions of man's struggle with the problem of *how* he should live. The last mentioned problem is obviously a vast one, its enormity reflecting not only man's inability to cope with his environment, but even more his increasing self-reflectiveness.

By problems in living, then, I refer to that truly explosive chain reaction which began with man's fall from divine grace by partaking of the fruit of the tree of knowledge. Man's awareness of himself and of the world about him seems to be a steadily expanding one, bringing in its wake an ever larger *burden of understanding* (an expression borrowed from Susanne Langer, 1953). *This burden,* then, *is to be expected and must not be misinterpreted.* Our only *rational* means for lightening it is *more understanding,* and appropriate *action* based on such understanding. The main alternative lies in acting as though the burden were not what in fact we perceive it to be and taking refuge in an outmoded theological view of man. In the latter view, man does not fashion his life and much of his world about him, but merely lives out his fate in a world created by superior beings. This may logically lead to pleading nonresponsibility in the face of seemingly unfathomable problems and difficulties. Yet, if man fails to take increasing responsibility for his actions, individually as well as collectively, it seems unlikely that some higher power or being would assume this task and carry this burden for him. Moreover, this seems hardly the proper time in human history for obscuring the issue of man's responsibility for his actions by hiding it behind the skirt of an all-explaining conception of mental illness.

CONCLUSIONS

I have tried to show that the notion of mental illness has outlived whatever usefulness it might have had and that it now functions merely as a convenient myth. As such, it is a true heir to religious myths in general, and to the belief in witchcraft in particular; the role of all these belief-systems was to act as *social tranquilizers*, thus encouraging the hope that mastery of certain specific problems may be achieved by means of substitutive (symbolic-magical) operations. The notion of mental illness thus serves mainly to obscure the everyday fact that life for most people is a continuous struggle, not for biological survival, but for a "place in the sun," "peace of mind," or some other human value. For man aware of himself and of the world about him, once the needs for preserving the body (and perhaps the race) are more or less satisfied, the problem arises as to what he should do with himself. Sustained adherence to the myth of mental illness allows people to avoid facing this problem, believing that mental health, conceived as the absence of mental illness, automatically insures the making of right and safe choices in one's conduct of life. But the facts are all the other way. It is the making of good choices in life that others regard, retrospectively, as good mental health!

The myth of mental illness encourages us, moreover, to believe in its logical corollary: that social intercourse would be harmonious, satisfying, and the secure basis of a "good life" were it not for the disrupting influences of mental illness or "psychopathology." The potentiality for universal human happiness, in this form at least, seems to me but another example of the I-wish-it-were-true type of fantasy. I do not believe that human happiness or well-being on a hitherto unimaginably large scale, and not just for a select few, is possible. This goal could be achieved, however, only at the cost of many men, and not just a few being willing and able to tackle their personal, social, and ethical conflicts. This means having the courage and integrity to forego waging battles on false fronts finding solutions for substitute problems—for instance, fighting the battle of stomach acid and chronic fatigue instead of facing up to a marital conflict.

Our adversaries are not demons, witches, fate, or mental illness. We have no enemy whom we can fight, exorcise, or dispel by "cure." What we do have are *problems in living*—whether these be biologic, economic, political, or sociopsychological. In this essay I was concerned only with problems belonging in the last mentioned category, and within this group mainly with those pertaining to moral values. The field to which modern psychiatry addresses itself is vast, and I made no effort to encompass it all. My argument was limited to the proposition that mental illness is a myth, whose function it is to disguise and thus render more palatable the bitter pill of moral conflicts in human relations.

REFERENCES

HOLLINGSHEAD, A. B., & REDLICH, F. C. *Social class and mental illness.* New York: Wiley, 1958.

JONES, E. *The life and work of Sigmund Freud.* Vol. III. New York: Basic Books, 1957.

LANGER, S. K. *Philosophy in a new key.* New York: Mentor Books, 1953.

PETERS, R. S. *The concept of motivation.* London: Routledge & Kegan Paul, 1958.

SZASZ, T. S. Malingering: "Diagnosis" or social condemnation? *AMA Arch Neurol. Psychiat.,* 1956, 76, 432–443.

SZASZ, T. S. *Pain and pleasure: A study of bodily feelings.* New York: Basic Books, 1957. (a)

SZASZ, T. S. The problem of psychiatric nosology: A contribution to a situational analysis of psychiatric operations. *Amer. J. Psychiat.,* 1957, 114, 405–413. (b)

SZASZ, T. S. On the theory of psychoanalytic treatment. *Int. J. Psycho-Anal.,* 1957, 38, 166–182. (c)

SZASZ, T. S. Psychiatry, ethics and the criminal law. *Columbia law Rev.,* 1958, 58, 183–198.

SZASZ, T. S. Moral conflict and psychiatry, *Yale Rev.,* 1959, in press.

PERSONALITY DISORDER *IS* DISEASE

DAVID P. AUSUBEL

IN two recent articles in the *American Psychologist*, Szasz (1960) and Mowrer (1960) have argued the case for discarding the concept of mental illness. The essence of Mowrer's position is that since medical science lacks "demonstrated competence . . . in psychiatry," psychology would be wise to "get out" from "under the penumbra of medicine," and to regard the behavior disorders as manifestations of sin rather than of disease (p. 302). Szasz' position, as we shall see shortly, is somewhat more complex than Mowrer's, but agrees with the latter in emphasizing the moral as opposed to the psychopathological basis of abnormal behavior.

For a long time now, clinical psychology has both repudiated the relevance of moral judgment and accountability for assessing behavioral acts and choices, and has chafed under medical (psychiatric) control and authority in diagnosing and treating the personality disorders. One can readily appreciate, therefore, Mowrer's eagerness to sever the historical and professional ties that bind clinical psychology to medicine, even if this means denying that psychological disturbances constitute a form of illness, and even if psychology's close working relationship with psychiatry must be replaced by a new rapprochement with sin and theology, as "the lesser of two evils" (pp. 302–303). One can also sympathize with Mowrer's and Szasz' dissatisfaction with prevailing amoral and nonjudgmental trends in clinical psychology and with their entirely commendable efforts to restore moral judgment and accountability to a respectable place among the criteria used in evaluating human behavior, both normal and abnormal.

Opposition to these two trends in the handling of the behavior disorders (i.e., to medical control and to nonjudgmental therapeutic attitudes), however, does not necessarily imply abandonment of the concept of mental illness. There is no inconsistency whatsoever in maintaining, on the one hand, that most purposeful human activity has a moral aspect the reality of which psychologists cannot afford to ignore (Ausubel, 1952, p. 462),

that man is morally accountable for the majority of his misdeeds (Ausubel, 1952, p. 469), and that psychological rather than medical training and sophistication are basic to competence in the personality disorders (Ausubel, 1956, p. 101), and affirming, on the other hand, that the latter disorders are genuine manifestations of illness. In recent years psychology has been steadily moving away from the formerly fashionable stance of ethical neutrality in the behavioral sciences; and in spite of strident medical claims regarding superior professional qualifications and preclusive legal responsibility for treating psychiatric patients, and notwithstanding the nominally restrictive provisions of medical practice acts, clinical psychologists have been assuming an increasingly more important, independent, and responsible role in treating the mentally ill population of the United States.

It would be instructive at this point to examine the tactics of certain other medically allied professions in freeing themselves from medical control and in acquiring independent, legally recognized professional status. In no instance have they resorted to the devious stratagem of denying that they were treating diseases, in the hope of mollifying medical opposition and legitimizing their own professional activities. They took the position instead that simply because a given condition is defined as a disease, its treatment need not necessarily be turned over to doctors of medicine if other equally competent professional specialists were available. That this position is legally and politically tenable is demonstrated by the fact that an impressively large number of recognized diseases are legally treated today by both medical *and* nonmedical specialists (e.g., diseases of the mouth, face, jaws, teeth, eyes, and feet). And there are few convincing reasons for believing that psychiatrists wield that much more political power than physicians, maxillofacial surgeons, ophthalmologists, and orthopedic surgeons, that they could be successful where these latter specialists have failed, in legally restricting practice in their particular area of competence to holders of the medical degree. Hence,

AMERICAN PSYCHOLOGIST, 1961, 16, pp. 69-74.

even if psychologists were not currently managing to hold their own vis-à-vis psychiatrists, it would be far less dangerous and much more forthright to press for the necessary ameliorative legislation than to seek cover behind an outmoded and thoroughly discredited conception of the behavior disorders.

THE SZASZ-MOWRER POSITION

Szasz' (1960) contention that the concept of mental illness "now functions merely as a convenient myth" (p. 118) is grounded on four unsubstantiated and logically untenable propositions, which can be fairly summarized as follows:

1. Only symptoms resulting from demonstrable physical lesions qualify as legitimate manifestations of disease. Brain pathology is a type of physical lesion, but its symptoms properly speaking, are neurological rather than psychological in nature. Under no circumstances, therefore, can mental symptoms be considered a form of illness.

2. A basic dichotomy exists between *mental* symptoms, on the one hand, which are subjective in nature, dependent on subjective judgment and personal involvement of the observer, and referable to cultural-ethical norms, and *physical* symptoms, on the other hand, which are allegedly objective in nature, ascertainable without personal involvement of the observer, and independent of cultural norms and ethical standards. Only symptoms possessing the latter set of characteristics are genuinely reflective of illness and amenable to medical treatment.

3. Mental symptoms are merely expressions of problems of living and, hence, cannot be regarded as manifestations of a pathological condition. The concept of mental illness is misleading and demonological because it seeks to explain psychological disturbance in particular and human disharmony in general in terms of a metaphorical but nonexistent disease entity, instead of attributing them to inherent difficulties in coming to grips with elusive problems of choice and responsibility.

4. Personality disorders, therefore, can be most fruitfully conceptualized as products of moral conflict, confusion, and aberration. Mowrer (1960) extends this latter proposition to include the dictum that psychiatric symptoms are primarily reflective of unacknowledged sin, and that individuals manifesting these symptoms are responsible for and deserve their suffering, both because of their original transgressions and because they refuse to avow and expiate their guilt (pp. 301, 304).

Widespread adoption of the Szasz-Mowrer view of the personality disorders would, in my opinion, turn back the psychiatric clock twenty-five hundred years. The most significant and perhaps the only real advance registered by mankind in evolving a rational and humane method of handling behavioral aberrations has been in substituting a concept of disease for the demonological and retributional doctrines regarding their nature and etiology that flourished until comparatively recent times. Conceptualized as illness, the symptoms of personality disorders can be interpreted in the light of underlying stresses and resistances, both genic and environmental, and can be evaluated in relation to *specifiable* quantitative and qualitative norms of appropriately adaptive behavior, both cross-culturally and within a particular cultural context. It would behoove us, therefore, before we abandon the concept of mental illness and return to the medieval doctrine of unexpiated sin or adopt Szasz' ambiguous criterion of difficulty in ethical choice and responsibility, to subject the foregoing propositions to careful and detailed study.

Mental Symptoms and Brain Pathology

Although I agree with Szasz in rejecting the doctrine that ultimately some neuroanatomic or neurophysiologic defect will be discovered in *all* cases of personality disorder, I disagree with his reasons for not accepting this proposition. Notwithstanding Szasz' straw man presentation of their position, the proponents of the extreme somatic view do not really assert that the *particular nature* of a patient's disordered beliefs can be correlated with "certain definite lesions in the nervous system" (Szasz, 1960, p. 113). They hold rather that normal cognitive and behavioral functioning depends on the anatomic and physiologic integrity of certain key areas of the brain, and that impairment of this substrate integrity, therefore, provides a physical basis for disturbed ideation and behavior, but does not explain, except in a very gross way, the particular kinds of symptoms involved. In fact, they are generally inclined to attribute the *specific* character of the patient's symptoms to the nature of his preillness personality structure, the substrate integrity of which is impaired by the lesion or metabolic defect in question.

16

Nevertheless, even though this type of reasoning plausibly accounts for the psychological symptoms found in general paresis, various toxic deleria, and other comparable conditions, it is an extremely improbable explanation of *all* instances of personality disorder. Unlike the tissues of any other organ, brain tissue possesses the unique property of making possible awareness of and adjustment to the world of sensory, social, and symbolic stimulation. Hence by virtue of this unique relationship of the nervous system to the environment, diseases of behavior and personality may reflect abnormalities in personal and social adjustment, quite apart from any structural or metabolic disturbance in the underlying neural substrate. I would conclude, therefore, that although brain pathology is probably not the most important cause of behavior disorder, it is undoubtedly responsible for the incidence of *some* psychological abnormalities *as well as* for various neurological signs and symptoms.

But even if we completely accepted Szasz' view that brain pathology does not account for any symptoms of personality disorder, it would still be unnecessary to accept his assertion that to qualify as a genuine manifestation of disease a given symptom must be caused by a physical lesion. Adoption of such a criterion would be arbitrary and inconsistent both with medical and lay connotations of the term "disease," which in current usage is generally regarded as including any marked deviation, physical, mental, or behavioral, from normally desirable standards of structural and functional integrity.

Mental versus Physical Symptoms

Szasz contends that since the analogy between physical and mental symptoms is patently fallacious, the postulated parallelism between physical and mental disease is logically untenable. This line of reasoning is based on the assumption that the two categories of symptoms can be sharply dichotomized with respect to such basic dimensions as objectivity-subjectivity, the relevance of cultural norms, and the need for personal involvement of the observer. In my opinion, the existence of such a dichotomy cannot be empirically demonstrated in convincing fashion.

Practically all symptoms of bodily disease involve some elements of subjective judgment—both on the part of the patient and of the physician. Pain is perhaps the most important and commonly used criterion of physical illness. Yet, any evaluation of its reported locus, intensity, character, and duration is dependent upon the patient's subjective appraisal of his own sensations and on the physician's assessment of the latter's pain threshold, intelligence, and personality structure. It is also a medical commonplace that the severity of pain in most instances of bodily illness may be mitigated by the administration of a placebo. Furthermore, in taking a meaningful history the physician must not only serve as a participant observer but also as a skilled interpreter of human behavior. It is the rare patient who does not react psychologically to the signs of physical illness; and hence physicians are constantly called upon to decide, for example, to what extent precordial pain and reported tightness in the chest are manifestations of coronary insufficiency, of fear of cardiac disease and impending death, or of combinations of both conditions. Even such allegedly objective signs as pulse rate, BMR, blood pressure, and blood cholesterol have their subjective and relativistic aspects. Pulse rate and blood pressure are notoriously susceptible to emotional influences, and BMR and blood cholesterol fluctuate widely from one cultural environment to another (Dreyfuss & Czaczkes, 1959). And anyone who believes that ethical norms have no relevance for physical illness has obviously failed to consider the problems confronting Catholic patients and/or physicians when issues of contraception, abortion, and preferential saving of the mother's as against the fetus' life must be faced in the context of various obstetrical emergencies and medical contraindications to pregnancy.

It should now be clear, therefore, that symptoms not only do not need a physical basis to qualify as manifestations of illness, but also that the evaluation of *all* symptoms, physical as well as mental, is dependent in large measure on subjective judgment, emotional factors, cultural-ethical norms, and personal involvement on the part of the observer. These considerations alone render no longer tenable Szasz' contention (1960, p. 114) that there is an inherent contradiction between using cultural and ethical norms as criteria of mental disease, on the one hand, and of employing medical measures of treatment on the other. But even if the postulated dichotomy between mental and physical symptoms were valid, the use of physical measures in treating subjective and relativisitic psychological symptoms would still be warranted. Once we accept the

17

proposition that impairment of the neutral substrate of personality can result in behavior disorder, it is logically consistent to accept the corollary proposition that other kinds of manipulation of the same neutral substrate can conceivably have therapeutic effects, irrespective of whether the underlying cause of the mental symptoms is physical or psychological.

Mental Illness and Problems of Living

"The phenomena now called mental illness," argues Szasz (1960), can be regarded more forthrightly and simply as "expressions of man's struggle with the problem of how he should live" (p. 117). This statement undoubtedly oversimplifies the nature of personality disorders; but even if it were adequately inclusive it would not be inconsistent with the position that these disorders are a manifestation of illness. There is no valid reason why a particular symptom cannot both reflect a problem in living *and* constitute a manifestation of disease. The notion of mental illness, conceived in this way, would not "obscure the everyday fact that life for most people is a continuous struggle . . . for a 'place in the sun,' 'peace of mind,' or some other human value" (p. 118). It is quite true, as Szasz points out, that "human relations are inherently fraught with difficulties" (p. 117), and that most people manage to cope with such difficulties without becoming mentally ill. But conceding this fact hardly precludes the possibility that some individuals, either because of the magnitude of the stress involved, or because of genically or environmentally induced susceptibility to ordinary degrees of stress, respond to the problems of living with behavior that is either seriously distorted or sufficiently unadaptive to prevent normal interpersonal relations and vocational functioning. The latter outcome—gross deviation from a designated range of desirable behavioral variability—conforms to the generally understood meaning of mental illness.

The plausibility of subsuming abnormal behavioral reactions to stress under the general rubric of disease is further enhanced by the fact that these reactions include the same three principal categories of symptoms found in physical illness. Depression and catastrophic impairment of self-esteem, for example, are manifestations of personality disorder which are symptomologically comparable to edema in cardiac failure or to heart murmurs in valvular disease. They are indicative of underlying pathology but are neither adaptive

nor adjustive. Symptoms such as hypomanic overactivity and compulsive striving toward unrealistically high achievement goals, on the other hand, are both adaptive and adjustive, and constitute a type of compensatory response to basic feelings of inadequacy, which is not unlike cardiac hypertrophy in hypertensive heart disease or elevated white blood cell count in acute infections. And finally, distortive psychological defenses that have some adjustive value but are generally maladaptive (e.g., phobias, delusions, autistic fantasies) are analogous to the pathological situation found in conditions like pneumonia, in which the excessive outpouring of serum and phagocytes in defensive response to pathogenic bacteria literally causes the patient to drown in his own fluids.

Within the context of this same general proposition, Szasz repudiates the concept of mental illness as demonological in nature, i.e., as the "true heir to religious myths in general and to the belief in witchcraft in particular" (p. 118) because it allegedly employs a reified abstraction ("a deformity of personality") to account in causal terms both for "human disharmony" and for symptoms of behavior disorder (p. 114). But again he appears to be demolishing a straw man. Modern students of personality disorder do not regard mental illness as a cause of human disharmony, but as a co-manifestation with it of inherent difficulties in personal adjustment and interpersonal relations; and in so far as I can accurately interpret the literature, psychopathologists do not conceive of mental illness as a cause·of particular behavioral symptoms but as a generic term under which these symptoms can be subsumed.

Mental Illness and Moral Responsibility

Szasz' final reason for regarding mental illness as a myth is really a corollary of his previously considered more general proposition that mental symptoms are essentially reflective of problems of living and hence do not legitimately qualify as manifestations of disease. It focuses on difficulties of ethical choice and responsibility as the particular life problems most likely to be productive of personality disorder. Mowrer (1960) further extends this corollary by asserting that neurotic and psychotic individuals are responsible for their suffering (p. 301), and that unacknowledged and unexpiated sin, in turn, is the basic cause of this suffering (p. 304). As previously suggested, however, one can plausibly accept the proposition that psychiatrists and clinical psychologists have erred in trying to divorce behavioral evaluation from ethical considerations, in conducting psychotherapy in an amoral setting, and in confusing the psychological explanation of unethical behavior with absolution from accountability for same, *without* necessarily endorsing the view that personality disorders are basically a reflection of sin, and that victims of these disorders are less ill than responsible for their symptoms (Ausubel, 1952, pp. 392–397, 465–471).

In the first place, it is possible in most instances (although admittedly difficult in some) to distinguish quite unambiguously between mental illness and ordinary cases of immorality. The vast majority of persons who are guilty of moral lapses knowingly violate their own ethical precepts for expediential reasons—despite being volitionally capable at the time, both of choosing the more moral alternative and of exercising the necessary inhibitory control (Ausubel, 1952, pp. 465–471). Such persons, also, usually do not exhibit any signs of behavior disorder. At crucial choice points in facing the problems of living they simply choose the opportunistic instead of the moral alternative. They are not mentally ill, but they are clearly accountable for their misconduct. Hence, since personality disorder and immorality are neither coextensive nor mutually exclusive conditions, the concept of mental illness need not necessarily obscure the issue of moral accountability.

Second, guilt may be a contributory factor in behavior disorder, but is by no means the only or principal cause thereof. Feelings of guilt may give rise to anxiety and depression; but in the absence of catastrophic impairment of self-esteem induced by *other* factors, these symptoms tend to be transitory and peripheral in nature (Ausubel, 1952, pp. 362-363). Repression of guilt, is more a consequence than a cause of anxiety. Guilt is repressed in order to avoid the anxiety producing trauma to self-esteem that would otherwise result if it were acknowledged. Repression per se enters the causal picture in anxiety only secondarily—by obviating "the possibility of punishment, confession, expiation, and other guilt reduction mechanisms" (Ausubel, 1952, p. 456). Furthermore, in most types of personality disorder other than anxiety, depression, and various complications of anxiety such as phobias, obsessions, and compulsion, guilt feelings are either not particularly prominent (schizophrenic reactions), or are conspicuously absent (e.g., classical cases of inadequate or aggressive, antisocial psychopathy).

Third, it is just as unreasonable to hold an individual responsible for symptoms of behavior disorder as to deem him accountable for symptoms of physical illness. He is no more culpable for his inability to cope with sociopsychological stress than he would be for his inability to resist the spread of infectious organisms. In those instances where warranted guilt feelings *do* contribute to personality disorder, the patient is accountable for the misdeeds underlying his guilt, but is hardly responsible for the symptoms brought on by the guilt feelings or for unlawful acts committed during his illness. Acknowledgment of guilt may be therapeutically beneficial under these circumstances, but punishment for the original misconduct should obviously be deferred until after recovery.

Lastly, even if it were true that all personality disorder is a reflection of sin and that people are accountable for their behavioral symptoms, it would still be unnecessary to deny that these symptoms are manifestations of disease. Illness is no less real because the victim happens to be culpable for his illness. A glutton with hypertensive heart disease undoubtedly aggravates his condition by overeating, and is culpable in part for the often fatal symptoms of his disease, but what reasonable person would claim that for this reason he is not really ill?

CONCLUSIONS

Four propositions in support of the argument for discarding the concept of mental illness were carefully examined, and the following conclusions were reached:

First, although brain pathology is probably not the major cause of personality disorder, it does account for *some* psychological symptoms by impairing the neural substrate of personality. In any case, however, a symptom need not reflect a physical lesion in order to qualify as a genuine manifestation of disease.

Second, Szasz' postulated dichotomy between mental and physical symptoms is untenable because the assessment of *all* symptoms is dependent to some extent on subjective judgment, emotional factors, cultural-ethical norms, and personal involvement of the observer. Furthermore, the use of medical measures in treating behavior disorders—irrespective of whether the underlying causes are neural or psychological—is defensible on the grounds that if inadvertent impairment of the neural substrate of personality can have distortive effects on behavior, directed manipulation of the same substrate may have therapeutic effects.

Third, there is no inherent contradiction in regarding mental symptoms both as expressions of problems in living *and* as manifestations of illness. The latter situation results when individuals are for various reasons unable to cope with such problems, and react with seriously distorted or maladaptive behavior. The three principal categories of behavioral symptoms—manifestations of impaired functioning, adaptive compensation, and defensive overreaction—are also found in bodily disease. The concept of mental illness has never been advanced as a demonological cause of human disharmony, but only as a co-manifestation with it of certain inescapable difficulties and hazards in personal and social adjustment. The same concept is also generally accepted as a generic term for all behavioral symptoms rather than as a reified cause of these symptoms.

Fourth, the view that personality disorder is less a manifestation of illness than of sin, i.e., of culpable inadequacy in meeting problems of ethical choice and responsibility, and that victims of behavior disorder are therefore morally accountable for their symptoms, is neither logically nor empirically tenable. In most instances immoral behavior and mental illness are clearly distinguishable conditions. Guilt is only a secondary etiological factor in anxiety and depression, and in other personality disorders is either not prominent or conspicuously absent. The issue of culpability for symptoms is largely irrelevant in handling the behavior disorders, and in any case does not detract from the reality of the illness.

In general, it is both unnecessary and potentially dangerous to discard the concept of mental illness on the grounds that only in this way can clinical psychology escape from the professional domination of medicine. Dentists, podiatrists, optometrists, and osteopaths have managed to acquire an independent professional status without rejecting the concept of disease. It is equally unnecessary and dangerous to substitute the doctrine of sin for illness in order to counteract prevailing amoral and nonjudgmental trends in psychotherapy. The hypothesis of repressed guilt does not adequately explain most kinds and instances of personality disorder, and the concept of mental illness does not preclude judgments of moral accountability where warranted. Definition of behavior disorder in terms of sin or of difficulties associated with ethical choice and responsibility would substitute theological disputation and philosophical wrangling about values for specifiable quantitative and qualitative criteria of disease.

REFERENCES

AUSUBEL, D. P. *Ego development and the personality disorders.* New York: Grune & Stratton, 1952.

AUSUBEL, D. P. Relationships between psychology and psychiatry: The hidden issues. *Amer. Psychologist,* 1956, 11, 99–105.

DREYFUSS, F., & CZACZKES, J. W. Blood cholesterol and uric acid of healthy medical students under the stress of an examination. *AMA Arch. intern. Med.,* 1959, 103, 708.

MOWRER, O. H. "Sin," the lesser of two evils. *Amer. Psychologist,* 1960, 15, 301–304.

SZASZ, T. S. The myth of mental illness. *Amer. Psychologist* 1960, 15, 113–118.

HUMAN LIFE GOALS IN THE
HUMANISTIC PERSPECTIVE*

CHARLOTTE BUHLER

Introduction

WITH the psychologists' attention having been concentrated for some time entirely on the need aspect of human motivation, the goal aspect has been almost completely neglected. Yet psychologists are beginning to realize the great importance of this aspect, especially within the frame of reference of psychotherapy. "All I hear is questions about goals," a psychoanalytically-oriented therapist said in a recent discussion in admitting that the handling of goals and values was an unresolved problem.

Research related to goals has been scarce and haphazard. There is no systematic description nor theory of the constituent and contributory *factors* to goalsetting.

From Narziss Ach's studies (1905) on "determining tendencies" at the beginning of this century, over Kurt Lewin's (1926) "aspiration levels," to more recent studies of decision making, of achievement, and of success, we have investigations of special aspects of goalsetting. Developmental aspects of goalsetting were discussed by the author (1962) in a study on "Genetic Aspects of the Self." Goal patterns of healthy, essentially happy, and effective individuals were demonstrated by A. Maslow (1954), while H. Otto (1963) found, on the other hand, that the majority of people who answered his questionnaire on personality strength and personal resources had never given any thought or time to an assessment or evaluation of their potentialities. In accordance with this, I find in my therapy groups that very few of these people chose careers or entered personal relationships under the aspect of their own potentialities or their self-actualization.

Everett Shostrom (1963) found, while standardizing his "Inventory for the Measurement of Self-Actualization," that the most self-actualizing person is the one who "is able to tie the past and the future to the present in meaningful continuity." His study throws some light on the healthy and unhealthy relationships of the individual to time.

But little is known about the continuity of pursuits of those who, in the end, found their lives to be fulfilled as against those who ended in failure. In fact, we know the barest minimum about what people seek in life and what they do with themselves. The whole field is full of speculation.

While this address cannot be the occasion for a systematic investi-

---
* This paper was read as the Presidential Address at the Fourth Annual Convention of the American Association for Humanistic Psychology in New York, 1966.

JOURNAL OF HUMANISTIC PSYCHOLOGY, 1967, 7, pp. 36-52.

gation of all factors entering goalsetting, I want to point to certain behavioral as well as experiential patterns which in the developmental progression seem to indicate advance in goalsetting. The twelve points which I will discuss are considered very tentative formulations and are not claimed to be final nor necessarily complete. The organizing principle for the twelve points is *developmental*; that is to say, I will enumerate them as I see them coming up in the individual's development.

Activity

The first behavior contributing to and involving, already from the start, certain characteristics of the individual's goalsetting is the *activity* with which the individual begins his existence even in the prenatal stage.

As Eiduson, Eiduson, & Geller (1962) establish in a careful survey of the most recent literature, the individual starts with a given genetic setup acting in and on a given environment. While this environment's influence becomes immediately a co-determinant of the individual's behavior, there is from the start selectivity in the way the individual responds to all given stimuli.

Some interesting details may be mentioned briefly with respect to the nature of the individual's primary activity.

This primary activity is known to occur in different *levels*, as M. Fries (1953) called it. She distinguished five activity levels, starting from very passive up to overactive behavior. Also some very recent observers, Thomas *et al.* (1963), establish consistency in the infant's activity level.

The activity level seems more or less coordinated with passivity and aggressiveness of approach. This passivity and aggressiveness is seen by L. W. Sontag (1950) as representing the infant's earliest approaches to working out the basic problem of dependency versus independence. This implies a very important assumption: namely, that the natural tendency to be passive or aggressive predisposes the baby, from birth on, to two fundamentally opposed human relationships. They are the *acceptance of dependency* or the *struggle for independence*. Of course, it must be said at once that passivity and aggressiveness could not possibly be the sole determinants of dependent or independent behavior, nor are passivity and aggressiveness themselves completely unalterable. But within limits, Sontag's theory, for which he brings considerable experimental evidence from the Fels Institute's research probjects, impresses this writer as sound. Kagan & Moss (1962) pursued this Fels Institute research study on a longitudinal range from infancy into adulthood. They found that the continuity of the previously mentioned traits was later influenced by the individual's sex role standard.

Another characteristic of the infant's primary activity is what the writer (1958) called degrees of curiosity or lack of it, and what Thomas *et al.* (1963) establish as consistently accepting or rejecting responses

22

to new stimuli and experiences. In this we can see roots of later preferences for adventure as against preference for familiar situations. Also
creativity and non-creativity — the interest in, or lack of interest in,
discovering and doing something new — may have here one of its roots.

Selective Perception

The second behavior, contributing also from the start to the individual's later goalsetting, is his selective perception.

Sensory perception, which begins in the intrauterine life, is for quite
some time partly vague, partly very specified, and becomes only
gradually organized. R. Spitz (1965) has, in continuing our earlier
Viennese research, brought systematic evidence for the way in which
the awareness of an object is gradually built up during the first year
of life.

All during this process, the infant responds in a very individual way
to the world of stimuli that he perceives. His responsiveness is selective
from the start, as is now widely acknowledged. Stirnimann (1940)
brings comprehensive data proving this selectivity. Tinbergen (1948)
speaks of an "innate perceptual pattern." Hilgard (1951) speaks of the
pursuit of "innate preferences."

Apart from preferences, there are also such individual features as
degrees of sensitivity in response to environmental stimuli. Hyper-
sensitivity is one of the most generally acknowledge inborn characteristics. The vulnerability of the hypersensitive child is one of those
conditions which are apt to induce neurotic development.

To what degree and in what way goalsetting is linked up with perception first, and later with imagery or phantasy, is still undecided.
Undoubtedly when a person decides to get an orange out of his
refrigerator, he must focus his imagination on an object which he
knows from his perception.

But when a person has a vague urge for some activity — he may
have imagined only vaguely one or another situation — he may phantasy about it, but the main thing in him may be this urge and a variety
of feelings. In the creative process, as described by some writers and
musicians, there may be a phase in which fleeting images pass through
the mind in colors and in a variety of feelings.

There we find a selective imagination brought to life under the
directive of an active mind which sets and pursues a goal.

In the two, the ability of *directive activity*, operating in unison with
a *selective perception and imagination*, I see the core of the person or
the individual's "rudimentary self." With this I mean the beginning of
a system of purposeful behavior in the direction of the development of
the individual's own potentials.

Reactions to Care and Contact

A basic goal, from the start, is *psychophysical needs*. However, this
satisfaction seems only to be beneficial if brought about in what R.

Spitz (1965) called the right "emotional climate." This emotional climate depends on the type of personal care which the mother or her substitute gives to the infant. While subconsciously so, the infant's need seems to be for psychophysical satisfactions received in an atmosphere of love and care. This shows us from the beginning an unconscious intent in the direction of human closeness.

There is more proof of that. We know that as early as from about three to six weeks on, the infant responds with a smile to another person's smile and that it initiates sounds. Piaget (1951) observed, the same as I did, a behavior which must be called "strenuous efforts" at imitating sounds and mouth movements. Here we find rudimentary stages of understanding and of identification.

Thus the earliest tendency to need-satisfaction is, from the start, one in which not only satiation is wanted, but care as well as contact.

Will, Conscience, Identity

The fourth behavior contributing to goalsetting becomes conscious in the experiences: *I want*. This getting into conflicts with the experiences, *I must, I should*, results in the two to four-year-old child's first inquiry into *who am I?* — an inquiry which from then on will plague the individual sometimes far into his adulthood or even all through life.

In his first "I want to" behavior, the child is quite arbitrary regarding his objective. He may say "yes" and "no" in short succession to the same offer or request. He tries out how it feels to make choices and decisions of his own. And he discovers himself, if allowed by his environment, as a person in his own right.

Here, then, is where the autonomous ego is set up, and where the child begins to discover his own self and the possibility of giving himself a direction of his own. Erikson (1959) speaks of the happenings of this period as of the "battle for autonomy."

But clinical studies show more recently how very individually different this period is being experienced. There are some children who, while having tantrums and resisting their environment, do not really set up goals of their own. They just fight submission, but remain in the end just as dependent on their environment as they were before. All they want to do is to be opposite of what their environment wants.

Some of my patients who are now in their thirties or forties, or even older, remember that all they ever wanted was to do the opposite of what was suggested to them. This, then, is the beginning of a completely neurotic self-determination. There are children who are set on neurotic love relationships with a parent and who do not want autonomy but possessive domination.

Besides this neurotic outcome of the battle for autonomy, there are also healthy solutions. Partly depending on the specific environment, partly on the child, the outcome may be a voluntary submission and identification with the adults' goals.

The opposite type, the child with much of a creative potential, begins at this point with his first attempts toward self-realization. The more or less creative child will, in this period, already have ideas of his own of how to set up his identity. This child may feel that she does not want to be like her mother, but like her aunt, whom she admires; or she may want to do things as the neighbor lady does, who can teach her something she wants to learn (Bühler, 1962).

These tentative early goals show us beginnings of the child's conscious attempts to identify with certain persons and with certain objectives in the humanistic perspective of values.

These first goals may have to do with aptitudes or with moral considerations. "Is he a good boy or is he a bad boy?" asks Peter, two, in talking thoughtfully to himself. "No, he is a bad boy," he concludes with a certain glee. Peter is too young to even speak of himself as "I," yet already conceives of a moral goal for himself. Of course, all this is partly playful, but still it is astonishing how many valid, lasting decisions are being made in this period.

Besides evaluation and identification there is, however, something more to be noted. Vascillating in their directives as these children's self-expressions may be, there is definitely the evidence of a degree of intentionality in them. They are not yet sure what exactly they want or should do with themselves, but they know vaguely there is something to be realized in some distant future.

If we jump from this age to the young adolescents whom Getzels & Jackson (1962) examined, we find a fully established self-awareness and dependently conforming or independently self-responsible identities. In this excellent study of "Creativity and Intelligence," we meet adolescents during their high school years who have very clear ideas about themselves.

There are those like Mary, a high IQ but non-creative girl, who has a positive image of her family and who states in her autobiography that she has "internalized" her mother's ideals and is very close to her (p. 163).

And there are those who, like John, declare, "If I could achieve one thing during my lifetime, I would want it to be 'independence.' "

And his equally original sister, Joan, says, "that, although she thinks of her parents as being pleasant enough, she has no intention of identifying with them. As to her mother, she feels that she need only make an assertive statement on the question of identification: 'When they try to get me to be like my mother, I . . . tell them that I am me.' And that is that" (p. 191).

These identity concepts go along with elaborate self-evaluations. Here we see the beginnings of certain features of long-range goal-setting.

The cases of this study will also serve as examples for the next factor determining goalsetting. That is the factor of potentialities in terms of abilities and aptitudes.

Mastery

The experience in this area begins with "I can" or "I cannot."

I agree with Lois Murphy (1962) that this "I can" or "I cannot" belongs to the earliest experiences of infancy. This four- to five-month-old baby who swings his rattle under good control, as against that one who hits himself or loses hold of the rattle — this 1½-year-old who successfully puts one block on the other so that it stands, as against that child whose towers always tumble before they are finished — of course these babies do not have a conscious awareness of their being able or unable to master these materials, but semiconsciously they have first realizations of success and of failure. Proofs of this are the happy smiles of the one and the unhappy rages of the other. Observations of the despair and helplessness of these failing children have been made thus far only in an incidental way. They are usually children with birth injuries or childhood schizophrenia, children who are uncoordinated and unintegrated.

Experiences in coping and in mastery contribute essentially to the setting up of a child's personality, as L. Murphy showed (1962) in her extensive observations.

Already, then, the more adaptively and the more creatively coping individual can be distinguished. This difference becomes very pronounced in Getzels & Jackson's studies (1962). And here we already see some distinctive characteristics of life goals.

In these well-known studies of creative versus highly intelligent, non-creative high school students, great pains were taken to establish all relevant variables that could codetermine the subjects' behavior.

The findings show us the creative and the high-achievement though non-creative type associated with different motivational patterns. The non-creative, moving toward conventional standards and conforming with what is expected of them, show themselves in dependency relationships with their environment. The creative group, on the other hand, which moves away from models provided by teachers and which seeks out careers that do not conform with what is expected of them, show themselves in independence relationships with their environment.

There are further related results regarding the social and moral orientation of these two groups. While both groups participate in activities that are expected and approved by the social order, the adaptive, non-creative group tends more to be what one usually calls socially "adjusted." They are "insiders;" they seem

to prefer social interaction to individual achievement, to seek experiences that are immediately enjoyable as against those that promise more remote gratification, to find more satisfaction in experiencing with others than in asserting their own autonomy, to be willing to sacrifice moral commitment in the interest of interpersonal harmony (p. 159).

The highly creative show the reverse of these trends. They tend to

26

be "outsiders" and stand up individualistically for highly moral principles.

All the described findings are suggestive of different innate tendencies of these two groups. But the possible role of environmental influence is not neglected by Getzels & Jackson ". . . irrespective of the possible role of genetic factors." To quote them further: The findings in this direction are that the high-IQ family "is one in which individual divergence is limited and risks minimized, and the overall impression of the high-creativity family is that it is one in which individual divergence is permitted and risks are accepted" (p. 76).

The cautious conclusion from all these findings would be that in his eventual goal structure and goal development, an individual's inherent tendencies to be more creative and independent or more non-creative and dependent are codetermined by the environment's goals and values. These enhance that "openness to experiences" and that willingness to take risks which were found in the creative child, as they also enhance that orientation toward security and success which are found in the non-creative child.

The question of how that child which is not creative and not as adaptive as the family might expect, will fare under these influences has not as yet been established in correspondingly thorough studies.

But from other studies, such as B. Eiduson's (1962) investigation on "Scientists," we gather how extremely complicated the picture becomes, as soon as the dynamics of very different individual lives are compared.

Constructiveness and Destructiveness

From the beginning, the infant is under the impact of his environment. Parents, siblings, peers, and other persons contribute essentially to the child's goalsetting by information, guidance, and by all social relationships that are being established. We already mentioned dependency and independence. But apart from these, there is a host of feelings of love and fear, of frustration and hostility, of acceptance, security — or the opposite — of belonging or being a loner and an outsider, of rivalry and jealousy, of submission and domination, of cooperation and opposition, friendships and crushes, and many more.

Apart from the impact which the child receives from his environment, he becomes increasingly aware of how the others — his elders and his peers — are handling themselves and their affairs. He begins to interpret their intents, their selfishness or their kindness. In responding to them and in coping with them, their demands, their rebuffs, their beatings, the eight- to twelve-year child develops ideas, methods, and directions of his own. He becomes an essentially constructive person who handles himself and his social relationships in the direction of goals that benefit him and others, as against the essentially destructive person, who is full of hostilities and whose mind is set on damaging others or even himself.

In introducing the concepts of constructiveness and destructiveness, I want to emphasize that I think of them as complex motivational patterns. Constructiveness is not a simple entity such as activity, but a complex unit, such as achievement. There may be the instinctual element of building in it. But constructiveness and destructiveness, as understood here, are developed under the influence of a person's interaction with his environment. Everybody probably harbors both constructive as well as destructive attitudes. But similar to the achievement attitude, constructiveness or destructiveness may under circumstances be all-pervasive.

Studies on this aspect of constructiveness or destructiveness as basic attitudes to life are not as yet available. Fritz Redl & David Wineman's (1951) studies on "Children Who Hate" come the closest to it in describing and analyzing an all-pervasive destructiveness of a group of preadolescent youngsters.

The definition of the term constructiveness would be that this is the basic orientation of a person who tries to work out things for himself and for others in such a way that there is a beneficial result. Beneficial might be a result that gives pleasure or is helpful or educational or contributory to any kind of growth and development. The opposite orientation of destructiveness is that of persons who harbor much hostility and who try to damage others or themselves. Such damaging might be consciously, or unconsciously, planned and might range from preventing happiness and success of others, or oneself, to actually trying to injure, to ruin, to eliminate people.

Harmful aggression with a destructive intent may be observed even in nursery school children. As a basic attitude of malevolence, it seems to begin to dominate a child from about eight to ten or twelve years on, the age in which some of the conflicts between children and their parents culminate.

In criminal adolescents and adults there is often evidence of a predominant orientation toward destructiveness.

At this point, the two basic goals, to be constructive or to be destructive, can only be introduced as concepts with the hope of later availability of appropriate evidence.

Achievement Motivation

In this period, all foregoing experiences of being able to master things and being successful against failures converge to generate an individual attitude to and concept of achievement. The idea of achievement as a goal has by then become more or less clearly established in the child's mind. Many factors contribute to how it is being conceived by the individual.

In the studies of D. McClelland and his collaborators (1953), the enormous impact of the parental attitude to achievement has not only been established, but also analyzed in its various characteristics.

Achievement styles are established which often remain the same all through life, styles in terms of work habits, of dependence or independence in goalsetting, orientation toward success or failure, and, particularly, attitudes to values and beliefs.

Evidence as accumulated by the McClelland group, by Getzels & Jackson (1962), by Eiduson (1962), by Goertzel & Goertzel (1962), show attitudes to achievement in their consistency and show them almost always linked up with beliefs and values.

Beliefs and Values

In the eight- to twelve-year-old period, in which a child begins to have some overview over his various personal relationships as well as his competence in life, he consolidates beliefs and values for himself. The constructive or destructive attitudes which he starts building, result from the experiences and evaluations which crystallize now to opinions and convictions. Eight- to twelve-year-old children often debate with others or with themselves issues such as honesty, fairness, popularity, power, being important, being accomplished, and being the best in everything.

In these beliefs and values, the growing child establishes ordering principles for himself. Like some other goal-determining principles which we see at work from the start — namely, need-satisfaction, self-limiting adaptation, creative expansion — the ordering principle is also noticeable from the infant's first attempts at coordination and organization on. I consider all these as basic tendencies and call this last one *tendency to the upholding of the internal order* (C. Bühler, 1959).

Love and Other Committing Relationships

We said previously that, from the beginning, the infant's need-satisfaction depends on care given within the framework of a warm, human relationship. Very early in life the infant not only responds to the "emotional climate" which the adult creates, but he also strains himself toward a contact of understanding.

In adolescence, two new goals of human relationships are discovered and aspired. They are intimacy and commitments. Healthy intimacy and commitments may be defined as freely chosen bonds. Their free choice distinguishes them from unfree dependency on the one hand, while on the other hand they represent a voluntary reduction of independence.

Intimacy and commitment in a sex and love-relationship, if shared by both partners, develops it beyond functional enjoyment to something new : namely, the ecstatic experience of a unity. The goal to achieve this is, as everybody knows, one of the, if not *the* most essential, life goals of the maturing person.

Maslow quotes it among his peak experiences. Also psychoanalysis recognizes in this a new step in the development of object relations. It is called the development of genitality. "Genitality," says Erikson

29

(1959, p. 96), "is the potential capacity to develop orgastic potency in relation to a loved partner of the opposite sex."

This sex-love unity is probably the most essential of the uniting experiences and goals of the person willing to commit himself, to give and to share. But in the same period, commitments to friends, to groups, to causes, become also freely chosen goals. These commitments bring the beliefs which the eight- to twelve-year-old child began to conceive of, into the sphere of reality.

The development in this whole area is, as we all know, full of problems and perils for the majority of youths. The degree to which they want to allow themselves the pleasure of sexual excitement is one of their problems. The finding of and commitment to a love-partner is a second, the accomplishment of self-dedication through intercourse a third. And the question to what degree these goals may preoccupy them in comparison with achievement goals and with the dedication to groups and causes is perhaps the most difficult to resolve. The pursuit of sexual and other pleasurable excitements easily becomes, for the adolescent, a goal which conflicts with other goals of life, especially achievement goals.

A great deal of conflict concerning the hierarchy of the different values that were developed up to this point, is practically unavoidable. A hierarchical order and integration of all the directions which we encountered up to now is a task of younger adulthood, if not of the rest of life.

Integration

We mentioned the word integration. All during childhood and adolescence, we saw goalsetting being developed in various and increasing directions. In this development, several factors are obviously of decisive influence. The complexity of the process of goalsetting is extraordinary, and the integrative task required is tremendous.

Very little research has been dedicated, up to now, to this whole question of integration. Thomas French (1952) has devoted a comprehensive investigation to this principle of integration. He has particularly dwelt on the factor of hope as an integrating principle. Hope is undoubtedly of fundamental importance in holding a person together and in keeping a person going.

However, before it comes to hope, there are problems regarding the inner organization of our goals. One principle of organizing seems to be given in the individually varying roles of different values and beliefs. G. Allport (1961) also sees a hierarchy of values as the organizing principles of the self. But what determines that hierarchy of values?

In the first instance, we must think of it as changing in time and being determined by age.

A second codeterminant is obviously the genetic factor, about which we know least of all. But, undoubtedly, a person's dispositions — his gifts and aptitudes, as well as his deficiencies — are codetermining the hierarchy of values and with it the structure of his goalsetting.

Thirdly, there is the host of environmental influences.

Emotional dynamics are nowadays the best-known factor of all which influence a person. However, as far as goalsetting is concerned, here, also, only recent clinical studies give us relevant information regarding the environmental impact.

The same is true of socio-cultural influences on goalsetting, a factor which recent social psychological studies have explored (Strodtbeck, 1958).

While we have increasing knowledge of all these factors, little is known regarding the integrating procedure by means of which the individual evaluates and orders all these codeterminants of his goalsetting. While much of this may take place in the unconscious, it still remains a question of how it is done.

How do people choose? Or how does it come about that in one case the impact of a mother's ambition — in another case a cultural prejudice acquired in a group — plays a decisive role in what a person believes and wants? It does not explain anything to say one factor was "stronger." Obviously, it is the individual who reacts more strongly to one or the other factor. And what determines his choices and decisions? A discussion of these factors of goalsetting has been prepared by the author and collaborators (in press).

Little has been done to investigate integration in its early stages. A. Weil (1956), who specialized in the study of childhood schizophrenias, comes to the conclusion that the unevenness of these children's maturational patterning, apart from their peculiarities, is the reason why their development lacks integration at all times. In this, she sees their basic pathology. And, indeed, the inability of integration seems part of the basic pathology of schizophrenia at any age.

But correspondingly, then, is an even and regular maturational progress a guarantee of successful integration?

It seems to me that we know far too little about people's inner organization, about decisions between preferences, about what ultimate needs they have as against more visible or more pressuring ones.

Very few people know themselves in this respect. Most subjects or patients whom I ask: What do you want ultimately? What is ultimately important to you? will give vague answers. "I wish I knew myself," they will say.

Direction, Purpose, and Meaning

The problem of integration entails the factor of direction, purpose, and meaning in a way, because it seems that we integrate ourselves with the view of certain goals in mind. These goals may be closer or farther away, shortsighted or seen under a big perspective; whatever they are, they have an influence on the way an individual organizes his behavior. The integrative process of the person who wants the "here and now" will undoubtedly be different from the one who has a long-

31

range plan. Some concrete answers as to how a great variety of determining factors may be absorbed and integrated into a specific way of life, with specific goals and purposes, result from B. Eiduson's study of "Scientists" (1962).

In this study, the development and personalities of forty scientists were examined by means of tests and interviews. All of these men, says Eiduson,

> whose early determining factors show a great variety, seem to have in common that their excellent intellectual abilities lead them to early concentration on intellectual interests, and they all turn away from their families during adolescence or when starting college (p. 66).

This independence factor which we found associated with creative abilities in earlier studies, also becomes apparent here.

These scientists show, as Eiduson (1962) states in summarizing her findings, "a great diversity of sources that fed the investment in the intellectual" (p. 89). Yet they are all men whose life goals, to an extraordinary degree, are identified with, and related to, their creative research.

From this and other research it appears that the creative person finds it easier to set a direction and goals for himself. Also, they are goals which lead the creative person in a more natural way to transcend himself, which V. Frankl (1966), as well as Maslow (1964), considers a specifically human accomplishment. It becomes increasingly evident that in dedicating himself to a self-transcending goal, a person feels his life to be meaningful, as V. Frankl pointed out. But to be meaningful, and, with this, to fulfill a basic existential human need, this goal must be chosen in accordance with a person's own best potentialities.

This concept of meaningfulness, which has a long history regarding its definition, occupied many thinkers, historically speaking, since Brentano and Husserl, W. Dilthey, E. Spranger, and K. Buhler, my own work — then in existentialistic writings like Paul Tillich's and recently V. Frankl's (1966) — in its application to psychotherapy. This concept seems to refer to the development of an existential quality of life which I think is best defined by two characteristics, one emphasized by K. Buhler (1927), who says, meaningful is what is a contributory constituent to a teleological whole; the other by P. Tillich (1952), whose discourse on the despair of meaningfulness calls for an act of faith by which to accept oneself in a meaningful act.

As for creative work, it also usually enhances a person's enthusiasm for life and his self-esteem. It helps him more quickly to find his identity and to establish himself as a person in his own right.

For all these reasons, the humanistic psychologist is greatly interested in awakening and increasing people's creative potentials. H. Otto (1962) has recently started systematic work with older persons in this direction. And, luckily, schools and parents begin to become aware of the fundamental importance of this factor of creativity, the existence of which, as Guilford (1950) observed, had been almost forgotten in psychology and education.

However, not everybody is primarily creative. What about the direction of those people who are primarily non-creative?

In Getzels & Jackson's previously mentioned studies, it is very apparent how the non-creative youngsters whom they examined and who were essentially healthy, non-neurotic persons, found it easy and natural to fall in with their families' and their teachers' guidance and ideas for their futures. That means they allowed their elders to help them find their direction in life.

A mutually satisfactory development under this kind of influence does, however, not only depend on the willingness and adaptability of the child. It depends perhaps even more on the wisdom and adequate understanding of the grown-up environment.

The questions that pose themselves at this point will be taken up from a different angle when we discuss our last factor.

Fulfillment and Failure

What is a human being living towards? The presumable end result has been described in different terms. Some think of no result at all and see only a growth and decline process with a peak somewhere in the earlier part or the middle. Some never see any other goal than the attainment or restoring of equilibrium. Some think of the full development of the self as the ultimate satisfaction. The humanistic psychologists, as you know, usually speak of self-realization as the goal.

I personally considered this concept at about the same time as K. Horney (1950) first introduced it into the literature. In discussing it, I rejected it in favor of the concept of fulfillment. I find that, while a good objective description of a very important aspect of a fulfilled life, self-realization is only one aspect, and, at that, it is one that only relatively few people are fully aware of.

What do people want to get out of their lives? Naïve people, as you know, speak of happiness and various goods that they think will bring it to them. More materialistic and/or ambitious people may speak of the success they want to end up with. But if one talks with older people, as I did in a study I am presently engaged in, one hears quite other things.

If not very analytical, the essentially fulfilled people may say : they had a good life and they would not want it any different or much different if they had to live it all over again.

In the opposite case of complete failure, they may say, "It all came to nothing," or they are tired and glad it is all over. Or as Sonja Kowalewska expressed it in the title of a drama she left after her suicidal death : "As it was and as it could have been."

In the case of a resigned ending, they may say, there were so many disappointments.

All this is to say people have, toward their end, inclusive feelings of fulfillment or failure or a kind of resignation in between. Even people who in earlier years lived with short-range goals or from day to day, seem to have toward the end an inclusive reaction to their life as a whole.

If, in talking with more analytically-minded people, one tries to let them specify the main aspects of their fulfillment or failure feelings, four major considerations could be distinguished.

The first is the aspect of *luck*. Practically always people mention that they had much luck, or lack of luck, in meeting the right persons or getting the right opportunities at the right time. This factor seems to contribute most to happiness or unhappiness, to the feeling of being a fortunate or an unfortunate person. In religious persons, this is an area where they see, most of all, God's hand.

The second may be called the aspect of the realization of *potentialities*. This is usually referred to in terms as these: "I did most of what I wanted to do," or "I did what was right for me," or "I did many things that were wrong for me," or "I could not really make the best out of myself."

The third is the aspect of *accomplishment*. Most people I talked with feel strongly about this aspect. They feel that their life should amount to something; it should have borne fruit; it should represent an accomplishment of some kind. There should be "something to show" for the past life. This factor contributes greatly to their ultimate satisfaction or dissatisfaction with their lives.

Finally, a fourth factor is that of a *moral* evaluation. Often persons emphasized that they had lived *right*, meaning in terms of their moral and/or religious convictions. Many persons mentioned objectives they had lived for in some form of self-dedication, be it the family or social groups, mankind, or progess in some field of endeavor.

The four aspects correspond essentially to the goals of the four tendencies which I assumed all to be basic tendencies toward fulfillment.

The most successful lives in terms of fulfillment I found to be those who were rather conscious of their life being something they ought to do something with and they were responsible for — be it in religious terms of relationship to a God, or in existential terms in relationship to the universal order, or simply in ethical terms of non-metaphysical convictions.

Religion, philosophy, and moral convictions are, of course, as we know, not sufficient to help a person live a healthy life and conquer his destructive neurotic tendencies. The essentially fulfilled lives that I studied seem to have been able to be essentially successful in sustaining an individually balancd equilibrium between their basic tendencies to *need-satisfaction, self-limiting adaptation, creative expansion*, and *upholding of the internal order*, and to be constructive under whichever aspect they believed in.

SUMMARY

Human goalsetting is, as you see, a very complex process emerging from a multiplicity of ingredients. I pointed out twelve main developmental advances on different levels and in different areas of personality functioning. Briefly summarized, they are : (1) *Activity* with a more passive or more aggressive approach; (2) selective *Perception*; (3) *Care and Contact*; (4) *Identity* and *Intentionality* beginnings with choice and direction of the person who feels he wants or he must or he should; (5) *Mastery* beginnings based on the experience "I can" or "I cannot," with success and failure, adaptive and creative behavior; (6) *Constructiveness* and *Destructiveness* developed in the dynamic interrelationships with the environment; (7) *Achievement* motivation; (8) *Beliefs and Values* with opinions and convictions; (9) *Love* and other committing relationships; (10) *Integration* of factors; (11) *Direction, Purpose, and Meaning*; (12) *Fulfillment, Resignation, and Failure*.

One of the results of the studies (in preparation) of lives which accomplished essential fulfillment as against lives ending in the resignation of a heap of unordered experiences, many disappointments, or in the despair of failure, is this :

Fulfillment seems to result primarily from a constructive and thoughtful way of living; constructive to the degree that even major tragedies as well as great misfortunes are overcome and used beneficially; thoughtful in the use of even mediocre potentialities for accomplishments and meaningful self-dedication; thoughtful also in attempting to look repeatedly backwards and forward at the whole of one's existence and to assess it in whatever terms one believes in.

REFERENCES

ACH, N. *Uber die Willenstätigkeit und das Denken* (About will and thinking). Göttingen : Vandenhock & Ruzprecht, 1905.

ALLPORT, G. *Pattern and growth in personality.* New York : Harper, 1961.

BUHLER, C. Earliest trends in goalsetting. *Rev. psychiat. Infantile,* 1958, *25*, 1-2, 13-23.

BUHLER, C. Theoretical observations about life's basic tendencies. *Amer. J. Psychother.*, 1959, *13*, 3, 561-581.

BUHLER, C. *Genetic aspects of the self.* New York : Acad. Sciences, 1962a.

BUHLER, C. *Values in psychotherapy.* Glencoe, Ill. : Free Press, 1962b

BUHLER, C. *Intentionality and fulfillment.* San Francisco : Jossey-Bass, in press.

BUHLER, C. & MASSARIK, F. (Eds.). *The course of human life. A study of life goals in the humanistic perspective.* New York : Springer, in press.

BUHLER, K. *Die Krise der Psychologie.* Jena : G. Fischer, 1927.

(Transl. *The crisis of psychology*. Cambridge : Schekman Publ. Co., in press.)

EIDUSON, B. *Scientists*. New York : Basic Books, 1962.

EIDUSON, B.; EIDUSON, S.; & GELLER, E. Biochemistry, genetics and the nature-nurture problem. *Amer. J. Psychiat.*, 1962, 58.

ERIKSON, E. *Identity and the life cycle*. New York : Interntl. Univer. Press, 1959.

FRANKL, V. Self-transcendence as a human phenomenon. *J. humanistic Psychol.*, 1966, 6, 2, 97-106.

FRENCH, T. *The integration of behavior*. Chicago : Univer. Chicago Press, 1952, 1954, 1956 (3 vols.).

FRIES, M. & WOOLF, P. Some hypotheses on the role of the congenital activity type in personality development. Vol. 8. *The psychoanalytic study of the child*. New York : Interntl. Univer. Press, 1953.

GETZELS, J. & JACKSON, P. *Creativity and intelligence, explorations with gifted students*. New York : J. Wiley & Sons, 1962.

GOERTZEL, V. & GOERTZEL, M. *Cradles of eminence*. Boston : Little, Brown & Co., 1962.

GUILFORD, J. P. *Fields of psychology*. New York : Van Nostrand, 1950.

HILGARD, E. The role of learning in perception. In R. R. Blake & G. V. Ramsey (Eds.), *Perception*. New York : Ronald, 1951.

HORNEY, K. *Neurosis and human growth*. New York : W. W. Norton, 1950.

KAGAN, J. Acquisition and significance of sex typing and sex role identity. *Child Development Research, Russel-Sage Foundation*. Philadelphia : Wm. F. Fell Co., 1964.

KAGAN, J. & MOSS, H. A. *Birth to maturity*. New York : Wiley, 1962.

LEWIN, K. Vorsatz, Wille und Bedürfris (Intention, will and need). *Psychol. Forschg.*, 1926, 7, 330-385.

MASLOW, A. *Motivation and personality*. New York : Harper, 1954.

MASLOW, A. *Religions, values, and peak-experiences*. Columbus : Ohio State Univer. Press, 1964.

McCLELLAND, D.; ATKINSON, W.; CLARK, R.; & LOWELL, E. *The achievement motive*. New York : Appleton-Century-Crofts, 1953.

MURPHY, L. *The widening world of childhood*. New York : Basic Books, 1962.

OTTO, H. The personal resource development research — the multiple strength perception effect. *Proceedings of Utah Acad. Sci., Arts, & Letters, 38*, 1961-62.

OTTO, H. Self-perception of personality strengths by four discrete groups. *J. humanistic Relations*, 1963, 12, 4.

PIAGET, J. *Dreams and imitation in childhood*. New York : Norton, 1951.

REDL, F. & WINEMAN, D. *Children who hate, the disorganization and breakdown of behavior controls*. Glencoe, Ill. : Free Press, 1951.

SHOSTROM, E. Personal orientation inventory. San Diego: Educational and Industrial Test Service, 1963.

SONTAG, L. The genetics of differences in psychosomatic patterns in childhood. *Amer. J. Orthopsychiat.*, 1950, *20*, 3.

SPITZ, R. Genese des premieres relations objectales. *Rev. franç. Psychanal.*, Paris, 1954.

SPITZ, R. *The first year of life.* New York : Internatl. Univer. Press, 1965.

STIRNIMANN, F. *Psychologie des neugeborenen Kindes.* Zurich und Leipzig : Rascher Verl., 1940.

STIRNIMANN, F. Psychologie des neugeborenen Kindes. In E. Schachtel (Ed.), *Metamorphosis.* New York : Basic Books, 1959.

STRODTBECK, F.; MCCLELLAND, D. *et al. Talent and society.* Princeton, N.J. : Van Nostrand Co., 1958.

THOMAS, A. *et al. Behavioral individuality in early childhood.* New York : N.Y. Univer. Press, 1963.

TILLICH, P. *The courage to be.* New Haven: Yale Univer. Press, 1952.

TINBERGEN, N. Social releases and the experimental method required for their study. *Wilson Bull.*, 1948, *60*, 6-51.

WEIL, A. Some evidences of deviational development in infancy and early childhood. Vol. 11. *Psychoanalytic study of the child.* New York : Internatl. Univer. Press, 1956.

TOWARD A CONCEPT OF THE NORMAL PERSONALITY[1]

EDWARD JOSEPH SHOBEN, JR.

CLINICAL practice and the behavioral sciences alike have typically focused on the pathological in their studies of personality and behavior dynamics. While much of crucial importance remains to be learned, there is an abundant empirical knowledge and an impressive body of theory concerning the deviant and the diseased, the anxious and the neurotic, the disturbed and the maladjusted. In contrast, there is little information and even less conceptual clarity about the nature of psychological normality. Indeed, there are even those (5, 13) who argue that there is no such thing as a normal man; there are only those who manage their interpersonal relationships in such a way that others are strongly motivated to avoid them, even by committing them to a mental hospital or a prison, as opposed to those who do not incite such degrees of social ostracism.

This argument has two characteristics. First, it disposes of the issue by simply distributing people along a dimension of pathology. All men are a little queer, but some are much more so than others. Second, it has affinities with the two major ideas that have been brought to bear on the question of what constitutes normal or abnormal behavior: the statistical conception of the usual or the average and the notion of cultural relativism. If pathology is conceived as the extent to which one is tolerated by one's fellows, then any individual can theoretically be described in terms of some index number that reflects the degree of acceptability accorded him. The resulting distribution would effectively amount to an ordering of people from the least to the most pathological. Similarly, if the positions on such a continuum are thought of as functions

of one's acceptance or avoidance by others, then they can only be defined by reference to some group. The implications here are twofold. First, the conception of pathology is necessarily relativistic, varying from group to group or culture to culture. Second, the degree of pathology is defined as the obverse of the degree of conformity to group norms. The more one's behavior conforms to the standards of the group, the less one is likely to be subject to social avoidance; whereas the more one's behavior deviates from the rules, the greater is the probability of ostracism to the point of institutional commitment.

STATISTICAL AND RELATIVISTIC CONCEPTS OF NORMALITY

Yet it is doubtful that the issues are fully clarified by these statistical and culturally relativistic ideas. Is it most fruitful to regard normality or integrative behavior as merely reflecting a minimal degree of pathology, or may there be a certain merit in considering the asset side of personality, the positive aspects of human development? This question becomes particularly relevant when one is concerned with the socialization process or with the goals and outcomes of psychotherapy or various rehabilitative efforts.

It seems most improbable that the family, the church, and the school, the main agents of socialization, exist for the minimizing of inevitable pathological traits in the developing members of the community. Rather, parents, priests, and educators are likely to insist that their function is that of facilitating some sort of positive growth, the progressive acquisition of those characteristics, including skills, knowledge, and attitudes, which permit more productive, contributory, and satisfying ways of life. Similarly, while psychotherapists may sometimes accept the limited goals of simply trying to inhibit pathological processes, there are certainly those (11, 16) who take the position that therapy

[1] This paper is revised from versions read on March 26, 1956, at the convention of the American Personnel and Guidance Association in Washington, D. C., and on November 16, 1956, at a conference on mental health research at Catholic University in Washington, D. C., under the joint sponsorship of Catholic University, the University of Maryland, and the U. S. Veterans Administration.

AMERICAN PSYCHOLOGIST, 1957, 12, pp. 183-189.

is to be judged more in terms of how much it contributes to a patient's ability to achieve adult gratifications rather than its sheer efficiency in reducing symptoms or shoring up pathological defenses.

A general concern for such a point of view seems to be emerging in the field of public mental health (26). Beginning with an emphasis on treatment, the concept of community mental health swung to a preventive phase with the main interest focused on identifying the antecedents of mental disease and on reducing morbidity rates by attacking their determinants. The vogue of eugenics was one illustrative feature of this stage. More recently, there has been a considerable dissatisfaction with the whole notion of interpreting psychological states in terms of disease analogues (15, 23). Maladjustive behavior patterns, the neuroses, and—perhaps to a lesser extent—the psychoses may possibly be better understood as disordered, ineffective, and defensive styles of life than as forms of sickness. In consequence, there seems to be a growing tendency to conceive of the public mental health enterprise as emphasizing positive development with the prevention and treatment of pathology regarded as vital but secondary.

But in what does positive development consist? The statistical concept of the average is not very helpful. Tiegs and Katz (27), for example, reported a study of college students who had been rated for fourteen different evidences of "nervousness." By and large, these traits were normally distributed, suggesting that those subjects rated low must be considered just as "abnormal" (unusual) as those rated high. This conception seems to provide a superficial quantitative model only at the expense of hopeless self-contradiction and violence to the ordinary categories of communication. Even in a case that at first blush seems to cause no difficulty, the problem remains. Criminal behavior, for example, is distributed in a J-shaped fashion with most cases concentrated at the point of zero offenses, ranging to a relatively few instances of many-time offenders. Few would argue that the usual behavior here is not also the most "positive." But one suspects that the sheer frequency of law-abiding behavior has little to do with its acknowledged integrative character. If conformity to social rules is generally considered more desirable than criminality, it is not because of its rate of occurrence but because of its consequences for both society and the individual.

Thus, a statistical emphasis on the usual as the criterion of positive adjustment or normality shades into a socially relativistic concept with an implied criterion of conformity. The terms "usual" or "most frequent" or "average" are meaningless without reference to some group, and this state of affairs poses two problems. First, conformity in itself, as history abundantly demonstrates, is a dubious guide to conduct. Innovation is as necessary to a culture's survival as are tradition and conservation, and conformity has frequently meant acquiescence in conditions undermining the maturity and positive development of human beings rather than their enhancement. On more personal levels, conformity sometimes seems related in some degree to personality processes that can quite properly be called pathological (2, 24). Second, relativistic conceptions of normality pose serious questions as to the reference group against which any individual is to be assessed. Benedict (3), for example, has made it quite clear that behavior which is considered abnormal in one culture is quite acceptable in others, that certain forms of abnormalities which occur in some societies are absent in others, and that conduct which is thought completely normal in one group may be regarded as intensely pathological in another. Such observations, while descriptively sound, can lead readily to two troublesome inferences. One is that the storm trooper must be considered as the prototype of integrative adjustment in Nazi culture, the members of the Politburo as best representing human normality Soviet–style, and the cruelest adolescent in a delinquent gang as its most positively developed member. The other is that any evaluative judgment of cultures and societies must be regarded as inappropriate. Since normality is conceived only in terms of conformity to group standards, the group itself must be beyond appraisal. Thus, the suspicion and mistrust of Dobu (10), the sense of resigned futility that permeates Alor (6), and the regimentation that characterizes totalitarian nations can logically only be taken as norms in terms of which individual behavior may be interpreted, not as indications of abnormal tendencies in the cultures themselves.

Wegrocki (28), in criticizing such relativistic notions, argues that it is not the form of behavior, the actual acts themselves, that defines its normal or pathological character. Rather, it is its function. What he calls the "quintessence of abnormality" lies in reactions which represent an escape from conflicts and problems rather than a facing of them. This formulation, implying that integrative adjustments are those which most directly confront conflicts and problems, seems essentially free of the difficulties inherent in statistical conceptions and the idea of cultural relativism. But it presents troubles of its own. For instance, what does it mean to "face" a problem or conflict? On what ground, other than the most arbitrarily moralistic one, can such confrontations be defended as more positive than escape? Finally, does this facing of one's problems have any relationship to the matter of conformity in the sense of helping to clarify decisions regarding the acceptance or rejection of group standards?

To deal with such questions requires coming to grips with certain problems of value. It is at this point that the behavioral sciences and ethics meet and merge, and it seems unlikely that any conception of normality can be developed apart from some general considerations that are fundamentally moral. Once the purely relativistic ideas of normality are swept away, it becomes difficult to avoid some concern for the issues of happiness and right conduct (*i.e.*, conduct leading to the greatest degree of human satisfaction) that are the traditional province of the literary interpreter of human experience, the theologian, and the moral philosopher. A primary challenge here is that of providing a rational and naturalistic basis for a concept of integrative adjustment that is at once consistent with the stance and contributions of empirical science and in harmony with whatever wisdom mankind has accumulated through its history.

SYMBOLIC AND SOCIAL ASPECTS OF HUMAN NATURE

One way to meet this challenge is by frankly postulating a basic principle of value. The fundamental contention advanced here is that behavior is "positive" or "integrative" to the extent that it reflects the unique attributes of the human animal. There are undoubtedly other ways of approaching a fruitful concept of normality. Nevertheless, this assertion is consistent with the implications of organic evolution, escapes the fallacy of the survival-of-the-fittest doctrine in its various forms, and permits a derivation of more specific criteria of positive adjustment from the distinctive characteristics of man. No discontinuity within the phylogenetic scale need be assumed. It seems clear, however,

that man, while certainly an animal, can hardly be described as "nothing but" an animal; and his normality or integration seems much more likely to consist in the fulfillment of his unique potentialities than in the development of those he shares with infrahuman organisms.

Foremost among these uniquely human potentialities, as Cassirer (4) and Langer (14) make clear, is the enormous capacity for symbolization. What is most characteristic of men is their pervasive employment of *propositional* language. While other organisms, especially dogs (22) and the higher apes (29), react to symbols, their faculty for doing so indicates only an ability to respond to mediate or representative as well as direct stimuli. Man, on the other hand, uses symbols designatively, as a vehicle for recollecting past events, for dealing with things which are not physically present, and for projecting experience into the future. Goldstein (12) makes the same point in his discussion of the "attitude toward the merely possible," the ability to deal with things that are only imagined or which are not part of an immediate, concrete situation. In patients whose speech has been impaired because of brain damage, this attitude toward the possible is disrupted. Thus, aphasics are typically unable to say such things as, "The snow is black" or "The moon shines in the daytime"; similarly, they are incapable of *pretending* to comb their hair or to take a drink of water, although they can actually *perform* these acts. Such patients appear to have lost the uniquely human capacity for thinking *about* things as well as directly "thinking things."

It is his symbolic ability, then, that makes man the only creature who can "look before and after and pine for what is not." Propositional speech makes it possible for him to learn from not only his own personal experience but from that of other men in other times and places, to forecast the consequences of his own behavior, and to have ideals. These three symbol-given attributes—the aptitude for capitalizing on experience, including the experience of others, over time, the capacity for foresight and the self-imposed control of behavior through the anticipation of its outcomes, and the ability to envision worlds closer than the present one to the heart's desire—constitute a basic set of distinctively human potentialities.

A second set of such potentialities seems related to the long period of helpless dependence that characterizes infancy and childhood. Made mandatory by the relative biological incompleteness of the human baby, this phase of development is likely to be lengthened as cultures become more complex. Thus, in such simpler societies as the Samoan (18), children can achieve a higher degree of independence at an earlier age than in the civilizations of the West, for example, where the necessity for learning complicated and specialized economic skills extends the period of dependence through adolescence and even into chronological young adulthood. The central point, however, is that unlike the young of any other species, human children in *all* cultural settings must spend a long time during which the gratification of their most basic needs is mediated by somebody else and is dependent on their relationship to somebody else.

This state of affairs exposes youngsters during their earliest and most formative stages of development to two fundamental conditions of human life. The first is that one's survival, contentment, and need fulfillment involve an inevitable element of reliance on other people. The second is that the relative autonomy, authority, and power that characterize the parent figures and others on whom one relies in childhood are always perceived to a greater or lesser extent in association with responsibility and a kind of altruism. That is, the enjoyment of adult privileges and status tends to occur in conjunction with the acceptance, in some degree, of responsibility for mediating, in some way, the need gratifications of others. Mowrer and Kluckhohn (20) seem to be speaking of a similar pattern when they describe the socialization process as progressing from childhood *dependency* through *independence* to adult *dependability*.

Moreover, this reciprocal relationship between reliance and responsibility seems to obtain on adult levels as well as between children and parents, with the degree of reciprocity a partial function of the complexity of the culture. In simpler societies, a relatively small number of persons may assume primary responsibility for virtually all of the needs of the group in excess of its bare subsistence demands. Under civilized conditions, however, the specialization made necessary by technology and the pattern of urban living means that each adult is dependent on some other adult in some way and that, conversely, he is responsible in some fashion for the welfare of some other adult. The difference between the simpler and the more complex cultures,

however, is only one of degree. The crucial point is that, throughout human society, men are in one way or another dependent on each other both in the familiar situation of parents and children and in the course of adult living. This pattern of interdependency gives to human life a social character to be found nowhere else in the animal kingdom. Even among the remarkable social insects, the patterns of symbiosis found there seem to be a result of a genetically determined division of labor rather than the fulfillment of a potentiality for the mutual sharing of responsibilities for each other.

It is in this notion of the fulfillment of distinctively human potentialities that a fruitful conception of positive adjustment may have its roots. From the symbolic and peculiarly social character of human life, it may be possible to derive a set of potential attributes the cultivation of which results in something different from the mere absence of pathology and which forms a standard against which to assess the degree of integration in individual persons. To accept this task is to attempt the construction of a normative or ideal model of a normal, positively developed, or integratively adjusted human being.

A MODEL OF INTEGRATIVE ADJUSTMENT

In the first place, it would seem that, as the symbolic capacity that endows man with foresight develops in an individual, there is a concomitant increase in his ability to control his own behavior by anticipating its probable long-range consequences. The normal person is, first of all, one who has learned that in many situations his greatest satisfaction is gained by foregoing the immediate opportunities for comfort and pleasure in the interest of more remote rewards. He lives according to what Paul Elmer More, the Anglican theologian, calls "the law of costingness":

. . . the simple and tyrannical fact that, whether in the world physical, or in the world intellectual, or in the world spiritual, we can get nothing without paying an exacted price. The fool is he who ignores, and the villain is he who thinks he can outwit, the vigilance of the nemesis guarding this law of costingness . . . all [one's] progress is dependent on surrendering one interest or value for a higher interest or value (19, p. 158).

Mowrer and Ullman (21) have made the same point in arguing, from the results of an ingenious experiment, that normality results in large part

41

from the acquired ability to subject impulses to control through the symbolic cues one presents to oneself in the course of estimating the consequences of one's own behavior. Through symbolization, the future outcomes of one's actions are drawn into the psychological present; the strength of more remote rewards or punishments is consequently increased; and a long-range inhibitory or facilitating effect on incipient conduct is thereby exercised.

This increase in self-control means a lessened need for control by external authority, and conformity consequently becomes a relatively unimportant issue. The integratively adjusted person either conforms to the standards of his group because their acceptance leads to the most rewarding long-range consequences for him, or he rebels against authority, whether of persons or of law or custom, on *considered* grounds. This considered form of revolt implies two things. The first is an honest conviction that rules or the ruler are somehow unjust and that the implementation of his own values is likely to lead to a more broadly satisfying state of affairs. Such an attack on authority is very different from revolts that occur out of sheer needs for self-assertion or desires for power or as expressions of displaced hostility. The main dimension of difference is that of honesty as opposed to deception. The normal person is relatively well aware of his motives in either conforming or rebelling. The pathological rebel, on the other hand, tends to deceive himself and others about his goals. His reasons for nonconformity amount to rationalizations, and his justifications are typically projections. This kind of self-defeating and socially disruptive deceptiveness is seen daily in clinical practice.

The second characteristic of nonconformity in the normal person is that it is undertaken with an essential acceptance of the possible consequences. Having considered the risks beforehand, he is inclined neither to whine nor to ask that his rebellious conduct be overlooked if he runs afoul of trouble. In keeping with the "law of costingness," he is willing to pay the price for behaving in accordance with his own idiosyncratic values. "We have the right to lead our own lives," John Erskine (8) makes Helen of Troy say to her daughter Hermoine, "but that right implies another—to suffer the consequences. . . . Do your best, and if it's a mistake, hide nothing and be glad to suffer for it. That's morality." A psychological paraphrase of this bit of belletristic wisdom is not inappropriate:

The assumption of responsibility [2] for one's actions is one of the attributes of personal integration.

But if personal responsibility and self-control through foresight can be derived as aspects of integrative adjustment from man's symbolic capacity, a third characteristic of interpersonal responsibility can be deduced from his social nature. If interdependency is an essential part of human social life, then the normal person becomes one who can act dependably in relation to others and at the same time acknowledge his need for others. The roots of the former probably lie, as McClelland (17) has pointed out, in the role perceptions which developing children form of parent figures and other agents of the socialization process. By conceiving of such people as at least in some degree the nurturant guides of others and through identification with them, the integratively adjusted individual "wants to be" himself trustworthy and altruistic in the sense of being dependable and acting out of a genuine concern for the welfare of others as he can best conceive it. Altruism in this context, therefore, means nothing sentimental. It certainly includes the making and enforcement of disciplinary rules and the imposition of behavioral limits, but only if these steps are motivated by an interest in helping others and express concern and affection rather than mere personal annoyance or the power conferred by a superior status.

Similarly, the acknowledgment of one's needs for others implies a learned capacity for forming and maintaining intimate interpersonal relationships. Erikson (7) refers to this aspect of the normal personality as the attitude of "basic trust," and it is not far from what can be meaningfully styled in plain language as the ability to love. One suspects that the origins of this ability lies in the long experience during childhood of having need gratifications frequently associated with the presence of another person, typically a parent figure. By this

---

[2] This conception of responsibility is by no means anti-deterministic. As Fingarette (8) points out, one can *understand* his own or another's behavior, in the sense of accounting for it or rationally explaining it, by the retrospective process of examining the past. Responsibility, on the other hand, is neither retrospective in orientation nor explanatory in function. It is future oriented and refers to the *act* of proclaiming oneself as answerable for one's own conduct and its consequences. Thus, "responsibility," in this context, is not a logical term, implying causation, but a behavioral and attitudinal one, descriptive of a class of human actions.

association and the process of generalization, one comes to attach a positive affect to others. But as the youngster develops, he gradually learns that the need-mediating behavior of others is maintained only by his reciprocating, by his entering into a relationship of mutuality with others. If this kind of mutuality is not required of him, he is likely to perpetuate his dependency beyond the period his biological level of development and the complexity of his culture define as appropriate; whereas if he is required to demonstrate this mutuality too soon, he is likely to form the schema that interpersonal relationships are essentially matters of traded favors, and that, instead of basic trust, the proper attitude is one of getting as much as possible while giving no more than necessary. The pursuit in research and thought of such hypotheses as these might shed a good deal of light on the determinants of friendship, marital happiness, and effective parenthood, the relational expressions of effective personal integration.

But there is still another interpersonal attitude relevant to a positive conception of adjustment that is somewhat different from that bound up with relationships of an intimate and personal kind. There is a sense in which each individual, even if he regards himself as unfortunate and unhappy, owes his essential humanity to the group which enabled him to survive his helpless infancy. As studies of feral children (25) have shown, even the humanly distinctive and enormously adaptive trait of propositional speech does not become usable without the stimulation and nurture of other people. A kind of obligation is therefore created for the person to be an asset rather than a burden to society. It is partly to the discharging of this obligation that Adler (1) referred in developing his concept of social interest as a mark of normality. While the notion certainly implies the learning of local loyalties and personal affections, it also transcends the provincial limits of group and era. Because man's symbolic capacity enables him to benefit from the record of human history and to anticipate the future, and because his pattern of social interdependency, especially in civilized societies, reaches across the boundaries of political units and parochial affiliations, it seems reasonable to expect the positively developed person to behave in such a fashion as to contribute, according to his own particular lights, to the general welfare of humanity, to take

as his frame of reference mankind at large as best he understands it rather than his own group or clan.

Ideologies are at issue here, but there need be neither embarrassment nor a lack of room for debate regarding the specifics of policy and values in the hypothesis that democratic attitudes are closely bound up with personality integration. After all democracy in psychological terms implies only a concern about others, a valuing of persons above things, and a willingness to participate in mutually gratifying relationships with many categories of persons, including those of which one has only vicarious knowledge. Departures from democratic attitudes in this psychological sense mean a restriction on the potentiality for friendship and imply both a fear of others and a valuation of such things as power over people, thus endangering the interpersonal rewards that come from acting on the attitude of basic trust. Democratic social interest, then, means simply the most direct route to the fulfillment of a distinctively human capacity derived from man's symbolic character and the inevitability of his social life.

Finally, man's ability to assume an attitude toward the "merely possible" suggests that the normal person has ideals and standards that he tries to live up to even though they often exceed his grasp. For an integrative adjustment does not consist in the attainment of perfection but in a striving to act in accordance with the best principles of conduct that one can conceive. Operationally, this notion implies that there is an optimum discrepancy between one's self concept and one's ego ideal. Those for whom this discrepancy is too large (in favor, of course, of the ideal) are likely to condemn themselves to the frustration of never approximating their goals and to an almost perpetually low self-esteem. Those whose discrepancies are too low, on the other hand, are probably less than integratively adjusted either because they are failing to fulfill their human capacity to envision themselves as they could be or because they are self-deceptively over estimating themselves.

This model of integrative adjustment as characterized by self-control, personal responsibility, social responsibility, democratic social interest, and ideals must be regarded only in the most tentative fashion. Nevertheless, it does seem to take into account some realistic considerations. It avoids the impossible conception of the normal person as one who is always happy, free from conflict, and without problems. Rather, it suggests that he may often fall short of his ideals; and because of ignorance, the limitations under which an individual lives in a complex world, or the strength of immediate pressures, he may sometimes behave in ways that prove to be shortsighted or self-defeating. Consequently, he knows something of the experience of guilt at times, and because he tries to be fully aware of the risks he takes, he can hardly be entirely free from fear and worry. On the other hand, a person who is congruent to the model is likely to be one who enjoys a relatively consistent and high degree of self-respect and who elicits a predominantly positive and warm reaction from others. Moreover, it is such a person who seems to learn wisdom rather than hostile bitterness or pathologically frightened withdrawal from whatever disappointments or suffering may be his lot. Guilt, for example, becomes a challenge to his honesty, especially with himself but also with others; and it signalizes for him the desirability of modifying his behavior, of greater effort to live up to his ideals, rather than the need to defend himself by such mechanisms as rationalization or projection. Finally, the model permits a wide variation in the actual behaviors in which normal people may engage and even makes allowance for a wide range of disagreements among them. Integrative adjustment does not consist in the individual's fitting a preconceived behavioral mold. It may well consist in the degree to which his efforts fulfill the symbolic and social potentialities that are distinctively human.

REFERENCES

1. ADLER, A. Social interest: A challenge to mankind. London: Faber & Faber, 1938.
2. ADORNO, T. W., FRENKEL-BRUNSWIK, ELSE, LEVINSON, D. J., & SANFORD, R. N. The authoritarian personality. New York: Harper, 1950.
3. BENEDICT, RUTH. Anthropology and the abnormal. J. gen. Psychol., 1934, 10, 59–82.
4. CASSIRER, E. An essay on man. New Haven: Yale Univer. Press, 1944.
5. DARRAH, L. W. The difficulty of being normal. J. nerv. ment. Dis., 1939, 90, 730–739.
6. DuBOIS, CORA. The people of Alor. Minneapolis: Univer. Minnesota Press, 1944.
7. ERIKSON, E. H. Childhood and society. New York: Norton, 1950.
8. ERSKINE, J. The private life of Helen of Troy. New York: Bobbs-Merrill Co., 1925.
9. FINGARETTE, H. Psychoanalytic perspectives on moral guilt and responsibility: A re-evaluation. Phil. phenomenol. Res., 1955, 16, 18–36.
10. FORTUNE, R. F. Sorcerers of Dobu. London: Routledge, 1932.
11. FROMM, E. The sane society. New York: Rinehart, 1955.
12. GOLDSTEIN, K. Human nature in the light of psychopathology. Cambridge, Mass.: Harvard Univer. Press, 1940.
13. HACKER, F. H. The concept of normality and its practical significance. Amer. J. Orthopsychiat., 1945, 15, 47–64.
14. LANGER, SUSANNE K. Philosophy in a new key. Cambridge, Mass.: Harvard Univer. Press, 1942.
15. MARZOLF, S. S. The disease concept in psychology. Psychol. Rev., 1947, 54, 211–221.
16. MAY, R. Man's search for himself. New York: Norton, 1953.
17. McCLELLAND, D. Personality. New York: William Sloane Associates, 1951.
18. MEAD, MARGARET. Coming of age in Samoa. New York: William Morrow, 1928.
19. MORE, P. E. The Catholic faith. Princeton: Princeton Univer. Press, 1931.
20. MOWRER, O. H., & KLUCKHOHN, C. A dynamic theory of personality. In J. McV. Hunt (Ed.), Personality and the behavior disorders. New York: Ronald Press, 1944. Pp. 69–135.
21. MOWRER, O. H., & ULLMAN, A. D. Time as a determinant in integrative learning. Psychol. Rev., 1945, 52, 61–90.
22. PAVLOV, I. P. Conditioned reflexes. London: Oxford Univer. Press, 1927.
23. RIESE, W. The conception of disease. New York: Philosophical Library, 1953.
24. RIESMAN, D. The lonely crowd. New Haven: Yale Univer. Press, 1950.
25. SINGH, J. A. L., & ZINGG, R. M. Wolf-children and feral man. New York: Harper, 1942.
26. SUBCOMMITTEE ON EVALUATION OF MENTAL HEALTH ACTIVITIES. Evaluation in mental health. Bethesda, Md.: Public Health Service, 1955.
27. TIEGS, E. W., & KATZ, B. Mental hygiene in education. New York: Ronald Press, 1941.
28. WEGROCKI, H. J. A critique of cultural and statistical concepts of abnormality. J. abnorm. soc. Psychol., 1939, 34, 166–178.
29. YERKES, R. M. Chimpanzees: A laboratory colony. New Haven: Yale Univer. Press, 1943.

THEORIES OF PERSONALITY

The articles selected for this section reflect the editors' interests in personality theory from an historical point of view.

Beginning with Freud's psychobiological theory, its key concepts appear in "Instincts and Their Vicissitues". The overestimation of sexuality led Freud to derive all kinds of social and cultural behaviors from disturbances in sexual development. This overestimation was born of the Victorian age and could hardly flourish in the climate of our current anti-reductionist philosophies.

Rapaport, in "The Conceptual Model of Psychoanalysis", attempts to construct a truly psychodynamic science, one in which motivational energy and controls play a primary role. Evoking the concept of differentiation, Rapaport describes the emergence of distinct structures and a synthesis of these structures. Within the last thirty years, structure and dynamics of the personality have been the avenues of interest of the Freudian school. Rapaport's work represents a clear advance on the basic tenets of Freudian theory in that it considers intentionality as one of the most important functions of the ego and a conflict-free sphere within the ego.

Several theories have made a radical break with Freud's, diverging in respect to factors of libido theory, environmental influences, sexuality. Foremost among them is Sullivan's, which concentrates the whole power of its arguments on 'interpersonal relations'. Yet for Sullivan, the individual is virtually non-existent and psychic activity can only be viewed from the position of interpersonal communication. The self possesses a structure although this structure is constantly in flux with the environment.

The notion of self, so overlooked in Freudian theory, has been investigated by the British school as well as by Sullivan; and here it is represented by Fairbairn. In "Endopsychic Structure Considered in Terms of Object-Relationships", Fairbairn insists that psychoanalytic characterology cannot be based on libido theory. Rather, by integrating Sullivan's notions of the self with a 'depth' psychology, Fairbairn sees man in an inner world burdened with early trauma impinging on an outer world of the here and now.

Among the many searches for more adequate explanations of human behavior which try to overcome Freudian positivism is the existential approach. Maddi's paper, "The Existential Neurosis", points to a fundamental fact that man is fully capable of transcendence of both object and self. His views are opposed to those of the pragmatist and sensualist although there is some danger that highly complex problems may be oversimplified and reduced to 'philosophy'.

Finally, Portes, "On the Emergence of Behavior Therapy in Modern Society", calls a warning to the current American movement towards Behaviorism. Our action-oriented culture is particularly receptive to this doctrine but fails to note that it is impossible to apply it literally to complicated psychic activity. Reflective self-awareness, empathy, trust, in the end, must be the qualities at work in the effectiveness of treatment within all theories.

Sigmund Freud

INSTINCTS AND THEIR VICISSITUDES

We have often heard it maintained that sciences should be built up on clear and sharply defined basic concepts. In actual fact no science, not even the most exact, begins with such definitions. The true beginning of scientific activity consists rather in describing phenomena and then in proceeding to group, classify and correlate them. Even at the stage of description it is not possible to avoid applying certain abstract ideas to the material in hand, ideas derived from somewhere or other but certainly not from the new observations alone. Such ideas— which will later become the basic concepts of the science— are still more indispensable as the material is further worked over. They must at first necessarily possess some degree of indefiniteness; there can be no question of any clear delimitation of their content. So long as they remain in this condition, we come to an understanding about their meaning by making repeated references to the material of observation from which they appear to have been derived, but upon which, in fact, they have been imposed. Thus, strictly speaking, they are in the nature of conventions—although everything depends on their not being arbitrarily chosen but determined by their having significant relations to the empirical material, relations that we seem to sense before we can clearly recognize and demonstrate them. It is only after more thorough investigation of the field of observation that we are able to formulate its basic scientific concepts with increased precision, and progressively so to modify them that they become serviceable and consistent over a wide area. Then, indeed, the time may have come to confine them in definitions. The advance of knowledge, however, does not tolerate any rigidity even in definitions. Physics furnishes an excellent illustration of the way in which even 'basic concepts' that have been established in the form of definitions are constantly being altered in their content.[1]

A conventional basic concept of this kind, which at the

[1] [A similar line of thought had been developed in the paper on narcissism (1914c, p. 77 above).]

INSTINCTS AND THEIR VICISSITUDES, Hogarth Press, 1957, 14, pp. 117-140.

moment is still somewhat obscure but which is indispensable to us in psychology, is that of an 'instinct'.[1] Let us try to give a content to it by approaching it from different angles.

First, from the angle of *physiology*. This has given us the concept of a 'stimulus' and the pattern of the reflex arc, according to which a stimulus applied to living tissue (nervous substance) *from* the outside is discharged by action *to* the outside. This action is expedient in so far as it withdraws the stimulated substance from the influence of the stimulus, removes it out of its range of operation.

What is the relation of 'instinct' to 'stimulus'? There is nothing to prevent our subsuming the concept of 'instinct' under that of 'stimulus' and saying that an instinct is a stimulus applied to the mind. But we are immediately set on our guard against *equating* instinct and mental stimulus. There are obviously other stimuli to the mind besides those of an instinctual kind, stimuli which behave far more like physiological ones. For example, when a strong light falls on the eye, it is not an instinctual stimulus; it *is* one, however, when a dryness of the mucous membrane of the pharynx or an irritation of the mucous membrane of the stomach makes itself felt.[2]

We have now obtained the material necessary for distinguishing between instinctual stimuli and other (physiological) stimuli that operate on the mind. In the first place, an instinctual stimulus does not arise from the external world but from within the organism itself. For this reason it operates differently upon the mind and different actions are necessary in order to remove it. Further, all that is essential in a stimulus is covered if we assume that it operates with a single impact, so that it can be disposed of by a single expedient action. A typical instance of this is motor flight from the source of stimulation. These impacts may, of course, be repeated and summated, but that makes no difference to our notion of the process and to the conditions for the removal of the stimulus. An instinct, on the other hand, never operates as a force giving a *momentary* impact but always as a *constant* one. Moreover, since it impinges not from without but from within the organism, no flight can avail against it. A better term for an instinctual stimulus is a

---

[1] ['*Trieb*' in the original. See Editor's Note, p. 111.]

[2] Assuming, of course, that these internal processes are the organic basis of the respective needs of thirst and hunger.

48

'need'. What does away with a need is 'satisfaction'. This can be attained only by an appropriate ('adequate') alteration of the internal source of stimulation.

Let us imagine ourselves in the situation of an almost entirely helpless living organism, as yet unorientated in the world, which is receiving stimuli in its nervous substance.[1] This organism will very soon be in a position to make a first distinction and a first orientation. On the one hand, it will be aware of stimuli which can be avoided by muscular action (flight); these it ascribes to an external world. On the other hand, it will also be aware of stimuli against which such action is of no avail and whose character of constant pressure persists in spite of it; these stimuli are the signs of an internal world, the evidence of instinctual needs. The perceptual substance of the living organism will thus have found in the efficacy of its muscular activity a basis for distinguishing between an 'outside' and an 'inside'.[2]

We thus arrive at the essential nature of instincts in the first place by considering their main characteristics—their origin in sources of stimulation within the organism and their appearance as a constant force—and from this we deduce one of their further features, namely, that no actions of flight avail against them. In the course of this discussion, however, we cannot fail to be struck by something that obliges us to make a further admission. In order to guide us in dealing with the field of psychological phenomena, we do not merely apply certain conventions to our empirical material as basic *concepts*; we also

---

[1] [The hypothesis which follows concerning the behaviour of a primitive living organism, and the postulation of a fundamental 'principle of constancy', had been stated in similar terms in some of the very earliest of Freud's psychological works. See, for instance, Chapter VII, Sections C and E, of *The Interpretation of Dreams* (1900a), *Standard Ed.*, 5, 565 ff. and 598 ff. But it had been expressed still earlier in *neurological* terms in his posthumously published 'Project' of 1895 (1950a, Part I, Section 1), as well as, more briefly, in his lecture on the Breuer and Freud 'Preliminary Communication' (1893h) and in the penultimate paragraph of his French paper on hysterical paralyses (1893c). Freud returned to the hypothesis once more, in Chapters I and IV of *Beyond the Pleasure Principle* (1920g), *Standard Ed.*, 18, 1 ff. and 26 ff.; and reconsidered it in 'The Economic Problem of Masochism' (1924c). Cf. footnote, p. 121 below.]

[2] [See further below, p. 134 ff. Freud dealt with the subject later in his paper on 'Negation' (1925h) and in Chapter I of *Civilization and its Discontents* (1930a).]

make use of a number of complicated *postulates*. We have already alluded to the most important of these, and all we need now do is to state it expressly. This postulate is of a biological nature, and makes use of the concept of 'purpose' (or perhaps of expediency) and runs as follows: the nervous system is an apparatus which has the function of getting rid of the stimuli that reach it, or of reducing them to the lowest possible level; or which, if it were feasible, would maintain itself in an altogether unstimulated condition.[1] Let us for the present not take exception to the indefiniteness of this idea and let us assign to the nervous system the task—speaking in general terms—of *mastering stimuli*. We then see how greatly the simple pattern of the physiological reflex is complicated by the introduction of instincts. External stimuli impose only the single task of withdrawing from them; this is accomplished by muscular movements, one of which eventually achieves that aim and thereafter, being the expedient movement, becomes a hereditary disposition. Instinctual stimuli, which originate from within the organism, cannot be dealt with by this mechanism. Thus they make far higher demands on the nervous system and cause it to undertake involved and interconnected activities by which the external world is so changed as to afford satisfaction to the internal source of stimulation. Above all, they oblige the nervous system to renounce its ideal intention of keeping off stimuli, for they maintain an incessant and unavoidable afflux of stimulation. We may therefore well conclude that instincts and not external stimuli are the true motive forces behind the advances that have led the nervous system, with its unlimited capacities, to its present high level of development. There is naturally nothing to prevent our supposing that the instincts themselves are, at least in part, precipitates of the effects of external stimulation, which in the course of phylogenesis have brought about modifications in the living substance.

When we further find that the activity of even the most highly developed mental apparatus is subject to the pleasure principle, i.e. is automatically regulated by feelings belonging. to the pleasure-unpleasure series, we can hardly reject the further hypothesis that these feelings reflect the manner in which the process of mastering stimuli takes place—certainly in the sense that unpleasurable feelings are connected with an increase

[1] [This is the 'principle of constancy'. See footnote 1 above, p. 119].

50

and pleasurable feelings with a decrease of stimulus. We will, however, carefully preserve this assumption in its present highly indefinite form, until we succeed, if that is possible, in discovering what sort of relation exists between pleasure and unpleasure, on the one hand, and' fluctuations in the amounts of stimulus affecting mental life, on the other. It is certain that many very various relations of this kind, and not very simple ones, are possible.[1]

If now we apply ourselves to considering mental life from a *biological* point of view, an 'instinct' appears to us as a concept

[1] [It will be seen that two principles are here involved. One of these is the 'principle of constancy' (see above, p. 120, and footnote 1, p. 119). It is stated again in *Beyond the Pleasure Principle*, 1920g, Chapter I (*Standard Ed.*, 18, 9), as follows: 'The mental apparatus endeavours to keep the quantity of excitation present in it as low as possible or at least to keep it constant.' For this principle Freud, in the same work (ibid., 56), adopted the term 'Nirvana principle'. The second principle involved is the 'pleasure principle', stated at the beginning of the paragraph to which this note is appended. It, too, is restated in *Beyond the Pleasure Principle* (ibid., 7): 'The course taken by mental events is automatically regulated by the pleasure principle. . . . [That course] takes a direction such that its final outcome coincides with . . . an avoidance of unpleasure or a production of pleasure.' Freud seems to have assumed to begin with that these two principles were closely correlated and even identical. Thus, in his 'Project' of 1895 (Freud, 1950a, Part I, Section 8) he writes: 'Since we have certain knowledge of a trend in psychical life towards avoiding unpleasure, we are tempted to identify that trend with the primary trend towards inertia [i.e. towards avoiding excitation].' A similar view is taken in Chapter VII (E) of *The Interpretation of Dreams* (1900a), *Standard Ed.*, 5, 598. In the passage in the text above, however, a doubt appears to be expressed as to the completeness of the correlation between the two principles. This doubt is carried farther in *Beyond the Pleasure Principle* (*Standard Ed.*, 18, 8 and 63) and is discussed at some length in 'The Economic Problem of Masochism' (1924c). Freud there argues that the two principles cannot be identical, since there are unquestionably states of increasing tension which are pleasurable (e.g. sexual excitement), and he goes on to suggest (what had already been hinted at in the two passages in *Beyond the Pleasure Principle* just referred to) that the pleasurable or unpleasurable quality of a state may be related to a *temporal* characteristic (or rhythm) of the changes in the quantity of excitation present. He concludes that in any case the two principles must not be regarded as identical: the pleasure principle is a *modification* of the Nirvana principle. The Nirvana principle, he maintains, is to be attributed to the 'death instinct', and its modification into the pleasure principle is due to the influence of the 'life instinct' or libido.]

on the frontier between the mental and the somatic, as the psychical representative of the stimuli originating from within the organism and reaching the mind, as a measure of the demand made upon the mind for work in consequence of its connection with the body.[1]

We are now in a position to discuss certain terms which are used in reference to the concept of an instinct—for example, its 'pressure', its 'aim', its 'object' and its 'source'.

By the pressure [*Drang*] of an instinct we understand its motor factor, the amount of force or the measure of the demand for work which it represents. The characteristic of exercising pressure is common to all instincts; it is in fact their very essence. Every instinct is a piece of activity; if we speak loosely of passive instincts, we can only mean instincts whose *aim* is passive.[2]

The aim [*Ziel*] of an instinct is in every instance satisfaction, which can only be obtained by removing the state of stimulation at the source of the instinct. But although the ultimate aim of each instinct remains unchangeable, there may yet be different paths leading to the same ultimate aim; so that an instinct may be found to have various nearer or intermediate aims, which are combined or interchanged with one another. Experience permits us also to speak of instincts which are 'inhibited in their aim', in the case of processes which are allowed to make some advance towards instinctual satisfaction but are then inhibited or deflected. We may suppose that even processes of this kind involve a partial satisfaction.

The object [*Objekt*] of an instinct is the thing in regard to which or through which the instinct is able to achieve its aim. It is what is most variable about an instinct and is not originally connected with it, but becomes assigned to it only in consequence of being peculiarly fitted to make satisfaction possible. The object is not necessarily something extraneous: it may equally well be a part of the subject's own body. It may be

[1] [See the discussion in the Editor's Note, pp. 111–13.]

[2] [Some remarks on the active nature of instincts will be found in a footnote added in 1915 to Section 4 of the third of Freud's *Three Essays* (1905*d*), *Standard Ed.*, 7, 219.—A criticism of Adler for misunderstanding this 'pressing' characteristic of instincts appears at the end of the second Section of Part III of the 'Little Hans' analysis (1909*b*), *Standard Ed.*, 10, 140–1.]

changed any number of times in the course of the vicissitudes which the instinct undergoes during its existence; and highly important parts are played by this displacement of instinct. It may happen that the same object serves for the satisfaction of several instincts simultaneously, a phenomenon which Adler [1908] has called a 'confluence' of instincts [*Triebverschränkung*].[1] A particularly close attachment of the instinct to its object is distinguished by the term 'fixation'. This frequently occurs at very early periods of the development of an instinct and puts an end to its mobility through its intense opposition to detachment.[2]

By the source [*Quelle*] of an instinct is meant the somatic process which occurs in an organ or part of the body and whose stimulus is represented in mental life by an instinct. We do not know whether this process is invariably of a chemical nature or whether it may also correspond to the release of other, e.g. mechanical, forces. The study of the sources of instincts lies outside the scope of psychology. Although instincts are wholly determined by their origin in a somatic source, in mental life we know them only by their aims. An exact knowledge of the sources of an instinct is not invariably necessary for purposes of psychological investigation; sometimes its source may be inferred from its aim.

Are we to suppose that the different instincts which originate in the body and operate on the mind are also distinguished by different *qualities*, and that that is why they behave in qualitatively different ways in mental life? This supposition does not seem to be justified; we are much more likely to find the simpler assumption sufficient—that the instincts are all qualitatively alike and owe the effect they make only to the amount of excitation they carry, or perhaps, in addition, to certain functions of that quantity. What distinguishes from one another the mental effects produced by the various instincts may be traced to the difference in their sources. In any event, it is only in a later connection that we shall be able to make plain what the problem of the quality of instincts signifies.[3]

What instincts should we suppose there are, and how many?

[1] [Two instances of this are given by Freud in the analysis of 'Little Hans' (1909*b*), *Standard Ed.*, 10, 106 and 127.]
[2] [Cf. below, p. 148.]
[3] [It is not clear what 'later connection' Freud had in mind.]

There is obviously a wide opportunity here for arbitrary choice. No objection can be made to anyone's employing the concept of an instinct of play or of destruction or of gregariousness, when the subject-matter demands it and the limitations of psychological analysis allow of it. Nevertheless, we should not neglect to ask ourselves whether instinctual motives like these, which are so highly specialized on the one hand, do not admit of further dissection in accordance with the *sources* of the instinct, so that only primal instincts—those which cannot be further dissected—can lay claim to importance.

I have proposed that two groups of such primal instincts should be distinguished: the *ego*, or *self-preservative*, instincts and the. *sexual* instincts. But this supposition has not the status of a necessary postulate, as has, for instance, our assumption about the biological purpose of the mental apparatus (p. 120); it is merely a working hypothesis, to be retained only so long as it proves useful, and it will make little difference to the results of our work of description and classification if it is replaced by another. The occasion for this hypothesis arose in the course of the evolution of psycho-analysis, which was first employed upon the psychoneuroses, or, more precisely, upon the group described as 'transference neuroses' (hysteria and obsessional neurosis); these showed that at the root of all such affections there is to be found a conflict between the claims of sexuality and those of the ego. It is always possible that an exhaustive study of the other neurotic affections (especially of the narcissistic psychoneuroses, the schizophrenias) may oblige us to alter this formula and to make a different classification of the primal instincts. But for the present we do not know of any such formula, nor have we met with any argument unfavourable to drawing this contrast between sexual and ego-instincts.[1]

I am altogether doubtful whether any decisive pointers for the differentiation and classification of the instincts can be arrived at on the basis of working over the psychological material. This working-over seems rather itself to call for the application to the material of definite assumptions concerning instinctual life, and it would be a desirable thing if those assumptions could be taken from some other branch of knowledge and carried over to psychology. The contribution which biology has to

[1] [See the Editor's Note, p. 115.]

make here certainly does not run counter to the distinction between sexual and ego-instincts. Biology teaches that sexuality is not to be put on a par with other functions of the individual; for its purposes go beyond the individual and have as their content the production of new individuals—that is, the preservation of the species. It shows, further, that two views, seemingly equally well-founded, may be taken of the relation between the ego and sexuality. On the one view, the individual is the principal thing, sexuality is one of its activities and sexual satisfaction one of its needs; while on the other view the individual is a temporary and transient appendage to the quasi-immortal germ-plasm, which is entrusted to him by the process of generation.[1] The hypothesis that the sexual function differs from other bodily processes in virtue of a special chemistry is, I understand, also a postulate of the Ehrlich school of biological research.[2]

Since a study of instinctual life from the direction of consciousness presents almost insuperable difficulties, the principal source of our knowledge remains the psycho-analytic investigation of mental disturbances. Psycho-analysis, however, in consequence of the course taken by its development, has hitherto been able to give us information of a fairly satisfactory nature only about the *sexual* instincts; for it is precisely that group which alone can be observed in isolation, as it were, in the psychoneuroses. With the extension of psycho-analysis to the other neurotic affections, we shall no doubt find a basis for our knowledge of the ego-instincts as well, though it would be rash to expect equally favourable conditions for observation in this further field of research.

This much can be said by way of a general characterization of the sexual instincts. They are numerous, emanate from a great variety of organic sources, act in the first instance independently of one another and only achieve a more or less complete synthesis at a late stage. The aim which each of them

[1] [See footnote, p. 78 above. The same point is made near the beginning of Lecture XXVI of the *Introductory Lectures* (1916–17).]

[2] [This hypothesis had already been announced by Freud in the first edition of his *Three Essays* (1905*d*), *Standard Ed.*, 7, 216 *n*. But he had held it for at least ten years previously. See, for instance, Draft I in the Fliess correspondence (1950*a*), probably written in 1895.]

strives for is the attainment of 'organ-pleasure'; [1] only when synthesis is achieved do they enter the service of the reproductive function and thereupon become generally recognizable as sexual instincts. At their first appearance they are attached to the instincts of self-preservation, from which they only gradually become separated; in their choice of object, too, they follow the paths that are indicated to them by the ego-instincts. [2] A portion of them remains associated with the ego-instincts throughout life and furnishes them with libidinal components, which in normal functioning easily escape notice and are revealed clearly only by the onset of illness. [3] They are distinguished by possessing the capacity to act vicariously for one another to a wide extent and by being able to change their objects readily. In consequence of the latter properties they are capable of functions which are far removed from their original purposive actions—capable, that is, of 'sublimation'.

Our inquiry into the various vicissitudes which instincts undergo in the process of development and in the course of life must be confined to the sexual instincts, which are the more familiar to us. Observation shows us that an instinct may undergo the following vicissitudes:—

Reversal into its opposite.
Turning round upon the subject's own self.
Repression.
Sublimation.

Since I do not intend to treat of sublimation here[4] and since repression requires a special chapter to itself [cf. next paper, p. 146], it only remains for us to describe and discuss the two first points. Bearing in mind that there are motive forces which

[1] ['Organ-pleasure' (i.e. pleasure attached to one particular bodily organ) seems to be used here for the first time by Freud. The term is discussed at greater length in the early part of Lecture XXI of the *Introductory Lectures* (1916–17). The underlying idea, of course, goes back much earlier. See, for instance, the opening passage of the third of the *Three Essays* (1905*d*), *Standard Ed.*, **7**, 207.]
[2] [Cf. 'On Narcissism', p. 87 above.]
[3] [Ibid., p. 82 f. above.]
[4] [Sublimation had already been touched upon in the paper on narcissism (pp. 94–5); but it seems possible that it formed the subject of one of the lost metapsychological papers. (See Editor's Introduction, p. 106.)]

work against an instinct's being carried through in an unmodified form, we may also regard these vicissitudes as modes of *defence* against the instincts.

Reversal of an instinct into its opposite resolves on closer examination into two different processes: a change from activity to passivity, and a reversal of its content. The two processes, being different in their nature, must be treated separately.

Examples of the first process are met with in the two pairs of opposites: sadism—masochism and scopophilia—exhibitionism. The reversal affects only the *aims* of the instincts. The active aim (to torture, to look at) is replaced by the passive aim (to be tortured, to be looked at). Reversal of *content* is found in the single instance of the transformation of love into hate.

The turning round of an instinct upon the subject's own self is made plausible by the reflection that masochism is actually sadism turned round upon the subject's own ego, and that exhibitionism includes looking at his own body. Analytic observation, indeed, leaves us in no doubt that the masochist shares in the enjoyment of the assault upon himself, and that the exhibitionist shares in the enjoyment of [the sight of] his exposure. The essence of the process is thus the change of the *object*, while the aim remains unchanged. We cannot fail to notice, however, that in these examples the turning round upon the subject's self and the transformation from activity to passivity converge or coincide.

To elucidate the situation, a more thorough investigation is essential.

In the case of the pair of opposites sadism—masochism, the process may be represented as follows:

(*a*) Sadism consists in the exercise of violence or power upon some other person as object.

(*b*) This object is given up and replaced by the subject's self. With the turning round upon the self the change from an active to a passive instinctual aim is also effected.

(*c*) An extraneous person is once more sought as object; this person, in consequence of the alteration which has taken place in the instinctual aim, has to take over the role of the subject.[1]

---

[1] [Though the general sense of these passages is clear, there may be some confusion in the use of the word 'subject'. As a rule 'subject' and 'object' are used respectively for the person in whom an instinct (or other

Case (c) is what is commonly termed masochism. Here, too, satisfaction follows along the path of the original sadism, the passive ego placing itself back in phantasy in its first role, which has now in fact been taken over by the extraneous subject.[1] Whether there is, besides this, a more direct masochistic satisfaction is highly doubtful. A primary masochism, not derived from sadism in the manner I have described, seems not to be met with.[2] That it is not superfluous to assume the existence of stage (b) is to be seen from the behaviour of the sadistic instinct in obsessional neurosis. There there is a turning round upon the subject's self *without* an attitude of passivity towards another person: the change has only got as far as stage (b). The desire to torture has turned into self-torture and self-punishment, not into masochism. The active voice is changed, not into the passive, but into the reflexive, middle voice.[3]

Our view of sadism is further prejudiced by the circumstance that this instinct, side by side with its general aim (or perhaps, rather, within it), seems to strive towards the accomplishment of a quite special aim—not only to humiliate and master, but, in addition, to inflict pains. Psycho-analysis would appear to show that the infliction of pain plays no part among the original purposive actions of the instinct. A sadistic child takes no account of whether or not he inflicts pains, nor does he intend to do so. But when once the transformation into masochism has taken place, the pains are very well fitted to provide a passive masochistic aim; for we have every reason to believe that sensations of pain, like other unpleasurable sensations, trench upon sexual excitation and produce a pleasurable condition, for the sake of which the subject will even willingly experience the unpleasure of pain.[4] When once feeling pains has become a masochistic aim, the sadistic aim of *causing* pains can arise also,

state of mind) originates, and the person or thing to which it is directed. Here, however, 'subject' seems to be used for the person who plays the active part in the relationship—the agent. The word is more obviously used in this sense in the parallel passage on p. 129 and elsewhere below.]

[1] [See last footnote.]

[2] (*Footnote added* 1924:) In later works (cf. 'The Economic Problem of Masochism', 1924c) relating to problems of instinctual life I have expressed an opposite view.

[3] [The allusion here is to the voices of the Greek verb.]

[4] [See a passage near the end of the second of the *Three Essays* (1905d), *Standard Ed.*, 7, 203–4.]

retrogressively; for while these pains are being inflicted on other people, they are enjoyed masochistically by the subject through his identification of himself with the suffering object. In both cases, of course, it is not the pain itself which is enjoyed, but the accompanying sexual excitation—so that this can be done especially conveniently from the sadistic position. The enjoyment of pain would thus be an aim which was originally masochistic, but which can only become an instinctual aim in someone who was originally sadistic.

For the sake of completeness I may add that feelings of pity cannot be described as a result of a transformation of instinct occurring in sadism, but necessitate the notion of a *reaction-formation* against that instinct. (For the difference, see later.)[1]

Rather different and simpler findings are afforded by the investigation of another pair of opposites—the instincts whose respective aim is to look and to display oneself (scopophilia and exhibitionism, in the language of the perversions). Here again we may postulate the same stages as in the previous instance:—(a) Looking as an *activity* directed towards an extraneous object. (b) Giving up of the object and turning of the scopophilic instinct towards a part of the subject's own body; with this, transformation to passivity and setting up of a new aim—that of being looked at. (c) Introduction of a new subject[2] to whom one displays oneself in order to be looked at by him. Here, too, it can hardly be doubted that the active aim appears before the passive, that looking precedes being looked at. But there is an important divergence from what happens in the case of sadism, in that we can recognize in the case of the

[1] [It is not clear to what passage this is intended to refer, unless, again, it was included in a missing paper on sublimation. There is in fact some discussion of the subject in 'Thoughts for the Times on War and Death' (1915b), p. 281 below. But this cannot have been what Freud had in mind, for it was originally published in a different volume. In a footnote added in 1915 (the year in which the present paper was written) to the *Three Essays* (1905d), Freud insists that sublimation and reaction-formation are to be regarded as distinct processes (*Standard Ed.*, 7, 178 n.).—The German word for 'pity' is '*Mitleid*', literally 'suffering with', 'compassion'. Another view of the origin of the feeling is expressed in the 'Wolf Man' analysis (1918b), *Standard Ed.*, 17, 88, which was actually written, in all probability, at the end of 1914, a few months earlier than the present paper.]

[2] [I.e. agent; see footnote on pp. 127-8.]

scopophilic instinct a yet earlier stage than that described as (a). For the beginning of its activity the scopophilic instinct is auto-erotic: it has indeed an object, but that object is part of the subject's own body. It is only later that the instinct is led, by a process of comparison, to exchange this object for an analogous part of someone else's body—stage (a). This preliminary stage is interesting because it is the source of *both* the situations represented in the resulting pair of opposites, the one or the other according to which element in the original situation is changed. The following might serve as a diagrammatic picture of the scopophilic instinct:—

(a) Oneself looking at a sexual organ = A sexual organ being looked at by oneself

(β) Oneself looking at an extraneous object (active scopophilia)

(γ) An object which is oneself or part of oneself being looked at by an extraneous person (exhibitionism)

A preliminary stage of this kind is absent in sadism, which from the outset is directed upon an extraneous object, although it might not be altogether unreasonable to construct such a stage out of the child's efforts to gain control over his own limbs.[1]

With regard to both the instincts which we have just taken as examples, it should be remarked that their transformation by a reversal from activity to passivity and by a turning round upon the subject never in fact involves the whole quota of the instinctual impulse. The earlier active direction of the instinct persists to some degree side by side with its later passive direction, even when the process of its transformation has been very extensive. The only correct statement to make about the scopophilic instinct would be that all the stages of its development, its auto-erotic, preliminary stage as well as its final active or passive form, co-exist alongside one another; and the truth of this becomes obvious if we base our opinion, not on the actions to which the instinct leads, but on the mechanism of its satisfaction. Perhaps, however, it is permissible to look at the matter

[1] (*Footnote added* 1924:) Cf. footnote 2, p. 128.

and represent it in yet another way. We can divide the life of each instinct into a series of separate successive waves, each of which is homogeneous during whatever period of time it may last, and whose relation to one another is comparable to that of successive eruptions of lava. We can then perhaps picture the first, original eruption of the instinct as proceeding in an unchanged form and undergoing no development at all. The next wave would be modified from the outset—being turned, for instance, from active to passive—and would then, with this new characteristic, be added to the earlier wave, and so on. If we were then to take a survey of the instinctual impulse from its beginning up to a given point, the succession of waves which we have described would inevitably present the picture of a definite development of the instinct.

The fact that, at this[1] later period of development of an instinctual impulse, its (passive) opposite may be observed alongside of it deserves to be marked by the very apt term introduced by Bleuler—'ambivalence'.[2]

This reference to the developmental history of instincts and the permanence of their intermediate stages should make the development of instincts fairly intelligible to us. Experience shows that the amount of demonstrable ambivalence varies greatly between individuals, groups and races. Marked instinctual ambivalence in a human being living at the present day may be regarded as an archaic inheritance, for we have reason to suppose that the part played in instinctual life by the active impulses in their unmodified form was greater in primaeval times than it is on an average to-day.[3]

We have become accustomed to call the early phase of the

---

[1] ['*Jener*'. In the first edition only, '*jeder*', 'every'.]

[2] [The term 'ambivalence', coined by Bleuler (1910*b*, and 1911, 43 and 305), seems not to have been used by him in this sense. He distinguished three kinds of ambivalence: (1) emotional, i.e. oscillation between love and hate, (2) voluntary, i.e. inability to decide on an action, and (3) intellectual, i.e. belief in contradictory propositions. Freud generally uses the term in the first of these senses. See, for instance, the first occasion on which he seems to have adopted it, near the end of his paper on 'The Dynamics of Transference' (1912*b*), and later in the present paper (pp. 133 and 139). The passage in the text is one of the few in which he has applied the term to activity and passivity. For another instance of this exceptional use see a passage in Section III of the 'Wolf Man' case history (1918*b*), *Standard Ed.*, 17, 26.]

[3] [See *Totem and Taboo* (1912–13), *Standard Ed.*, 13, 66.]

61

development of the ego, during which its sexual instincts find auto-erotic satisfaction, 'narcissism', without at once entering on any discussion of the relation between auto-erotism and narcissism. It follows that the preliminary stage of the scopophilic instinct, in which the subject's own body is the object of the scopophilia, must be classed under narcissism, and that we must describe it as a narcissistic formation. The active scopophilic instinct develops from this, by leaving narcissism behind. The passive scopophilic instinct, on the contrary, holds fast to the narcissistic object. Similarly, the transformation of sadism into masochism implies a return to the narcissistic object. And in both these cases [i.e. in passive scopophilia and masochism] the narcissistic *subject* is, through identification, replaced by another, extraneous ego. If we take into account our constructed preliminary narcissistic stage of sadism, we shall be approaching a more general realization—namely, that the instinctual vicissitudes which consist in the instinct's being turned round upon the subject's own ego and undergoing reversal from activity to passivity are dependent on the narcissistic organization of the ego and bear the stamp of that phase. They perhaps correspond to the attempts at defence which at higher stages of the development of the ego are effected by other means. [See above, pp. 126-7.]

At this point we may call to mind that so far we have considered only two pairs of opposite instincts: sadism—masochism and scopophilia—exhibitionism. These are the best-known sexual instincts that appear in an ambivalent manner. The other components of the later sexual function are not yet sufficiently accessible to analysis for us to be able to discuss them in a similar way. In general we can assert of them that their activities are *auto-erotic*; that is to say, their object is negligible in comparison with the organ which is their source, and as a rule coincides with that organ. The object of the scopophilic instinct, however, though it too is in the first instance a part of the subject's own body, is not the eye itself; and in sadism the organic source, which is probably the muscular apparatus with its capacity for action, points unequivocally at an object other than itself, even though that object is part of the subject's own body. In the auto-erotic instincts, the part played by the organic source is so decisive that, according to a plausible suggestion of Federn (1913) and Jekels (1913), the form and function of the organ determine the activity or passivity of the instinctual aim.

The change of the *content* [cf. p. 127] of an instinct into its opposite is observed in a single instance only—the transformation of *love into hate*.[1] Since it is particularly common to find both these directed simultaneously towards the same object, their co-existence furnishes the most important example of ambivalence of feeling. [See p. 131 *n*. 2.]

The case of love and hate acquires a special interest from the circumstance that it refuses to be fitted into our scheme of the instincts. It is impossible to doubt that there is the most intimate relation between these two opposite feelings and sexual life, but we are naturally unwilling to think of love as being some kind of special component instinct of sexuality in the same way as the others we have been discussing. We should prefer to regard loving as the expression of the *whole* sexual current of feeling; but this idea does not clear up our difficulties, and we cannot see what meaning to attach to an opposite content of this current.

Loving admits not merely of one, but of three opposites. In addition to the antithesis 'loving—hating', there is the other one of 'loving—being loved'; and, in addition to these, loving and hating taken together are the opposite of the condition of unconcern or indifference. The second of these three antitheses, loving—being loved, corresponds exactly to the transformation from activity to passivity and may be traced to an underlying situation in the same way as in the case of the scopophilic instinct. This situation is that of *loving oneself*, which we regard as the characteristic feature of narcissism. Then, according as the object or the subject is replaced by an extraneous one, what results is the active aim of loving or the passive one of being loved—the latter remaining near to narcissism.

Perhaps we shall come to a better understanding of the several opposites of loving if we reflect that our mental life as a whole is governed by *three polarities*, the antitheses

Subject (ego)—Object (external world),
Pleasure—Unpleasure, and
Active—Passive.

[1] [In the German editions previous to 1924 this reads 'the transformation of *love and hate*'.]

63

The antithesis ego—non-ego (external), i.e. subject—object, is, as we have already said [p. 119], thrust upon the individual organism at an early stage, by the experience that it can silence *external* stimuli by means of muscular action but is defenceless against *instinctual* stimuli. This antithesis remains, above all, sovereign in our intellectual activity and creates for research the basic situation which no efforts can alter. The polarity of pleasure—unpleasure is attached to a scale of feelings, whose paramount importance in determining our actions (our will) has already been emphasized [pp. 120–1]. The antithesis active—passive must not be confused with the antithesis ego-subject—external world-object. The relation of the ego to the external world is passive in so far as it receives stimuli from it and active when it reacts to these. It is forced by its instincts into a quite special degree of activity towards the external world, so that we might bring out the essential point if we say that the ego-subject is passive in respect of external stimuli but active through its own instincts. The antithesis active—passive coalesces later with the antithesis masculine—feminine, which, until this has taken place, has no psychological meaning. The coupling of activity with masculinity and of passivity with femininity meets us, indeed, as a biological fact; but it is by no means so invariably complete and exclusive as we are inclined to assume.[1]

The three polarities of the mind are connected with one another in various highly significant ways. There is a primal psychical situation in which two of them coincide. Originally, at the very beginning of mental life, the ego is cathected with instincts and is to some extent capable of satisfying them on itself. We call this condition 'narcissism' and this way of obtaining satisfaction 'auto-erotic'.[2] At this time the external world

[1] [This question is discussed at much greater length in a footnote added in 1915 (the year in which the present paper was written) to the third of Freud's *Three Essays* (1905d), *Standard Ed.*, 7, 219 f.—See also p. 55 above.]

[2] Some of the sexual instincts are, as we know, capable of this auto-erotic satisfaction, and so are adapted to being the vehicle for the development under the dominance of the pleasure principle [from the original 'reality-ego' into the 'pleasure-ego'] which we are about to describe [in the next paragraphs of the text]. Those sexual instincts which from the outset require an object, and the needs of the ego-instincts, which are never capable of auto-erotic satisfaction, naturally

64

is not cathected with interest (in a general sense) and is indifferent for purposes of satisfaction. During this period, therefore, the ego-subject coincides with what is pleasurable and the external world with what is indifferent (or possibly unpleasurable, as being a source of stimulation). If for the moment we define loving as the relation of the ego to its sources of pleasure, the situation in which the ego loves itself only and is indifferent to the external world illustrates the first of the opposites which we found to 'loving'.[1]

In so far as the ego is auto-erotic, it has no need of the external world, but, in consequence of experiences undergone by the instincts of self-preservation, it acquires objects from that world, and, in spite of everything, it cannot avoid feeling internal instinctual stimuli for a time as unpleasurable. Under the

disturb this state [of primal narcissism] and so pave the way for an advance from it. Indeed, the primal narcissistic state would not be able to follow the development [that is to be described] if it were not for the fact that every individual passes through a period during which he is helpless and has to be looked after and during which his pressing needs are satisfied by an external agency and are thus prevented from becoming greater.—[This very condensed footnote might have been easier to understand if it had been placed two or three paragraphs further on. It may perhaps be expanded as follows. In his paper on the 'Two Principles of Mental Functioning' (1911b) Freud had introduced the idea of the transformation of an early 'pleasure-ego' into a 'reality-ego'. In the passage which follows in the text above, he argues that there is in fact a still earlier *original* 'reality-ego'. This original 'reality-ego', instead of proceeding directly into the *final* 'reality-ego', is replaced, under the dominating influence of the pleasure principle, by a 'pleasure-ego'. The footnote enumerates those factors, on the one hand, which would favour this latter turn of events, and those factors, on the other hand, which would work against it. The existence of auto-erotic libidinal instincts would encourage the diversion to a 'pleasure-ego', while the *non*-auto-erotic libidinal instincts and the self-preservative instincts would be likely instead to bring about a direct transition to the final adult 'reality-ego'. This latter result would, he remarks, in fact come about, if it were not that parental care of the helpless infant satisfies this second set of instincts, artificially prolongs the primary state of narcissism, and so helps to make the establishment of the 'pleasure-ego' possible.]

[1] [On p. 133 Freud enumerates the opposites of loving in the following order: (1) hating, (2) being loved and (3) indifference. In the present passage, and below on pp. 136 and 139, he adopts a different order: (1) indifference, (2) hating and (3) being loved. It seems probable that in this second arrangement he gives indifference the first place as being the first to appear in the course of development.]

dominance of the pleasure principle a further development now takes place in the ego. In so far as the objects which are presented to it are sources of pleasure, it takes them into itself, 'introjects' them (to use Ferenczi's [1909] term[1]); and, on the other hand, it expels whatever within itself becomes a cause of unpleasure. (See below [pp. 184 and 224], the mechanism of projection.)

Thus the original 'reality-ego', which distinguished internal and external by means of a sound objective criterion,[2] changes into a purified 'pleasure-ego', which places the characteristic of pleasure above all others. For the pleasure-ego the external world is divided into a part that is pleasurable, which it has incorporated into itself, and a remainder that is extraneous to it. It has separated off a part of its own self, which it projects into the external world and feels as hostile. After this new arrangement, the two polarities coincide once more: the ego-subject coincides with pleasure, and the external world with unpleasure (with what was earlier indifference).

When, during the stage of primary narcissism, the object makes its appearance, the second opposite to loving, namely hating, also attains its development.[3]

As we have seen, the object is brought to the ego from the external world in the first instance by the instincts of self-preservation; and it cannot be denied that hating, too, originally characterized the relation of the ego to the alien external world with the stimuli it introduces. Indifference falls into place as a special case of hate or dislike, after having first appeared as their forerunner. At the very beginning, it seems, the external world, objects, and what is hated are identical. If later on an object turns out to be a source of pleasure, it is loved, but it is also incorporated into the ego; so that for the purified pleasure-ego once again objects coincide with what is extraneous and hated.

Now, however, we may note that just as the pair of opposites love—indifference reflects the polarity ego—external world, so the second antithesis love—hate[3] reproduces the polarity pleasure—unpleasure, which is linked to the first polarity. When

---

[1] [This seems to be the first occasion on which Freud himself used the term. Cf. the footnote on p. 241 below.]

[2] [See above p. 119 and footnote 2. The 'reality-ego' and the 'pleasure-ego' had already been introduced in the paper on the two principles of mental functioning (1911b).]

[3] [See footnote 1, p. 135.]

66

the purely narcissistic stage has given place to the object-stage, pleasure and unpleasure signify relations of the ego to the object. If the object becomes a source of pleasurable feelings, a motor urge is set up which seeks to bring the object closer to the ego and to incorporate it into the ego. We then speak of the 'attraction' exercised by the pleasure-giving object, and say that we 'love' that object. Conversely, if the object is a source of unpleasurable feelings, there is an urge which endeavours to increase the distance between the object and the ego and to repeat in relation to the object the original attempt at flight from the external world with its emission of stimuli. We feel the 'repulsion' of the object, and hate it; this hate can afterwards be intensified to the point of an aggressive inclination against the object—an intention to destroy it.

We might at a pinch say of an instinct that it 'loves' the objects towards which it strives for purposes of satisfaction; but to say that an instinct 'hates' an object strikes us as odd. Thus we become aware that the attitudes[1] of love and hate cannot be made use of for the relations of *instincts* to their objects, but are reserved for the relations of the *total ego* to objects. But if we consider linguistic usage, which is certainly not without significance, we shall see that there is a further limitation to the meaning of love and hate. We do not say of objects which serve the interests of self-preservation that we *love* them; we emphasize the fact that we *need* them, and perhaps express an additional, different kind of relation to them by using words that denote a much reduced degree of love—such as, for example, 'being fond of', 'liking' or 'finding agreeable'.

Thus the word 'to love' moves further and further into the sphere of the pure pleasure-relation of the ego to the object and finally becomes fixed to sexual objects in the narrower sense and to those which satisfy the needs of sublimated sexual instincts. The distinction between the ego-instincts and the sexual instincts which we have imposed upon our psychology is thus seen to be in conformity with the spirit of our language. The fact that we are not in the habit of saying of a single sexual instinct that it loves its object, but regard the relation of the ego

---

[1] [German '*Beziehungen*', literally 'relations'. In the first edition this word is printed '*Bezeichnungen*', 'descriptions' or 'terms'—which seems to make better sense. The word 'relations' in the later part of the sentence stands for '*Relationen*' in the German text.]

to its sexual object as the most appropriate case in which to employ the word 'love'—this fact teaches us that the word can only begin to be applied in this relation after there has been a synthesis of all the component instincts of sexuality under the primacy of the genitals and in the service of the reproductive function.

It is noteworthy that in the use of the word 'hate' no such intimate connection with sexual pleasure and the sexual function appears. The relation of *unpleasure* seems to be the sole decisive one. The ego hates, abhors and pursues with intent to destroy all objects which are a source of unpleasurable feeling for it, without taking into account whether they mean a frustration of sexual satisfaction or of the satisfaction of self-preservative needs. Indeed, it may be asserted that the true prototypes of the relation of hate are derived not from sexual life, but from the ego's struggle to preserve and maintain itself.

So we see that love and hate, which present themselves to us as complete opposites in their content, do not after all stand in any simple relation to each other. They did not arise from the cleavage of any originally common entity, but sprang from different sources, and had each its own development before the influence of the pleasure—unpleasure relation made them into opposites.

It now remains for us to put together what we know of the genesis of love and hate. Love is derived from the capacity of the ego to satisfy some of its instinctual impulses auto-erotically by obtaining organ-pleasure. It is originally narcissistic, then passes over on to objects, which have been incorporated into the extended ego, and expresses the motor efforts of the ego towards these objects as sources of pleasure. It becomes intimately linked with the activity of the later sexual instincts and, when these have been completely synthesized, coincides with the sexual impulsion as a whole. Preliminary stages of love emerge as provisional sexual aims while the sexual instincts are passing through their complicated development. As the first of these aims we recognize the phase of incorporating or devouring— a type of love which is consistent with abolishing the object's separate existence and which may therefore be described as ambivalent.[1] At the higher stage of the pregenital sadistic-anal

[1] [Freud's first published account of the oral stage was given in a paragraph added to the third (1915) edition of his *Three Essays, Standard*

organization,[1] the striving for the object appears in the form of an urge for mastery, to which injury or annihilation of the object is a matter of indifference. Love in this form and at this preliminary stage is hardly to be distinguished from hate in its attitude towards the object. Not until the genital organization is established does love become the opposite of hate.

Hate, as a relation to objects, is older than love. It derives from the narcissistic ego's primordial repudiation of the external world with its outpouring of stimuli. As an expression of the reaction of unpleasure evoked by objects, it always remains in an intimate relation with the self-preservative instincts; so that sexual and ego-instincts can readily develop an antithesis which repeats that of love and hate. When the ego-instincts dominate the sexual function, as is the case at the stage of the sadistic-anal organization, they impart the qualities of hate to the instinctual aim as well.

The history of the origins and relations of love makes us understand how it is that love so frequently manifests itself as 'ambivalent'—i.e. as accompanied by impulses of hate against the same object.[2] The hate which is admixed with the love is in part derived from the preliminary stages of loving which have not been wholly surmounted; it is also in part based on reactions of repudiation by the ego-instincts, which, in view of the frequent conflicts between the interests of the ego and those of love, can find grounds in real and contemporary motives. In both cases, therefore, the admixed hate has as its source the self-preservative instincts. If a love-relation with a given object is broken off, hate not infrequently emerges in its place, so that we get the impression of a transformation of love into hate. This account of what happens leads on to the view that the hate, which has its real motives, is here reinforced by a regression of the love to the sadistic preliminary stage; so that the hate acquires an erotic character and the continuity of a love-relation is ensured.

The third antithesis of loving, the transformation of loving into being loved,[3] corresponds to the operation of the polarity

Ed., 7, 198. The preface to that edition is dated 'October 1914'—some months before the present paper was written. See also below, p. 249 ff.]
[1] [See 'The Disposition to Obsessional Neurosis' (1913*i*).]
[2] [See footnote 2, p. 131.]
[3] [See footnote 1, p. 135.]

of activity and passivity, and is to be judged in the same way as the cases of scopophilia and sadism.[1]

We may sum up by saying that the essential feature in the vicissitudes undergone by instincts lies in *the subjection of the instinctual impulses to the influences of the three great polarities that dominate mental life.* Of these three polarities we might describe that of activity—passivity as the *biological,* that of ego—external world as the *real,* and finally that of pleasure—unpleasure as the *economic* polarity.

The instinctual vicissitude of *repression* will form the subject of an inquiry which follows [in the next paper].

[1] [The relation between love and hate was further discussed by Freud, in the light of his hypothesis of a death-instinct, in Chapter IV of *The Ego and the Id* (1923*b*).]

ON THE PSYCHO-ANALYTIC THEORY OF AFFECTS

By DAVID RAPAPORT, PH.D.

I

We do not possess a systematic statement of the psycho-analytic theory of affects.[1] The attempt I shall here make to piece together the existing fragments of this theory encounters two major difficulties. The first is that we have to deal with formulations originating from all three phases of the development of psycho-analysis: the beginning phase in which the theory of catharsis and the theory of psycho-analysis were not as yet sharply separated; the middle phase in which the id was in the centre of interest; and the recent phase in which interest is increasingly concerned with the ego. The treatment of the formulations of three such disparate origins is the more difficult partly because each of them persists into the later phases, and partly because most of the later formulations are to some extent anticipated in the earlier phases. The second difficulty is that the fragments to be put together are only too familiar, and culling them will thus appear to many just as superfluous as their systematization will seem unpalatable and unacceptable officiousness to others.

In view of these difficulties it will be worthwhile to remind ourselves, before going on to the task set for this paper, that an attempt at systematizing the theory of affects is not merely a theoretical nicety, but has eminent practical importance. Freud (28) wrote (p. 109):

If the instinct did not attach itself to an idea, or manifest itself as an affective state, we could know nothing about it.

Indeed, it goes without saying that in his everyday work the transference affects are the guide of the therapist, and that, though affect-storms of abreaction and catharsis are no longer the aims of psycho-analytic therapy, 'recall' and 'insight' without affective experience do not usually yield therapeutic advance. But it is less obvious how we can explain theoretically that affects serve as such guides and that without them insight is ineffective. We know that when —in therapy in general, and particularly in 'working through'—defences are 'undone', affects arise as indicators of the drive discovered and 'liberated' from its defence-shackles. Freud (26, p. 376) wrote:

Theoretically one may correlate . . . [working through] with the 'abreaction' of quantities of affects pent up by repression, without which the hypnotic treatment remained ineffective.

We also know that 'liberation' of drives in the form of abreaction, i.e. massive affective outburst, is not as a rule therapeutically effective. Fenichel (15), criticizing Kaiser's resistance-analysis, wrote:

. . . there is a 'taking distance' from the affect, which seems to me—in contrast to Kaiser—desirable. The judging ego of the patient should take distance from its affect, should recognize it untimely and should remember its origins affectively. An 'affect breakthrough' without such 'taking distance' is —as Freud has put it once—' an outright calamity'. Kaiser's comment that 'after a "genuine break-through of drives" there is nothing left for the analyst to explain', or clarify, or add to the contents

---

[1] The term affect will in this paper be used to stand for the terms 'emotion' and 'feeling' also, since there is no clear distinction in the literature in the use of these terms. For a suggested terminology, see Rapaport (60, Chap. II).

INTERNATIONAL JOURNAL OF PSYCHOANALYSIS, 1953, 34, pp. 177-198.

expressed by the patient ' makes us suspect that he actually does not recognize this ' calamity ' for what it is, that he neglects ' working through ', does not understand its essential role in the actual elimination of repressions, and that thus he is after a sort of ' neo-catharsis '—instead of analysis.

A. Freud (17a, p. 42), in discussing the use of mechanisms of defence against affects, points to the importance of the understanding of affects for the technique of child analysis, and her point seems to have a validity beyond the confines of the latter also:

The analysis and bringing into consciousness of the specific form of this defence against affect—whether it he reversal, displacement or complete repression—teaches us something of the particular technique adopted by the ego of the child in question and, just like the analysis of resistance, enables us to infer his attitude to his instincts and the nature of his symptom-formation. It is therefore a fact of peculiar importance in child-analysis that, in observing the affective processes, we are largely independent of the child's voluntary co-operation and his truthfulness or untruthfulness in what he tells us. His affects betray themselves against his will.

Clearly, S. Freud, Fenichel and A. Freud imply that the liberation of drives from repression is necessarily accompanied by an appearance of affects, and therapy is dependent upon effecting the appearance of these affects in certain forms and handling the emerged affects in certain ways. But we are not so clear theoretically about the relationships between drive and effect implied in these propositions derived from therapeutic experience. Therefore clarification of the theory of affects should be a step towards the theory of psycho-analytic technique and therapy. It might even be asked whether a metapsychological theory of technique and therapy is altogether conceivable before the metapsychological status of affects, which occupy a central position in the processes of therapy, has been clarified.

Their central role in therapy, however, does not exhaust the clinical significance of affects.

We have. come to label as affect such a wide variety of phenomena that both in diagnostic and therapeutic work we are in danger of being led astray by the term, as long as we lack a systematic view of the relationships of all the phenomena to which we apply it.[2] A brief survey will show the complexity of the situation. We call affect not only the infant's rage (encountered later on in temper tantrums and in the destructive outbursts of some catatonics) and the adult's anger accompanied by the corresponding expressive movements and other physiological concomitants, but also the subjective feelings of those well-controlled adults who show little or no affect-expression, as well as the anger of over-controlling compulsive persons who just ' know ' that they ' could be ' or ' should be ' angry. We also call affects those displays which impress the onlooker as histrionic or affectations, and which certain character-types are prone to produce, either in exaggeration of experienced, or as substitutes for not-experienced, affects. It is not quite clear how these are related to the ' as if ' affects of those schizoid personalities described by Helene Deutsch (8, p. 123).[3] Nor is their relation clear to those oversensitive incipient and ambulatory schizophrenics who appear to wallow in their affects, which on closer inspection turn out to be restitution-products following a total withdrawal of object cathexes;[4] these patients are affectively moved by anything that seems to promise them the experience of affects, because it proves to them that they are still capable of feeling.[5] Nor is there clarity about the relation of both these latter types to those more crudely obvious schizophrenic affect-phenomena termed ' flat affect ' and ' inappropriate affect '. We need not dwell on displaced affects, somatic affect-equivalents without conscious affect-experience, or the relation of these to conversion-symptoms and psychosomatic disorders and all the rest that belong to the chapter of ' unconscious emotion'; they have been variously discussed (Fenichel,

---

[2] While all the phenomena discussed below have to do with affects, and are time and again so referred to in the literature, my listing them here does not imply that they are correctly labelled as affects nor that the theory of affects alone must account fully for all of them. Indeed some of the phenomena to be listed are most complex, and more than the theory of affects will have to be invoked for their explanation. What I imply by listing them here is that they constitute an important problem for the theory of affects also.

[3] ' . . . outwardly he conducts his life as if he possessed a complete and sensitive emotional capacity. To him there is no difference between his empty forms and what others actually experience . . . [this] is no longer an act of repression but a real loss of object cathexis.'
[4] Here the subjective experience of lack of affect in depersonalization (Schilder, 65, Fenichel, 17) and in certain allied syndromes of organic etiology (Buerger-Prinz and Kaila, 7, and Schilder, 65) is also relevant.
[5] Compare Federn on narcissistic affect (12, p. 13).

17; Alexander, 1; Rapaport, 60). But we must mention the related phenomena of 'frozen affects' which find expression—without conscious affect-experience—in stereotyped postures, facial expressions, tones of voice, motility, etc., to which Reich (63) called attention. And we must take notice of such affects as anxiety, guilt, elation, depression, which—in contrast to the momentary affects so far mentioned—may take pathological chronic forms; even more important, they may take characterological chronic forms, as in anxious people, gay people, gloomy people, bashful people, etc. (cf. Landauer, 54). Furthermore, we must mention a special group of affects, namely those grouped around the experiences of the comic, wit, humour, etc., which are apparently related to a specific kind of saving of cathectic expenditure, rather than to any specific kind of cathectic tension. It is noteworthy that a proclivity to elicit and/or experience such affects may also take a chronic form and structuralize into a character trait (cf. Brenman, 4). Finally we must mention such specific and complex affective states as apathy, nostalgia, boredom, etc., which are also relatively chronic affect-formations (cf. 3a).

To make even more glaring the complexity of what a theory of affect must account for, we might add that, on the one hand, neurotic inhibition and ego-limitation cuts down the range of intensity and variability of affect-experiences; on the other, regression-processes bring to the fore unbridled and unmodulated affective attacks in which, while intensity is formidable, range and variability are minimal.

II

I shall now review the concepts of affect of each of the three phases of the development of psycho-analysis.

The dominant concept of affect of the beginning phase of psycho-analysis, in which no sharp differentiation between the theory of cathartic-hypnosis and that of psycho-analysis had as yet occurred, equates affect with the quantity of psychic energy, which was later conceptualized as drive-cathexis. But while later the cathexis of affects is distinguished from drive-cathexis proper and from bound-(ego-) cathexes, here affect stands for all of these. Freud (19, p. 75) wrote:

. . . among the psychic functions there is something which should be differentiated (*an amount of affect*, *a sum of excitation*[*]), something having all the attributes of a quantity . . . a something which is capable of increase, decrease, displacement, and discharge, and which extends itself over the memory traces of an idea like an electric charge over the surface of the body.

Accordingly, the role of affects in symptom-formation is that affects prevented from discharge remain on the one hand fixed to the pathogenic idea or phantasy, and on the other find outlet in the innervations of conversion symptoms. Freud (5, pp. 7–8) wrote:

The ideas which have become pathogenic are preserved with such freshness and affective force because the normal process of absorption by abreaction and by reproduction in a state of unrestrained association is denied them.

And Breuer (*ib.*, pp. 151–2) wrote:

The 'hysterical conversion' is then complete, for the original intercerebral excitement of the affect was changed into the process of excitement of the peripheral path, and the original affective idea no longer evokes the affect, but only the abnormal reflex.

Correspondingly, the role of affects in therapy is that the discharge of the dammed-up affect drains the pathogenic idea of its force and influence. Freud (18, pp. 40–41) wrote:

By providing an opportunity for the pent-up affect to discharge itself in words the therapy deprives of its effective power the idea which was not originally abreacted.

Simultaneously the anxiety-affect was explained as affect or libido (these terms were at this point still interchangeable) transformed by being repressed. Freud (19, pp. 96–7) wrote:

. . . an accumulation of excitation is involved. . . . Anxiety . . . probably represents . . . the deflection of somatic sexual excitation from the psychical field, and . . . an abnormal use of it, due to this deflection. (20, pp. 96–7).
Libido will therefore subside . . . and the excitation will express itself instead subcortically as anxiety (20, p. 99).

Freud also (22, p. 227) wrote:

. . . anxiety actually was libido diverted from its usual course.

---

[*] Italics mine (D. R.).

This concept of affect and anxiety persisted into the second phase of the development of psycho-analysis which, as we shall see, already contains fragments of a more advanced theory of affects and anxiety. Freud (23, p. 537) wrote:

The fulfilment of these wishes would no longer produce an affect of pleasure, but one of pain; *and it is just this conversion of affect that constitutes the essence of what we call ' repression '.*

Even later Freud (24, p. 178) wrote:

When once a state of anxiety establishes itself, the anxiety swallows up all other feelings; with the progress of repression, and the more those ideas which are charged with affect and which have been conscious move down into the unconscious, all affects are capable of being changed into anxiety.

Indeed the use of the term affect as though it were psychic energy (cathexis) in general—aided and abetted by Bleuler's (3), Jung's (46), and Schilder's (64, 66) usage—persists in psycho-analytic literature to our own day. Academic psychology, psychosomatic medicine, and psychiatry at large lent a hand in perpetuating it and making it general usage, when psycho-analytic theoretical development had long since abandoned it.

Before turning to the affect-concept of the next phase in the development of psycho-analysis, we must point out that already in the *Studies in Hysteria* (published 1895) and in Freud's posthumously published *Outline of a Psychology* (written 1895)—which will not be discussed here—there are traces of the later conception of affects. For instance, the relation between drive and affect is indicated for the first time, though not theoretically further developed; the affective state of ' being-in-love ' is derived from the ' sexual instinct '. Freud (5, pp. 145–6) wrote:

This is glaringly observed in the wonderful phenomenon of being in love . . . [The object] becomes endowed with the whole quantity of excitement set free by the sexual instinct; she becomes . . . an ' affective idea '. That is, in assuming actuality in consciousness, she sets free the increased excitement which really originates in another source, namely, in the sexual glands.

Even traces of a distinction between disposal of tension by action, by affect, and by binding through the work of thought (association), are already present, though still clouded by the affect-terminology. Freud (18, pp. 30–31) wrote:

The fading of a memory or of its affect depends . . . foremost on whether an energetic reaction (discharge of feeling) supervened on the affective experience or not. By *reaction* we here mean the whole range of voluntary and involuntary reflexes, by which . . . affects are habitually worked off— from weeping up to an actual act of revenge . . . the reaction . . . to the trauma has a . . . complete cathartic effect only if it takes the form of a fully adequate reaction, such as an act of revenge. But man finds a surrogate for such an act in speech. . . . Abreaction is, however, not the only kind of solution at the disposal of the normal psychic mechanism . . . the normal man succeeds by means of associations in dissipating the accompanying affect.

III

The second phase of the development of psycho-analytic theory begins with *The Interpretation of Dreams* (23, 1900); it is characterized by the metapsychological systematization of psycho-analytic discoveries in general and by the development of the economic point of view, the theory of cathexes, in particular. It is a familiar fact that, while the dynamic point of view was highly developed by the time this phase of the theory opened, and while the economic point of view was developed in this phase, the structural point of view—the third of the metapsychological triad—was still lagging behind, taking the form of the topographical point of view. Metapsychology as we find it in Freud's main writings devoted to it (23, Chap. VII, and ' Metapsychological Papers ', 1911–17) is an incomplete theory preparatory to the developing of the structural point of view, the advent of which ushers in ego-psychology and completes the formal framework of metapsychology.

The Interpretation of Dreams already breaks sharply with the previous conception of affect as psychic (drive) energy proper, and considers affects to be motor and secretory (discharge) processes which are controlled from the unconscious. Freud (23, p. 521) wrote:

We here take as our basis a quite definite assumption as to the nature of the development of affect. This is regarded as a motor or secretory function, the key to the innervation of which is to be found in the ideas of the Unconscious.

But this sharp break was not noted at the time; only well in the third phase of the development:

of psycho-analysis did Kulovesi (52) come back to it, noting and attempting to clarify the relation between the James-Lange and the psycho-analytic theories of affects.[7] The break is sharp, the dynamic is no longer that of affects but rather that of the energy (drive-cathexis) inherent in wishes. Affects are released by, and are indicators of, unconscious wishes. The complex relation of affects to the other class of indicators (representations) of drives—i.e. ideas—is also considered. Freud (23, p. 537) wrote:

The memories from which the unconscious wish evokes a liberation of affect have never been accessible to the Preconscious, and for that reason this liberation cannot be inhibited. It is precisely on account of this generation of affect that these ideas are not now accessible even by way of the preconscious thoughts to which they have transferred the energy of the wishes connected with them.

and:

. . . the ideational contents have undergone displacements and substitutions, while the affects have remained unchanged. No wonder, then, that the ideational content which has been altered by dream-distortion no longer fits the affect which has remained intact (ibid., p. 434).

The realization of the theoretical programme forecast in the *Studies in Hysteria*—to differentiate between tension-disposal by means of action on the one hand, and by means of affect-discharge on the other—was ushered in by regarding affects as motor and secretory functions controlled from the unconscious. But not until eleven years later, in the ' Formulations Regarding the Two Principles in Mental Functioning' (25), did Freud take the next step, when in delineating the development of the reality-principle he formulated that, with its advent, the role of motility changes: while hitherto it fulfilled, in the main, a safety-valve discharge-function for drive-tensions (affect-discharge), it now becomes an apparatus used in action designed to alter reality. This view co-ordinates affect-discharge with the pleasure-principle and with alteration of the internal environment, and contrasts it with action, which it co-ordinates with the reality-principle and with the alteration of the external environment so as to make the drive-object ultimately available. Affect-discharge is then the short-cut to tension-decrease, while action is the

realistic detour towards it. Freud (25, p. 16) wrote:

A new function was now entrusted to motor discharge, which under the supremacy of the pleasure-principle had served to unburden the mental apparatus of accretions of stimuli, and in carrying out this task had sent innervations into the interior of the body (*mien*, expressions of affect); it was now employed in the appropriate alteration of reality. It was converted into *action*.

Freud (28, p. 111, footnote) returned to this point to clarify it further:

Affectivity manifests itself essentially in motor (i.e. secretory and circulatory) discharge resulting in an (internal) alteration of the subject's own body without reference to the outer world; motility, in actions designed to effect changes in the outer world.

The tension which is diminished by affect-discharge is that of drives. More specifically, affect-expression is the final outcome of the discharge of a specific part of drive-cathexes, termed ' affect-charge '. ' Affect-charge ' and ' ideas ' are both drive-representations; they had to be theoretically distinguished because their fate under repression is different. They may both be repressed, as in severely inhibiting hysterical neuroses; ideas may be repressed while affects remain amenable to consciousness, as in hysterias characterized by affect-outbursts; or ideas (or their derivatives) may remain amenable to consciousness while affects are repressed, displaced, or isolated from them, as in obsessional neuroses. Freud (27, p. 91) wrote:

In our discussion hitherto we have dealt with the repression of an instinct-presentation, and by that we understood an idea or group of ideas which is cathected with a definite amount of the mental energy (libido, interest) pertaining to an instinct. Now clinical observation forces us further to dissect something that hitherto we have conceived of as a single entity, for it shows us that beside the idea there is something else, another presentation of the instinct to be considered, and that this other element undergoes a repression which may be quite different from that of the idea. We have adopted the term *charge of affect* for this other element in the mental presentation; it represents that part of the instinct which has become detached from the idea, and finds proportionate expression, according to its quantity, in processes which become observable

---

[7] Note also Landauer (53).

to perception as affects. From this point on, in describing a case of repression, we must follow up the fate of the idea which undergoes repression separately from that of the instinctual energy attached to the idea.

In comparing the two kinds of drive-representations, Freud points out that affect-expression and -experience are related to discharge of cathexes; ideas, to cathecting of memory traces. He makes this distinction to explain that ideas when repressed—when their cathexis is withdrawn, or when they are counter-cathected—persist as actualities (as memory traces) while affects when repressed (decathected or counter-cathected) persist only as potentialities. Freud (28, p. 111) wrote:

The whole difference arises from the fact that ideas are cathexes—ultimately of memory-traces—whilst affects and emotions correspond to processes of discharge, the final expression of which is perceived as feeling. In the present state of our knowledge of affects and emotions we cannot express this difference more clearly.

I believe that here Freud as yet lacked the observations which could have indicated to him (as they did to him as well as to Brierley and Jacobson later) that discharge-thresholds of drives and affects are indispensable concepts of an affect-theory. But such thresholds heightened (presumably by counter-cathexis) to attain repression of affect would render the repressed 'affect-charge' just as actual as memory-traces render unconscious ideas. Freud's conception here shows the limitations of a pure discharge-theory of affects which has no place in it for threshold-structures.

In this discharge-theory, all affects, including the anxiety-affect, are partial vicissitudes of drives. Thus, though the earlier 'toxic' or 'transformation' theory of anxiety still persists, it no longer implies that undischarged affects can be transformed into anxiety, but only that repressed drive-cathexis can be so transformed. Freud (27, pp. 91–2) wrote:

The fate of the quantitative factor in the instinct-presentation may be one of three, as we seĕ by a cursory survey of the observations made through psycho-analysis: either the instinct is altogether suppressed, so that no trace of it is found, or it appears in the guise of an affect of a particular qualitative tone, or it is transformed into anxiety. With the two last possibilities we are obliged to focus our attention upon the *transformation* into

affects, and especially into *anxiety,* of the mental energy belonging to the *instincts,* this being a new possible vicissitude undergone by an instinct.

Let us now fit this theory into the psychoanalytic model of psychic processes. This model [8] is formed on the following observational (or hypothetical) sequence: the restlessness of the hungry infant → the appearance of the mother, i.e., breast, and sucking → subsidence of restlessness. We conceptualize this sequence as: drive-tension → appearance of, and action on, drive-object → gratification. In the absence of the drive-object, restlessness will persist and/or a hallucinatory image of past gratification will appear. We conceptualize the restlessness as *expression* of affect and refer it to an ' affect-charge ', that is, to a part of the drive-cathexis which would be discharged if the drive-object were present and drive-action on it could take place. We conceptualize the hallucinatory gratification as *idea,* and refer it to the drive-cathecting of the memory traces of past gratification situations. Idea and affect-charge are both conceptualized as *drive-representations,* safety-valves of drive tensions. The quantitative relations that appear to obtain are: drive-cathexis → affect-charge → cathexis of memory-trace.

It seems to be assumed that if drive-action—discharge of drive-cathexes—were possible, no separating off of a cathectic amount in the form of affect-charge, or disposal of it in the form of affect-discharge, would take place. This proposition contains on the one hand a crucial implication for the theory of affect and on the other a factual fallacy. The *implication for theory* may be formulated as the ' conflict theory ' of affects. *The fallacy* lies in the untenable assumption of immediate and complete discharge by drive-action. Let us discuss these, keeping in mind that our framework at this moment is that of drive-cathexes and drive-representations, that is, mobile cathexes and primary processes. In other words, we are still considering that hypothetical state of affairs which is supposed to obtain before definitive ego-formation, before the establishment of bound cathexes and secondary processes, before the internalization of the *delay* of drive-discharge and of the *detour*-behaviour towards the drive-object, and before they become guaranteed by psychic structure-formation, that is, before the fami-

---

[8] Freud, 23, Chap. VII, pp. 508–509; 25, p. 14. See also Rapaport, 61, Part VII; and Rapaport, 62.

liar advanced defensive and adaptive mechanisms are established. Or, in other terms, we are considering the state of affairs in which the pleasure-principle is supposed to hold full sway before the establishment of the reality-principle.

The 'conflict-theory' of affects. The major implication of the affect-theory of the second phase of psycho-analysis is that affect-expression is the outcome of the discharge of part of the accumulated drive-cathexes when direct discharge in drive-action *cannot* take place. This conception of affects was forecast already by Spinoza (68, p. 129):

By emotions (*affectus*) I understand the modification of the body by which the power in action of the body is increased or diminished, aided or restrained and at the same time the ideas of these modifications.

and by Dewey:

When there is no inhibition there is no overflow and no affect.

The psychologist Drever (9a) saw the necessity for such a conflict (for him, 'obstacle') theory of affect, but realized its insufficiencies for the explanation of continuous pleasurable affects.

One of the finest Anglo-Saxon psychiatric observers and thinkers, MacCurdy, influenced by psycho-analysis, by his studies of circular psychoses, and by the theories of James, Lange, Dewey, Cannon, MacDougall, etc., stated this conception in 1925—before Freud's 'The Problem of Anxiety'—and concluded that affects are products of conflict. He wrote (56, p. 65):

[Affects] . . . appear both objectively and subjectively when instinct is aroused but not in operation as such. The function of emotion is to warn oneself or others of the nature of behaviour that is likely to develop.

In the psycho-analytic literature too—though only after 'The Problem of Anxiety'—we find a tendency to state the conflict-theory of affects explicitly. Landauer (54, p. 390) interpreted Freud's 'The Problem of Anxiety' to imply such a conflict-theory. He wrote:

The affective process is not a simple response to a stimulus . . . there are at work at least two directly conflicting tendencies. . . Freud thinks we must assume in all affects an inherited compro-

mise of this sort between conflicting tendencies . . . the affects are inherited hysterical attacks.

In a discussion of the state of affairs obtaining *after* definitive ego-formation, after *delay* of drive-discharge has been internalized—that is, after drives and discharge-controlling structures clash intrapsychically—such a conflict theory would be a matter of course for us;[9] it seems less obvious at this point, where drives conflict with reality—i.e. where the absence of the drive-object is what prevents drive-action. Several considerations recommend themselves at this point: (1) To consider affects which derive from the clash between mounting drive-tension and the reality-absence of the drive-object as a prototype of conflict (namely, of that conflict which gives rise to affect-discharge) has a precedent in our theorizing: the derivation of anxiety from reality-danger. Freud (33, p. 116) wrote:

. . . instinctual demands often become an (internal) danger only because . . . their gratification would bring about an external one.

(2) In discussing the concept of 'unconscious affects' Freud inferred from his observations that the 'affect-charge' cathexis is *not* segregated in a persisting fashion from drive-cathexes proper; when repression (or other defence?) blocks its discharge it has—unlike the idea—no actual unconscious existence but only a potential one, in that when the discharge-channels are unblocked affect-discharge again serves as a safety-valve to mounting drive-tension. Freud wrote (28, pp. 110–11):

. . . we apply the term 'unconscious' to those affects that are restored when we undo the work of repression. So . . . the use of the term . . . is logical; but a comparison of the unconscious affect with the unconscious idea reveals the significant difference that the unconscious idea continues, after repression, as an actual formation in the system Unconscious, whilst to the unconscious affect there corresponds in the same system only a potential disposition which is prevented from developing further.

Thus in this conception 'affect-charge' would be defined simply as that amount of drive-cathexis which the constitutional nature—that is, thresholds—of the affect-discharge channels (motor, secretory, etc.), permits them to carry off. This is a pure 'dynamic theory' in which affects are created always *de novo*.[10]

---

[9] Federn's affect-theory (12, p. 14 ff.), which is part of his ego-psychology, also implies such a conflict theory.

[10] Cf. Freud, 33, pp. 19–20.

It will be discussed later whether or not such a conception can be sustained for the state of affairs that obtains after discharge-controls and delay are internalized and become the preventers of drive-discharge—that is whether or not ' affect-charge ' remains always an unsegregated and *ad hoc* discharged part of drive-cathexis even when, with the advancement of psychic development, structuralization of other psychic functions becomes the typical form. It is clear here, however, that in this phase of his theorizing Freud considered affect-discharge a dynamic product (that of the conflict between mounting tension and discharge-preventing reality) and saw only its direction as determined by inborn discharge-avenues. A consideration of these discharge-avenues leads to the *factual fallacy* mentioned above.

The *fallacy* in question seems not to vitiate the core of the ' conflict-theory ', but only to point up its limitations. It is a fallacy inherent in a purely dynamic—i.e. drive-cathexis—theory of affect. To bring this into sharp relief, let us remind ourselves that the stress we have put in our discussion on inborn discharge-channels of affects is in part ' borrowed ' from Freud's *The Problem of Anxiety*,[11] that is, from the third phase of the development of psycho-analytic theory. In the second phase, motor and secretory channels are neither treated with a stress on their inborn character, nor built into the theory. The very existence of inborn discharge-channels raises several questions: Does discharge in drive-action not itself have channels and thresholds? Or in other words: to what point (threshold) must drive-tension mount before discharge in action becomes imperative? Do inborn drive-discharge thresholds—as structures—prevent drive-discharge before the absence of the drive-object in reality prevents it, and thus before defences—or more generally: internalized delay-mechanisms—prevent it? Is it possible that such drive-discharge thresholds (disposition to frustration-tolerance?) have decisive influence on how the experience of the absence of the drive-object will affect psychic structure-formation? Does the relation of affect-discharge thresholds to drive-discharge thresholds explain why drive-action too (e.g. sexual intercourse, cf. Jacobson, 42)—and not only its delay—is accompanied by affect-discharge and affect-experience? Does

the relation of these two kinds of thresholds to each other influence decisively the development of controlling and defensive structures? These questions lead into the most obscure and least explored areas of psychic organization to which we refer by such terms as ' disposition to anxiety ', ' constitutional intensity of drives ' (Reich, 63; Freud, 35), etc. There are but a few facts known which are relevant to these questions:

(1) Affect-discharge can and does occur not only when the drive-object is absent, but also before the drive-tension has reached the point where its discharge is imperative, and even parallel with actual drive-discharge. These familiar phenomena cannot be explained by the dynamic—i.e. conflict—theory of affects. They indicate that a conflict and drive-safety-valve (dynamic-economic) theory of affect is insufficient and has to be supplemented by a structural theory, which must take into consideration affect-discharge and drive-discharge thresholds[12] (cf. Jacobson, 42, 43).

(2) It seems that we can conceive of two kinds of such thresholds: inborn ones (Freud's —30, 32—' stimulus barrier ' is of this type), and defensive counter-cathexes (repression is of this type). It is possible that a structural theory will explain the relations between drives and affects—pointed to in the questions above and in (1)—by the conflict of thresholds of defensive and controlling organizations of counter-cathexes with discharge-bent drive-tensions for which affects serve as safety-valves and indicators. It is, however, just as—indeed even more—possible that a structural theory will have to take *inborn* discharge-thresholds also into consideration. In doing so it would have a precedent in Hartmann's treatment of memory, motility, perceptual organs, as ego-apparatuses: that is, structures which unlike some other ego-structures do not grow from conflict, and are in this sense ' autonomous '; rather, being innate they are pre-existent to the differentiation of the ego and the id from their undifferentiated matrix, and become—once the ego is fully developed—apparatuses in the service of the ego. Thus drive- and affect-discharge thresholds would be added to the so far familiar list of those inborn apparatuses which have primary autonomy from conflict (though these, too,

---

[11] Cf. Freud, 33, pp. 70–71, 117.
[12] It is not implied here that consideration of thresholds will alone make the theory a structural one, nor that a structural theory considering thresholds is necessarily an adequate theory of affects.

---

like other such apparatuses, may become secondarily involved in conflict).

(3) These considerations are not pure theoretical niceties: there are clinical phenomena necessitating some such assumption. (*a*) The psychosomatic symptoms appearing in the first days of life, such as infantile exemata, inclination to colics, and also the early manifest individual differences, e.g. of hypo- and hypermotility, suggest the crucial role of differential thresholds in channelling the discharge of tensions into specific individually varying directions (10). (*b*) The observations of autistic disorders of infancy and childhood (Kanner, 47; Putnam, 59; Mahler, 57; Bergman and Escalona, 2) show hypersensitivities and affect-phenomena which are relevant in this context. Bergman and Escalona (2) felt that their observations could be explained by assuming that the discharge thresholds are low in these cases, giving rise to high sensitivity, with the result that a precocious, partial and uneven ego-development sets in, in order—as it were—to establish new and higher thresholds to compensate for the low inborn thresholds.

Summing up: The affect theory of the second phase of the development of psycho-analysis is a *cathectic* (*economic*) *theory* in that affect-discharge (affect-expression and affect-felt) is a discharge of a definite part of the accumulated drive-cathexis, termed *affect-charge*. It is a *dynamic theory* in that affect-charge is discharged as a safety-valve function when discharge of drive-cathexes by drive-action meets opposition (‘ conflict ’). It is, however, also a *topographical theory* in that *affect-charge* is conceptualized as a drive-representation of the same order as the *idea*. It contains also traces of a *structural theory*, in that it stresses the importance of discharge-channels by characterizing affect-expression as discharge into the interior of the body, in contrast to action which is discharge into the external reality. As a structural theory it is quite unsatisfactory, in that it deals exclusively with primary affects carrying fully mobile drive-cathexes which strive to discharge with full intensity. This theory remains an id-theory of affects, not exploring their relation to, and function in the service of, the ego and its role in the development and release of the broad range and variety of what Fenichel (16, 17) has called ‘ tamed ’ affects. It was left to the third phase of the development of psycho-analytic theory to make the first systematic moves towards coping with these problems, partly with the aid of the budding concepts of the structural point of view and ego-psychology, which were available for the first time, and partly as a means and a by-product of its attempts to develop these very concepts.

IV

The discussion of the affect-theory of the third phase of psycho-analytic theory must begin with the admission that here too the development of affect-theory has remained scanty, and received little attention; the beginnings we do possess have not been made very explicit, and are even less integrated with the rest of the theory than were the previous affect-theories. The discussion of this third affect-theory is even more difficult than that of the first two, because it presupposes a metapsychological theory of psycho-analysis, complemented by the structural point of view (absorbing the topographical one), a systematic presentation of which is simply not extant. Hartmann’s (38, 39), Hartmann, Kris, and Loewenstein’s (40, 41), and my own (61, 62) efforts to develop such a systematic presentation remain incomplete; they will not be reviewed here, since the more incomplete a theory, the less it lends itself to concise restatement.

Though the systematic status of this third theory is still deplorable, its roots go back to *The Interpretation of Dreams* (23). There the conversion-theory of affects (particularly of anxiety) still persists in the framework of the cathectic (second phase) theory. Freud wrote (23, p. 521):

. . . the suppression of the Unconscious becomes necessary . . . [because] if the movement of ideas in the Unconscious were allowed to run its course, it would develop an affect which originally had the character of pleasure, but which, since the process of repression, bears the character of pain.

Nevertheless, traces of the third theory of affects already appear. Even then Freud recognized that one of the concomitants of the development of the secondary process and reality-testing is the ‘ taming ’ of affects to the point of changing them into signals, though he was never cognizant of the fact that this process is never crowned by complete success.

Thought must concern itself with the connecting-paths between ideas without allowing itself to be misled by their intensities. But it is obvious that condensations of ideas and intermediate or compromise-formations are obstacles to the attainment of [this] . . . Such procedures are, therefore, carefully avoided in our secondary thinking. It will readily be seen, moreover, that the pain-principle, although at other times it *provides the thought-process with its most important clues*,[13] may also put difficulties in its way in the pursuit of identity of thought. Hence, the tendency of the thinking process must always be to free itself more and more from exclusive regulation by the pain-principle, and *to restrict the development of affect through the work of thought to the very minimum which remains effective as a signal* . . . [13] But . . . this refinement is seldom completely successful, even in normal psychic life, and . . . our thinking always remains liable to falsification by the inter-vention of the pain-principle (23, pp. 535–6).

Thus affects appear here as ' most important clues ' and ' signals ' of the secondary process, but also as ' falsifiers ' of it, since this ' refine-ment is seldom completely successful ', and therefore actually—to use Fenichel's term—affects of all degrees of '.taming ' appear in consciousness.

Furthermore, defences directed against affects (in the example below: reaction-formation) are already noted and attributed to the ' secondary system ' [14] which binds cathexes—that is, delays and regulates discharge, instead of directly discharging mobile cathexes. Defence against affects is a part of the complex structural view of affects, and will be further discussed below. Freud wrote (23, p. 537):

. . . such a conversion of affect occurs in the course of development (one need only think of the emergence of disgust . . .) and that is connected with the activity of the secondary system.

It is in accord with this that in *The Interpre-tation of Dreams*, and even more in ' The Unconscious ' (28), there are indications of the conception that it is not repression which gives rise to anxiety (affect) but rather anxiety which is a motive of repression. Freud (28, p. 110) wrote:

. . . to suppress the development of affect is the true aim of repression and . . . its work does not terminate if this aim is not achieved.

But let us turn now from these predecessors to the third phase of the theory. *The Ego and the Id*, which officially ushers in the third phase

of psycho-analytic theory, contains a simile which paraphrases well the portent of the third phase of the theory of affects also; it forecasts the view that, owing to structure-development, processes which are originally related to the conflicts of the id recur and involve higher levels of psychic structure. Freud (31, p. 53) wrote:

The struggle that once raged in the deepest strata of the mind . . . is now carried on in a higher region, like the Battle of the Huns which in Kaulbach's painting is being fought out in the sky.

Otherwise, we find in *The Ego and the Id* little about affects in general, but much about guilt and unconscious guilt. I cannot discuss the complex issue of guilt here, since it would lead us far afield. I will restrict myself to pointing out—crudely simplifying matters—that Freud represents the guilt-affect as arising from a conflict of the ego with the super-ego; and that his discussion of ' unconscious guilt ' again implies the conception of ' defence against affects. Thus a structural conflict theory of affects is already forecast here, and so is a hier-archic layering of affects. But at the same time Freud holds fast to the previous drive-theory of affects, though he has to invoke the death-instinct to do so. He writes (31, p. 77):

If we turn to melancholia first we find that the excessively strong super-ego which has obtained a hold upon consciousness rages against the ego with merciless fury as if it had taken possession of the whole of the sadism in the person concerned . . . The destructive component had entrenched itself in the super-ego and turned against the ego. What is now holding sway in the super-ego is, as it were, a pure culture of the death instinct. . . .

This conception of the guilt affect [15] was further extended, in regard to both its origin in conflict and its multiple layering, by Jones in his ' Fear, Guilt and Hate ' (45), which already makes use of Freud's major contribution to the third phase of affect-theory, i.e. *The Problem of Anxiety* (33). It is to my knowledge the first study of affects in the literature to make use of this advance in affect-theory. Jones shows that fear, hate, and guilt are mul-tiple-layered, in that any one of them may

---

[13] Italics mine (D. R.).
[14] This point was then taken up first by Grueninger (37c).
[15] Federn (11, 12) presents a different theory of guilt and of affects in general. His theory is not only the earliest but also the most extensive attempt to develop a theory of affects which takes the structural point of view

into account, and most of the problems and phenomena of affects touched on in the contributions here discussed have been noted and tackled in it; I will not discuss it here because its idiosyncratic character and terminology divides it from the mainstream . of psycho-analytic thinking, and makes its presentation (short of a most extensive review) impossible.

appear not only under the basic dynamic conditions which usually give rise to it, but also as an outcome of defence against any of the others. This conception implies, besides the conflict origin of these ' secondary affects ' and their hierarchic layering, the concept of defence against affects. Regrettably, Jones makes no clear distinction between the defence against the underlying drives and the defence against the affects; nor does he point up that these three affects are, even in their basic forms, of different orders of complexity (and thus imply even before the ' secondary defence ' a hierarchic order) in the ascending sequence: fear, hate, guilt—although in the adult individual there are fears, hates and guilts of equivalent orders of complexity also. Jones (**45**, p. 396) wrote in his summary:

. . . I called attention to the various layers of secondary defence that covered the three attitudes of fear, hate and guilt, and pointed out that the defences themselves constituted a sort of ' return of the repressed '. We have seen how deep must be the primary layers of these three emotional attitudes, and also that two stages can be distinguished in the development of each of them. The relationship of the secondary layers would appear to be somewhat as follows. Any one of these primary attitudes may prove to be unendurable, and so secondary defensive reactions are in turn developed, these being derived, as was just indicated, from one of the other attributes. Thus a secondary hate may be developed as a means of coping with either fear or guilt, a secondary fear attitude (' signal ' anxiety) as a means of coping with guilty hate, or rather the dangers that this brings, and occasionally even a secondary guilt as a means of coping with the other two. These secondary reactions are therefore of a regressive nature, and they subserve the same defensive function as all other regressions.

As we see, Jones leaves it rather indefinite whether these secondary affects are *the* defences pitted against the primary ones, or whether they issue from the defences that are brought to bear. This type of uncertainty—implying also the uncertainty of distinction between defences against drives and those against affects to be touched on below—is characteristic for the psycho-analytic theory of both defences and affects.

After this excursion on guilt, for the sake of which we have broken the chronological order, we come to Freud's *The Problem of Anxiety* (**33**), which by its treatment of anxiety and defences ushered in ego-psychology, gave substance to the programme of the structural approach presented in *The Ego and the Id*, and constitutes the most important advance of the third phase of psycho-analytic theory in regard to the theory of affects.

In the first theory, affects were equated with drive-cathexes; in the second theory, they appeared as drive-representations, serving as safety-valves for drive-cathexes the discharge of which was prevented; in the third theory they appear as ego-functions, and as such are no longer safety-valves but are used as signals by the ego. Freud wrote:

Anxiety . . . [as any] affective state . . . can . . . be experienced only by the Ego (**33**, p. 80). [Anxiety is] not to be explained on an economic basis; [16] . . . is not created *de novo* in repression but is reproduced as an affective state . . . (*ibid.*, p. 20).

This is then a structural view of affects. ' Affect-charge ' if prevented from discharge does not become merely ' potential ', as was asserted in the discussion of ' unconscious emotion '; it is structuralized and thus it can be reproduced as a signal without its ' economic basis ', i.e. without ' affect discharge ' actually taking place. The ego, which before the affect was ' tamed ' into a signal endured it passively, now produces it actively.

Brierley's (**6**) was the first attempt to state the ego-theory of affects here implied. She did this partly by stressing the role of affects in the interplay between internal and external reality, and partly by insisting that affects are tension-, rather than discharge-, phenomena. Basically, however, she persisted with the second (cathectic) theory. She wrote (**6**, p. 259):

All our modern conceptions of the relation of anxiety to symptom-formation and of its role in development contradict the idea that affect is itself a discharge and support the view that it is a tension-phenomenon impelling to discharge either in the outer or the inner world. . . . Affects which appear to arise spontaneously always have unconscious stimuli and, in practice, we find affectivity tends to be high where frustration, particularly internal frustration, is marked.

In considering affects as tension-phenomena and in bringing up the question of thresholds, she touches on issues crucial to the structural

[16] That is, the affect is no longer a cathectic discharge-process; it does not serve as a safety valve for drive-tension dammed up by repression.

approach, but she does not make the transition from the cathectic- to the signal-theory. She wrote (*ibid.*, pp. 259–60):

The conception of affects as tension-phenomena is, of course, in line with Freud's earliest formulations of the working of the psychic apparatus and the pleasure-pain principle (*The Interpretation of Dreams*). On the quantitative side we have, I think, to conceive of some threshold above which instinct-tension becomes appreciable as affect, and of a higher threshold, which may be attained either by the strength of the stimulus itself or by damming due to frustration, above which affect becomes intolerable and necessitates some immediate discharge, either outwards or inwards.

—Brierley's viewing of affects as tension-phenomena is certainly in keeping with the general conception of ego-psychology: the ego, the secondary process, strives on the one hand to bind mobile cathexes, and on the other to control and delay their discharge. But even in terms of the cathectic (second) theory one might consider affects as tension-phenomena, as phenomena of drive-tension mounting to threshold-intensity; though—since this theory is concerned with mobile cathexes and deals with the safety-valve role of affects—this distinction of tension *versus* discharge has little theoretical meaning in it. However, it has much theoretical meaning on the level of the third, the ego-theory, of affects. Yet it is possible that a *pure* tension-concept of affect (Brierley's is not quite that: note again the quote from pp. 259–60) empties out the baby with the bath water, by laying the foundations of an ego-theory of affects at the price of disregarding the indispensable elements of the superseded id-theory. Indeed Landauer (54) and Fenichel (16) referred to genetic (developmental) observations, showing how massive affect-discharge recedes with maturation, and thus began to lay the foundations of a theory which takes both the discharge and tension aspects of affect into consideration. Landauer (54, pp. 396–7) wrote:

Thus it is really only in children that we see affective attacks in an approximately pure form. But we see too how phylogenetically older affects are overlaid by others more recent and more complicated, which in their turn become obsolete and are gradually surmounted. Thus in a new-born baby fright can still be very easily and extensively mobilized, especially in the form of starting. It is only gradually that fright is increasingly pushed aside by anxiety.

and (*ibid.*, p. 401):

I have described anxiety as a secondary hysterical attack, which serves as a means of escape from the primary hysterical attack of fright. The affects of gaiety and sadness have been evolved as a means of escape from despair; they have absorbed the latter affect and amalgamated it with many other tendencies. In melancholic and manic seizures the two affects become to a large extent disintegrated and then certain characteristic features of despair become prominent.

Fenichel described the role of increasing ego-mastery in the decreasing discharge-character and increasing tension-character of affects during the course of development, as well as the consequences in affect-phenomena of pathological impairments of ego-mastery. Just as ideation is tamed into 'trying out' experimental action in thought, so, according to him, affect-discharge is tamed into anticipatory signals in the service of the ego. Fenichel (16, pp. 49–50) wrote:

. . . children and 'neurotic personalities', i.e. persons with many repressions, and therefore greater tensions, in general have more frequent emotional spells than normal adults. It is obvious that the normal adult does not lack emotions. But he does not have overwhelming emotional spells. Apparently the ego's increasing strength enables it somehow to get the upper hand of the affects at the moment when they arise. The ego is no longer overwhelmed by something alien to it, but it senses when this alien something begins to develop and simultaneously upon this recognition it re-establishes its mastery, binding the affects, using them for its purposes, 'taming' them as it were. To be sure, even the most adult ego can do this only to a certain degree. Too much excitement is emotionally upsetting for everyone. Thus we see that the first stage, in which the ego is weak and the affects dominant, is followed by a second in which the ego is strong and has learned to use the affects for its purposes. But a third state is always possible in which once more an elemental affect may overwhelm the organism.

Furthermore, Fenichel (17, p. 43) wrote:

When the child learns to control his motility, purposeful actions gradually take the place of mere discharge reactions; the child can now prolong the time between stimulus and reaction and achieve a certain tolerance of tension. The characteristic capacity for 'trying out' that is thus acquired changes the ego's relation to its affects. Affects are originally archaic discharge syndromes that supplant voluntary actions under certain exciting conditions. Now the growing ego learns to 'tame' affects and to use them for its own anticipating purposes.

—Indeed, the very fact that Freud in his *The Problem of Anxiety* envisaged two forms of anxiety production—on the one hand, anxiety issuing from economic conditions, i.e. as safety-valve drive-discharge, and on the other, anxiety being issued by the ego as a signal (pp. ·108–9)—already foreshadows Landauer's and Fenichel's views.

Most recently Jacobson (42) has criticized sharply both the tension-, and the discharge-theory of affects. She argued justly:

MacCurdy [56] and even Brierley [6] and Rapaport [60] [17] seem to ignore . . . that not only all normal ego functions, but particularly direct instinct gratifications, such as the sexual act or eating, are accompanied by intensive affective expression (42, ms. p. 29).

Analysing the course of the pleasure-experience in orgasm, she concluded that (*a*) the orgastic experience includes alternating increases of tension and partial discharges accompanying the rise of tension to a climax and its drop after the climax; (*b*) the affect-experience corresponds neither to tension nor to discharge *per se*, but rather to the change (increase or decrease) in tension. Thus, too, is a combined tension- and discharge-theory of affect. But this theory leaves us with the questions: (*a*) does it not limit itself to considering only the conscious experience of affect? (*b*) does it not equate the concepts of pleasure-pain as defined in the pleasure-principle with subjectively experienced affect? But more about this later. Jacobson (42, p. 39) wrote:

If what we perceive as feelings is not ' tension ' —in contradistinction to ' discharge '—but the flux of mobile psychic energy released, the changes in the level of tension—or in the amount of excitation respectively—above a certain threshold, then Brierley's tension-concept would become more meaningful. But her argument against the discharge idea would be senseless, because what we would ' feel ' would be the rises as well as the drops of tension in the course of a discharge process.

The recent closely reasoned and stimulating manuscript of M. Schur (67) concerning the

theory of anxiety centres also on this discharge *versus* signal (tension) dichotomy, and proposes a theory to resolve it. His theory—as I see it—stresses that the ego is always passive in anxiety experiences, and that anxiety is always a regression phenomenon. He therefore negates the ' signal-theory ' and explains the role of the ego in anxiety by means of Kris's (51) concept of ' regression in the service of the ego.' Though Schur's theory appears to have a primarily id-psychological slant, actually it touches on the least clear, yet central issues of the ego-psychology of affects, and it treats of ego-aspects of the anxiety and affect problem not heretofore discussed in the literature.

But let us return to the affect theory of *The Problem of Anxiety*, to outline further features of it. Freud takes cognizance there of the innate factors in affect-formation.[18] He characterizes affects as congenital hysterical attacks and suggests that even the obscure phobias of early childhood are remnants of congenital equipment commonly observed in animals. Freud (33, pp. 70–71) wrote:

For we hold that other affects as well are reproductions of past experiences of a character vital to the organism, experiences possibly even antedating the individual; and we draw a comparison between these, as universal, specific, congenital hysterical attacks, and the seizures of the hysterical neurosis, later and individually acquired, the genesis and significance of which as memory symbols have been made clearly manifest by analysis. It would of course be most desirable to be able to demonstrate the validity of this conception for a number of other affects, but at the present time we are far from being in a position to do this.

and further (*ibid.*, p. 117):

The enigmatic phobias of early childhood deserve mention once again at this point. Certain of them —the fear of being alone, of the dark, of strangers —we can understand as reactions to the danger of object loss; with regard to others—fear of small animals, thunderstorms, etc.—there is the possibility that they represent the atrophied remnants of an innate preparedness against reality dangers such as is so well developed in other animals. It is the part of this archaic heritage having to do with object loss which alone has utility for man. If such childhood phobias become fixed, grow more intense, and persist into a later period of life,

---

[17] Jacobson's criticism applies to my discussion in *Emotions and Memory* (60), which at the time failed to consider the structural ego-psychological issues. Cf., however, my discussions in *Organization and Pathology of Thought* (61), and in ' The Conceptual Model of Psy-

choanalysis ' (62).

[18] In doing so, he returns to a conception expressed already in *Studies in Hysteria* (pp. 151–2), according to which hysterical attacks are abnormal expressions of affects.

analysis demonstrates that their content has become connected with instinctual demands, has become the representative of internal dangers also.

Thus Freud's ego-theory of affects implies the recognition of the innate character of some basic affect-discharge channels, and even the innate character of their thresholds and of their relation to releasing stimuli. It seems safe to assert that any theory of affects which implies the structural point of view will consider these innate aspects of affects as its point of departure. But Freud's theory also shows how these innate structures are to be embedded into the rest of the theory. These preformed affect-discharge channels are made use of for safety-valve discharge by a whole series of conflicted drives on various levels of structure-formation in the course of development. In the case of anxiety, for instance, the series of conflicts has the common denominator of helplessness, and some of the situations in which conflicts leading to helplessness use anxiety as a safety-valve are: birth, separation from the mother, castration threat, etc. Furthermore, Freud points up that these inborn discharge-channels and thresholds—as well as new ones formed in the course of development—come progressively, with advancing psychic structure-formation, under the control of the ego. Freud (**33**, pp. 114–5) wrote:

The danger situation is the recognized, remembered and anticipated situation of helplessness. Anxiety is the original reaction to helplessness in the traumatic situation, which is later reproduced as a call for help in the danger situation. The ego, which has experienced the trauma passively, now actively repeats an attenuated reproduction of it with the idea of taking into its own hands the directing of its course.

and further (*ibid.*, pp. 108–9):

The anxiety felt in the process of birth now became the prototype of an affective state which was obliged to share the fate of other affects. It was reproduced either automatically in situations which were analogous to that of its origin and as an inexpedient type of reaction, after having been an appropriate one in the initial situation of danger; or else the ego acquired control over this affect and reproduced it itself, making use of it as a warning of danger and as a means of rousing into action the pleasure-pain mechanism. . . . To anxiety in later life were thus attributed two modes of origin: the one involuntary, automatic, economically justified when-

ever there arose a situation of danger analogous to birth; the other, produced by the ego when such a situation merely threatened, in order to procure its avoidance.

Fenichel (**17**, pp. 133–4) states some aspects of this view of the development of affects concisely:

This triple stratification of anxiety may be summarized in a short table:
(1) Trauma Anxiety automatic and unspecific.
(2) Danger Anxiety in the service of the ego, affect created by anticipation, controlled and used as a warning signal.
(3) Panic [19] Ego control fails, affect becomes overwhelming, regression to state (1); anxiety spell in anxiety hysteria.
The same triple stratification of anxiety will be found again in all other affects.

While as a schema this triple stratification appears to be correct, in actuality there is a fluid transition between the three; Fenichel's emphasis on ego-control also seems to imply that there are transitions of all shades between these three strata, depending on the availability of the synthetizing forces of the ego (and these, of course, vary in the course of individual development, show inter-individual variations, and fluctuate in the adult individual also). On the one hand, there occur normally, even at sustained ego-control, automatic affect-phenomena; on the other, affect-attacks due to pathological failing of ego-controls have many shades short of panic. This, too, seems to be the implication of Fenichel's phrase concerning the ego's ' taming ' of affects. One facet of this process is described in Jones' discussion of the various layers of hate, fear, and guilt affects, and of their relation to defensive operations. Further light is thrown on it by the process of binding of affects by processes of thought, pointed out already by Freud and Breuer. They (**18**, p. 31) wrote:

Abreaction is . . . not the only . . . solution. . . . The normal man succeeds by means of associations in dissipating the accompanying affect.

This process of binding affects by processes of thought is elucidated in Freud's description of the work of mourning. He (**29**, p. 154) wrote:

The task is now carried through bit by bit, under great expense of time and cathectic energy, while

---

[19] Fenichel (**13**) likes to use the analogy that panic occurs when the drive-tension is excessive, and thus the anxiety signal acts as a lighted match in a powder keg.

all the time the existence of the lost object is continued in the mind. Each single one of the memories and hopes which bound the libido to the object is brought up and hypercathected, and the detachment of the libido from it accomplished. Why this process of carrying out the behest of reality bit by bit, which is in the nature of compromise, should be so extraordinarily painful is not at all easy to explain in terms of mental economics. It is worth noting that this pain seems natural to us. The fact is, however, that when the work of mourning is completed the ego becomes free and uninhibited again.

Glover's characterization of certain obsessional systems, too, seems to be relevant and to elucidate this process of binding. Indeed it seems to link ' binding ' and ' taming ' of affects, and to suggest that their end-products are variable and modulated affects instead of massive affect-attacks. Glover (36, p. 137) wrote:

. . . we see that apparently complicated rituals . . . provide an ever more complicated meshwork of conceptual systems through which affect may pass in a. finely divided state. When . . . these rituals are interfered with, we observe once more the existence of massive affects.

Fenichel's and A. Freud's discussions of defences against affects elucidate this taming process. Fenichel's discussion (14) of defence against anxiety, and of anxiety as a motive of defence, is a particularly instructive analysis of the hierarchic layering of gradually tamed affects. Anna Freud's (17a) discussion centres on the relation between defences against drives and defences against affects, and states sharply the relative independence of these two. She wrote (pp. 34–5):

We know that the fate of the affect associated with an instinctual demand is not simply identical with that of its ideational representative. Obviously, however, one and the same ego can have at its disposal only a limited number of possible means of defence. At particular periods in life and according to its own specific structure the individual ego selects now one defensive method now another— it may be repression, displacement, reversal, etc.— and these it can employ both in its conflict with the instincts and in its defence against the liberation of affect. If we know how a particular patient seeks to defend himself against the emergence of his instinctual impulses, i.e. what is the nature of his habitual ego-resistances, we can form an idea of his probable attitude towards his own unwelcome affects. If, in another patient, particular forms of affect-transformation are strongly in evidence, such as complete suppression of emotion, denial,

etc., we shall not be surprised if he adopts the same methods of defence against his instinctual impulses and his free associations. It is the same ego, and in all its conflicts it is more or less consistent in using every means which it has at its command.

Fenichel pursues further Anna Freud's distinction between defences against drives and defences against affects; his treatment of blocking, postponement, displacement, equivalents, reaction-formations, change of quality, isolation, projection and introjection, and the varieties of defences against guilt (16 and 17, p. 161 ff.) appears to be singular in the literature. Yet even this discussion leaves the concept of ' defence against affects ' with some of the same lack of clarity as Jones' (45) contribution left it. (a) Fenichel speaks of defences against affects as ' primitive defences ', a phrase suggesting a relation to ' pre-stages of defence '. ' Pre-stages of defence ' in turn seems at least in part to imply for Fenichel (17) inborn mechanisms; it certainly implies for Hartmann (38) such inborn mechanisms of ' primary autonomy ' which determine the subsequent choice of defence-mechanisms used against drives. If these ' primitive defences ' against affects are indeed to be so understood, then they must be closely linked to, or identical with, the thresholds and other propensities of inborn affect discharge-channels. (b) Fenichel does not shut the door on interpreting ' defence against affects ' as defence against the drive-impulse which gave rise to them; though (c) in the main he seems—in agreement with A. Freud—to suggest that signal-affect just like thought, and affect-charge just like ideas, and all of these just like drives, are subject to defensive operations. It is possible that this lack of clarity arises because all these three forms of defence are extant and used on the various levels of the motivational and structural hierarchy in all kinds of complex combinations.

Landauer pointed out another aspect of the ' taming of affects ', namely their changing their ' attack ' character to one of a continuous state, and attributed it to continuous superego stimulation, as Freud did for grief (29), guilt (31), and certain forms of anxiety (33). Landauer (54, p. 389) wrote:

Are the affects really reactions? In children we still see them as such. But in later life anxiety is apparently continuous in the anxious-minded, the pessimist is permanently melancholy and the cheerful man consistently buoyant. How does an isolated reaction become a continuous state? Freud has solved this problem in the theory of the affects by demonstrating the function of the super-ego in their release. He illustrated his remarks chiefly from the example of anxiety.

Landauer expressed the conception of continuous affect-stimulation in a different way also, implying—as did Jones (45)—a conception of hierarchic layering of affects arising from defensive operations, directed against more basic affects. Landauer (54, p. 402) wrote:

Some of the affects have been relegated to subordinate egos, whilst the ego-in-chief addresses itself to reality in a manner at once reasonable and good, affectionate and defensive. These affects have gradually become shut off, have dwindled into mere reflexes. But the converse process may take place and super-affects be formed. Thus there arises embarrassment, i.e. fear of shame, and prudence, i.e. fear of anxiety. Since a prohibited affect threatens to return again and again, the super-affect, once formed, seems to be continuously present. A mood or a certain type of temperament is created. The commonest super-affect is certainly anxiety, but there are quite a number of other super-affects. Embarrassment may mean not only that we fear shame but that we are ashamed of fear. Next to anxiety sadness is, I think, the commonest super-affect. Since it may bring about a real loss of love or, later, forestalling the condemnation of the super-ego, an endopsychic loss of love, sadness becomes itself an occasion for sadness.

While Landauer's terminology (subordinate egos, super-affects) is not easy to follow and his documentation is insufficient, he certainly points more than any other psycho-analytic author—excepting perhaps Flügel (1948)—to the need to explain continuous affects which take the form of structuralized affective states and even of character traits. Flügel (1948)—like Drever—notes the insufficiencies of a purely dynamic conflict-theory of affect for the explanation of sustained pleasurable affects, and advances a theory of hierarchically layered derivative needs to explain these. Landauer's suggestion that continous affects are to be explained by continuous stimulation by one of the three structural divisions of the psyche

seems to fit certain cases (e.g. certain forms of sadness and guilt). But studies of boredom (Fenichel, 14; Greenson, 1951), apathy (Greenson, 1950), teasing (Sperling, 1951), Freud's (34) discussion of humour, Kris's (48, 49, 50) various papers on the comic, and particularly Bibring's (3a) discussion of depression and Brenman's (4) discussion of teasing, suggest that in general such affective states are too complex to be so accounted for, and though they are ego-reactions or ego-states, yet in them ego, id, and super-ego contributions are integrated into complex quasi-stable substructures.[20]

The attempt to develop a definitive psycho-analytic theory of affects has culminated in two attempts at a classification of affects. The first of these, Glover's (37, p. 300), brought the great variety and complexity of affect phenomena most clearly to the fore:

. . . affective phenomena call for a greater variety of approaches than any other mental manifestation. This is borne out by the fact that affects can be classified in a great variety of ways. They can be described in crude qualitative terms, e.g. of subjective pleasure or ' pain ', or labelled descriptively according to the predominant ideational system associated with them in consciousness. They can be classified by reference to the instinct or component instinct from which they are derived, or they can be considered as either ' fixed ' or ' labile '. They can be divided into primary affects and secondary affects, more precisely into ' positive ' and ' reactive ' affects, or they can be considered as tension and discharge phenomena. Finally, they can be grouped as simple or compound (' mixed ' and/or ' fused ') affects.

Otherwise, however, Glover's theory failed to pass from the second (cathectic) to the third (signal) level of affect-theory, and remained—as Jacobson (42, p. 21) implied in her discussion of it—a fragmentary drive-theory without significant application of the structural point of view. The second of these classifications implying an affect theory—Jacobson's—is founded on the structural point of view and succeeds in restating the ' conflict theory ' of affects in structural terms. In this theory, affects arise from tensions in the id or ego, or

---

[20] By this comparison I do not imply that Landauer's super-affects, moods, affect-attitudes crystallized into character-traits, apathy, etc., are of the same order of complexity. I mean only that all these, though they must be dealt with by a theory of affects, are complex integrated formations which cannot be accounted for by an affect-theory alone. Kris's contributions are well known, thus only his theory of the affective reaction to the becoming conscious of daydreams (51) should be particularly pointed to. Bibring's (3a) and Brenman's (4) contributions are, however, little known and the reader's attention is called to their far-reaching implications for the extension of the structural point of view in general and that of the theory of affective states in particular. It would lead too far afield to discuss them here.

from tensions between id and ego, or ego and super-ego. Jacobson (**42**, pp. 22–3) wrote:

We may consider replacing . . . [Glover's] with a classification that employs our current structural concepts. Even though all affects are ego experiences and develop in the ego, one of their qualitative determinants must be the site of the underlying energetic tension by which they have been induced and which may arise anywhere within the psychic organization. Practically, certain affects have always been characterized in this way; guilt feelings, for instance, are commonly defined as arising from a tension between ego and super-ego. There is no reason why we should not introduce this kind of classification for affect types in general. Thus we might distinguish:

(1) simple and compound affects arising from intrasystemic tension:

    (a) affects that represent instinctual drives proper, i.e. that arise directly from tensions in the id (e.g. sexual excitement, rage);

    (b) affects that develop directly from tensions in the ego [21] (e.g. fear of reality and physical pain, as well as components of the more enduring feelings and feeling attitudes, such as object love and hate or thing interest);

(2) simple and compound affects induced by intersystemic tensions:

    (a) affects induced by tensions between the ego and the id (e.g. fear of the id, components of disgust, shame, and pity);

    (b) affects induced by tensions between ego and super-ego (e.g. guilt feelings, components of depression).

As will be noticed, I have not included tensions between ego and reality. These represent conflict, that is, affective responses to reality. The underlying energetic psychic tension can only arise within the psychic organization and not between it and the outside world. (This is another example of the prevailing lack of distinction between affective and energetic processes.)

The problems Jacobson's theory leaves us with are these: (a) One wonders whether or not her structural theory is achieved at a price of disregarding some of the insights (drive representation, affect-charge, affect-discharge) of Freud's previous drive-theory of affects without which an affect-theory cannot be complete, since it

would disregard the hierarchic continuum discussed above. (b) One is left uncertain whether her treatment of pleasure and pain (referred to earlier in this paper) means to subsume pleasure and pain as affects, and if so, whether or not so doing disregards the fact that in the conception of the '*pleasure-pain principle*' *pleasure* and *pain* are *neither affects* subjectively felt nor ' affect-charges ', *but concepts* the referent of which is the process of discharge regulation; the various phases of this may or may not be experienced as pleasure or pain, and if they are so experienced, they *are not just pleasure or pain in general but specific qualities of pleasure and pain.*[22] (c) It is difficult to be sure whether or not Jacobson, by limiting her discussion to the conscious subjective experience of affect, has neglected affect-discharge and affect-equivalents, for which it is hard to account without incorporating the second (the cathectic) theory into the definitive one. An affect-theory centred on the conscious experience of affects runs into yet another difficulty: the very act of becoming conscious is dependent on a complex balance involving more than just the affect-process (cf. Kris, **51**, and Brenman, **4**). (d) One wonders whether in its classificatory simplicity it may not preclude a theoretical accounting of the many shades and varieties of affects arising in the taming process, as well as those varieties of continuous ' affective states' which we referred to above and which appear to be quasi-stable formations integrating complex id, ego, and super-ego contributions and their shifting balances into something like a sub-structure. In passing, it may be mentioned that the structural point of view does not seem to stop at the analysis of ego, id, super-ego factors; it enters upon the study of structuralization within each of these, as well as upon the study of structuralization of functions uniting components from all (Hartmann, **38**; Kris, **51**; Brenman, **4**).

V

The complexity of the phenomena and of the theoretical implications of affects which I have attempted to unfold here in the fashion of a review makes a definitive formulation of an up-to-date psycho-analytic theory of affects certainly ill-advised, if not impossible. Yet I

---

[21] Federn (**12**) has dealt with these extensively and, indeed, attempted to reduce all affects to this category.

[22] The same difficulty is particularly clear in a paper by Jelgersma (**44**) dealing with the psycho-analytic theory of feelings.

should like to sketch the outlines of a theory as it seems to emerge from this review, because even though necessarily characterized by gaps and assumptions easily proved to be unwarranted, it will give us one possible interpretation of where we stand and thus may facilitate orientation for future observation and theorizing.

The following outline of a theory attempts to integrate the affect theories of the second and third phase, and uses some contribution from the theory of the first phase.

(1) Affects use—to begin with—inborn channels and thresholds of discharge. These may be considered apparatuses pre-existing the differentiation of ego and id from their undifferentiated matrix (Hartmann, Kris, Loewenstein, 40). This is the referent of the phrase ' affects are inherited hysterical attacks '. In this respect affects are common properties of the species, and this may have to do with the roots of their social role in communication and empathy (Schilder, 65). Yet even in this respect there are already at birth great interindividual differences (Bergman and Escalona, 2; Escalona and Leitch, 10) which seem to have to do with what develops into ' predisposition to anxiety ' and into various affect-equivalents in psychosomatic pathology, as well as into various 'frozen affects' taking the form of character traits (Reich, 63).

(2) At the reconstructed hypothetical stage (see p. 182 ff., above) where the pleasure-principle holds full sway, drive- (mobile-) cathexes strive for immediate discharge; affects arise as safety-valve functions when drive-discharge by drive-action is not possible because of the absence of the drive-object in reality. This stage is hypothetical because drive-tension, too, has thresholds and before these are reached no discharge occurs; thus these set limits to the full success of the pleasure-principle, i.e. they prevent a completely tension-less state. At this stage affects appear as discharge-phenomena of a part (a determinate quantity) of drive-cathexis, which is conceptualized as ' affect-charge ' and is probably determined by the amount of cathexis the various inborn affect-discharge channels can carry.

(3) ' Affect charge ' and ' idea ' are drive-representations, both still operating with mobile cathexes, abiding by the pleasure-principle. Affect-discharges are massive affect-storms, which discharge into the interior of the body through secretory and motor innervations, instead of discharging in action on to the drive-object.

(4) The general development of psychic structure begins with innate discharge-regulating thresholds, is fostered by delays of discharge enforced by reality conditions, and progresses by internalization of the delay of discharge caused by reality, establishing an *ability to delay*. This ability is achieved by defences (counter-cathectic energy-distributions), which may be regarded as alterations of discharge-thresholds. The damming up of drives by defences makes for more intensive and more varied use of the affect-discharge channels and of the corresponding ' affect-charges '.

The establishment of counter-cathectic energy distributions, however, has other crucial consequences. It gives rise to varied derivative and partial drives (the latter particularly in conjunction with somatic maturation), some of which arise as modifications of the drives defended against, others as modifications of drives to which the counter-cathectic energy-distributions generalized (that is, spread or were displaced), others as motivating forces originating from the counter-cathectic energy-distributions themselves (cf. Rapaport, 61, pp. 699–701). These all have their thresholds of discharge, and when prevented from discharging by reality conditions or by the counter-cathectic energy-distributions which developed as internalizations of these reality conditions, they apparently use and modify the thresholds of the existing affect-discharge channels. This process is repeated variously for the derivative and partial motivations also in the course of development, giving rise to a hierarchy of motivations ranging from drives to interests and preferences. This process is apparently synonymous with that of binding (Freud, 23; see also Rapaport, 62) and/or neutralization (Hartmann, Kris, Loewenstein, 41) of mobile cathexes. Another aspect of this process is the development of the secondary thought-process from the primary one, that of experimental action in thought by means of small amounts of bound (neutralized) cathexes and memory traces, from hallucinatory gratification by means of drive-cathecting of memory traces to perceptual (hallucinatory) intensity (see Freud, 25; also Rapaport, 61). The drive-representing idea tends to become reality-representing thought. Drive-discharge is delayed and becomes action using thought as preparation, and the tension dammed up by delay is discharged through the safety-valve of affect-discharge. But affects do not remain inborn discharge-channels used by dammed up-drives as safety-valves; they too partake in the development sketched: they become progressively tamed. This is achieved by various means: (a) At each level of the motivational hierarchy the derivative motivations use affects as safety-valve discharge-channels, but the cathexes of these motivations are more and more neutralized with the ascent of the hierarchy; consequently the cathexes of the affect-charges too become less and less peremptory, and the affect-discharges less automatic and massive. (b) It appears that not only are the discharge-thresholds of the drive-derivatives and of the affects altered with the ascent of the hierarchy, but also new, more complex, and subtle affect discharge-channels are created with general maturation, ascending hierarchy, and psychic structure-formation. (c) Furthermore, affect-charges themselves also seem to become subject to defensive counter-cathecting, that is, to direct modification of their discharge-thresholds.

(5) This hierarchic development has a dual outcome: (a) On the one hand, since various drives and derivative drives (motivations) from all levels of the hierarchy remain effective in psychic life, we find in the normal adult also affect-phenomena of quite mobile cathexes, akin to massive affect-attacks, just as we find in his conscious thought primary-process phenomena too. (b) On the other hand we find affects of highly neutralized cathexes, which serve as signals and means of reality-testing for orientation to both external reality (danger) and internal reality (drive-inundation). The continuum of affects extends in all shadings from massive affect-attacks to mere signals and even signals of signals (Fenichel, 13). The development of the motivational- and affect-hierarchy is one aspect of structure-formation and ego-development. In the course of it the ego, which originally endured affects passively, obtains control of them and comes to release them in tamed forms of anticipatory signals. Massive affect-attacks may come about either owing to weakening of ego-control or with the 'consent' of the ego as 'regressions in the service of the ego' (Kris, 51); Schur (67)

suggests that affect-signals too are such 're-gressions in the service of the ego'. To be sure, there are great differences within the normal range as to which end of the affect-continuum, and which qualities of affect within it, are emphasized in the individual. On the whole, the less rich the hierarchic development of controlling counter-cathectic energy-distributions, the less the variability and modulation and the greater the intensity of massive affect-outburst; the less flexible and more excessively rigid these controls, the more meagre both in intensity, variability, and modulation affects become; and, as so often in life-phenomena, the optimum is not the maximum. Rich and modulated affect-life appears to be the indicator of a 'strong ego'.

(b) 'Affect-charge' if discharged may arouse further tensions. To prevent the development of these, the underlying drive as well as the 'affect-charge' must be defended against. Thus affects (e.g., anxiety) become motives of defence (Fenichel, 17). It appears that otherwise also, under special conditions, affect-charge as energy-quantity may come to play the role of motivation. But these conditions are not well understood and it is not certain that, if understood, they cannot be accounted for by assuming that the drive underlying the affect rather than the affect itself acts as motivation. Should this way out not prove feasible, we are faced with a return—true, only a limited and partial one—of the first phase of affect-theory, in the framework of the third-phase theory.

(7) The development of the ascending hierarchy of motivations appears to be one aspect of psychic structure-formation, id-ego-superego differentiation. On each level of the hierarchy the conflict of discharge-bent cathexes with innate thresholds, or with reality (absent object), or with counter-cathexes, is the dynamic aspect of affect-formation. The economic aspect of affect-formation is the partial discharge of motivational cathexes of ever-increasing neutralization. The structural aspect and the adaptive aspect [23] of affect-formation are more complex.

(8) Structurally the integration of the ascending motivational systems into id, ego, and super-ego amounts to the creation of mutually

---

[23] The 'adaptive aspect' is not of the same order as the dynamic, economic and structural. Actually it may be regarded as part of the structural aspect. It is here separated and singled out thus because of its singular importance, which has been already stressed by Hartmann (38).

controlling systems of organization, continuous conflicts among which also give rise to tensions and to their discharge, i.e. to affects which may thus become continuous. This is what Landauer (54) and Jacobson (42) conceptualized, following Freud's (31, 33) lead. But such enduring affective states are mostly not outcomes of a conflict within one, or between two, of the three institutions; rather they often come about as integrations of complex balances and conflicts of components from all three major structural divisions of the psyche. The closer study of these complex affect-states and of their chronic characterological forms (see e.g. Brenman, 4) may lead to an important advancement of the structural point of view.

(9) From the *point of view of adaptation*: On the one hand, affects seem to start even in human beings to some extent—and certainly in animals—as what Hartmann called states of adaptedness: that is, the affect-discharge apparatus has a limited attunement to certain external reality stimuli, such as is seen in startle (Landis, 55) and smile (Spitz, 69). On the other hand, affects as signals are just as indispensable a means of reality-testing as thoughts. Indeed, they are more indispensable for reality-testing in all except successfully intellectualizing and obsessional characters. Reality-testing without the contribution of affect-signal readily changes into obsessional or paranoid magic. The expelled affect-signal returns through the back door: there is no warning of the impending affect-formation which may therefore, unimpeded, appear as mobile cathexis and disturber of the secondary process.

VI

The theory of affects, the bare outlines of which seem to emerge, integrates three components: *inborn affect discharge-channels* and discharge-thresholds of drive-cathexes; the use of these inborn channels as safety-valves and indicators of drive-tension, the modification of their thresholds by drives and derivative motivations prevented from drive-action, and the formation thereby of *the drive-representation termed affect-charge*; and the progressive ' taming ' and advancing ego-control, in the course of psychic structure-formation, of the affects which are thereby turned into *affect-signals* released by the ego.

BIBLIOGRAPHY

(1) ALEXANDER, F., ' Fundamental Concepts of Psychosomatic Research: Psychogenesis, Conversion, Specificity ', *Psychosom. Med.*, **5**, 205–210, 1943.

(2) BERGMAN, P. and ESCALONA, S. ' Unusual Sensitivities in Very Young Children.' In: *The Psychoanal. Study of the Child*, 3/4, New York, Int. Univ. Press, 1949, pp. 333–352.

(3a) BIBRING, E. ' On Depression '. Unpublished ms., 1947.

(3) BLEULER, E. ' Affectivity, Suggestibility, Paranoia ', *State Hosp. Bull.*, **4**, 481–601,1912.

(4) BRENMAN, M. ' On Teasing and Being Teased: and the Problem of " Moral Masochism",' *The Psychoanal. Study of the Child*, **7.**

(5) BREUER, J. and FREUD, S. (1895). *Studies in Hysteria.* Trans. by A. A. Brill, New York, Nerv. and Ment. Dis. Monographs, 1937.

(6) BRIERLEY, M. ' Affects in Theory and Practice ', *Int. J. Psycho-Anal.*, **18**, 256–268, 1937.

(7) BÜRGER-PRINZ, H. and KAILA, M. ' Über die Struktur des amnestischen Symptomenkomplexes ', *Z. Neurol. Psychiat.*, **124**, 553–595, 1930. ' On the Structure of the Amnesic Syndrome.' In: *Organization and Pathology of Thought*, ed. by David Rapaport, New York, Columbia Univ. Press, 1951, pp. 650–686.

(8) DEUTSCH, H. ' Some Forms of Emotional Disturbance and Their Relationship to Schizophrenia', *Yearb. of Psa.*, **1**, 121–136, 1945.

(9) DEWEY, J. ' The Theory of Emotion ', *Psa. Rev.*, **1**, 553–569, 1894; **2**, 13–32, 1895.

(9a) DREVER, J. *Instinct in Man.* Cambridge, Cambridge Univ. Press, 1917.

(10) ESCALONA, S. and LEITCH, M. ' Progress Report: Early Phases of Personality Development; A Non-Normative Study of Infant Behavior ', Report to the U.S. Public Health Service, Project MH–27, 1951.

(11) FEDERN, P. ' Das Ich als Subjekt und Objekt im Narzissismus ', *Int. Z. Psa.*, **15**, 393–425, 1929.

(12) —— ' Zur Unterscheidung des gesunden und krankhaften Narzissismus ', *Imago*, **22**, 1–40, 1936.

(13) FENICHEL, O. ' Über Angstabwehr, insbesondere durch Libidinisierung ', *Int. Z. Psa.*, **20**, 476–489, 1934. ' Concerning Defense Against Anxiety, Particularly by Libidinization.' In: *The Collected Papers of Otto Fenichel*, New York, Norton, in press.

(14) FINICHEL, O. 'Zur Psychologie der Langeweile', *Imago*, 20, 270-281, 1934. 'On the Psychology of Boredom.' In: *Organization and Pathology of Thought*, ed. by David Rapaport, New York, Columbia Univ. Press, 1951, pp. 349-361.

(15) —— 'Zur Theorie der psychoanalytischen Technik', *Int. Z. Psa.*, 21, 78-95, 1935. 'Concerning the Theory of Psychoanalytic Technique.' In: *The Collected Papers of Otto Fenichel*, New York, Norton, in press.

(16) —— 'The Ego and the Affects', *Psa. Rev.*, 28, 47-60, 1941.

(17) —— *The Psychoanalytic Theory of Neurosis*, New York, Norton, 1945.

(17a) FREUD, A. (1936). *The Ego and the Mechanisms of Defense*. New York, Int. Univ. Press, 1946.

(18) FREUD, S. (1893). 'On the Psychical Mechanism of Hysterical Phenomena', *Col. Pap.*, Vol. I, London, Hogarth, 1946, pp. 24-41.

(19) —— (1894). 'The Defence Neuro-Psychoses', *Col. Pap.*, Vol. I, London, Hogarth, 1946, pp. 59-75.

(20) —— (1894). 'The Justification for Detaching from Neurasthenia a Particular Syndrome: The Anxiety-Neurosis', *Col. Pap.*, Vol. I, London, Hogarth, 1946, pp. 76-106.

(21) —— (1895). 'Entwurf einer Psychologie', *Aus den Anfängen der Psychoanalyse*, London, Imago Publishing Co., 1950, pp. 373-466.

(22) —— (1898). 'Sexuality in the Ætiology of the Neuroses', *Col. Pap.*, Vol. I, London, Hogarth, 1946, pp. 220-248.

(23) —— (1900). 'The Interpretation of Dreams', *The Basic Writings*, New York, Modern Library, 1938, pp. 179-548.

(24) —— (1909). 'Analysis of a Phobia in a Five-Year-Old Boy', *Col. Pap.*, Vol. III, London, Hogarth, 1946, pp. 149-289.

(25) —— (1911). 'Formulations Regarding the Two Principles in Mental Functioning', *Col. Pap.*, Vol. IV, London, Hogarth, 1946, pp. 13-21.

(26) —— (1914). 'Further Recommendations in the Technique of Psycho-Analysis. Recollection, Repetition and Working Through', *Col. Pap.*, Vol. II, London, Hogarth, 1946, pp. 366-376.

(27) —— (1915). 'Repression', *Col. Pap.*, Vol. IV, London, Hogarth, 1946, pp. 84-97.

(28) —— (1915). 'The Unconscious', *Col. Pap.*, Vol. IV, London, Hogarth, 1946, pp. 98-136.

(29) —— (1917). 'Mourning and Melancholia', *Col. Pap.*, Vol. IV, London, Hogarth, 1946, pp. 152-170.

(30) —— (1920). *Beyond the Pleasure Principle*, London, Int. Psa. Press, 1922.

(31) —— (1923). *The Ego and the Id*, London, Hogarth, 1927.

(32) —— (1925). 'A Note upon the "Mystic Writing-Pad",' *Col. Pap.*, Vol. V, London, Hogarth, 1950, pp. 175-180.

(33) —— (1926). *The Problem of Anxiety*, New York, Norton, 1936.

(34) —— (1928). 'Humour', *Col. Pap.*, Vol. V, London, Hogarth, 1950, pp. 215-221.

(35) —— (1937). 'Analysis Terminable and Interminable', *Col. Pap.*, Vol. V, London, Hogarth, 1950, pp. 316-357.

(36) GLOVER, E. 'A Developmental Study of the Obsessional Neuroses', *Int. J. Psycho-Anal.*, 16, 131-144, 1935.

(37) —— 'The Psycho-Analysis of Affects', *Int. J. Psycho-Anal.*, 20, 299-307, 1939.

(37a) GREENSON, R. 'The Psychology of Apathy', *Psa. Quart.*, 18, 290-302; 1949.

(37b) GREENSON, R. 'Apathetic and Agitated Boredom'. Unpublished ms., 1950.

(37c) GRÜNINGER, U. *Zum Problem der Affektverschiebung*. Zürich, Buchdruckerei, des Schweizerischen Grütlivereins, 1917.

(38) HARTMANN, H. 'Ich-Psychologie und Anpassungsproblem', *Int. Z. Psa. and Imago*, 24, 62-135, 1939. 'Ego Psychology and the Problem of Adaptation.' In: *Organization and Pathology of Thought*, ed. by David Rapaport, New York, Columbia Univ. Press, 1951, pp. 362-396.

(39) HARTMANN, H. 'Technical Implications of Ego Psychology', *Psa. Quart.*, 20, 31-43, 1951.

(40) HARTMANN, H., KRIS, E., and LOEWENSTEIN, R. 'Comments on the Formation of Psychic Structure.' In: *The Psychoanal. Study of the Child*, 2, New York, Int. Univ. Press, 1946, pp. 11-38.

(41) —— 'Notes on the Theory of Aggression.' In: *The Psychoanal. Study of the Child*, 3/4, New York, Int. Univ. Press, 1949, pp. 9-36.

(42) JACOBSON, E. 'The Psychoanalytic Theory of Affects', ms., 1951.

(43) —— 'The Influence of the Speed Factors on the Pleasure-Unpleasure Qualities of Feelings and Their Relations to the Psychic Discharge Processes', ms., 1952.

(44) JELGERSMA, G. 'Psychoanalitischer Beitrag zu einer Theorie des Gefühls', *Int. Z. Psa.*, 7, 1-8, 1921.

(45) JONES, E. 'Fear, Guilt and Hate', *Int. J. Psycho-Anal.*, 10, 383-397, 1929.

(46) JUNG, C. (1906). *The Psychology of Dementia Præcox*, New York, Nerv. and Ment. Dis. Pub., 3, 1944.

(47) KANNER, L. 'Early Infantile Autism', *J. Pediatrics*, 25, 211-217, 1944.

(48) KRIS, E. 'The Psychology of Caricature', *Int. J. Psycho-Anal.*, 17, 285-303, 1936.

(49) —— 'Ego Development and the Comic', *Int. J. Psycho-Anal.*, 19, 77-90, 1938.

(50) —— 'Das Lachen als Mimischer Vorgang; Beiträge zur Psychoanalyse der Mimik', *Int. Z. Psa. and Imago*, 24, 146-148, 1939.

(51) —— 'On Preconscious Mental Processes', *Psa. Quart.*, 19, 540-560, 1950. Also in: *Organization and Pathology of Thought*, ed. by David

Rapaport, New York, Columbia Univ. Press, 1951, pp. 474-493.

(52) KULOVESI, Y. 'Psychoanalytische Bemerkungen zur James-Langeschen Affekttheorie', *Imago*, **17**, 392-398, 1931.

(53) LANDAUER, K. 'Die Gemütsbewegungen oder Affekte.' In: *Das psychoanalytische Volksbuch*, Vol. 2, Pt. 1, ed. by Paul Federn and Heinrich Meng, Stuttgart, Hyppokrates-Verlag, 1928, pp. 136-151.

(54) —— 'Affects, Passions and Temperament', *Int. J. Psycho-Anal.*, **19**, 388-415, 1938.

(55) LANDIS, C., and HUNT, W. A. *The Startle Pattern*, New York, Farrar and Rinehart, 1939.

(56) MACCURDY, J. T. *The Psychology of Emotion, Morbid and Normal*, New York, Harcourt, 1925.

(57) MAHLER, M. . 'Remarks on Psychoanalysis with Psychotic Children', *Quarterly J. of Ch ild Behavior*, **1**, 18-21, 1949.

(58) MAHLER, M. S., ROSS, J. R., JR., and DE FRIES, Z. 'Clinical Studies in Benign and Malignant Cases of Childhood Psychosis (Schizophrenialike)', *Amer. J. of Orthopsychiatry*, **19**, 295-305, 1949.

(59) PUTNAM, M. C. 'Case Study of an Atypical Two-and-a-Half-Year-Old', *Am. J. of Orthopsychiatry*, **18**, 1-30, 1948.

(60) RAPAPORT, D. *Emotions and Memory*, Baltimore, Williams and Wilkins, 1942.

(61) —— *Organization and Pathology of Thought*, New York, Columbia Univ. Press, 1951.

(62) —— 'The Conceptual Model of Psychoanalysis', *J. of Personality*, **20**, 56-81, 1951.

(63) REICH, W. *Charakteranalyse*, Vienna, Selbstverlag des Verfassers, 1933.

(64) SCHILDER, P. 'Über Gedankenentwicklung', *Z. Neurol. Psychiat.*, **59**, 250-263, 1920.

(65) —— *Medizinische Psychologie*, Berlin, Springer, 1924. *Medical Psychology*, trans. by David Rapaport, New York, Int. Univ. Press, in press.

(66) —— *Studien zur Psychologie und Symptomatologie der progressiven Paralyse*, Berlin, Karger, 1930. 'Studies Concerning the Psychology and Symptomatology of General Paresis.' In: *Organization and Pathology of Thought*, ed. by David Rapaport, New York, Columbia Univ. Press, 1951, pp. 519-580.

(67) SCHUR, M. 'Some Modifications of Freud's Theory of Anxiety', ms., 1952.

(67a) SPERLING, S. 'On Teasing'. Unpublished ms., 1950.

(68) SPINOZA, B. DE. *Improvement of the Understanding, Ethics, and Correspondence*, New York, Willey, 1901.

(69) SPITZ, R. A., and WOLF, K. M. 'The Smiling Response: A Contribution to the Ontogenesis of Social Relations', *Genetic Psychol. Monog.*, **34**, 57-125, 1946.

92

Harry Stack Sullivan's Theory of Schizophrenia

PATRICK MULLAHY

THROUGH THE YEARS, beginning in 1924, Sullivan published numerous papers on schizophrenia. Apparently his ideas on this "grave psychosis," as he called it, first began to take shape while he worked at Sheppard and Enoch Pratt Hospital. He went to Sheppard in 1923 as an Assistant Physician. In 1925 he was appointed Director of Clinical Research, retaining this post until June, 1930. It was there that he established his special receiving ward that became a spectacular success, not only under Sullivan's supervision but under the supervision of his successor, William V. Silverberg.

Many of the papers Sullivan wrote on schizophrenia during the years he spent at Sheppard have recently been collated and republished in *Schizophrenia as a Human Process*.[1]

Throughout his professional life he continued to develop his theory of schizophrenia as a grave disorder of living. In the lecture series published under the title of *Conceptions of Modern Psychiatry*, it is considerably elaborated and described in a language that, to my knowledge, has never been equaled in any psychiatric textbook.

Anxiety and Dynamic Balance. A major innovation in *Conceptions of Modern Psychiatry* is the conception of anxiety as a dynamic process, first acquired in infancy, and developing through the various phases of personality growth. In the case of potential male schizophrenic patients, it evolves or passes over into terror or literal panic, usually during the adolescent phase, under circumstances which cannot always be exactly specified, though they are amply illustrated. Sullivan believed that in women the onset of schizophrenia often occurs several years later than in men due to cultural factors which he did not attempt to pinpoint.

Anxiety may be characterized variously. In Sullivan's more mature formulations, it is a felt threat to, or actual loss of, self-esteem due to the actual, anticipated, or imaginary disapproval of significant other

This paper is based on a chapter of Mr. Mullahy's forthcoming book on the theories and therapeutic methods of Harry Stack Sullivan, tentatively entitled *Psychoanalysis and Interpersonal Psychiatry*, scheduled for publication by Science House in 1968.

[1] Harry Stack Sullivan, *Schizophrenia as a Human Process*. With Introduction and Commentaries by Helen Swick Perry. New York: W. W. Norton & Co. Inc., 1962.

INTERNATIONAL JOURNAL OF PSYCHIATRY, 1967, 4, pp. 492–521.

people or of disapproval of one's self, owing to the values and ideals one has acquired or developed. Its roots may be traced back to infancy when various activities of the baby may be intensely disturbing to the mother (or her surrogate). But an emotional disturbance in the mothering one need not arise from her observation of the infant's activities. Apparently any current emotional upset she suffers gets "communicated." Thus, according to Sullivan, various upset states in the mothering one may induce in the infant a tension state which may gradually develop into anxiety, a condition which may generalize increasingly as the youngster approaches the adolescent era.

Concomitantly, various other unfortunate experiences, maldevelopments and distortions which the individual suffers may all combine to render him abnormally vulnerable to the demands and stresses of the adolescent stage in Western Society—demands and stresses which he cannot successfully negotiate. It appears that in such cases, a powerful motivational system exists in dissociation which is contradictory to the self-dynamism and which is entirely unsuited to the type of life for which the self has been organized.

Sullivan uses the notion of a dynamic balance between the self-system and the dissociated elements or processes of the personality. In people who, owing to the evil effects of their education or acculturation, are destined or predisposed to become schizophrenic, the balance between the two is uneasy, a condition which may have been obscurely manifest for a considerable period. Some specific event may happen which destroys the equilibrium. Hours or days later panic may ensue, an experience that includes extremely unpleasant visceral sensations with a boundless and contentless (objectless) terror.

This may be illustrated by a brief account of one of Sullivan's patients, an only boy with five sisters who led "as sheltered a life as that situation would permit." [2] Soon after having been inducted into the armed forces, he was "prowling around" Washington, D.C. and one day was "gathered up" by a very well-dressed and charming dentist. This man took the boy to his office and performed fellatio on him. The following day he found himself, quite absent-mindedly, returning to the immediate vicinity of the dentist's office, whereupon he could no longer exclude from his awareness that he wanted to continue to have such experiences as he had had the day before. He became conscious of what Sullivan called abhorrent cravings, i.e., increasingly intense, because unsatisfied, longings to engage in performances that are abhorrent to one. Though the day before, his encounter may have seemed to be only a new kind of experience, now the realization burst upon him that he was a prey to homosexual desires, a realization that was attended by all sorts of revulsions and a feeling that it was infrahuman to have such interests. Presumably he then underwent panic for he arrived at (or was taken to) the hospital shortly afterward in what is called a schizophrenic disturbance.

Schizophrenia occurs upon the collapse of the self-system. This collapse frequently manifests itself as panic. Panic, in turn, represents failure of the *dissociative power* of the self.

The essence of the self, which is determined by its primary functions, namely, the fulfillment of needs and the preservation and maintenance of emotional security, represents a meaningful organization of life experience. Roughly speaking, this self includes one's habitual thoughts about the world and about oneself, one's everyday

[2] Harry Stack Sullivan, *The Interpersonal Theory of Psychiatry.* Edited by Helen Swick Perry and Mary Ladd Gawel with an Introduction by Mabel Blake Cohen, M.D. W. W. Norton & Co., Inc., 1953, p. 326.

perceptions (and misperceptions), one's more or less recognizable and familiar emotions and motives, one's attitudes about life in general, one's moral code, one's hopes and expectations about the future, and one's philosophy of life, if any. These may be said to constitute the stuff of life. Unless we are inclined toward reflection we tend to take them for granted. And, since we are, as a rule, products of our "culture," others share these meanings too, in the sense that the self of each of us is built up from widely held attitudes, beliefs, ideas, emotional patterns and norms of conduct. Thus, typically, our way of life, which the self-conscious personality structure embodies, is reinforced by the attitudes and behavior of members of our society and social class, aided and abetted nowadays by mass media of communication.

While it is perfectly true that every self, and every personality, is uniquely structured, Sullivan believed that this aspect of the person has been over-emphasized and is, in any event, beyond the grasp of science. Science deals with uniformities, with recurrent patterns. Furthermore, personality is not self-actional. Human experiences and activities require the cooperation of the environment, either directly or mediately. No matter how much "ego-autonomy" one may possess, he can exercise it only in conjunction with the powers or abilities and actions of other people, who embody widespread uniformities of behavior and dispositions or traits more or less common to people in the culture. Human life is a history of "transactions."

Because man is a social and moral being, nothing in the world is more horrifying to most of us—perhaps not even the prospect of imminent death, which some people, at least, can face with stoicism and unfaltering resolution—than the abrupt or insidious disorganization or disintegration of the self-conscious personality. An experience, or train of experiences, that undermines the structure of the self strikes at the very heart of whatever is meaningful, worthwhile or "good" in one's way of life. The pattern of one's thinking, imagining, perceiving, feeling is abruptly (or sometimes insidiously) torn apart so that the world has become "wholly irrational and incomprehensible."

Panic: Initial Phase of the Schizophrenic Process. When panic occurs, all organized activity is lost and all thought is paralyzed. Panic, according to Sullivan, is disorganization of the personality arising from the utterly unforeseen failure of something completely trusted and vital for one's safety; [3] it occurs when some essential aspect of the universe which one had long taken for granted suddenly collapses. The disorganization which follows is probably the most appalling state that man can undergo, and one that is entirely incompatible with life. It is, however, a transitory state.

Consider the experience of one young man whom Sullivan had interviewed. Parenthetically, I shall mention that for certain reasons (discussed in a general way in Sullivan's formulations of personality development and its distortions) this patient had sublimated all recognized manifestations of lustful (genital) integrative tendencies or motives. In general, sublimation is "the unwitting substitution, for a behavior pattern which encounters anxiety or collides with the self-system, of a socially more acceptable activity pattern which satisfies part of the motivational system that caused trouble." [4] In more fortunate circumstances the rest of the unsatisfied need or "motivational system" is discharged through the symbol processes occurring in sleep and in reverie. In dreams, impulses

[3] Harry Stack Sullivan, *Conceptions of Modern Psychiatry*. With a Foreword by the author and a Critical Appraisal of the Theory by Patrick Mullahy. New York: W. W. Norton & Co., Inc., 1953, p. 134.
[4] *The Interpersonal Theory of Psychiatry*, p. 193.

which in waking life are dissociated are said to make their appearance and play out dramas of interpersonal relations with more or less purely fictitious people. (For this reason, among others, one should never forget the immensely significant psychological role of sleep.) Sullivan believed that under certain circumstances the self is able to dissociate lust and the impulses to genital behavior. Even so, one can dissociate the "genital lust dynamism" only at grave risk to effective living. It is so powerful a dynamism that in most people it cannot be dissociated at all. If an individual can dissociate lust, he can accomplish it only by the unwitting development of new and elaborate stratagems and techniques of living.

For the purposes of this exposition, imagine the young man who had sublimated lust having met an extremely attractive and most forthright young woman "who firmly believes that lust should be satisfied and that its satisfaction is unqualifiedly good." [5] Assume also that he is attractive and suitable for "genital integration." Imagine, furthermore, that he, so to speak, succumbs and enters "quite effectively into the integration." In the titillating language of popular discourse, they have "an affaire," though of brief duration. [6] Even though the young man has "a shockingly good time," he does not, like a Hollywood moving picture idol, emerge triumphant and joyful. In the aftermath he suffers self-recrimination and severe conflict because "evil" early life experience has done its work. To make matters worse, a good deal of his distress gets communicated to the partner, who is upset and repelled by his behavior. She may say

---

[5] *Conceptions of Modern Psychiatry*, p. 132.
[6] In a footnote (footnote 44) to pages 132–133 of the *Conceptions of Modern Psychiatry* Sullivan points out that the illustration is defective because a person who found the young man so attractive and suitable for genital integration could not be so "healthy." Analogously, the young man would not be motivated by simple, uncomplicated lust.

> "*If an individual can dissociate lust, he can accomplish it only by the unwitting development of new and elaborate stratagems and techniques of living.*"

something which makes him feel that he has not only done the wrong thing but made a fool of himself. His conviction of personal worth has been gravely shaken if not shattered.

One possible outcome of this occurence is "ecstatic absorption," a transitory state, though one which may result in an "end state" similar to that ensuing upon panic. [7] In ecstatic absorption, Sullivan says, the patient regresses rapidly to a condition in which dream-like processes pertaining to a God-like state solve his acute feelings of abasement. One must bear in mind that a person who suffers such a threat to the integrity of the self and such an injury to his already fragile self-esteem has usually, if not always, been subjected from infancy onward to intense anxiety-tensions and suffered painful feelings of inadequacy at some phase or phases of his development, e.g., isolation from his peers during the juvenile era, overt disparagement from his parents and others, inability to have a close friend, or failures in school or on the job. The fragmentary case histories which Sullivan has published and his illustrative comments on the development of mental disorder are replete with examples of such misfortunes. Puberty brings added difficulties. The young man cannot learn to re-

---

[7] *Ibid.*, p. 133.

late to the other sex in an intimate fashion, or finds it overwhelmingly difficult to effect "genital integrations" with them. Perhaps he is reduced to treating all his female acquaintances like sisters—treatment that not all of them will appreciate. Everyone else he knows seems to be enjoying "dates," conquests and, exciting experiences. What, he may ask himself, is wrong with him? Given the current "obsessional" preoccupation with sex, he is likely to be subjected to intense pressures to go with a girl, if only to prove his manliness, by his parents (who are perhaps dimly aware that they have proved inadequate) and others. The outcome of the encounter mentioned may be the crowning blow to his already shaky feeling of self-worth. The dream-like reverie processes pertaining to a God-like state in ecstatic absorption appear to be reaction to the acute feelings of abasement.

The regression is said to be facilitated by the person's increasingly ineffectual attempts to remedy his interpersonal situation involving the sexual partner by conversational efforts that are becoming increasingly autistic and correspondingly puzzling to her or to others to whom they are addressed. Sullivan asserts that the state of ecstatic absorption has its root-experiences in earlier performances connected with falling asleep when one was feeling very insecure. The person's attempts to maintain relations with actual people fail partly because of the increasing inutility of speech (for he has become increasingly incoherent and incomprehensible) and partly because of the "prehended" disconcertion of his auditors, who are likely to be baffled or dismayed; so he abandons all efforts to talk to anyone. "His awareness is now that of a twilight state between waking and dreaming; his facial expression is that of absorption in ecstatic 'inner' experiences, and his behavior is peculiar to the degree that he no longer eats or sleeps, or tends to any of the routines of life." [8]

If one recognizes that the evil effects of early experience have not merely necessitated a "sublimatory reformulation" of all genital drives but have also resulted in a barrier to women, with corresponding homosexual motivation existing in dissociation, the ecstatic absorption can be understood to accomplish a double function by isolating the young man from either woman or man. The repercussion on the dissociative power of the self is what has made the distressing aftermath of his unexpected sexual engagement so dangerous.

The sudden failure of sublimation may follow a different course that bears more directly on the topic of this exposition. Assume the young man leaves his partner without any painful discussion. By becoming preoccupied, he will put the thought of the experience out of mind. The following night he sleeps poorly, tossing and turning in his bed through the night while harassed by unpleasant dreams. The next afternoon, with fatigue increasing due to insufficient rest and mounting inner pressures, he takes a long walk. Wandering with no conscious destination in mind, without warning he suddenly discovers that he is returning to see his sexual partner and burning with desire to repeat the experience. He is terrified. Panic, or a condition bordering on panic, supervenes.

As I have mentioned, panic is disorganization of the personality—a state which cannot last long if one is to survive—involving failure of the dissociative power of the self. "The mental state," Sullivan says, "is best suggested by referring to a sort of experience which may have befallen anyone. If you have walked each day for years across a little bridge in the sidewalk, and it one

[8] *Ibid.,* p. 133.

morning yields under your feet, suddenly gives way and sinks a few inches, the eruption into awareness that accompanies this experience . . . *is* panic." [9] It results from temporary total failure of the functional efficiency of the self dynamism.

The personality in such a situation reintegrates as swiftly as possible; often, according to Sullivan, through a transitory state of terror with extreme concentration of attention on escape from the poorly envisaged danger. All of one's energies are directed to flight. Sullivan asserts that if the flight response is impossible, panic enventuates in circus movements, random activity, and finally incoordination of the skeletal muscles. In terror, he says, the perception of the source of the threat is primitive, having the cosmic quality of the very early (infantile) formulation of the Bad Mother. (The Bad Mother is a "complexus of impressions" of the mothering one by the infant resulting from her interference with the satisfaction of needs and her association with the induction of anxiety.) The sufferer of this dreadful state experiences the whole world as threatening and everyone as dangerous, hostile and bent on one's destruction. "The terror-stricken person is alone among deadly menaces, more or less blindly fighting for his survival against dreadful odds." [10] (However, this experience is very different from that of "paranoid schizophrenia", to be discussed subsequently, where there is a wholesale transference of blame.)

An extreme restriction and distortion of perception occurs, illustrated by the typical delusionary conviction that one is being watched and followed. After panic has passed into terror, many patients, before they are admitted to the hospital, believe they are followed by people in automobiles.

In this delusion, the person walking along the street notices only the cars that are behind him. As a car passes, it immediately disappears from notice and is no longer perceived. Hence no cars are perceived to pass by. And as long as the cars are behind one, and remain behind one, it must be that they are menacing. This is an extreme example of a process Sullivan subsequently formulated as selective inattention. One fails to perceive or to grasp relevant factors in certain situations and to "forget" them instantly even when one may have *noticed* them.

Phenomena which arise from the autonomous function of a specific zone of interaction, such as the auditory or oral, or the oral supported by the auditory, are even more disturbing than the sort of delusionary belief previously mentioned. To say that a zone of interaction becomes autonomous means that it is no longer under the control of the self-conscious personality, serving instead as the channel for the expression of a dissociated "system." The sufferer may notice but does not comprehend such phenomena. Sullivan states that in the phase of terror following panic it is usually the auditory zone which becomes intermittently autonomous. "One hears voices, spoken statements which pertain to the experiential structure of the dissociated integrating tendency." [11] These hallucinated utterances are said to carry with them many indications of the non-existent speaker's personality. They are, in fact, disguised, symbolic "representations" of the dissociated processes of the patient's personality. Hallucinated statements rather quickly become expressions of particular illusory persons or personifications: God, the Devil, the President, one's deceased mother, and various legendary figures one has learned about (which

9 *Ibid.*, p. 134.
10 *Ibid.*, p. 137.

11 *Ibid.*, p. 138.

C. G. Jung might regard as expressions of a collective unconscious). Though initially these hallucinatory experiences are profoundly disturbing, to patients' who have suffered them for years the "voices" may become commonplace occurrences, having about the same significance as ordinary conversation.[12]

Other forms of automatism besides hallucination, such as the tic and automatic writing, are of great significance in psychiatry but not relevant here.[13]

Certain stratagems or security operations are used by many persons to handle (though not to comprehend) a dissociated tendency that manifests itself in certain obscure ways *within awareness*. But in the schizophrenic state ensuing upon panic this is not possible. Not only has the dissociative power of the self failed completely, its ability to employ security operations—which both normal people and, to an even greater extent, "neurotic" persons may employ when their self-esteem is threatened—have largely failed as well. All that remains of security operations ("defense mechanisms") by the self dynamism is a disowning of the now far too meaningful symptoms. While in all other conditions or states of mental illness the self maintains a monopoly of awareness, a more or less exclusive control of consciousness, in schizophrenic states there is a functional splitting of the control of awareness, covering that which is part of the self and also that which attends the

autonomous activities of the hallucinating zones of interaction. "In schizophrenic states . . . a state of conflict has as it were been universalized, the conflict-provoking tendency systems being accorded independent personality with power greater than that of the self." [14] According to Sullivan, the schizophrenic is unable to accept the manifestations of the dissociated tendencies, disowned through projection as the performances of others. "They" communicate abuses and disturbing suggestions to him, making him experience disagreeable and disgusting sensations, and otherwise (through the hallucinosis) destroying his peace of mind, perplexing and puzzling him, and (by fatigue and other interferences) reducing him to deeply regressed states of being. To the degree that the self functions, the person engages in regressive magic operations in an attempt to protect himself, that is, to regain some measure of security in a world that has become nightmarishly terrifying, irrational and incomprehensible.

A psychologically unsophisticated individual might wonder why the patient does not accept the dissociated tendency system as part of him, or in other words, incorporate it into his self and learn to live with it. Would not that be better, less harrowing, than the present ghastly situation? One must bear in mind that such a course would entail an extreme change in personality, a reorganization of the sorts of interpersonal relations according to which one has lived and had his being—a prospect that would not even be acceptable to most normal human beings who have maintained a more or less intact personality structure. Because of the limitations imposed by the organization of the self dynamism—because, in other words, of the limitations imposed or set by past experiences, which act like

---

[12] In *The Interpersonal Theory of Psychiatry*, pp. 360–361, Sullivan claims that autochthonous ideas precede the occurrence of hallucinations: "Thus while the self-system excludes from awareness clear evidences of a dissociated motivational system, that which is dissociated is represented in awareness by some group of ideas or thoughts which are marked uncannily with utter foreignness—they have nothing to do with oneself."

[13] For a discussion of automatisms, see *Conceptions of Modern Psychiatry* and *Clinical Lectures in Psychiatry*.

---

[14] *Conceptions of Modern Psychiatry*, p. 142.

blinders—the schizophrenic has no foresight as to the direction and extent of such a change. Nor can he foretell that such a radical change would be tolerable. Practically, he has no choice. He is enmeshed in the present course of events and cannot strike out on a course which seems to entail all the terrors and anxieties of the unknown —even if he were able to contemplate such a possibility. And he is bedeviled by an awful driving urgency, always hovering on the fringes of awareness, until sleep brings a respite. But, Sullivan says, it returns when he awakens in the morning and remains until he has again fallen asleep. One might say that "the schizophrenic suffers an almost unceasing fear of becoming an exceeding unpleasant form of nothingness by collapse of the self." [15]

Hence he cannot easily reestablish (reintegrate) a unitary awareness, and rebuild an integral, unified self. He cannot accept any suggestion that his terrible experiences are no more real than a nightmare or that they arise from his own inner unrecognized needs and desires.

Sullivan claims that if the patient has fortunate experiences with the "more real" people whom he encounters in his disturbed state, the fury of the hallucinosis may decrease, the welter of delusional perceptions may diminish, and a condition approximating a stable maladjustment of a deeply regressive sort may ensue. In these "fairly quiescent" states the regression of the patient's personality is such that he lives in a world and participates in interpersonal relations that are, in varying degrees, dreamlike.

Schizophrenic processes do not always ap-

> *"Schizophrenic processes do not always appear suddenly and dramatically. In the incipient schizophrenic state they may appear gradually, even insidiously."*

pear suddenly and dramatically. In the *incipient* schizophrenic state they may appear gradually, even insidiously.[16] According to Sullivan's account, a patient may feel unhappy for a long time over his inadequacies, believing that others do not respect him, dislike his company, and perhaps talk about him in a derogatory way. In order to avoid further hurts to self-esteem, he becomes more and more seclusive, which in turn causes him to suffer increasingly from loneliness. His efforts at communication begin to fail. "He appears more and more preoccupied, inattentive, or given to puzzlement, misunderstanding, and misinterpretation." [17] His responses to questions become more and more autistic. Sooner or later he will withdraw from efforts to deal with his peers. He remains more and more indoors, if he is living at home; often he appears to need the company of one of his parents though he becomes decreasingly communicative and increasingly morose and unpleasant.

15 Harry Stack Sullivan, *Clinical Studies in Psychiatry.* Edited by Helen Swick Perry, Mary Ladd Gawel and Martha Gibbon. With a Foreword by Dexter M. Bullard, M.D. New York: W. W. Norton & Co., Inc., 1956, p. 318.

16 Compare Harry Stack Sullivan, "The Relation of Onset to Outcome in Shizophrenia," *Schizophrenia (Dementia Praecox): An Investigation of the Most Recent Advances,* 10:111–118; Baltimore: Williams & Wilkins, 1931. Reprinted in *Schizophrenia as a Human Process,* pp. 236–244; "The Onset of Schizophrenia," *American Journal of Psychiatry* (1927–28) 84:105–134. Reprinted in *Schizophrenia as a Human Process,* pp. 104–136.
17 *Conceptions of Modern Psychiatry,* p. 154.

At this point, a definite persecutory formula is apt to erupt into the patient's awareness: "His mother has been putting poison in his food; a friend is trying to make him homosexual; people are reading his mind and printing stories about him in the newspaper." [18] Thus, fleeting convictions that one is being subjected to persecutory or destructive influences almost invariably occur in the incipient schizophrenic state. This "paranoid coloring" is found in catatonic schizophrenic states as well, but it is not a true paranoid development because it does not relieve immensely depressed self-esteem nor does it remove chronic and recurrent anxiety. The paranoid coloring is due to the loss of the more refined referential processes; it is a mistaken explanation for puzzling events.

A Disorder of living. Having presented a general introductory outline of Sullivan's theory of schizophrenia, I shall now give a more detailed exposition of it. Schizophrenia is a *disorder of living,* not of the organic substrate. One becomes schizophrenic for situational reasons, and this may happen more or less abruptly or gradually. The disorder is an "episode," or series of episodes, in one's career among people, a career which begins at birth and ends at death. Such an episode may be preceded by months or years of maladjustment. It is often precipitated by a disaster to self-esteem, resulting in a grave, though temporary, disorganization of the personality. Frequently the "victim" has gotten himself involved in a situation that he entered more or less blindly—without foresight as to its meaning and outcome for him. Increasingly intense—because unsatisfied—deeply unconscious longings have caused him to engage in something which is abhorrent to him. He has stumbled into a situation that

provoked the eruption of abhorrent cravings, such as homosexual desires. The conscious realization of such tendencies, as illustrated by the experiences of the patient whose encounter with the dentist proved disastrous, may result in a fateful disaster to the person's self-esteem and collapse of the self dynamism. "At some particular time which he will never forget, the structure of his world was torn apart and dreadful, previously scarcely conceivable, events injected themselves." [19]

Though some readers may wonder if Sullivan has not overemphasized schizophrenic disorders of sudden onset, this possibility is not vital for the purposes of this paper and will not be discussed.

Sullivan concluded, from his own studies of schizophrenia, that whether or not one shall continue to be typically schizophrenic is wholly determined by *situational* factors. Thus he believed—contrary to received psychiatric opinion, which recognizes at least four types of schizophrenia: simple, catatonic, paranoid and hebephrenic—that there are *no* "types" of schizophrenia, only some typical courses of events to be observed in schizophrenic conditions.

The prevailing climate of psychiatric opinion in Sullivan's day—an orientation which he bitterly fought against—was radically at variance with this approach. The author of a psychiatric textbook published in 1936 wrote that many "cases" of schizophrenia are "youths who are not disposed to accept the social restrictions and the cultural demands of their environment; they resent situations which interfere with their gratification of natural impulses, or which jeopardize their security and restrict their opportunities for gaining recognition and achieving pleasurable satisfaction. Instead of putting forth intelligent and con-

---

[18] *Ibid.,* p. 154.

[19] *Ibid.,* p. 149.

structive efforts to unify personality and achieve self-realization in the midst of such difficult situations, they adopt what to them appears to be a more ready avenue of escape and revert to this technique of creating an inner compensatory world of fantasy and romance." [20]

In contrast to such views, Sullivan held that the schizophrenic has not gradually and inattentively drifted into a world of vague philosophizings in lieu of interpersonal relations, or into a world of more or less pleasant fantasy reminiscent of early childhood. He has arrived at his present state by a course that has been fraught with "fear, terror, or literal panic."

Sullivan says that if the course of one's interpersonal relations comes to a schizophrenic state that continues without complication, one manifests a peculiar pattern of behavior which may be called the catatonic state. In this state the patient as a self-conscious person is assumed to be profoundly preoccupied with regaining a feeling of security. Since he is in a profoundly demoralized, regressed condition, he pursues the goal of security by means of activities rarely manifested after early childhood, except in sleep. But since an indefinitely great part of the patient's previous experience relevant to the pursuit of security is still in evidence, the picture is complicated. The integrations which the self dynamism manifests include parataxic illusions on the pattern of the Good Mother (originally a personification of the mothering one who behaves tenderly toward the infant), the Bad Mother (originally a personification of the mothering one who interfers with the satisfaction of needs and provokes anxiety-tension), the Good Father (a personification analogous to the Good Mother) and the

Bad Father (a personification analogous to the Bad Mother). In general these illusory personifications or "me-you patterns" are symbolic representations derived from experiences with significant people, chiefly the parents or their surrogates during infancy and early childhood. Additionally, insofar as education subsequent to early childhood continues to be effective, it provides the parataxic illusions with attributes acquired from the myths, folklore or religion which the patient has acquired. Although the goal of these integrations involving illusory figures is security, the performances in these fantastic interpersonal situations are exclusively power operations (analogous to the magical performances of infancy and early childhood) designed to gain dominance or control over them.

The experience which the patient undergoes in the catatonic state is said to be of the most awesome, universal character. He "seems to be living in the midst of struggle between personified cosmic forces of good and evil, surrounded by animistically enlivened natural objects which are engaged in ominous performances that it is terribly necessary—and impossible—to understand. He is buffeted about. He must make efforts. He is incapable of thought. The compelling directions that are given him are contradictory and incomprehensible. He clings to life by a thread. He finally thinks that he is dead; that this is the state after death; that he awaits resurrection or the salvation of his soul." [21]

Sullivan states that acts and ideas reminiscent of the whole history of man's elaboration of magic and of religion appear in such states, including ancient myths of redemption and rebirth. Though the patient believes he is dead, he "clearly is not

[20] William S. Sadler, M.D. *Theory and Practice of Psychiatry.* St. Louis: The C. V. Mosby Company, 1936; p. 818.

[21] *Conceptions of Modern Psychiatry*, pp. 151–152.

through with life." As an explanation for this state of affairs, he may hit upon surviving remnants of religious teachings. He will be absolved from the faults and failures of his past. Then he will be reborn. This "archaic" thinking reflects his deep regression to a state in which only primitive prototypes of "abstract" thought processes can be active, *not* the tapping of a "collective unconscious." The driving force is an "abysmal insecurity."

As Sullivan describes it, in the midst of this dreadful experience the patient is beyond the commonplace necessities of living, taking neither food nor drink, noticing nothing of the excretory processes, silent, uncomprehending of the meaning of others' efforts on his behalf. He may manifest little overt activity, lying nude with his eyes closed, his mouth "finally shut," hands clenched, and most of the skeletal muscles in a condition of tonic contraction. The catatonic may engage in strange motions: often these motions are rythmical. He may experience sudden eruptions of excitement. From mute catatonic stupor he may occasionally pass into violent excitement with apparently random activity. Though he may harm others or kill himself, there is

"According to Sullivan, the minimum [a catatonic patient] may expect is that only one pair of contradictory ideas or propositions shall occur to him at a time. No wonder he is often 'blocked' or totally inhibited in the act of speaking. . ."

said to be no personally oriented hostility (directed toward any particular person) and no self-destructive motivation.

The interpersonal relations of the catatonic are of great "parataxic complexity," i.e., they are dominated by, or composed of, numerous illusory me-you patterns. Such a patient is unable to relate to real persons for varying lengths of time, being driven to integrate situations with imaginary others endowed with various, and probably incongruous, attributes absorbed during an earlier period of life. Hence, little experience or behavior is manifested in a simple, conventional manner. Any impulse is likely to be followed at once by some opposing or negating impulse. "In the act of expressing an idea, a whole series of contradictory or otherwise complicating ideas may occur." [22] According to Sullivan, the minimum such a patient may expect is that only one pair of contradictory ideas or propositions shall occur to him at a time. No wonder he is often "blocked" or totally inhibited in the act of speaking or that he sometimes abandons the struggle to talk and becomes entirely mute. Nor is it difficult to understand why the stress of this way of life is so great.[23]

The referential thought processes of the catatonic schizophrenic also become "primitive," or analogous to the symbol activity of infancy and early childhood. The earliest type of thinking, or symbol formation, occurs in what Sullivan eventually called the *prototaxic mode*, which is succeeded by the parataxic mode of symbol activity. The infant originally has no self. He may be conscious in a rudimentary sense but he is not self-conscious. Nor has he any awareness of himself as an entity separate from the rest of the world. There is no "I" in contrast to "Thou." His felt experience is

[22] *Conceptions of Modern Psychiatry*, p. 155.
[23] For a discussion of *stupor, mutism, blocking* and *neologisms*, see *Clinical Studies in Psychiatry*.

an undifferentiated whole; he receives impressions and reacts, as Allport puts it, but no mediating self intervenes.[24] Distinctions of time and place are lacking. His experience is timeless and cosmic. The alternation of need and satisfaction, of anxiety-tension and security, is experienced in the prototaxic mode; the infant does not realize any serial connection between them.

The parataxic mode of experience develops during late infancy and early childhood. ("Parataxic" is also a grammatical term which refers to the ranging of clauses or propositions one after another without connectives—such as "and," "or," "since," "for," "because"—to show the relations between them.) In the parataxic mode of experience, the infant makes elementary discriminations between himself and the rest of the world—he no longer reaches out to touch the moon. The original, undifferentiated wholeness of experience is broken up, but the diverse aspects, the "parts" of experience, are not related or connected in an orderly, logical fashion. They are experienced as concomitant. In the most literal sense, they are *associated* rather than logically connected. There is no logical movement of "thought" from one idea or experience to the next.

The autistic speech of a child is a verbal manifestation of the parataxic mode of experience. A word such as "cat" may "refer" to the animal running around the house, the picture of a cat in a picture book, and a toy that resembles the "kitty." For the child, the meaning of "cat" has very broad reference. In the child's mind, "cat" is associated with several different kinds of things though he is not aware of any incongruity in this type of symbol activity. And so it is with a great many other things in the child's life. Obviously this limitation

makes communication often imprecise and difficult.

The referential processes of the catatonic patient seem to be similar to these early modes of symbol activity. For considerable periods of time, he is unable to employ the communicative, consensually validated speech he began to learn in childhood. His referential processes are of a less focused, less precise character than communicative speech. A spread of meaning occurs. Many things that have not seemed meaningful since the patient's childhood again "become important ingredients of the relevant universe of the schizophrenic." The distinction between "thee" and "me," as a result of language operations in the interest of the self, is undermined. The boundary between the patient and the universe, particularly the world of people, undergoes a "diffusion" similar to the "extravasation" of meaning. The schizophrenic tries to communicate by means of these primitive referential processes. "And when the schizophrenic tries to communicate in this way, it sounds as if he has become involved with the whole universe, or as if he has become involved with vast entities whose performance is, as it were, a cosmic drama which struggles to find the solution for a life problem in the same way that a nightmare does." [25] For such reasons, according to Sullivan, communication between therapist and patient is often extraordinarily difficult.

The Paranoid Solution. Hence, says Sullivan, the elaboration of a *paranoid* distortion of the past, present and future, for those whose personal history permits it, occurs as a welcome relief. Compared to the exhausting and extremely "embarrassing" flood of the sorts of experience mentioned, the paranoid systematization of experience is relatively firm and dependable for the patient—though it also takes a heavy toll.

---

24 Gordon Allport, *Pattern and Growth in Personality.* New York: Holt, Rinehart and Winston, Inc. 1961, p. 112.

25 *Clinical Studies in Psychiatry*, p. 316.

To systematize a belief is to suppress (selectively inattend, in this context) all negative or doubt-provoking instances, and to bolster an inherently inadequate account of one's experience with rationalizations in the service of an unrecognized purpose. In the paranoid transformation of personality, a massive transfer of blame is made to the (supposedly) evil people among whom one lives. Next the patient invents a specific "transcendental" or psychotic explanation of why people are persecuting him or plotting against him. In this fashion he discovers an "explanation" for his own inadequacies and difficulties. More accurately, since it has become impossible to maintain dissociation, that which was dissociated is now personified as *not-me*, or as *others*. These others now carry the blame for those tendencies formerly maintained in dissociation as intolerable aspects of one's own personality, and they are (in the patient's view) very evil creatures. Thus the paranoid person arrives at the following formula: "I'm a very important person against whom certain devilish people are engaged in a destructive plot." [26]

Many people have a "paranoid slant on life" without being psychotic or schizophrenic. I shall discuss this point presently. But my main task is to elucidate the differences—which are by no means absolute—between paranoid states and paranoid schizophrenic states. The much more common type of paranoid person is said to be the paranoid schizophrenic. Paranoid schizophrenia is a "mixture" of elements of the systematized paranoid state and of elements of schizophrenia.

Sullivan observes that the onset of paranoid schizophrenic illnesses, that is, *schizophrenic illnesses that are likely to wind up as chronic paranoid states which are in turn more or less schizophrenic,* statistically

date from a much later chronological age than the durable catatonic or the hebephrenic states. For the sake of greater clarity, one should bear in mind that he believed absolute "types" of schizophrenia do not occur, only certain more or less typical courses of events characterizing the schizophrenic process. Analogously, the distinctions "between paranoid schizophrenia, paranoid states, and paranoia will not . . . stand up under any very intensive study of individual patients." [27] To make this clear, I must try to clarify Sullivan's explanation of the "paranoid dynamism." The paranoid dynamism is said to be rooted in (1) an awareness of some inferiority—which is a manifestation or expression of insecurity or low self-esteem—and (2) a transference of blame onto others, necessitated by the awareness of inferiority. These two alone constitute merely "a paranoid slant on life," not a paranoid state or paranoid schizophrenia. The awareness of inferiority entails the formulation in consciousness of some chronic feeling of "profound insecurity," either anxiety or, perhaps worse, jealousy. The dread that others can disrespect one because of something one manifests and cannot "fix" entails a constant insecurity in his relations with others. Such a disability represents an almost fatal deficiency of the self-system for one is unable to disguise from oneself, or exclude from awareness, a definite conviction or formulation which says: "I am inferior. Therefore people will dislike me and I cannot be secure with them." [28] Such a loss of self-esteem is hardly to be borne for it can bedevil one night and day, depriving one of any happiness or contentment.

Just as unresolved needs for satisfaction and security evoke certain processes in sleep, the failure of the self dynamism to

[26] *Ibid.*, p. 149.

[27] *Ibid.*, p. 311.
[28] *Ibid.*, p. 145.

protect self-esteem causes the person to re-double his efforts to redeem himself from the tortured awareness of inferiority. Effective efforts follow the precise pattern of the self operations anyone uses in making careful, consensually valid statements which communicate precisely what he means. According to Sullivan it is by means of refined cognitive operations that the self system develops the group of processes that constitute the paranoid dynamism, which appears suddenly with all the trappings of a great insight and illumination. One suddenly sees that one is the victim of a devilish environment, which is to blame for all one's troubles. So the essence of the paranoid dynamism can be said to be the wholesale transference of blame. Still, we have not yet arrived at an adequate explanation of the paranoid state.

The operation of blaming others in order to relieve painful insecurity is not "bomb-proof." A psychiatrist can demonstrate to the patient, by skillful interview technique, that his explanation is unsound, not based on solid fact. As yet, the patient has merely arrived at what one might call a "paranoid slant on life," though a formidable one. He is still at the mercy of anyone who is not deceived and can inquire into the true state of affairs, a position that can be very awkward, and threatening for the patient who has not yet achieved an unshakable feeling of power and certainty. He has another fork in the road to choose before he reaches a point from which there is rarely a way back.

The last turning in the road, the final step, toward a grave psychosis occurs when the paranoid person invents "a specific, rather transcendental (in the sense of thoroughly psychotic) explanation of why these people do this." [29] He now "knows" of a conspiracy against him, a conviction he substantiates with a vast amount of intro-spective falsification. The plot may be an exquisitely built up, as illustrated in *Conceptions of Modern Psychiatry*. Sullivan one day interrogated a patient at Sheppard and Enoch Pratt Hospital who on entering the office drew an odd diagram on a piece of paper. According to the patient, the diagram symbolized the patient's intricate association with a scientist with whom he had had casual contact abroad on one occasion. "I learned," Sullivan says, "that these two people were about the most important people on earth. They exercised vast powers achieved by command over natural forces through the instrumentality of hypnotism, and were soon to achieve . . . hegemony of the world. They were in constant communion, across the continent, by telepathy. Both were imperiled by a horde of secret agents who were all around us." [30] This patient's behavior exemplifies a well-systematized paranoid state, with only incidental schizophrenic remnants in its structure.

At the beginning of the paranoid transformation of personality (following upon the schizophrenic episode), "the only impression one has is of a person in the grip of horror, of uncanny devastation that makes everyone threatening beyond belief. But if the person is not utterly crushed by the process, he can begin rather rapidly to elaborate personifications of evil creatures. And in this process of personifying the specific evil, the transformation begins to move fast, since it's wonderfully successful in one respect: it begins to put the blame on these others—people who are outside of him, his enemies—everything which he has clearly formulated in himself as defect, blamable weakness, and so on. Thus as the process goes on, he begins to wash his hands of all those real and fancied unfortunate aspects of his own personality which

[29] *Ibid.*, p. 148.

[30] *Conceptions of Modern Psychiatry*, p. 159.

he has suffered for up to this time. Under those circumstances, needless to say, he arrives at a state which is pretty hard to remedy—by categorical name, a paranoid state." [31]

Sullivan observes in *Clinical Studies in Psychiatry* that a highly systematized paranoid state may appear either under the guise of litigious paranoia, or it may be a nightmare of practically "transcendental" persecution. The paranoid dynamism works because the person has discovered a substitute activity that is a completely adequate occupation of the self: one scrutinizes every event that impinges on him and gains his attention to see how it is part of the plot to injure him, that is, to make him feel anxious or insecure or inferior. Such substitutive activity functions primarily to avoid clear, conscious certainty about one's own situation and motivations.

The term paranoid implies the premise that people around one are dangerous and ill-disposed toward one; that transcendental superhuman powers, or persons endowed

with such powers, who may be malignant or punitive, are at large. The person who entertains such ideas of hovering malignant power becomes blameless, ennobled and expanded in worth.[32] In varying degrees and nuances, these are the attitudes and ideas which the psychiatrist encounters in paranoid states and in markedly paranoid schizophrenia.

Since there are certain almost sacrosanct explanations in psychiatric circles of paranoid processes, it may be well to turn briefly to Sullivan's interpretation of their genesis. He claims that the extent to which explanatory "doctrines" which make other people responsible for one's own shortcomings are utilized varies from family to family. One particular family may be very ingenious at discovering how other people are to blame for its members' sins of omission and commission, while another family may be much less clever at finding scapegoats, that is, people whom one can blame for the deeply shameful or contemptible things in one's own make-up. Thus, apparently, the beginnings of the paranoid process are first learned in the family, where a child learns from the adults in his home to make other people a basis for self-ennobling or self-excusing explanations of behavior of his which has no real causal connection with the behavior of the people who are blamed. Subsequently, the child fails to encounter or to benefit from corrective experience, which would demonstrate that blaming others does not work satisfactorily because it evokes hostility, ridicule or even ostracism, or that there are potentially kind people who will respect him if he can give them a fair chance.

It seems that a paranoid person acquires the blaming strategem as a youngster by first having been the victim of it himself. Significant people blamed him at times, or

[31] *The Interpersonal Theory of Psychiatry*, pp. 361–362.

"... *a paranoid person acquires the blaming stratagem as a youngster by first having been the victim of it himself. Significant people blamed him at times, or took out their disgruntlements and shortcomings on him—an experience that certainly lowers one's self-esteem."*

[32] *Clinical Studies in Psychiatry*, p. 335.

took out their disgruntlements and short-comings on him—an experience that certainly lowers one's self-esteem. A more or less cruel parent may enjoy piling blame on the child. Or a professionally inadequate teacher may gain a certain pleasure from making the child suffer for her (or his) embarrassments while concealing her inadequacies as a teacher by blaming—and perhaps ridiculing—the child for being stupid or lazy.

To be sure, the origins of security or insecurity go further back into infancy in connection with empathically experienced significant people. The roots of the self and the primitive origins of anxiety can be traced to infancy and early childhood. But the person cannot reach back that far, cannot recall that period of life and say, "I would be perfectly happy and content if it were not for the significant people in my infancy and their evil effect on me." That is one of the inescapable limitations of human living: the nucleus of the self is established long before one can reason or understand what is happening or why. But one can reach back into late childhood, whether or not one can recall all the attendant circumstances when significant people blamed him unfairly. Even if one was able to attack their unfairness, they "compounded the felony" by defending themselves, claiming that they were not unfair. This, according to Sullivan, is ultimately reassuring because the child eventually perceives that a person who cannot admit a fault is obviously not as secure as he seems and concludes that he is superior to his detractors. So, Sullivan says, the following thought, easily accessible to awareness at any time in the experiences of everyone, occurs to the child: "I wouldn't have this horrible feeling of discomfort with others if *they* weren't there, and if I hadn't been taught the way I've been taught by other people." Another thought, based on real experiences in the person's earlier years

under certain circumstances, occurs to him: "I wouldn't have this sense of discomfort if other people didn't treat me unfairly." [33] As I have already pointed out, in some families blaming others for one's own shortcomings becomes a way of life. A child in such a family may be subjected to increasing insecurity and blame as he proceeds, stage by stage, with ever growing feelings of inadequacy, toward adolescence.

But it is not until he has reached the preadolescent era that paranoid developments appear. Paranoid processes result to a high degree from incomplete development in the preadolescent and adolescent phases, which in turn is apparently to a large degree an outcome of previous very unfortunate experiences. They appear "very commonly" in the "mid-adolescent" stage of personality development, which extends up to the patterning of sexual (genital) behavior. The paranoid person does not progress through a patterning of sexual behavior. He has failed to establish workable sexual habits. In fact this failure, "this final defeat," according to Sullivan, is the situation in which the paranoid state usually appears, though it is generally preceded by a schizophrenic episode. In other words failure to establish workable sexual relations, constituting the final defeat in a life already pervaded by excruciating thwartings, defeats, and failures, has precipitated a *schizophrenic episode* which may be quickly replaced by a substitutive state traditionally labeled paranoid schizophrenia.

However, this exposition of paranoid processes is incomplete and must be pressed further. They do not appear until preadolescence owing largely to the results of incomplete development of personality in this era continuing into adolescence—a phase of development which in some people may persist into the senium. Sullivan gives

33 *Ibid.*, p. 147.

an illuminating account of a "paranoid preadolescent" who had had "an appalling life." Very early in his life a distant relative who had been compelled to live in the boy's unhappy home for a time treated him "like a human being" though she finally "escaped." Sullivan says that everything else that happened to him was as unfriendly and frustrating and savagely cruel as one might expect. In school the boy was a holy terror, hated and feared by teachers and schoolmates, and "quite a gifted thorn" at home. Then at preadolescence he discovered that all the available youngsters toward whom he felt any tendency to be friendly shied away from him because they were repelled by his "problem character," which amounted to a lack of humanity. Though he tried hard, by serious application and much self-disciplinary planning, to convince his peers that he *was* human—an acceptable human being—he failed in his efforts. Under some circumstances, an emotionally distorted preadolescent, whose behavior may be obnoxious to more normal youngsters, will team up with other "sick" preadolescents. But in this instance there were no other such people available. The boy soon "came out with a fine paranoid system." Sullivan relates that this unfortunate youth would detail to unsuspecting youngsters a story about how he was really quite an important individual, who had been stolen from a hospital for purposes of blackmail by the woman who now claimed to be his mother, elaborating much alleged evidence for his story.[34]

Some psychiatrists might interpret this boy's situation to mean that he got bogged down by his intense hatred of his mother, who had been extremely thwarting and cruel to him, when he thought of "moving" toward women; in short, that he was paranoid owing to a homosexual conflict. Sulli-

van had no patience with this style of interpretation, which he thought was not only incorrect but destructive of therapeutic efforts. In Sullivan's opinion, the psychiatrist who "attacks" a paranoid state on the basis of an attempt to interpret to the patient his alleged homosexuality, where such experience is missing, is effecting an atrocious miscarriage of the therapeutic process. He destroys any possibility of establishing rapport with the patient, for the therapist in effect agrees with or fosters the patient's conviction that there is essentially a revolting difference between him and good, estimable people. Hence the psychiatrist unwittingly strengthens the victim's paranoid state.[35]

The Need for Intimacy. Anyway, Sullivan held that what the youngster suffered from was *an inescapable barrier to intimacy with man, woman, or beast.* He had failed in his almost frantic efforts to achieve intimacy with *someone.* From other people's avoidance of him he was forced to conclude, "they have no use for me." Over and over, he was forced to tell himself, in effect if not in so many words, "I am too inferior to get what I must have." This driving, poignant, excruciating awareness of inferiority became so intolerable that he at length reached the solution of blaming others, a solution bolstered of necessity by his compensatory explanation of why he was persecuted.

Statistically, it seems to be true that the great majority of "paranoid cases" emerge around the ages of 25, 26 and 27. However, these people are still, psychologically, in early (or mid-) adolescence, the phase which *precedes* the patterning of sexual behavior. They have failed to establish workable sexual habits. And this final defeat has culminated in a paranoid development.

In Sullivan's view, while such a final de-

[34] *Ibid.*, p. 152.

[35] *Ibid.*, pp. 163–164.

feat may often be the *presenting* difficulty in therapy, it is *not* the real difficulty. The real problems, the basic problems, of any patient in therapy have to do with interpersonal relations, with living as happily as circumstances allow with others.

Sometimes those "mid-adolescents" (or early adolescents, according to Sullivan's subsequent division of adolescence into early and late stages) have been able to establish a measure of intimacy with someone during preadolescence. Sullivan says that those who are not too badly warped may have been quite close to some other person for a time. They then have attempted to comport themselves like other young men—"which too often in this culture means abandoning real happiness in favor of heterosexual prestige." [36] But owing to the barrier against women, they are unable to achieve successfully comfortable relations of an intimate nature with them.

Such an adolescent may become convinced that no woman would have anything to do with him. This notion in turn becomes generalized into the conviction that other men know that women would not put up with him, that he is no good with women. The next step is that he believes men think he is sexually interested in them—that they ascribe his failure with women to homosexuality. So his perception of self includes an intolerable awareness of defect, of inferiority, of not being fully human that can, if no positive experience intervenes, set off a schizophrenic episode followed by a paranoid development.

In summary, Sullivan believed that it is *the need for intimacy*, coupled with the inescapable awareness of a fatal incapacity for that intimacy, that evokes "this desolating paranoid dynamism." [37] One should also bear in mind that failure to develop

---

[36] *Clinical Studies in Psychiatry*, p. 155.
[37] *Ibid.*, p. 158.

workable sexual *habits* does not lessen the intensity of the genital lust dynamism. Such a failure implies an added burden to be borne. Frustration of the sexual drive itself impairs one's sense of well-being, becoming an additional source of unpleasant tension.

As I have pointed out, under the heading of the paranoid dynamism Sullivan includes those processes which he labels the paranoid slant on life, characterized by a profound feeling of insecurity and inferiority and a transfer of blame onto others for the troubles and difficulties insecurity entails, such as severe anxiety and jealousy. At this stage, a merely intellectual, cognitive transference of blame is attempted. Such people work out a faith, making a "religion" of how wretchedly others treat them, falsely and derogatorily misinterpreting their most benevolent actions. But this operation or strategem of blaming others fails when one attempts to validate it consensually. One cannot employ it effectively since it includes factors he does not understand. The real causes for the feelings of inadequacy and inferiority which spur one on to blaming others originate in late infancy and early childhood, beyond the reach of cognition. Blaming others is a primarily intellectualistic operation which is not sufficiently potent to cope with the deeply buried roots of insecurity. The wretched feelings of inferiority and ineffectuality remain, and they compel the sufferer to redouble his efforts. Then comes the third step, whereby he feels persecuted or conspired against. Typically he engages in such paranoid interpersonal relations as writing bitter, troublesome letters to his Congressman, starting lawsuits, pestering psychiatrists or intimidating neighbors.

The overt, diagnosed paranoid patient is said to be an intellectually gifted individual whose systematizations make his self system impregnable to any disturbing influences emanating from his psychiatrist.

> *"By his skill at reasoning (though on false assumptions), [the paranoid] is usually able to divest any communication from the therapist of its power to stir dissociated tendencies and thus bring conflict into awareness."*

By his skill at reasoning (though on false assumptions), he is usually able to divest any communication from the therapist of its power to stir dissociated tendencies and thus bring conflict into awareness. Nevertheless his is a far from comfortable way of life. His ability to obtain the satisfactions he needs is reduced, sometimes gravely so. As a rule, if not always, warm, intimate relationships are beyond him. Unless he is integrated into paranoid interpersonal relations, wherein he can blame others, real and imagined, for his troubles, the power of the dissociated tendencies of his personality come to exceed the dissociating power of the self. In the latter case, he becomes prey to anxiety, conflict erupting within awareness, or panic, followed by the outburst of schizophrenic processes previously described.

Parenthetically, Sullivan believed that it is not much use for the psychiatrist to assume that he has engaged a markedly paranoid schizophrenic in the curative process as long as the latter's history continues to reveal no markedly schizophrenic onset of the illness. The patient has too much skill at reasoning convincingly against one. Only when he can be induced to admit that he has experienced a phase in living which

Sullivan labeled the schizophrenic episode —an episode which the patient *cannot* understand or explain away—is there hope for therapeutic progress. "If the patient cannot be gotten to review a period when he was thoroughly schizophrenic, then I do not think the psychiatrist can do much with any of the later content. Only people who are quite gifted in referential operations, argument, and rationalization can sustain so complicated a distortion of reality as is the paranoid position. And so, when you encounter a person who can do so, there is no use in struggling with his interwoven blend of facts, misinterpretations and slightly fraudulent distortion of events." [37]

The Catatonic-Paranoid Polarity. Sullivan distinguishes pure paranoia and pure schizophrenia as two absolute poles, never fully realized in actuality. He says that a person who approached pure paranoia would be one who handles all his difficulties by transferring any feeling of blame in any connection out of his awareness and onto the persons making up his environment. The nearer a patient approaches this (imaginary) pole of absolute paranoia, the more highly systematized his delusions of persecution and grandeur become as an explanation of why he is persecuted.[38]

Sullivan believed that the essential schizophrenic condition is catatonia.[39] Although he does not explicitly draw the comparison, it appears that pure schizophrenia is similar to catatonia as previously described. In this condition control of conscious awareness is lost—often following upon a disaster to self-esteem—with the eruption into awareness of unorganized and primitive referential processes, to the profound mystification of the person affected. These reverie processes and subverbal or autistic verbal

---

[37] *Ibid.*, p. 307.
[38] *Ibid.*, pp. 304 f.
[39] *Ibid.*, p. 313.

operations escape the excluding devices of the self. Control of the *content* of consciousness is lost. A "regressive divestment" of the later acquisitions of personality occurs. The schizophrenic disaster, involving the collapse of the self, may occur hours or days after some event has precipitated very grave conflicts between one's need for satisfactions and one's need for security and self-esteem. If a capacity for intimacy with another person has never been consolidated, the schizophrenic disaster follows a course which quickly eliminates a great many of the more recent additions to the self. If the person has experienced a need for and succeeded in the consolidation of intimacy, regression is not so swift. In the latter case, the schizophrenic disaster is more likely to follow a course characterized primarily by its close relationship to the nightmares experienced by adolescents and some chronological adults. The conflict between the need for satisfaction and the need for security is said to lower the threshold of awareness to a level where the earlier, more primitive, referential processes escape the excluding devices of the self and erupt into consciousness. Sullivan claims that this waking conflict is also a problem-solving effort similar to that operating in troubled dreams and nightmares: a considerable effort at solution of a problem at the level of high orders of reverie processes and subverbal or autistic verbal operations. "As long as this sort of process continues, the patient can be called catatonic." [40] If the person despairs the hebephrenic change may ensue, or a change into paranoid schizophrenia or the paranoid state may occur.

It may be helpful for the understanding of paranoid schizophrenia if one realizes that the schizophrenic (when his condition is not complicated by elements of paranoia) is *not* concerned with problems of blame. According to Sullivan, schizophrenics are especially vulnerable to having blame transferred *to them*. Usually they have not understood people, and how to deal with them, well enough to make others scapegoats.

It happens, however, that in the course of schizophrenic stupor, a patient's non-validated thinking processes—the primitive type of referential processes—may randomly hit on the notion of his being Jesus Christ and, perhaps, the world's being made up of people (such as Jews) bent on crucifying him. If this is sufficient to contain the schizophrenic disturbances at the level of awareness, the patient rapidly goes into a bitter, highly systematized paranoid state. However, this is not the usual outcome; if the paranoid development had sufficed, it would have occurred sooner. If the patient had succeeded in the past at making someone else the scapegoat, he would not stay schizophrenic very long.

A certain group of patients, according to Sullivan, do show Christ identifications, yet remain catatonic. They are not paranoid. Often paranoid attitudes do not suffice. Even the catatonic Christ identification may progress to a paranoid phase, but under skillful therapeutic pressure, the Christ identification collapses, and the patient "is again lost in the whole welter of universal patterns and is again definitely stuporous." [41] Sullivan points out that the paranoid schizophrenic can sometimes relapse into stupor, revert to simple schizophrenia, and from that emerge as a social, if not real, recovery. Sullivan believes this shows that the transfer of blame does not really solve the problems of schizophrenics, as is also indicated by the "shocking character" of the persecutions many of them complain of. Paranoid schizophrenics still have a very hard time. When the paranoid state

---

40 *Ibid.*, p. 313.

41 *Ibid.*, p. 338.

becomes a durable maladjustment, perhaps of years' duration, it remains very unpleasant even though it brings a relative security.

In short, the more paranoid a person is the less schizophrenic are his interpersonal relations. However, every patient who had undergone the paranoid state whom Sullivan encountered had in his personal history a period of "schizophrenic content," though the latter condition was sometimes hard to discover. Only the patient who has encountered blaming stratagems in his parents or teachers and other such significant people in the culture, and from them learned successfully how to scapegoat others, may elaborate a paranoid distortion of the past, present and future. But the cost of such a paranoid systematization of experience is "an adoption of hate in the place of a never-quite-realized love. The result of this substitution of hate in place of love as the goal of interpersonal relations is the gradual disintegration of the patient." [42]

The Hebephrenic Outcome. The other outcome of the schizophrenic state is hebephrenic dilapidation. While the essentially schizophrenic person is pretty well demoralized, with slight expectation of a brighter, more pleasant future, he is not utterly hopeless, as indicated by many of his utterances and some of his behavior. But a certain proportion of schizophrenics do become hopeless: they despair of becoming human beings acceptable to others. And then, with few exceptions, they leave the field of human relations for good. The hebephrenic "has had such disastrous experiences in his initial, rather frantic, schizophrenic attempt at doing something that he has given it all up as a bad job. That is conspicuously shown by the avoidance of interpersonal contacts and the very disturbing effect of

interpersonal pressure on the person with the hebephrenic change." [43] An attitude of resigned separation or alienation from life and an utter hopelessness seems to be the essence of the hebephrenic state. The patient has abandoned the effort at living, and exists on a sort of autobiological level. At the same time he has relinquished, or escaped from, the stress and turmoil and the painfully deep pessimistic expectations of the true schizophrenic state. Condemned to despair, he suffers a feeling of total, utter isolation, and of utter incapacity to do anything which might remedy his situation. Any tie, or even a life line, with the real interpersonal world is finally and usually irretrievably broken.

Sullivan claimed that the person who suffers a schizophrenic episode, without having had a genuinely meaningful experience of the preadolescent era, will be characterized by a much prompter appearance of the hebephrenic development. Normally, during preadolescence one first learns to become intimate with another human being, which entails a considerable expansion and deepening of one's values, and thereby a relatively firm attachment to the real interpersonal world—the world of real people. [44] On the other hand, this very tie is conspicuously troublesome to schizophrenics who have experienced some preadolescent intimacy, and who can not dilapidate immediately because, despite their anguish, they still retain a modicum of hope regarding the world.

Not only does the hebephrenic divest himself of, or abandon, the interpersonal abilities developed during the early stages of personality development (truncated and warped though they may be), he is driven to occupying himself with "amusing" zones of

[42] *Conceptions of Modern Psychiatry*, p. 156. Compare *Clinical Studies in Psychiatry*, pp. 160–163.

[43] *Clinical Studies in Psychiatry*, p. 353.
[44] Compare Kurt Haas, *Understanding Ourselves and Others*. Englewood Cliffs, New Jersey: Prentice-Hall, Inc. 1965; pp. 36–84.

interaction to keep himself from being trapped into very disturbing relations with others. However gravely deteriorated he may be, he still retains the various impulses or drives which make up a part of living and cannot be eradicated. Normally they are satisfied in and through interpersonal situations. But the hebephrenic wants no more of the latter and must fall back upon unsocial modes of satisfaction. The satisfaction of needs can be gained without great difficulty in a mental institution (if it is tolerably rational and humane) with minimal contact with people, and in relative contentment. The hebephrenic can eat, drink, rest, sleep in this fashion. He can more or less continuously manipulate his penis and thus avoid being disturbed by lust, which could be troublesome since it might involve him with another person. And he may possibly "have a wonderful time with the feces."

To further clarify the situation of the hebephrenic, impulses that were once a part of the prepsychotic self, which played a part in the conflict and chaos of the catatonic state, and which were *then* opposed to the impulses whose eruption into consciousness horrified or terrified him, are now *themselves* in much the same relationship to the patient's awareness as were the originally dissociated impulses. The impulses of the prepsychotic self are no longer "on the side of the angels" because they tend to involve him with others. "If they tend strongly to integrate an interpersonal situation, the patient becomes acutely anxious, often becomes seriously disturbed, perhaps acutely hallucinated, excited, assaultive, and more or less randomly destructive." [45]

However, two kinds of experience remain which cannot be handled in the unsocial fashion of the satisfaction of bodily drives. One is loneliness, which the hebephrenic

[45] *Conceptions of Modern Psychiatry*, p. 164.

has little or no resources left to deal with. The other is the need for security. Sullivan thought that the hebephrenic deteriorates as the self and its security operations are progressively and rapidly abandoned. The individual is left with a rather constant, unchanging feeling that people regard him with indifference, contempt, scorn or other negative attitudes. But he gets more or less used to this twilight existence because it is uniform, more or less unchanging without threat of novelty; it has the relative reassurance of the habitual. This is the end-state of the hebephrenic change.

This change may appear very early in the course of a schizophrenic episode or it may occur as the termination of a prolonged catatonic state. In any long-continued schizophrenic condition that has not tended markedly to recovery, hebephrenia appears. According to Sullivan, the condition of most patients who have suffered paranoid schizophrenic states eventually becomes indistinguishable from the condition of those in whom the hebephrenic change appeared early.

The outstanding characteristics of the hebephrenic state, that is, the signs ordinarily enumerated as its description, are said to be a marked seclusiveness and avoidance of any companionship; a disintegration of language processes (manifested in speech that is "scattered," incoherent, vague, unconnected or expressing poverty of ideas); and a marked diminution of emo-

> "Sullivan thought that the hebephrenic deteriorates as the self and its security operations are progressively and rapidly abandoned."

tional rapport, so that the patient impresses one as having undergone a dilapidation or impoverishment of the emotional aspects of interpersonal behavior. Sullivan's explanation of the causes of seclusiveness and the reduction of emotional rapport has been described previously: The disintegration of language processes can be explained as concomitants of the disintegration of the self, a very important dimension of which is communicative speech. Psychologically two of the most important functions of language are the communication of ideas and attitudes and the expression of feeling and emotion. And the hebephrenic, for reasons mentioned previously, wants no part of either: they are too threatening to his (relative) "peace of mind," to whatever security he can manage to retain.

While Sullivan discusses a few other signs of the hebephrenic state, I omit them since they are not vital to an understanding of his theory of schizophrenia.

According to Sullivan, the "paranoid maladjustment" and the hebephrenic change are *not* part of schizophrenia but are very unfortunate outcomes of schizophrenic episodes; the essential schizophrenic condition is catatonic schizophrenia.[46] By and large Sullivan's therapy of schizophrenia is oriented toward the treatment of the latter.

Dissociation. Sullivan's ideas on dissociation are relevant to a fuller understanding of schizophrenia. In his Foreword to *Conceptions of Modern Psychiatry* Sullivan wrote that in this lecture series he had ascribed undue importance to dissociation to the neglect of selective inattention, which he had not yet formulated in 1939 when the lectures were delivered. But I think this qualification does not materially alter his conception of dissociation as a functionally separate part of the personality. Selective

---
[46] *The Interpersonal Theory of Psychiatry*, p. 328.

inattention is an instrumentality of the self by which dissociated dynamisms are kept unconscious, though selective inattention is not the only instrumentality employed for this purpose.

Selective inattention does *not* pertain to the inhibition of motives and hence is quite different from the *suppression* or *repression* of classical psychoanalysis. Its function is the control of consciousness in situations where anxiety might be aroused. Its clearest formulation is in *Clinical Studies in Psychiatry*. One might call it a misuse of concentration or attention in the traditional sense of those ideas. When one concentrates or attends, he focuses on the relevant aspects of a situation or problem and ignores or inattends everything else, including any distracting elements that might intrude. When one selectively inattends something, he may notice it but does not focus on it or concentrate on it; he therefore fails to perceive or to understand relevant and significant aspects of a situation or problem in order to avoid or minimize anxiety. Of course, very often this operation occurs at the cost of learning highly illuminating aspects of situations which would otherwise be educative. Selective inattention, as I previously mentioned, is an instrumentality of the self; it is part of the restrictive "machinery" of the self. And since the self may also stand in the way of *unfavorable* change, selective inattention must be regarded as at times serving a constructive function when it acts as a barrier against dissociated processes, the emergence of which into consciousness may precipitate panic.

Dissociation is used by Sullivan in two major senses. In one sense, it refers to the inhibition of motives or impulses, with a concomitant exclusion from consciousness of any recognition of their existence. In this sense it is somewhat similar to Freud's concept of repression, though Sullivan said he had never "encountered anything as simple and as comprehensive as the repression of orthodox psychoanalysis." To dissociate is actually to keep some deeply unconscious tendency—or motivational system —functionally split off from the self or, if it has become conscious, to put it out of consciousness in such a fashion that it is isolated from the self system.

In the second, and related meaning of dissociation, it refers to an aspect of the personality that is functionally separate from and often intensely antipathetic to the self and its values. Some degree of dissociation is ubiquitous. Some impulses are "choked off" in large measure very early in anyone's education. Western culture "does not use part of our impulse equipment . . . part of our adjustive potentialities. . . . But they are not choked-off utterly—it is probably impossible to do so. Like the trees growing at the edge of the Grand Canyon, something happens, however terribly distorted." [47] If the impulses constitute a major integrative tendency, a major motivational system, they are not completely divorced from the development which occurs during any stage of growth. "But if a major integrative tendency gets very little place in socialized life, so that it has no material satisfaction in the operations of the self-conscious person, then all that happens is that it is never, in any way, represented in the self-system." [48] Since such a tendency system was never part of the self, it does not require "any great machinery" (such as selective inattention or obsessive substitutive processes) to keep it out. It operates as a separate organization of processes, running on and on, in and out of season, whenever the self system is not making its presence felt; that is, whenever the self is not alerted, in some interpersonal situation, to any behavior of the self, however obscure, which

might arouse the disapproval of significant others, or of one's self.

But other impulse systems which have been a part of the self may, because of some unfortunate experience or series of experiences, cease to be known to the person and vanish into the region where he does things that he never notices or attends. When they vanish (become dissociated) in this fashion the person no longer accepts them as his. In the course of personality development, a "massive dissociation of impulse systems" before adulthood may occur. The classic psychoanalytic example of such a massive dissociation pertains to sexuality, but almost any impulse system can be ejected from consciousness and functionally isolated from the self. The peculiarities of anyone's development combined with the restrictions of his socio-cultural environment determine what drives and motives are acceptable and what must be dissociated.

Since dissociated processes have a significant relation to sleep, I shall briefly discuss it. According to Sullivan the functional importance of sleep, from a psychiatric viewpoint, is the marked relaxation of security operations that occurs in sleep. Sleep is the one phase of life in which one is more or less relieved of the necessity of maintaining security. Many unsatisfied needs and unsatisfied components of needs which cannot be discharged in waking life are, to a degree, satisfied in the "symbolic devices" of sleep. People who are denied sleep for a period of time manifest signs of mental disturbance and their ability to deal with troublesome motivations deteriorates rapidly.

Even in sleep the self system is not completely in abeyance. Sometimes a person who is severely anxious while awake may have a frightful nightmare one night which he cannot shake off even when he wakes up; not long after that he becomes overtly schizophrenic. Normally, one maintains dis-

[47] *Clinical Studies in Psychiatry*, p. 66.
[48] *Ibid.*, p. 66.

sociation during sleep by a continued vigilance of the dissociative apparatus in the self system. And the more of the personality that exists in dissociation, the less restful and more troubled by unpleasant dreams and nightmares will one's sleep be. A person in this plight will often not be able to obtain adequate returns from sleep even if he sleeps long hours. In other words, when certain powerful motivational systems are dissociated, the person is unable to relax the self sufficiently to have deep, restful sleep. In general, the tensions of needs and of anxiety are "oppositional" to the tensions of sleeping.

On occasion Sullivan was able to save an incipient schizophrenic from grave disorganization by administering a liberal dose of alcohol, which temporarily enfeebles the "higher centers," making deep sleep possible and thus ensuring a relatively intact personality more amenable to therapy, if it is quickly available.

On the other hand, once the dissociative power of the self has failed and the contents of consciousness have escaped from its control, the sleep of schizophrenics tends to be profound. But the sleep of those patients is said to be very different from relatively normal sleep because it is a "regressive

"Sullivan believed that schizophrenia occurs in people who are 'fixed' at the preadolescent or early adolescent level of personality development when sex and problems of intimacy with others are pressing problems."

phenomenon." By this Sullivan seems to mean a state reminiscent of early childhood or infancy.

While the self is said to be relatively dormant in sleep it does not disappear.[49] It is what Sullivan calls a perduring aspect of personality. So these dissociated aspects, he says, tend, by fantastic means, to follow a principle which is very markedly manifested in the waking life of those who suffer one of the mental disorders. He claims that the character of the interpersonal phenomena manifested in their sleep is often regressive to archaic modes of awareness. The awareness of the infant is diffuse and nonspecific, for it exists in either the prototaxic or parataxic mode of experience. "We may, therefore, say that the maximum regression of prehending processes is to a sort of an amorphous universe in which one has one's being—doubtless, a fairly early infantile mental state. If there were necessity, one could revert in dreams to that sort of attack upon one's problems."[50] In those who do not suffer from major interpersonal difficulties, regression is not usually "anything like so deep."

Sullivan's Therapeutic Innovations. I shall close with a brief and hence necessarily superficial account of Sullivan's method of treatment.

First, one must bear in mind that mature people do not suffer schizophrenic illness (with the possible exception of times of catastrophic social change). Sullivan believed that schizophrenia occurs in people who are "fixed" at the preadolescent or early adolescent level of personality development when sex and problems of intimacy with others are pressing problems. During these stages problems of intimacy and problems connected with the sexual drive often

[49] Compare *Clinical Studies in Psychiatry,* pp. 175–177.
[50] *Conceptions of Modern Psychiatry,* p. 71.

take on an almost "preternatural importance," particularly in American society. Failure to handle them successfully constitutes a great social liability, which may in turn have grave consequences for the individual's conviction of personal worth. Other, but probably related, factors such as approaching marriage may help to precipitate a schizophrenic episode.[51] However they are not the causes of schizophrenia. The variables in the etiology of schizophrenia are apparently multiple. In Sullivan's theory, these variables pertain chiefly to interpersonal relations.

Sullivan believed that the prognosis of a sudden onset of schizophrenia—the "acute dramatic divorcement from more or less commonplace living"—is much better than the insidious onset in which a sudden dramatic break is not seen. The insidious onset implies that personality development has been arrested long before the hospital admission, so that the available human ability and emotional resources useful for a reintegration or resynthesis of anything like an average life situation and normal interpersonal relations are more limited.

In an early paper published in 1924, Sullivan sought to combat the pessimism of many psychiatrists regarding schizophrenia.[52] He attempted to insure a new measure of interest in schizophrenic patients so that they would "cease to be regarded by so many as *a priori* inexplicable and hopeless." At the same time he warned against dilettantish, thoughtless, or insensitive behavior on the part of the physician, nurse, or attendant. Sullivan claimed that the general attitude of the physician towards the patient determines his value far more

than any single action. The schizophrenic patient appreciates "all too definitely" the physician's attitude toward the life situation presented by the patient. In this connection, certain philosophical and speculative anthropological notions (such as solipsism and Jung's "collective unconscious") or an allegedly scientific outlook which eliminates purpose from human life and "reduces the individual to organismic cravings in pitched battle," that influence the attitude of the physician have a destructive effect on the patient much like those to which he was previously subjected in the world, in various guises.

Sullivan reiterated William Alanson White's dictum that the psychiatrist must understand what the patient is trying to do. To Sullivan, the element of motivation seemed logically fundamental in attacking the problem of understanding and treatment of schizophrenia.

In the same paper he offered a technique for treating acute and subacute states of schizophrenia which differs from orthodox psychoanalytic method. In dealing with schizophrenics, Sullivan rejected free association at least until they had reached some measure of insight into their situation or a significant degree of improvement. He

"Sullivan reiterated . . . that the psychiatrist must understand what the patient is trying to do. To Sullivan, the element of motivation seemed logically fundamental in attacking the problem of understanding and treatment of schizophrenia."

---

[51] Compare Robert W. White. *The Abnormal Personality*. New York: The Ronald Press Company, 1956; Chapter 15.

[52] Harry Stack Sullivan, "Schizophrenia: Its Conservative and Malignant Features," *American Journal of Psychiatry* (1924–1925) 81:77–91. Reprinted in *Schizophrenia as a Human Process*, pp. 7–22.

reported that in some instances, the careful use of questions addressed to the patient or to a trained assistant within hearing of the patient, was effective in stimulating perception, analysis, and resynthesis of psychotic content.

When, toward the end of his career as Director of Clinical Research at Sheppard and Enoch Pratt Hospital, he was able to establish a special ward there, he stressed to his assistants the importance of the first 24 hours on the ward for any patient. Data from the first 24 hours were carefully noted because the patient's initial encounter with the daily round in the institution might turn out to be crucial for his entire stay. Sullivan encouraged his assistants to spend a great deal of time with the new patient in a close and reassuring way. The patient's life on the ward was regarded as in many ways more crucial to his progress than the single hour a day that he spent with the doctor, partly because the patient's daily living provided more complex and varied, in many ways more rewarding, data.

Sullivan summarized his procedures in "The Modified Psychoanalytic Treatment of Schizophrenia," published in 1931:

> The procedure of treatment begins with removing the patient from the situation in which he is developing difficulty to a situation in which he is encouraged to renew efforts at adjustment with others. . . The sub-professional personnel with whom the patient is in contact must be aware of the principal difficulty; viz., the extreme sensitivity underlying whatever camoflage the patient may use. They must be activated by a well-integrated purpose of helping in the re-development or development de novo of self-esteem as an individual attractive to others. They must possess sufficient insight into their own personality organization to be able to avoid marked or unconscious sadism, jealousies, and morbid expectations of results. They must be free from the more commonplace ethical delusions and superstitions . . .
> Given the therapeutic environment, the

first stage of therapy by the physician takes the form of providing an orienting experience. After the initial, fairly searching interview, the patient is introduced to the new situation in a matter of fact fashion, with emphasis on the personal elements. In other words, he is made to feel that he is now one of a group, composed partly of sick persons—the other patients—and partly of well folk—the physician and all the others concerned. Emphasis is laid on the fact that something is the matter with the patient, and—once this is at least clearly understood to be the physician's view—that regardless of the patient's occasional or habitual surmise to the contrary, everyone who is well enough to be a help will from thenceforth be occupied in giving him a chance to get well. From the start, he is treated as a *person among persons*.[53]

Sullivan adds that there is to be no acceptance of the patient's thought as outré or crazy, and no use of a "never-mind" technique that ignores the obvious. Everyone in this milieu is expected to regard the patient's outpourings of thought and his actions as valid for him, at least, and worthy of serious consideration as communications that should be understood. Sullivan also asserts that the "individualism" of the patient's performances is neither to be discouraged nor encouraged, but instead, when they seem clearly morbid, to be noted and perhaps questioned. The questioning must be based on a desire to center the patient's attention on the discovery of the factors concerned in his performances. Violence, if it occurs, is to be discouraged *unemotionally* and in the clearly stated interest of "the general or special good." Violence by the patient often arises from panic, and such a state of affairs must be dealt with by the physician. On the other hand, if the patient seems obviously to increase in comfort (emotional security)

53 "The Modified Psychoanalytic Treatment of Schizophrenia," *American J. Psychiatry*, (1931–1932) 88:519–540. Reprinted in *Schizophrenia as a Human Process*, pp. 272–294.

without professional attention after his introduction to care, the physician may profitably await developments. Sullivan claimed that a considerable proportion of such patients proceed, in this "really human environment," to a degree of social recovery that permits analysis without much contact with the supervising physician. Furthermore patients who experienced this (as far as I know, unprecedented) form of therapy often became aware of their need for insight into their previous difficulties and somewhat cognizant of the nature of the procedures to be used for that purpose, thus becoming prepared for psychoanalytically oriented treatment procedures as well as ready to accept them.

Sullivan emphasizes that in analytically oriented treatment, the physician attempts a more direct and thorough approach, chiefly by reconstructing the actual chronology of the psychosis as the patient improves and his acceptance of his need for help increases. The therapist discourages all the patient's attempts to smooth over, or glide over, relevant past experiences. He employs free associational techniques when apparent failures of memory occur, while he emphasizes the role of significant persons, their activities in the patient's life, and their influence on the etiology of his problems. Sullivan tried to impress the patient in therapy with the principle that, however mysteriously the pathological phenomena originated, everything that has befallen him is related to his actual living among a relatively small number of significant people, in a relatively simple way. In this treatment situation, he subjected psychotic phenomena recalled from the patient's more disturbed periods to study in regard to their relation to those significant others. Sullivan studied the patient's dreams by this principle.

The dynamics of the patient's difficulty thus become apparent to the physician whether or not they are grasped by the patient. The physician scrupulously avoids forcing interpretations on him and preferably offers none except as "statistical findings." That is, if the patient seems to be gaining insight at a considerable pace, the therapist can *occasionally* offer, " 'thus-and-so' has, in some patients, been discovered to be the result of 'this-and-that,' " and can request the patient's associations to the proferred comment.

Sullivan claimed that one of three situations will develop. The family may insist on taking the patient home, particularly if he is doing very well, while ignoring advice as to further treatment. Second, under certain circumstances when the patient has great difficulty in gaining insight, he is discharged for regular treatment by a psychoanalyst who is experienced in the psychiatry of schizophrenia but not too rigid in devotion to technique. Or, finally, the stage of "chronology-perfecting" may be accompanied by so much insight that the therapy is gradually shifted to a close approximation to regular analytic sessions which follow Sullivan's "liberal variant" of classical psychoanalysis.[54]

The special receiving service which Sullivan set up in Sheppard and Enoch Pratt Hospital around 1929 he has described in a paper entitled, "Socio-Psychiatric Research".[55] Mrs. Helen S. Perry, a former managing editor of *Psychiatry*, has investigated Sullivan's setting up of the special receiving service. She reports that the social structure of the ward was drawn to his specifications, based on certain changes he had already partially incorporated on other wards at Sheppard after he was made Direc-

---

54 Compare *Clinical Studies in Psychiatry*, Chapter 15, "Therapy with Schizophrenic Patients."
55 Harry Stack Sullivan, "Socio-Psychiatric Research," *American Journal of Psychiatry*, (1930–1931) 87:977–991. Reprinted in *Schizophrenia as a Human Process*, pp. 256–270.

tor of Clinical Research in 1925. The six-bed ward consisted of two three-bed rooms separated by intercommunicating sitting rooms and a corridor and housed in a fairly new building separate from the other buildings. Perry says there were several wards in this building—75 beds in all—and Sullivan's influence on the other wards, she thinks, was probably also considerable. But Sullivan ran the ward in such a way that it was uniquely cut off from various hierarchical structures that exist in any hospital. The freedom with which Sullivan was allowed to run this ward is said to have been quite remarkable. For one thing, the special ward was wholly removed from the supervision of the Nursing Service. On this ward no woman could set foot. It is said there were six attendants (plus various relief personnel) who worked two 12-hour shifts. According to Perry's account, the day shift was composed of four attendants, the night of two. Sullivan handpicked these attendants from the hospital at large, and he may have directly hired some of them. Despite the fact that they were low in the hierarchy, as all attendants were and are to this day in mental hospitals, these attendants were trained in an intensive way by Sullivan to become full-fleged assistants.

"As Perry says, to expect an individual who had suffered humiliation in his family and the world at large to find a cure in an institution riddled with outworn codes of hierarchical values seemed nonsensical to Sullivan."

Under Sullivan's tutilage and inspiration they apparently developed a remarkable esprit de corps, possessed unusual integrity and devotion to the patients. This is partly indicated by the fact that for considerable periods of time the latter were entrusted to their care without direct intervention by Sullivan, whose dedication to his patients was unlimited. Thus the ward became a testing ground of carefully supervised interpersonal relations.

The special ward was created, in part, for the purpose of sealing off the patients from the hierarchical values of any mental hospital—values which largely reflect the social world outside. As Perry says, to expect an individual who had suffered humiliation in his family and the world at large to find a cure in an institution riddled with outworn codes of hierarchical values seemed nonsensical to Sullivan. Since his patients were male schizophrenics, female nurses were excluded, at least partly because "the registered female nurse may become the prototype of the high status female in an inferior male society" of patients as in almost all state hospitals where the high-status doctor seldom appears. Also the profession of nursing has certain inherent superordinate-subordinate standards which may obstruct the establishment of a sympathetic personal environment for the patient—a vital necessity in Sullivan's view.

There were other innovations. "At Sheppard, Sullivan installed a microphone on his desk, concealed by an ornamental device, so that his conversations with the patient could be recorded. At the time of the establishment of the special ward, this material was sound-tracked down to another floor where recordings were made by Sullivan's secretary. Even before the establishment of the special ward, however, Sullivan had transcriptions made of conversations with patients and collected various kinds of documents from the patients.

. . . This is probably one of the early instances of verbatim records being made of interviews with schizophrenic patients." [56]

The milieu of the ward was modeled on the preadolescent society, Perry points out, so that the schizophrenic patient might have what Sullivan thought was the crucial experience needed for recovery. In his theory of personality development, preadolescence is the time when the capacity for intimacy matures and when one's mental horizon expands immeasureably. This idea may no longer seem plausible due to the vast social changes which have occurred during the past 40 years. In any case it needs more study than it has received.

Sullivan's success with the patients in the special ward was spectacular and unprecedented. His successor, Dr. William V. Silverberg, of New York City, spent a year at Sheppard, making no essential changes in the organization which Sullivan created there. Silverberg in 1931 summarized his own work as follows: During the year he was at Sheppard he dealt with 16 schizophrenics in the special 6-bed ward. "Of

these 16 patients, 12 either recovered or improved. Of the 12 cases that had been cured or improved, nine were discharged and three remained under care at the end of the period. Of the 4 unimproved cases, three were discharged and one remained under care. Of the three unimproved, discharged cases, two turned out to be patients who had been ill for some time, without its being known by their families. They had been paranoid for at least two years before coming to the hospital.

"On the basis of these statistics, one sees that 75 percent of the cases going through this organization has been either recovered or improved. If one omits the two chronic cases for whom, as Dr. Sullivan has already said, such a method of treatment, or any method of treatment, seems to be of no great value, it will be seen that about 85 percent of these 14 cases have been either recovered or improved." [57]

[56] Schizophrenia as a Human Process, p. xxi.

[57] Harry Stack Sullivan, "The Modified Psychoanalytic Treatment of Schizophrenia." Discussion in American J. Psychiatry, (1931–1932) 88:519–540. Reprinted in Schizophrenia as a Human Process, pp. 290–291.

ENDOPSYCHIC STRUCTURE CONSIDERED IN TERMS OF OBJECT-RELATIONSHIPS

By W. RONALD D. FAIRBAIRN

OBJECT-RELATIONSHIP PSYCHOLOGY AS THE RATIONALE OF THE INTERNALIZATION OF OBJECTS

In a previous article (1941) I attempted to formulate a new version of the libido theory and to outline the general features which a systematic psychopathology based upon this re-formulation would appear to assume. The basic conception which I advanced on that occasion, and to which I still adhere, is to the effect that libido is primarily object-seeking (rather than pleasure-seeking, as in the classic theory), and that it is to disturbances in the object-relationships of the developing ego that we must look for the ultimate origin of all psychopathological conditions. This conception seems to me not only to be closer in accord with psychological facts and clinical data than that embodied in Freud's original theory of the libido, but also to represent a logical outcome of the present stage of psycho-analytical thought and a necessary step in the further development of psycho-analytical theory. In particular, it seems to me to constitute an inevitable implication of the illuminating conception of internalized objects, which has been so fruitfully developed by Melanie Klein, but which traces its scientific origin to Freud's theory of the super-ego (an endopsychic structure which was, of course, conceived by him as originating in the internalization of objects).

Quite apart from the considerations advanced in my previous paper or various other considerations which could be adduced, it may be claimed that the psychological introjection of objects and, in particular, the perpetuation of introjected objects in inner reality are processes which by their very nature imply that libido is essentially object-seeking; for the mere presence of oral impulses is in itself quite insufficient to account for such a

pronounced devotion to objects as these phenomena imply. A similar implication would appear to arise out of the mere possibility of an Œdipus situation being perpetuated in the unconscious ; for unceasing devotion to an object constitutes the very essence of this situation. Nevertheless the conception of internalized objects has been developed without any significant modification of a libido theory with which there is no small reason to think that it is incompatible. Freud himself never saw fit to undertake any systematic re-formulation of his original theory of libido, even after the introduction of his theory, of the super-ego. At the same time there are innumerable passages in his works in which it appears to be taken for granted that libido is specifically object-seeking. Indeed it is possible to find passages in which this implicit view becomes explicit—as, for example, when he states quite simply (1929) : ' Love seeks for objects.' This statement occurs in a paragraph in which, referring to his original theory of instincts, he writes as follows : ' Thus first arose the contrast between ego instincts and object instincts. For the energy of the latter instincts and exclusively for them I introduced the term libido ; an antithesis was then formed between the ego instincts and the libidinal instincts directed towards objects.' As Freud proceeds to point out, the distinction between these two groups of instincts was abandoned upon his ' introduction of the concept of narcissism, i.e. the idea that libido cathects the ego itself ' ; but in the light of the passage quoted it would appear no very revolutionary step to claim that libido is primarily object-seeking, especially if, as I have suggested in my previous article, we conceive of narcissism as a state in which the ego is identified with objects.[1]

---

[1] Quite apart from this suggestion, there is no necessary incompatibility between the view that libido is primarily object-seeking and the conception of libido cathecting the ego, since there is always the possibility of one part of the ego structure treating another part as an object—a possibility which cannot be ignored in the light of what follows regarding the splitting of the ego.

INTERNATIONAL JOURNAL OF PSYCHOANALYSIS, 1944-45, 25/26, pp. 70-93.

Nevertheless the ever increasing concentration of psycho-analytical research upon object-relationships has left unmodified the original theory that libido is primarily pleasure-seeking, and with it the related conception that ' the course of mental processes is automatically regulated by " the pleasure principle " ' (Freud, 1920 ; 1). The persistence of this view has raised various problems which might otherwise have proved easier of solution. Prominent amongst these is the problem for which Freud set out to find a solution in *Beyond the Pleasure Principle* (1920) itself, viz. how it comes about that neurotics cling to painful experiences so assiduously. It was the difficulty of accounting for this phenomenon in terms of the pleasure principle that led Freud to fall back upon the conception of a ' repetition compulsion '. If, however, libido is regarded as primarily object-seeking, there is no need to resort to this expedient ; and in a recent article (1943) I attempted to show how the tendency to cling to painful experiences may be explained in terms of relationships with bad objects. In the same article I also attempted to show how the difficulties involved in the conception of primary ' death instincts ' (in contrast to the conception of primary aggressive instincts) may be avoided if all the implications of libidinal relationships with bad objects are taken into account.

IMPULSE PSYCHOLOGY AND ITS LIMITATIONS

In actual fact, the ' object-relationship ' standpoint which I have now come to adopt has resulted from an attempt, imposed upon me by circumstances, to gain a better understanding of the problems presented by patients displaying certain schizoid tendencies, i.e. a class of individuals for whom object-relationships present an especial difficulty ; and here, in parenthesis, I venture to express the opinion that psycho-analytical research in its later phases has suffered from too great a preoccupation with the problems of melancholia. Previous to my reaching the above mentioned standpoint, however, I had already become very much impressed by the limitations of ' impulse psychology ' in general, and somewhat sceptical of the explanatory value of all theories of instinct in which the instincts are treated as existing *per se*. The limitations of impulse psychology make themselves felt in a very practical sense within the therapeutic field ; for, whilst to reveal the nature of his ' impulses ' to a patient by painstaking analysis is one proposition, to enable him to know what to do with these ' impulses ' is quite another. What an individual shall do with his ' impulses ' is clearly a problem of object-relationships. It is equally a problem of his own personality : but (constitutional factors apart) problems of the personality are themselves bound up with object-relationships. These problems are bound up with the relationships of the ego to its internalized

objects—or, as I should prefer to say for reasons which will shortly appear, the relationships of various *parts* of the ego to internalized objects and to one another as objects. In a word ' impulses ' cannot be considered apart from the endopsychic structures which they energize and the object-relationships which they enable these structures to establish ; and, equally, ' instincts ' cannot profitably be considered as anything more than forms of energy which constitute the dynamic of such endopsychic structures.

From a practical psychotherapeutic standpoint the analysis of impulses considered apart from structures proves itself a singularly sterile procedure, and particularly so in the case of patients with well-marked schizoid tendencies. By means of interpretations couched more or less exclusively in terms of impulses, it is sometimes quite easy in such cases to release a flood of associations (e.g. in the form of oral-sadistic phantasies), which appear singularly impressive as manifestations of the unconscious, but which can be maintained indefinitely without any real movement in the direction of integration and without any significant therapeutic development. The explanation of this phenomenon would appear to be that the ego (or, as I should prefer to say, *the central ego*) does not participate in the phantasies described except as a recording agent. When such a situation arises, the central ego, so to speak, sits back in the dress-circle and describes the dramas enacted upon the stage of inner reality without any effective participation in them. At the same time it derives considerable narcissistic satisfaction from being the recorder of remarkable events and identifying itself with the analyst as observer while asserting a superiority over the analyst as mere observer by reason of the fact that it is not merely observing, but also furnishing the material for observation. This procedure is really a masterpiece of defensive technique—one to which schizoid individuals are only too ready to resort at the best of times, but which constitutes an almost irresistible temptation to them when the analyst's interpretations are couched too exclusively in terms of ' impulses '. Such a technique provides the best of all means of enabling the patient to evade the central therapeutic problem, viz. how to release those dynamic charges known as ' impulses ' in the context of reality. This problem is clearly one of object-relationships within the social order.

My point regarding the inadequacy of impulse psychology may be illustrated by a reference to one of the cases in the light of which my present views were developed. This patient was an unmarried woman with schizoid features which were none the less present because the clinical picture was dominated by well-marked phobic and hysterical symptoms, as well as by generalized anxiety. She was repressed in proportion to a high degree of unrelieved libidinal tension. When this libidinal tension rose during a session, it was no uncommon occurrence for her to complain of feeling sick. This sense of nausea was undoubtedly a transference phenomenon based upon an attitude towards her mother and her mother's breast mediated by her father and her father's penis, all as internalized objects ; and it readily lent itself to interpretation in terms of oral impulses in so far as her associations had been characterized from the first by a considerable amount of oral material. Nevertheless the chief significance of her nausea seemed to reside, not so much in the oral nature of the reaction as in the influence shown by this reaction to be exercised upon her object-relationships (1) by a libidinal fixation upon her mother's breast, and (2) by an attitude of rejection towards the object of her libidinal need. It was true, of course, that the oral nature of her reaction was related to a severe repression of genital sexuality ; and she was probably right when, on more than one occasion, she hazarded the opinion that she would be frigid in intercourse, although the correctness of this surmise had never been put to the test. At the same time, her difficulty in achieving a genital attitude seemed best understood, not in terms of any fixation at an oral stage, but rather in terms of a rejection of her father's penis based partly on an identification of this object with the bad breast, partly on a preferential fixation on the breast, and partly on the emotional ' badness ' of her father as a whole object. The scales were further weighted against a genital attitude by the fact that an oral attitude involves a lesser degree of commitment to the object whilst conferring a greater measure of power over it. It was not uncommon for the same patient to say during a session : ' I want to go to the lavatory.' In the first instance this statement had quite a literal significance ; but later in the analysis it came increasingly to mean that she was experiencing a desire to express libidinal feelings mobilized by the transference situation. Here again, it was not in the nature of the ' impulse ' considered in terms of phases (this time urinary and anal) that the chief significance of the phenomenon lay. It lay rather in the quality of the object-relationship involved. ' Going to the lavatory ', like ' being sick ', undoubtedly signified a rejection of the libidinal object considered as contents. Nevertheless, as compared with ' being sick ', it signified a lesser measure of rejection ; for, although in both cases a cathartic discharge of libidinal tension was also involved, the discharge of contents represented by ' going to the lavatory ', being a discharge of assimilated contents, indicated a greater willingness to express libidinal feelings *before* an external object, albeit falling short of that direct discharge of feelings *towards* an object, which characterizes the genital attitude.

The scientific validity of a psychological theory cannot. of course, be assessed solely in terms of psychotherapeutic success or failure ; for the scientific significance of therapeutic results can only be judged when it is known exactly how these results are obtained. Impulse psychology cannot be regarded as providing any exception to this general rule ; but it is significant that, where psycho-analysis is concerned, it is now generally recognized that therapeutic results are closely related to the phenomenon of transference, i.e. to the establishment of an object-relationship of a special kind with the analyst on the part of the patient. On the other hand, it is an accepted article of the psycho-analytical technique that the analyst should be unusually self-effacing. As we know, there are very good reasons for the adoption of such an attitude on his part ; but it inevitably has the effect of rendering the object-relationship between patient and analyst somewhat one-sided from the patient's point of view and thus contributing to the resistance. A certain one-sidedness in the relationship between patient and analyst is, of course, inherent in the analytical situation ; but it would appear that, when the self-effacing attitude of the analyst is combined with a mode of interpretation based upon a psychology of impulse, a considerable strain is imposed upon the patient's capacity for establishing satisfactory object-relationships (a capacity which must be regarded as already compromised in virtue of the fact that the patient is a patient at all). At the same time, the patient is placed under a considerable temptation to adopt, among other defences, that to which reference has already been made, viz. the technique of describing scenes enacted on the stage of inner reality without any significant participation on the part of the central ego either in these scenes or in an effective object-relationship with the analyst. One of my patients, who was a past master in this technique, said to me one day, after providing a comprehensive intellectual description of the state of impulse-tension in which he felt himself to be placed : ' Well, what are you going to do about it ? ' By way of reply I explained that the real question was what he himself was going to do about it. This reply proved highly disconcerting to him, as indeed it was intended to be. It was disconcerting to him because it faced him abruptly with the real problem of the analysis and of his life. How an individual is going to dispose of impulse-tension is clearly a problem of object-relationships : but it is equally a problem of the personality, since an object-relationship necessarily involves a subject as well as an object. The theory of object-relationships thus inevitably leads us to the position that, if impulses cannot be considered apart from objects, whether external or internal, it is equally impossible to consider them apart from ego structures. Indeed it is even more impossible to consider impulses apart from ego structures, since it is only ego structures that can seek relationships with objects. We are thus brought back to the conclusion, already recorded, that 'impulses' are but the dynamic aspect of endopsychic structures and cannot be said to exist in the absence of such structures, however immature these may turn out to be. Ultimately 'impulses' must be simply regarded as constituting the forms of activity in which the life of ego structures consists.

STRUCTURE PSYCHOLOGY AND THE REPRESSION OF STRUCTURES

Once the position now indicated has been reached, it obviously becomes incumbent upon us to review afresh our theory of the mental apparatus. In particular, it becomes a question how far Freud's description of mental structure in terms of id, ego and super-ego can be retained without modification. The moment this question is raised, it is, of course, plainly in relation to the status of the id that doubts will first arise ; for, if it be true that no 'impulses' can be regarded as existing in the absence of an ego structure, it will no longer be possible to preserve any psychological distinction between the id and the ego. Freud's conception of the *origin* of the ego as a structure which develops on the surface of the psyche for the purpose of regulating id-impulses in relation to reality will thus give place to a conception of the ego as the source of impulse-tension from the beginning. This inclusion of the id in the ego will, of course, leave essentially unaffected Freud's conception of the *function* served by the 'ego' in regulating the discharge of impulse-tension in deference to the conditions of outer reality. It will, however, involve the view that 'impulses' are oriented towards reality, and thus to some extent determined by the 'reality principle', from the very beginning. Thus, for example, the child's earliest oral behaviour will be regarded as oriented *ab initio* towards the breast. In accordance with this point of view, the pleasure principle will cease to be regarded as the primary principle of behaviour and will come to be regarded as a subsidiary principle of behaviour involving an impoverishment of object-relationships and coming into operation in proportion as the reality principle fails to operate, whether this be on account of the immaturity of the ego structure or on account of a failure of development on its part. Questions regarding the extent to which the reality principle has superseded the pleasure principle will then give place to questions regarding the extent to which an originally immature reality principle has progressed towards maturity ; and questions regarding the capacity of the ego to regulate id-impulses in deference to reality will give place to questions regarding the measure in which the ego structure within which impulse-tension arises has been organized in accordance with the reality principle, or, in default of this, has resorted to the pleasure principle as a means of organization.

If, then, 'impulse' is to be regarded as inseparably associated with an ego structure from the beginning, what becomes of Freud's conception of repression as a function exercised by the ego in its dealings with impulses originating in the id ? I have already elsewhere (1943) considered the implications of my theory of object-relationships for the concept of repression. There I advanced the view that repression is primarily exercised, not against impulses which have come to appear painful or 'bad' (as in Freud's final view) or even against painful memories (as in Freud's earlier view), but against *internalized objects* which have come to be treated as bad. I still feel justified in regarding this view as correct ; but in certain other respects my views regarding repression have undergone a change. In particular, I have come to regard repression as exercised, not only against internalized objects (which, incidentally, must be regarded as endopsychic structures, albeit not ego structures), but also against parts of the 'ego' which seek relationships with these internal objects. Here it may occur to the reader to pass the criticism that, since repression is a function of the 'ego', this view involves the anomaly of the ego repressing itself. How, it may be asked, can the ego be conceived as repressing the ego ? The answer to this question is that, whilst it is inconceivable that the ego as a whole should repress itself, it is not inconceivable that one part of the 'ego' with a dynamic charge should repress another part of the 'ego' with a dynamic charge. This is, of course, quite a different proposition from one set of impulses repressing another set—a conception rightly rejected by Freud when engaged in the task of formulating his theory of the mental apparatus. In order to account for repression Freud found himself compelled to postulate the existence of a *structure* capable of instigating repression—viz. the super-ego. It is, therefore, only another step in the same direction to postulate the existence of structures which are repressed. Apart from any theoretical reasons such as those already advanced, there are very good clinical reasons for making such an assumption. Prominent among these is the difficulty experienced in effecting the sublimation of libidinal 'impulses'. This difficulty cannot be adequately explained as due to an inveterate and inherent obstinacy on the part of 'impulses' themselves, especially once we have come to regard 'impulses' as just forms of energy at the disposal of the ego structure. On the contrary, it can only be satisfactorily explained on the assumption that the repressed 'impulses' are inseparable from an ego structure with a definite pattern. The correctness of this assumption is confirmed by the phenomena of multiple personality, in which the linkage of repressed 'impulses' with a submerged . ego structure is beyond question ; but such a linkage may also be detected in the less extensive

126

forms of dissociation, which are so characteristic of the hysterical individual. In order to account for repression, we thus appear to be driven to the necessity of assuming a certain multiplicity of egos. This should not really prove a particularly difficult conception for any one familiar with the problems presented by schizoid patients. But here, as so often, we are reminded of the limitations imposed upon psycho-analytical theory in some of its later developments by a preoccupation with the phenomena of melancholia.

THE SCHIZOID POSITION

That Freud's theory of mental structure is itself based in no small measure upon a consideration of the phenomena of melancholia can hardly escape the notice of any reader of *The Ego and the Id* (1923), the work which contains the classic exposition of the theory ; and, in conformity with this fact, it is in his paper entitled ' Mourning and Melancholia ' (1917) that we find the final link in the chain of thought which culminated in the exposition in question. Correspondingly the ' depressive position ' is accorded a place of central importance in the views of Melanie Klein and her collaborators. Here I must confess that the accordance of such a central place to the depressive position is difficult to reconcile with my own experience. It would be idle, of course, to deny the importance of the depressive position in individuals suffering from true depression or, for that matter, in individuals of a depressive type. So far as my experience goes, however, such individuals do not constitute any appreciable proportion of the analyst's clientèle, although, of course, they are common enough in ordinary psychiatric practice. So far as concerns the usual run of patients suffering from anxiety states, psychoneurotic symptoms and character difficulties, the central position seems to me to be schizoid rather than depressive in the vast majority of those who embark upon and persist in analytical treatment ; and it is not very often that I find a patient under analysis displaying what I should regard as an incontrovertibly depressive (i.e. melancholic) reaction. By contrast I find schizoid reactions relatively common.

At this point I feel it necessary to refer to the distinction which I have already drawn (1941) between the characteristically melancholic affect of ' depression ' and the ' sense of futility ' which I have come to regard as the characteristically schizoid affect. From the point of view of the observer there is, admittedly, sufficient superficial similarity between the two affects to render the distinction difficult to draw in many cases, especially since the schizoid individual so commonly describes himself as ' depressed ' ; and consequently the familiar term ' depressed ' is frequently applied in clinical practice to patients who should properly be described as suffering from a sense of futility. In this way a confusion of classification is liable to occur, with the result that a number of patients with psychoneurotic symptoms come to be regarded as belonging to the depressive type when the type to which they belong is really schizoid. Apart from this source of confusion, however, it is a common thing for a basic schizoid position to escape notice in the case of ' psychoneurotic ' patients owing to the strength of psychoneurotic defences and the resulting prominence of psychoneurotic (e.g. hysterical) symptoms in the clinical picture. Yet, when we consider the cases cited by Janet in illustration of the material upon the basis of which he formulated the conception of hysteria as a clinical entity, it is difficult to avoid concluding that quite a number of the individuals concerned displayed remarkably schizoid characteristics ; and indeed it may be surmised that an appreciable proportion would actually be diagnosed as frank schizophrenics if they appeared in a modern psychiatric clinic. Here it may be added that my own investigations of patients with hysterical symptoms leave me in no doubt whatever that the dissociation phenomena of ' hysteria ' involve a split of the ego fundamentally identical with that which confers upon the term ' schizoid ' its etymological significance.

' BACK TO HYSTERIA '

At this point it seems apposite to recall that Freud's earliest researches within the realm of psychopathology were concerned almost exclusively with hysterical (and *not* with melancholic) phenomena, and that it is upon a basis of these phenomena, accordingly, that psycho-analytical theory and practice were originally founded. It would doubtless be idle to speculate to what extent the development of psycho-analytical theory would have pursued a different course if hysterical phenomena had retained the central place which they originally occupied in Freud's researches ; but it may at least be surmised that the importance subsequently assumed by the depressive position would have been assumed in large measure by the schizoid position. It was, of course, when Freud turned from the study of the repressed to a study of the agency of repression that the problems of melancholia began to oust problems of hysteria from the central position which the latter had hitherto occupied. That this should have been the case is not difficult to understand in view of (a) the close association which appears to exist between guilt and repression, on the one hand, and (b) the outstanding prominence which guilt assumes in the melancholic state, on the other. Be that as it may, Freud's theory of the super-ego certainly represents an attempt to trace the genesis of guilt and the instigation of repression to a common source in the Œdipus situation. This fact gives rise to a serious incompatibility between Freud's views regarding the origin of repression and Abraham's ' phase ' theory of libidinal development ; for, whilst Freud conceived the Œdipus situation, to which he looked for the rationale of repression, as essentially a genital situation, his account of the origin of the super-ego, which he regarded as the instigator of repression, is conceived in terms of an oral situation, i.e. a situation corresponding to a stage which, according to the ' phase ' theory, must necessarily be pregenital. Melanie Klein has, of course, come to regard the Œdipus situation as originating at a very much earlier stage than was formerly supposed. Her resolution of the difficulty must accordingly be interpreted as having been achieved at the expense of the ' phase ' theory. This theory has already been the subject of detailed criticism on my part (1941). At the same time I have now come to look for the source of repression not only beyond the genital attitude, but also beyond the Œdipus situation, and even beyond the level at which the super-ego is established. Thus I not only attempted elsewhere (1943) to show that *repression* originates primarily as a defence against ' bad ' internalized objects (and not against impulses, whether incestuous in the genital sense or otherwise), but also that *guilt* originates as an *additional* defence against situations involving bad internalized objects. According to this view, guilt originates on the principle that the child finds it more tolerable to regard himself as conditionally (i.e. morally) bad than to regard his parents as unconditionally (i.e. libidinally) bad. To describe the process whereby the change from the latter to the former attitude is effected, I introduced the term ' moral defence ' ; and, according to my view, it is only at the instance of the ' moral defence ' that the super-ego is established.[2] The establishment of the super-ego accordingly represents the attainment of a new level of structural organization, beneath which the old level persists. Thus, in my opinion, beneath the level at which the central ego finds itself confronted with the super-ego as an internal object of moral significance lies a level at which parts of the ego find themselves confronted with internal objects which are, not simply devoid of moral significance, but unconditionally bad from a libidinal standpoint (amoral internal persecutors of one kind or another). Whilst, therefore, the main phenomenon of melancholia may be regarded as receiving a relatively satisfactory explanation at the super-ego level, some of the accompanying phenomena are not so easily explained. Thus the paranoid and hypochondriacal trends which so frequently manifest themselves in melancholics represent an orientation towards

internal objects which are in no sense ' good ', but are unconditionally (i.e. libidinally) bad. The same may be said of the obsessional features which are so characteristic of individuals in the initial stages of depression ; for the obsessional defence is not primarily moral. On the contrary, this defence is essentially a defence against the ' unlucky ', i.e. against situations involving relationships with unconditionally bad (internal) objects. It is equally difficult to find a satisfactory explanation of the symptoms of ' hysteria ' at the super-ego level—if for no other reason than that in ' hysteria ' the libidinal inhibitions which occur are out of all proportion to the measure of guilt which is found to be present. Since, therefore, it was in an effort on Freud's part to explain hysterical phenomena that psycho-analysis originated, it may not be without profit to return to a consideration of this material, encouraging ourselves, if encouragement be needed, with the slogan ' Back to hysteria '.

A MULTIPLICITY OF EGOS

Attention has already been drawn to the fact that, whereas the repressed was eventually described by Freud as consisting essentially of impulses, he found it necessary to fall back upon structural conceptions (the ego and the super-ego) when he came to seek an explanation of the agency of repression. Reduced to its simplest terms, Freud's conception of repression is to the following effect :—(a) that the agency of repression is the ego, (b) that repression is instigated and maintained by the pressure of the super-ego (an internalized parental figure) upon the ego, (c) that the repressed consists essentially in libidinal impulses, and (d) that repression arises as a means of defence against impulses involved in the Œdipus situation and treated by the ego as ' guilty ' in terms of the pressure of the super-ego. That the agent and the instigator of repression should both be regarded as structures whilst the repressed is regarded as consisting of impulses involves a certain anomaly which appears so far to have escaped attention. The extent of this anomaly may perhaps best be appreciated in the light of the fact that the super-ego, which is described as the instigator of repression, is itself largely unconscious ; for this raises the difficult question whether the super-ego itself is not also repressed. Freud himself was by no means oblivious to this problem ; and he expressly envisages the possibility of the super-ego being in some measure subject to repression. Repression of the super-ego would, of course, represent the repression of a structure. It would thus appear

---

[2] I should add that, in my opinion, it is always ' bad ' objects that are internalized in the first instance, since it is difficult to find any adequate motive for the internalization of objects which are satisfying and ' good '. Thus it would be a pointless procedure on the part of the infant to internalize the breast of a mother with whom he already had a perfect relationship in the absence of such internalization, and whose milk proved sufficient to satify his incor-porative needs. According to this line of thought it is only in so far as his mother's breast fails to satisfy his physical and emotional needs and thus becomes a bad object that it becomes necessary for the infant to internalize it. It is only later that good objects are internalized to defend the child's ego against bad objects which have been internalized already ; and the super-ego is a ' good object ' of this nature.

that the general possibility of the repression of a structure is recognized by Freud ; and, in the light of the considerations already advanced, it becomes reasonable to ask whether the repressed is not invariably and inherently structural. In this event the anomaly to which I have referred would be avoided.

That the repressed is essentially structural in nature is implicit in the view which I have already advanced (1943) to the effect that repression is primarily directed against internalized objects which are treated as bad ; for, unless it is assumed that internalized objects are structures, the conception of the existence of such objects becomes utterly meaningless. In the light of further experience, my view that repression is primarily directed against bad internalized objects has proved to require considerable elaboration in a direction which has eventually led me to a revised conception of psychical structure. What actually provided the occasion of my chief step in this direction was the analysis of a dream recorded by one of my patients. This patient was a married woman who originally came to me for analysis on account of frigidity. Her frigidity was unquestionably a phenomenon of hysterical dissociation (hysterical anæsthesia combined with hysterical paresis of the vagina) ; but, like all such phenomena, it represented but one part of a general personality problem. The dream itself was simple enough ; but it struck me in the light of one of those simple manifestations which have so often in the history of science been found to embody fundamental truths.

The (manifest) dream to which I refer consisted in a brief scene in which the dreamer saw the figure of herself being viciously attacked by a well-known actress in a venerable building which had belonged to her family for generations. Her husband was looking on ; but he seemed quite helpless and quite incapable of protecting her. After delivering the attack the actress turned away and resumed playing a stage part, which, as seemed to be implied, she had momentarily set aside in order to deliver the attack by way of interlude. The dreamer then found herself gazing at the figure of herself lying bleeding on the floor ; but, as she gazed, she noticed that this figure turned for an instant into that of a man. Thereafter the figure alternated between herself and this man until eventually she awoke in a state of acute anxiety.

It came as no great surprise to me to learn from the dreamer's associations that the man into whom the figure of herself turned was wearing a suit closely resembling one which her husband had recently acquired, and that, whilst he had acquired this suit at her instigation, he had taken ' one of his blondes ' to the fitting. This fact, taken in conjunction with the fact that in the dream he was a helpless spectator of the attack, at once confirmed a natural suspicion that the attack was directed no less against him than against herself. This suspicion was amply confirmed by further associations which need not be detailed. The course followed by the associations also confirmed an additional suspicion that the actress who delivered the attack belonged as much to the personality of the dreamer as did the figure of herself against which the attack was delivered. In actual fact, the figure of an actress was well suited to represent a certain aspect of herself ; for she was essentially a shut-in and withdrawn personality who displayed very little genuine feeling towards others, but who had perfected the technique of presenting façades to a point at which these assumed a remarkably genuine appearance and achieved for her a remarkable popularity. Such libidinal affect as she experienced had, since childhood, manifested itself predominantly in a secret phantasy life of masochistic complexion ; but in the life of outer reality she had largely devoted herself to the playing of rôles—e.g. the rôles of good wife, good mother, good hostess and good business woman. From this fact the helplessness attributed to her husband in the dream derived additional significance ; for, although she played the rôle of good wife with conspicuous success, her real personality was quite inaccessible to him and the good wife whom he knew was for the most part only the good actress. This held true not only within the sphere of emotional relationships, but also within the sphere of marital relations ; for, whilst she remained frigid during intercourse, she had acquired the capacity of conveying the impression of sexual excitement and sexual satisfaction. Further, as the analysis revealed beyond all question, her frigidity represented not only an attack upon the libidinal component in herself, but also a hostile attitude towards her husband as a libidinal object. It is clear, therefore, that a measure of hidden aggression against her husband was involved in her assumption of the rôle of actress as this was portrayed in the dream. It is equally clear from the dream that, in a libidinal capacity, she was identified with her husband as the object of her own aggression. At this point, it should be mentioned that, when the dream occurred, her husband was a member of one of the combatant Services and was about to return home on leave. On the eve of his return, and just before the occurrence of the dream, she had developed a sore throat. This was a conjunction of events which had occurred so frequently in the past as to preclude coincidence on this occasion, and which accordingly served to confirm her identification with her husband as the object of her aggression. The situation represented in the dream is thus one in which the dreamer in one capacity, so far unspecified, vents her aggression directly against herself in another capacity, viz., a libidinal capacity, whilst, at the same time, venting her aggression indirectly against her husband as a libidinal object. At a superficial level, of course, this situation readily lent itself to being interpreted in the sense that the dreamer, being ambivalent towards her husband, had diverted the aggressive component in her ambivalent attitude from her husband to herself at the instance of guilt over her aggression in conformity with the melancholic pattern. Nevertheless, during the actual session in which the dream was recorded this interpretation did not commend itself to me as exhaustive, even at a superficial level.

It is obvious, of course, that the situation represented in the dream lent itself to a deeper interpretation than that to which reference has just been made. The situation was described a moment ago as one in which the dreamer in a capacity so far unspecified vented her aggression directly against herself in a libidinal capacity, whilst, at the same time, venting her aggression indirectly against her husband as a libidinal object. This description is, of course, incomplete in that it leaves unspecified the capacity in which she expressed her aggression ; and it is when we come to consider the nature of this unspecified capacity that the deeper significance of the dream becomes a matter of moment. According to the manifest content of the dream, it was as an actress that she delivered the attack ; and we have already seen how well suited the figure of an actress was to represent an aspect of herself hostile to libidinal relationships. However, abundant material had already emerged during the analysis to make it plain that the figure of an actress was at least equally well suited to represent the dreamer's mother—an artificial woman who had neither displayed any natural and spontaneous affection towards her children nor welcomed any such display on their part towards herself, and for whom the fashionable world provided a stage upon which she had spent her life in playing parts. It was thus easy to see that, in the capacity of actress, the dreamer was closely identified with her mother as a repressive figure. The introduction of her mother into the drama as an apparently ' super-ego ' figure at once raises the question whether the deeper interpretation of the dream should not be couched in terms of the Œdipus situation ; and it becomes natural to ask whether her father is not also represented. In reality her father had been killed on active service during the war of 1914–18, at a time when she was only six years of age ; and analysis had revealed the presence of considerable resentment towards him as a libidinal object who had proved at once exciting and rejecting (this resentment being focussed particularly upon the memory of an early dressing-room scene). If then we are to look for a representation of her father in the dream, our choice is obviously limited to a single figure—the man who alternated with the figure of the dreamer as the object of attack. We

have seen, of course, that this figure represented her husband ; but analysis had already revealed how closely her husband was identified by transference with her father. For this, as well as for other reasons which need not be detailed, it was safe to infer that the man who was involved in the attack represented her father at the deeper level of interpretation. At this level, accordingly, the dream was capable of being interpreted as a phantasy in which both she and her father were portrayed as being killed by her mother on account of a guilty incestuous relationship. At the same time the dream was equally capable of being interpreted in terms of psychical structure, and thus as representing the repression of her libido on account of its incestuous attachment to her father at the instigation of a super-ego modelled upon her mother. Nevertheless, neither of these interpretations seemed to me to do justice to the material, although the structural interpretation seemed to offer the more fruitful line of approach.

At this point I feel it necessary to make some reference to the development of my own views regarding phantasy in general and dreams in particular. Many years ago I had the opportunity to analyse a most unusual woman whom, in retrospect, I now recognize to have been a schizoid personality, and who was a most prolific dreamer. Among the dreams recorded by this woman were a number which defied all efforts to bring them into conformity with the ' wish-fulfilment ' theory, and which she herself came to describe quite spontaneously as ' state of affairs ' dreams, intending by this description to imply that they represented actually existing endopsychic situations. Doubtless this made an impression on me. At any rate, much later, after Freud's theory of psychical structure had become familiar, after Melanie Klein had elaborated the conceptions of psychical reality and internal objects and after I myself had become impressed by the prevalence and importance of schizoid phenomena, I tentatively formulated the view that all the figures appearing in dreams represented either parts of the dreamer's own personality (conceived in terms of ego, super-ego and id) or else identifications on the part of the ego. A further development of this view was to the effect that dreams are essentially, not wish-fulfilments, but snapshots, or rather ' shorts ' (in the cinematographic sense), of situations existing in inner reality. To the view that dreams are essentially ' shorts ' of situations existing in inner reality I still adhere in conformity with the general line of thought pursued in this article ; but, so far as the figures appearing in dreams are concerned, I have now modified my view to the effect that such figures represent either parts of the ' ego ' or internalized objects. According to my present view, therefore, the situations depicted in dreams represent relationships existing between endopsychic structures ; and the same applies to situations depicted in waking phantasies. This conclusion is the natural outcome of my theory of object-relationships taken in conjunction with a realization of the inescapable fact that internalized objects must be regarded as endopsychic structures if any theoretic significance whatever is to be attached to them.

After this explanatory digression I must return to the specific dream under discussion with a view to giving some account of the conclusions which I subsequently reached, in no small measure as the result of an attempt to solve the theoretic problems which it raised in my mind. As I have already stated, none of the obvious interpretations seemed to me entirely satisfactory, although the structural type of interpretation seemed to offer the most fruitful line of approach. The reader will, of course, bear in mind what I have already said regarding psychical structures ; and he will also recall my having already formulated the view that all psychopathological developments originate at a stage antecedent to that at which the super-ego develops and proceed from a level beneath that at which the super-ego operates. Thus no reference will be made in what follows either to the super-ego or to the id as explanatory concepts. On the contrary, whilst adopting a structural approach, I shall attempt to elucidate the significance of the dream quite simply in terms of the data which it itself provides.

In the manifest dream the actual drama involves four figures :—(1) the figure of the dreamer subjected to attack, (2) the man into whom this figure turns, and who then alternates with it, (3) the attacking actress, and (4) the dreamer's husband as a helpless onlooker. In our preoccupation with the actual drama, however, we must not forget our only witness of its occurrence —the dreamer herself, the observing ego. Including her, there are five figures to be reckoned with. At this juncture I venture to suggest that, if the dream had ended a few seconds earlier, there would only have been four figures, even on the assumption that the ' I ' of the dream is taken into account ; for it was only in the fifth act, so to speak, that a man began to alternate with the figure of the dreamer as the object of attack. This is an interesting reflection ; for we must conclude that, up to the point of the emergence of this man, the object of attack was a composite figure. The special interest of this phenomenon resides in the fact that, as we have seen, there is good reason to regard a second figure as composite ; for the attacking actress undoubtedly represented both another figure of the dreamer and the dreamer's mother. I venture, therefore, to hazard a further suggestion—that, if the dream had lasted a few seconds longer, there might well have been six figures, instead of five. It is safe, at any rate, to infer that there were six figures in the latent content ; and this, after all, is what matters for purposes of interpretation. Assuming then that six figures are represented in the dream, let us proceed to consider the nature of these figures. When we do so, our first observation is that the figures fall into two classes—ego structures and object structures. Interestingly enough there are three members of each class. The ego structures are (1) the observing ego or ' I ', (2) the attacked ego, and (3) the attacking ego. The object structures are (1) the dreamer's husband as an observing object, (2) the attacked object, and (3) the attacking object. This leads us to make a second observation—that the ego structures naturally lend themselves to be paired off with the object structures. There are three such pairs :— (1) the observing ego and the dreamer's husband, who also figured as an observer ; (2) the attacking ego and the attacking object representing her mother, and (3) the attacked ego and the attacked object representing her father (for at this point it is to the deeper level of interpretation that we must adhere).

Bearing these two main observations in mind, let us now consider the conclusions to which I was led in an attempt to interpret the dream to my satisfaction. They are as follows. The three ego figures which appear as separate in the dream actually represent separate ego structures in the dreamer's mind. The dreamer's ' ego ' is therefore split in conformity with the schizoid position ; and it is split into three separate egos—a central ego and two other subsidiary egos which are both, relatively speaking, cut off from the central ego. Of these two subsidiary egos, one is the object of aggression on the part of the other. Since the ego which is attacked is closely related to the dreamer's father (and by transference to her husband), it is safe to infer that this ego is highly endowed with libido ; and it may thus be appropriately described as a ' libidinal ego '. Since the attacking ego is closely related to the dreamer's mother as a repressive figure, its behaviour is quite in accord with that traditionally ascribed to the super-ego in the setting of the Œdipus situation. Since, however, the attack bears all the marks of being vindictive, rather than moral, and gives rise to an affect, not of guilt, but of plain anxiety, there is no justification (apart from preconceptions) for equating the attacking ego with the super-ego. In any case, as I have already indicated, there is reason to attach overriding psychopathological importance to a level beneath that at which the super-ego functions. At the same time, it was shown by the circumstances in which the dream occurred that the dreamer's libidinal relationship with her husband was severely compromised ; and, so far as the dream is concerned, it is clearly to the operation of the attacking ego that we must look for the compromising factor. Consequently, the attacking ego may perhaps be most appropriately described as an ' internal saboteur '. In an

131

attempt to discover what this dream was stating and to determine the structural significance of what was stated, I was accordingly led to set aside the traditional classification of mental structure in terms of ego, id and super-ego in favour of a classification couched in terms of an ego-structure split into three separate egos—(1) a central ego (the ' I '), (2) a libidinal ego, and (3) an aggressive, persecutory ego which I designate as the internal saboteur. Subsequent experience has led me to regard this classification as having a universal application.

THE OBJECT-RELATIONSHIPS OF THE CENTRAL EGO AND THE SUBSIDIARY EGOS

Such being my conclusions regarding the ego structures represented in the dream, let us now pass on to consider my conclusions regarding the object-relationships of these ego structures. As already indicated, each of the three egos in question naturally lends itself to being paired off with a special object. The special object of the central ego was the dreamer's husband ; and it is convenient to begin by considering the nature of the attitude adopted by the dreamer's central ego towards him. Since the central ego was the observing ' I ' of the dream, who was felt to be continuous with the waking ' I ' by whom the dream was subsequently described, it is safe to infer that this ego is in no small measure pre-conscious—which is, in any case, what one would naturally expect of an ego deserving the title of ' central '. This inference gains further support from the fact that the dreamer's husband was a supremely important object in outer reality and was very much in the dreamer's conscious thoughts on the eve of the dream. Although the figure representing him in the dream must be regarded as an internalized object, this object must obviously occupy a much more superficial position in the psyche than the other objects represented (parental objects internalized in childhood) ; and it must correspond comparatively closely to the relative object in outer reality. Accordingly, the dreamer's attitude to her husband as an external object assumes considerable significance for our present purpose. This attitude was essentially ambivalent, especially where marital relations were concerned. Active manifestations of aggression towards him were, however, conspicuously absent. Equally, her libidinal attachment to him bore the marks of severe repression ; and, in associating to the dream, she reproached herself over her lack of deep feeling towards him and her failure to give to him of herself, albeit her conscious capacity to remedy these deficiencies was restricted to an assumption of the rôle of ' good wife '. The question therefore arises whether, since her hidden aggression towards him and her hidden libidinal need of him do not declare themselves directly in the dream, they may not manifest themselves in some indirect fashion.

No sooner is this question raised than we are at once reminded of the metamorphosis undergone by the figure of the libidinal ego after this was attacked by the figure of the internal saboteur. The libidinal ego changed into, and then began alternating with, a man who, whilst representing the dreamer's father at a deep level, was nevertheless closely associated with her husband. It is thus evident that, instead of being directed against her husband as an external object, a considerable proportion of her aggression was absorbed in an attack directed, not simply against the libidinal ego, but also against an internal object closely connected with the libidinal ego. It is likewise evident that this volume of aggression had come to be at the disposal, not of the central ego, but of the internal saboteur. What then of the libidinal component in her ambivalence ? As we have seen, her libidinal attitude to her husband showed signs of considerable impoverishment in spite of good intentions at a conscious level. It is obvious, accordingly, that what held true of her aggression also held true of her libido. A considerable proportion had ceased to be at the disposal of the central ego. The object towards whom this volume of libido is directed can hardly remain in doubt. In terms of the dream, it must surely be the man who alternated with the libidinal self as the object of aggression. Unlike the aggression, however, this libido is not at the disposal of the internal saboteur. On the contrary we must regard it as being at the disposal of the libidinal ego ; and indeed it is precisely for this reason that the term ' libidinal ego ' has come to commend itself to me for adoption. At this point it becomes desirable to formulate a suspicion which must be already present in the mind of the reader—that, although it is represented otherwise in the dream, the attack delivered by the internal saboteur is only secondarily directed against the libidinal ego and is primarily directed against the libidinal object which alternates with this ego. Assuming this suspicion to be correct, we must regard the ordeal to which the libidinal ego is subjected as evidence of a very complete identification with, and therefore a very strong libidinal attachment to, the attacked object on the part of the libidinal ego. It is evidence of the measure of ' suffering ' which the libidinal ego is prepared to endure out of devotion to its object. The anxiety experienced by the dreamer on waking may be interpreted in a similar sense ; and indeed I venture to suggest that this anxiety represented an irruption into consciousness of such ' suffering ' on the part of the libidinal ego. Here we are at once reminded of Freud's original conception of neurotic anxiety as libido converted into suffering. This is a view which at one time presented the greatest theoretic difficulty to me, but which I have now come to appreciate in the light of my present standpoint, and substantially to accept in preference to the modified view which Freud later (and, as I think, rather reluctantly) came to adopt.

The position regarding the object-relationships of the three egos represented in the dream has now been to some extent clarified ; but the process of clarification is not yet complete. Up to date, the position which has emerged would appear to be as follows. The dreamer's preconscious attitude towards her husband is ambivalent ; and this is the attitude adopted by her central ego towards its external object, as well as towards the internalized representative of this object. However, both the libidinal and the aggressive components in the object-relationship of the central ego are predominantly passive. On the other hand, a considerable proportion of the dreamer's active libido is at the disposal of the libidinal self and is directed towards an internalized object which, for purposes of nomenclature, may perhaps best be described as ' the (internal) needed object '. At the same time, a considerable proportion of her aggression is at the disposal of the internal saboteur and is directed (a) towards the libidinal self, and (b) towards the needed object (i.e. towards the object of the libidinal self). It cannot fail to be noticed, however, that this summary of the position leaves out of account certain endopsychic relationships which may be presumed to exist—notably (1) the relationship of the central ego to the other egos, and (2) the relationship of the internal saboteur to the internalized object with which it is so closely associated, and which is represented by the maternal component in the actress figure. Taking the latter relationship first, we have no difficulty in seeing that, since the actress in the dream was a composite figure representing both the dreamer's mother and herself, the internal saboteur is closely identified with its object and must therefore be regarded as bound to this object by a strong libidinal attachment. For purposes of description we must give the object a name ; and I propose to describe it as ' the (internal) rejecting object '. I have chosen this term primarily for a reason which will emerge later ; but meanwhile my justification will be that the dreamer's mother, who provided the original model of this internalized object, was essentially a rejecting figure, and that it is, so to speak, in the name of this object that the aggression of the internal saboteur is directed against the libidinal self. As regards the relationship of the central ego to the other egos, our most important clue to its nature lies in the fact that, whereas the central ego must be regarded as comprising preconscious and conscious, as well as unconscious, elements, the other egos must equally be regarded as essentially unconscious. From this we may infer that the libidinal ego and the internal saboteur are both rejected by the central ego ; and this inference is confirmed by the fact that, as we have seen, the considerable volume of libido and of aggression which has ceased to be at the disposal of the central

ego is now at the disposal of the subsidiary egos. Assuming then that the subsidiary egos are rejected by the central ego, it becomes a question of the dynamic of this rejection. Obviously the dynamic of rejection cannot be libido. So there is no alternative but to regard it as aggression. Aggression must, accordingly, be regarded as the characteristic determinant of the attitude of the central ego towards the subsidiary egos.

I have now completed the account of my attempt to reconstruct, in terms of dynamic structure, the endopsychic situation represented in a patient's dream. The account has been cast in the form of a reasoned statement ; and, as such, it should serve to give some indication of what is involved in my view that dreams are essentially ' shorts ' of inner reality (rather than wish-fulfilments). However, it is not primarily with the aim of substantiating my views on dreams in general that I have claimed so much of the reader's attention for a single dream. On the contrary, it is because the dream in question seems to me to represent an endopsychic situation of a classic order, and indeed of a basic character which entitles it to be regarded as the paradigm of all endopsychic situations. For convenience, the general features of this situation are illustrated in the accompanying diagram.

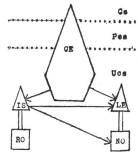

CE, Central Ego ; IS, Internal Saboteur ; LE, Libidinal Ego ; RO, Rejecting Object ; NO, Needed Object. Cs, Conscious ; Pcs, Preconscious ; Ucs, Unconscious. ⟶, Aggression ; =, Libido.

THE BASIC ENDOPSYCHIC SITUATION AND A REVISED THEORY OF MENTAL STRUCTURE FOUNDED THEREON

I myself feel convinced that the basic endopsychic situation above described is the situation underlying Freud's description of the mental apparatus in terms of ego, id, and super-ego. It is certainly the endopsychic situation upon which I deliberately base the revised theory of mental structure which I now submit, and which is couched in terms of central ego, libidinal ego and internal saboteur. As it would, of course, be natural to expect, there is a general correspondence between Freud's concepts and those which I have now come to adopt. In the case of ' the central ego ' the correspondence to Freud's ' ego ' is fairly close from a functional standpoint ; but there are important differences between the two concepts. Unlike Freud's ' ego ', the ' central ego ' is not conceived as originating out of something else (the ' id '), or as constituting a passive structure dependent for its activity upon impulses proceeding from the matrix out of which it originated, and on the surface of which it rests.[3] On the contrary, the ' central ego ' is conceived as a primary and dynamic structure, from which, as we shall shortly see, the other mental structures are subsequently derived. The ' libidinal ego ' corresponds, of course, to Freud's ' id ' ; but, whereas according to Freud's view the ' ego ' is a derivative of the ' id ', according to my view the ' libidinal ego ' (which corresponds to the ' id ') is a derivative of the ' central ego ' (which corresponds to the ' ego '). The ' libidinal ego ' also differs from the ' id ' in that it is conceived, not as a mere reservoir of instinctive impulses, but as a dynamic structure comparable to the ' central ego ', although differing from the latter in various respects, e.g. in its more infantile character, in a lesser degree of organization, in a smaller measure of adaptation to reality and in a greater devotion to internalized objects. The ' internal saboteur ' differs from the ' super-ego ' in a number of respects. For one thing it is in no sense conceived as an internal object. It is wholly an ego structure, although, as we have seen, it is very closely associated with an internal object. Actually, the ' super-ego ' corresponds not so much to the ' internal saboteur ' as to a compound of this structure and its associated object (like the figure of the actress in the dream). At the same time, the ' internal saboteur ' is unlike the ' super-ego ' in that it is conceived as, in itself, devoid of all moral significance. Thus I do not attribute the affect of guilt to its activity, although this activity is unquestionably a prolific source of anxiety. Such anxiety may, of course, merge with guilt ; but the two affects are theoretically distinct. Here it should be noted that, whilst introducing the conception of the internal saboteur, I am not prepared to abandon the conception of the super-ego as I have now come to abandon that of the id. On the contrary, it seems to me impossible to offer any satisfactory psychological explanation of guilt in the absence of the super-ego ; but the super-ego must be regarded as originating at a higher level of mental organization than that at which the internal saboteur operates. Exactly how the activities of the two structures are related must in the meantime remain an open question ; but for the most recent expression of my views regarding the origin and the function of the super-

ego I must refer the reader to another article (1943).

SPLITTING OF THE EGO AND REPRESSION CONSIDERED AS ASPECTS OF AN IDENTICAL PROCESS OPERATIVE IN BOTH SCHIZOID AND HYSTERICAL CONDITIONS

Before proceeding to consider the origin of what I have called ' the basic endopsychic situation ', I feel it necessary to record some general conclusions which seem to follow from the inherent nature of the situation itself. The first and most obvious of these conclusions is that the ego is split. In this respect, therefore, the basic endopsychic situation which has now emerged conforms to the pattern of the schizoid position—a position which, as already indicated, I have come to regard as central (in preference to the depressive position). Freud's theory of the mental apparatus was, of course, developed upon a basis of the depressive position ; and it is on a similar basis that Melanie Klein has developed her views. By contrast, it is the schizoid position that constitutes the basis of the theory of mental structure which I now advance. It is to be noted, further, that, whilst conforming to the pattern of the schizoid position, the endopsychic situation revealed in my patient's dream also provided a satisfactory explanation of the dreamer's hysterical frigidity in terms of dynamic structure. Here we are reminded of the common association of hysterical symptoms with an underlying schizoid attitude—an association to which reference has already been made. There would, accordingly, appear to be good grounds for our second conclusion—that hysterical developments are inherently based upon an underlying and fundamental schizoid position. Our third conclusion follows from what has already been said regarding the aggressive attitude of the central ego towards the subsidiary egos. It is to the effect that the splitting of the ego observed in the schizoid position is due to the operation of a certain volume of aggression which remains at the disposal of the central ego. It is this aggression that provides the dynamic of the severance of the subsidiary egos from the central ego. The subsidiary egos are, of course, ordinarily unconscious ; and their unconscious status at once raises the suspicion that they are subject to repression. This is obviously so in the case of the libidinal ego (which corresponds to Freud's id) ; but, if one of the subsidiary ego structures can be repressed, there is no reason for regarding the other as immune from similar treatment at the hands of the central ego. Consequently our fourth conclusion is that the internal saboteur (which largely corresponds to Freud's super-ego in function) is repressed no less than the libidinal ego. This conclusion may at

---

[3] Freud's conception of the ego was, of course, borrowed from Groddeck ; but, if there is any truth in the conclusions which will shortly be recorded, it is a conception based upon an endopsychic situation resulting from repression, and therefore is anomalous in terms of Freud's own views, since it implies that repression is responsible for the origin of the ego.

first sight appear to be in conflict with the theory which I previously advanced (1943), to the effect that repression is primarily directed against bad internalized objects. There is no real inconsistency, however : for I regard the repression of the subsidiary egos, which I now envisage, as secondary to the repression of bad internalized objects. Here we find a helpful analogy in the attack of the internal saboteur on the libidinal ego ; for, as we have seen, the aggression involved in this attack is primarily directed against the needed object to which the libidinal ego is related, and only secondarily against the libidinal ego itself. Similarly, I regard repression of the libidinal ego on the part of the central ego as secondary to repression of the needed object. Our fifth conclusion needs no elaboration in the light of what precedes. It is to the effect that the dynamic of repression is aggression. Our sixth, and last, conclusion, which follows equally from preceding conclusions, is that splitting of the ego, on the one hand, and repression of the subsidiary egos by the central ego, on the other, constitute essentially the same phenomenon considered from different points of view. Here it is apposite to recall that, whilst the concept of splitting of the ego was formulated by Bleuler in an attempt to explain the phenomena of what was known as ' dementia præcox ' until he introduced the term ' schizophrenia ' to take its place, the concept of repression was formulated by Freud in an attempt to explain the phenomena of hysteria. Our final conclusion thus serves to substantiate the view that the position underlying the development of hysterical symptoms is essentially a schizoid position.

The Origin of the Basic Endopsychic Situation and of the Multiplicity of Egos

It is now time for us to turn our attention to questions regarding the origin of the basic endopsychic situation which found a classic expression in my patient's dream. In the light of considerations which have already emerged, it will be obvious that whatever explanation we may reach regarding the origin of this situation will also serve as an explanation of the origin of the schizoid position, the origin of repression and the differentiation of the various fundamental endopsychic structures. As we have seen, the patient whose dream has occupied so much of our attention was essentially ambivalent towards her husband as an external object ; and it is from the establishment of a state of ambivalence towards external objects in early life that the basic endopsychic situation springs. The first libidinal object of the infant is, of course, his mother's breast, although there can

be no doubt that the form of his mother as a person soon begins to take shape round the original nucleus of this maternal organ. Under theoretically perfect conditions the libidinal relationship of the infant to his mother would be so satisfactory that a state of libidinal frustration could hardly arise ; and, as I see it, there would consequently be no ambivalence on the part of the infant towards his object. At this point I must explain that, whilst I regard aggression as a primary dynamic factor in that it does not appear capable of being resolved into libido (as Jung, for example, sought to resolve it), at the same time I regard it as ultimately subordinate to libido, not only metaphysically, but also psychologically. Thus I do not consider that the infant directs aggression spontaneously towards his libidinal object in the absence of frustration ; and my observation of the behaviour of animals confirms me in this view. It should be added that in a state of nature the infant would never normally experience that separation from his mother which appears to be imposed upon him increasingly by conditions of civilization. Indeed, it may be inferred that in a state of nature it would be rare for the infant to be deprived of the shelter of his mother's arms and of ready access to her breast until, in the ordinary course of development, he himself became increasingly disposed to dispense with them.[4] Such perfect conditions are, however, only theoretically possible for the human infant born into a cultural group ; and in actual fact the libidinal relationship of the infant to his mother is disturbed from the first by a considerable measure of frustration, although, of course, the degree of such frustration varies in different cases. It is the experience of libidinal frustration that calls forth the infant's aggression in relation to his libidinal object and thus gives rise to a state of ambivalence. To content ourselves with saying simply that the infant becomes ambivalent would, however, be to give an incomplete and partial picture of the situation which now arises ; for it would be a picture conceived exclusively from the point of view of the observer. From the point of view of the infant himself it is a case of his mother becoming an ambivalent object, i.e. an object which is both good and bad. Since it proves intolerable to him to have a good object which is also bad, he seeks to alleviate the situation by splitting the figure of his mother into two objects. Then, in so far as she satisfies him libidinally, she is a good object, and, in so far as she fails to satisfy him libidinally, she is a bad object. The situation in which he now finds himself placed proves, however, in its turn to be one which imposes a severe strain upon his capacity for endurance and his power of adjust-

---

[4] It must be recognized, of course, that, under any conditions, a profound sense of separation and loss of security must be experienced by the infant at the time of birth ; and it may be presumed that some measure of aggression, in addition to anxiety, is called forth by this experience. There is no reason, however, to think that this experience in itself would give rise to a state of ambivalence in the absence of further experience of libidinal frustration during infancy.

ment. Being a situation in outer reality, it is one which he finds himself impotent to control, and which, accordingly, he seeks to mitigate by such means as are at his disposal. The means at his disposal are limited ; and the technique which he adopts is more or less dictated by this limitation. He accordingly follows the only path open to him and, since outer reality seems unyielding, he does his best to transfer the traumatic factor in the situation to the field of inner reality, within which he feels situations to be more under his own control. This means that he internalizes his mother as a bad object. Here I would remind the reader that, in my opinion, it is always the bad object (i.e., at this stage, the unsatisfying object) that is internalized in the first instance ; and as already indicated in a footnote) I find it difficult to attach any meaning to the primary internalization of a good object which is both satisfying and amenable from the infant's point of view. There are those, of course, who would argue that it would be natural for the infant, when in a state of deprivation, to internalize the good object on the wish-fulfilment principle ; but, as it seems to me, internalization of objects is essentially a measure of coercion and it is not the satisfying object, but the unsatisfying object that the infant seeks to coerce. I speak here of ' the satisfying object ' and ' the unsatisfying object ', rather than of ' the good object ' and ' the bad object ', because I consider that, in this connection, the terms ' good object ' and ' bad object ' tend to be misleading. They tend to be misleading because they are liable to be understood in the sense of ' desired object ' and ' undesired object ' respectively. There can be no doubt, however, that a bad object may be desired. Indeed it is just because the infant's bad object is desired as well as felt to be bad that it is internalized. The trouble is that it remains bad after it has been internalized, i.e. it remains unsatisfying. At this point an important consideration arises. Unlike the satisfying object, the unsatisfying object has, so to speak, two facets. On the one hand, it frustrates ; and, on the other hand, it tempts and allures. Indeed its essential ' badness ' consists precisely in the fact that it combines allurement with frustration. Further, it retains both these qualities after internalization. After internalizing the unsatisfying object, accordingly, the infant finds himself in the quandary of ' out of the frying-pan into the fire '. In his attempts to control the unsatisfying object, he has introduced into the inner economy of his mind an object which not only continues to frustrate his need, but also continues to whet it. He thus finds himself confronted with another intolerable situation—this time an internal one. How does he seek to deal with it ? As we have seen, in his attempt to deal with the intolerable external situation with which he was originally faced his technique was to split the maternal object into two objects, (a) the ' good ' and (b) the ' bad ',

and then proceed to internalize the bad object ; and in his attempt to deal with the intolerable internal situation which subsequently arises he adopts a technique which is not altogether dissimilar. He splits the bad internal object into two objects—(a) the tempting or needed object and (b) the frustrating object ; and then he represses both these objects (employing aggression, of course, as the dynamic of repression). Here a complication arises, however ; for his libidinal attachment to the undivided object is shared, albeit not in equal proportions, by the objects resulting from division. The consequence is that, in the process of repressing the resultant objects, the ego, so to speak, develops pseudopodia by means of which it still maintains libidinal attachments to the objects undergoing repression. The development of these pseudopodia represents the initial stage of a division of the ego. As repression of the objects proceeds, the incipient division of the ego becomes an accomplished fact. The two pseudopodia are rejected by the part of the ego which remains central on account of their connection with the rejected objects ; and with their associated objects they share the fate of repression. It is in this way that the two subsidiary egos, the libidinal ego and the internal saboteur, come to be split off from the central ego, and that a multiplicity of egos arises.

THE DIVIDE ET IMPERA TECHNIQUE FOR THE DISPOSAL OF LIBIDO AND AGGRESSION

It will be noted that the situation resulting from the sequence of processes which has just been described has now assumed the *structural* pattern of what I have called ' the basic endopsychic situation '. It has also assumed the *dynamic* pattern of this situation except in one important respect—that the aggressive attitude adopted by the internal saboteur towards the libidinal ego and its associated object (the needed object) is still left out of the picture. In order to explain the origin of this feature of the situation, we must return to the original ambivalence of the child towards his mother and consider from a fresh angle what this involves. This time we shall consider the child's reactions, less in their conative, and more in their affective aspect. It is natural for the child, not only to be impulsive, but also to express his feelings in no uncertain terms. Moreover, it is through the expression of his feelings that he makes his chief impression upon his objects. Once ambivalence has been established, however, the expression of feeling towards his mother involves him in a position which must seem to him singularly precarious. Here it must be pointed out that what presents itself to him from a strictly conative standpoint as *frustration* at the hands of his mother presents itself to him in a very different light from a strictly affective standpoint. From the latter standpoint, what he experiences is a sense of lack of love, and indeed emotional *rejection* on his mother's part. This being so, the expression of hate towards her as a rejecting object becomes in his eyes a very dangerous procedure. On the one hand, it is calculated to make her reject him all the more, and thus to increase her ' badness ' and make her seem *more real* in her capacity of bad object. On the other hand, it is calculated to make her love him less, and thus to decrease her ' goodness ' and make her seem *less real* (i.e. destroy her) in her capacity of good object. At the same time, it also becomes a dangerous procedure for the child to express his libidinal need, i.e. his nascent love, of his mother in face of rejection at her hands : for it is equivalent to discharging his libido into an emotional vacuum. Such a discharge is accompanied by an affective experience which is singularly devastating. In the older child this experience is one of intense humiliation over the depreciation of his love, which seems to be involved. At a somewhat deeper level (or at an earlier stage) the experience is one of shame over the display of needs which are disregarded or belittled. In virtue of these experiences of humiliation and shame he feels reduced to a state of worthlessness, destitution or beggardom. His sense of his own value is threatened ; and he feels bad in the sense of ' inferior '. The intensity of these experiences is, of course, proportionate to the intensity of his need ; and intensity of need itself increases his sense of badness by contributing to it the quality of ' demanding too much '. At the same time his sense of badness is further complicated by the sense of utter impotence which he also experiences. At a still deeper level (or at a still earlier stage) the child's experience is one of, so to speak, exploding ineffectively and being completely emptied of libido. It is thus an experience of disintegration and of imminent psychical death.

We can understand accordingly how precarious a matter it becomes for the child, when confronted with the experience of rejection by his mother, to express either aggressive or libidinal affect towards her. Reduced to its simplest terms, the position in which he finds himself placed would appear to be one in which, if, on the one hand, he expresses aggression, he is threatened with loss of his good object, and, if, on the other hand, he expresses libidinal need, he is threatened with the loss of his libido (which for him constitutes his own goodness) and ultimately with loss of the ego structure which constitutes himself. Of these two threats by which the child feels menaced, the former (i.e. loss of the good object) would appear to be that which gives rise to the affect of depression, and which provides a basis for the subsequent development of a melancholic state in individuals for whom the disposal of aggression presents greater difficulties than the disposal of libido. On the other hand, the latter threat (i.e. loss of libido and of ego structure) would appear to be that which gives rise to the affect of futility, and which provides a basis for the subsequent development of a schizoid state in individuals for whom the disposal of libido presents greater difficulties than the disposal of aggression.

So far as the ætiology of depressive and schizoid states is concerned, views similar to those just indicated have already been developed by me at some length previously (1941). In the present instance, however, our immediate concern is with the measures adopted by the child to circumvent the various dangers which appear to him to attend the expression of affect, whether libidinal or aggressive, towards his mother when he is faced with the experience of rejection at her hands. As we have already seen, he attempts to deal with the ambivalent situation successively (1) by splitting the figure of his mother into two objects, a good and a bad, (2) by internalizing the bad object in an endeavour to control it, (3) by splitting the bad internalized object in turn into two objects, viz. (*a*) the tempting or needed object, and (*b*) the rejecting object, (4) by repressing both these objects and employing a certain volume of his aggression in the process, and (5) by employing a further volume of his aggression in splitting off from his central ego and repressing two subsidiary egos which remain attached to these respective internalized objects by libidinal ties. These various measures, based upon the techniques of internalization and splitting, serve to mitigate the asperities of the situation resulting from the child's experience of frustration in his relationship with his mother and his sense of rejection at her hands ; but, except in the most extreme cases, they do not succeed in eliminating the child's need of his mother as an object in outer reality, or in robbing her of all significance—which, after all, is just as well. In conformity with this fact, his libido and his aggression are very far from being wholly absorbed in the processes so far described ; and, consequently, the risks involved in the expression of libidinal and aggressive affect towards his mother as a rejecting object still remain to be met. The measures so far described thus require to be supplemented. Actually they are supplemented by a very obvious technique which is closely akin to the well-known principle of ' *Divide et impera* '. The child seeks to circumvent the dangers of expressing both libidinal and aggressive affect towards his object by using a maximum of his aggression to subdue a maximum of his libidinal need. In this way he reduces the volume of affect, both libidinal and aggressive, demanding outward expression. As has already been pointed out, of course, neither libido nor aggression can be considered as existing in a state of divorce from structure. Accordingly, what remains for us to decide is to which of the ego structures already described the child's excess of libido and excess of aggression are to be respectively allotted. This is a question to which the answer can be in no doubt. The excess of libido is taken over by the libidinal ego ; and the excess of aggression is taken over by the internal saboteur. The child's technique of using aggression to subdue libidinal need thus resolves itself into an attack by the internal saboteur upon the libidinal ego. The libidinal ego in its turn directs the excess of libido with which it becomes charged towards its associated object, the needed object. On the other hand, the attack of the internal saboteur upon this object represents a persistence of the child's original resentment towards his mother as a temptress inciting the very need which she fails to satisfy and thus reducing him to bondage—just as, indeed, the attack of the internal saboteur upon the libidinal ego represents a persistence of the hatred which the child comes to feel towards himself for the dependence dictated by his need. It should be added that the processes just described take place simultaneously with those which they are designed to supplement, although, in the interests of clarity of exposition, they have been described separately.

DIRECT REPRESSION, LIBIDINAL RESISTANCE AND INDIRECT REPRESSION

Now that the origin of the aggressive attitude adopted by the internal saboteur towards the libidinal ego and the needed object has been described, our account of the processes which determine the dynamic pattern of the basic endopsychic situation is complete. At this point, however, something requires to be added to what has already been said regarding the nature and origin of repression. In terms of the line of thought so far developed, repression is a process originating in a rejection of both the needed object and the rejecting object on the part of the undivided ego. This primary process of repression is accompanied by a secondary process of repression whereby the ego splits off and rejects two parts of itself, which remain attached respectively to one and the other of the repressed internal objects. The resulting situation is one in which the central ego (the residue of the undivided ego) adopts an attitude of rejection, not only towards the needed object and the rejecting object, but also towards the split off and subsidiary egos attached to these respective objects, i.e. the libidinal ego and the internal saboteur. This attitude of rejection adopted by the central ego constitutes repression ; and the dynamic of the rejection is aggression. So far so good. But this explanation of the nature and origin of repression is incomplete in so far as it has not yet taken into account what is involved in the technique of reducing the volume of libido and aggression available for expression towards external objects by employing a maximum of aggression to subdue a maximum of libido. As we have seen, this technique resolves itself into a process whereby (a) the excess of aggression is taken over by the internal saboteur and devoted to an attack upon the libidinal ego, and (b) the excess of libido is

taken over by the libidinal ego and directed towards the needed object. When the full significance of this process is considered, it becomes at once plain that the relentless attack of the internal saboteur upon the libidinal ego must operate as a very powerful factor in furthering the aims of repression. Indeed, so far as dynamic is concerned, it seems more than likely that this is the most important factor in the maintenance of repression. Obviously it is upon the phenomenon just mentioned that Freud's conception of the super-ego and its repressive functions is based ; for the uncompromising hostility which, according to Freud, characterizes the attitude of the super-ego towards id impulses coincides exactly with the uncompromisingly aggressive attitude adopted by the internal saboteur towards the libidinal ego. Similarly, Freud's observation that the self-reproaches of the melancholic are ultimately reproaches directed against the loved object falls readily into line with the aggressive attitude adopted towards the needed object by the internal saboteur.

There is no need at this point to repeat the criticisms already passed upon Freud's conceptions of the super-ego and the id, and upon all that is involved in these conceptions. It does, however, seem desirable to draw attention to the fact that, in his description of repression, Freud left completely out of account all that is involved in the phenomenon which I have described as the attachment of the libidinal ego to the needed object. As we have seen, this attachment comes to absorb a considerable volume of libido. Further, the volume of libido in question is directed towards an object which is both internal and repressed ; and, in conformity with this fact, it is inevitably oriented away from outer reality. Such being the case, the object-seeking of the libidinal ego operates as a resistance which powerfully reinforces the resistance directly resulting from repression, and which is thus no less in conflict with therapeutic aims than is the latter resistance. This is a theme which I have already developed, *mutatis mutandis*, elsewhere (1943). I add the proviso ' *mutatis mutandis* ' here, because, at the time when I wrote the article referred to, I had not yet formulated my present views regarding endopsychic structures ; but the effect of these latter views is to give greater point, rather than otherwise, to the original theme. This theme is, of course, in direct conflict with Freud's statement (1920 ; 19) : ' The unconscious, i.e. the " repressed " material, offers no resistance whatever to curative efforts.' It is, however, a theme which develops naturally out of the view that libido is primarily object-seeking, once we come to consider what happens when the object sought is a repressed internal object ; and, in terms of my present standpoint, there can be no room for doubt that the obstinate attachment of the libidinal ego to the needed object and its reluctance to renounce this object constitute a particularly formidable source of resistance—and one which plays no small part in determining what is known as the negative therapeutic reaction. The attachment in question, being libidinal in character, cannot, of course, be regarded as in itself a repressive phenomenon ; but, whilst itself a resultant of repression exercised by the central ego, it also functions as a powerful aid to this process of repression. The attack of the internal saboteur upon the object of the libidinal ego (the needed object) serves, of course, to perpetuate the attachment of the libidinal ego to its object by virtue of the fact that this object is being constantly threatened. Here we catch a glimpse of the original wolf under its sheep's clothing, i.e. we catch a glimpse of the original ambivalent situation persisting underneath all its disguises ; for what the obstinate attachment of the libidinal ego to the needed object and the equally obstinate aggression of the internal saboteur towards the same object really represent is the obstinacy of the original ambivalent attitude. The truth is that, however well the fact may be disguised, the individual is extremely reluctant to abandon his original hate, no less than his original need, of his original objects in childhood. This holds particularly true of psychoneurotic and psychotic individuals, not to mention those who fall into the category of psychopathic personality.

If the attachment of the libidinal ego to the needed object serves as a powerful aid to repression, the same may equally be said of the aggressive attitude adopted towards this internal object by the internal saboteur. So far as the actual process f repression is concerned, however, the latter differs from the former in one important respect ; for not only does it forward the aim of repression, but it also actually operates in the same manner as repression. In its attack upon the needed object it performs a function which constitutes it a co-belligerent, albeit not an ally, of the central ego, whose repression of the needed object represents, as we have seen, a manifestation of aggression. The internal saboteur functions further as a co-belligerent of the central ego in respect of its attack upon the libidinal ego—an attack which serves to supplement that involved in the repression of this ego by the central ego. There is a sense, therefore, in which it would be true to say that the attacks of the internal saboteur upon the libidinal ego and upon its associated object represent an *indirect form of repression*, whereby the direct repression of these structures by the central ego is both supplemented and facilitated.

As we have already seen, the subsidiary egos owe their origin to a split of the undivided ego : but, as we have also seen, what presents itself from a topographic standpoint as simply a split of the ego presents itself from a dynamic standpoint as an active rejection and repression of both the subsidiary egos on the part of the central ego. It

thus becomes a matter for some comment that, whilst both the libidinal ego and the internal saboteur share a common fate so far as direct repression is concerned, only one of the subsidiary egos, viz. the libidinal ego, should be subjected to the process of indirect repression. When the difference between direct and indirect repression is considered in the light of what has already been said, it is, of course, plain that the process of repression described by Freud corresponds very much more closely to what I have described as indirect repression than to what I have described as direct repression. Nevertheless, when Freud's conception of repression is compared with my conception of the total phenomenon of repression, both direct and indirect, this common feature may be detected—that the libidinal components in the psyche are subjected to a much greater measure of repression than the aggressive components. There can be no doubt, of course, that the repression of aggressive components does occur : but it is difficult to see how this fact can be consistently explained in terms of Freud's theory of the mental apparatus. This theory, conceived as it is in terms of a fundamental divorce between impulse and structure, would appear to permit only of the repression of libido : for, in terms of Freud's theory, the repression of aggression would involve the anomaly of aggression being used to repress aggression. By contrast, if, in conformity with the point of view which I advocate, we conceive of impulse as inseparable from structure and as representing simply the dynamic aspect of structure, the repression of aggressive components in the psyche is no more difficult to account for than the repression of libidinal components. It then becomes a question, not of aggression repressing aggression, but of one ego structure using aggression to repress another ego structure charged with aggression. This being so, my view to the effect that the internal saboteur, no less than the libidinal ego, is repressed by the central ego provides a satisfactory explanation of the repression of aggressive components. At the same time, the fact that libidinal components are subject to a greater measure of repression than aggressive components is satisfactorily explained by means of the conception of indirect repression. The truth would appear to be that, if *the principle of repression* governs the disposal of *excess libido* in greater measure than it governs the disposal of excess aggression, *the principle of topographical redistribution* governs the disposal of *excess aggression* in greater measure than it governs the disposal of excess libido.

THE SIGNIFICANCE OF THE ŒDIPUS SITUATION

I have already said enough to indicate that the technique whereby aggression is employed to subdue libido is a process which finds a common place in Freud's conception of ' repression ' and my own conception of ' indirect repression '. At the same time, my views regarding the origin of this technique differ from those of Freud. According to Freud, the technique originates as a means of averting the expression of libidinal (incestuous) impulses towards one parent and aggressive (parenticidal) impulses towards the other parent in the setting of the Œdipus situation. According to my view, on the other hand, the technique originates in infancy as a means of averting the expression of both libido and aggression on the part of the infant towards his mother, who at this stage constitutes his only significant object, and upon whom he is wholly dependent. This discrepancy of views will be interpreted, quite correctly, in the sense that I have departed from Freud in my evaluation of the Œdipus situation as an explanatory concept. For Freud, the Œdipus situation is, so to speak, an ultimate cause ; but this is a view with which I no longer find it possible to agree. So far from agreeing, I now consider that the rôle of ultimate cause, which Freud allotted to the Œdipus situation, should properly be allotted to the phenomenon of infantile dependence. In conformity with this standpoint, the Œdipus situation presents itself, not so much in the light of a causal phenomenon as in the light of an end-product. It is not a basic situation, but the derivative of a situation which has priority over it not only in the logical, but also in the temporal sense. This prior situation is one which issues directly out of the physical and emotional dependence of the infant upon his mother, and which declares itself in the relationship of the infant to his mother long before his father becomes a significant object. The present is no occasion for an elaboration of the views which I have now reached regarding the Œdipus situation—views which have been in some measure adumbrated already (1941). Nevertheless, in view of the comparison which I have just drawn between my own conception of repression and Freud's conception, formulated as it is in terms of the Œdipus situation, it seems desirable that I should indicate briefly how I propose to introduce this classic situation into the general scheme which I have outlined. It will hardly be necessary to remind the reader that I have dispensed with the Œdipus situation as an explanatory concept not only in my account of the origin of repression, but also in my account of the genesis of the basic endopsychic situation and in my account of the differentiation of endopsychic structure. These accounts have been formulated exclusively in terms of the measures adopted by the child in an attempt to cope with the difficulties inherent in the ambivalent situation which develops during his infancy in his relationship with his mother as his original object. The various measures which the child adopts in his attempt to deal with this ambivalent situation have all been adopted before the Œdipus situation develops. It

is in the setting of the child's relationship to his mother that the basic endopsychic situation is established, that the differentiation of endopsychic structure is accomplished and that repression is originated ; and it is only after these developments have occurred that the child is called upon to meet the particular difficulties which attend the Œdipus situation. So far from furnishing an explanatory concept, therefore, the Œdipus situation is rather a phenomenon to be explained in terms of an endopsychic situation which has already developed.

The chief novelty introduced into the child's world by the Œdipus situation, as this materializes in outer reality, is that he is now confronted with two distinct parental objects instead of with only one as formerly. His relationship with his new object, viz. his father, is, of course, inevitably fraught with vicissitudes similar to those which he previously experienced in his relationship with his mother—and, in particular, the vicissitudes of need, frustration and rejection. In view of these vicissitudes, his father becomes an ambivalent object to him, whilst at the same time he himself becomes ambivalent towards his father. In his relationship with his father he is thus faced with the same problem of adjustment as that with which he was originally faced in his relationship with his mother. The original situation is reinstated, albeit this time in relation to a fresh object ; and, very naturally, he seeks to meet the difficulties of the reinstated situation by means of the same series of techniques which he learned to adopt in meeting the difficulties of the original situation. He splits the figure of his father into a good and a bad object, internalizes the bad object and splits the internalized bad object into (a) a needed object associated with the libidinal ego and (b) a rejecting object associated with the internal saboteur. It should be added that the new paternal needed object would appear to be partly superimposed upon, and partly fused with the old maternal needed object, and that similarly the paternal rejecting object is partly superimposed upon, and partly fused with the maternal rejecting object.

The adjustment which the child is called upon to make in relation to his father differs, of course, in one important respect from that which he was previously called upon to make in relation to his mother. It differs in the extent to which it has to be achieved upon an emotional plane. The new adjustment must be almost exclusively emotional ; for in his relationship with his father the child is necessarily precluded from the experience of feeding at the breast. We are thus introduced to a further important respect in which his adjustment to his father must differ from his previous adjustment to his mother. His father is a man, whereas his mother is a woman. It is more than doubtful, however, whether the child at first appreciates the genital difference between the two parents. It would appear rather that the difference which he does appreciate is that his father has no breasts. His father thus first presents himself to the child as a parent without breasts ; and this is one of the chief reasons that his relationship with his father has to be established so much more on an emotional plane than his relationship with his mother. On the other hand, it is because the child does have the experience of a physical relationship with his mother's breast, while also experiencing a varying degree of frustration in this relationship, that his need for his mother persists so obstinately beneath his need for his father and all subsequent genital needs. When the child comes to appreciate, in some measure at least, the genital difference between his parents, and as, in the course of his own development, his physical need tends to flow increasingly (albeit in varying degrees) through genital channels, his need for his mother comes to include a need for her vagina. At the same time, his need for his father comes to include a need for his father's penis. The strength of these physical needs for his parents' genitals varies, however, in inverse proportion to the satisfaction of his emotional needs. Thus, the more satisfactory his emotional relations with his parents, the less urgent are his physical needs for their genitals. These latter needs are, of course, never satisfied, although substitutive satisfactions may be sought, e.g. those of sexual curiosity. Consequently, some measure of ambivalence necessarily develops in relation to his mother's vagina and his father's penis. This ambivalence is reflected, incidentally, in sadistic conceptions of the primal scene. By the time the primal scene is envisaged, however, the relationships of his parents to one another have become a matter of moment for the child ; and jealousy of each of his parents in relation to the other begins to assert itself. The chief incidence of his jealousy is, of course, partly determined by the biological sex of the child ; but it is also in no small measure determined by the state of his emotional relationships with his respective parents. Be this as it may, the child is now called upon to meet the difficulties of two ambivalent situations at the same time ; and he seeks to meet these difficulties by the familiar series of techniques. The result is that he internalizes both a bad maternal genital figure and a bad paternal genital figure and splits each of these into two figures, which are embodied respectively in the structures of the needed object and the rejecting object. It will thus be seen that, before the child is very old, these internal objects have already assumed the form of complex composite structures. They are built up partly on a basis of the superimposition of one object upon another, and partly on a basis of the fusion of objects. The extent to which the internal objects are built up respectively on a basis of layering and on a basis of fusion differs, of course, from individual to individual ; and the extent to which either layering or fusion predominates would

appear to be a matter of no small importance. Thus, in conjunction with the proportioning of the various component objects, it would appear to play an important part in determining the psycho-sexual attitude of the individual in so far as this is not determined by biological sexual factors. Likewise, in conjunction with the proportioning of the component objects, it would appear to be the chief determining factor in the ætiology of the sexual perversions. We may thus envisage an ætiology of the perversions conceived in terms of object-relationship psychology.

It will be noticed that in the preceding account the personal pronoun employed to indicate the child has been consistently masculine. This must not be taken to imply that the account applies only to the boy. It applies equally to the girl ; and the masculine pronoun has been used only because the advantages of a personal pronoun of some kind appear to outweigh those of the impersonal pronoun, however non-committal this may be. It will also be noticed that the classic Œdipus situation has not yet emerged. The stage which was last described was one at which, whilst the relations of his parents with one another had become significant to the child, his position was essentially one of ambivalence towards both parents. We have seen, however, that the child seeks to deal with both ambivalent situations by a series of processes in consequence of which genital figures of each of his parents come to be embodied both in the structure of the needed object and in that of the rejecting object. It must be recognized, of course, that the biological sex of the child must play some part in determining his attitude to his respective parents ; but that this is very far from being the sole determining factor is obvious from the frequency of inverted and mixed Œdipus situations. Considered in terms of the views which I have outlined, these inverted and mixed Œdipus situations must necessarily be determined by the constitution of the needed object and the rejecting object. It is, therefore, only taking a further step in the same direction to conclude that the same consideration applies to the positive Œdipus situation. The fact then would appear to be that *the Œdipus situation is not really an external situation at all, but an internal situation*—one which may be transferred in varying degrees to the actual external situation. Once the Œdipus situation comes to be regarded as essentially an internal situation, it is not difficult to see that the maternal components of both the internal objects have, so to speak, a great initial advantage over the paternal components ; and this, of course, applies to children of both sexes. The strong position of the maternal components is, of course, due to the fact that the nuclei of both the internal objects are derivatives of the original ambivalent mother and her ambivalent breasts. In conformity with this fact, *a sufficiently deep analysis of the Œdipus situation invariably reveals that this situation is built up around the figures of an internal needed mother and an internal rejecting mother.* It was, of course, on a basis of hysterical phenomena that Freud originally formulated the concept of the Œdipus situation ; and according to Abraham's 'phase' theory the origin of hysteria is to be traced to a fixation in the genital (phallic) phase. I have already (1941) passed various criticisms on Abraham's 'phase' theory ; and so I shall be merely passing a further criticism, if only by implication, when I say that I have yet to analyse the hysteric, male or female, who does not turn out to be an inveterate breast-seeker at heart. I venture to suggest that the deep analysis of a positive Œdipus situation may be regarded as taking place at three main levels. At the first level the picture is dominated by the Œdipus situation itself. At the next level it is dominated by ambivalence towards the heterosexual parent ; and at the deepest level it is dominated by ambivalence towards the mother. Traces of all these stages may be detected in the classic drama of *Hamlet* ; but there can be no doubt that, both in the rôle of needed and tempting object and in that of rejecting object, the Queen is the real villain of the piece. The position then would appear to be this. The child finds it intolerable enough to be called upon to deal with a single ambivalent object ; but, when he is called upon to deal with two, he finds it still more intolerable. He, therefore, seeks to simplify a complex situation, in which he finds himself confronted with two needed objects and two rejecting objects, by converting it into one in which he will only be confronted with a single needed object and a single rejecting object ; and he achieves this aim, with, of course, a varying measure of success, by concentrating upon the needed aspect of one parent and the rejecting aspect of the other. He thus, for all practical purposes, comes to equate one parental object with the needed object, and the other with the rejecting object ; and by so doing *the child constitutes the Œdipus situation for himself.* Ambivalence to both parents persists, however, in the background ; and at rock bottom both the needed object and the rejecting object remain what they originally were, viz. figures of his mother.

NEUROTIC ANXIETY AND HYSTERICAL SUFFERING

I have spoken of the *divide et impera* technique as a means of reducing the volume of affect (both libidinal and aggressive) which demands outward expression ; and at this point it would be both relevant and profitable to consider in some detail what happens when the attack of the internal saboteur upon the libidinal ego fails to subdue libidinal need sufficiently to meet the requirements of the central ego, i.e. sufficiently to reduce the volume of available libidinal affect to manageable proportions. It is impossible, however, to embark upon so large a theme on the present occasion. Suffice it to say that, when the technique in question does not succeed in reducing the volume of libidinal affect sufficiently and so fails to fulfil its primary function, it appears to assume a secondary function, in virtue of which it imposes a change of quality upon such libidinal affect as insists upon emerging and thereby disguises the quality of the original affect. Thus, when the dynamic tension within the libidinal ego rises above a certain threshold value and an excess of libidinal need threatens to assert itself, the emergent libidinal affect is converted into (neurotic) *anxiety* by the impact of the aggression which is directed against the libidinal ego by the internal saboteur. When the dynamic tension within the libidinal ego continues to rise until it reaches a further threshold value, it becomes no longer possible for a libidinal discharge to be averted ; and the attack of the internal saboteur upon the libidinal ego then has the effect of imparting a *painful* quality to the libidinal affect accompanying the inevitable discharge. Such, at any rate, would appear to be the process involved in the hysterical mode of expressing affect—a process which demands that the expression of libidinal need shall be experienced as suffering.

THE PSYCHOLOGY OF DYNAMIC STRUCTURE AND ITS GENERAL SCIENTIFIC BACKGROUND

In the light of what has just been said regarding the genesis of (neurotic) anxiety, it will be noted that my conception of the nature of anxiety is closely in accord with Freud's original conception, viz. that anxiety is a converted form of undischarged libido. Here we find but one example of the somewhat remarkable fact that, if the general standpoint which I have now come to adopt represents a departure from some of Freud's later views, it has had the effect of revivifying some of Freud's earlier views (views which, in some cases, have latterly been in abeyance). The explanation of this general phenomenon would appear to be that, whilst at every point there is a recognizable analogy between my present views and those of Freud, the development of my views follows a path which diverges gradually from that followed by the historical development of Freud's views. This divergence of paths itself admits of only one explanation—a difference in certain basic theoretic principles. The central points of difference are not difficult to localize. They are two in number. In the first place, although Freud's whole system of thought was concerned with object-relationships, he adhered theoretically to the principle that libido is primarily pleasure-seeking, i.e. that it is directionless. By contrast, I adhere to the principle that libido is primarily object-seeking, i.e. that it has direction. For that matter, I regard aggression as having direction also, whereas, by implication at any rate, Freud regards aggression as, like libido, theoretically directionless. In the second place, Freud regards impulse (i.e. psychical energy) as theoretically distinct from structure, whereas I do not accept this distinction as valid and adhere to the principle of dynamic structure. Of these two central points of difference between Freud's views and those which I have now come to adopt, the latter is the more fundamental ; and indeed the former would appear to depend upon the latter. Thus Freud's view that libido is primarily pleasure-seeking follows directly from his divorce of energy from structure ; for, once energy is divorced from structure, the only psychical change which can be envisaged as other than disturbing, i.e. as pleasant, is one which makes for the establishment of an equilibrium of forces, i.e. a directionless change. By contrast, if we conceive of energy as inseparable from structure, then the only changes which are intelligible are changes in structural relationships and in relationships between structures ; and such changes are essentially directional.

No man, even the greatest and most original, can remain wholly independent of the scientific background of his day ; and it cannot be claimed that even Freud provides an exception to this rule. Here we must remind ourselves of the scientific atmosphere of the nineteenth century in which Freud was nurtured. This atmosphere was dominated by the Helmholtzian conception that the physical universe consisted in a conglomeration of inert, immutable and indivisible particles to which motion was imparted by a fixed quantity of energy separate from the particles themselves. The energy in question was conceived as having been, for some unknown reason, unevenly distributed at the beginning and as subsequently undergoing a gradual process of redistribution calculated to lead eventually to an equilibrium of forces and an immobilization of the solid particles. Such being the prevailing conception of the contemporary physicist, it is not difficult to understand how it came about that, when Freud, in advance of his time, set himself the arduous task of introducing order into the hitherto confused realm of psychopathology, he should have remained sufficiently under the influence of the scientific atmosphere of his day to conceive impulse (psychical energy) as separate from structure and to cast his libido theory in an equilibrium-seeking mould. In my opinion, however, this feature constitutes a limitation imposed by outside influences upon his thought, which otherwise represented an historic advance upon prevailing conceptions in the psychological field, and which was much more in the spirit of the new scientific outlook at present emerging ; for during the twentieth century the scientific conception of the physical universe has already undergone a profound change. The inert and indivisible particles or atoms, of which the physical universe was formerly thought to be composed, are now known to be structures of the greatest complexity embodying almost incredible quantities of energy—energy in the absence of which the structures themselves would be unintelligible, but which is equally difficult to explain in the absence of the structures. This intra-atomic energy has effects which not only determine intra-atomic relationships, but also influence bodies at enormous distances. The most remarkable of these effects is radiation ; and it has been found necessary to call in radiation to explain certain of the phenomena of light, which defied explanation on the basis of the wave theory of the previous scientific epoch. Interestingly enough, radiation has proved to possess at least one of the properties formerly regarded as a prerogative of solid matter, viz. mass ; and the occurrence of radiation affects the structure of both the emitting and the receiving atoms. Further, the universe itself is conceived as undergoing a process of change other than that involved in the establishment of an equilibrium within a closed system. Thus it would appear that the universe is expanding at a terrific speed. The major forces at work are attraction and repulsion (cf. libido and aggression) ; but, although attraction has the effect of producing local condensations of matter, the dominant force, at any rate during the present phase, is repulsion. So far from being in process of establishing a non-directional equilibrium, therefore, the universe is in process of expanding towards a limit at which no further expansion will be possible and everything will be so attenuated that no further mutual influences will occur and nothing more will be able to happen. The change which the universe is undergoing is thus a directional change. Such being the general scientific background of the present day, it seems to me a demand of the times, if nothing else, that our psychological ideas should be reformulated in terms of a relationship psychology conceived on a basis of dynamic structure.

THE PSYCHOLOGY OF DYNAMIC STRUCTURE AS AN EXPLANATORY SYSTEM

As an explanatory system, the psychology of dynamic structure which I envisage seems to me to have many advantages, among which by no means the least is that it provides a more satisfactory basis than does any other type of psychology for the explanation of group phenomena. However, this is a theme which, like certain others touched upon in this article, must be left for another occasion. It remains for me, in my concluding remarks, to say something regarding the advantages which appear to accrue from the particular theory of mental structure which I have advanced in place of Freud's classic theory. It is obvious, of course, that, from a topographic standpoint, Freud's theory only admits of the operation of three factors (id, ego and super-ego) in the production of the variety of clinical states with which we are familiar. By contrast, my theory admits of the operation of five factors (central ego, libidinal ego, internal saboteur, needed object and rejecting object)—even when the super-ego as I conceive it is left out of account. My theory, accordingly, offers a greater range of ætiological possibilities. In actual practice, the difference between the two theories as regards ætiological possibilities is even greater than at first appears ; for, of the three factors envisaged in Freud's theory, only two (the ego and the super-ego) are structures properly speaking—the third (viz. the id) being only a source of energy. The energy proceeding from the id is, of course, conceived by Freud as assuming two forms—libido and aggression. Consequently, Freud's theory admits of the operation of two structural and two dynamic factors in all. Freud's two dynamic factors find a place, of course, in my own theory ; but, according to my theory, the number of the structural factors is not two, but five. Thus, with five structural factors and two dynamic factors to conjure with, my theory permits of a much greater range of permutations and combinations than does Freud's theory. Actually, however, the possibilities left open by Freud's theory in the abstract are still further limited by his conception of the function of the super-ego, which he regards not only as characteristically aggressive, but also as characteristically anti-libidinal. According to Freud, therefore, the endopsychic drama largely resolves itself into a conflict between the ego in a libidinal capacity and the super-ego in an anti-libidinal capacity. The original dualism inherent in Freud's earliest views regarding repression thus remains substantially unaffected by his subsequent theory of mental structure. Such a conception of the endopsychic drama is unduly limiting, not only as far as its implications for social psychology are concerned (e.g. the implication that social institutions are primarily repressive), but also so far as concerns its explanatory value within the psychopathological and characterological fields. Within these fields explanation reduces itself to an account of the attitudes adopted by the ego in a libidinal capacity vis-à-vis the super-ego. By contrast, my theory possesses all the features of an explanatory system enabling psychopathological and characterological phenomena of all kinds to be described in terms of the patterns assumed by a complex of relationships between a variety of structures. It also possesses the advantage of enabling psychopathological symptoms to be explained directly in terms of structural conformations, and thus of doing justice to the unquestionable fact that, so far from being independent phenomena, symptoms are but expressions of the personality as a whole.

At this juncture it becomes necessary to point out (if indeed it has not already become sufficiently obvious) that the basic endopsychic situation which I have described, and to which I have attached such importance, is by no means conceived as immutable from the economic standpoint. From the topographic standpoint, it must be regarded as relatively immutable, although I conceive it as one of the chief aims of psycho-analytical therapy to introduce some change into its topography by way of territorial adjustment. Thus I conceive it as among the most important functions of psycho-analytical therapy (a) to reduce the split of the original ego by restoring to the central ego a maximum of the territories ceded to the libidinal ego and the internal saboteur, and (b) to bring the needed object and the rejecting object so far as possible within the sphere of influence of the central ego. The extent to which such changes can be effected appears, however, to be strictly limited. In its economic aspect, by contrast, the basic endopsychic situation is capable of very extensive modification. In conformity with this fact, I conceive it as another of the chief aims of psycho-analytical therapy to reduce to a minimum (a) the attachment of the subsidiary egos to their respective associated objects, (b) the aggression of the central ego towards the subsidiary egos and their objects, and (c) the aggression of the internal saboteur towards the libidinal ego and its object. On the other hand, the basic endopsychic situation is undoubtedly capable of considerable modification in a psychopathological direction. As I have already indicated, the economic pattern of the basic endopsychic situation is the pattern which prevails in hysterical states. Of this I have no doubt whatsoever in my own mind. I have, however, come across cases of hysterical individuals who displayed remarkably paranoid traits (even to the point of having been previously diagnosed as paranoid), and who were found, on analysis, to oscillate between paranoid and hysterical attitudes. Such oscillations appeared to be accompanied by changes in the economic pattern of the endopsychic situation—the paranoid phases being characterized by a departure from the economic pattern of what I have called the *basic* endopsychic situation. What economic pattern the endopsychic situation assumes in the paranoid state I do not feel in a position to say ; but I do venture to suggest that corresponding to every distinguishable clinical state there is a characteristic pattern of the endopsychic situation. It must be recognized, of course, that various patterns may exist side by side or be superimposed one upon the other. It must also be recognized that patterning of the endopsychic situation may either be rigid or flexible—extreme rigidity and extreme flexibility being alike unfavourable features. At the same time, it must be stressed that the *basic* (and original) endopsychic situation is that which is found in hysterical states. In conformity with this consideration, I take the view that the earliest psychopathological symptoms to manifest themselves are hysterical in character ; and I interpret the screaming fits of the infant in this sense. If I am right in this, Freud showed no mean insight in choosing hysterical phenomena as the material out of which to build the foundations of psycho-analytical theory.

In the light of considerations already advanced it will be understood, of course, that, although the basic endopsychic situation is the situation underlying hysterical states, it is itself the product of a split of the original ego and is, therefore, a schizoid phenomenon. Thus, although the earliest psychopathological *symptoms* are hysterical, the earliest psychopathological *process* is schizoid. Repression itself is a schizoid process ; and splitting of the ego is a universal phenomenon, although, of course, the degree of such splitting varies in different individuals. It is not to be inferred, however, that overt schizoid states are the earliest psychopathological states to develop. On the contrary, the earliest of such states are hysterical in nature. An actual schizoid state is a much later development —one which only materializes when the schizoid process is pushed to a point at which a massive repression of affect occurs and even an hysterical expression of affect is thereby precluded. Thus it is only when a massive repression of affect occurs that the individual becomes unduly detached and experiences a pronounced sense of futility. What is involved in the development of schizoid states cannot, however, be discussed further on the present occasion.

THE DYNAMIC QUALITY OF INTERNALIZED OBJECTS

The feature of Freud's theory of the mental apparatus presenting the greatest anomaly is one to which reference has not yet been made. It is this—that the only part of the psyche which he describes in terms at all approximating to those of dynamic structure is the super-ego. The id is, of course, described as a source of energy without structure ; and the ego is described as a passive structure without energy except such as invades it from the id. By contrast, the super-ego is described as a structure endowed with a fund of energy. It is true that the energy in question is conceived as being ultimately derived from the id ; but this in no way alters the fact that Freud attributes to the super-ego a considerable measure of independent functional activity. So much is this the case that he speaks of the super-ego and the id as diametrically opposed to one another in the aims of their activities, and of the ego as buffetted beween these two endopsychic entities. The odd thing about all this is that the super-ego is really only a naturalized alien, as it were, within the realm of the individual mind, an immigrant from outer reality. Its whole significance resides in the fact that it is essentially an internalized object. That the only part of the psyche which Freud treats as a dynamic structure should be an

internalized object is, to my mind, an anomaly sufficient in itself to justify my attempt to formulate an alternative theory of psychical structure. It will be observed that, in formulating such an alternative theory, I have so far followed a line opposite to that followed by Freud in that, whereas an internalized object is the only part of the psyche which Freud treats as a dynamic structure, the internalized objects which I envisage are the only parts of the psyche which I have *not* treated as dynamic structures. I have treated the internalized objects simply as *objects* of the dynamic ego structures, i.e. as endopsychic structures which are not themselves dynamic. I have done this deliberately in order to bring into focus the activity of the ego structures which I find it necessary to postulate, and in order to avoid all risk of under-rating the primary importance of this activity ; for, after all, it is only through this activity that objects ever come to be internalized. However, in the interests of consistency, I must now draw the logical conclusion of my theory of dynamic structure and acknowledge that, since internal objects are structures, they must necessarily be, in some measure at least, dynamic. In drawing this conclusion and making this acknow ledgment, I shall not only be here following the precedent of Freud, but also, it would seem, conforming to the demands of such psychological facts as are revealed, e.g. in dreams and in the phenomena of paranoia. This further step will enhance the explanatory value of my theory of mental structure by introducing additional possibilities into the endopsychic situation by way of permutation and combination. It must be recognized, however, that, in practice, it is very difficult to differentiate between the activity of internalized objects and the activity of the ego structures with which they are associated ; and, with a view to avoiding any appearance of demonology, it seems wise to err, if anything, on the side of overweighting the activity of the ego structures rather than otherwise. It remains true, nevertheless, that under certain conditions internalized objects may acquire a dynamic independence which cannot be ignored.

REFERENCES

FAIRBAIRN, W. R. D. (1941). 'A Revised Psychopathology of the Psychoses and Psychoneuroses ', *Int. J. Psycho-Anal.*, 22, 250.

—— (1943). 'The Repression and the Return of Bad Objects ', *Brit. J. med. Psychol.*, 19, 327.

FREUD, S. (1917). (*Trans.* 1925.) ' Mourning and Melancholia ', *Collected Papers*, IV, 152.

—— (1920). (*Trans.* 1922.) *Beyond the Pleasure Principle.*

—— (1923). (*Trans.* 1927.) *The Ego and the Id.*

—— (1929). (*Trans.* 1930.) *Civilization and its Discontents*, 95 f.

THE EXISTENTIAL NEUROSIS

SALVATORE R. MADDI

Social critics, philosophers, sociologists, and psychotherapists are raising the cry that alienation and the problems of existence form the sickness of our times. Even though a significant proportion of the statements has been vague and polemical, more and more people are hanging on every word. I do not think this is merely the new fad. There is too much insistence and desperation in people's attempts to understand the commentaries that have been made in some terms that will make a difference in their lives. It is too hard to overlook the evidence that people seeking psychotherapy do so in ever increasing numbers because they are deeply dissatisfied with the nature and bases of their living. It is too obvious that even those who do not seek psychotherapy often feel alone and empty.

Under the circumstances, the best thing serious students of the human condition can do is try for clarity and precision in thinking about alienation and the problems of existence. My task in this paper falls within this category of endeavor. What I will do is offer a model for the understanding of psychopathology and then use the model in ordering the various themes common in existential writings. Sometimes I will agree with writers in this field, and sometimes I will be reinterpreting their views. My basic aim in all this is to attempt to bring order and structure to an amorphous and complex literature in a way that clarifies the parts of it bearing on psychopathology and on mental health.

A MODEL FOR NEUROSIS

At the outset we need a model for neurosis that can serve as a heuristic device, a thread of Ariadne, lest we lose our way in the labyrinth of words that has been created. The model I suggest we adopt represents fairly standard thinking in the area, happily enough. It starts with the notion of a neurosis as a set of symptoms that can be distinguished not only from mental health but also from other psychopathological states. So the hysterical neurosis, for example, can be described as a set of cognitive and motor symptoms that are absent not only in the healthy state, but also in other classes of illness, like psychosis, and other neuroses, like obsessive-compulsiveness. When we discuss the existential neurosis, then, we will be searching for a set of relevant symptoms that are clearly different both from whatever we consider to be mental health and from other forms of psychopathology.

Further, the model distinguishes between the neurosis itself and the premorbid personality out of which the neurosis may come through a process of breakdown. For example, if you are working within a psychoanalytic framework, you would say that the obsessive-compulsive neurosis represents the breakdown of the anal character type. While the anal character type bears some strong

JOURNAL OF ABNORMAL PSYCHOLOGY, 1967, 72, pp. 311-325.

resemblances to the obsessive-compulsive neurosis (e.g., the reliance upon defense mechanisms of intellectualization, isolation, and undoing), the latter includes symptoms (e.g., obsessions and compulsions) that are considered pathological and that appear in only minimal form in the former. The premorbid personality is within the category of normality, though like the neurosis it can be distinguished from other types of premorbid personality. As there is an anal character type, so also are there phallic and oral character types. The differences between the premorbid personalities define predispositions to different kinds of neuroses. The significance of all this for discussion of the existential neurosis is that we will want to define a premorbid personality for which the neurosis itself is a believable breakdown product.

Premorbid personalities define predispositions to particular neurotic manifestations because they incorporate vulnerabilities to particular kinds of stress. The next aspect of the model, stress, is best considered to be something objectively describable, whether originating inside or outside the person, that represents a comprehensive enough threat to the personality to disrupt the premorbid balance or adjustment. Obviously, stress has to be defined with the characteristics of premorbid personality in mind. Loss of a strong loved one may be especially stressful to the person with an oral character, because in that character satisfaction of dependency is especially important for adequate functioning. Stress can be a sudden occurrence, or an accumulation of undermining events, as long as what is called stress is reasonably specifiable.

The model states that neurosis is some joint function of premorbidity and stress. Without attempting to state the exact nature of the function, some facets of the relationship are apparent. If there is zero stress, there should be no neurosis. Further, the amount of stress necessary to precipitate a neurosis should depend upon the intensity of the vulnerability constituted by the premorbid characteristics. But it should be kept in mind that the stress must match the nature of the vulnerability if undermining of the premorbid adjustment is to be possible. In considering the existential neurosis, I will try to identify the kinds of stress that are relevant, though it will be very difficult to make any qualitative statements about how much stress is too much.

Any model which involves the notion of premorbidity, or that which predisposes to illness, also involves the notion of what the ideal personality would be. What I am saying is not very mysterious or new. In psychoanalytic thinking, the ideal is genital personality, whereas in Rogerian thinking, the ideal is the fully functioning person. The ideal personality is usually a null class, which nonetheless has the very important theoretical function of permitting specification of what it is about the premorbid personality that predisposes to illness. In discussing the existential neurosis, we should expect to understand at least those aspects of the ideal personality that insure against the likelihood of that disorder. It may, in addition, be possible to gain an even more comprehensive sense than that of what is ideal.

The rest of the model refers to development. There is first ideal development, or that series of early life experiences that culminate in the ideal personality. Second, there is what might be called deviant development—a series of life experiences leading to premorbidity. It should be possible to specify the particular developmental deviancy that accounts for particular premorbid personalities. It will be important in this article to consider the developmental vicissitudes producing the premorbid state out of which the existential neurosis may come, and, in this consideration, a sense of what would be developmentally more ideal will necessarily be gained.

Without a doubt there are vexing questions that can be raised concerning this model. But rather than raise them here, let me encourage you to consider the general outlines of the model as no more than an interesting and plausible heuristic device. In that spirit, let us plunge in.

The Symptoms Called Existential Neurosis

Like all neuroses, we should expect the existential neurosis to have cognitive, affective, and actional components. Once we have accepted the heuristic notion that there are existential manifestations some of which are neurotic and some of which are not, we have already begun to find the road to clarity. The cognitive component of the existential neurosis is meaninglessness, or chronic inability to believe in the truth, importance, usefulness, or interest value of any of the things one is engaged in or can imagine doing. The most characteristic features of affective tone are blandness and boredom, punctuated by periods of depression which become less frequent as the disorder is prolonged. As to the realm of action, activity level may be low to moderate, but more important than amount of activity is the introspective and objectively observable fact that activities are not chosen. There is little selectivity, it being immaterial to the person what if any activities he pursues. If there is any selectivity shown, it is in the direction of ensuring minimal expenditure of effort and decision making.

It is important to recognize that the syndrome described above refers to a chronic state of the organism. I do not refer to stabs of doubt, in the cognitive domain, or occasional indifference and passivity, in the affective and actional domains. Rather, I refer to the settled state of meaninglessness, apathy, and aimlessness, such that contradictory states of commitment, enthusiasm, and activeness are the exception rather than the rule. The temporary state of doubt, though an existential manifestation, is not here defined as part of the existential neurosis. Indeed, doubt is a by-product of vigorous mental health, I shall argue later, no matter how painful it may be.

If my model is to be served, the existential neurosis must be distinguished from other forms of illness. I take it that the obviousness of its difference from such psychotic states as schizophrenia and senile psychosis, such character disorders as homosexuality and psychopathy, and such neuroses as obsessive-compulsiveness and hysteria, is clear without further attention. Of the traditional states of psychopathology, the existential neurosis probably most nearly resembles neuraesthenia and depression. It is from these two disorders that distinctions are important. The major difference between neuraesthenia and the existential neurosis is that the dreadful lack of energy and somatic decreptitude of the former is not present in the latter. There is certainly listlessness in existential neurosis, but it is not experienced as a primarily somatic disability. In addition, the cognitive state of meaninglessness is virtually absent in neuraesthenia.

The distinction between depression and the existential neurosis is harder to make, specifically because the latter state sometimes includes sadness, and usually includes low activity level. But in existential neurosis, depressive affect is the exception rather than the rule, with apathy—an actual absence of strong emotion—being the usual state. Apathy is not typical of depression, though it may occur occasionally in that disorder. In traditional terms, what I am calling the existential neurosis might actually be called depression, but this would involve an unwarranted stretching of the latter concept, taking some such form as inferring depressive affect hidden by defenses such that apathy was the visible resultant. But once we have decided that traditional terminology is not necessarily exhaustive in describing psychopathology, the syndrome I have called the existential neurosis is very likely to emerge as discriminably different from depression.

The way I have defined it, the existential neurosis is characterized by the belief that one's life is meaningless, by the affective tone of apathy and boredom, and by the absence of selectivity in actions. This symptom cluster is, to judge from the writing of many psychotherapists, sociologists, and social critics (e.g., Fromm, 1955; Josephson & Josephson, 1962; May, Angel, & Ellenberger, 1958; Sykes, 1964), rampant in contemporary life. It may seem as if what I am talking about as existential neurosis is much closer to alienation from self, than it is to alienation from society. But on reflection, it should be clear that the existential neurotic would be separated from deep interaction with others as well as from his own personal vitality. Therefore, I find the existential neurotic to be alienated both from self and from society. Indeed, the notions of self-alienation and societal alienation represent little more to me than biases reflecting whether the theorist considers the individual or the group to be the most important unit of analysis.

Nonetheless, it is true that traits sometimes considered under the rubric of alienation are not covered by my definition of the existential neurosis. Such things as anguish, rebelliousness, acute dissatisfaction, and civil disobedience are sometimes considered evidence of alienation. Alienation in such cases is usually taken to be from society and not at all from self. First, I should affirm that such traits are not to be considered part of the existential neurosis. The symptoms of the neurosis all point to a rather comprehensive psychological death, where there is no longer even anguish or anger to remind the person that he is a person, and a very dissatisfied one at that. But what can be said in understanding these traits that I have excluded? Sometimes, what is meant is doubt of the kind that I will later argue is quite healthy. Even when this is not the case, I have difficulty understanding why the traits are considered evidence of alienation in the first place. After all, a person acutely dissatisfied with society, and actively trying to change it through his own actions, is hardly alienated in any important sense. He is accepting the importance of society by the stance that it is worth changing, and feeling perhaps even more powerfully than most of us that he can produce a change. There is little here of the meaninglessness and powerlessness that are supposed to characterize alienation. The person with these traits may well have some psychological malady, but unless his social protest masks an underlying tendency toward meaninglessness, apathy, and aimlessness, the malady bears little relationship to either existential neurosis or what has been called alienation.

The character of Meursault in Camus' (1946) *The Stranger* is a perfect example of the existential neurotic. He frequently says, and even more frequently implies, that he believes life to be meaningless and his activities to be arbitrary. He is virtually always bored and apathetic. He never imagines or daydreams. He has no goals. He makes only the most minimal decisions, doing little more than is necessary to keep a simple job as a clerk. He walks in his mother's funeral cortege and makes love to a woman with the same apathy and indifference. He frequently says, "It's all the same to me." His perceptions are banal and colorless. The most difference anything makes is to be mildly irritating. He has this reaction, for example, to the heat of the sun, but then does nothing about it. Although it might seem remarkable that a novel about such a person could have any literary power at all, it is precisely because of the omnipresence of the symptom cluster we have been calling existential neurosis that the reader is intrigued and shocked. When Meursault finally murders a man without any emotional provocation or reaction, without any premeditation or reason, without any greater decision than is involved in resolving to take a walk, the reader is not even surprised. Anything is possible for Meursault, specifically because nothing is anything of importance. His is a vegetative existence that amounts to psychological death. Some writers have called this a state of nonbeing (e.g., May et al., 1958; Sartre, 1956).

THE PREMORBID PERSONALITY

Turning to the premorbid personality out of which the existential neurosis can come through a process of breakdown precipitated by appropriate stress, I find that the concept of central importance is that of *identity*. I define identity in phenomenological terms, as that which you consider yourself to be. Although a person's identity is not necessarily expressed in verbal terms at any given time, it can be so stated if the person reflects upon the question of what he thinks he is. In focusing upon identity, therefore, I am not implying something that is barred from awareness.

Theorists having recourse to this kind of concept of identity or self have frequently considered of importance the discrepancy between one's sense of identity and one's natural potentialities as a human being. In following that lead, I would say that the premorbid personality corresponding to the existential neurosis is one in which the identity includes only some of the things that express the true nature of man. I will not discuss the true nature of man until the section of this paper on the ideal personality. It will suffice for initial purposes to say that the premorbid identity can be considered overly *concrete* and *fragmentary*. These are certainly ideas that are, in one form or another, common enough in the existential literature (e.g., Fromm, 1955; Kierkegaard, 1954; May et al., 1958). But to say this and nothing more is to fall short of the precision really necessary for adequate understanding of the etiology of existential neurosis. We must ask in what ways is the premorbid identity overly concrete and fragmentary?

The best way to summarize the problem is that the premorbid identity stresses qualities of man that are, among those he has, the ones least unique to him both as opposed to other species and to other men. In other words, the identity is insufficiently humanistic. For our society at this point in time, it is easy to say what an insufficiently humanistic identity looks like. Such an identity leads the person to consider himself to be nothing more than *a player of social roles and an embodiment of biological needs*. I must stress that the difficulty is not so much that man is not these two things, but that what he is in addition to them finds little representation in identity. Considering yourself to be an embodiment of biological needs certainly does not set you apart from other species. Neither does the view of yourself as a player of social roles, for most subhuman species have social differentiation of at least a rudimentary sort. And there is little in either of the two components of identity that permits much sense of difference between individual men, except in the trivial sense that the particular social roles played this moment may be different for me than for you, and the biological needs that I have right now may happen to be different than those you have. But tomorrow, or an hour from now, the situation may change, and we may not even have that small basis for distinguishing ourselves from one another. The overarching fact of life for a person with the premorbid personality I have described is that all men play a small number of social roles and all men embody a few biological needs, and that is that.

Consider what it means to view yourself as a player of social roles. First, you accept the idea that the social system—a set of interrelated institutions operating according to a different group of laws than those that govern individual existence—is a terribly real and important force in living. Second, you believe that the way you presently perceive the social system and have been taught it to be is its real and unchangeable nature. Finally, you consider it not only inevitable, but proper, that you conform to the pressures of the social system. A major aim in life becomes playing the roles that are necessarily yours as well as you can.

Also imagine what it means to consider yourself an embodiment of biological needs. First, you believe that such needs as that for food, water, and sex are terribly important and real forces in living. Second, you are convinced that an important gauge of the adequacy of the life is the degree to which these needs are satisfied. Finally, you believe that any alternative to direct expression of these needs, if an alternative were possible, would be unwise because it would constitute a violation of the true nature of man. All this means that a major aim in life becomes biological survival and satisfaction.

A person who has only these two themes represented in his identity would feel powerless in the face of social pressures from without, and powerless in the face of biological pressures from within. Both social and biological pressures would be considered independent variables, that is, variables that influence the behavior of the person without themselves being influenced by him. Naturally he tries to play his social roles well and to insure physical satisfaction and survival. Indeed, he *is* his social roles and biological needs. In other words, his identity is overly concrete. The goals of serving social roles and biological needs often lead in different, if not incompatible, directions. Generally speaking, the person will try to serve social and biological pressures at different times, or in different places, keeping possible incompatibilities from the eyes of others and from direct confrontation in his own awareness. In other words, this kind of identity is overly fragmentary.

For vividness, consider further the cognitive and affective state of the person with the premorbid personality under discussion. In the cognitive realm, the person would be rather consistently pragmatic and materialistic in his outlook on life. The pragmatism would come primarily from accepting the necessity of playing certain social roles. How often one hears that the world is the way it is, so one might as well be practical about it! The materialism would come primarily from the view that man is an embodiment of biological needs. The pursuit of material things is given the status of a natural process. How often one hears that narrow self-interest is the only real motivating force outside of society! Superimposed upon the fairly consistent pragmatism and materialism would be more transitory states of fatalism, cynicism, and pessimism. These transitory cognitive states would presumably mirror the moment-to-moment economy of social system and biological rewards and punishments. There is a final implication contained in the premorbid personality that is extremely important. If you consider yourself bound by certain rules of social interaction, on the one hand, and in need of certain material goods for satisfaction and survival, on the other hand, relationships between yourself and other people will be made on contractual grounds, rather than on the grounds of tradition or intimacy. The person with a premorbid personality will tend to look upon relationships as serving some specific social or biological end. His view of relationship will be rather cold-blooded.

Turning to the affective realm, the person with a premorbid identity would tend to worry about such things as whether he is considered by others to be conscientious, whether he is seen to be a nice person, whether he is admired, whether people can guess the animal lusts within him, whether he can satisfy his needs without interfering too much with social role playing. His predominant affective states would be fear and anxiety, and these would be only aggravated by the frequent incompatibility between serving other-directed social aims and self-interested biological aims. The other affective states typical of the premorbid state stem from the continual emphasis upon contractual relationships. Since relationships are defined in terms of limited, specific goals, and in terms of the economic considerations of who is getting what out of interaction, social life will be rather structured and superficial. Contractual relationships are devoid of intimacy, commitment, and spontaneity because of the preemptiveness of role playing and need expression. Thus, important affective states associated with premorbidity would be loneliness and disappointment. On the one hand, the person feels anxious and afraid a good deal of the time, while on the other hand, he feels alone and as if something were missing from his life.

You will have recognized in the discussion of the premorbid personality many of the features common in writings on alienation. There is much in what I have said that is reminiscent of Fromm's (1955) marketing personality and Sartre's (1956) idea of bad faith, to name only two sources. I want to encourage you to think of the premorbid personality not as a sickness in itself, but rather as a predisposition to sickness of an existential sort. What I have described as premorbidity is simply too common and livable to be considered frank neurosis, though it is a state with its own characteristic sufferings and limitations. The premorbid person is still too much enmeshed in the problems of his living, still too much concerned with having a successful life, to be considered existentially neurotic, given the implications of detachment from life included in that idea.

PRECIPITATING STRESS

For the person with a premorbid identity, life may go on in a rather empty, though superficially adequate, way for a long time. He may even be reasonably successful in objective terms, keeping his vague dissatisfactions and anxieties to himself. But he may also be precipitated into an existential neurosis if he encounters stress of the right content and sufficient intensity to be undermining.

The stresses that will be effective are those that have content that strikes at the vulnerabilities inherent in defining yourself as

151

nothing more than a player of social roles and an embodiment of biological needs. The stronger this self-definition the weaker can the stress be and still produce breakdown. In speaking of precipitating stress, I do not mean the things that merely make the person worry. The threat of social censure or biological deprivation are potent sources of concern for the premorbid personality we are discussing, but these things do not ordinarily cause the kind of comprehensive breakdown involved in the existential neurosis. *The stresses that can produce the neurosis are ones that disconfirm the premorbid identity by forcing recognition of its overly concrete, fragmentary, and nonhumanistic nature.*

Three stresses come readily to mind, though there are bound to be others as well. Perhaps the most effective of them is the concrete threat of imminent death. It is my impression that this threat must be to your own life in order to be very effective. Even the threatened death of someone reasonably close to you may not have the force I am about to describe. Perhaps those of you who have faced the threat of death to yourself and to others will know what I mean. If the threat of death actually does lead to death, people with the premorbid identity tend to die The Death of Ivan Ilych, in the great novella by Tolstoi (1960). Ilych knows he is dying of a horrible disorder, and this colors all his perceptions and judgments. Most of the visitors to his bedside are business associates who, he comes to realize, are only performing what they experience as a distasteful obligation of their social role. Then he realizes that the same thing is true of his own family! None of these people is deeply touched by his drift toward death, for theirs is a contractual rather than intimate relationship to him. And even more horrible, he realizes the appropriateness of their behavior because he too has thought of and experienced them only in contractual, superficial terms. The triviality and superficiality of their materialism and social conformity—and his own—are thrown into sharp relief by the threat of death. He becomes acutely aware of his wasted life and can tell himself nothing that will permit a peaceful death. He realizes that he has always felt deprived

of intimacy, love, spontaneity, and enthusiasm. By renouncing himself and the people around him, he is finally able to feel truly human and alive just at the point where he dies physically. This story is didactically and literarily powerful because this is a tragic way to die. What bankruptcy when it is death that frees us from the impoverishing shackles of social conformity and biological needs!

If the person with a premorbid identity who is faced with the threat of imminent death should actually recover rather than die he is likely to experience an existential neurosis. Before he dies, Ilych is certainly a good example of this. If the threat of death disconfirms your previous identity, then you have no identity to work with, and in an adult this is virtually the same as psychological death. The adequacy of recovery from the existential neurosis will be determined by whether the person can use, or be helped to use, the knowledge gained through facing death to build a more comprehensive, abstract, humanistic identity.

The second stress that can precipitate existential neurosis is gross disruption of the social order, through such things as war, conquest, and economic depression, leading to disintegration of social roles and even of the institutionalized mechanisms for satisfying biological needs. Such catastrophe has two effects on people with the premorbid identity. First, it makes it difficult to continue to obtain the usual rewards for playing social roles and expressing biological needs. Second, and more important, disruption of the social order demonstrates the relativity of society to someone who has been treating it as absolute reality. The premorbid person is left without much basis for living and an existential neurosis may well ensue. Thinking along very similar channels, Durkheim (1951) saw social upheaval, or anomie, as a factor increasing suicide rates.

The final stress is difficult to describe because it is less dramatic than threat of death and social upheaval. Not only is this stress less dramatic, but it is usually an accumulation of events rather than something that need happen only once. And yet, this final stress is probably the most usual precipitating factor in the existential neurosis. The stress I mean is the repeated confrontation with the limitation on deep and comprehensive experiencing produced by the premorbid identity. These confrontations usually come about through other people's insistence on pointing out the person's existential failures. The aggressive action of other people is more or less necessary because the person with the premorbid identity usually avoids self-confrontation. But let there be a close relative who is suffering because of the person's premorbidity, and confrontations will be forced.

A good example of this kind of stress and its effects is to be found in Arthur Miller's (1964) *After the Fall*. During the first two-thirds of the play, Quentin discovers that his is what I would call a premorbid identity. The discovery is a terribly painful stress. It begins when his first wife, working up the courage for a separation and divorce, tries, after a long period of docility, to force him to recognize the limitations in their relationship and her deep dissatisfaction with him. In listening to his own attempts to answer her charges, and in considering her attacks, he begins to recognize that his has been little more than a contractual commitment to her. He has been merely conforming to social roles in being husband and father. Under her scrutiny, he begins to recognize his superficial sexuality—a biological need—as well. He feels at fault for his limitations, but can do little about them, instead asking pathetically for understanding. His wife is also important in forcing recognition that his offer to defend his old law professor in court is not out of deep affection, or intimacy, or even loyalty, but rather out of an attempt to convince people that he feels these ways toward this man. Frightened and distraught by what he is learning about himself, Quentin finally begins to envy his wife for her ability to experience deeply and know what she wants.

After the breakup of his first marriage, Quentin moves impulsively into a second. His second wife, Maggie, idealizes him, and he feels reassured about himself, though he has not really changed much. It is only after they have been married for some time that Quentin begins to appreciate Maggie's extraordinary neediness and lack of differentiation as a person. Her adulation of him can no longer serve to reassure him, and to make matters worse, he has new evidence of his superficiality in his inability to reach her in any significant way. He must stand by and let her commit suicide, having decided that the most he can do is to save his own life! Whatever depth of personality could have saved her in a husband, he simply did not have.

After Maggie's death, Quentin spends 2 years or so in a state of meaninglessness, apathy, and aimlessness. He does not work, he does not relate to people, he merely drifts. This period is clearly one of existential neurosis, and can be seen as precipitated by a person's being forced repeatedly to confront the limitations on living produced by social conformity and expression of biological need.

THE IDEAL PERSONALITY

From the discussion of the premorbid personality, it will come as no surprise that ideal identity from my point of view is abstract, unified, and humanistic. I would remind you of Emerson's (Atkinson, 1940) elegant plea for such an identity at the beginning of *The American Scholar*:

It is one of those fables which out of an unknown antiquity convey an unlooked-for wisdom, that the gods, in the beginning, divided Man into men, that he might be more helpful to himself; just as the hand was divided into fingers, the better to answer its end.

The old fable covers a doctrine ever new and sublime; that there is One Man—present to all particular men only partially, or through one faculty; and that you must take the whole society to find the whole man. Man is not a farmer, or a professor, or an engineer, but he is all. Man is priest, and scholar, and statesman, and producer, and soldier. In the *divided* or social state these functions are parcelled out to individuals, each of whom aims to do his stint of the joint work, whilst each other performs his. The fable implies that the individual, to possess himself, must sometimes return from his own labor to embrace all the other laborers. But, unfortunately, this original unit, this fountain of power, has been so distributed to multitudes, has been so minutely subdivided and peddled out, that it is spilled into drops, and cannot be gathered. The state of society is one in which the members have suffered amputation from the trunk, and strut about so many walking monsters —a good finger, a neck, a stomach, an elbow, but never a man.

Man is thus metamorphosed into a thing, into many things. The planter, who is Man sent out into the field to gather food, is seldom cheered by any idea of the true dignity of his ministry. He sees his bushel and his cart, and nothing beyond, and sinks into the farmer, instead of Man on the farm. The tradesman scarcely ever gives an ideal worth to his work, but is ridden by the routine of his craft, and the soul is subject to dollars. The priest becomes a form; the attorney a statute-book; the mechanic a machine; the sailor a rope of the ship.

In this distribution of functions the scholar is the delegated intellect. In the right state he is *Man Thinking*. In the degenerate state, when the victim of society, he tends to become a mere thinker, or still worse, the parrot of other men's thinking [pp. 45–46].

This quote criticizes concretizations (e.g., when a man is a farmer, instead of man on the farm) and fragmentation (e.g., one can find a good finger, neck, etc., but never a man), and implies that the antidote to this ill is humanistic-in nature (e.g., note the capitalization of man). Rousing and emotionally convincing though Emerson is, he does not give us a theory of man that makes this ideal identity rationally understandable. I shall try to present the rough outlines of such a theory, which is based on Emerson's intuitive lead and the writings of many other people concerned with the problems of existence.

First, let us assume that there are three sides to man's nature—social, biological, and psychological. The social side refers to interpersonal relationships, the biological side to physical survival and satisfaction, and the psychological side to mental processes, primarily symbolization, imagination, and judgment. Assume further that all three sides are of equal importance for successful living, and that curtailment of expression of any of them sets up some kind of premorbidity.

When you express your psychological side fully and vigorously, you generate symbols that represent concrete experiences in the general form that makes clear their similarities to and differences from other experiences. You also have an active and uninhibited imagination, which you use as a guide rather than substitute for action. In other words,

you let your imagination reveal what you want your life to be, and then attempt to act on that knowledge. The psychological faculty of judgment functions as a check upon the validity of your imagination. When you act upon imagination, you can evaluate the nature of your ensuing experience in order to determine whether it is really what you seem to want. Does the action lead to satisfaction, or is it frightening or boring? Hence the knowledge gained through exercising judgment is also used as a guide to living.

Of the psychological, biological, and social sides of man, it is the psychological side that is most human. All subhuman species have biological requirements for survival and satisfaction, and these requirements are generally acted upon in a straightforward and simple manner. Most subhuman species have patterned social relationships. Indeed, sometimes subhuman society is quite complex and extensive. But even then it tends to be rigidly organized and characterized by social roleship. Only in man is it reasonable to consider the psychological side of life to be of much importance. Indeed, when social and biological behavior is unusually subtle and complex in man it is because of his most human, or psychological, side.

Let me make my position more vivid by contrasting the lives of people with premorbid and ideal identities. Whereas both premorbid and ideal identities involve expression of the social and biological sides of man, only the ideal identity shows much representation of the psychological side. Because the premorbid person does not have available to him the generalizing, unifying, humanizing effect of psychological expression, encompassing as it does symbolization, imagination, and judgment, he achieves only the most obvious, common, superficial forms of social and biological expression. He accepts social roles as given, tries to play them as well as he can, and sees himself quite literally as the roles he plays. He accepts biological needs as given and acts on them in a way that is isolated and unreflective, however straightforward it may be. The best example of such biological expression is with regard to the sexual need. The premorbid person considers sexuality to be no more than an animalistic urge, and satisfies it as simply as possible, with little consideration of relationship, affection, or even comprehensiveness of attraction. Little wonder that though he seems very social, he frequently feels insecure, lonely, and without intimacy, and that though he seems very active in expressing biological needs, he frequently feels incompletely satisfied. The loneliness and incomplete satisfaction are signs that he is deprived of psychological expression.

As the premorbid person does not rely upon the processes of symbolization, imagination, and judgment, favoring instead the view that life is determined by social and biological considerations, he not only feels powerless to influence his actions, but also does indeed lead an existence that is rather stereotyped and unchanging. As no human being is completely without psychological expression, the premorbid person often has a glimmer of awareness that his life is not what it might be. This accumulated sense of missed opportunity is what May et al. (1958, pp. 37–91) have called ontological guilt.

With vigorous psychological expression, would come social and biological living that is more unified, subtle, deep, and rewarding than that I have described above. The person with the ideal identity would not feel powerless in the face of social and biological pressures, because he puts heavy reliance in living on his own processes of symbolization, imagination, and judgment. He would perceive many alternatives to simple role playing and isolated biological satisfaction. Because he sees himself to be the "fountain of power," to use Emerson's excellent phrase, his social and biological living transcend the concrete instance and involve anything that he can imagine and anything that is evaluated by him as worthwhile.

So, if contractual relationships leave him unsatisfied, he can choose to relate otherwise, such as on the basis of shared personal experience. He can even make a start on this by talking with others about his dissatisfaction with merely playing social roles. Once he does this, he will undoubtedly find some people who will be encouraged to share their own feelings of loneliness with him, and the road to more subtle, myriadly rewarding

social relations has already been found. If simple, unreflective expression of biological urges leaves him unsatisfied, he can choose to explore other forms of expression. For example, instead of merely seeking food, he can make hunger the basis for more comprehensive satisfaction by cooking especially tasty dishes, or by eating in the company of people with whom he feels intimate. And the same with sex. He can make sexual expression a subtle, complex, changing thing, indulged in with people toward whom he feels intimate and affectionate on other than simply sexual grounds. There will be many more parts to the life of the person with an ideal identity, and the parts will achieve much closer integration than is true for the premorbid person.

One important consequence of reliance upon his imagination and judgment as guides to living is that the ideal person is not a conformist. Some critics of my position would argue that it amounts to advocating the unleashing of monsters on the world. What is to stop a person from murdering, or robbing, if he feels so free to put his imagination into operation? Psychologists like Rogers (1961) would answer this criticism by contending that there is nothing basic to the organism that would lead in the direction of such monstrosities. As the individual is oriented toward survival, so too does his natural functioning support the survival of his species. One can easily develop an evolutionary argument for this position. Rogers would believe that only an imagination already perverted by psychopathogenic social pressures would lead the person in the direction of terrible aggressions toward his fellow men. I have considerable sympathy for this position, but would like to add to it the notion that judgment is a maturing supplement to imagination. Your imagination might even include the bases for catastrophic action, perhaps at a time when someone has hurt you badly, and still you might not act on the imagination if judgment provided some balance. I sincerely feel that although the ideal person might well make mistakes in life, he will not be a monster simply because he does not conform to the most obvious societal pressures.

It should be remembered that Emerson's (Atkinson, 1940, p. 148) conclusion that "whosoever would be a man must be a nonconformist" is echoed by many of the world's finest thinkers. If a critic responds by claiming that this kind of thinking permits such abominations as Hitler, I would suggest that he was a badly twisted man who showed less imagination than repetitive, compulsive preoccupations, and less judgment than megalomanic overconfidence. It is only by losing the usual standards of what is meant by imagination and judgment that Hitler and the ideal identity can be discussed in the same breath! But a secondary argument could be made that the position I am taking makes it at least possible for some twisted person like Hitler to gain dangerous power because those around him believe enough in imagination and judgment as guides to living that they may not see that he is only a pseudo-example of this in time to do anything about it. This is a terribly weak argument. Indeed, it is much more likely that people who define themselves as social role players and embodiments of biological needs will not recognize or be able to stop a man like Hitler. It is to the point that Hannah Arendt (1964) subtitled her treatise on the enacting of the final solution to the "Jewish problem" *a report on the banality of evil.* To judge from reports, the rank-and-file Germans were simply following rules when they gassed people!

Another consequence of relying upon imagination and judgment as guides to action is that the life of the ideal person will be a frequently changing, unfolding thing. New possibilities will be constantly developing, though it is unlikely that the process of change will be without pattern or continuity. The reliance upon judgment insures that there will be values and principles represented in the personality, and these would be slow to change. But more concrete experiential possibilities would change, presumably in an orderly fashion, due to the abstract view of experience and the play of imagination. The person with an ideal identity would not, then, be beset by boredom or by ontological guilt. Indeed, he would feel emotions deeply and

spontaneously, be they pleasant or unpleasant. He would be enthusiastic and committed.

But his life would not be quite that rosy. When you are in a rather continual process of change, you cannot predict what existential outcomes will be. Interestingly enough, we find that doubt (Frankl, 1955) or existential anxiety (May et al., 1958, pp. 37–91) is a necessary concomitant of the ideal identity. When you stop to think about it, it is quite understandable that someone who is his own standard of meaning would be unsure and anxious at times when he was changing.

Looked at in this way, doubt (existential anxiety) is actually a sign of strength, rather than illness. This is precisely what was meant by Camus (1955) when he said, "I cherish my nights of despair," and Tillich (1952) when he designated doubt to be the "god above God." Powerful expression to doubt as an aspect of humanism, and therefore strength, is given by Frankl (1955) when he says:

Challenging the meaning of life can . . . never be taken as a manifestation of morbidity or abnormality; it is rather the truest expression of the state of being human, the mark of the most human nature in man. For we can easily imagine highly developed animals or insects—say ants or bees—which in many aspects of their social organization are actually superior to man. But we can never imagine any such creature raising the question of the meaning of its own existence, and thus challenging this existence. It is reserved for man alone to find his very existence questionable, to experience the whole dubiousness of being. More than such faculties as power of speech, conceptual thinking, or walking erect, this factor of doubting the significance of his own existence is what sets man apart from animal [p. 30].

On logical grounds alone, nothing so basic to man's nature as doubt could ever be defined as psychopathological, for to do so would be to call everyone sick by virtue of his true nature. This logical argument is made more psychologically compelling by recognizing that when one is one's own standard of meaning, that will entail accepting and even valuing doubt because it is the necessary concomitant of the uncertainty produced by personal change. To avoid doubt is to avoid change and to give over the power in living to social and biological considerations.

This is too big a price to pay for comfort alone. In avoiding the tragedies, you also lose the potentiality of triumphs.

PRECIPITATING STRESS AND THE IDEAL PERSONALITY

If the ideal identity is truly an improvement over the premorbid identity, then the stresses that precipitate breakdown in the latter should be ineffective in the former. You will recall that the three stresses mentioned earlier are the threat of imminent death, social upheaval, and the accumulated sense of failure in living deeply and commitedly.

The ideal person would be so actively and enthusiastically enmeshed in living socially, biologically, and psychologically that the therapeutic effect of threat of imminent death would be markedly diminished. You simply do not need the threat of death to remind you to take life seriously and live in the immediate moment, if you are already doing these things. To the ideal person, such a threat could be frightening to some degree, but it would not be helpful. A definite implication of my saying this is the belief that the emphasis on death as what makes life important, which appears in one form or another in so much existential writing, is only of relative importance. Only when you think in terms of premorbidity as the true nature of man and the world, do you celebrate the purifying effects of threat of imminent death.

If the ideal person actually does come to the point of death, he will die a much more graceful death than that of Ivan Ilych. Death for the ideal person will be no more than a very unfortunate interruption of an intense and gratifying life process. I contend that someone who is living well will more easily face death than someone who senses that he has not even lived at all. In any event, it seems clear that the threat of imminent death will hardly precipitate an existential neurosis in a person with the ideal identity.

As to social upheaval, it is interesting to note in detail Durkheim's (1951) point of view on anomic suicide:

It is not true . . . that human activity can be released from all restraint. Nothing in the world can enjoy such a privilege. All existence being a part of the universe is relative to the remainder; its nature and method of manifestation accordingly depend not only on itself but on other beings, who consequently restrain and regulate it. Here there are only differences of degree and form between the mineral realm and the thinking person. Man's characteristic privilege is that the bond he accepts is not physical but moral; that is, social. He is governed not by a material environment brutally imposed on him, but by a conscience superior to his own, the superiority of what he feels. Because the greater, better part of his existence transcends the body, he escapes the body's yoke, but is subject to that of society.

But when society is disturbed by some painful crisis . . . it is momentarily incapable of exercising this influence; thence come the sudden rises in the curve of suicides which we have pointed out [p. 252].

Durkheim clearly believes that man's animalistic, self-interested urges must be held in check by societal regulation of life. Naturally, then, social upheaval would lead to a rise in suicide and, incidentally, in existential neurosis. But it is also likely that times of social upheaval involve intense creativity. While some people are committing suicide, others are using to good advantage the freedom achieved by the breakdown of monolithic social institutions. We should remember that the Italian Renaissance was a time of extraordinary social upheaval, and while suicide must have been high, so too was creativity. That the increase in creativity might have been due to the existence of ideal persons, for whom freedom from social pressures was helpful, is suggested by the following quote from the *Oration on the Dignity of Man,* written by Pico della Mirandola (1956), a most Renaissance man:

Neither heavenly nor earthly, neither mortal nor immortal have we created thee, so that thou mightest be free according to thy own will and honor, to thy own creator and builder. To thee alone we gave growth and development depending on thy own free will. Thou bearest in thee the germs of a universal life [p. 17].

Rather than constituting a stress, social upheaval may well be a boon for the person with the real identity.

Finally, there is the matter of an accumulated sense that your life is a failure in terms of depth and committedness of experience. Actually, I am speechless here. It is simply incomprehensible that a person with an ideal identity would ever experience the painful course of self-revelation leading to existential neurosis seen in Arthur Miller's Quentin. The person with an ideal identity will certainly make mistakes, and suffer for them, but will not go for as long as Quentin with no cognizance for his superficiality and attendant frustration, and, hence, will not be in the position of condemning his life.

IDEAL AND DEVIANT DEVELOPMENT

It is natural at this point to raise the question of how ideal and premorbid identities develop. But before launching into considerations of early experience and their effects on later personality, one obviously relevant and thorny problem should be raised. It is the problem of free will.

Some of you may have long since decided that I have left the scientific fold with all this emphasis upon the person himself as the "fountain of power." Does this not mean, you will ask, that according to me man's actions are not determined by anything but his own will? And is this not a view antithetical to science? Let me try to explain why I think what I am saying is quite scientific. *I am explicating the way in which a particular set of beliefs about oneself and the nature of the world can lead to actions that are more varied, active, and changeable than is true when that set of beliefs is absent.* In the psychologist's terms, I am focusing upon proactive and reactive behavior, and attempting to explain the differences between them on the basis of differences in sense of identity. The functioning of the ideal person is well summarized by the concept of proactive behavior, with its emphasis on the person as an influence on his environment. In contrast, reactive behavior, which is influenced by the environment, is very descriptive of the premorbid person. But just because proactive behavior is more varied, flexible, and original is no reason to presume it is not caused in a scientifically specifiable way. In my view, proactive behavior is caused by the characteristics of the ideal personality, namely, the humanistic belief in oneself as the fountain of power, and the associated preparedness to exercize fully the psychological as well as social and biological sides of man. Further, the ideal personality is not a mysterious implant of God, like the concept of soul. The ideal personality, like the premorbid personality, is formed out of early life experiences. I propose to sketch these experiences in the paragraphs that follow. Clearly, my position assumes that all action is determined in a specifiable scientific way. My approach amounts to availing oneself of the value in recognizing that some behavior is active while some is passive without assuming anything about a soul, or divine inspiration, or mysterious freedom.

In developing an ideal identity it certainly helps to start out with a minimum of average intelligence, but once having this, the rest depends upon the parent-child relationship, and the supplementation of this in later relationships that are significant. Even relationship of child to teacher needs to be considered. One route to ideal development is for the person to experience in his relationships with significant people in his life what Rogers (1959) has called unconditional positive regard. This means that the person is appreciated as a human being and knows it. With such appreciation, the person comes to value his own humanness, and is able to act without fear and inhibition from all three sides of himself. But unconditional positive regard is not enough. There must be something better suited to point the young person in particular directions rather than others. The people around him must value symbolization, imagination, and judgment and encourage and support the child when he shows evidence of these psychological processes. But in this, the emphasis must be upon the child's own psychological processes, rather than on his parroting those of others. In addition, the child's range of experience must be broad, so that the generalizing function of symbolization, and the ordering function of judgment will have raw material with which to work. A broad range of experience may also have the secondary value of firing the imagination. Finally, it is crucial that the significant people in the child's life recognize the importance of social and biological functioning as well, so that they can encourage him in such expression. Their encouragement, however, should not be in the service of accepting social roles and animalistic urges, so much as in the conviction that social and biological living is what you make it, and, in the final analysis, these two sides of man are not so separate from each other and from the life of the mind.

From this brief statement, it is easy to see what would be deviant development leading to premorbidity. All you need to develop a premorbid identity is to grow up around people in significant relationship to you who value only some aspects of you, who believe in social roles and biological needs as the only defining pressures of life, and who are either afraid of active symbolization, imagination, and judgment, or see no particular relevance of these processes to living. Have these significant people act on their views in interactions with the child, and he will develop a premorbid identity.

While my brief remarks may seem somewhat flippant, I urge you to recognize that the two kinds of identity are almost that simply caused.

Concluding Remarks

If I have succeeded in my purpose, you should have a clearer, potentially research-oriented sense of existential disorder, its precursors, and its opposite, than you did before. In addition, you should have found documented here aspects of your own life and those of the people you know well.

If I have drawn the outlines of premorbid identity at all well, you will have recognized its great frequency in our contemporary Western world. While one can point to a set of early experiences in explaining the development of premorbidity, this does not help very much in understanding why this type of personality should be so prevalent these days. Inevitably, the question is raised of why so many parents and significant people in the life of modern-day youngsters instill in them the seeds of premorbidity. This question requires an answer concerning the general cultural milieu in which both adult and child exist. It is as products of their culture that adults influence the young.

Much has been written about the cultural causes of conformity, materialism, and shallow living, and I do not intend to review that literature here. But I would like to point to three broad views, of special interest to psychologists, that have gone far toward creating a cultural climate congenial to premorbidity. The men usually associated with these views are Darwin, Weber, and Freud.

Darwin argued a kinship between all animals, and this view has been sloppily interpreted by many to mean that man is very little different from lower animals. Any characteristics of man that do not seem amply represented in lower animals must be epiphenomenal, or reducible to simpler, animalistic things. Inevitably, such a view undercuts the importance of psychological processes and humanistic doctrines. And that is just what happened. I would like to point out, however, that there is nothing in the concept of a phylogenetic scale that justifies overlooking the importance of characteristics that seem to emerge at one level, having appeared in what may be only minimal prototypical form at lower levels. Add this to the reasonable view that man is really quite far on the scale from his next lower kin, and you have a form of Darwinism that is not so incompatible with my view of the ideal identity, and that would not be a cultural seed for the existential neurosis. To those psychologists who have rashly made what Murray (1954, p. 435) calls "the audacious assumption of species equivalence" between man and white rat I would say that a meaningful comparative psychology is as much interested in the differences as the similarities between species.

The sociologist Weber was certainly among the first to formally specify that modern, industrial society is necessarily bureaucratic in nature. This view has been considered to mean that the social roles a person is delegated are the most important things about him. Indeed, many a modern sociologist will define personality as the sum total of the social roles played by a person. Anyone who accepts such a view of himself without looking more deeply into the matter will very likely either be on the road to premorbidity himself, or be the kind of parent that breeds premorbidity in his children. In trying to show that there is an alternative to this view, let me agree that all behavior can be analyzed as social role playing, but point out that this does not necessarily mean that the social system is unchangeable and an irresistible shaper of individual living. The first step in convincing yourself of this is recognizing that there are different types of social roles. Social roles differ in their rigidity, preemptiveness, status, initiative requirements, and even in the degree to which they involve the person in changing existing social roles. The import of all this is that some social roles encourage the expression of symbolization, imagination, and judgment. Clear examples are roles of leadership, power, and aestheticism. The second step in convincing yourself that the social system is not necessarily the prime mover of individual life is to ask yourself the question of how any person comes to play certain types of roles as opposed to others. In any society that does not restrict competition for roles, the roles that a person actually does come to play will be determined in part by his view of the good life and his sense of personal identity. The person with the ideal identity will gravitate toward roles involving symbolization, imagination, and judgment, while the person with the premorbid identity will avoid these roles. Indeed, the sense of powerlessness and despair pointed to by Marx in people playing social roles that are inhuman may be a psychological problem as much as a sociological one.

Finally, we come to Freud. It may not have escaped your recognition that Freud, in classical libido theory, gives expression to the belief that life represents a compromise between the necessity of playing social roles and of expressing biological needs. He makes what I have called premorbidity the ideal! Further, for Freud the psychological processes are defensive in nature, reflecting at most no more than a pale shadow of the truth. It is not hard to believe that our current-day outlook that thought processes are not to be trusted and that man's self-interested sexual nature needs to be checked by society was given great impetus by

Freud's theory. Interestingly enough, his theory may well have served as a necessary corrective in his day, when thought had become arid through neglect of the biological side of man and too heavy in emphasis upon judgment to the detriment of imagination. But because his theory was a corrective rather than something more comprehensively adequate, its acceptance into the general culture has contributed to setting the stage for a new emphasis in psychopathology, namely, the existential neurosis.

REFERENCES

ARENDT, H. Eichmann in Jerusalem—a report on the banality of evil. New York: Viking, 1964.

ATKINSON, B. (Ed.) The selected writings of Ralph Waldo Emerson. New York: Modern Library, 1940.

CAMUS, A. The stranger. New York: Knopf, 1946.

CAMUS, A. The myth of Sisyphus and other essays. (Trans. by J. O'Brien) New York: Knopf, 1955.

DELLA MIRANDOLA, P. Oration on the dignity of man. (Trans. by A. R. Caponigri) Chicago: Gateway, 1956.

DURKHEIM, E. Suicide. Glencoe, Ill.: Free Press, 1951.

FRANKL, V. The doctor and the soul. (Trans. by R. Winston & C. Winston) New York: Knopf, 1955.

FROMM, E. The sane society. New York: Rinehart, 1955.

JOSEPHSON, E., & JOSEPHSON, M. (Eds.) Man alone. New York: Dell, 1962.

KIERKEGAARD, S. The sickness unto death. (Trans. by W. Lowrie) New York: Doubleday, 1954.

MAY, R., ANGEL, E., & ELLENBERGER, H. F. (Eds.) Existence. New York: Basic Books, 1958.

MILLER, A. After the fall. New York: Viking, 1964.

MURRAY, H. A. Toward a classification of interaction. In T. Parsons & E. A. Shils (Eds.), Toward a general theory of action. Cambridge, Mass.: Harvard University Press, 1954. Pp. 435 ff.

ROGERS, C. R. A theory of therapy, personality, and interpersonal relationships, as developed in the client-centered framework. In S. Koch (Ed.), Psychology: A study of a science. Vol. 3. New York: McGraw-Hill, 1959. Pp. 184–256.

ROGERS, C. R. On becoming a person. Boston: Houghton Mifflin, 1961.

SARTRE, J. P. Being and nothingness. (Trans. by H. Barnes) New York: Philosophical Library, 1956.

SYKES, G. (Ed.) Alienation. New York: Braziller, 1964.

TILLICH, P. The courage to be. New Haven: Yale University Press, 1952.

TOLSTOI, L. The death of Ivan Illych. New York: Signet, 1960.

ON THE EMERGENCE OF BEHAVIOR THERAPY
IN MODERN SOCIETY

ALEJANDRO PORTES [1]

In the last few years, there has been an impressive series of applications of the principle of academic psychology to the demands of modern life. One of the most significant developments has taken place in the field of psychiatry and clinical psychology with the emergence of behavior therapy. Though little noticed at present outside clinical and academic circles, the growth of behavior therapy may be an important indicator of the direction in which social processes and cultural developments are evolving. It is the purpose of this paper to examine, from a social psychological standpoint, some of the elements which account for its success, and to comment on the meaning of its emergence in modern society.

What exactly is behavior therapy? Gelfand and Hartmann (1968) define it as a group of "treatment techniques derived from theories of learning and aimed at the direct modification of one or more problem behaviors rather than at effecting more general and less observable personality or adjustment changes [p. 205]." This general definition encompasses several different techniques. Patterson (1969) distinguishes between modeling, operant, and complex "social system" approaches, the latter being a new development of the second. Bijou

and Sloane (1966) differentiate classical conditioning from operant analysis therapies. Wolpe and Lazarus (1967) distinguish between counterconditioning, or reciprocal inhibition, positive reconditioning, and experimental extinction. Gelfand and Hartmann (1968) adopt a more functional classification of behavior therapies with children, referring to deceleration of maladaptive behaviors, acceleration of prosocial behavior, and multiple treatment techniques, the latter being similar to Patterson's "complex" approach.

Without a doubt, the principles of classical and operant conditioning have been dominant in behavior therapy. Yet other points of view have also found application. The social imitation, or "vicarious learning," theories of Miller and Dollard (1941) and, more recently, of Bandura and Walters (1963) have been implemented through the technique of "modeling" (Bandura, Grussec, & Menlove, 1967; Coffey & Wiener, 1967; Straughan, Potter, & Hamilton, 1965).

A new development in behavior therapy is the attempt to use operant conditioning theory for the modification of relationships in social systems. So far the social theory most commonly employed by behavior therapists has been the very simple notion of "reciprocity," or "distributive justice" (Homans, 1961; Thibaut & Kelley, 1966). Other principles, such as the diminishing marginal value of social rewards (Blau, 1966; Homans, 1961) and the determinants of conflict, cooperation, and cohesiveness in groups (Cartwright & Zander, 1953), have not been employed.

[1] The author is thankful to John Reid, Warren Hagstrom, and Burton Fisher of the Departments of Psychology and Sociology at the University of Wisconsin for their most helpful comments on earlier drafts of this paper. The contents, nevertheless, are my sole responsibility.

JOURNAL OF CONSULTING AND CLINICAL PSYCHOLOGY, 1971, 36, pp. 303-313.

In general, the action-dependent approach of behavior therapies has limited most of its uses to simple behaviors and to noncomplex patients, such as children, retardates, psychotics, and autistic individuals. As Grossberg (1964) has pointed out, cases of clear, well-defined behaviors, such as tantrums, bedwetting, and phobias, are the ones which behavior therapy most successfully treats. As the generality and perceptual-cognitive character of the disease increases and as the cognitive complexity of the patient grows, behavior therapies seem to decrease in usefulness. Yet some of the most brilliant behavior therapists, such as Wolpe, Lazarus, and Patterson, have gone beyond simple instances to treat quite complex cases—social inadequacies, sexual problems, and group maladjustments. It is their work which interests the writer primarily throughout the rest of the paper.

The ensuing comments attempt to answer two questions:

1. How adequate is behavioristic theory for understanding and curing complex mental disturbances?

2. What is there in behavior therapy that cures when applied to complex human problems?

CHARACTERISTICS OF BEHAVIOR THERAPY: A CRITIQUE

Theory and Practice

Psychoanalysis was initially a method of therapy which later attempted to become a science; behaviorism was initially a scientific theory which only recently has tried its hand at therapy. The beginnings of psychoanalysis were ideographic, those of behaviorism nomothetic. From here derives the "badness" of psychoanalysis as scientific theory, and the elegance and simplicity of learning principles. However, this same theoretical "goodness" of learning theories leads to potential shortcomings in their application.

Behaviorism as a nomothetic approach tends to stress general scientific principles over individual phenomena. As a rational approach to conduct, it tends to deduce syllogistically individual instances from universal laws. This deduction is facilitated by the fact that these laws are few and easy to comprehend. The

inevitable tendency to subsume complex singularities under simple universals is counterbalanced in other therapeutic systems by their emphasis on individual uniqueness, by their understanding of the plural causality of any phenomenon, and even by their vagueness, or theoretical "badness," which prevents straightforward deductions. This is not the case with behaviorism, which conceptualizes human phenomena as eminently rational and as fundamentally simple. There ensues a process of scientific stereotyping in which human manifestations, be they normal conduct or pathological symptoms, are rigidly defined as derivations, not of the person's own dynamic, but of an abstract theory. Thus Bachrach (1965, p. 62), in his comparative scheme of psychoanalysis and behavior therapy, characterizes the former as having an "emphasis on individual," while the latter is depicted as a "study of individual but [with] emphasis on general laws of behavior." Salter (1965) tells us,

The concepts with which we approach the patient's material, and the concepts with which we direct the patient's ability are all objective . . . psychological events are physiological events, and conditioning is the modification of tissue by experience [p. 23]."

Science does not adapt to the patient; on the contrary, the patient must adapt to science. In the process he may be changed from a problem-ridden subject to a quasi-object whose symptoms, regardless of individual characteristics, exemplify the same standard principles.

Psychoanalysis, of course, is not free from the same tendencies. However, the individual-oriented tradition of psychoanalytic therapy and the complications, vagueness, and general "badness" of the theory prevent, in most cases, the automatic conceptualization of symptoms as simple rational products of inadequate learning and encourage a more personal approach to the patient's problems.

The above comments should not be taken as a criticism of individual behavior therapists. In fact, the main point of the following section is the functional transformations that take place in behavioral theory when put into therapeutic practice. The crucial point I am attempting to make here is that a "good" psychological theory does not necessarily lead to good therapy. Exclusive training in learning theories has three main negative effects. First, it may desensitize the therapist from awareness of the fact that the theories he is learning are no more than a partial approach to human phenomena. Imposing the rational and simplified principles of behaviorism on these phenomena may help in heuristically ordering a multiplicity of aspects, but believing that these principles exhaust the meaning content of all variations and types of human manifestations is clearly absurd.

Second, it fails to convey the point that human phenomena add to the usual complexity of empirical reality the fact that they already have a meaning for the actors. This is not to posit another hidden subjectivist trait, but simply to say that individuals are capable of *knowing* they have a problem and what this problem is, and that the way they grasp it will have important consequences for their ensuing behavior.

Third, behaviorism suggests, by its strong scientific leanings, the framing of the therapeutic situation in experimental terms: As psychological phenomena must be observable in order to be studied in the behavioral lab, so mental illness must be externalized in specific symptoms to be cured behaviorally. This easily blurs the crucial distinctions between patient and subject, and between experiments with behavior and control of behavior, on the one hand, and therapy on the other. Bachrach (1965) tells us that

Fundamental to any behavioristic system is the recognition of the necessity for the clear specification of the behavior to be studied and controlled. One of the difficulties with a *psychodynamic* approach to behavior is that it does not clearly specify the responses demanded from the individual [p. 64].

Some may believe that experimentalizing therapy is not negative. I will argue that its advantages are not self-evident. Curing and hypothesis testing follow qualitatively different paths, though the subtle changes in social interaction which occur during the process may be unnoticed by the sociologically naive. It is questionable whether the increasing remoteness of therapist–patient interactions and the casting of heavily emotional disorders in the rationalistic mold of scientific research will result in any improved ability to care for the disturbed individual.

Therapy and Social Standards

The psychoanalytic model has at its roots a vision of the person as locked in perpetual and inevitable conflict with his society and its demands. This basic conflictive view has led psychoanalysts away from the attempt to mold persons in their society's image and likeness. Psychoanalysis (and most of its modified versions) has been dynamic enough to preserve the goal of helping men to achieve their own unique integration even against societal standards. This characteristic has been preserved despite the institutionalization and relative popularity of psychoanalysis as a legitimate form of therapy.

Such is not the case with behavoir therapy. Behaviorism has nothing at its core that prevents its practitioners from becoming behavior controllers at the service of whatever groups happen to have power in the society. If this sounds too extreme, another point seems inescapable: Behavior therapy is one of the therapeutic approaches most inclined to confuse mental health with conformity to social standards. As sociology has only recently discovered through the work of Becker (1966), an individual may be characterized as "deviant" or "disturbed" only because he was "caught," while thousands of others participating in the same activities continue to lead normal lives. If such a "disturbed" person is brought before a behavior therapist, the latter has no element in his conceptual scheme to question the adequacy of the social judgment. His past training would have left him as wholly unsensitized to the distinction between the social deviant and the truly ill as to that between the patient and the experimental subject. As a behavior technician, the only thing left for him to do would be to accept the social label and try to change the behavioral "disorder."

The permeability of behavior therapy to the standards set up by society is clearly evidenced in the behavioral definition of "symptom." Some of the most perceptive behavior therapists define symptom in a personal manner. Thus, for Wolpe (1965), "symptomatic improvement simply means that the patient has less discomfort [p. 6]." Others, however, explicitly add to the personal definition of symptoms the statement that they are also "maladaptive behaviors rejected by the society" (Cahoon, 1968; Goldiamond, 1965; Krasner & Ullmann, 1965).

Since the individual (especially the adult) is not a completely malleable object, the attempt, ensuing from the above definition, to fit the person into an "adjustive" social mold may often prove painful, if not actually harmful.

Images of Man

There are two crucial elements missing in the behavioristic image of man: (*a*) a systematic understanding of meanings and (*b*) an explicit recognition of self-reflectiveness in human beings. In Meadian terms, what behaviorism lacks is a theory of mind and a theory of self. An examination of each of them follows.

Meanings. Above we have employed the term "objective" in referring to the experimentalization of behavior therapy success criteria. Yet, strictly speaking, behaviorism is not objective. No description of any phenomenon whatsoever is objective. Description employs language and language is simply a set of arbitrary rules developed through the psychological interaction of a group of individuals to order quasi-arbitrarily the chaos of empirical reality. In the case of descriptions of human phenomena, objectivity is further limited.

Heider (1958) had no trouble showing how any characterization of human behavior must ultimately refer to underlying psychological dispositions. To make sense of such empirical phenomena, we attribute intentions, desires, perceptions, ignorances, abilities, etc., to the person. Any attempt, even the most careful artificial efforts of behaviorists, to describe human (and, for that matter, animal) conduct objectively will inevitably end in absurdity.

Take the behaviorist concept of "punishment." Have we "seen" a punishment? Can a punishment be grasped as we grasp a stone? Is there a single set of motions or acts connected with punishment? Clearly, the word punishment is intrinsically tied to a specific feeling on the part of the sufferer. It is his dislike, repugnance, or pain—all psychological states— which gives meaning to the term and which unifies the infinity of actual or potential empirical occurrences which we could characterize as "punishment."

The same set of considerations could be applied to the concept of "reward" or "rein-forcement." The best attempt to eliminate "subjectivist connotations" from the word reinforcement has been provided by Sidman (1960); he defines reinforcement as "any event, contingent upon the response of the organism, that alters the future likelihood of that response [p. 396]." This definition, though apparently brilliant, is an invitation to tautology: The independent variable, a reinforcing event, is defined in terms of the dependent variable, "likelihood of that response"; thus, if an event reinforces, it is reinforcing. A second point is that when the psychologist abandons the territory of abstract definitions, he will certainly not go around searching at random for reinforcing events; he will proceed by asking himself what his subject likes, that is, what are his psychological desires.

The issue of meanings in the description of human conduct is important enough to deserve further consideration. Below I reproduce a series of terms employed by Wolpe and Lazarus (1967, p. 108) in describing a case of sexual inadequacy. As seen above, these most prominent behavior therapists are among the first to stress the need for clear, objective specification of symptoms. I reproduce here the terms in their 17-line description which seem to me to possess an indisputable psychological content: "had suffered," "satisfaction," "conscious," "(sexual) fulfillment," "interest in other men," "irritating," "general confidence," "felt," "received on sufferance," "humiliation," "stage fright," "(feelings of) being hurt," "assertiveness." These 13 terms plus the general tone of the description clearly show that the only objectivity attained by Wolpe and Lazarus is to employ a set of underlying psychological dispositions which are more in the realm of common sense, and thus more widely shared, than the involved elaborations of psychoanalytic theory. The same could be shown in many other clinical descriptions of behavior therapy.

Thus, it is evident that man cannot go out of himself to check the objectivity of his perceptions. We perceive in a certain way, we use language to describe, and we attribute intentions, desires, and knowledge to living things. The procedure, varying in content but unchangeable in form, of understanding the infinite nuances in the conduct of other humans by reference to fewer underlying psychological elements is the only way we have of making sense out of such infinity. Behaviorism, despite itself, does the same thing.

Self. The absence of an explicit recognition that persons are aware of their own existence is a related problem in the behaviorist image of man. Rather than restating the theory of self already developed by Mead (1934) and Cooley (1922), I will try to demonstrate the impossibility of disregarding man's self-image in behavioral treatments of human problems by presenting three contradictions.

The first is embodied in the notion of *generalization*, as employed by behavior therapists. Therapeutic results in one area are supposed to generalize to others, forming a "virtuous circle." Similarly, a maladjustment in one situation may generalize to others in a "vicious circle." We may ask, Can this happen automatically? Is there a mysterious mediating mechanism? Nothing of the kind. It is evident that good results generalize because the person is aware of his improvement and he carries this new sense of well-being and self-confidence to other areas. Similarly, failures, punishments, and humiliations generalize negatively because again the person, aware of this negative feedback, transmits it to other areas of his life. There is no hidden mechanism; the individual, because he is reflectively aware of what he does and what happens to him, is his own mediator effecting generalization.

Concerning this issue, Wolpe and Lazarus (1967) give the example of a case of claustrophobia which "also had claustrophobic reactions in situations that had the mere 'feel' of enclosement, e.g., a tight zipper, or wanting to remove nailpolish while having no access to remover [p. 7]." How could such physically dissimilar stimuli have the same "feel" in a person unless they were endowed with the same or similar meaning(s) to him? Obviously, a physicalistic or mechanistic interpretation of why these stimuli are "the same," or "similar," would be absurd. It is the perception the person has of himself in relation to his environment that gives to widely separated instances their functional similarity.

The second contradiction appears in the notion of *social reinforcements*. The evident fact that expressions of approval, esteem, sym-

pathy, etc., can be as rewarding as material things has been employed by "operant" therapists, such as Patterson (1965, 1969), with consistent success. One may ask, How can social reinforcements work if the individual is not aware of himself and, consequently, cannot value his own image? To reward someone by praising his good qualities, that someone must know that he has qualities or else the praise falls on deaf ears. We can tell our lab rat how much we appreciate his last trick or how much we love him and yet the likelihood of repetition of that act will not increase.

The third contradiction is linked with the common behavior therapy procedure of asking patients to participate in one way or the other in their own reconditioning. Thus, in "assertive training" (Wolpe & Lazarus, 1967, Ch. 4) patients are asked to make a certain type of response in a situation that has previously proved disturbing or threatening. Again, we will be lucky indeed if we succeed in convincing our experimental rat to take a hand in his own conditioning. Only organisms that are aware of themselves, who can realize that they are being conditioned and why this conditioning is taking place, could participate in the process of shaping their own behavior.

WHAT CURES?

The Therapeutic Situation

The various contradictions presented in the above section implicitly contain what is intended to be the main point of this paper. This point can be summarized in two statements:

1. Effective therapy in complex cases only employs behaviorism by analogy. It is used as a helpful but partial heuristic device for understanding pathological disorders and guiding corrective measures. The therapist uses it analogically, "as if" the patient were a simple, semimechanical entity, but this simple ordering frame is de facto transcended both in the understanding of the patient's problems and in the therapeutic procedures applied.

2. The true final goal of therapy in such cases is psychological, and not observable, in nature. The therapist uses manipulations—rewards, punishments, reinforcement schedules, and contingencies—that have, for him and for the patient, meaning only in terms of psycho-

logical states. Similarly, a patient is cured, not when he performs certain mechanical motions, but only when a set of such motions has an underlying, unifying meaning for the patient and for the therapist: when the patient is not afraid of enclosed places, when he acquires self-confidence, when he enjoys sex, when he is less aggressive, when he has less discomfort, or simply when he feels better.

Thus, in a strict sense a therapist does not apply behaviorism to complex disorders. What he applies is his implicit commonsense understanding of persons with their affects, self-perceptions, and outlooks on the world; behaviorism functions as a basic ordering device. However, neither does the therapist interpret in strict behavioristic terms, nor does he cure or assess his results in "objective" terms. This only restates the well-known fact that the essential, or one of the essential, causes of a therapist's effectiveness lies in the depth and accuracy of his perceptions and the appropriateness of his commonsense approach to other humans.

Yet, being basically no different in interpretations and goals from other therapeutic systems, behavior therapy seems to have proved itself more effective in handling some types of mental disturbances. At least, this is what can be concluded from the numerous reports of success with which behavior therapists have filled the journals in the past few years. Accepting the available evidence at face value, we may ask what it is that gives behaviorism this extra margin of efficiency, especially in the case of phobias, sexual inadequacies, social inhibitions, and group maladjustments. Answering, at least partially, this question is the topic of the next section.

The Language of Actions

An evident distinction between behavior therapists and followers of other therapeutic schools is the former's emphasis on doing rather than on talking. The therapist does not merely interpret for the patient or support his ego, he makes the latter act in ways that will positively alter the underlying psychological structure. The therapist acts not as a subtle commentator, but as a skillful manipulator of situations. From the patient's point of view, the perception of his therapist as not merely a talker but as a man who confidently acts, constructs challenging situations, and uses concrete (and presumably expert) procedures, from desensitization to drugs, is in itself positive. As Frank (1961) has shown, a relationship in which the therapist is able to mobilize the patient's expectation of help and give him confidence in the relief of his suffering is, in and of itself, a powerful therapeutic instrument. Somehow it seems that, at least in an action-oriented society such as ours, the man who acts is regarded with more confidence than the man who merely talks. The added confidence of the patient in his therapist thus may itself be beneficial.

More important, however, is the fact that actions in real-life situations drive their intended meaning much more clearly than interpretations and discussions in a protected setting. The conventional therapeutic situation is not "for real" and the patient knows it; what may take a therapist months to convey to the psychological core of his patient may be profoundly impressed on the individual by a casual remark in a real-life interaction. Similarly, his own actions in a crucial existential situation may change the patient's perception of himself, his capabilities, and the world outside much more than analyzing for months all the fine nuances of his mental life. Our own acts and remarks and the feedback we receive from others in everyday life tell us things about ourselves and the world with as much clarity and with far greater power than discussions in an artificially protected environment. The effectiveness of behaviorism thus lies in the directness with which it impresses a new outlook on things and self.

Wolpe and Lazarus (1967, pp. 48–50) present the case of a pathologically timid man whose professional career had stagnated at a very low level despite excellent qualifications. The therapist trained him in a few assertive skills and sent him out into the world. Obviously, nothing could change this person's image of himself more than perceiving that he could act differently and that his new way of acting brought much more rewarding feedbacks from others. Because these new developments changed his self-image significantly, he was able to maintain the gains and generalize them to other areas.

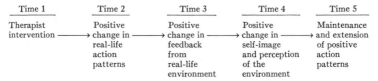

Time 1	Time 2	Time 3	Time 4	Time 5
Therapist intervention ⟶	Positive change in ⟶ real-life action patterns	Positive change in ⟶ feedback from real-life environment	Positive change in ⟶ self-image and perception of the environment	Maintenance and extension of positive action patterns

FIG. 1. The causal sequence of successful behavior therapy.

Another case depicts a sexual maladjustment in a married couple because of premature ejaculation by the husband (Wolpe & Lazarus, 1967, pp. 108–110). Again, training husband and wife in techniques to avoid this problem resulted in complete elimination of the disorder in a matter of weeks. The techniques were clearly designed to define the lovemaking situation as a relaxed, easy one; this new outlook permitted a more satisfactory sexual relationship which in turn changed their perception of sex and increased their sexual confidence even further.

We see, then, that the effectiveness of behavior therapy in action-linked complex disorders is not due to "objectivity" or to its concern with conduct, but to the fact that it affects the person's view of himself and his outlook on the environment in a compelling manner by conveying the message through real-life situations and actions. It is not the newly acquired social skill, but the person's perception of it that cures him; it is not in terms of the motions of the patient and the responding sounds of an alter that therapy is effected and evaluated, but in terms of what they mean psychologically to the patient, his alters, and the therapist.

Real-life actions as language, and the perceptual interpretation of behavioristic cures derived from them, can be represented by a scheme such as that in Figure 1. This interpretation, besides sounding less "forced" to the mind, has the theoretical advantage of accounting for all the problems and contradictions encountered with behavioral interpretations of therapeutic results: the generalization of positive or negative results to other areas of the patient's life, the effectiveness of social reinforcements, the possibility of asking patients to help in their own desensitization or conditioning, the impossibility of escaping psychological interpretations, and the fact that behavior therapy appears to be more effective with action-linked problems (even of the complex variety) than with generalized, nonspecifically behavioral disorders.

Affect

There is an all-important base of affection underlying the actions of effective parents. Such affection is neither limited to, nor conditional on, certain child responses. In the view of Ferenczi (1925), children who are not loved just do not live; and that all-important, unconditional, and often (from a behavioristic viewpoint) "dysfunctional" love is conveyed through an infinity of imperceptible gestures and passing remarks in the child's everyday life. More superficial actions of a rewarding or punishing character can be employed in rational schedules of behavior control, but that underlying substratum of "irrational" affection is a key element of which, I believe, not even the most committed behaviorists will deprive their own children. Through similarly imperceptible actions throughout the extended period of socialization, a successful parent also conveys, even involuntarily, other fundamental components of personality—his positive general outlook on the world, his basic sense of confidence, and the inner integration of desires, attitudes, and self-image. No possible reinforcement schedule could account for the absorption of these general traits by children and the way their own sense of confidence and inner integration reflects that of their parents.

Reading the work of Wolpe, of Patterson, and of other prominent behavior therapists shows that they are very much aware of the importance of affect. Rational behavioristic theory does not explicitly recognize what is evident in the work of these men: that they surround their work with behavioristic tools within a frame of strong emotional support. Klein, Dittman, Parloff, and Gill (1969) have recently observed, with reference to the work

167

of Wolpe and Lazarus, that a crucial characteristic of their clinical approach is the imagination and unorthodoxy with which they adapt behavioristic techniques to each individual's emotional needs. This only restates the point that effective practitioners use behaviorism only as a loose guiding scheme. In practice, even if not in theory, the dangers of taking behaviorism too seriously in the therapeutic situation are recognized. In some passages of their work, Wolpe and Lazarus (1967) have made this point explicit:

Whatever the measures decided upon, it is of first importance to display empathy and establish a trustful relationship. At this point we take leave to chide some fellow behavioral scientists who, espousing notions of rigid behavioral engineering, imagine that one can do without such personal influencing processes [pp. 28–29].

FINAL COMMENT

So far two arguments have been made: first, that literal application of behavioristic theory to complex human disorders is absurd and, if attempted, will yield meaningless results; second, that use of behaviorism in successful therapy in these cases is essentially analogical. Analysis of the current high status of behavior therapy has been made in terms of certain features its best practitioners have introduced or maintained in the therapeutic situation: the action orientation of the therapist, the use of confrontations in everyday life, and the implicit, but real, basis of affective support. This analysis would be incomplete if not accompanied by a view of behavior therapy in the context of the more general cultural setting in which it is taking place. Such is the purpose of this final section.

As contemporary as behaviorism is the point of view of the sociology of knowledge. Above I have already employed Max Weber's (1949) approach to the subject, which stresses the heuristic, tentative, temporary character of every intellectual effort to understand the infinite manifestations of social and physical reality. In these last lines I want to make use of another sociologist of knowledge, Karl Mannheim (1952, 1967) as they apply to our subject.

Unless one still believes in the imminent development of ideas and theories, one will not fail to ask himself what changes in the relationships and roles of men in the modern world, what transformations in the prevailing beliefs and values, have brought about the increasing acceptance of behavioristic theory and of its applications.

Here I may bring in the first concept of Mannheim's argument, "relativism." Relativism simply means that the main intellectual systems and beliefs of an era are conditioned by the different dimensions of the existing socio-economic structure and by the experiences of men enacting roles within that structure. Thus, the assertion of universal, timeless truth is an impossibility. The organization of the society influences decisively men's needs, perceptions, and beliefs, which are in turn projected on their intellectual productions.

Attempting to use empirical research to lend permanent objectivity to intellectual productions is somewhat futile. If a behaviorist presents us with a rat that follows automatically S–R patterns, a gestaltist can lead us to a most insightful Tenerife monkey. The question of why experimental psychologists have stressed one line of study rather than the other cannot be answered on the basis of their relative merits. The needs of men, their points of view, and even their mental disorders follow different culturally and structurally influenced channels. Changes in these underlying elements point today to the growth of one approach and the decadence of another. True, many contemporary experimental techniques and results are likely to be preserved in future times, but again they will be interpreted and applied within a significantly different framework. As different, perhaps, as is that in which we interpret Aristotle's, Thomas', and Machiavelli's discoveries from the ones in which they were originally understood.

Here, we may introduce Mannheim's second concept, what he calls "relationism." The term tells us that the fact that intellectual orientations are largely products of the socioeconomic structure does not mean that they are false; their truth is not universal but they are certainly true, real, and valid for their time and place. The doctrines of behaviorism have grown to be more and more appropriate for the needs and perceptual outlook of modern man. Today behavior therapy may even "fit" the nature of his disorders better than any other therapeutic system.

This should not be confused with an assertion that the structure and functioning of the human mind are radically altered by cultural changes. Such a view would take the impact of culture to an absurd extreme. The above sections have examined the impossibilities of applying behaviorism literally to the treatment of complex problems precisely because of permanent, basic features in the nature of human perceptual processes and behavior. These features do not change, what changes with social structural arrangements is the way men perceive themselves, the traits they impute to their own minds (or no minds), and the manner in which they define their disorders. The structure of human thinking and behavior is not altered, its content is.

Early in the century, Weber (1958, 1965, Part III) envisioned, as Sorokin (1937) was to do a few years later, the main character of the era as an inexorable trend toward rationalism. Scientificism, bureaucratism, and impersonal legalism were aspects of this process. Their predictions were particularly valuable because they included charismatic and irrational explosions and humanistic rebellions—which many are prone to identify with "turning points"—as mere temporary interruptions of a long-term development.

Max Weber (1964) gives us an insight present neither in Marx nor in Mannheim nor Sorokin: The structure of basic socioeconomic relations among men does not lead directly to intellectual orientations; its influence lies in producing differential receptivities to the various intellectual systems. Intellectual prophets and systems have been always present and abound especially in our era, from Freud to Pavlov, from Mead to Sartre, from Marx to Chardin. But the crucial question is, Which ones will fit best the mood of the era? A mood, to repeat, that did not arise at random. Our modern world seems to have been increasingly receptive to the point of view of behaviorism and to its applications.

Behavior therapy's claims to objective success alone do not seem to justify its emergence and rapid acceptance. From the standpoint of the sociology of knowledge, the question is what factors in the surrounding cultural context have determined the preference by those involved, therapists and patients alike, for the image of man conveyed by behavior therapy over competing ones. Its better "fit" into existing social structural arrangements seems a function of its rational simplicity (the person as a consequence of a few logically consistent principles) and its greater claim to scientific status (its principles as derived from experimental research).

The appeal of such characteristics is contingent: If overwhelming to a style of thought imbedded in extreme rationality, it would also be insignificant in other cultural settings. The willingness in modern society to treat and seek cure on the basis of an approach which, at least in theory, denies subjectively obvious thought processes and emotional complexes just because of its scientific claim points to new heights in the process anticipated by Sorokin and Weber.

Today reactions against the unrelenting rationalization of individual life and society are occurring everywhere. Psychology is certainly not the exception. We have already witnessed the enthusiastic emergence of group therapy, existential therapy, and similar schools. Whether they form a true "turning point" or will be remembered as mere interruptions of a dominant trend remains to be seen. Whatever the outcome, it will not take place in isolation from other cultural developments and will certainly not be independent of processes of stability and change in the underlying socioeconomic structure. For reasons too long to be presented here, this writer believes that the "fit" between behaviorism and dominant cultural themes is likely to be maintained, or even improved, in the near future. However, it is important to note a final trend, this one taking place within behaviorism. Essentially, the trend may be labeled "passage from pure to applied science."

As long as theories remain at the pure level, either speculative or observational–experimental, there are no extremes of implausibility they cannot reach. Yet, when they come down to systematic applications in practical tasks, a series of uninterrupted, often unnoticeable, but eventually fundamental, changes take place. The basic features which common sense has persisted in calling "human nature" unfailingly succeed in modifying the theory and, with amazing resilience, remaining the same. This has been true of early Christianity as well as Calvinism, of Fourierism and Marxism, of Freudianism and Behaviorism. The more extreme the theory, the greater the changes that will take place and the more significant its implicit or explicit adaptation to the demands of human realities. Behavioristic theory has caught the mood of the era to the extent of being called into practical action; behavioristic practice has changed, and will continue to change, the theory wherever it does not meet the requirements of its task.

This paper has tried to couple a critique of behaviorism as a theory of human nature with an examination of some of the implicit and often nonobvious modifications already endured by the theory in its passage from abstractions to practice. These modifications and other nonintended consequences of the application of behaviorism to human disorders were seen as major causes in the effectiveness reached by behavior therapy. Like some other observers, I tend to believe these and future therapy-propelled changes to be for the best.

REFERENCES

BACHRACH, A. J. Some applications of operant conditioning to behavior therapy. In J. Wolpe, A. Salter, & J. L. Reyna (Eds.), The conditioning therapies, the challenge of psychotherapy. New York: Holt, Rinehart & Winston, 1965.

BANDURA, A., & WALTERS, R. H. Social learning and personality development. New York: Holt, Rinehart & Winston, 1963.

BANDURA, A., GRUSSEC, J. E., & MENLOVE, F. L. Vicarious extinction of avoidance behavior. Journal of Personality and Social Psychology, 1967, 5, 16–23.

BECKER, H. S. Outsiders, studies in the sociology of deviance. New York: Free Press, 1966.

BIJOU, S. W., & SLOANE, H. N. Therapeutic techniques with children. In I. S. Berg & L. A. Pennington (Eds.), An introduction to clinical psychology. New York: Ronald Press, 1966.

BLAU, P. M. Exchange and power in social life. New York: Wiley, 1966.

CAHOON, D. D. Symptom substitution and the behavior therapies: A reappraisal. Psychological Bulletin, 1968, 69, 149–156.

CARTWRIGHT, D., & ZANDER, A. Group dynamics. Evanston, Ill.: Row, Peterson, 1953.

COFFEY, H. S., & WIENER, L. L. Group treatment of autistic children. Englewood Cliffs, N. J.: Prentice-Hall, 1967.

COOLEY, C. H. Human nature and the social order. New York: Scribners, 1922.

FERENCZI, S., & RANK, O. The development of psychoanalysis. New York: Nervous and Mental Disease Publishing, 1925.

FRANK, J. D. Persuasion and healing. New York: Schocken, 1961.

GELFAND, D. M., & HARTMANN, D. P. Behavior therapy with children: A review and evaluation of research methodology. Psychological Bulletin, 1968, 69, 204–215.

GOLDIAMOND, I. Self-control procedures in personal behavior problems. Psychological Reports, 1965, 17, 851–868.

GROSSBERG, J. M. Behavior therapy: A review. Psychological Bulletin, 1964, 62, 73–88.

HEIDER, F. The psychology of interpersonal relations. New York: Wiley, 1958.

HOMANS, G. C. Social behavior: Its elementary forms. New York: Harcourt, Brace & World, 1961.

KLEIN, M. H., DITTMAN, A. T., PARLOFF, M. B., & GILL, M. M. Behavior therapy: Observations and reflections. Journal of Consulting and Clinical Psychology, 1969, 33, 259–266.

KRASNER, L., & ULLMANN, L. P. (Eds.) Research in behavior modification. New York: Holt, Rinehart & Winston, 1965.

MANNHEIM, K. Essays on the sociology of knowledge. (P. Kecskemeti, Ed.) London: Routledge & Kegan Paul, 1952.

MANNHEIM, K. Ideology and utopia. New York: Harcourt, Brace & World, 1967.

MEAD, G. H. Mind, self, and society. Chicago: University of Chicago Press, 1934.

MILLER, N. E., & DOLLARD, J. Social learning and imitation. New Haven, Conn.: Yale University Press, 1941.

PATTERSON, G. R. An application of conditioning techniques to the control of a hyperactive child. In L. P. Ullmann & L. Krasner (Eds.), Case studies in behavior modification. New York: Holt, Rinehart & Winston, 1965.

PATTERSON, G. R. Behavior techniques based upon social learning: An additional base for developing behavior modification technologies. In C. M. Frank (Ed.), Behavior therapy appraisal and status. New York: McGraw-Hill, 1969.

SALTER, A. The theory and practice of conditioned reflex therapy. In J. Wolpe, A. Salter, & J. L. Reyna (Eds.), The conditioning therapies, the challenge of psychotherapy. New York: Holt, Rinehart & Winston, 1965.

SIDMAN, M. Tactics of scientific research: Evaluating experimental data in psychology. New York: Basic Books, 1960.

SOROKIN, P. A. Social and cultural dynamics. Vol. 2. New York: American Book, 1937.

STRAUGHAN, J. H., POTTER, W. K., & HAMILTON, S. H. The behavioral treatment of an elective mute. Journal of Child Psychology and Psychiatry, 1965, 6, 125–130.

THIBAUT, J. W., & KELLEY, H. H. The social psychology of groups. New York: Wiley, 1966.

WEBER, M. Objectivity in social science. In M. Weber (Ed.), The methodology of the social sciences. (Trans.

by E. A. Shils & H. A. Finch) New York: The Free Press, 1949.

WEBER, M. Bureaucracy. In H. H. Gerth & C. W. Mills (Eds.), *From Max Weber: Essays in sociology.* New York: Oxford University Press, 1958.

WEBER, M. *The sociology of religion.* (Trans. by E. Fischoff) Boston: Beacon Press, 1964.

WEBER, M. *The theory of social and economic organization.* (Trans. by A. M. Henderson & T. Parsons) New York: The Free Press, 1965.

WOLPE, J. The comparative clinical status of conditioning therapies and psychoanalysis. In J. Wolpe, A. Salter, & J. L. Reyna (Eds.), *The conditioning therapies, the challenge of psychotherapy.* New York: Holt, Rinehart & Winston, 1965.

WOLPE, J., & LAZARUS, A. A. *Behavior therapy techniques, a guide to the treatment of neuroses.* New York: Pergamon Press, 1967.

171

There is a basic premise we all accept.....i.e., the importance of a warm, satisfying relationship between the mother and her child during infancy and early childhood. We believe this is necessary in order to foster good personality development. How then do the patterns of disturbed behavior take root? At what point is the child moving into the territory of the abnormal? What physiological, social and cultural forces contribute to the abnormal state? The ensuing chapters touch upon these issues although little resolution occurs.

Bowlby, in "The Nature of the Child's Tie to His Mother", views the extent of this relationship from both maternal aspects (separation and other deviations in maternal care) and child aspects (his role in the attachment to the mother). Bowlby's work is important, even though it is somewhat loose and overgeneralized, because it has stimulated psychologists, psychiatrists and social workers to institute reforms in medical and social agency procedures and to carry out much need research.

Although she appreciates Bowlby's work, Murphy tries to go beyond his frame of reference with, "Some Aspects of the First Relationship". Here, she emphasizes social rather than ethological concepts, describing 'contact with an object', 'communication', 'approach', and 'exploration'. The mother is the facilitator of eventual separateness, the supporter of the undeveloped self, rather than an object for complete reliance or an object in instinctual development.

According to both Bowlby and Murphy it appears that human development is complex and most pervious to averse events at the beginning of life. Searles, too, agrees that early thwarting of ego development is a strong factor in the etiology of schizophrenia; schizophrenic communication, both verbal and non-verbal, reflects the individual's attempt to establish a link with significant others. His paper, "Schizophrenic Communication", provides dramatic clinical examples of the deep understanding which exists in the mother-child relationship.

Beall's paper also brings excellent clinical material to the student. Here the fundamental change in modern neuroses emerges,according to Beall, in that there is no boundary 'personality' and its symptoms. The social and environmental influences are primary, so that the individual not only uses his character as a defense against further symptoms but character may also provide the structure for the development of new symptoms. Contemporary neurotics then, behave in their characteristic ways rather than function as a result of a single, traumatic event. They reflect their own particular histories in interaction with a specific milieu.

Finally, Frieda Fromm-Reichmann's paper on "Loneliness" represents a milestone in the understanding of human behavior. In it are many of her ideas about the various levels of this experience, its relationship to anxiety and to the development of psychosis.

This section, then, goes beyond the concept of instinct in explaining abnormal development. It implies that experiences with significant others, contact with the environment, capacity to be alone, may be the necessary ingredients which must interact with biological needs so that a whole personality may emerge.

THE NATURE OF THE CHILD'S TIE TO HIS MOTHER [1]

By

JOHN BOWLBY

Psycho-Analysts are at one in recognizing the child's first object relations as the foundation stone of his personality: yet there is no agreement on the nature and dynamics of this relationship. No doubt because of its very importance, differences are sharp and feelings often run high. In this paper I am taking it for granted that today we are all agreed on the empirical fact that within 12 months the infant has developed a strong libidinal tie to a mother-figure [2] and that our differences lie in how this has come about. What in fact are the dynamics which promote and underlie this tie?

My plan will be to begin by describing very briefly four alternative views which in greater or less degree of purity are to be found in the psycho-analytic and other psychological literature and to sketch a fifth which I believe may account more adequately for the data. I shall then attempt to assess what have been and are the views advanced in their writings by a number of leading analysts.

Before elaborating the view which I favour it will be necessary to discuss in rather summary fashion, first, some notions, including those of Piaget, regarding the development of perception and cognition and, secondly, some of the more recent theories of instinctual behaviour. Indeed, in writing it I have wondered whether this paper should not have been preceded by three others —one on cognitive development, a second on instinct, and a third on the comparative advantages and disadvantages on the one hand of direct observation of infants and on the other of reconstructions based on the psycho-analysis of older subjects. However, I have not taken this course, and instead am presenting a paper in which, I am acutely aware, despite its length a number of crucial matters are treated both controversially and cursorily.

The four theories regarding the positive aspects of the child's tie which are to be found in the literature can be described briefly. They are: —

(i) The child has a number of physiological needs which must be met, particularly for food and warmth, but no social needs. In so far as a baby becomes interested in and attached to a human figure, especially mother, this is the result of the mother meeting the baby's physiological needs and the baby in due course learning that she is the source of gratification. I propose to call this the theory of *Secondary Drive*, terminology which is derived from Learning Theory. It has also been called the cupboard-love theory of object relations.

(ii) There is in infants an in-built need to relate themselves to a human breast, to suck it and to possess it orally. In due course the infant learns that, attached to the breast, is a mother and so relates to her also. I propose to call this the theory of *Primary Object Sucking*.

(iii) There is in infants an in-built need to be in touch with and to cling to a human being. In this sense there is a need for an object independent of food which is as primary as the need for food and warmth. I propose to call it *Primary Object Clinging*.

(iv) Infants resent their extrusion from the womb and seek to return there. This I shall call the theory of *Primary Return-to-Womb Craving*.

In this nomenclature, it should be noticed, the terms primary and secondary refer to whether the response is regarded as built-in and inherited or acquired through the process of learning; throughout the paper they will be used in this sense. The terms have no reference either to the period of life when the response appears or to the primary and secondary processes postulated by Freud.

---

[1] An abbreviated version of this paper was read before the British Psycho-Analytical Society on 19th June, 1957.
[2] Although in this paper I shall usually refer to mothers and not mother-figures, it is to be understood that in every case I am concerned with the person who mothers the child and to whom he becomes attached rather than to the natural mother.

INTERNATIONAL JOURNAL OF PSYCHOANALYSIS, 1958, 39, pp. 350-371.

The hypothesis which I am advancing incorporates the theories of Primary Object Sucking and Primary Object Clinging. It postulates that the attachment behaviour which we observe so readily in a baby of 12 months old is made up of a number of component instinctual responses which are at first relatively independent of each other. The instinctual responses mature at different times during the first year of life and develop at different rates; they serve the function of binding the child to mother and contribute to the reciprocal dynamic of binding mother to child. Those which I believe we can identify at present are sucking, clinging, and following, in all of which the baby is the principal active partner, and crying and smiling in which his behaviour serves to activate maternal behaviour. (By 'following' I mean the tendency not to let mother out of sight or earshot, which is readily observed in human infants during the latter half of their first year and throughout their second and third years of life and in the young of other species sometimes almost from birth.) Whereas sucking is closely related to food-intake and crying may be so, the remaining three are non-oral in character and not directly related to food. In the normal course of development they become integrated and focused on a single mother figure: as such they form the basis of what I shall call 'attachment behaviour'.

In certain essential features I believe this theory to have much in common with the views advanced by Freud in his *Three Essays on Sexuality*, in which he advanced the view that mature adult sexuality is to be conceived as built up of a number of individual component instincts which in infancy 'are upon the whole disconnected and independent of one another', but which in adult life come to 'form a firm organization directed towards a sexual aim attached to some extraneous sexual object' (*S.E.* VII, pp. 181, 197). Partly because of this similarity, but also because I believe it to be apt, I propose to call it the theory of *Component Instinctual Responses*.

The data which have influenced me in framing this hypothesis are culled less from the analysis of older subjects and more from the direct observation of babies and young children. I have also been deeply influenced by the accounts given me by mothers, both those whose children were prospering and those whose children were causing anxiety. The longer I contemplated the diverse clinical evidence the more dissatisfied I became with the views current in psychoanalytical and psychological literature and the more I found myself turning to the ethologists for help. The extent to which I have drawn on concepts of ethology will be apparent.

Although the hypothesis advanced incorporates the theories of Primary Object Sucking and Primary Object Clinging, it is essentially different from the theory of Secondary Drive. The theory of Primary Return-to-Womb craving is regarded as both redundant and biologically improbable.

It may be worth mentioning that this paper deals neither with ego nor superego. By confining itself to the instinctual roots of the child's tie, it is concerned only with an examination of certain parts of the id.

Review of Literature

The hypotheses advanced during the past fifty years by psycho-analysts are numerous and diverse. As usual, we cannot understand Freud's evolving views without tracing them historically. In reading his works we are at once struck by the fact that it was not until comparatively late that he appreciated the reality of the infant's close tie to his mother, and that it was only in his last ten years that he gave it the significance we should all give it today. You will recall the passage in his paper of 1931 on *Female Sexuality* in which he confesses how elusive everything connected with the first mother-attachment had seemed to him in his analytic work and how he had found it difficult to penetrate behind the strong father-transference which his women patients made to him. What then struck him as new, he tells us, was the 'equally great attachment to the mother' which precedes the dependence on the father and the length of time this attachment lasts (*C.P.*, V, pp. 254–255). Freud's failure to give due weight to this early tie until the last phase of his work has had (and I believe is still having) far-reaching effects on psychoanalytic theorizing. His first serious discussion of the matter was not until 1926 (28).

Realization of the tremendous importance of this first attachment seems to have been reached by Freud in a number of steps. Up to the early twenties he had held the view that, apart from a fleeting moment during which the oral component has the mother's breast as an object, all the components of libido start by being auto-erotic. This view, stemming from the *Three Essays on Sexuality*, is succinctly expressed in his encyclopædia article titled *Psycho-Analysis*, written as late as 1922. 'In the first instance the oral component instinct finds satisfaction by attaching itself to the sating of the desire for nourishment; and its object is the mother's breast. It then detaches itself, becomes independent and at the same time *auto-erotic*, that is, it finds an object in the child's own body. Others of the component instincts also start by being auto-erotic and are not until later directed on to an external object.' Between the ages of two and five years 'a convergence of sexual impulses occurs' the object of which is the *parent of the opposite sex* (*S.E.*, XVIII, p. 245). In this account the phase we all now recognize when in both sexes there is a strong tie to the mother is conspicuous by its absence. Indeed, in the *Interpretation of Dreams* there is a passage in which he expresses the view that 'When people are absent, children do not miss them with any great intensity, [which] many mothers have learnt to their sorrow', a passage that, a little surprisingly, remains unamended and unqualified throughout later editions (*S.E.*, IV, p. 255).

Nevertheless there are in various of Freud's earlier writings, statements suggesting that the infant is not so exclusively auto-erotic as his principal formulations assert. Thus in the *Three Essays*, after referring to the child sucking at his mother's breast as the prototype of later love relations, he writes, ' But even after sexual activity has become detached from the taking of nourishment, an important part of this first and most significant of all sexual relations is left over . . . All through the period of latency children learn to feel for other people who help them in their helplessness and satisfy their needs, a love which is on the model of, and a continuation of, their relation as sucklings to their nursing mother . . . A child's intercourse with anyone responsible for his care affords him an unending source of sexual excitation and satisfaction from his erotogenic zones ', and he proceeds to praise the mother who ' by stroking, kissing and rocking him is fulfilling her task in teaching the child to love ' (*S.E.*, VII, pp. 222–223). We find a similar passage in his paper on Narcissism (1915) where he refers to the persons who have to do with the feeding, care and protection of the child becoming his earliest sexual objects. This type of object choice he terms the ' anaclitic ', because in this phase the sexual instincts find their satisfaction through ' leaning up against' the self-preservative instincts (*S.E.*, XIV, p. 87).

By 1920, we know, Freud had observed that an infant of 18 months dislikes being left alone (*Beyond the Pleasure Principle, S.E.*, XVIII, pp. 14–16), and six years later we find him discussing why the infant desires the presence of his mother and fears losing her (*Inhibitions, Symptoms and Anxiety*, pp. 105–107). There remains, however, a disinclination to postulate any primary socially-oriented drive. Instead, he interprets the infant's anxiety that he may lose his mother as due to the danger that his body needs will not be gratified and that this will lead to ' a growing tension due to need, against which it [the baby] is helpless.' The real essence of the danger, he tells us, is the

' economic disturbance caused by an accumulation of amounts of stimulation which require to be disposed of.' That the infant fears the loss of his mother is, therefore, to be understood as a displacement: ' When the child has found out by experience that an external, perceptible object can put an end to the dangerous situation which is reminiscent of birth, the nature of the danger it fears is displaced from the economic situation on to the condition which determined that situation, viz. the loss of the object ' (pp. 106–108).

By 1931, as already remarked, the full significance of the phase during which the libidinal object is the mother has been grasped. However, in the paper on *Female Sexuality* no account is attempted of how this relationship develops. In his final synthesis we find a pregnant highly condensed paragraph (*An Outline of Psycho-Analysis*, 1938, p. 56). One notes at once the dramatic and colourful terms in which the relationship to the mother is described, terms which, so far as I know, are not found elsewhere in his writings on the subject. He describes it as ' unique, without parallel, laid down unalterably for a whole lifetime, as the first and strongest love-object and as the prototype of all later love relations—for both sexes.'

In delineating the dynamics of this newly evaluated relationship, Freud begins, as formerly, by telling us that ' a child's first erotic object is the mother's breast which feeds him ' and that ' love in its beginning attaches itself to the satisfaction of the need for food.' He proceeds to indicate that, because the child ' makes no distinction between the breast and his own body ', part of the ' original narcissistic cathexis ' is carried over on to the breast as an outside object. ' This first object subsequently becomes completed into the whole person of the child's mother who not only feeds him but looks after him and thus arouses in him many other physical sensations pleasant and unpleasant. By her care of the child's body she becomes his first seducer. In these two relations lies the root of a mother's importance.' This passage refers to the same dynamic that in his early writings he had attributed to the period of latency but which since the 'twenties he had realized to be active in a much earlier phase of life.

Had he said no more we should have concluded with confidence that to the end of his life Freud espoused the theory of Secondary Drive ; (although we should have been wise to note that he held it in a special form ; in Freud's view the mother becomes important not only because she gratifies physiological needs but also because in so doing she stimulates the infant's erotogenic zones). These, however, are not his last words on the subject. Almost it might seem as an afterthought, at the end of this significant paragraph he expresses an opinion which differs radically from any previously expressed by him and which seems to contradict much of the earlier explanation. 'The phylogenetic foundation', he writes, 'has so much the upper hand in all this over accidental experience that it makes no difference whether a child has really sucked at the breast or has been brought up on the bottle and never enjoyed the tenderness of a mother's care. His development takes the same path in both cases.' Our most conservative conclusion is that Freud was not wholly satisfied with his earlier accounts. A more radical one is that, towards the end of his life and imbued with a newly-found but vivid appreciation of the central importance of the child's tie to his mother, Freud was not only moving away from the theory of Secondary Drive but developing the notion that special drives built into the infant in the course of evolution underlie this first and unique love relationship.

I confess I would like to believe that this was so. My speculations are encouraged by a passage in his *Three Essays* which, so far as I know, he never expanded. In discussing the activity of thumb-sucking and the independence of the sucking from the taking of nourishment Freud proceeds 'In this connection a grasping-instinct may appear and may manifest itself as a simultaneous rhythmic tugging at the lobes of the ears or a catching hold of some' part of another person (as a rule the ear) for the same purpose.' (*S.E.*, VII, pp. 179–180). Plainly here is a reference to a part-instinct even more independent than sucking of the taking of nourishment. It is a theme to which the Hungarian school has given particular attention and to which I shall be referring more fully when expounding my own views.

Whether or not we are right in thinking that in his later years Freud was in process of developing new ideas, it is evident that at most they were still no more than germinal when he died. That members of the Viennese school should have been little influenced by them is hardly surprising. In fact, as is well-known, Anna Freud and those who trained in Vienna before the war have continued to favour the theory of Secondary Drive. In a number of publications in the past ten years she has expressed the view with welcome clarity. 'The relationship to the mother', she writes in a recent publication (1954), 'is not the infant's first relationship to the environment. What precedes it is an earlier phase in which not the object world but the body needs and their satisfaction or frustration play the decisive part . . . In the struggle for satisfaction of the vital needs and drives the object merely serves the purpose of wish fulfilment, its status being no more than that of a means to an end, a " convenience ". The libidinal cathexis at this time is shown to be attached, not to the image of the object, but to the blissful experience of satisfaction and relief.' In an earlier paper (1949) she describes how in the first year of life 'the all-important step from primary narcissism

to object-love should be taking place, a transition which happens in small stages.' In accounting for this transition she follows Sigmund Freud in regarding the mother as a 'seducer'. 'By means of the constantly repeated experience of satisfaction of the first body needs', she writes, 'the libidinal interest of the child is lured away from exclusive concentration on the happenings in his own body and directed towards those persons in the outside world (the mother or mother substitute) who are responsible for providing satisfaction.' In this same article, which is concerned with the origin of certain forms of social maladjustment, she describes how, when for any reason the mother fails to be a steady source of satisfaction, 'the transformation of narcissistic libido into object-libido is carried out inadequately' and how as a result auto-erotism persists and the destructive urges remain isolated.

Although in her theoretical expositions Anna Freud seems unequivocal in her endorsement of the theory of Secondary Drive, there are passages in her clinical writings which hint at something different. The accounts which she and Dorothy Burlingham have given of the children in the Hampstead Nurseries include one of the few descriptions of the development of the child's tie which have been written by analysts on the basis of empirical observations (11). Two of their conclusions I wish to single out because I believe them to have been given too little weight in analytic theory. The first is their insistence that it is not until the second year of life that 'the personal attachment of the child to his mother . . . comes to its full development' (p. 50). The second is that 'children will cling even to mothers who are continually cross and sometimes cruel to them. The attachment of the small child to his mother seems to a large degree independent of her personal qualities' (p. 47). Indeed, their observations make it plain that the potential for attachment is ever-present in the child and ready, when starved of an object, to fix on almost anyone. In the nursery setting, they tell us, 'the emotions which [the child] would normally direct towards its parents . . . remain undeveloped and unsatisfied, but . . . are latent in [him] and ready to leap into action the moment the slightest opportunity for attachment is offered' (12) (p. 43). The extent to which the attachment seems to be independent of what is received, which is very plain in these records (e.g. (12) p. 52) and which will be a main theme of this paper, emerges again in another report of the behaviour of young children for which Anna Freud is jointly responsible (26). This describes the behaviour of six children from a concentration camp, aged between three and four years, whose only persisting company in life had been each other. The authors emphasize that 'the children's positive feelings were centered exclusively in their own group . . . they cared greatly for each other and not at all for anybody or anything else.' Was this, we may wonder, a result of one infant being instrumental in meeting the physiological needs of others? It is observations such as these that led Dorothy Burlingham and Anna Freud to describe the child's need ' for early attachment to the mother ' as an ' *important instinctual need* ' (12) (p. 22, my italics)—a formulation which hardly seems compatible with the theory of Secondary Drive advanced elsewhere.

A discrepancy between formulations springing direct from empirical observations and those made in the course of abstract discussion seems almost to be the rule in the case of analysts with first-hand experience of infancy—for example Melanie Klein, Margaret Ribble, Therese Benedek, and Rene Spitz. In each case they have observed non-oral social interaction between mother and infant and, in describing it, have used terms suggesting a primary social bond. When they come to theorizing about it, however, each seems to feel a compulsion to give primacy to needs for food and warmth and to suppose that social interaction develops only secondarily and as a result of instrumental learning.

Melanie Klein's basic theoretical concepts have their origin in ideas current before 1926. Although these basic concepts have persisted in her theorizing largely unmodified, first-hand observations of infants, made later, have resulted in a number of more empirically oriented concepts, often divergent in character, being juxtaposed.

In contrast to Anna Freud, Melanie Klein has for some years been an advocate of the view that there is more in the infant's relation to his mother than the satisfaction of physiological needs. Yet there is a very pronounced tendency for her theoretical formulations to be dominated by the inter-related themes of food, orality and the mother's breast. As regards food, she writes in the second of two chapters in which she discusses the matter (41) (chapters 6 and 7): ' The infant's relations to his first object, the mother, and towards food are bound up with each other from the beginning. Therefore the study of fundamental patterns of attitudes towards food seems the best approach to the understanding of young infants ' (p. 238). She elaborates this in a number of passages where she relates particular attitudes toward food to particular forms taken later by psychic organization and development.

This concentration on orality and food, which has been such a conspicuous feature of Melanie Klein's theories since her early paper on *Infant Analysis* (1926), seems in large measure to be due to the influence exerted on her thinking by Abraham's important papers on *The First Pregenital Stage* (1916) and *The Development of the Libido* (1924). In these works, as is well-known, Abraham gave special attention to orality. Nevertheless, his papers date from the period before the signifi-

cance of the child's tie had been recognized and their basic concepts are little different from those of Freud's 1922 encyclopædia article (see p. 245). Looking back at Melanie Klein's paper, it seems, the importance of the child's attachment is missed and only the oral component perceived. As a result, I believe, its influence has led to excessive emphasis being placed on orality and the first year of life and, as a consequence, to an underestimation of other aspects of the tie and events of the second and third years.

Turning again to the 1952 publication of Melanie Klein and her group, it is in keeping with her oral theory that we find her advancing the view that ' the relation to the loved and hated—good and bad—breast is the infant's first object-relation ' (p. 209) and that ' the close bond between a young infant and his mother centres on the relation to her breast ' (p. 243). Indeed, in an important note she postulates an inborn striving after the mother's breast: ' the newborn infant unconsciously feels that an object of unique goodness exists, from which a maximal gratification could be obtained and that this object is the mother's breast ' (p. 265). In discussing this notion she quotes approvingly Freud's statement regarding the significance of a phylogenetic foundation for early object relations which, it has already been observed, suggests that at the end of his life Freud was moving towards a formulation different from the theory of Secondary Drive which he had hitherto espoused.

Yet, despite this preoccupation in her theory with food, orality, and the mother's breast, Melanie Klein reports observations of infants from which she herself draws a different conclusion. Thus in one of the same chapters from which I have been quoting we find the following passage: ' Some children who, although good feeders, are not markedly greedy, show unmistakable signs of love and of a developing interest in the mother at a very early stage—an attitude which contains some of the essential elements of an object-relation. I have seen babies as young as three weeks interrupt their sucking for a short time to play with the mother's breast or to look towards her face. I have also observed that young infants—even as early as in the second month—would in wakeful periods after feeding lie on the mother's lap, look up at her, listen to her voice and respond to it by their facial expression ; it was like a loving conversation between mother and baby. Such behaviour implies that gratification is *as much related to the object which gives the food as to the food itself* ' (p. 239, my italics).

Up to this point in Melanie Klein's writings (1952) the overall impression given is that, although she believes that the infant's first relation to the mother comprises more than one component instinct, she believes the oral component plays an overwhelmingly dominant part. As a result of this and her tendency to equate good breast and good mother, many of her formulations and those of her colleagues have given the impression of subscribing to the theory I have termed Primary Object Sucking. Nonetheless, perhaps the most accurate description is to say that she has oscillated between a foreground exposition of a theory of Primary Object Sucking and a variety of background references to a broader theory to which she had not then given systematic attention.[3]

In the opening pages of her most recent publication (Klein, 1957, pp. 3–5) we find the same oscillation. On the one hand is emphasis on the primacy of the breast and orality: there are references to ' the primal good object, the mother's breast ', to ' the dominance of oral impulses ', and to the feeling of security in relation to the mother being dependent ' on the infant's capacity to cathect sufficiently the breast or its symbolic representative the bottle. . . .' On the other hand the belief is expressed that there is from the first an awareness in the infant of something more: ' there is in his mind ', writes Melanie Klein, ' already some indefinite connection between the breast and other parts and aspects of the mother. I would not assume that the breast is to him merely a physical object. The whole of his instinctual desires and his unconscious phantasies imbue the breast with qualities going far beyond the actual nourishment it affords.'

Whereas, formerly, Melanie Klein had said little about the nature of this ' something more ', in her new publication she has ventured an hypothesis to explain it. She has in fact drawn upon the theory of Primary Return-to-Womb Craving. ' This mental and physical closeness to the gratifying breast ', she suggests, ' in some measure restores, if things go well, the lost prenatal unity with the mother and the feeling of security which goes with it . . . It may well be that his having formed part of the mother in the pre-natal state contributes to the infant's innate feeling that there exists outside him something that will give him all he needs and desires.' Later she refers to ' the universal longing for the pre-natal state ' as though it were something self-evident. Thus Melanie Klein's most recent hypothesis regarding the dynamic underlying the child's tie seems to be that it combines a primary oral need to suck a breast with a primary craving to return to the pre-natal state of unity with the mother.

In advancing the theory of Primary Return-to-Womb Craving to account for a tie which she believes to be more broadly founded than on orality alone, Melanie Klein has resuscitated a theory which has led an egregious existence in psycho-analysis for many years. So far as I know, it was advocated first in 1913 by Ferenczi in his *Stages in the Development of the Sense of Reality*. It is interesting to note, however, that Ferenczi did not advance the theory to account for the vigour with which the infant relates to his mother, but as an explanation of the fantasy of omnipotence.[4] When during its long history it was first borrowed by an analyst to account for the child's attachment to his mother I do not know, but we find it in Fairbairn (1943).[5] In any case, despite its place of origin, it does not seem to have played a major part in the thinking of the Hungarian school.

No doubt inspired by Ferenczi's interest in the mother-child relation, members of the Budapest Society gave much thought to our problem and during the nineteen-thirties published a number of papers about it. Hermann (1933, 1936) had noted that infant apes spend the early weeks of their lives clinging to their mother's bodies and also that there are many clasping and grasping movements to be seen in human babies, especially when they are sucking or feel threatened. As a result of these observations, and resuscitating the early and virtually discarded idea from Freud's *Three Essays,* he postulated as a primary component instinct in human beings an instinct to cling. It appears, however, that Hermann was reluctant to regard this as an object-relationship, so that it would probably be incorrect to say that he subscribed to the theory of Primary Object Clinging (see discussion in Appendix A).

Michael and Alice Balint (5, 4) express their indebtedness to Hermann, but go further than he does. Starting from Ferenczi's concept of passive object love, both reject the theory of primary narcissism and insist that from the first there is a primitive object relationship. Influenced, however, as they were by Hermann's work as well as by their own observations, they came to conceive of the infant as active in the relationship. Alice Balint in the appendix to her paper gives a vivid description of the development of their thought:

. . . The starting point of these ideas is Ferenczi's well-known concept of ' *passive object love* '. In

<hr />

[3] Following the discussion of this paper Mrs. Klein drew my attention to the rôle which she attributes to anal and urethral impulses in the infant's relation to his mother. Although in her writings it is the hostile components of those impulses which seem to be most emphasized (an aspect of the relationship which lies outside the scope of this paper), it is evident that she also attaches importance to the pleasure in mastery and possession which are commonly attributed to anal erotism.

[4] Ferenczi suggests that the foetus ' must get from his existence the impression that he is in fact omnipo-

tent ' and that the child and the obsessional patient, when demanding that their wishes be at once fulfilled, are demanding no more than a return to those ' good old days ' when they occupied the womb.

[5] Freud (1926) is struck by the functional similarity of mother's womb and mother's arms as modes of infant care (p. 109), which is a different matter. However, in postulating that the need for companionship in agoraphobia is due to ' a temporal regression to infancy, or, in extreme cases, to pre-natal days ' (p. 89), he comes near to postulating a return-to-womb craving.

my paper on this subject—printed in the Ferenczi memorial volume—I used only this term. Later, under the influence of M. Balint's ideas on the 'new beginning' in which he emphasizes the active features in early infantile behaviour, as well as partly under that of I. Hermann's work on the instinct to cling—I thought that the term *passive* was not a suitable description of a relation in which such markedly *active* tendencies as the instinct to cling play a paramount rôle. Since then I have used—as in the present paper—in place of ' *passive object love* ' mainly the terms ' *archaic* ' or ' *primary object relation* ' (*object love*).

In describing this primitive but active object relationship, the Balints lay emphasis on two points. The first is the egoism of the relationship. After rejecting other notions Alice Balint concludes: ' We come nearest to it with the conception of egoism. It is in fact an archaic, egotistic way of loving, originally directed exclusively at the mother ', its main characteristic being a lack of any appreciation of the mother's own interests. The second point, though more controversial, is more germane to the present thesis. It is that the relationship is wholly independent of the erotogenic zones. ' This form of object relation ', writes M. Balint (1937), ' is not linked to any of the erotogenic zones ; it is not oral, oral-sucking, anal, genital, etc., love, but is something on its own. . . .'

Reading these papers it seems clear that Primary Object Clinging is regarded as a major component in the Balints' conception of Primary Object Love but that, just as Melanie Klein's earlier views implied some dynamic beyond Primary Object Sucking, the views of the Balints go beyond Primary Object Clinging. Nevertheless in their work there is little discussion of the nature of other components.

It is curious, and to me disappointing, that in publications by British and American analysts during the past decade there has been so little interest shown in the ideas advanced in Budapest. One of the very few references to them is to be found in a footnote by Paula Heiman (41) (p. 139). There, speaking in the name of the four authors of the book, she expresses agreement with Michael Balint's detailed critique of the theory of primary narcissism. She also records briefly that, with regard to the nature of the destructive impulses and the rôle of introjection and projection in early infancy, there is some disagreement. She fails, however, to note that, whilst the Hungarian group lays special emphasis on the non-oral components in the early object relation, the Kleinian group sees orality as dominating the relationship. The divergence plainly requires more attention than it has yet been given. Furthermore, it must be emphasized, in so far as Melanie Klein has now dealt more fully with the non-oral component and has explained it as stemming from a primary craving to return to the womb, she is advocating a theory radically different from that of the Hungarians.

Winnicott's conception of the relationship seems always to have been far less dominated by food and orality than Melanie Klein's. Thus in a paper dated 1948 he lists a number of things about a mother which stand out as vitally important. His first two items refer to the fact that ' she exists, continues to exist . . . is *there* to be sensed in all possible ways ' and that ' she loves in a physical way, provides contact, a body temperature, movement and quiet according to the baby's needs.' That she also provides food is placed fourth. In an important note to his paper on *Transitional Objects* (1953) he discusses his usage of the term ' mother's breast '. ' I include the whole technique of mothering. When it is said that the first object is the breast, the word ' breast ' is used, I believe, to stand for the technique of mothering as well as for the actual flesh. It is not impossible for a mother to be a good enough mother (in my way of putting it) with a bottle for the actual feeding.' Food and mother's breast, therefore, are not in Winnicott's view central in the technique of mothering. Yet it is not clear how Winnicott conceptualizes the dynamic internal to the infant. In the note quoted above he hazards the view that ' If this wide meaning of the word " breast " is kept in mind, and maternal technique is seen to be included in the total meaning of the term, then there is a bridge forming between the wording of Melanie Klein's statement of early history and that of Anna Freud. The only difference left is one of dates.' In this comment, it seems to me, Winnicott has failed to distinguish between a theory invoking primary instinctual responses and a theory of secondary drive.

Margaret Ribble (1944) also puts much emphasis on non-oral components, emphasizing that there is in infants an ' innate need for contact with the mother ', which she likens to that of hunger for food. This need, however, she relates very closely to the satisfactory functioning of physiological processes, such as breathing and circulation, and seems hardly to conceive as constituting a social bond in its own right. Indeed, in a separate section she discusses the development of the child's emotional attachment to his mother and appears to adopt a theory of Secondary Drive: ' This attachment or, to use the psycho-analytic term, cathexis for the mother grows gradually out of the satisfactions it derives from her.' Thus, like Klein and Winnicott, Ribble makes no reference either to a primary need to cling, or to a primary need to follow.

Like others who had their initial training in Budapest, Therese Benedek is also keenly alive to the emotional bond between mother and child, and has coined the term ' emotional symbiosis ' to

181

describe it. She refers to 'the need to be smiled at, picked up, talked to, etc.' (1956, p. 403) and recognizes, further, that a crying fit may be caused, not 'by a commanding physiologic need such as hunger or pain, but by the thwarting of an attempt at emotional (psychologic) communication and satisfaction' (p. 399): Nevertheless, as she herself admits, she finds this fact very difficult to understand. The upshot is that her theory is phrased in terms of what she describes as 'the dominant tendency of childhood—the need to be fed' (p. 392)—an outcome which seems alien to her clinical descriptions. As a prisoner of orality theory she even postulates that the mother's bond to her child, about which she writes so insightfully, is also oral. Advancing the view (I believe rightly) that when a woman becomes a mother many of the same forces which bound her, as an infant, to her own mother are mobilized afresh to bind her, as a mother, to her infant, she cannot escape formulating the resulting relationship as reciprocally oral: 'the post-partum symbiosis is oral, alimentary for both infant and mother' (p. 398).

Erikson, Sullivan and Spitz are similarly trapped —an expression intended to convey that I believe their clinical appreciation of the facts to be nearer the truth than their conventional theorizing. Erikson (1950), like Melanie Klein concerned to trace the origin of ambivalence in infancy, conceives it largely in terms of sucking and biting. Basic trust, on which he rightly places so much emphasis, has its origins, he believes, in orality: 'The oral stages, then, form in the infant the springs of the *basic sense of trust*' (p. 75). Erikson, however, never formulates a Secondary Drive theory and seems at times to be assuming a theory of Primary Object Sucking.

Sullivan (1953), on the other hand, is very explicit about the primacy of physiological needs: 'I regard the first needs that fall into the genus of the need for tenderness [from the mother] as needs arising in the necessary communal existence of the infant and the physico-chemical universe. [They] are direct derivatives of disequilibrium arising in the physico-chemical universe inside and outside the infant' (p. 40). Later, he thinks, infants may develop a primary need for contact and human relationships. The curious thing, however, is that he (or his editor) is so uncertain about it that discussion of this crucial issue is relegated to a footnote:

'The only nonphysicochemically induced need that is probably somewhere near demonstrable during very early infancy and which certainly becomes very conspicuous not much later than this, is the *need for contact* . . . The very young seem to have very genuine beginnings of purely human or interpersonal needs in the sense of requiring manipulations by and peripheral contact with the living, such as lying-against, and so on. But, when I talk as I do now of the first weeks

and months of infancy, this can only be a speculation. . . .' (p. 40 note).

Spitz is also keenly alive to the need for contact and laments that 'throughout the Western world skin contact between mother and child has been progressively and artifically reduced in an attempted denial of the importance of mother-child relations' (1957, p. 124). Nevertheless, in his theorizing he does not give it primacy and, instead, throughout adheres to Freud's formulation of primary narcissism and the theory of Secondary Drive. True object relations, he holds, stem from the need for food: 'The anaclitic choice of object is determined by the original dependence of the infant on the person who feeds, protects and mothers him . . . the drive unfolds anaclitically, that is by leaning onto a need for gratification essential for survival. The need which is gratified is the need for food' (1957, p. 83).

As we noted when describing Michael Balint's position, Freud's theory of primary narcissism has not gone unchallenged. Another who has given it much critical attention and who, also like Balint, centres his psycho-pathology on the child's relation to his mother is Fairbairn (1941, 1943). Fairbairn pictures infants partly in terms of a primary identification with the object (an idea mooted by Freud in his Group Psychology (1921, *S.E.,* XVIII, p. 105) but never developed by him) and partly in terms of primary drives oriented towards social objects. In trying to explain the genesis of primary identification, Fairbairn invokes the theory of Primary Return-to-Womb Craving. In his concern with primary object seeking drives, on the other hand, he emphasizes the infant's real dependence on the mother and stresses orality. His belief that 'infantile dependence is equivalent to oral dependence' (1952, p. 47) underlies much of his theorizing and leads him, like Melanie Klein, to infer that the crucial events in personality development take place in the first year of life. He admits, however, that this conclusion is not consistent with his clinical experience which is that schizoid and depressive psychopathology occur 'when object-relationships continue to be unsatisfactory during the succeeding years of early childhood.' To explain this he is forced to lean heavily on a theory of 'regressive reactivation' (p. 55). In the most recent of his papers (1956), however, he appears to have changed his ground in some measure and to have moved nearer the position advanced in this paper: he protests against the 'assumption that man is not by nature a social animal' and refers to ethology as demonstrating that object seeking behaviour is exhibited from birth.

It happens that one of the most systematic presentations of this last view was advanced in *The Origins of Love and Hate* (1935), the work of a British psychotherapist, Suttie, who, although much influenced by psycho-analysis, was not himself an analyst. Conceived and written at the same

182

time as the work of the Hungarian school, Suttie and others of the pre-war Tavistock group postulated that 'the child is born with a mind and instincts *adapted to infancy*', of which 'a simple attachment-to-mother' is predominant. This need for mother is conceived as a primary 'need for company' and a dislike of isolation, and is independent of the bodily needs which mother commonly satisfies. Had Suttie linked his ideas to those which Freud was advancing from 1926 onwards they might have been given attention in analytical circles and have led to a valuable development in theory. As it was, he couples them with a polemical attack on Freud which inevitably led to resentment of his book and neglect of his ideas.

In this paper I shall deal rather briefly with the views of others who are not psycho-analysts. First we may note that non-analysts are as divided in their views on this crucial issue as analysts. On the one hand is the powerful school of Learning Theorists, adherents of which have long made the assumption that the only primary drives are those related to the physiological needs and that, in so far as an animal becomes interested in members of its own species, it is a result of a Secondary Drive. Although they claim legitimately that such assumptions fulfil the scientific demand for parsimony, it cannot be said that their explanations, in terms of instrumental response, social stimuli as conditioned or secondary reinforcers, and conditioned drives, are anything but complex and inelegant. One of them indeed (29), admits that Learning Theory has been elaborated to account for phenomena which are relatively simpler and has, therefore, still to prove its relevance to our problem.

Holding an opposite view are the ethologists, who have never assumed that the only primary drives were those related to physiological needs. On the contrary, all their work has been based on the hypothesis that in animals there are many in-built responses which are comparatively independent of physiological needs and responses, the function of which is to promote social interaction between members of a species. In discussing the relation of young to parents in lower species, most if not all ethologists regard the theory of Secondary Drive as inadequate, and, though they are reluctant to commit themselves as 'regards a species they have not studied systematically, it is probably fair to say that no ethologist would expect the human infant's tie to his mother to be wholly explicable in terms of Learning Theory and Secondary Drive.

Empirical research workers such as Shirley (1933),, Charlotte Bühler (1933), and Griffiths (1954), tend to side with this view. Each of them has been struck by the specificity of the responses babies show to human beings in the first weeks of life: they respond to the human face and voice

in a way different to the way they respond to all other stimuli. Already in the first week, Shirley observed, some babies soberly watch an adult's face; by five weeks half of her sample of twenty odd babies were quietened by social interaction, such as being picked up, talked to, or caressed. It was similar observations which led to Bühler to advance the view that there was something in the human face and voice which had a peculiar-significance for the infant. Amongst her many published enquiries are those of her associates, Hetzer and Tudor-Hart (1927), who made a systematic study of the various responses which babies show to sounds of different kinds. As early as the third week of life the human voice was observed to evoke responses, for example sucking and expressions indicative of pleasure, which were unlike those evoked by any other sound. Griffiths has used some of these very early social responses in constructing her normative scale.

Plainly such observations do not rule out the possibility that the baby's early interest in human face and voice are the result of his learning that they are associated with the satisfaction of physiological needs: they cannot be taken to prove that there is an in-built interest. Nonetheless they support the contention of Melanie Klein and other analysts that even in the earliest weeks there is some special interest in human beings as such and at least raise the question whether learning accounts for all of it.

A review of the many formulations which have been advanced shows them to fall into three main classes. On the one hand are those who commit themselves clearly to the Learning Theory standpoint. Next are the many who, whilst plainly dissatisfied with the theory of Secondary Drive, nonetheless find it difficult to put anything very explicit or plausible in its place. Finally, at the other end of the spectrum, are those, notably the Hungarian school of psycho-analysis and the ethologists, who postulate primary drives of clinging and/or following which are capable potentially of tying infant to mother. It is this third view which I believe will prove the right one.

Perceptual and cognitive aspects of the child's tie

Yet, even though there is good evidence that the human face and voice hold some special interest for the infant even in his earliest weeks, it is probably mistaken to suppose that at this age he entertains anything which remotely resembles the concept of 'human being'. This raises the question of the perceptual and cognitive aspects of the child's tie. Although this is as difficult and controversial a matter as is the dynamic aspect, I do not propose to deal with it in the same degree of detail. Whilst refering briefly to some of the current views, my main purpose in this section will be to describe my own views as a necessary preliminary to giving detailed attention to the problem of the dynamics of the relationship, which is the main theme of this paper.

All who have given thought to the subject seem agreed that it is only through a series of stages that the infant progresses to a state where he can order his cognitive world in terms of the concepts ' human being' and ' mother'. There is wide agreement, too, that the earliest phase of all is probably one in which there is a total lack of differentiation between subject and object and that subsequently the infant passes through a phase during which he relates to part-objects, namely parts only of a complete human object. Beyond this, however, there is much difference of opinion.

Amongst analysts who have given special attention to these problems are Alice Balint, Melanie Klein, Winnicott, and Spitz.

A distinction to which several have drawn attention is between a phase of development when there is no concern for the object's own interests and a later one when there is. Thus Alice Balint (1939), Melanie Klein (1948), and Winnicott (1955), have all postulated a phase during which a primitive form of object relation is present without there being concern for the object. Alice Balint termed it a phase of ' primary archaic object relation', for Melanie Klein it is the phase which precedes the attainment of the depressive position, and Winnicott characterizes it as one of ' pre-ruth'.

Spitz (1954) has introduced another distinction. On the one hand, there is a later phase when the infant enjoys a relationship with a libidinal object; in his opinion the essential qualities of such an object are that it is conceived as anticipating needs, protecting and satisfying, and continuing to do so despite its changing exterior attributes. On the other there is an earlier phase, revealed by Spitz's own experiments on the smiling response, in which it appears that what the infant is responding to is merely a gestalt signal, a superficial attribute of an object and not a conceptualized object at all. Here the distinction lies between the older infant who is responding to stimuli which he interprets as coming from a world of permanent objects existing in time and space and the younger infant who responds only to the stimulus presented in the here and now and without reference to any complex cognitive

world. Referring to his work on the smiling response Spitz writes: ' This research led me to the conclusion that we are not justified in saying that perception of the human smile at three months is a real object relation. I have established that what the baby sees is not a partner, is not a person, is not an object but solely a signal.' Nonetheless Spitz holds that, in so far as the gestalt signal belongs to and is derived from the face of the mother, it has a place in the ' genealogy' of the libidinal object. For this reason he terms the response a pre-object relation (*une rélation pré-objectale*) and the signal a precursor of the object (pp. 494–496). In thus qualifying his terminology for the earliest form of object relation, Spitz is following the lead given by Alice Balint who, in her term ' primary archaic object relation', was plainly groping after a similar concept.

He is also on a track which Piaget has pioneered in his two important volumes on early cognitive development (44, 45). Basing his theories on the results of innumerable little experiments conducted on his own three children during their first 18 months of life, Piaget has developed a detailed account of how we may suppose the human infant gradually constructs his conceptual world. In particular he has given attention to how the infant progresses from a phase in which he appears to be influenced only by stimuli, familiar or unfamiliar, acting in the here and now, to a phase where he appears to conceptualize the world as one of permanent objects existing in time and space and interacting with each other, of which he is one. Like Freud and others, Piaget supposes that the initial phase is one in which there is no differentiation between subject and object. In the next phases, he suggests, although the infant is certainly responding to objects in the external world there is no reason to suppose that he is organizing his impressions of them in terms of permanently existing objects. Instead, he suggests, the infant is witness to a procession of images, visual, auditory, tactile, and kinaesthetic, each of which exists only in the here and now and belongs to nothing more permanent. As such it is a piecemeal world and responded to only by a series of *ad hoc* responses. This is a notion identical with that advanced by Spitz.

In my view the evidence that the infant in fact passes through such a phase is convincing. Further, pending other evidence, I am inclined to accept Piaget's conclusion that it is not much before the age of 9 months that the infant has finally constructed for himself a world of permanent objects, and that it is, therefore, not until after about this age that he is able to conceive of objects as endowed with certain of the attributes of human beings. This raises the question whether the infant can feel concern for his mother before he conceives of her as a human being existing in time and space. It may be that he can; but if he does so these feelings are likely to be at only a rudimentary level.

Nonetheless, even if Piaget proves right in putting the final construction as late as 9 months, it is evident that there is an important intermediate phase which starts at about 6 months. Prior to this the infant's differentiation, as measured by his responsiveness between familiar mother-figure and stranger is present but only evident on careful observation. After this phase has been reached, however, differential responses are very striking. In particular there is fear and avoidance of strangers and a pronounced turning to mother. This has been shown in a number of studies by Spitz (e.g. 1946) and confirmed recently by Schaffer (in press). Infants who lose their mothers after this point in development fret; those who lose them earlier do not.

This leads on to important and controversial issues regarding the age at which the child passes through the depressive position; or, putting it into a wider theoretical context, the age during which the child passes through one of the critical phases in the development of his modes of regulating the conflict of ambivalence —for it seems likely that there is more than one. Since there is no space to discuss this issue at length I will remark only that, whilst I regard the stage in development when the infant first relates together his concepts of ' good-mother-to-be-loved ' and ' bad-mother-to-be-hated ' as a critical one for his future, I regard the dating of it suggested by Melanie Klein as debatable.

In constructing our picture of the infant's cognitive world I believe there are two fallacies into which it is easy to fall. The first is that because an infant responds in a typically ' sociable ' way he is aware of the human characteristics of the object to which he is responding; the second that because an infant recognizes a person (or a thing) he therefore perceives and thinks of him (or it) as something having a permanent existence in time and space. Let us consider them serially.

As already described, many observers have recorded how from the earliest weeks onward infants respond in special ways to the sight of a human face and the sound of a human voice; in particular we know that after about 6 weeks of age infants smile readily at the sight of a face. Is this not evidence, it may be thought, that they are aware of another human being? The answer is certainly in the negative. Both Spitz & Wolf (1946) and Ahrens (undated) have shown that they also smile at a mask painted with little more than a couple of eyes. Furthermore they do not smile at a real human face when it is in profile. These facts strongly support Spitz's view, described earlier, that in the second to fourth months the infant, on these occasions at least, is responding to the perception not of a human being but only of a visual gestalt signal.

The second fallacy is that of supposing that recognition of a person or thing requires the person or thing to be conceived as having existence in time and space. When we say that an infant recognizes a person as familiar we are basing our judgement on the fact that he responds differently to that person from the way he responds to others. In the same way we can say that ants recognize members of their own colony (by smell) when we observe that they respond to such members differentially. Yet, just as we should be rash to attribute to ants a capacity for perceiving the world in terms of many different ant colonies each with its own history and future, so should we be rash without further evidence to attribute to infants of 6 weeks [6] or even 6 months a capacity for perceiving the world in terms of a number of different human beings each with his or her own history and future. In this connexion, we should also remember, even machines can be constructed to recognize visual and auditory patterns.

The fact, therefore, that in the second half of the first year infants are able readily to recognize familiar figures by sight and hearing cannot be taken by itself to indicate that the figures recognized are endowed by the infants with specific human characteristics. In my view it is quite possible that infants aged 6–9 months do not so endow them. This does not imply, however, that

---

[6] The age at which an infant differentiates reliably between individuals is uncertain. Griffiths (1954) states there is visual discrimination in the second month.

in this period there are no organized psychological processes relating them to the external world. On the contrary, I believe it is evident that throughout these early months psychic organization is developing apace and that much of it has the function of relating the infant to a mother-figure.

It is now time to outline the view of the infant's perceptual and cognitive world which I favour and which I shall assume when I come to discuss the dynamics of the infant's tie to his mother. There appears to me good evidence for postulating a phase, which begins almost immediately after birth, when the infant responds in certain characteristic ways to certain inherently interesting stimulus patterns, by no means all of which are related to food. Thus, thanks to the human nature he inherits, the infant is predisposed to be interested, amongst other things, in the feel at his lips of something warm, moist, and nipple-like. or the sight of a pair of sparkling eyes, and is so made that he responds to them in certain characteristic ways, to the one by sucking and to the other by smiling. As the weeks and months pass he develops, first, an increasing capacity to recognize fragments of the perceptual world by one or another sense modality (probably starting with the kinaesthetic) and, secondly, a capacity to relate the fragments perceived and recognized by one sense modality to those perceived and recognized by another, so that ultimately all the fragments perceived in the here and now are attributed to one and the same source. There is reason to believe that this occurs at about five or six months. Only after this point has been reached is it possible for him to take the next steps, first to conceive of the source as existing outside himself, and secondly, for the familiar fragments to be attributed to a familiar object which has the rudiments of a past and a future. The age at which this finally occurs is uncertain; according to Piaget it may be as late as nine months.

These views I advance with much diffidence since I believe we still lack the data on which to base any which can be held with more confidence. My purpose in advancing them is to provide a sketch map of the perceptual and cognitive aspects of the child's ties as a background against which to consider its dynamic aspects, to which we will now return.

Theories of 'Instinct' and 'Instinctual Response'

Since in constructing the hypothesis of Component Instinctual Responses I am leaning heavily on the work of the ethological school of animal behaviour studies, it is necessary to refer briefly to some of the ideas on instinct which have been developed in recent years. It must be recognized that these ideas differ in many significant respects from the theories of instinct which have for long been current in psychoanalysis. Yet it would be short-sighted were we not to avail ourselves of ideas stemming from other disciplines, particularly on this topic, about which Freud wrote forty years ago: ' I am altogether doubtful whether any decisive pointers for the differentiation and classification of the instincts can be arrived at on the basis of working over the psychological material. This working-over seems rather itself to call for the application to the material of definite assumptions concerning instinctual life, and it would be a desirable thing if those assumptions could be taken from some other branch of knowledge and carried over to psychology ' (*Instincts and their Vicissitudes, S.E.,* XIV, p. 124). As is well known, Freud looked to biology for help in this matter. It seems best that, before attempting to relate these more recent theories of instinct to those advanced by Freud, a brief account is given of their basic principles.

Their most striking feature is a concentration of attention on certain limited and relatively precise behaviour patterns which are common to all members of a species and determined in large measure by heredity. They are conceived as the units out of which many of the more complex sequences are built. Once activated the animal of which they form a part seems to be acting with all the blind impulsion with which, as analysts, we are familiar.

Zoologists first became interested in these behaviour patterns because of the light they throw on taxonomy, namely the ordering of species with reference to their nearest relations alive and dead. For it has been found that, despite potential variability, the relative fixity of these patterns in the different species of fish and birds is such that they may be used for purposes of classification with a degree of reliability no less than that of anatomical structures. This interest goes back to Darwin (1875). In the *Origin of Species* he gives a chapter to *Instinct*, in which he notes that each species is endowed with its own peculiar repertoire of behaviour patterns in the same way that it is endowed with its own peculiarities of anatomical structure. Emphasizing that ' instincts are as important as corporeal structure for the welfare of each species', he advances the hypothesis that 'all the most complex and wonderful instincts' have originated through the process of natural selection having preserved and continually accumulated variations which are biologically advantageous.

Since Darwin's time zoologists have been concerned to describe and catalogue those patterns of behaviour which are characteristic of each species and which, athough in some degree variable and modifiable, are as much the hallmark of the species as the red breast of the robin or the stripes of the tiger. We cannot mistake the egg-laying activity of the female cuckoo for that of the female goose, the urination of the horse for that of the dog, the courtship of the grebes with that of the farmyard fowl. In each case the behaviour exhibited bears the stamp of the particular species and is, therefore, species-specific, to use a convenient if cumbersome term. Ethologists have specialized in the study of these species-specific behaviour patterns, or instincts as Darwin called them, the term deriving from the Greek 'ethos' which signifies the nature of the thing.

It will be my thesis that the five responses which I have suggested go to make up attachment behaviour—sucking, clinging, following, crying, and smiling—are behaviour patterns of this kind and specific to Man. I propose to call them 'instinctual responses' which I equate with the more cumbersome term 'species-specific behaviour pattern.'

My reason for preferring the term 'instinctual response' to 'instinct' or 'part-instinct' will perhaps be clear. In psycho-analysis the term 'instinct' (an unfortunate translation from the German 'Trieb') has been used to denote a *motivating force*. The term 'instinctual response' used here describes something very different: it denotes an *observable pattern of behaviour*. Although this pattern results from the activation of a structure (which, since we know next to nothing of its neurological basis, is best conceived in purely psychic terms), the question of the nature and origin of the energy involved is deliberately left open.

This leads to a consideration of the dynamic of instinctual responses. Whereas Freud, with many earlier biologists, postulated instincts of sex and self-preservation to explain the motive force behind certain types of behaviour, ethologists point out that this is unnecessary—as unnecessary in fact as to postulate an instinct to see in order to explain the existence of the eye. Instead, just as the present efficiency of the eye as a seeing instrument can be explained as due to the process of natural selection having favoured the accumulation of variations leading to better vision, so the present efficiency of instinctual responses as the instruments of self-preservation and reproduction can be explained as due to similar processes having favoured the accumulation of favourable variations in these responses. In the same way that the eye can be said to have the function of sight, instinctual responses can be said to have the function, amongst other things, of safeguarding the individual and mediating reproduction.

It is contended, therefore, that it is redundant and misleading to invoke hypothetical instincts of sex and self-preservation as causal agents. Instead we may look to the conditions found necessary to activate a pattern as being in fact their causes.

In considering the conditions necessary to activate an instinctual response it is useful to distinguish between conditions internal to the organism and those external to it. Conditions internal to the organism which may be necessary before it will be exhibited include physiological conditions such as the hormonal state and stimuli of interoceptive origin. In Man they include also conditions such as thoughts and wishes, conscious and unconscious, which can be conceptualized only in psychological terms. All of these together put the organism into a responsive mood and sometimes lead to 'seeking' behaviour well designed to lead to the next links in the chain of behaviour. It is on the nature of the conditions activating succeeding links that the ethologists have thrown a flood of light. What they have demonstrated is that, for most instinctual responses, activation only occurs in the presence of particular external conditions.

Heinroth was probably the first to point out that species-specific behaviour patterns may often be activated by the perception of fairly simple visual or auditory gestalts to which they are innately sensitive. Well-known examples of this, analysed by means of experiments using dummies of various shapes and colours, are the mating response of the male stickleback, which is elicited by the perception of a shape resembling a pregnant female, the gaping response of the young herring-gull, which is elicited by the perception of a red spot similar to that on the beak of an adult gull, and the attack response of the male robin which is

187

elicited by the perception in his own territory of a bunch of red feathers, similar to those on the breast of a rival male. In all three cases the response seems to be elicited by the perception of a fairly simple gestalt, known as a ' sign-stimulus '.

A great deal of ethological work has been devoted to the identification of the sign-stimuli which elicit the various species-specific behaviour patterns in fish and birds. In so far as many of these behaviour patterns mediate social behaviour—courtship, mating, feeding of young by parents and following of parents by young— much light has been thrown on the nature of social interaction. In dozens of species it has been shown that behaviour subserving mating and parenthood is controlled by the perception of sign-stimuli presented by other members of the same species, such as the spread of a tail or the colour of a beak, or a song or a call, the essential characteristics of which are those of fairly simple gestalten. Such sign-stimuli are known as social releasers. They play an essential rôle in the activation of a response.

Oddly enough stimuli of a comparable kind often play an essential rôle also in the *termination* of a response. Psycho-analysis has for long thought of instinctive behaviour in terms of the flow of a hypothetical psychic energy. According to this view behaviour is activated when energy has accumulated within the organism and terminates when it has flowed away. So deeply is our thinking coloured by such concepts that it is by no means easy instead to conceive of an activity coming to an end because a set of stimuli, either internal or external to the organism, switch it off, much as the referee's whistle terminates a game of football. Yet this is a concept which has been elaborated during recent years and will, I believe, prove immensely fruitful.

Sometimes the stimuli which have a terminating effect, and which are conveniently termed consummatory stimuli, arise within the animal. Thus experiments using oesophagostomized dogs have demonstrated that the acts of feeding and drinking are terminated by proprioceptive and/or interoceptive stimuli which arise in the mouth, the oesophagus, and the stomach and which in the intact animal are the outcome of the performances themselves. Such cessation is due neither to fatigue nor to a satiation of the need for food or drink: instead the very act gives rise to the feed-back stimuli which ter-

minate it. (For discussion see Deutsch, 1953, and Hinde, 1954.)

In the case of other responses, it can be shown, termination results from stimuli arising in the organism's environment; for instance, Hinde has observed that in early spring the mere presence of a female chaffinch leads to a reduction of the male's courtship behaviour, such as singing and searching. When she is present he is quiet, when she is absent he becomes active. In this case, where a socially relevant behaviour pattern is terminated by consummatory stimuli emanating from another member of the same species, we might perhaps speak of a ' social suppressor ' as a term parallel to social releaser. I believe it to be a concept extremely valuable for helping us understand the problem before us.

The basic model for instinctive behaviour which this work suggests is thus a unit comprising a species-specific behaviour pattern (or instinctual response) governed by two complex mechanisms, one controlling its activation and the other its termination. Although sometimes to be observed active in isolation, in real life it is usual for a number of these responses to be linked together so that adaptive behaviour sequences result. For instance sexual behaviour in birds can be understood as a sequence of a large number of discrete instinctual responses, in greater or less measure modified by learning, and so oriented to the environment, including other members of the species, and linked in time that reproduction of the species is commonly achieved. There are a large number of responses which, strung together in the right way, eventually lead to copulation; many others lead to nest-building, others again to brooding, and others again to care of young. It is interesting to note that, even in birds, those leading through courtship to copulation are far from few and fully confirm Freud's view that sexual activity is best understood in terms of the integration of a number of component ' part-instincts '.

Plainly this integration occurs under the influence of forces operating at a high level and is proceeding in the perceptual as well as the motor field. Moreover it has a complex ontogeny. For instance it has been shown that, as in Man, during the development of members of lower species there are many hazards which must be avoided if co-ordinated and effective functioning is to be achieved in adult life. An example of failure is the case of the turkey cock, who, although he could copulate with turkey hens, could only court human males. Another is the case of the gander, all of whose sexual responses were fixated on a dog-kennel and who, moreover, behaved as though mourning when his dog-kennel was turned on its side.

In considering groups of instinctual responses patterned into behaviour sequences, concepts such as hierarchical structure and the availability of one and the same response for integration into more than one sequence are both of great interest; but their discussion would lead us too far afield on this occasion.

Two further points, however, need mention. First, to ensure survival of the individual and the species, it is necessary for the organism to be equipped with an appropriately balanced repertoire of instinctual responses at *each stage* of its ontogeny. No only must the adult be so equipped, but the young animal must itself have a balanced and efficient equipment of its own. This will certainly differ in many respects from that of the adult. Furthermore, not only do individuals of different sexes and at different stages of development require specialized repertoires, but in certain respects these need to be reciprocal. Male and female mating responses need to be reciprocal, and so also do those mediating on the one hand parental care and on the other parent-oriented activity in the young. It is my thesis that, as in the young of other species, there matures in the early months of life of the human infant a complex and nicely balanced equipment of instinctual responses, the function of which is to ensure that he obtains parental care sufficient for his survival. To this end the equipment includes responses which promote his close proximity to a parent and responses which evoke parental activity.

Not very much study has yet been given by ethologists to the process of transition from the infantile equipment to that of the adult (though there is one valuable paper by Meyer-Holzapfel, 1949). Let us hope this will be remedied, since it appears to me that it is precisely this transition in the human being which provides a main part of the subject matter of psycho-analysis.

My second point concerns how as human beings, we experience the activation in ourselves of an instinctual response system. When the system is active and free to reach termination, it seems, we experience an urge to action accompanied, as Lorenz (1950) has suggested, by an emotional state peculiar to each response. There is an emotional experience peculiar to

smiling and laughing, another peculiar to weeping, yet another to sexual foreplay, another again to temper. When, however, the response is not free to reach termination, our experience may be very different: we experience tension, unease and anxiety. As observers when these responses are activated in another, we commonly think and speak of the individual as the subject of conscious and unconscious wishes and feelings.

All instinctual response systems which are not active are so potentially. As such they go to make up what has been described earlier as psychic structure. It is here, I believe, that concepts derived from ethology may link with those in regard to infantile phantasy which have been elaborated by Melanie Klein and her colleagues. Nevertheless, in making such linkages we need to walk warily, since there may well be processes in Man, such as imitation and identification, with their associated ego structures, which need for their understanding a different and complementary frame of reference. A full correlation of the two sets of concepts will be a long and difficult task.

In this brief account of ethological instinct theory I have concentrated on three main concepts: (*a*) the presence of species-specific behaviour patterns, or instinctual responses as I have called them; (*b*) the activation and termination of these responses by various conditions internal and external to the organism; and (*c*) their integration into more complex behaviour sequences. As such the approach starts with limited and observed behaviour and attempts to understand more complex behaviour as due to a synthesis, more or less elaborate, of these simpler units into greater wholes. In this respect it resembles Freud's earlier view of instinct as expressed in his *Three Essays on Sexuality* and *Instincts and their Vicissitudes*. It is the antithesis, however, of the approach he favoured later. In his essay *Beyond the Pleasure Principle* (1920) and later works, Freud starts with purely abstract concepts, such as those of psychic energy and Life and Death Instincts, and attempts to understand particular examples of behaviour as expressions of these hidden forces. Put briefly we might say that, whereas Freud's later theories conceive of the organism as starting with a quantum of unstructured psychic energy which during development becomes progressively more structured, ethology conceives of it as starting with a number of highly structured responses (some of which are active at birth and some of which mature later), which in the course of development become so elaborated, through processes of integration and learning, and in Man by imitation, identification and the use of symbols, that the resulting behaviour is of amazing variety and plasticity.[7] This picture of Man's behaviour may appear incredible to some, but before dismissing it we should be wise to recall that in other spheres we are used to the idea that from relatively few and simple components rich and varied structures may be created.

Indeed, in advocating the ethological approach, it is my hope that I am not underestimating the extraordinary complexities of behaviour characteristic of Man. By his skill in learning and his mastery of symbol he so conducts himself that the comparatively stereotyped behavioural units may well seem to have disappeared; and this may seem to be as true of the two-year-old as of the adult. Yet I believe this conclusion will prove false and that there will be found active beneath the symbolic transformations and other trappings of humanity, primeval dynamic structures which we share in common with lower species. Furthermore, I believe they will be found playing a dominant rôle in early infancy. As we go down the phylogenetic scale to simpler organisms we find instinctual responses increasingly in evidence; in the same way, I believe, as we trace Man back to his ontogenetic beginnings we shall find them responsible for an increasing proportion of his behaviour.

I emphasize that at present this is no more than my belief and that whether or not ethology will prove a fruitful approach to psycho-analytic problems is yet to be shown. Speaking for myself, a main reason for preferring it to other approaches is the research which it suggests. With ethological concepts and methods it is possible to undertake a far-reaching programme of experimentation into the social responses of the preverbal period of infancy, and to this I attach much importance. Thus the repertoire of instinctual responses may be catalogued and the range of ages when each matures identified. Each response may be studied to discover the nature of the conditions which activate it and the nature of those which terminate it (often

called consummatory stimuli), and why in some individuals responses come to be activated and terminated by unusual objects. The conditions which lead to certain responses being manifested at abnormal levels, either too low or too high an intensity, and the conditions which lead to a perpetuation of such a state may be explored. Other main interests will be the study of the conflicts arising when two or more incompatible responses are activated at once and the modes by which conflict is regulated. Finally, we may be interested to investigate the critical phases through which the modes of regulating conflict develop and the conditions which in an individual lead to one mode of regulation becoming dominant.

Even this brief sketch describes an extensive programme. Analysts will differ in their evaluation of it and in how they perceive its relatedness to the traditional research method of reconstructing early phases of development from the investigation of later ones. Since, however, we have yet to see the fruits of this new approach, it is perhaps premature to attempt to judge its likely value. For me it carries with it the hope that, by introducing experimental method to the investigation of early emotional development, we may be entering a phase when more reliable data will be available to us in our consideration of crucial theoretical issues.

The dynamic aspects of the child's tie—comparative studies

In presenting this brief and inadequate account of recent theories of instinctive behaviour I am keenly aware that they will be unfamiliar to many and controversial to all. I hope, in due course, time will be found when we can examine them in their own right and that meanwhile the account given will provide a background to my hypothesis.

Before proceeding I wish to emphasize again that I am discussing only the positive aspects of the child's tie and leaving an examination of its negative side to another occasion. My main thesis is that the positive dynamic is expressed through a number of instinctual responses, all of which are primary in the sense used in this paper and, in the first place, relatively independent of one another. Those which

---

[7] The many good theoretical reasons for being dissatisfied with Freud's notion of an unstructured id have been discussed by Fairbairn (1952) and Colby (1955). Moreover, Anna Freud (1951) in her empirical approach to child development has reached conclusions consistent with those advanced in the text.

Discussing the theoretical implications of her Hampstead Nursery observations, she advances the view that 'there exist in the child innate, preformed attitudes which are not originated, merely stimulated and developed by life experience.'

I am postulating are sucking, clinging, following, crying, and smiling, but there may well be many more.[8] In the course of the first year of life, it is suggested, these component instinctual responses become integrated into attachment behaviour. How this process of integration is related to the parallel process in the cognitive sphere is difficult to know. It seems not unlikely, however, that there are significant connexions between the two and that a disturbance in the one will create repercussions in the other.

The five responses postulated fall into two classes. Sucking, clinging, and following achieve their end, in the one case food and in the other close proximity to mother, with only a limited reciprocal response being necessary on the mother's part. Crying and smiling on the other hand depend for their results on their effect on maternal behaviour. It is my belief that both of them act as social releasers of instinctual responses in mothers. As regards crying, there is plentiful evidence from the animal world that this is so: probably in all cases the mother responds promptly and unfailingly to her infant's bleat, call, or cry. It seems to me clear that similar impulses are also evoked in the human mother and, furthermore, that the infant's smile has a comparable though more agreeable effect on her.

Since a main point of my thesis is that no one of these responses is more primary than another and that it is, therefore, a mistake to give pre-eminence to sucking and feeding, it may be useful to consider the evidence for such a view. Unfortunately, studies of human infants are inadequate for our purpose and the hypothesis, therefore, remains untested. In respect of other species, however, the data are unequivocal. In sub-human primates, as Hermann insisted twenty-five years ago, clinging is manifested independently of the oral response and food. The same is certainly true of following and 'crying' in certain species of birds. Such observations are of great theoretical interest and merit detailed attention.

Clinging appears to be a universal characteristic of Primate infants and is found from the lemurs up to anthropoid apes and human babies. In every species save Man during the early weeks the infant clings to its mother's belly.

Later the location varies, the mother's back being preferred in certain species. All accounts of infant-parent relations in sub-human Primates emphasize the extraordinary intensity of the clinging response and how in the early weeks 'it is maintained both day and night. Though in the higher species mothers play a rôle in holding their infants, those of lower species do little for them; in all it is plain that in the wild the infant's life depends, indeed literally hangs, on the efficiency of his clinging response.

In at least two different species, one of which is the chimpanzee, there is first-hand evidence that clinging occurs before sucking. As soon as it is born the infant either climbs up the ventral surface of the mother or is placed by her on her abdomen. Once there it 'clings tenaciously with hands and feet to the hair or skin.' Only later, sometimes after some hours, does it find the nipple and start to suck (14, 60). We may conclude, therefore, that in sub-human Primates clinging is a primary response, first exhibited independently of food.[9]

Similarly the response of following; which in nature is focused on a parent-figure, is known in certain species of birds to be independent of any other satisfactions and once again, therefore, primary. Although this response has the same function as clinging, namely to keep the infant animal in close proximity to its mother, it would be a mistake to regard the two as identical. Whereas clinging is virtually confined to Primates (and a few other mammals including bats and anteaters, see (13)), the following response is to be observed in a very great variety of species both of mammals, and birds.

The species in which the following response is certainly primary include many ground-nesting birds, such as ducks, geese, and rails, the young of which are not fed by their parents but start foraging for themselves a day or so after birth. In systematic experiments Hinde, Thorpe, and Vince (1956) have shown that the mere experience of following an object reinforces the response; in other words the response increases in strength without any other reward being given.

The fact that clinging and following are undoubtedly primary responses in some species, it should therefore be noted, robs the theory

[8] It has been suggested to me that cooing and babbling may represent a sixth.
[9] In 1957, Professor Harlow of the University of Wisconsin began a series of experiments on the attachment behaviour of young rhesus monkeys. Removed from their mothers at birth, they are provided with
the choice of two varieties of model to which to cling and from which to take food (from a bottle). Preliminary results (Harlow, in press) strongly suggest that the preferred model is the one which is most 'comfy' to cling to rather than the one which provides food.

that, as in the case of following, clinging waxes, reaches a zenith, and then wanes, or that, again like following, the course of its development may be influenced by experience. In the short term, we know, anxiety and a period of separation both lead to its exhibition at high intensity.

In the account of the human infant's repertoire of positively directed mother-oriented instinctual responses, I have left *sucking* to the last. My reason is that psycho-analytical theory has tended to become fixated on orality and it is a main purpose of this paper to free it for broader development. Nevertheless sucking is plainly of great importance both in infancy and later and must be studied systematically. Furthermore, the phase during which sucking is one of the dominant responses continues for far longer than is sometimes supposed, a fact remarked upon by Anna Freud (1951). In my experience most infants through much of the second year of life need a great deal of sucking and thrive on milk from a bottle at bedtime. It is regrettable that, in Western culture, arm-chair doctrines regarding weaning at 9 months or earlier have led to a neglect of this obvious fact.

In this exposition I have emphasized the endogenous aspects of these instinctual responses. Their development in the individual, however, can never be free of change through processes of learning. In respect of smiling in infants aged 14–18 weeks, this has already been demonstrated experimentally by Brackbill (1956). What is of particular interest in her work is that the ' reward ' given was no more than a little social attention.

At this point I wish to emphasize that it is a main part of my thesis that each of the five instinctual responses which I am suggesting underlie the child's tie to his mother is present because of its survival value. Unless there are powerful in-built responses which ensure that the infant evokes maternal care and remains in close proximity to his mother throughout the years of childhood he will die—so runs the thesis. Hence in the course of our evolution the process of natural selection has resulted in crying and smiling, sucking, clinging and following becoming responses species-specific to Man. Their existence, it is claimed, is readily intelligible on biological grounds. In this respect they differ sharply from the hypothetical craving to return to the mother's womb. It is difficult to imagine what survival value such a desire might have and I am not aware that any has been suggested.

Indeed, the hypothesis of Primary Return-to-Womb Craving has been advanced on quite other grounds and, so far as I know, lays no claim to biological status. I emphasize this to make clear my own position. The theory of Component Instinctual Responses, it is claimed, is rooted firmly in biological theory and requires no dynamic which is not plainly explicable in terms of the survival of the species. It is because the notion of a primary desire to return to the womb is not so rooted and because I believe the data are more readily explained in other ways that this theory is rejected.

In stressing the survival value of the five component instinctual responses we are put in mind of Freud's concepts of libido and Life instinct. Not only is there the same emphasis on survival, but the means of achieving it—a binding together—is the same: ' Eros desires contact because it strives to make the ego and the loved object one, to abolish the barriers of distance between them ' (1926, p. 79). Despite the starting points of the two theories being so different, and their having different implications, the themes appear to be the same.

Although I have described these five responses as mother-oriented, it is evident that at first this is so only potentially. From what we know of other species it seems probable that each one of them has the potential to become focused on some other object. The clearest examples of this in real life are where sucking becomes directed towards a bottle and not to the mother's breast, and clinging is directed to a rag and not to the mother's body. In principle it seems likely that an infant could be so reared that each of his responses was directed towards a different object. In practice this is improbable, since all or most of the consummatory stimuli which terminate them habitually come from the mother-figure. No matter for what reason he is crying—cold, hunger, fear, or plain loneliness—his crying is usually terminated through the agency of the mother. Again, when he wants to cling or follow or to find a haven of safety when he is frightened, she is the figure who commonly provides the needed object. It is for this reason that the mother becomes so central a figure in the infant's life. For in healthy development it is towards her that each of the several responses becomes directed, much as each of the subjects of the realm comes to direct his loyalty towards the Queen; and it is in relation to the mother that the several responses become integrated into the complex behaviour which I have termed

' attachment behaviour ', much as it is in relation to the Sovereign that the components of our constitution become integrated into a working whole.

We may extend the analogy. It is in the nature of our constitution, as of all others, that sovereignty is vested in a single person. A hierarchy of substitutes is permissible but at the head stands a particular individual. The same is true of the infant. Quite early, by a process of learning, he comes to centre his instinctual responses not only on a human figure but on a particular human figure. Good mothering from any kind woman ceases to satisfy him —only his own mother will do.[11]

This focusing of instinctual responses on to a particular individual, which we find but too often ignored in human infancy, is found throughout the length and breadth of the animal kingdom. In very many species, mating responses are directed to a single member of the opposite sex, either for a season or for a lifetime, whilst it is the rule for parents to be solicitous of their own young and of no others and for young to be attached to their own parents and not to any adult. Naturally such a general statement needs amplification and qualification, but the tendency for instinctual responses to be directed towards a particular individual or group of individuals and not promiscuously towards many is one which I believe to be so important and so neglected that it deserves a special term. I propose to call it ' monotropy ', a term which, it should be noted, is descriptive only and carries with it no pretensions to causal explanation.[12]

In the case of human personality the integrating function of the unique mother-figure is one the importance of which I believe can hardly be exaggerated; in this I am at one with Winnicott who has constantly emphasized it (e.g. 56). I see the ill-effects stemming from maternal deprivation and separation as due in large part to an interference with this function, either preventing its development or smashing it at a critical point. This is a view I have advanced in the past (8, p. 54) and to which I hope to give further attention.

In the final synthesis of these many responses into attachment behaviour directed towards a single mother-figure, it may well be that certain component responses play a more central part than others. Without much further research we cannot know which they may be. However, the ease with which sucking is transferred to objects other than the mother's breast leads me to think it will not prove the most important. Clinging and following seem more likely candidates for the rôle.

This view is strengthened by clinical observation. My impression in taking the histories of many disturbed children is that there is little if any relationship between form and degree of disturbance and whether or not the child has been breast-fed. The association which constantly impresses itself upon me is that between form and degree of disturbance and the extent to which the mother has permitted clinging and following, and all the behaviour associated with them, or has refused them. In my experience a mother's acceptance of clinging and following is consistent with favourable development even in the absence of breast feeding, whilst rejection of clinging and following is apt to lead to emotional disturbance even in the presence of breast feeding. Furthermore, it is my impression that fully as many psychological disturbances, including the most severe, can date from the second year of life when clinging and following are at their peak as from the early months when they are rudimentary. I am, of course, aware that these views contrast with those expressed by many other analysts and I make no special claim for their truth: like those of others, they rest only on a collection of not very systematic clinical impressions. In the long run this, like other scientific issues, will be decided on the quality of the empirical data presented.

---

[11] I am hesitant to name an age for this development. The studies of Spitz (1946) and Schaffer (in press) make it clear that it has already occurred by six or seven months.

[12] Excellent examples of monotropy in young children are given in *Infants without Families*. For example ' Bridget (2–2½ years) belonged to the family of Nurse Jean of whom she was extremely fond. When Jean had been ill for a few days and returned to the nursery, she constantly repeated: " My Jean, my Jean." Lillian (2–2½ years) once said " my Jean " too, but Bridget objected and explained: " It's my Jean, it's Lillian's Ruth and Keith's very own Ilsa." ' (Burling-

ham and Freud, 1944, p. 44).

Robert Hinde has drawn my attention to the emphasis which William James gives to this process. In his chapter on Instinct, James (1890) discusses two processes which lead to great variations in the manifestation of instinctual responses in different individuals. The first is the tendency for them to become focused on one object, and therefore to be inhibited in respect of other objects, which he terms ' the law of inhibition of instincts by habits.' The second refers to critical phases in the development of instinct. James' treatment of the whole problem is remarkably perspicacious.

This completes our review of the quintet of responses through which, it is suggested, the dynamic of the child's tie to his mother is expressed. It may be noted that all of them, even smiling, seem to reach a zenith and then to decline. As the years roll by first sucking, then crying, then clinging and following all diminish. Even the smiley two-year-old becomes a more solemn school-child. They are a quintet comprising a repertoire which is well adapted to human infancy but, having performed their function, are relegated to a back seat. Nevertheless none disappear. All remain in different states of activity or latency and are utilized in fresh combinations when the adult repertoire comes to mature. Furthermore, some of them, particularly crying and clinging, revert to an earlier state of activity in situations of danger, sickness, and incapacity. In these rôles, they are performing a natural and healthy function and one which there is no need to regard as regressive.[13] Like old soldiers, infantile instinctual responses never die.

Conclusion

It will be noticed that in this account I have carefully avoided the term 'dependence', although it is in common use. My reason is that to be dependent on someone and to be attached to them are not the same thing. The terms 'dependence' and 'dependency' are appropriate if we favour the theory of Secondary Drive, which has it that the child becomes oriented towards his mother because he is dependent on her as the source of physiological gratification. They are, however, inappropriate terms if we believe that dependence on physiological satisfactions and psychological attachment, although related to one another, are fundamentally different phenomena. On this view, we observe on the one hand that in the early weeks the infant is in fact dependent on its mother, whether or not there are forces in him which attach him to her, and on the other that

he is attached to her by dynamic forces, whether or not, as in hospital, he is dependent on her physiologically. On this view, psychological attachment and detachment are to be regarded as functions in their own right apart altogether from the extent to which the child happens at any one moment to be dependent on the object for his physiological needs being met. It is interesting to note that, despite their adherence to the theory of Secondary Drive, both Sigmund Freud and Anna Freud nonetheless employ the term 'attachment' (Freud, *C.P.*, V, p. 252–3; Burlingham and Freud, 1944).

Other terminological issues also arise. Thus we shall no longer regard it as satisfactory to equate breast and mother, to identify good feeding and good mothering, or even to speak of the earliest phase as oral and the first relationship as anaclitic. To some these may seem revolutionary consequences but, if the hypothesis advanced here is correct, terminological change is inescapable.

The hypothesis advanced, however, can be no more than tentative. Data are still scarce and it may well be many years before crucial evidence is available. Meanwhile I advance it as a working hypothesis, both as the best explanation of the facts as we now know them and above all as a stimulus to further research.

———

The author is much indebted to Robert Hinde and Anthony Ambrose for discussions in which these ideas were clarified. The enquiry was undertaken as part of the work of the Tavistock Child Development Research Unit, which is at present supported by the National Health Service and by grants from the Josiah Macy Jr. Foundation, the Foundations Fund for Research in Psychiatry and the Ford Foundation, to all of which our thanks are due. The review of literature was extensively revised whilst the author held a Fellowship at the Center for Advanced Study in the Behavioral Sciences.

REFERENCES

In most cases references to the works of Sigmund Freud are given in the text, wherever possible to the Standard Edition. *S.E.* = Standard Edition ; *C.P.* = Collected Papers.

(1) ABRAHAM, K. (1916). 'The first pregenital stage of the libido.' *Selected Papers on Psycho-Analysis.* (London: Hogarth, 1927.)

(2) —— (1924). 'A short study of the development of the libido, viewed in the light of mental disorders.' *Selected Papers on Psycho-Analysis.* (London: Hogarth, 1927.)

[13] In much theorizing (e.g. Benedek, 1956), all manifestations of attachment behaviour after infancy are conceived as 'regressive'. Since this term inevitably carries with it the connotation pathological or, at least, undesirable, I regard it as misleading and failing to do justice to the facts.

(3) AHRENS, R. (Undated). 'Beitrag zur Ent-wicklung des Physiognomie- und Mimikerkennens.' *Zeitschrift fur experimentelle und angewandte Psychologie*, II/3, 412–454.

- (4) BALINT, A. (1939). *Int. Z. f. Psa. u. Imago*, **24**, 33–48. English Translation (1949): 'Love for the Mother and Mother-Love.' *Int. J. Psycho-Anal.*, **30**, 251–259.

(5) BALINT, M. (1937). *Imago*, **23**, 270–288. English Translation (abbreviated) (1949): 'Early Developmental States of the Ego. Primary Object Love.' *Int. J. Psycho-Anal.*, **30**, 265–273.

(6) BENEDEK, T. (1938). 'Adaptation to reality in early infancy.' *Psycho-Anal. Quart.*, **7**, 200–215.

(7) —— (1956). 'Toward the biology of the depressive constellation.' *J. Amer. Psa. Assn.*, **4**, 389–427.

(8) BOWLBY, J. (1951). *Maternal Care and Mental Health*. (Geneva: W.H.O. Monograph No. 2.)

(9) BRACKBILL, Y. (1956). *Smiling in infants : relative resistance to extinction as a function of reinforcement schedule*. (Ph.D. Thesis: Stanford University.)

(10) BUHLER, Ch. (1933). 'The Social Behavior of Children.' *A Handbook of Child Psychology*. (Worcester, Mass.: Clark Univ. Press.)

(11) BURLINGHAM, D., and FREUD, A. (1942). *Young Children in War-time*. (London: Allen and Unwin.)

(12) —— (1944). *Infants without Families*. (London: Allen and Unwin.)

(13) BURTON, M. (1956). *Infancy in Animals*. (London: Hutchinson.)

(14) CARPENTER, C. R. (1934). 'A field study of the behaviour and social relations of howling monkeys (*Alouatta palliata*).' *Comp. Psychol. Monograph*, **10**, No. 48.

(15) COLBY, K. M. (1955). *Energy and Structure in Psycho-Analysis*. (New York: Ronald Press.)

(16) DAANJE, A. (1950). 'On locomotory movements in birds and the intention movements derived from them.' *Behaviour*, **3**, 48–98.

(17) DARWIN, C. (1875). *The Origin of Species*. Sixth Edition. (London: Murray.)

(18) DEUTSCH, J. A. (1953). 'A new type of behaviour theory.' *Brit. J. Psychol. (General Section)*, **44**, 304–317.

(19) ERIKSON, E. H. (1950). *Childhood and Society*. (New York: W. W. Norton.)

(20) FAIRBAIRN, W. R. D. (1941). 'A revised psychopathology of the psychoses and psycho-neuroses.' *Int. J. Psycho-Anal.*, **22**. Reprinted in *Psycho-Analytic Studies of the Personality*. (London: Tavistock, 1952.)

(21) —— (1943). 'The war neuroses—their nature and significance.' *Psycho-Analytic Studies of the Personality*. (London: Tavistock, 1952.)

(22) FERENCZI, S. (1916). 'Stages in the develop-ment of the sense of reality.' *Contributions to Psycho-Analysis*. (Boston: Badger.)

(23) FREUD, A. (1949). 'Certain types and stages of social maladjustment.' *Searchlights on Delinquency*, ed. K. R. Eissler. (London: Imago Pub. Co.)

(24) —— (1951). 'Observations on child development.' *Psycho-Anal. Study of the Child*, **6**, 18–30.

(25) —— (1954). 'Psycho-analysis and educa-tion.' *Psycho-Anal., Study of the Child*, **9**.

(26) FREUD, A., and DANN, S. (1951). 'An experiment in group upbringing.' *Psycho-Anal. Study of the Child*, **6**, 127–168.

(27) FREUD, S. (1926, English trans. 1936). *Inhibitions, Symptoms and Anxiety*. (London: Hogarth.)

(28) —— (1938). *An Outline of Psycho-Analysis*. (London: Hogarth.)

(29) GERWITZ, J. L. (1956). 'A program of research on the dimensions and antecedents of emotional dependence.' *Child Development*, **27**, 205–221.

(30) GRIFFITHS, R. (1954). *The Abilities of Babies*. (London: Univ. of London Press.)

(31) HARLOW, H. (In press.) *American Psycho-logist*.

(32) HAYES, Cathy, (1951). *The Ape in our House*. (London: Gollancz.)

(33) HERMANN, I. (1933). 'Zum Triebleben der Primaten.' *Imago*, **19**, 113, 325.

(34) —— (1936). 'Sich-Anklammern—Auf-Suche-Gehen.' *Int. Z. Psa.*, **22**, 349–370.

(35) HETZER, H., and TUDOR-HART, B. H. (1927). 'Die frühesten Reaktionen auf die menschliche Stimme.' *Quellen und Studien zur Jugendkunde*, **5**.

(36) HINDE, R. A. (1954). 'Changes in respon-siveness to a constant stimulus.' *Brit. J. Animal Behaviour*, **2**, 41–45.

(37) HINDE, R. A., THORPE, W. N., and VINCE, M. A. (1956). 'The following response of young coots and moorhens.' *Behaviour*, **9**, 214–242.

(38) JAMES, W. (1890). *Textbook of Psychology*. (New York: Holt.)

(39) KELLOGG, W. N., and KELLOGG, L. A. (1933). *The Ape and the Child*. (New York: Whittlesey House.)

(40) KLEIN, M. (1948). *Envy and Gratitude*. (London: Tavistock.)

(41) KLEIN, M., HEIMANN, P., ISAACS, S., and RIVIERE, J. (1952). *Developments in Psycho-Analysis*. (London: Hogarth.)

(42) LORENZ, K. Z. (1950). 'The Comparative Method in Studying Innate Behaviour Patterns.' *Physiological Mechanisms in Animal Behaviour*, No. IV of Symposia of the Society for Experimental Biology, Cambridge University Press.

(43) MEYER-HOLZAPFEL, Monika. (1949). 'Die Beziehungen zwischen den Trieben Junger und Erwachsener Tiere.' *Schweiz. Z. für Psychol. und ihre Anwendungen*, **8**, 32–60.

(44) PIAGET, J. (1936). *La Naissance de l'intelligence chez l'enfant.* English translation: (1953). *The Origin of Intelligence in the Child.* (London: Routledge, 1953.)

(45) —— (1937). *The Child's Construction of Reality.* English translation: (London: Routledge, 1955.)

(46) RIBBLE, M. A. (1944). 'Infantile experience in relation to personality development.' Hunt (ed.), *Personality and the Behavior Disorders.* (New York: Ronald Press.)

(47) SCHAFFER, H. R. (In press). 'Observations on personality development in early infancy.' *Brit. J. Med. Psych.*

(48) SHIRLEY, M. M. (1933). *The First Two Years.* Vols. II and III. (Minneapolis: Univ. of Minnesota Press.)

(49) SPITZ, R. A. (1946). 'Anaclitic depression.' *Psycho-Anal., Study of the Child, 2.*

(50) —— (1954). 'Genèse des premières relations objectales.' *Revue française de psychanalyse,* **18,** 479–575.

(51) —— (1957). *No and Yes.* (New York: Int. Univ. Press.)

(52) SPITZ, R. A., and WOLF, K. M. (1946). 'The smiling response: a contribution to the onto-genesis of social relations.' *Genetic Psychology Monographs,* **34,** 57–125.

(53) SULLIVAN, H. S. (1892–1949). *The Interpersonal Theory of Psychiatry,* (ed. Perry and Gawel). (New York: Norton, 1953.)

(54) SUTTIE, Ian D. (1935). *Origins of Love and Hate.* (London: Kegan Paul.)

(55) TOMILIN, M. I., and YERKES, R. M. (1935). 'Chimpanzee twins: Behavioral relations and development.' *J. Genet. Psychol.,* **46,** 239–263.

(56) WINNICOTT, D. W. (1945). 'Primitive emotional development.' *Int. J. Psycho-Anal.,* **26,** 137–143.

(57) —— (1948). 'Pediatrics and Psychiatry.' *Brit. J. Med. Psychol.,* **21,** 229–240.

(58) —— (1953). 'Transitional objects and transitional phenomena.' *Int. J. Psycho-Anal.,* **34,** 1–9.

(59) —— (1955). 'The depressive position in normal emotional development.' *Brit. J. Med. Psychol.,* **28,** 89–100.

(60) YERKES, R. M., and TOMILIN, M. I. (1935). 'Mother-infant relations in chimpanzees.' *J. Comp. Psychol.,* **20,** 321–348.

(61) ZUCKERMAN, S. (1933). *Functional Affinities of Man, Monkeys and Apes.* (London: Kegan Paul.)

SOME ASPECTS OF THE FIRST RELATIONSHIP[1]

By

LOIS B. MURPHY

THE early months of the infant's life are of course but dimly reflected in psycho-analytic data; hypotheses and speculations about the development of the infant himself, and his relation to his mother, are sometimes based on reconstructions from analysis, but often on deductions from the abstract conceptual framework of psycho-analysis. In the fields of developmental and experimental psychology dynamic processes aside from the processes of growth and the simplest forms of learning have hardly been studied at all. Perhaps some gaps in both areas can be filled by bringing the dynamic and observational approaches together. Without going into descriptive detail within the limited space of this paper, I shall make use constantly of both experimental results and observations by Escalona (Escalona et al., 1953) and also Shirley (1931–33), Bernfeld (1929), Buhler (1930), and others; and I shall also use data from my own observations and photo-records over many years. This is an area which has attracted much attention in both Great Britain and the United States, owing to wartime separations, problems of placement of infants and young children in infants' and foster homes, and many difficulties in understanding failures in normal development. There is moreover no area more basic for the understanding of personality and development and socialization of the child than the development of his relation to the mother, that is, the first relationship.

The Initial Situation of the Infant and Mother

In order to understand the development of the relationship between baby and mother, we must look at each in the situation in which they begin that relationship, and the observable phenomena of these beginnings. The infant is born into an environment from which he must gain sustenance for his vegetative life, adequate stimulation for the development of all his sensory, motor and intellectual functions, and through which he must gradually find a place in human society. He is equipped with certain assimilative functions such as breathing and sucking, which provide for his intake from the environment. Also he has the faculties of sneezing, coughing, spitting out, or ' riddance ' reflexes as Rado (1939) calls them—which help him to get rid of irritating mucous or unwanted tastes; and reflexes for urinating and eliminating faeces to expel waste products. He reacts visibly to conditions of excessive warmth, cold, etc., but cannot do very much about such discomforts. He can, with crudely directed efforts, push away unpleasant objects impinging on his face or some part of it, and some neonates can even wriggle themselves into a comfortable corner of the crib, or in some other way adjust their posture. He cries when hungry or in distress, but he cannot run for help or shelter until the end of the first year has brought maturation of locomotion. He soon ceases to cry when picked up. But unlike the infants of sub-human species such as the monkey, he cannot cling to the mother for some months; he has to be held, and usually likes to be cradled or cuddled in his mother's arms. Like the monkey he prefers softness.

Although his sensory equipment is still immature, the neonate shows the ' orienting reflex ' (Sokolov, 1958), according to Soviet psychologists, and ' orientation ' is so basic that he will stop sucking to attend to a loud sound. He also looks at bright lights or other conspicuous visual stimuli. He shows reactions vividly by movements of head or hands, or a severe ' startle reflex ' at sudden loud sounds, or sudden loss of support. These imply tendencies to be sensitive to and to react to stimuli from the external world not connected with the oral or contact needs mentioned above.

His mother is biologically prepared to provide milk, and also to respond to his behaviour. While the infant can suck, he cannot get the

---

[1] The first version of this paper was presented at a Menninger Foundation Forum, 13 January, 1960.

INTERNATIONAL JOURNAL OF PSYCHOANALYSIS, 1964, 45, pp. 31–45.

milk without the breast or bottle to suck; this must be offered by a mother who in many instances actively helps the infant to solve his sucking and swallowing problems. The reflexes mentioned above, especially crying, but also spitting up, coughing, etc. attract the mother's attention and initiate her maternal care.

In most cultures the mother 'instinctively' shelters the newborn baby from excessive or harmful stimulation and after a few weeks of his healthy development she offers stimulation within limits suitable to his needs and capacities. The normal baby learns—after repeated experiences over many weeks—to recognize the mother's voice or footsteps as a signal of approaching food or comfort and becomes able to wait for her arrival when he hears these.

The mother is warmly rewarded by the baby's smile (Jones, 1926; Spitz, 1946b; Wolff, 1959), which begins to appear after the first weeks or months in situations of satisfaction or in response to pleasurable stimulation such as tickling, hugging, rhythmic play, and the mother's smile or that of others. The baby's response, in turn, evokes from the mother more of these loving expressions as well as her delighted verbal responses, which also stimulate the infant's vocalizations. Long before the infant clearly differentiates the mother from other adults he participates in mutually gratifying basic love experiences.

Motor capacities begin with diffuse tension-discharge patterns, a capacity to reach the mouth with the thumb, and steadily grow into a range of visual-motor skills, body management and locomotor resources (Mittelmann, 1954); these follow an innate timetable for maturation (Gesell, 1940; McGraw, 1943), but are rapidly involved in multiple motor interactions with all aspects of the environment including the mother, who is both a sensorimotor and social stimulus object and also a mediator of stimulation. Thus she has an important role in supporting ego development as well as in meeting basic needs for survival, and support for libidinal development.

The human infant has from birth capacities to learn through conditioning, which has been experimentally demonstrated (Marquis, 1931) and a tendency for active responses to produce configurated patterns or structures, a process closely related to channelling or familiarization. These processes soon add learned preferences, learned ' integration of skills, and learned organism-environment interaction patterns to his innate ones. In the early months, preferred foods, and a little later, preferred toys, are recognized (Escalona et al., 1953). The development of preferences involves the development of capacities to differentiate within all the modalities involved (and) concurrently with the processes of familiarization just mentioned. The development of clear-cut preference for the mother as distinct from other human beings, and consciousness of a special relationship to her, takes some months, but there are wide differences in different babies. Some babies are disturbed by strange people at as early as two months (Escalona et al., 1953).

All this can be seen as employing the phylogenetically developed equipment and needs of both human baby and mother to guarantee survival of an infant which cannot fend for itself, cannot obtain food or needed sensory stimulation through its own efforts, cannot keep warm or clean or protect itself adequately from harm or pain or excessive stimulation. Since it takes some years before a child is able to accomplish these necessary prerequisites for survival and normal development he is dependent upon prolonged adult care, which, however, gradually decreases as the child's resources increase. The patent fact of this dependence, visible and expressed through cries and through difficulties in managing for himself, constantly rearouses the normally responsive mother's attention and help.

The almost total dependence of the baby upon the mother during the first six months of life, the outstanding role of the baby's need to be fed, and the symbiotic relation of nursing baby and nursing mother led to a common practice of equating oral needs with dependence (although oral drives continue to provide gratification throughout life), and to focus upon vicissitudes in oral drives as the central dynamic factor in infantile life and in the relation of the infant to the mother (Freud, 1905).

The emphasis on orality has, in turn, led to certain balancing efforts to point up or to emphasize exclusively other instinctual drives and equipment which contribute to the development of an attachment of the baby to the mother by the end of the first half-year. Of these contributions, that of Bowlby (1951, 1953, 1958) is especially comprehensive.

He reviewed the literature dealing with this problem thoroughly (Bowlby, 1958), but also formulated a controversial hypothesis regarding the dynamics of the development of the infant's tie to the mother. In the following pages

I shall review Bowlby's questions, his summary of the hypotheses of Freud and others, his reasons for rejecting them, and his own hypothesis; I shall briefly summarize criticisms of his hypothesis by others and then add my own comments on Bowlby's use of ethology. From this point on I shall discuss (a) those contributions from Bowlby which seem to me valid, (b) the validity of hypotheses by Freud, Anna Freud, Winnicott, the Balints, Hoffer, and Greenacre as they concur with experimental and observational data on infant behaviour, (c) the implications of the latter for some aspects of ego development which have not been much discussed but can provide additional help to explain the phenomena from which Bowlby took his departure.

Bowlby's criticisms of theories of the infant's attachment to the mother and his multi-instinct hypothesis:

Bowlby's question is, How do we explain the attachment or tie of the child to the mother? He wants to explain this in order to understand the separation anxiety, grief, and, in extreme cases, anaclitic depression, marasmus or death which occurs when a child of nine months to two years is separated from the mother, without a familiar adequate mother-surrogate. He also emphasizes the child's demand for the mother to stay in sight. Why does the young child run after mother? Why should the child be so dependent for its development, and mental health if not survival, on the presence of the mother?

Since his formulation postulates several factors in the child's tie to the mother, it is important for us to consider these in turn. Inspired by the observations of the ' clinging ' pattern in chimpanzees and ' following ' pattern in geese, Bowlby (1958) has come to the conclusion that a human baby has an instinct to ' cling to its mother ' and an instinct to ' follow '. He invokes the vestigial grasping reflex of the baby as some evidence of the clinging instinct, and the observed tendency of toddlers to follow their mothers, especially when anxious, as important evidence for the ' following ' instinct. These he sees as two components of the baby's intense attachment to the mother, along with sucking, crying, and smiling. In order to lay a careful foundation for this hypothesis as contrasted with others, Bowlby reviews a series of remarks by Freud on the child's attachment to the mother, including his early emphasis on the importance of the mother as love-object and

source of many sensations. He notes both the ways in which his thinking is congruent with Freud's and points at which he differs.

It is important to review his outline of Freud's major comments here.

He notes that Freud's awareness of the importance of the attachment to the mother developed late and was reported only in his 1931 paper on ' Female Sexuality ', where he recognizes that the mother attachment precedes dependence on the father, but does not explain how this develops. Quoting Freud's (1922) encyclopedia article on *Psychoanalysis* he notes that Freud then believed that the ' oral component instinct finds satisfaction by attaching itself to the sating of the desire for nourishment; and its object is the mother's breast. It then detaches itself, becomes independent and at the same time auto-erotic, that is, finds an object in the child's own body. Others of the component instincts also start by being auto-erotic and are not until later directed on to an external object.' (This still does not tell us how the latter takes place; but it confirms the tendency to find the roots of attachment in orality, as Freud also did in the *Three Essays* (1905). There Freud stated that ' even after sexual activity has become detached from the taking of nourishment, an important part of this first and most significant of all sexual relations is left over. . . . All through the period of latency children learn to feel for other people who help them . . . and satisfy their needs a love which is on the model of, and a continuation of, their relation as sucklings to their nursing mother. . . .' But he went a bit further there, proceeding to praise the mother who by stroking, kissing and rocking him is ' fulfilling her task in teaching the child to love.')

In *Beyond the Pleasure Principle* (1920), Freud observed that an infant of eighteen months dislikes being left alone (but factors in this were not discussed). But six years later he dealt further with this observation originally discussed in terms of the infant's way of handling the loss. In *Inhibitions, Symptoms and Anxiety* (1926) he discussed anxiety as dread of loss of the mother due to the danger that his body needs will not be gratified and that this will lead to growing tension due to need, against which it (the baby) is helpless. The real danger is the ' economic disturbance caused by an accumulation of amounts of stimulation which require to be disposed of.'

In 1938 Freud described the relation to the mother as ' unique, without parallel, laid down unalterably for a whole lifetime, as the first and strongest love-object and as the prototype of all later love relations.' Continuing his emphasis on the dynamic importance of the mother's breast, Freud maintained that in addition to the satisfaction of the need for food, part of the baby's narcissistic cathexis of his own body is carried over to the breast as an outside object, which subsequently becomes completed into the whole person of the mother. She not only feeds him but looks after him and ' thus arouses in him many other physical sensations pleasant and unpleasant. By her care of the infant's body she becomes his first seducer.' This is a third point which, however, restates his position in the *Three Essays*, that the mother teaches the child to love.

Bowlby quotes Freud's 1938 addition that the ' phylogenetic foundation has so much the upper hand in all this . . . that it makes no difference whether the child has really sucked at the breast and never enjoyed the tenderness of a mother's care. His development takes the same path in both cases.' (Empirical data since that statement have challenged this.) Bowlby uses this as indication of Freud's inclination to entertain the notion that ' special drives built into the infant in the course of evolution underlie this first and unique love relationship.' To support this he refers to Freud's mention of the activity of a grasping instinct which ' may manifest itself as a simultaneous rhythmic tugging at the lobes of the ears, or a catching hold of some part of another person . . . for the same purpose ' (1958). Bowlby relates this to the concepts of the Hungarian school.

He is influenced by the Balints' concept of ' primary object relation ' (Balint, 1952), but he uses it chiefly to add weight to his emphasis on other non-oral components than the early need for an object. And he refers to Winnicott's (1960) remark that among the things that make the mother vitally important are the fact that ' she exists, continues to exist . . . is there to be sensed in all possible ways ' and that ' she loves in a physical way, provides contact, a body temperature, movement, and quiet according to the baby's need.' Bowlby also discusses Ribble's (1943) emphasis on the infant's innate need for contact with the mother. But he feels

dissatisfied with both Winnicott and Ribble because of their reliance, as he sees it, upon the theory that the child's tie to the mother is the result of gratifications from her satisfaction of his needs, rather than its own instinctive drives.

In particular Bowlby rejects what he refers to as ' secondary drive theory ' as expressed by Anna Freud: ' By means of the constantly repeated experience of satisfaction of the first body needs, the libidinal interest of the child is lured away from exclusive concentration on the happenings in his own body and directed toward those persons in the outside world (the mother or mother substitute) who are responsible for providing satisfaction ' (A. Freud and Burlingham, 1944). He claims that Anna Freud's observations on the child's tendency to cling even to mothers who are cross and sometimes cruel to them, suggest that the attachment of the small child to his mother is to a large degree independent of her personal qualities.[2]

Rejecting this ' secondary drive theory ', he proposes, then, that the child's tie is a resultant of five instinctive responses: sucking, clinging, following, crying, and smiling, which he thinks of in the sense in which ethologists have talked about ' species-specific behaviour patterns '. Bowlby is especially interested, and rightly, in what comes from the child himself, the active role of the child in contributing to the development of the attachment to the mother.

Schur (1960) in criticizing Bowlby distinguishes correctly between the ethologists' definition of instinct as a preformed behaviour pattern and the psycho-analytic concept of instinctual drive. Bowlby really uses the concept of instinct in the way in which it was used long before the development of psycho-analysis; psycho-analysis developed a special adaptation of the concept, using it to refer to psychic tendencies, drives, or wishes, for which Schur suggests that the term instinctual drive be adhered to, so as to avoid confusion with the biologists' term ' instinctive '.

Schur offers a formulation which fits with the current position both of ethology and of psychoanalysis; he emphasizes the complementary series of innate and acquired or learned factors, and the difficulty in man of discriminating between the two.

We can add that certainly by the second year

---

[2] It is important to note here the observational reports on children, and experimental reports on animals, where periods of gratifying response from the adult, alternating with some periods of frustration or pain, do not lead to withdrawal by the child; as long as there is a good chance of gratifying response, the child continues to maintain the relationship. We must also not forget the role of familiarity in these instances and the basic feeding, cleaning, and other necessary nurture carried on by even the cross mother.

of life when the child is able to 'follow' the mother we are dealing with a very complex level of functioning in which learning, memory, wish, and awareness of perception of need, however vague, are all involved in the child's response. We agree with Schur's statement that 'this vitally important relationship is the result of a long, immensely complex development, of an interaction which takes place at every psychological and physiological level'. When it comes to a more detailed view of this process, there is room for revision of his approach. While Schur succinctly implies the range of libidinal and ego development during the oral phase, to which the mother contributes, he does not deal with the role of the 'mother-baby relation' in contributing to other aspects of the child's development, particularly in transitional phases or when the child is faced with threat. In the most general terms, he asserts that the development of the tie to the mother is . . .'the result of an Anlage, its maturation and development in an unbelievably complex interaction.' This seems to imply that the tie to the mother simply evolves or unfolds in the setting of the complex interaction, rather than making a fundamental contribution to various aspects of the child's development. But later he says that the infant 'learns to connect a "mother" figure with a source of all these "physiological" and psychological nutriments'. This agrees with Freud's statement, but adds the role of perceptual differentiation of the mother. It enters the 'symbiotic phase' where 'self awareness and body image start to develop—where, however, self and object are not really yet differentiated.'

Schur does not point out the demands, stresses, frustrations, challenges presented to the infant by the simultaneous development of differentiation and the increased exposure to the strange which this development brings, and which reinforces the symbiotic need. He does refer to the many 'developmental reasons the child experiences anxiety in the absence of its mother', but these reasons need to be specified in relation to the processes of differentiation and what the latter contribute to strangeness anxiety.

We have seen that Schur includes the role of learning on the side of the infant; we can add also the role of learning by the mother as to the individual needs of the particular infant; these learnings from both sides lead to complex mutual adjustments, which contribute to or shape the symbiotic phase. (The learning processes are of many kinds; not only conditioning, canalization

(Murphy, 1947), and the structuring which results from functioning (Piaget, 1936), but the development of cognitive maps (Tolman, 1948) and the sorting out process by which a child in any culture learns *not* to use certain available sounds or gestures as Sullivan (1953) observes.) Thus while Schur refers to the role of familiarity, implied by Freud (1920), he does not develop the implications of this for the child's problem of orientation, the mother's contribution to this, and the relation between this and the child's reaction to the strange as factors in separation anxiety. However, Schur's position seems adequate to much of the data now available to us; and is in general agreement with the formulations of Spitz as well as those of Anna Freud.

These authors do not deal with that aspect of the relation between the child's tie to the mother and of his own development which leads to gradual *loosening* of the tie to the mother, a development which is in turn dependent on the emergence of an increasingly autonomous ego. Long before he is two a child will spontaneously crawl or run away from the mother if he is in a familiar area. Many a mother will say any time after crawling is well established, 'I have to chase him all day long'. By the time he is 4 or 5 years of age it is comfortably possible for the child to be separated from the mother for a major part of his waking day, provided he is in a secure environment suited to his needs. The omission of this tendency of the infant and young child to roam away from the mother is doubtless a natural outcome of the fact that these authors have observed children chiefly under extreme or stressful conditions; they have not reported the flexible process of normal alterations of loosening and tightening of the tie to the mother which we see under normal conditions (dependent upon need at the time and the vicissitudes and interrelations of ego and libido development).

Limitations of ethological concepts applied to human infants

I have noted above that in humans we are dealing with complex psychic resultants of drive tendencies and learning processes.

The infant cannot accurately be said to have an instinct to cling or to follow. The ethologist's concept of the process of developing a 'following' relationship is simple: the baby goose soon becomes 'imprinted' or attached to a moving object at the critical period of about 17 hours of age (Lorenz, 1950).

If we pause to reflect on why this might be so we see that the young goose, like some other infrahuman species, can feed itself, move about and do much that is needed to sustain life. It ' needs ' to follow the mother for a short time to learn where to go, to avoid danger, and a few other patterns necessary to survival. It does not have to learn much to learn how to be a goose. The infant by contrast can do much less and has to learn infinitely more, in order to become a socialized human being.

The young baby cannot cling effectively to its mother, although it has a vestigial capacity to support its weight on a rod (for a short period after birth). It cannot follow its mother as does the 17-hour-old goose, and when it does begin to follow at the age of 8 months or so, it is quite as likely to run off in the opposite direction. By the time it is capable of following, thousands of conditioning experiences have woven a web of meaning into the relation to its mother, so that we deal with a totally different level of response from what we see in the following of a little goose.

Babies at birth can *follow only with their eyes,* and they look at or *follow anybody or anything* bright, colourful and interesting at first. By the time they can differentiate mother from other people, thousands of visual, auditory, tactual, kinaesthetic and oral experiences with her have taken place; by the time the infant demands only or chiefly the mother or actually follows her, ample conditioning has gone on through these thousands of experiences, conditioning which, as we know from experimental work, begins from birth. Whether or not there is such a thing as a following instinct in a human baby, we cannot leave out the fact that this conditioning has occurred.

Clinging is an everyday normal pattern characteristic of chimpanzees and some other species. Hayes (1951), in describing her experiences with the baby chimpanzee she adopted and treated completely like a baby, comments convincingly at one point on how nearly intolerable it was to have this little creature physically clinging to her in exactly the way it would have constantly clung to its own mother. Human babies moreover are unable to do this, and in primitive groups are held in slings or strap-like supports on the mother's back or hip, when not supported by the mother's arm.

If the infant became ' imprinted ' directly as the result of an inborn drive, instinct, or pre-formed action pattern to ' follow ', released by the presence of a suitable object—according to the process of imprinting ethologists have observed in newly hatched geese—additional processes would not have to be involved in the development of an attachment any more than they do for geese.

Actually there are ample data to show that while there are wide individual differences in different infants, no human infant shows such an attachment before many weeks of complex, varied experiences with a mother have been lived through (generally six to nine months) which slowly lead to the perceptual differentiation of the need-gratifying mother from similar persons. In other words, it is not accurate to speak of *imprinting in the ethological sense* at all when a variety of processes of gratification by, cooperation with, conditioning to, channelling, and adaptation to a mother figure have to go on not for hours but for a couple of hundred days and nights or more.

All comparisons between infrahuman species and human infants have to be made in the light of the developmental differences as well as similarities between human and infrahuman babies. The fact that it takes the baby one or two years to develop the locomotor skills which a little gosling has in the first few minutes is not the only important difference. This locomotor skill does not develop in the human baby until other slow processes of sensory development and development of eye-hand coordination have taken place. Thus it is that developmental sequences and the sequences in experience, and the parallel process of developing relationships with the impersonal and personal objects of the environment are different for the baby from those seen in species whose newborn are soon able to run around and feed themselves.

Another major difference between gosling or baby chimpanzee and the human baby lies in the human potential for signals, communication, symbol-formation, speech, and abstract thought. These make possible an infinitely greater complexity of relationships with the environment, as well as more complex integrations of sensory, motor, and cognitive resources of the baby. Early needs and drives for interaction, play, differentiated communication, have to be met in order to make possible these later complex relationships. Thus in many ways beyond the different conception of instinct the ethological approach is inadequate for understanding the human infant's relation to the mother, and the mother's role in helping the primitive organism to become a ' human ' being.

I emphasized earlier my appreciation of the multi-factor approach which Bowlby wishes to emphasize, and the readiness which this includes to deal with a complex process in a complex way. I also agreed 'with his emphasis on the active impulses from the infant himself which contribute to the relation to the mother. Beyond this, I would like to suggest that what he is calling attention to, with his emphasis on clinging and following, is in essence the infant's need for *contact with an object*; and what he is calling attention to in his emphasis on crying and smiling, is the infant's need for *communication* with the mother. But in line with my remarks just above, I think these have been and can be discussed in more accurate and useful ways than his terms allow.

Instead of the ' clinging ' and ' following ' instinct, I would rather talk about the multiple reaching out or *approach* patterns of babies as they explore the mother's body visually and tactually as well as orally in the earliest weeks before they are able to explore other objects. These approaching, exploring activities are precursors of capacities for manipulating which develop after thumb, finger, forefinger, prehension and visual-tactual coordination have matured. All of these have to do with the infant's need for the object, for the outside world, for stimulation (Jacobson, 1954). These approach activities bring the infant into multiple kinds of contact with the mother.

Here the contributions of Winnicott and Greenacre are relevant. Winnicott, with an emphasis on other than oral needs, discusses (1960) the role of the infant's need for skin contact in his concept of the ' holding phase '. In this early holding phase, Winnicott says, the ego moves gradually from an unintegrated state to a structured integration. One concomitant of this is that the infant becomes able to experience anxiety associated with disintegration. The result of healthy progress is that he attains to what might be called ' unit status '. The infant becomes a person, an individual in his own right.

Winnicott, moreover, provides a welcome balance when he says that ' one-half of the theory of the parent-infant relationship concerns the infant, and is the theory of the infant's journey from absolute dependence through relative dependence to independence. . . . The other half of the theory of the infant-child

relationship concerns maternal care, that is to say the qualities and changes in the mother that meet the specific and developing needs of the infant. . . .' This includes the needs for active support of the developing ego.

Winnicott is concerned here with these residues for ego development: ' As a result of success in maternal care (early empathy, then accurate response to signals) there is built up in the infant a *continuity of being which is the basis of ego strength.*' This continuity of being, we can add, is supported by stability and balance within the baby itself, with important individual differences within the individual baby, in the initial balance with which it starts life and goes through the stages of development, and also in the capacity to use support from the mother in achieving this balance. He comments on effects of failure of environmental provision for support for the ego development of the child and adds that ' the work of Klein on the defence mechanisms and on projections and introjections is an attempt to state ' the effects of this failure.

Winnicott does not discuss those specific ego processes and functions which begin in the earliest weeks and are an expression of the activity of the developing innate structures— the looking, listening, touching and so forth which can be seen in many babies even during the earliest weeks. Although these ego functions are autonomous in the sense that they emerge spontaneously, without training, and without extraneous gratification, they are also dependent on adequate environmental support in terms of appropriate stimuli. The work of Hebb (1949) and others has well established the dependence of even the mature organized mind on sensory intake. This offers one link that we needed in order to see the meaning of data from Spitz (1945, 1946a), and others also, on hospitalization; that is, the failure of adequate development of babies aseptically screened from multiple sensory stimulation. Moreover, without the stable presence of objects the infant cannot develop a concept of a constant object. The mother is the agent through whom many aspects of normal ' autonomous ego development ' are supported, as well as the mediator of libidinal gratification.

As ego development proceeds, ego functions serve libidinal demands, and while the mother supports ego and drive development independently she also supports their interaction. The mother's assistance to the child's autonomous efforts begins at birth, in her ways of facilitating his first sucking, burping, even eliminating, then in holding him in a position to see; she soon offers a variety of stimuli to activity with rattles to touch, then bang, and other toys. The fact that the mother not only meets nutritional and other bodily needs and gives and evokes love, but also supports the development of the specific ego functions and the integrative functions of the ego is important for understanding the seriousness of separation problems in the second year of life before the child has achieved stable autonomy.

The mother's role in supporting the ego development of the child also includes helping him to deal with anxiety and to modulate anger, frustration feelings, and the aggressive impulses aroused by these. Greenacre (1960) recently discussed certain aspects of the ego-development of the child and the place these have in the development of his relation with the mother; she focusses chiefly on the active protest, resistance, 'fighting' by the infant against unwanted procedures, and angry throwing away of objects not accepted as substitutes when the child is frustrated. In very active infants we also see what Greenacre describes as the vigorous bouncing, moving against the mother, but this is by no means typical of all infants. These encounters probably all contribute to the experience of separateness and the achievement of awareness of self over against the environment, including the possibility of a relationship which consists of the interaction of two egos rather than the utter dependence of the baby on the mother.

The role of ego development in the child's relation to the mother

I have touched on some aspects of the role of ego development in the child's relation to the mother in referring to Winnicott's position and that of Greenacre, but there is room for further clarification of some of the aspects of ego development to be included here.

Each new advance in the ego development of the infant makes possible new areas of autonomy and thus the possibility of a little more separation from the mother at least for a limited time within the limits of that achievement, and more awareness of self and mother as distinct. Each new area of skill reduces by so much the child's need to rely on the mother. But these ego functions do not add up to an organized and organizing ego, or awareness of a separate body ego. We saw above that Winnicott (1960), Hoffer (1950), and others have seen the development of the continuous, coherent, and organized

ego as dependent upon the reliability of inner experiences of comfort and satisfaction.

Here we may suggest that a variety of both negative, neutral, and positive experiences are involved. Freud suggested that bad feelings tend to be referred to the outside (1937). If this is true, it would appear that any disturbing encounter with the environment, conflict, or other painful experience would tend to produce awareness of outside versus self.

Experiences produced by startle or fear reactions; painful stimuli such as bumps or other rough encounters with the external world; or painful handling by adults including the use of any instruments that are painful; experiences of rough uncomfortable textures or vehicles—all these would tend to interfere on the one hand with the continuity of the comfortable inner equilibrium and to stimulate negative feelings about the outside and to separate the outside from the self.

In view of the fact that even the newborn discriminates between acceptable and unacceptable tastes (Carmichael, 1946) we have to recognize that differentiation of some pleasurable and unpleasurable stimuli begins at least from birth. The frown on the face of a 4-week-old-baby first experiencing a bottle after a month of breast feeding indicates that this differentiation is very soon accompanied by affect and some sort of rudimentary puzzlement, or effort to come to terms with the strange stimulus, which we assume may be vaguely referred to the outside.

Aside from the clearly unpleasant experiences which tend to detach the ego from the environment we also have to include the primary basic interactions between the baby and the environment, especially the orienting reflex, noted above, studied most extensively and intensively by scientists in the USSR (Sokolov, 1958). The orienting reflex is present from birth and is a reaction to a new stimulus or to a change and occurs even when the baby is nursing, as when he hears a new sudden sound.

It is just a step from this very first expression of mobilization for orientation, to the sustained listening and looking at what is out there as the baby achieves visual focus; the orientation process as we have described it from direct observation is elaborated and supported by various devices and steps as the child grows older.

While looking and listening are first visible as expressions of the effort to get oriented to the environment, as fast as manual coordination develops, activities of touching and handling objects begin to multiply (Shirley, 1931–33). In various ways the infant discovers the many different experiences which different kinds of encounters with different kinds of objects can provide.

The 8-week-old baby batting at a rattle or looking around the room is beginning to ' amuse himself ' and to tolerate absence of the mother. The 8-month-old baby who bangs a spoon in a cup, crumples paper to make new sounds and textures, is experiencing a capacity to create stimulation, which also extends his autonomy.

Along with these first most simple sensory encounters with the environment we find evidences of *selective* actions, *efforts to change the relationship of the self and the environment.* From the first days with some babies, or the first weeks with others we see actions of avoiding, and turning away or refusing. The baby who wants no more milk, or no more of whatever has been put into his mouth, may clamp his mouth shut, or spit out what was put into it. The baby who finds the light too bright may turn his head away. Many times in the Escalona-Leitch records we see young babies deliberately avoiding a particular stimulus or avoiding all further stimuli after a certain number have been presented.

At the earliest level we see some babies protesting by crying, terminating, fending off, pushing away and pushing against objects. These have all been observed within the first four weeks of life, although the capacity of babies' for this group of active efforts to deal with the environment varies greatly with individuals.

Increasingly after the first two months or so we also see efforts to evoke or stimulate a response from the environment: by crying for, smiling for, reaching for, or in other ways attracting attention. Activities of this sort are very vivid at three to four months, although they vary greatly with different babies, as does every aspect of development.

The capacity to manage the body in space or in relation to other objects so as to avoid painful bumps, uncomfortable postures, etc. is extended through the first year until the child is able to reach his own goal through his own locomotor efforts, steering in order to deal with obstacles between himself and the goal. Some children from the earliest weeks are able to adjust their posture to the mother's body or to the bed to make their own body comfortable;

most babies achieve this ability by the age of 4 or 5 months. By 8 or 10 months many babies physically resist all unpleasant or constraining handling, including those dressing and diapering activities which they find a nuisance. These manoeuvres towards, through, against, or away from the environment express and further sharpen the awareness of separateness. Between the age of a year and 18 months various self-care activities develop, including self-feeding, use of the spoon and pulling off clothes.

All these directed interactions with the environment, or executive actions, which have the effect of (*a*) avoiding pain, (*b*) reaching gratification, (*c*) increasing orientation and mastery, (*d*) making increasing use of objects in the environment in relation to these aims, also have the effect of helping the child to outgrow a tendency to be dominated by what we might call the omnipotence-helplessness axis. The more his capacity to make himself comfortable and avoid distress, get the help of the environment and also to help himself, increases, the more the omnipotence-helplessness axis yields to an attitude of effort toward realistic mastery; to this end the baby repetitiously and effortfully practises and perfects new motor skills, both within the area of eye-hand coordination and within the area of locomotion, and integrations of these in the direction of reaching goals. From these the ego feelings of mastery develop (Bernfeld, 1929).

In the process of all these developments of different ego functions and their increasingly directed use by the ego, we can assume an increasing awareness of the environment as ' out there ', to be used at times, at other times presenting barriers or difficulties.

If this is a sound approach it can help us to understand some of the difficulties in achievement of autonomy from the mother which we can observe in certain babies. Those infants with *low* motor drive, activity level, and related drive to explore the environment would have fewer encounters of the kind which contribute to awareness of self as distinct from the environment and also as able to manage the space and objects of the environment. This awareness probably also underlies specific differentiation of self from mother. Thus, passive babies would be expected to be slower to achieve differentiation of self from mother, and slower to develop autonomous ways of obtaining gratification from and protecting themselves in the environment. They would need to maintain closeness longer, that is to ' cling ', in the general sense of depending upon the mother for orientation, facilitation of gratification, safety, and the like. These are the children of low muscle tonus, markedly ' fragile ' appearance, whom we may see clinging to the mother at a later age than active children.

Similarly, children with very low sensory thresholds, high autonomic reactivity, developmental imbalance and other constitutional tendencies which contribute to vulnerability to overstimulation, could be expected to need to reduce encounters with the environment, retain more protection, and use the mother longer as an ego support or even surrogate. Reduced exploratory manipulation of the environment limits reality-testing and mastery; and the need to keep stimulation within low limits would interfere with depth of cathexis of stimuli other than those associated with safety and freedom from pain. These processes in turn reduce the resources which the more active or sturdy child utilizes and which gradually free him from the mother.

The development of ego functions which gradually free the child from the mother not only needs the support, stimulation, and protection of the mother to provide necessary material for sensory and motor experiencing and activity, as we saw above. Her help is also needed, especially at transition periods of new emerging functions, to keep the child from being overwhelmed by quantities or qualities of stimulation which he cannot handle. In this process, the mother, who is object of libido and aggression, who is familiar, and the source of major basic gratifications and satisfactions of needs, carries a basic role in the process of orientation, familiarization, and development of the infant's capacity to make new uses of the environment, and to integrate new relationships to it.

In pointing to the aspect of familiarity of the mother as basic in the child's tie to the mother, Freud by implication includes the problem of the *strange* in the infant's and the young child's problems of adaptation. It is significant that the two-year-old stage of sensitivity to strangers is the one which recurs, in the study of the child going to the hospital (Robertson, 1952), in Anna Freud and Dorothy Burlingham's observations (1944), in Bowlby's description of the small child following its mother (1958). These various authors, impressed by the child's anxiety at separation (in this phase, in threatening situations) do not fully scrutinize the developmental situation of the child at this time, or ask why strangeness and separation are especially stressful to the child at this state, as contrasted with its situation in a new place two or three years later; or what relation this has to the phenomena of ' attachment ' as illustrated by anxious clinging to the mother chiefly in these strange or threatening situations, while the same child roams away from his mother in a more secure situation.

Let us now look again at the child's situation in the sensitive phase of the second year of life. He has come to learn that things have names and purposes, most of which he does not know; he relies on his mother to tell him these names of things, places, processes, and events. Other people generally cannot easily understand the child's expressions and communications at this stage, so that he is dependent upon his mother's understanding of his questions to help in this basic process of clarification and familiarization. He is expanding his diet, but is often still squeamish about new foods, as well as having less appetite than formerly. He is in the process of outgrowing his diapers. Even at home these transitions are not easy; help from the familiar mother in getting used to strange things is crucial.

Thus not only, as Freud says, is the mother familiar, but she is his chief ally in the *process of familiarization* and making transitions from the very first steps in orientation to the point of relative autonomy when he goes to school.

Since this is an area which has attracted special study, consider the child in the hospital: there are new garments to be put on, new beds and coverings; new light fixtures; a different kind of brush to brush his hair; and endless new objects, medical tools and apparatus. Even with mother present a sensitive child may be overwhelmed by this massive newness.

Mutual expressions of love are also part of the familiar context and the daily emotional diet and are lost in the hospital setting. In other words, it is not just the loss of the love-object, in addition to the helpful role in meeting needs for familiarization with new aspects of the environment, it is the loss of the familiar way of loving, of expressing deep instinctual responses. The fact that the second year of life is a period of dramatic emergence of a sense of identity (expressed in response to his name, ability to use ' I ', to point to parts of his body) probably adds to the severity of the sense of loss of his own ways of expressing intense affects.

If his mother is available when he confronts

strangeness, he uses her in a variety of ways, cuddling, clinging, seeking body contact and loving help to restore the most basic and fundamental memories of security and contentment. If she is there, he has some confidence that the timing and pace of demands in the new situation will be modified to his coping capacity; she will understand his questions, will help him manage; and she will probably offer him rewards for cooperating in addition to the gratification of her presence.

The mother knows what the baby likes, what will appeal to him, how to motivate him, how fast he can be expected to make a new response, and what allowances or assistance he needs in order to be able to deal with the new situation; she helps to mediate the environment, to keep it within his limits of tolerance. In other words, mother and baby have a complex workable relationship in which each knows what to count on from the other.

Separation, then, is stressful at any time before the child has achieved secure locomotion, speech, self help and the capacity to evoke help from others when needed, to orient himself in strange places by his own efforts, to make new relationships with satisfaction and to get and maintain the level of stimulation he needs and protect himself comfortably from excessive demands from the environment.

In other words, the child's tendency to cling to, and to follow the mother in a situation like this is not merely an expression of innate instincts to behave in certain ways. It is both a deep cathexis of a gratifying love-object, and an expression of the child's urgent need to be able to manage, or to have help in familiarizing himself in and dealing with a strange world. We can use the concept of drive to mastery here, and the need to conquer the sense of helplessness which is brought by the child's feelings of inability to manage so much that is strange.

From the point of view which I have gradually reached, the clinging and following behaviour of the toddler referred to by Bowlby and seen chiefly in a strange or threatening situation, represents a complex response to anxiety: the child is using relatively new and only partially achieved functions of locomotion, climbing, etc. in order to reach and maintain an earlier secure infantile position of being held. This position represents protection to the child and reinstates his previous station in the arms of his mother, from which he can safely orient himself and familiarize himself with a new situation. He needs to use his mother again as an auxiliary ego and also get comfort. Clinging and following behaviour do not produce the attachment; they are an expression of the infant's reliance upon the need-gratifying, protecting, helping and soothing mother-figure.

In presenting this view of the mother's supportive role during the period of immaturity of the ego, we see this as congruent with and chiefly amplifying the emphasis by Freud, Anna Freud, Winnicott and others on the dependence of the infant and the young child, the role of need-gratifying activities of the mother, her role as object and source of much rich stimulation. I agree that we need to recognize all the active reaching out and effort to come to terms with the environment and to evoke what it needs, brought by the infant itself. I consider the feeding and loving aspects of the mother-baby relation as important not only in their own right but also for the massive and deep reinforcement they provide to the basic structuring and ego-development which goes on in the course of every aspect of the mother-baby experience.

In other words, an adequate review of the development of the mother-child relation is multilateral; it needs to look at the contribution and the problems each brings to the other, in ego terms, as well as in terms of the instinctual development of the baby and the libidinal contributions of the mother. This applies as well to the fuller understanding of the process of identification, which will require a separate discussion.

REFERENCES

BALINT, A. (1939). 'Love for the Mother and Mother Love.' In: *Primary Love and Psycho-Analytic Technique*, ed. M. Balint (1952).

BALINT, M. (1952). *Primary Love and Psycho-Analytic Technique*. (London: Hogarth.)

BERNFELD, S. (1929). *The Psychology of the Infant*. (New York: Brentano.)

BOWLBY, J. (1951). *Maternal Care and Mental Health*. (Geneva: W.H.O.)

—— (1953). 'Some Pathological Processes Engendered by Early Mother-Child Separation.' In: *Infancy and Childhood*, ed. M. J. Senn. (New York: Josiah Macy Jr. Fdn.)

—— (1958). 'The Nature of the Child's Tie to his Mother.' *Int. J. Psycho-Anal.*, 39.

BUHLER, C. (1930). *The First Year of Life.* (New York: John Day.)

CARMICHAEL, L. (1946). *Manual of Child Psychology.* (New York: Wiley, 1946.)

DEWEY, EVELYN (1935). *Behavior Development in Infants.* (New York: Columbia Univ. Press.)

ESCALONA, S. *et al.* (1953). *Earliest Phases of Personality Development.* (Child Res. Mono. No. 17. Evanston, Ill: Ch. Development Publications.)

—— Infant Records. (Filed at Topeka, Kansas: Menninger Foundation.)

FEDERN, P. (1952). *Ego Psychology and the Psychoses.* (New York: Basic Books.)

FREUD, A., and BURLINGHAM, D. (1942). *War and Children.* (New York: Int. Univ. Press, 1943.)

—— (1944). *Infants without Families.* (New York: Int. Univ. Press.)

FREUD, S. (1905). *Three Essays on the Theory of Sexuality.* *S.E.*, 7.

—— (1915). 'Instincts and their Vicissitudes.' *S.E.*, 14.

—— (1920). *Beyond the Pleasure Principle.* *S.E.*, 18.

—— (1921). *Group Psychology and the Analysis of the Ego.* *S.E.*, 18.

—— (1922). 'Psycho-Analysis.' *S.E.*, 18.

—— (1925). 'Psycho-Analysis: Freudian School.' *S.E.*, 20.

—— (1926). *Inhibitions, Symptoms and Anxiety.* *S.E.*, 20.

—— (1931). 'Female Sexuality.' *C.P.*, 5.

—— (1932). *New Introductory Lectures on Psychoanalysis.* (New York: Norton, 1933.)

—— (1937). 'Analysis Terminable and Interminable.' *C.P.*, 5.

—— (1938). *An Outline of Psychoanalysis.* (New York: Norton, 1949.)

GESELL, A. (1940). *The First Five Years.* (New York: Harper.)

GREENACRE, P. (1960). 'Considerations regarding the Parent-Infant Relationship.' *Int. J. Psycho-Anal.*, 41.

HARLOW, H. (1958). 'The Nature of Love.' *Amer. Psychol.*, 15.

HARTMANN, H. (1939). 'Ego Psychology and the Problem of Adaptation.' In: *Organization and Pathology of Thought*, ed. D. Rapaport. (New York: Columbia Univ. Press, 1951.)

HAYES, C. (1951). *The Ape in our House.* (New York: Harper.)

HEBB, D. O. (1949). *The Organization of Behavior: A Neuropsychological Theory.* (New York: Wiley.)

HENDRICKS, I. (1942). 'Instinct and the Ego During Infancy.' *Psychoanal. Quart.*, 11.

HOFFER, W. (1950). 'Development of the Body Ego.' *Psychoanal. Study Child*, 5.

JACOBSON, E. (1954). 'The Self and the Object World.' *Psychoanal. Study Child*, 9.

JONES, M. C. (1926). 'The Development of Early Behavior Patterns in Young Children.' *J. Genet. Psychol.*, 33.

KLEIN, M., and RIVIERE, J. (1937). *Love, Hate, and Reparation.* (London: Hogarth.)

LEVY, D. (1930). 'The Strange Hen.' *Amer. J. Orthops.*, 20.

—— (1937). 'Primary Affect Hunger.' *Amer. J. Psychiat.*, 94.

LORENZ, K. Z. (1950). 'The Comparative Method in Studying Innate Behaviour Patterns.' No. 4, Symposia Soc. for Exp. Biol. (London: Cambridge Univ. Press.)

McGRAW, M. (1943). *The Neuromuscular Maturation of the Human Infant.* (New York: Columbia Univ. Press.)

MAHLER, M. S. (1958). 'Autism and Symbiosis: Two Extreme Disturbances of Identity.' *Int. J. Psycho-Anal.*, 39.

MARQUIS, D. P. (1931). 'Can Conditioned Reflexes be Established in the Newborn Infant?' *J. Genet. Psychol.*, 39.

MITTELMANN, B. (1954). 'Motility in Infants, Children and Adults: Patterning and Psychodynamics.' *Psychoanal. Study Child*, 9.

MURPHY, G. (1947). *Personality.* (New York: Harper.)

PETERSON, F., and RAINEY, L. H. (1910). 'The Beginnings of Mind in the Newborn.' *Bull. Lying-In Hosp. of New York*, 7.

PIAGET, J. (1936). *The Origins of Intelligence in Children.* (New York: Int. Univ. Press, 1952.)

PRATT, K. C. *et al.* (1930). 'The Behavior of the Newborn Infant.' *Ohio State Univ. Stud. Confr. Psychol.*, No. 10.

PROVENCE, S., and LIPTON, R. C. (1962). *Infants in Institutions.* (New York: Int. Univ. Press.)

RADO, S. (1939). 'Developments in the Psychoanalytic Conception and Treatment of the Neuroses.' In: *Psychoanalysis of Behavior.* (New York: Grune & Stratton, 1956.)

RIBBLE, M. (1943). *Rights of Infants.* (New York: Columbia Univ. Press.)

ROBERTSON, J., and BOWLBY, J. (1952). 'Responses of Young Children to Separation from their Mothers. II. Observation of Sequences of Response of Children aged 16 to 24 Months during Course of Separation.' *Courrier de Centre International de l'Enfance*, 2.

SCHAFFER, H. R. (1958). 'Objective Observations of Personality Developments in Early Infancy.' *Brit. J. med. Psychol.*, 31.

SCHUR, M. (1960). 'Discussion of Dr Bowlby's Paper.' *Psychoanal. Study Child*, 15.

SHIRLEY, M. (1931–33). *The First Two Years of Life.* (Minneapolis: Univ. of Minnesota Press.)

SOKOLOV, E. N. (1958). *Perception and the Conditioned Reflex.* (Moscow: Univ. of Moscow.)

SPITZ, R. (1945). 'Hospitalism: An Inquiry into the Genesis of Psychiatric Conditions in Early Childhood.' *Psychoanal. Study Child*, 1.

210

—— (1946a). 'Hospitalism: Follow-up Report.' *Psychoanal. Study Child*, **2**.

—— (1946b). 'The Smiling Response: A Contribution to the Genesis of Social Relations.' *Genet. Psychol. Mono.*, **34**.

—— (1954). 'Infantile Depression and the General Adaptation Syndrome.' In: *Depression*, ed. P. M. Hoch and J. Zubin. (New York: Grune & Stratton.)

SPITZ, R., and WOLF, K. (1946). 'Anaclitic Depression.' *Psychoanal. Study Child*, **2**.

SULLIVAN, H. S. (1953). *Interpersonal Theory of Psychiatry*. (New York: Norton.)

TOLMAN, E. (1948). 'Cognitive Maps in Rats and Men.' *Psychol. Rev.*, **55**.

WINNICOTT, D. W. (1960). 'The Theory of the Parent-Infant Relationship.' *Int. J. Psycho-Anal.*, **41**.

WOLF, K. M. (1952). 'Observation of Individual Tendencies in the First Year of Life.' In: *Problems of Infancy and Childhood*. Trans. 6th Conference. (New York: Josiah Macy Jr. Fdn.)

WOLFF, PETER (1959). 'Observations on Newborn Infants.' *Psychosom. Med.*, **21**.

YARROW, L. J. (1955). 'Research on Maternal Deprivation.' A.A.A.S. Annual Meeting Section I. Atlanta, Ga.

—— (1956). 'The Development of Object Relationships during Infancy, and the Effects of a Disruption of Early Mother-Child Relationships.' *Amer. Psychol.*, **11**.

211

SCHIZOPHRENIC COMMUNICATION*

Harold F. Searles

Although communication with his fellow men is one of the basic goals to which every person's life is dedicated, it is for the schizophrenic individual an even more absorbing activity. Unlike his relatively healthy fellows, who possess reliable tools of communication in both verbal and non-verbal media, tools to which they can confidently turn as the need arises, he has few if any such dependable techniques. Thus in his activities the communicational facet which is, perhaps, present in every human activity, is the facet which takes precedence over other aspects, or motives, of his behavior. Rarely if ever can he "just" eat, or walk, or read, or listen to music, or whatever, immersed in this as an immediate experience having an end in itself; instead, for him, it presents itself as primarily another front in the unceasing battle for communication with others—or sometimes, for a prevention of disturbing delusional communication with others—a front on which a breakthrough may at last be achieved. The following comments by Ruesch, concerning two of the varieties of nonverbal language in human beings generally, are particularly applicable to the schizophrenic individual and, in my opinion, are proportionately less applicable to the person who has developed reliable modes of communication and who can afford, therefore, to "just live" as a subjectively separate entity at least a fair share of the time:

> . . . *Action language* embraces all movements that are not used exclusively as signals. Such acts as walking and drinking, for instance, have a dual function; on the one hand, they serve personal needs, and on the other, they constitute statements to those who may perceive them. *Object language* comprises all intentional and non-

* This research was supported by a grant from the Ford Foundation to the Chestnut Lodge Research Institute.

PSYCHOANALYSIS AND THE PSYCHOANALYTIC REVIEW, 1961, 48, pp. 3-50.

intentional display of material things such as implements, machines, art objects, architectural structures, and last but not least, the human body and whatever clothes it. . . .[12a]

In this paper I shall present what I have learned of schizophrenic communication in the course of more than eleven years of working predominantly with chronic schizophrenic patients. The paper attempts neither to explore the subject comprehensively nor to do justice to the relevant literature; it is devoted primarily, though not exclusively, to matters of *verbal* communication; and it is more clinical than theoretical in orientation. I have little hope of conveying original concepts to my fellow specialists in this field, but much hope of helping those therapists or analysts who are somewhat less at home here, who feel more baffled and lost here than on sure and familiar ground, to see and understand various aspects of this subject which became clear to me only in the course of years—one or two, seven or eight, ten or eleven, variously, in the instances of certain of the points I shall make—of working with schizophrenic patients.

First, I shall describe the more overt features of schizophrenic communication; next, various aspects of the patient's psychodynamics which account for these modes of communication; and, lastly, a number of points concerning relevant psychotherapeutic technique.

A. OVERT FEATURES

In our attempt to pierce the obscurity, and unravel the indirectness, of schizophrenic communication, it is useful to become acquainted with the various forms of disguise—that is to say, mental mechanisms or modes of defense—which are commonly at work. These are the same as those which constitute the various disguises found in dreams. In my experience these are the most common ones:

1. *Displacement*: Here the patient's comment has reference to a different person, and often is couched in terms of a different temporal era, than is intended by the preconscious or unconscious impulse which is striving for expression. For example, one of my first schizophrenic patients, a single young hebephrenic woman, ruminated for months on end, both throughout her therapeutic sessions with me and in her daily life on the ward, about the social rejections she had suffered in previous years, in her home city, prior to her

hospitalization. It took a number of months for me to realize that, though she was consciously thus immersed in events which had happened years ago and hundreds of miles away, innumerable of her comments could be understood, now, as preconscious or unconscious responses to events in her current life in the hospital. For instance, when she pressed her psychiatric administrator for an explanation of "Why did those two men give me the go-by?", I now understood this to mean, "Why are you and Dr. .... [another member of our staff; she showed indications of being romantically interested in each of them] giving me the go-by?" And, after approximately two more years, I developed the necessary courage to see that there was still another level of displacement involved in such comments: her remarkably intense libidinal feelings had been intended, evidently from the first, primarily for me as a father-figure in the transference, but had been almost totally displaced, in their overt expression, onto the young men in her history, and, more recently, onto my colleagues on the hospital staff.

This woman loved to wear unconventional and ever-changing costumes, and I had some reason to think that she found me boringly unimaginative in my attire, though she had never made as yet any direct statement to this effect. One day, after I had worn the same plain brown suit for many days in succession, she glanced at me as she came in and, to my amusement, said with annoyance, "I had a dream last night about Dr. .... [one of the above-mentioned colleagues]. He was wearing that damned brown suit."

This was one of the occasions when the displacement seemed almost consciously contrived. Another such incident occurred in an hour when, after having received some stiffening of the backbone from one of my supervisors, I resolved to delete from my psychotherapeutic approach to this young woman certain of my more obsequious responses; this was not an easy thing to do, for there was in her not merely a recurrently-jilted young thing, but also an arrogant, tyrannical *grande dame,* who was not accustomed to any trifling with her imperiousness. This time, as I went to close the door for her after she had entered my office, I behaved not like an effortless doorman but, one might say, like a well-oiled one: I said, sarcastically, "Grace, if you ever *feel like* closing the door as you come in, feel free to—and you won't lose any status as a woman, either, as far as I'm concerned, if you do."

Scarcely had these solicitous words ceased purring from my lips than she expostulated, in an unusually loud, outraged voice, full of scathing contempt, something about a play she had seen in New York (several years previously) in which "they had Eddie Landon's [a personal acquaintance of the patient] sister come out with her hair up and powder on her face. It was *stupid*," she exclaimed, practically spitting her contempt, "It was *stupid* as all hell!" On hearing this, I said firmly, "If you thought my suggestion that you close the door was stupid—", whereupon she interrupted, "I *did* think it was stupid," flatly and emphatically. I asserted, "I *don't* think it was stupid," and proceeded to bawl her out for not taking more responsibility for herself.

Here again, the displacement of her anger and contempt may have been in large part a conscious maneuver, since it was so easily cut through with my comment. But I encountered thousands of instances with her in which the displacement was a largely, or wholly, unconscious operation; she evidently genuinely *experienced* the communicated feelings in their displaced context. As with all the forms of distorted communication which one encounters with schizophrenic patients, one fairly soon learns that any particular patient shows considerable variability, from moment to moment, as to whether the distorted form of communication is only a "manner of speaking," or whether, instead, it is a faithful reflection of a distorted "manner of experiencing." The less experienced therapist is apt to assume, too frequently, that it is only a highly distorted form of *communication*, which springs out of a subjective experience, on the part of the patient, not widely different from his own experience of what is happening at the moment. It seems usually to require any therapist some years of work in this field to dare to see how remarkably distorted is the subjective experience of the patient itself.

In the instance of the patient I have just been describing, for example, it required more than four years for me to realize that she experienced *similar* persons or things as being *identical*—a phenomenon to which Arieti[1a] has applied the term "paleologic." This became evident during an hour in which she commented, "Dr. Edwards and Dr. Michaels [two of the other psychiatrists on the staff*] are the same," after having touched upon some similarities between them;

* Pseudonyms, as are all the names used in the clinical material in this paper.

215

and when, later in the hour, she said in a tone first of genuine puzzlement, then of discovery, "I always think my stockings are my glasses. Well, I don't *always* think so; but I often do." A few days before, she had mentioned that she derived the same feeling of security from her stockings (which she wore not on her legs but stuffed, wadded up, under the soles of her feet) as she did from her glasses (which she always wore, because of severe myopia). This revelation came a few days after her eccentricity about the stockings, a symptom which had persisted for many months, had finally been relinquished. Three months later on, she described in retrospect an incident during that era when her administrative psychiatrist "Told me, 'You ought to get along without your stockings!' I felt just as if he'd said, 'You ought to get along without your glasses!' " It is small wonder that schizophrenic patients whose perceptual-conceptual experience is so poorly differentiated would be prone, in innumerable instances, to the unconscious use of displacement.

Another young woman, whose ego-fragmentation was so extreme that she was incapable, for years, of more than fleeting moments of relatedness, revealed even less often any friendly feelings. I was touched, therefore, to learn that after she had been bathed by a student nurse whom she liked, she expressed her appreciation by saying, "I love your brother." She could not yet dare to say it—or, perhaps, even to experience it—in the direct, undisplaced form, "I love you." This woman used occasionally to ply me with the question, "Do you like ....?", giving the name of some person or other from her home city, a city with which I am almost totally unacquainted. One day she asked, "Do you like Roger O'Neill?", and, for the nth time, I tiredly responded, "Roger O'Neill. I never heard the name before. Any thoughts about him, as to how you feel about him?" She made no direct answer to this; but after some apparently unrelated, fragmentary comments from her, it dawned on me to comment, "When you asked if I like Roger O'Neill, maybe you were wondering if I like *you*," gently. Tears came into her eyes, and I felt confirmed in my interpretation of her meaning. I had noticed a few moments before this interchange, that when I addressed her by her first name, in a friendly, close way, she turned around with sudden hopefulness on her face, as if her heart had lifted.

Since then I have come gradually to see how very much of the time the schizophrenic patient is absorbed with the question of whether the therapist (=mother, in most such instances) likes him; and that he ventures to inquire about this in dozens of different questions which are couched in contexts involving displacement.

One becomes impressed, even more, by the extent to which he is concerned, basically (whether consciously or unconsciously), with what is transpiring *at the moment* between the doctor and himself, although his communications may involve, persistently, so much displacement to distant persons and remote temporal eras that the therapist will be slow to realize this. One of the many incidents which helped to convey this point to me occurred in a session with a hebephrenic man. He had grown up in a beautiful home but had been hospitalized now for a dozen years on wards which, because of the severity of his illness, were far indeed from duplicating the beauty of his home surroundings. In one session he graphically described his being in a beautiful, happy, peaceful and secure home, filled with lovely furnishings; then suddenly, with a gesture of his arm, he spoke of its being all swept away by some catastrophe which he seemingly refused to describe. At first I thought how graphic a description this was of his having been ejected, by force of circumstances, from the nest of his family home, into a world where he had become caught up in increasing rootlessness, deterioration of his personal identity, and eventual schizophrenia. But some time later—just how and when, I did not record—it dawned on me that this had been his way of experiencing the loss, probably only a moment before, of some unusually rich sense of relatedness with me, a loss attributable to some catastrophe which he could not possibly conceptualize as yet. Many times, subsequently, I had occasion to see that it required but a shift in my position in the chair, an ill-timed word, or a distracting gesture of my hand while speaking, to disrupt a stream of nonverbal relatedness between us, a stream in which he had evidently been happily immersed.

2. *Projection*: Of this much-discussed process, I wish to mention only two features: the extent to which the patient reveals, in statements based upon his projections, the feelings and ideas which are at work in his own unconscious; and the extent to which he projects his own unconscious utilization of nonverbal modes of communication.

His verbalizations of his projection-ridden subjective experience often fill in, in a remarkably detailed and precise way, gaps in our knowledge of what is going on in him.

A woman suffering from chronic paranoid schizophrenia experienced her interpersonal world as being comprised not of whole persons but of anatomical and psychological fragments of persons controlled, through holes in their heads, by vaguely-defined beings who held omnipotent power; and she felt herself to be likewise fragmented and victimized. She devoted the hours with me, for many months, to expressions of physical anguish, protestations of despair, and castigations of me for being responsible for the hellish state of the world in which she existed. It was largely through projection-ridden utterances of hers that I gradually became aware of how much she was, at an unconscious level, enjoying all this—enjoying a sense of omnipotent power over others, and, with this, a freedom from all controls.

This revelation came in such accusations of hers as, "The doctors have holes put in their heads and enjoy their not having any control!"; ". . . people who love to sit up in garrets and split personalities!" (said at a time when she was housed within a dormer roof, in the upper storey of one of the hospital buildings, and was speaking often, in the hours, of the persons—experienced by her as personality-fragments—she saw walking past on the road below); and, "They [referring to the family of her childhood] wanted a dream world, and they've *got* one; how do we get *free?*", said at a time when she perceived me as being, like herself, imprisoned within the dream world which "they" had wanted to create. These statements came, with others in the same vein, over widely-scattered hours; the last-quoted one occurred long before she, subjectively the most down-to-earth of women, could admit to herself any wish to create, and confine herself to, any such dream world as the luxuriantly delusional one in which she existed.

Her positive feelings toward me first found verbal expression in this same unconscious, projective fashion. In one hour she screamed at me, "I'm *not* going to marry you, and I don't care how many people are trying to *make* me marry you!" This, coming at a time when I had not realized that there was any such depth of positive feeling in her toward me, I found a very touching statement from this woman who generally presented herself to me as a kind of lioness encased in chain mail. Two or three weeks later these positive feelings were much closer to awareness, though not fully acknowledged yet as her own: she conjectured about the dilemma a married woman—and she was a married woman—would find herself in if a man other than her husband saved her life and she fell in love with him in the process.

Eight months later, as her infantile-dependent feelings toward me began to come to the fore, she told me scornfully, "You live only to have an hour with me every day." I was quite aware that the hours with her meant a great deal to me; but she could not yet acknowledge any such emotional investment in them. It was only a few weeks later that the following significant interchange occurred. I went to see her for the regularly-scheduled Wednesday hour and was greeted with an abrupt, "Why are you up here today, anyway? I don't have an hour on Tuesday." I replied, "This is Wednesday," whereupon she looked puzzled and said, "What happened to Tuesday?" I distinctly felt that she was unconsciously revealing the fact that those days in which she had no hour with me (and she had none on Tuesdays) were so desolate that they did not exist, for her, in her memory; that, in this quite striking sense, she indeed lived only for the hours with me. My impression was abundantly documented by her increasingly open expressions of dependency during subsequent months.

Lidz and Lidz, in a paper in 1952, called attention to the schizophrenic patient's projection, onto the therapist, of his own proclivity for nonverbal communication:

> ... The patient further projects, not only feelings, but his own attitudes of passive communication through symbols and indications rather than by words. Therapy is often hindered or endangered more by what the patient believes the therapist is covertly conveying than by anything actually said.[11a]

I have seen innumerable instances of the phenomenon which Lidz and Lidz describe. One such instance occurred only a few days ago, during a session with a man suffering from chronic schizophrenia with both hebephrenic and paranoid features, who after several years of therapy is apparently still unable to recapture more than occasional memory-fragments of his past. Most of the hours are spent, still, in silence. During this particular session, in the course of a prolonged silence as we were seated in chairs rather near one another, I began drumming on my chair, lightly and unthinkingly, with the fingers of my right hand—the hand nearer to him. His eyes lit up and he promptly broke his silence by saying in a tone of discovery, "You used to be light-fingered when you were young; I understand, Sweetie."

On the basis of my work with other patients I have little doubt that, as his memory improves and he becomes able to confide more fully in me, we shall discover that petty stealing was one of the aspects of his boyhood behavior. Another of my patients, a paranoid woman, was long convinced that the people about her (including myself) in the hospital were trying, by their behavior, to "show me" or "tell me" that this action in which they were engaged—an action always to her offensive—or this soiled garment they were wearing, or whatever, was typical of her own upbringing. In at least one instance which I recorded, she interpreted an action of mine not as a communication about the past, but as a warning about the future: she felt that my accidental dropping of an ash-tray was my way of telling her that I was going to drop her. I was interested to find, in the subsequent course of her therapy, that she became able to recognize the great extent to which she herself, all along, had been trying in comparably indirect and nonverbal ways to convey reproach to others. For example, she told me, in one of the later sessions, that earlier in the day she had gone into the combined living-room and kitchenette where there were a number of patients and personnel-members, had seen a banana peel lying on the sink, and had put it into the Disposall. "I wanted to show them that they shouldn't leave things lying around," she explained. Dozens of times in earlier years she had expressed, in a stingingly insulted tone, the conviction that I, or some nurse or aide, was "trying to show me that . . .", and she had evidently been unaware, until recently, of the extent to which she had been projecting, onto the rest of us, her own nonverbal and largely unconscious reproachfulness.

Another paranoid woman expressed the conviction that various of the daily-life activities on her ward were "tableaux" which were being presented to her for the purpose of illuminating, for her, the poorly-remembered and chaotically confused events of her past life. It only slowly dawned upon me how frequently her own room, where my sessions with her were long held, could be seen to be a tableau, unconsciously arranged by her for the purpose of conveying to me some unexplored facet of her past life. For example, there was a period of some weeks in which her room, equipped with opened suit-cases and little in the way of anything "homey", was her unconscious portrayal of a time which she was struggling to remember, when she had made a coast-to-coast auto trip, many years before, with her mother and brother; I eventually came to realize that her room had grown to look much like a hotel room where one stays only overnight. In a later phase of our work, there was a period of several weeks during which her room looked very like a boiler-filled basement; this was a time when memories of childhood experiences in the basement of her family home were beginning, bit by bit, to emerge into her awareness. Always, in such phases, her conscious reasons for so ar-ranging her room were quite other, and very delusional reasons; and always it dawned on me only belatedly that another meaningful tableau had presented itself.

A hebephrenic woman, upon entering my office after I had rearranged some of my furniture, asked in an irritated, disconcerted, anxious tone, "What's happened to the office?" When I explained that I had switched the furniture around so that it would harmonize better with a new picture which I had acquired, she said irritatedly, "I don't care anything about the picture." She was more restlessly anxious than usual throughout the hour; but near the end of it she laughed briefly and said, in a tone of realization, "Hilda [her current roommate] was making a take-off on me—I change my clothes a lot, so she moved her furniture around." It was apparent that, in this displaced fashion—displaced from me to her roommate—she was expressing the conviction that, in rearranging my furniture, I had been "making a take-off on" her several-times-a-day changing of her clothes—or, more accurately, costumes.

This woman, throughout the early years of her unusually pro-longed therapy, seemed never to experience any one in her current environment as *reminding her* of someone from her past; always, instead, the other person, or occasionally a pair of interacting persons were, she was immediately convinced, "doing a take-off on" some person(s) from her past. In later years of our work, it became clear that such misinterpretations had been based, in part, upon projection of what she could now acknowledge as her own zest for doing take-offs on—for mimicking in a caricatured fashion—other persons in either her present or her past life. In one session during the fifth year of our work, for instance, she described her having "put on a George White's Scandals show" for her administrative psychiatrist, was hurt that he had been angered rather than pleased by it, and was quite unaware, at that phase of our work, that she had unconsciously been trying to reproach him, by this "Scandals" show, about something concerning which she seriously disapproved of him. Later in this session, significantly, she said in an incensed tone that "it's *scandalous*" that these doctors (using her administrative psychiatrist as a prime example) "aren't more formal than the patients." Later in her therapy she became quite freely able to acknowledge, and enjoy, her doing take-offs on various people, often including me, during many of our sessions. These proved, incidentally, not only great fun for her, but very instructive to me; they showed, much better than could mere verbal descriptions, how I appeared to her currently, or, for example, how her parents had appeared to her during this or that significant incident in her childhood. But my main point here is that, earlier in her therapy, her projection of a then-unconscious tendency to do take-offs—mimicking which involved a high degree of non-verbal communication—had been one of the causes of her misconstruing the activities of those about her in the hospital.

3. *Introjection*: In a recent paper[14] I described in detail some of my experiences with manifestations of introjection on the part of schizophrenic patients; here I shall be brief and shall not repeat what the interested reader can find in that earlier paper. This discussion will be seen to be simply another frame of reference for viewing, or another level of viewing, those clinical phenomena which I have just been describing in terms of the patient's "doing a take-off on" the therapist or other persons. But in the instances presently under scrutiny, the patient's ego is so little in command, either consciously or unconsciously, of that which is being expressed, that one does not sense it as his trying to show us, by caricatured mimicry, this other person. Rather, his behavior seems so completely in command of the introjected other person, from present or past life, that his ego is quite overwhelmed by the introject which is manifesting itself, now, in the verbal or nonverbal communications we are receiving from him.

So far as the patient's subjective experience of these introjective phenomena is concerned, the more de-differentiated is his ego, the less able is he to distinguish between the introject and his own self; basically, he experiences, as an indistinguishable part of his self, some quality which "belongs" primarily in the therapist or some one else in his current surroundings, or in some one from his past.

It is not easy for the therapist to discern when, in the patient's communicating, an introject has appeared and is holding sway. One learns to become alert to changes in his vocal tone—to his voice's suddenly shifting to a quality not like his usual one, a quality which sounds somehow artificial or, in some instances, parrotlike. The content of his words may lapse back into monotonous repetition, as if a phonograph needle were stuck in one groove; only seldom is it so simple as to be a matter of his obviously parroting some timeworn axiom, common to our culture, which he has evidently heard, over and over, from a parent until he experiences it as part of him.

One hebephrenic woman often became submerged in what felt to me like a somehow phony experience of pseudo-emotion, during which, despite her wracking sobs and streaming cheeks, I felt only a cold annoyance with her. Eventually such incidents became more sporadic, and more sharply demarcated from her day-after-day behavior, and in one particular session, after several minutes of such behavior—which, as usual, went on without any accompanying words from her—she asked, eagerly, "Did you see Granny?" At first I did not know what she meant; I thought she must be seeing me as some one who had just come from seeing her grandmother, in their distant home-city. Then I realized that she had been deliberately showing me, this time, what Granny was like; and when I replied in this spirit, she corroborated my hunch.

At another phase in the therapy, when a pathogenic mother-introject began to emerge more and more upon the investigative scene, she muttered in a low but intense voice, to herself, "I hate that woman inside me!" I could evoke no further elaboration from her about this; but a few seconds later she was standing directly across the room from me, looking me in the eyes and saying in a scathingly condemnatory tone, "Your father despises you!" Again, I at first misconstrued this disconcertingly intense communication, and I quickly cast through my mind to account for her being able to speak, with such utter conviction, of an opinion held by my father, now several years deceased. Then I replied, coldly, "If you despise me, why don't you say so, directly?" She looked confused at this, and I felt sure it had been a wrong response for me to make. It then occurred to me to ask, "Is that what that woman told you?" She clearly agreed that this had been the case. I realized, now, that she had been showing me, in what impressed me as being a very accurate way, something her mother had once said to her; it was as if she was showing me one of the reasons why she hated that woman inside her. What had been an unmanageably powerful introject was now, despite its continuing charge of energy disconcerting to me, sufficiently within control of her ego that she could use it to show me what this introjected mother was like.

Earlier, this woman had been so filled with a chaotic variety of introjects that at times, when she was in her room alone, it would sound to a passerby as though there were several different persons in the room, as she would vocalize in various kinds of voice. A somewhat less fragmented hebephrenic patient of mine, who used to often seclude herself in her room, often sounded through the closed door—as I would find on passing by, between our sessions—for all the world like two persons, a scolding mother and a defensive child.

Particularly hard for the therapist to grasp are those instances in which the patient is manifesting an introject traceable to something in the therapist, some aspect of the therapist of which the latter is himself only poorly aware, and the recognition of which, as a part of himself, he finds distinctly unwelcome. I have found, time and again, that some bit of particularly annoying and intractable behavior on the part of a patient rests, in the final analysis, on this basis; and only when I can acknowledge this, to myself, as being indeed an aspect of my personality, does it cease to be a prominently troublesome aspect of the patient's behavior. For example, one hebephrenic man used to annoy me, month after month, by saying, whenever I got up to leave and made my fairly steoreotyped comment that I would be seeing him on the following day, or whenever, "You're welcome," in a notably condescending fashion—as though it were his due for me to thank him for the privilege of spending the hour with him, and he were thus pointing up my failure to utter a humbly grateful, "thank you" to him at the end of each session. Eventually it became clear to me, partly with the aid of another schizophrenic patient who could point out my condescension to me somewhat more directly, that this man, with his condescending, "You're welcome," was very accurately personifying an element of obnoxious condescension which had been present in my own demeanor, over these months, on each of these occasions when I had bid him good-bye with the consoling note, each time, that the healing Christ would be stooping to dispense this succor to the poor suffered again on the morrow.

Another patient, a paranoid woman, for many months infuriated not only me but the ward-personnel and her fellow patients by arrogantly behaving as though she owned the whole building, as though she were the only person in it whose needs were to be met. This behavior on her part subsided only after I had come to see the uncomfortably close similarity between, on the one hand, her arranging the ventilation of the common living room to her own liking, or turning the television off or on without regard to the wishes of the others, and on the other hand, my own coming stolidly into her room despite her persistent and vociferous objections, bringing my big easy chair with me, usually shutting the windows of her room which she preferred to keep in a very cold state, and plunking myself down in my chair—in short, behaving as if I owned her room.

4. *Condensation*: Here a variety of meanings and emotions are concentrated, or reduced, in their communicative expression, to some comparatively simple-seeming verbal or nonverbal statement.

One finds, for example, that a terse and stereotyped verbal expression, seeming at first to be a mere hollow convention, reveals itself over the months of therapy as the vehicle for expressing the most varied and intense feelings, and the most unconventional of meanings. More than anything, it is the therapist's intuitive sensing of these latent meanings in the stereotype which helps these meanings to become revealed, something like a spread-out deck of cards, on sporadic occasions over the passage of the patient's and his months of work together.[17,18] one cannot assume, of course, that all these accumulated meanings were inherent in the stereotype at the beginning of the therapy, or at any one time later on when the stereotype was uttered; probably it is correct to think of it as a matter of a well-grooved, stereotyped mode of expression—and no, or but a few, other communicational grooves, as yet—being *there,* available for the patient's use, as newly-emerging emotions and ideas well up in him over the course of months. But it is true that the therapist can sense, when he hears this stereotype, that there are at this moment many emotional determinants at work in it, a blurred babel of indistinct voices which have yet to become clearly delineated from one another.

225

Sometimes it is not a verbal stereotype—a "How are you now?" or an "I want to go home", or whatever—but a nonverbal one which reveals itself, gradually, as the condensed expression of more than one latent meaning. A hebephrenic man used to give a repetitious wave of his hand a number of times during his largely-silent hours with his therapist. When the therapist came to feel on sufficiently sure ground with him to ask him, "What is that, Bill—hello or farewell?", the patient replied, "Both, Dearie—two in one."

Of all the possible forms of nonverbal expression, that which seems best to give release, and communicational expression, to complex and undifferentiated feelings is laughter. It is no coincidence that the hebephrenic patient, the most severely dedifferentiated of all schizophrenic patients, shows, as one of his characteristic symptoms, laughter—laughter which now makes one feel scorned or hated, which now makes one feel like weeping, or which now gives one a glimpse of the bleak and empty expanse of man's despair; and which, more often than all these, conveys a *welter* of feelings which could in no way be conveyed by any number of words, words which are so unlike this welter in being formed and discrete from one another. To a much less full extent, the hebephrenic person's belching or flatus has a comparable communicative function; in working with these patients the therapist eventually gets to do some at least private mulling over of the possible meaning of a belch, or the passage of flatus, not only because he is reduced to this for lack of anything else to analyze, but also because he learns that even these animal-like sounds constitute forms of communication in which, from time to time, quite different things are being said, long before the patient can become sufficiently aware of these, as distinct feelings and concepts, to say them in words.

As I have been intimating, in the schizophrenic—and perhaps also in the dreams of the neurotic; this is a question which I have no wish to take up—condensation is a phenomenon in which one finds not a condensed expression of various feelings and ideas which are, at an unconscious level, well sorted out, but rather a condensed expression of feelings and ideas which, even in the unconscious, have yet to become well differentiated from one another. Freeman, Cameron and McGhie, in their description of the disturbances of thinking found in chronic schizophrenic patients, say, in regard to condensation, that

. . . the lack of adequate discrimination between the self and the environment, and the objects contained therein . . . in itself is the prototypical condensation.[7]

In my experience, a great many of the patient's more puzzling verbal communications are so for the reason that concrete meanings have not become differentiated from figurative meanings in his subjective experience. Thus he may be referring to some concrete thing, or incident, in his immediate environment by some symbolic-sounding, hyperbolic reference to transcendental events on the global scene. Recently, for example, a paranoid woman's large-scale philosophizing, in the session, about the intrusive curiosity which has become, in her opinion, a deplorable characteristic of mid-twentieth-century human culture, devolved itself, before the end of the session, into a suspicion that I was surreptitiously peeking at her partially exposed breast, as indeed I was. Or, equally often, a concretistic-seeming, particularistic-seeming statement may consist, with its mundane exterior, in a form of poetry—may be full of meaning and emotion when interpreted as a figurative expression: a metaphor, a smile, an allegory, or some other symbolic mode of speaking.

Of such hidden meanings the patient himself is, more often than not, entirely unaware. His subjective experience may be a remarkably concretistic one. One hebephrenic women confided to me, "I live in a world of words," as if, to her, words were fully concrete objects; Burnham,[4] in his excellent article (1955) concerning schizophrenic communication, includes mention of similar clinical material. A borderline schizophrenic young man told me that to him the various theoretical concepts about which he had been expounding, in a most articulate fashion, during session after session with me, were like great cubes of almost tangibly solid matter up in the air above him; as he spoke I was reminded of the great bales of cargo which are swung, high in the air, from a docked steamship. Another borderline schizophrenic young man experienced the beginning stirrings of de-repression of feelings, early in his analysis when, for example, he would be strolling along the street in an unguarded moment, as though he had suddenly bumped into, or been struck by, some massive but invisible object; it proved later to be thus that important emotional insights had first been presaged. Many schizophrenic patients, when presented with a penetrating but premature interpretation, evidently feel not that they have heard a meaningful figurative concept from their therapist, but rather that they have been struck a physical blow, or, in some instances I have seen, that they are being shot at from various quarters.

The therapist, too, may unconsciously long protect himself from seeing the poignant meanings latent in these patients' communications by hearing their statements as having purely concrete, or otherwise mundane, meanings. A paranoid man who had gradually become overwhelmed with psychosis in the course of a solitary Caribbean cruise used to bore me, in the sessions, by mentioning time and again, another and yet another of the titles of the almost innumerable motion pictures he had attended during the cruise; only after some weeks did it dawn upon me that the titles of the pictures formed symbolic expressions of the terror, the loneliness, and other warded-off emotions which had been building up in him as the cruise had progressed. A therapist during a supervisory hour with me recounted, boredly, what to him seemed the almost endlessly detailed description, by a paranoid woman who had recently returned from a visit to her children, of an afternoon's hike with them in the hills along the seashore. I heard this account, as he listlessly quoted it, as constituting an allegory filled with the most poignant statements of the patient's whole life-experience with her children and her years of separation from them during her hospitalization, and larded with echoes of her own childhood. Moreover, when I called these meanings to the therapist's attention, he could immediately accept them as being, indeed, there. It is not uncommon for the therapist, in daily contact with the patient's great but much-concealed grief and loneliness, to need to so ally himself with the strength of a colleague in order to perceive these meanings. Recently, in a session with a hebephrenic man—about whom I have many times received the just-mentioned kind of help from various colleagues—he said, "Hello" to me in the middle of the session. This struck me as a bit incongruous, and I expressed my curiosity to him. He replied, simply, by way of explanation, "A friendly hello as we pass on the avenue." At first I reacted to this as being only another of the familiar indications of his fantasying himself to be a tourist in this or that city; then the metaphorical impact of the whole statement hit me—its implications about the fleetingness of life, the impossibility for us as human beings to overcome our innate separateness from one another, the rarity with which we can enjoy a moment of simple and uncomplicated friendliness with one another.

5. *Isolation*: The content of the patient's speech may be descriptive of incidents or situations which seem to the listener as though these *must* be charged with intense emotion; but the words are astonishingly, and often maddeningly, isolated from—divorced from—any affective tone. Over the course of years of working with schizophrenic patients, the therapist gradually comes to realize how rarely is the patient aware, in such instances, of emotion and consciously withholding its expression. As the therapist becomes aware of this he desists from pressuring the patient to express that of which the latter is unaware, and dares to look at these various incidents and situations more and more from the patient's own point of view, a point of view from which feelings are elusive or completely shrouded in fog.

With great regularity, as I have seen it, this isolation—or, from the patient's point of view, inability to discern and experience any emotions about the subject at hand—is a defense erected primarily against the awareness of intensely *ambivalent* feelings. The comparatively lengthy discussion of ambivalence, in the next section of this paper, will serve as an extension of these brief remarks.

Various of the above-enumerated defenses are of course found, in actual clinical practice, *in combination with one another* more often than not, to that degree complicating the decipherment of many of the patient's communications.

For example, when I had just entered the room of a hebephrenic woman, for my usual therapeutic session with her, she said, while pressing her lower abdomen searchingly, "It feels as though there's a crazy shit in here that's going to the left." I had already acquired, from previous sessions, sufficient knowledge of her distorted modes of experience and of communication to surmise that this was a much-disguised way of her experiencing this unconscious feeling and idea: "I feel that my crazy shit of a therapist, who has just come into this room, is becoming a Communist." Her comments during the remainder of this session, and in the immediately subsequent one, strongly supported such an interpretation. Space does not allow my adducing sufficient of these data to "prove" my hunch; let me say only that for many hours there had been indications that my intrusive presence in her room was experienced by her as a stubborn "shit" that would not "get out" of her body, and that in the session following this one she confided to me some passages in a letter from her teen-age son (whom I often represented to her in the transference) in which he described

229

his interest, in a current course in college, in reading about the "Communist revolution" in Russia.

Here was a triply-disguised communication in which the defenses of both introjection and condensation (specifically, concretization) were at work. The percept of the therapist was condensed into the concrete representation of a "crazy shit"; the room—the "in here"—was introjected by the patient and felt as being within her abdomen; and the figurative concept of a political "going to the left" was experienced by her in a concretistic, geographical sense, as the moving to the left, in her abdomen, of the "crazy" fecal mass.

A paranoid woman whom I had been treating for several years bewildered me by saying, abruptly, "If you turned me into a gnat or mosquito, then the trees would have safe passage!" She of course behaved as though the meaning of this comment should be crystal clear to me; but she did rather impatiently give a bit of elucidation: she reminded me that the trees (on the hospital grounds outside her window) "have been allowed to stay here so long they're about to split and divide." My further pressing for information clarified "split and divide" as meaning "explode". When I asked for further elaboration upon the idea of her being turned, for example, into a mosquito, she replied, "Then I could go around and bite everybody," in a charming tone. I commented, "That wouldn't hurt people very much, would it?", to which she agreed. In earlier phases of our work, she had been terrified of her murderousness.

Much corollary data from my long previous experience with this woman made me fairly sure that this initially so bewildering communication was a much-disguised expression of this unconscious idea: "My life-functioning is paralyzed by my fear that I will seriously hurt other people. If only you would detoxify my destructiveness, then I could get out of the immobility of this long hospitalization, and safely get moving again as a functioning person." Both her state of paralysis, and the powerful energy pent up by this paralysis, she projected upon the immobile trees. Further, to her at this stage of her therapy, the concept of her being turned into a relatively innocuous insect was not a figurative concept, but a process which, she was convinced, was quite concretely possibly and, in fact, rife in the world about her.

A session during the following month produced, from this same woman, another example of a remarkably multiply-disguised communication. We were sitting on benches on the lawn near her building.

She was in the midst of expressing an unusual upsurge of memories, laden with much feeling—with, in particular, fondness and nostalgia —about the persons and places from out of a long-forgotten era of her past, when, by a seeming effort of her will, she discontinued this line of talk, saying, "Do you know that woman over there (gesturing toward the building where she roomed; I never became sure whom she meant by "that woman") who has that strange head? I think it's about to explode. What do they do—do they take people out of the pipes and then put them in someone's head like that until they mature? I think it would be dangerous if the person isn't able to feel." She explained that it would be dangerous if the person were unable to feel, because he (or she) would be unaware of the presence of these people in his head; she also elaborated enough to make fairly clear that she visualized the maturation-process as a biological one, a change from an embryonic into an eventually adult state.

All this had at first an eerie, ugly, anxiety-provoking effect upon me. But data from my long experience with her delusional perceptions, coupled with the fact that she had just been manifesting anxiety in the face of the upsurge of memories, enabled me to decipher this in a way which, although met with her usual resistiveness when I verbalized the translation to her, proved durably meaningful to me. In essence, it seemed that she was communicating an unconscious protest at this upsurge of memories from her unconscious (the "pipes", which in many preceding sessions she had located as being underground), a protest that, because she was not yet able to cope with the feelings associated with these memories, these feelings might cause her "strange head"—projected upon "that woman over there"—to explode. The agency of the unconscious, which of course did not feel subjectively part of her or within her control, she projected into the outer world; all this was, to her, something that "they" do. The process of a bio-logical maturation of these people in the host's brain, as she concep-tualized it, was a symbolic representation of a psychological process at work in her unconscious—a process whereby her remembered images of these persons were becoming more filled out, richly differ-entiated—in a sense, therefore, matured. As in the first-described example from my work with her, the defenses of both projection and condensation (specifically, here, concretization of figurative concepts) can be seen to be at work, when one retrospectively analyzes the com-munication.

Thus far, I have been describing various forms of the overt features of schizophrenic communication; the various forms which it takes, depending upon whatever unconscious defense(s) the patient is utilizing. Next I shall try to portray something of the underlying psychodynamic state of affairs which necessitates the patient's use of these various pathological forms of communication. Both the depth and breadth of this portrayal will be limited by the need to couch the discussion in general terms; I am attempting, here, to describe psychodynamics which hold true for schizophrenic patients in general, whereas only a thoroughgoing account of any one individual patient's psychodynamics could clarify, reasonably deeply and fully, the nature of his particular illness and, by the same token, the roots of his particular forms of communication.

1. *Regression*: The circumstance of the patient's having regressed to a more or less early level of ego-functioning is explanatory of many of the idiosyncrasies of schizophrenic communication. The clinical picture is complicated, in most instances, by the fact that the level of regression varies unceasingly, at times from one moment to the next, and there are even instances where the patient is functioning upon more than one developmental level simultaneously.

The fact of the patient's regressed mode of psychological functioning helps to account for the "concretization", or contrariwise the seeming oversymbolization, of his communications; these phenomena represent his having regressed, in his thinking (and over-all subjective experiencing), to a developmental level comparable with that in the young child who has not yet become able to differentiate between concrete and metaphorical (or similar forms of highly symbolic) thinking.[20]

Similarly, the patient may prattle in a way which gives us to know that the content of his speech is relatively unimportant to him at the moment; rather, he is immersed in the pleasure of saying the words and hearing the sound of them, very like the young child who has not yet learned to talk but loves to babble and to hear the sound of his babbling. A nonverbal patient may usefully be regarded as having regressed even further, to the pre-verbal era of infancy or very early childhood.

The matter of regression, in various ramifications, will come up again and again in the remainder of this discussion.

2. *Lack of self-esteem*: A very low self-esteem, generally accepted as one of the characteristics of the schizophrenic patient, is another psychodynamic feature basic to his pathological forms of communication.

So frequently, one feels that the schizophrenic patient is making a most forceful and effective communication, but that for a healthy person to so communicate would exact an unbearable toll in self-abasement.

Ferenczi, in his paper in 1913 entitled, "Stages in the Development of the Sense of Reality," says that during the animistic period in the developing apprehension of reality, the child "learns to represent by means of his body the whole multifariousness of the outer world."[6] To just such an all-encompassing degree is the behavior of the adult schizophrenic individual, partly by reason of his previously-mentioned regression, given over to a communicational representation —a representation much more distorted, however, than that which one sees in the healthy young child—of the events of his perceived outer and inner worlds.

One patient's drooping shoulders, stubble of beard, and hobo's mode of dress vividly convey his felt unbelongingness, and his reproach to those about him for not making him a part of their society. A woman's idiotic laughter and simpering demeanor toward her therapist, as they walk across the hospital grounds to his office, serve powerfully to communicate her derision toward him. Another woman's freakish demeanor and her mouthing of confused and half-inaudible sentences serve, eventually, to tell her therapist graphically how grotesque in appearance, and unintelligible in speech, she perceives him to be. Another woman's cosmeticizing herself, dressing, and in general, behaving like a prostitute more than adequately communicates her contempt for those about her, as does another man's frequent belching, passing of flatus, and generally porcine behavior.

But all these communicated acts are predicated upon, as well as being expressive of, an abysmally low self-esteem. It is as though, in fact, the regressed patient's need to communicate in such ways—in ways which involve the use of body posturings and other forms of nonverbal caricature—his need to communicate in such ways because more adult, verbal-symbolic ways are not as yet available to him, forms one of the *determinants of* the low state of his self-esteem. It is as though even greater, at the moment, than his need for self-esteem is his need to communicate with a fellow man.

3. *Ambivalence*: The strikingly intense ambivalence, another fundamental aspect of the schizophrenic individual's psychodynamics, contributes to a number of different typical kinds of schizophrenic communications.

(a) *Indirect communications*—A hebephrenic woman whom I had been treating for two years managed to convey to me, in her usual very indirect, hinting fashion, that she wanted to subscribe to her home-town newspaper. I felt much moved when I realized the import of this message; I sensed how poignantly left out she had felt, all along during her stay at the Lodge, through her not having received this. I suggested to her that she ask Dr. Jones, her administrative psychiatrist, to arrange for such a subscription; but she immediately said that there were several Dr. Joneses, and that it was so hard to talk to them. I felt that she could not manage, at this stage in her therapy when any direct communicating was still very difficult or impossible for her, to bring this up to Dr. Jones herself, and told her that I would mention this matter to him.

But no sooner had I said that I would tell him, than she proceeded to make clear that she felt, on the other hand, that were she to start receiving that newspaper it would be a great burden to her, and that she would rather forget all about her home town, and not have to worry about what this person and that person were doing there. After having heard this (as usual, indirectly-couched) communication, I changed my position, telling her that I would not speak to Dr. Jones about it, and suggesting that she do so if she wished. To this she made no, or at most a non-committal, reply.

The above incident is reminiscent of a general principle expressed by Burnham concerning the schizophrenic man with whom his paper on communication with schizophrenic patients is mainly concerned:

> The obscurity of his language could be thought of as a compromise between his intense desire for, and equally intense fear of, an extraordinarily intimate relationship.[4a]

(b) *Self-contradictory* verbal-and-nonverbal communications— On occasion, the patient may make a statement, or series of statements, in which both content and vocal tone switch suddenly in such a way as to give a self-contradictory effect. For instance, one hebephrenic woman commented to me, concerning another woman patient, "She has a beautiful face," in an admiring tone. But then without a pause her words switched to scorn in both tone and content, "She looks like a bulldog." Another hebephrenic woman said to me an eight-word statement in which the first seven words were uttered in a tone of heartfelt adoration and, with no pause whatever, the eighth word was spoken in a tone of equally profound contempt: "You should have the Congressional Medal of Spit." The person with a reasonably well-integrated ego is quite incapable of reproducing her spoken words—of making so rapid and complete a switch in expressed affect.

(c) Verbal communications in which there is a *split between content and vocal feeling-tone*—A number of examples from one hebephrenic woman will suffice to illustrate this very common type of schizophrenic communication. On one occasion, she said to me, "If you don't like it, sit down and have a drink!", in an antagonistic and defiant tone which clearly conveyed the meaning, "If you don't like it, get the hell out!" On another occasion, after she had been struggling for some time to convey intelligible words to me, while I had been listening silently, she said disgustedly, *"You* dirty *your* hands on the candy for a while!" The word "candy" in no way interfered with her getting across, in this, the message, "You lazy slob—you roll up your sleeves and take a hand at this work of ours, for a change!" On an occasion when I had correctly deciphered the meaning of one of her indirectly-put communications, and succinctly "read it back" to her, to see if this was not what she was wanting me to understand, she replied with partially-irrelevant words, but with a thoroughly confirming vocal tone, by saying, "You got the tickets!" delightedly. On still another occasion she said, "You're such a darling!" with a peculiarly hostile vocal tone such that I felt that, despite the complimentary words themselves, she was cutting off my head.

In assessing the meaning of such communications, one soon learns to brush aside the content, and attend to the feeling-tone—or, in still more complex instances, tones—in which the words are said.

Incidentally, a patient sometimes evidences a quite accurate grasp of the true import of such communications when they come from the therapist. At the end of each of the maddeningly silent sessions I spent with a hebephrenic man, I would constrain my fury and scorn toward him and politely say, as he started toward the door, "so long, Mr. Bryant—I'll see you to-morrow," to which he would mutter a furious reply, "Go to hell, you son of a bitch!" After this had happened several times, it dawned on me that he was very accurately expressing the covert message contained in my "polite" parting comment to him.

(d) *Nonverbal expression of a feeling contradictory to the one being verbalized*—A paranoid woman verbalized to me, for many months, her impatient wish to have her hospitalization and her work with me completed. Meanwhile, as the months passed, she developed a deep fondness for me which was quite evident to others but, at the time of which I am writing, not yet to herself. Toward the end of one session she said, "You know I want to live away from here more than anything in the world—you know that, don't you?", to which I made a noncommital reply. When I indicated, a few minutes later, that the time was up, she seemed as usual reluctant to leave, and this time, as she moved toward the door, instead of opening it she turned her back to it and stretched both arms across it, exactly as if she were determined to hold me captive there, in my office, and simultaneously broke into her usual verbal demands that I should let her go. Despite her words, I had rarely felt so intensely desired by, and desirable to, anyone.

A hebephrenic woman who frequently verbalized her wish to live in the refined atmosphere of a fine hotel (such, presumably, as the one in which her wealthy grandmother had lived throughout the girl's upbringing, in the same city), said in one of her therapeutic sessions, "I don't see any reason why I can't live in a hotel," going on to indicate that she thought her behavior entirely refined. Simultaneously, however, she had raised the front of her skirt and was wiping her genitals with Kleenex—as, for many months, she frequently did. In my experience it is particularly frequent for a patient to verbalize a desire to move out of the sanitarium, but to simultaneously communicate nonverbally a fear of, or unreadiness for, such a move.

A hebephrenic woman, in one of my earliest sessions with her, was verbally disclaiming any interest in sex, while squirming about in her chair in a markedly seductive, sexually excited manner. In a session sixteen months later she said to me, in a tone of intense loathing, "God, you're freakish! . . . . slimy . . . . dopey!", pausing repeatedly to hug her pillow to her, with grief-stricken tears, long before she was to become able, eventually, to acknowledge her wishes to similarly hug and cherish me. During the following month the daily nurses' report contained the following item written by a student nurse.

> . . . She grabbed my hand and put it on her and said "Don't touch me." I said, "Judy, I am not touching you." She said, "You are," and kicked me. . . .*

Four years later in my work with this same deeply ill woman, I came into her room, on a very warm summer day, with the top button of my shirt unbuttoned and without a coat. She soon began behaving, both in her postures and in various indirect verbal comments, in a coarsely sexual fashion. The particularly memorable instance of ambivalence occurred a bit later on in the session when she sat down in a chair directly across from me, about five feet away, put her knees far apart, pulled her skirt up to the middle of her thighs and said, looking at my collar, "Put your collar up, will you?" I asked her bluntly whether she were wishing that I would put my penis up her. To this she made no direct reply but, after some indirect references with sexual overtones, she made some quite sardonic but direct reference to my collar, harshly conveying to me that she felt that it was untidy. In this deeply disorganized and often animalistic woman I had seen clear evidence, on a number of earlier occasions, of a remarkably severe perfectionism, concerning behavior and, particularly, dress, reminiscent of each of her perfectionistically tidy parents; I had been reprimanded by her about such matters more than once before. But I was astonished, here, to realize that her "Put your collar up, will you?" had been simultaneously (1) a very gross sexual overture and (2) a measure of her perfectionistic prissiness. Each of these had had as strong a feeling-impact upon me as the other.

(e) *Expression of contradictory feelings at an entirely nonverbal level*—A brief example will suffice to illustrate this kind of communication; I have already mentioned on Page 17 the two-in-one, hello-and-farewell, wave which the hebephrenic man gave to his therapist.

A woman was describing to me in detail, and in a strikingly

---

* Here, as in some of the other clinical examples reported, one sees the element of the patient's projecting, upon the other person, the feeling or attitude or behavioral act which he himself is unconsciously communicating, or doing, at a nonverbal level.

matter-of-fact tone of voice, her having attempted to kill herself during a visit to her parental home, from which she had just been returned to the sanitarium. As her measured, precise words continued their unemotional cadence, her eyes were filled with tears of—so I distinctly sensed it—grief and despair, while her mouth was fixed in a smile of sadistic triumph—triumph at, I surmised, the anguish and anxiety which her near-suicide had aroused in others.

4. *Superego*: The archaically harsh, forbidding superego of the patient is another basic factor which helps to account for his heavily disguised and often fragmentary communications.

For example, the same hebephrenic woman who figured in the collar-incident, described above, during the early years of our work communicated with me in a fashion which suggested that she felt as though we were a couple of Yanks in a Japanese prison camp, or in some similarly repressive atmosphere wherein her words must be so disguised, and often so muted, that the oppressors would not overhear them and catch on to their meaning. Very frequently, her speech would consist in a few tersely-abbreviated colloquialisms, or mention of names and places which would be meaningful (as I learned from some discussion with her family-members) to a person from her home city, and from her social circle in that city, but to no one else. Maddeningly often, key words in her few sentences would be unsaid, or muttered inaudibly and not repeated. At times she referred uneasily to "the woman in the ceiling" who evidently must not be allowed to overhear what was transpiring between us—reminiscent to me of much earlier data, from her as well as from the other family-members, indicative of a kind of pal-relationship with her father, from which the mother had been excluded.

On many subsequent occasions, when I was now a predominantly hated, despised, and feared mother in the transference, I would feel hurt when she would abruptly turn from a seemingly close interchange with me to check with, seemingly, a hallucinatory image of her father, saying some variation of, "It's O.K., Bill—I'm onto this guy." This reminded me of the father's undisguised pleasure in telling me, at the time of his daughter's admission to Chestnut Lodge, that she always had liked him better than any of her succession of boy-friends; and I came to realize that the mother, portrayed for a long time in the transference-relationship as a severe person whom one must avoid provoking—by, for example, avoiding an almost infinite number of touchy subjects—had been shut out, like the boy-friends, from the apparently easygoing relatedness between father and daughter.

Later on, still, in the therapy, it became evident that this easygoing relatedness was not actually such, but could be preserved only if one avoided subjects about which the father, whose easygoing demeanor clothed a cruel rejectingness and harsh perfectionism, felt defensive. Thus this hebephrenic woman's superego, which contributed so heavily toward making communication between us desperately difficult, and which was projected variously in the form of concentration-camp rulers, or "the woman in the ceiling," or her seemingly easygoing father, "Bill", (to mention only a few of the forms which this projection assumed), was a superego which clearly had derived a pathological harshness from *each* of her parents.

But it was particularly interesting to see, as the therapy developed still further, that this harshly-forbidding superego apparatus, experienced apparently by her as something quite outside herself which interdicted any free and prolonged communicational exchange between us, resolved itself into a more and more clearly-acknowledged sensitivity on her *own* part, in reaction to innumerable key words among my comments, which happened—often quite unexpectedly to me—to touch upon areas of hostility, terror, or grief in herself. It became relatively easy to discern when a word or a phrase from me had suddenly blundered into such an area, and it required much determination on my part to go ahead into, as it were, a field mined with these unseen charges of rage, grief, and so forth. Had I deferred unduly, however, to such areas of sensitivity in her as I already knew of, my speech would have been precisely as disjointed and incomplete as her own had been, earlier in our work, when she had evidently been experiencing it that, for instance, the presence of the disapproving "woman in the ceiling" made it necessary for her to punch out many of the key words from her own sentences, and otherwise render them cryptic.

5. *The attempt to achieve, or to perpetuate, a symbolic infant-mother relatedness with the therapist*: I have come to believe that one can say, quite generally, that the various forms of verbal and non-verbal communication characteristic of schizophrenia are reflective of the patient's effort to foster, or to maintain, a symbolic relatedness

with the therapist (and, apart from the therapeutic sessions, with—in Sullivan's phrase—significant other persons), a relatedness such as normally holds sway between the young infant and his mother, in which the participants are subjectively at one with each other. I have reported elsewhere[17,18,21] my experience that such a mode of relatedness marks a therapeutically essential phase in the evolution of the schizophrenic patient's transference to his therapist—that his ego-fragmentation must gradually be resolved into such an interpersonal relatedness, before a more healthy ego-differentiation can subsequently develop out of this basic healthy-infant-and-loving-mother oneness in the transference-relationship. I have made careful studies to explain that this is a mode of relatedness which is not within the power of the therapist to wield manipulatively as a deliberate psychotherapeutic technique, but rather that it tends inevitably to *happen* over the long course of the therapy, after an earlier phase of intense and mutual ambivalence between patient and therapist has been traversed, and that the cue for the therapist is to try to see whether this is occurring, and to try not to interfere with its development, rather than feeling guilty, ashamed, or afraid about this state of affairs.

The obscurity of the patient's communications is such that his therapist tends to become the sole expert, or in any case the leading expert, in deciphering his communications. This circumstance contributes greatly to the private aura which their relationship develops, an aura of uniquely close communion as contrasted to their subjective distance from an outer world which "does not understand." Moreover, the therapist progressively moves into a position where he translates the communications of the confused schizophrenic patient even for the latter himself; in this, as well as in other ways, he functionally does the patient's thinking and feeling for him, to a considerable degree—he comes to personify the patient's externalized ego.

The prolonged silences which characterize the sessions foster abundant projection-and-introjection on the part of each participant. Thus not only does the patient maintain the quiet conviction that his therapist knows what he is thinking and feeling, without the need for any explicit communication—that, in essence, the therapist can read his mind—but the therapist also comes without realizing it to assume, much of the time, that the patient is sharing his thoughts and feelings as the quiet minutes pass. He, the therapist, may find himself quite disconcerted when the silent patient does resume speaking, for it then becomes unmistakable, more often than not, that his thought-content has been pursuing a course, a subject, widely different from the thoughts which have been running through the therapist's mind. Each of them finds painful such reminders that they are separate beings. One of my patients said, after I had broken a silence with some words which he evidently found alien and unsharing of his own feeling-state, "There's no friendly intuition here." Much of the time, however, their communion is genuinely close, and it is not without reason that the therapist, as well as the patient, develops the conviction that the other knows him better and more intimately than does any one else in the world.

In the instance of most of the chronic schizophrenic patients with whom I have worked, there has been a predominantly nonverbal phase extending over a number of (in some instances, over many) months. This is evidently the phase which Eissler[5] terms the "phase of relative clinical muteness" in the patient's psychotherapy. Invariably, when the patient has gone on eventually to the solid establishment of verbal interaction with me, this has been experienced by me, and so far as I could determine by the patient also, as not an unalloyed triumph of increasing maturation, but a step which involves also a marked sense of loss—the loss of the subjective sense of therapist-patient (mother-infant) oneness, so akin to the infant's coming to lose, with advancing individuation as his ego-boundaries become established, his erstwhile oceanic world-self.

The transference-evolution which I have outlined makes heavy demands upon the therapist's—as well, of course, as the patient's—feeling-capacities. He tends to be afraid of the intimacy involved in a genuine symbiotic relatedness with the patient; for example, he tends to be afraid of the deep communion which the silent hours often involve, and to be concerned lest the patient matters more than he should to him. And later, when it is time for both persons to relinquish their symbiotic relatedness, it is tempting for the therapist to try somehow to preserve this subjective oneness overly long, in order, first, not to have to experience the pain and anxiety of the sense of separateness and, secondly, to avoid facing all kinds of negative feelings, in himself as well as in the patient, against which the symbiosis can serve so effectively as an unconscious defense, just as did the pathology-ridden symbiosis in the patient's background. Whereas the therapist earlier had the task of learning to understand the patient's communications,

241

now he must help him learn to communicate in terms which are understandable to the other people in his environment. The therapist who earlier had dared to accept a Pygmalion feeling-orientation toward his Galatea, an orientation at first awesome in its power and later deeply enjoyable, must come to accept this far humbler-seeming role in order to have the satisfaction of helping the patient to achieve a healthy and durable maturity.

C. PSYCHOTHERAPEUTIC TECHNIQUE

The above paragraphs have already opened up the subject to which the remainder of this paper is devoted: the therapist's technique in coping with those difficulties in communication which are a function of the schizophrenic process.

Innumerable instances of the therapist's uncertainty as to how to respond to the patient's communication turn upon the question of whether the communication is to be "taken personally"—to be taken as primarily designed, for instance, toward filling the therapist with perplexity, confusion, anxiety, humiliation, rage, or some other negatively-toned affective state; or whether it is to be taken, rather, as primarily an effort to convey some basically unhostile need on the patient's part. Just as it is often essential that the therapist become able to sense, and respond to, personal communications in a patient's ostensibly stereotyped behavior or utterances, so, too, is it frequently essential that he be able to see, behind the overt "personal" reference to himself—often a stinging or otherwise emotionally-evocative reference—some fundamental need which the patient is hesitant to communicate openly.

A hebephrenic woman and I had, for years, great capacity to rub one another the wrong way; whole sessions would be spent in mutually vindictive comments and nonverbal torture-operations. In one period of the therapy during which she was often described by the ward-personnel as sitting in her bed, or in a chair in the hallway, crying for hours on end, her first comment as I came into her room was, "Do you know you're Dr. Searles?" She asked this in a matter-of-fact, rather than a taunting, tone; but, on the basis of abundant past experience with her taunts I felt needled, as usual, and thought to myself, with irritation and impatience, "Of course I know I'm Dr. Searles."

This time I replied, however, with a measure of friendliness and

242

matter-of-factness, "Yes—either Dr. Searles or Harold Searles," wanting her to know that it was all right for her to call me by my first name if she wished. It was perhaps twenty minutes later in the session, after much other talk—most of it fragmentary, as usual—from her that she said, "Thelma Foster [a name I had never before heard] is a nice person," in a tone of forced enthusiasm. She added, in the same tone, "Diana Kendall [another such name] is a nice person, too." She then added in a noncommittal tone, "She sits and cries all the time." I said, "I wonder what she is crying about." She replied, in a tone I found very poignant, "She's crying because she doesn't know who she is."

This came to me as a deeply moving revelation for, despite the fact that she clearly had misidentified me on innumerable occasions, I had failed to realize that she was often unaware of her own identity. I understood now that her initial question, "Do you know you're Dr. Searles?", indeed had not been intended as a jeering commentary on my stupidity, but had been an indirect way of trying to reveal a grief-laden, but to her also humiliating aspect of her self-experience.

It continued for long after that, however, to be a difficult thing for me to sense, in the face of her remarkable facility for making me feel insulted, the painful feelings about which she was covertly asking me for help. Another of the times when I became able to sense these occurred five months later.

On this second occasion I had been feeling exasperated, anxious, and perhaps more than anything worn down, by her having misidentified me, most of the time for more than two years, as being one or another person—sometimes several changing persons in any one session—from Philadelphia, her home city, while mentioning in her fragmentary way innumerable names of persons and places which she evidently assumed were well-known to me, but which to me were unadorned names only; she would keep looking to me to know all the background details that went with the names of these persons and places. When I went into her room for this particular session, she was sitting on her bed, looking through some torn-out sheets from an I. Magnan advertising brochure, sheets showing pictures of women's clothing. I commented that this store is in California; she agreed. I asked her whether she had ever been shopping there; to this, she gave no clear reply. But then she asked me, "Have you ever been shopping?" At first I started to feel derogated by this question; so many times before I had smarted at her treating me like an imbecile.

It occurred to me, however, that perhaps she was not sure she had ever been shopping; so I simply said, "Yes." She soon said, "You've been shopping—I've been shopping," but in an unconvincing tone as though reciting something. I asked, "But do you feel so out of touch with shopping that it's hard for you to believe that you've ever *been* shopping?" She clearly agreed that this was so, and went on to say, after having just spoken the names of two or three New York department stores, "Names mean me little."

With this, the realization dawned on me that for over two years now, in the previously-described kind of relatedness wherein she had been simultaneously misidentifying me and inundating me with names which I found meaningless and bewildering, actually these had been, all along, little but names to her also, and that she had been trying desperately to perceive me as some one (various persons at various times) who could fill in the details for her. With this I felt once again, of course, much more receptivity, kindliness, and patience with her.

On the other hand, as I have said, it is often crucial for the therapist to be able to sense a covert interpersonal communication in schizophrenic behavior which seems, on the face of it, utterly stereotyped and autistic. For example, the stereotyped military salute with which a hebephrenic man greets me—just as he greets other persons in his environment, including each of the passersby who speaks to him—has at times, as I have come to see and feel it, a defiant, contemptuous little additional jerk to it, after his hand has snapped up to his brow, a jerk which clearly conveys something translatable in words as, "Up your ass, you stuffed shirt!" At other moments, the salute conveys equally strong feelings of (a) fondness, (b) genuine respect, and (c) a pleading for help. In earlier papers[17,18] I presented other clinical examples of this nature. Some comments by Ruesch, although concerned primarily with nonverbal communication, are beautifully descriptive of the process which occurs in such patients as the transference evolves over the course of the therapy:

> . . . the primitive and uncoordinated movements of patients at the peak of severe functional psychoses . . . may be viewed as attempts to re-establish the infantile system of communication through action. It is as if these patients were trying to relive the patterns of communication that were frustrating in early childhood, *with the hope*

that this time there will be another person who will understand and reply in nonverbal terms. This thesis is supported by observations of the behavior of psychotic children who tend to play with their fingers, make grimaces, or assume bizarre body positions. Their movements rarely are directed at other people but rather at themselves, sometimes to the point of producing serious injuries. *As therapy proceeds, interpersonal movements gradually replace the solipsistic movements* [*], and stimulus becomes matched to response. Once these children have been satisfied in nonverbal ways, they become willing to learn verbal forms of codification and begin to acquire mastery of discursive language.[12b]

A hebephrenic woman, in two successive therapeutic sessions, made strikingly clear the presence of two contrasting feeling-states, one of helplessness and the other of hostility, which lay behind the fragmentation that had characterized her communications to me for many months.

In the first of these two sessions she helped me to see with unprecedented clarity the fact that her own perceptual world was a fragmentary, chaotically confused one. She conveyed this to me by reading aloud to me, first from a two-paged typewritten letter she had just received from a home-town friend, and then from a chewing-gum wrapper. As she read from the letter, she spoke only isolated words, some of which (I later found upon reading it myself, with her permission) were actually in the letter, and many others of which were not; these latter were evidently welters of associations which certain of the words touched off in her mind, associations experienced by her not as such but rather as words on the page. In reading the gum wrapper she read, "Wrigley's-keys-trees-," the second and third words being klang associations, arid then read the remainder of the brief sentence correctly, except for the word "manufacturer", which she read as "maintainer-maintainer". The letter, in particular, evidently came through to her as utterly meaningless gibberish—reminiscent to me of the nature of most of her verbalizations to me and, I presumed, comparable with the way most of my comments sounded to her. Her demeanor, throughout this, conveyed her anguish as finding her own mental processes so impossibly hampered. At one point she said in a low, intense voice, "I'm crazy!", as if the stunning realization of this were coming home to her more deeply than ever before. This whole

---

* All italics mine.—H.S.

245

hour left me feeling unprecedentedly patient with her and devoted to helping her.

Then in the session on the following day she was her more usual antagonistic self toward me and, although not having to be propelled to the hour—as was often necessary—she came to her room most reluctantly. Her verbalizations in the first few minutes were sparse and utterly fragmentary; she addressed me by various different names; and her over-all demeanor was that which I had found, so very often in the preceding many months, hate-engendering in me. After about five or ten minutes of this she said, "How would *you* like to see a different doctor every morning—all these *doctors!*" in utter resentment and disgust, making it very clear with this and subsequent fragmentary comments that she felt thoroughly fed up. Then she said, with unprecedented directness (so far as this particular subject was concerned), "I hate doctors! That's why I make things [clearly referring, as I felt it, to her communications] mush!" As the hour progressed, it became very clear to me that one of the prices she was paying for "making things mush" was that her own experience became mush in the same process. Just as I had felt nearly overwhelmed, on the preceding day, at seeing the depth of her helpless despair, now I felt the comparably awesome impact of her hatred.

The therapist must rely, in the far more numerous instances than the above two unusually clear-cut ones, upon his own intuition to tell him which kind of feeling is striving for expression behind the patient's utterances; but his intuition can develop the necessary breadth only in proportion as he can bear to be attuned to such intense, and extremely contrasting, feelings as these.

There are certain constraints under which the therapist must at times labor. Frequently, the patient's anxiety and proneness to confusion may be such that any verbal communication must be couched in a very few words; one of the patients I am treating currently, for example, usually can attend to no more than the first three or four words of a sentence.

Almost as frequently, one finds that figures of speech which are in everyday usage in our culture will have, for the schizophrenic individual, a bewilderingly concretistic meaning; so that for extended periods of time, with some of these persons, one learns to be sparing with the use of metaphor and allied modes of expression.

In occasional instances, one may find that the suspicious and confused patient attaches so much more significance to the nonverbal accompaniments—the manual gestures, for example—of one's speaking, than to one's words themselves, that one learns deliberately to keep such distracting physical movements to a minimum in saying something which one wants particularly much to get across to the patient.

Incidentally, in these last-mentioned instances it would be quite erroneous, of course, as well as technically unwise for the therapist to deny that his gestures have revealed inadvertently some significant, but to him unconscious, feeling or attitude toward the patient. The therapist, so much of whose professional activity is dedicated to helping the patient to explore the preconscious and unconscious realms in the latter's personality-functioning, must be able freely to acknowledge the existence of such realms in his own personality. Thus when a patient whom I am seeing in her room notes, while I am speaking to her, that my hand has gestured (inadvertently) toward her nearby bed, and she, seated across the room from me, quite disregards my words and expresses her conviction that I am trying, with my gesture, to tempt her into sexual activity, I do not brush aside the possibility that she may be quite correct. For one thing, I have long since learned that schizophrenic patients are, however unadept at interpreting the therapist's *conscious* communications, extremely perceptive of what is transpiring in his unconscious—extremely alert, that is to communications which he is *unconscious* of conveying. To deny, out of hand, that such perceptions possess validity is to deny such accurate reality-testing as the ill patient does possess.

So instead I reply in such an instance something as follows: "You may be quite correct about that; all I can say is that I was not aware of trying to say that. Try to listen to my words, for my words, rather than the movements of my hands—which much of the time I don't even notice—represent what I am conscious of and am trying to get across to you." Then I will repeat what I had earlier attempted to convey, this time deliberately avoiding the distracting gesticulations. If, by the way, the patient has pointed out something revealed by me in such a nonverbal manner, and which was so close to consciousness that I now become aware of it when it is thus called to my attention, I confirm the patient's suspicious hunch, but indicate that this matter which I had earlier begun to express verbally to her must still be explored. Such a response is reassuring, rather than alarming, to her:

it both reassures her that she has perceived correctly a bit of outer reality, and it reassures her that the therapist dares to face his own unconscious processes and to remain responsible for them, rather than having to deny their presence in himself and burden her with the main brunt of seeing them and coping with them, as did her mother and father during her upbringing.

There is one other communicational restraint to be mentioned, and this is a quite general one: schizophrenic patients, for so many of whom the other person's nonverbal communications take precedence over the accompanying verbal communications, are themselves likely to react, when their own nonverbal accompaniments to speech are called to their attention by the therapist, only with increased anxiety. Here, even more than in the analysis of neurotic individuals, it is well for the therapist to wait until the patient has become able to reveal *in words* an at least partial awareness of this or that conflict before calling it more explicitly to his attention. That which the patient reveals gesturally and by other nonverbal avenues provides the therapist with, of course, abundant and invaluable data; but it is usually best to store up this information privately and wait for the patient's *verbalizations* to indicate that these data are beginning, now, to reach the level of his own consciousness. To call them to his attention earlier disturbs, in too many instances, his precarious sense of personal identity.[21]

So much for the matter of constraints upon the therapist's communications and upon his utilization of those of the patient. These restrictions upon our modes of participation with the patient are, even when taken altogether, minor in contrast to the considerations which render it not only legitimate, but imperative for the curative process, that the therapist enjoy a relatively great measure of freedom.

Only if the forces of liberation and growth in the therapist are more powerful than those tending toward constriction, stasis, and psychological paralysis, can the patient by turn—partially through identification with the therapist—live, grow, and become progressively well. Such a statement as the following one by Arieti would deny to the therapist the inner freedom to experience as wide a range of feelings as possible toward the patient—the freedom to accept himself as a human being with hatred as well as love in his make-up—which in my opinion is a most essential ingredient of the therapeutic interaction:

... If at the beginning of the treatment the therapist has a feeling of hostility, or even a feeling of non-acceptance for the patient, any attempted treatment will be doomed to failure.[1b]

Similarly Hill, in his book which for the most part I consider unexcelled, implies in the following passage that the therapist who works with schizophrenic patients must somehow delete any real hostility from his make-up (and, to apply this to the subject of the present paper, from his communications to his patients) in order to be genuinely qualified for this work:

... Even in moments of warm appreciation and grateful cooperation, the patient may suddenly block everything because of his fear and distrust, even his strong belief that the therapist is an enemy. It may be, unfortunately, that at this moment he eliminates him forever from the company of those who can be useful to him. This may be the beginning of the end of reality for him. Some patients probably are beyond effective co-operation when first seen, but there is a painful suspicion that such a sudden rejection is usually based upon the patient's recognition of something in the doctor's or the nurse's attitude which is in psychological reality destructive to him.[10]

Such counsel underestimates the unquenchable power of the human being's—including the schizophrenic human being's—striving to live and grow. It is reminiscent to me of a description given by Fromm-Reichmann, in one of her later papers, of how fragile the schizophrenic patient was considered to be, relatively early (1939)[8] in the history of our work at Chestnut Lodge with these patients; and of how much more strength they were now seen, at the time of her writing that later paper (1948),[9] to possess.

Related to the therapist's readiness to condemn himself for any strongly negative feelings he experiences toward the patient is his concern lest he make irreparable errors of technique. Here it is well to remember that, since the patient's needs are usually so deeply ambivalent, any single response on the therapist's part is apt at best to meet reasonably well one need or set of needs, while inevitably thwarting the conflicting ones. Further, I have come to think it a useful rule of thumb to assume that the deeper is the patient's confusion, the more unquestioningly does he attribute omniscience to his therapist; evidently it would be intolerably anxiety-provoking to him to realize that there are many occasions when *both* persons in the therapeutic situation are feeling confused and helpless. Burnham puts it that the schizophrenic patient tends to "asume that the therapist understands much more than he actually does . . . to the point of believing that all of his inner thoughts are known by the doctor. . . ."[4b] When the therapist comes to realize how entirely beyond human attainment is this godlike understanding which the patient needs to attribute to him, his appraisal of his own efforts becomes less perfectionistic, he no longer perceives his mistakes as being catastrophic, and he dares to rely more upon his intuition—his preconscious and unconscious processes which are his strongest tool for seeing to the heart of the bewilderingly complex interaction taking place between himself and the patient, and for communicating with the latter. This interaction, much of the time, must switch its affective tone and ideational content too rapidly for any consciously-well-thought-out verbal responses from the therapist to meet the patient's needs.

I very much like, and found occasion to quote in an earlier paper,[13] comments by Leo Berman and by Lidz and Lidz concerning the role of the therapist's mistakes in the treatment of schizophrenic patients. Berman says that the therapist's

> . . . 'failing,' if it does not become too marked, probably . . . plays a part in the therapeutic process. The patient has occasion to experience the reality of a person who dedicates himself to the task of helping him to grow up and who comes through reasonably well in spite of obvious difficulties.[2]

Lidz and Lidz point out that

> The strength in the therapist that must be conveyed to the patient may well derive from sufficient integrity not to need to be infallible.[11b]

There is still another reason why it is well for the therapist to become able to desist from a perfectionistic striving toward omniscience in response to the schizophrenic patient's puzzling or confusing communications: such a striving on the therapist's part plays into the hands, at some phase in the work with almost any one of these persons, of the patient's sadism. On innumerable occasions, as I have seen both in my own work and in that of therapists whose work I have supervised, it comes about that the therapist reaches a point of desperation in his efforts to rescue the schizophrenic damsel (female or male; this is a figure of speech) from the scaly dragon of confusion which, as evidenced by the unceasing torrent of unintelligible words which issue from the patient's mouth, has this poor sufferer in its grip. Eventually, in those instances where the psychotherapy succeeds in breaking through this deadlock, it dawns upon the therapist that the patient is not only the poor struggling victim but the dragon also, and he realizes to what a degree he himself has been impaled, all along, upon the patient's sadistic effort—usually a genuinely unconscious effort—to drive him crazy with these maddeningly unintelligible utterances.[16] It seems as though in most instances this effort has been pushed within striking distance of its goal before the therapist, with his own sanity subjectively at stake, develops sufficient "callousness" to step back and take a somewhat dispassionate look at what has been going on all along, here, with this dragon and its victim.

The precise way in which the above-described development becomes therapeutic is, I think, as follows. The patient has indeed been in the grip of a "crazy" introject—usually, as Hill[10] describes in beautifully vivid detail, an introject of a crazy mother—which disrupts his own ego-functioning with crazy utterances and malicious counsel, coming to him oftentimes in the form of auditory hallucinations. In many instances, I think, the words which the patient conveys to the therapist are a fairly faithful repeating of the confusing words which this introject showers upon the poor patient's head. But, on the other hand, this introject has long ago become the vehicle, also, for the patient's own repressed sadism, and by exposing the therapist to the destructive force of the introject he is, in the same process, venting upon the latter his "own"—but unacknowledged—sadism. Eventually, the therapist becomes aware of the part which the patient's sadism is playing in the interaction, and thereby becomes able to immure himself against the destructive effect of the patient's communications—primarily by desisting from the self-tormenting rescue effort as described above. The result of this change in the therapist's mode of participation is that the patient's dissatisfaction and, eventually, rage against him becomes more and more explicit and therefore therapeutically investigatable. Then, through identification with the steadfast therapist who can ignore the crazy distractions, the patient in turn is able finally to ignore them and to go ahead with exercising his healthier ego-functions in spite of them. All this is no mere conjecture as to the course which psychotherapy with a schizophrenic patient should ideally follow in this particular regard, but is, rather, the course which I have actually seen it to follow in successful instances.

Closely related to the above development, and overlapping with it, is the gradual realization on the part of the therapist, previously so caught up in a deadly serious endeavor to rescue the poor struggling patient, that all this is not so desperately serious, now, as he had long felt it to be; that the patient's maddeningly confusing communications, once the emergence of their sadistic "driving-crazy" significance has helped him to see them in a different perspective, have a healthily playful quality at their root. Now, whereas he used to be the sober target of the patient's partially sadistic, but also partially genuinely playful, teasing *via* the bewildering communications, he becomes able instead to join the patient more and more often in mutually enjoyable plays on words, contributions of chaotically nonsensical verbalizations, and uninhibited flights of fancy. Here has become restored, I believe, what was best and healthiest in the patient's very early relationship with the mother;[15] and it is upon this kind of playful and unfettered interaction, historically traceable to the beginnings of verbal relatedness in the young child's life, that the patient's gradual development of firm ego-boundaries, and use of more logically organized, adult forms of thought and communication, can be founded. The therapist learns to his surprise that there is a kind of chaos and confusion which is not anxiety-provoking and destructive, but thoroughly pleasurable —the playful chaos which a mother and a little child can share, or which two little children can share, where mutual trust prevails to such a degree that there is no need for self-defensive organization.

Another way of viewing schizophrenic communication, in such a way as to help ourselves become free from undue self-demandingness, is this: we have the job of becoming more skillful at deciphering the patient's disguised communications; but *he* has the task of becoming able, over the long course of therapy, to express himself in more conventional terms. Thus we find that our therapeutic dedication is on several counts misplaced if it is persistently directed toward a sober and selfless wracking our brains to unravel the confusing communications: not only does an unvarying orientation of that sort prevent us from assessing fully the patient's sadism, and from participating subsequently with him in a therapeutically valuable phase of playfulness with communicational devices, but also it tends to maintain him in a regressive position where he is not held basically responsible for the development of increasingly mature forms of communication.

In my work with an initially highly autistic, though verbal, woman it was only after a number of years of therapy that she had become sufficiently in tune with her own emotions and ideational content, and had become sufficiently tolerant of interpersonal intimacy, to become able to clarify the meanings of various puzzling verbalizations which she had been uttering, from time to time, all along. I realized, in retrospect, how utterly impossible it would have been for me to divine their meaning earlier in the therapy. Experiences of this sort, over the years during which the work with such a patient necessarily extends, help one to develop more realistic, and therefore more comfortable, self-expectations.

Without exception in my experience, the psychotherapy with each schizophrenic patient includes a phase, sometimes at the very outset and sometimes only after years of work, in which the whole realm of verbal communication must gradually be relinquished by both participants in the therapeutic interaction, as it becomes clear that there is a need for the establishment of reliable communication in the developmentally earlier, nonverbal, mode before really effective verbal communication can develop in the patient. I am in full accord with Ruesch's statements that

> . . . the patient has to gain communicative experience in the non-verbal mode before he can engage in verbal exchange.[12c]

and

> . . . It is only through nonverbal replies that a nonverbal patient can be influenced; and once such nonverbal interaction has been established, the organization of the patient's experiences gradually can be translated into words.[12d]

Space allows me to give only one brief sample of this therapeutic evolution which I believe to be so generally true of the work with these patients. A paranoid woman had been in therapy with me for several years. The work had been, much of the time, stormy indeed and, during the first few years, highly verbal; she used to assert spontaneously that she could not stand, and never had been able to stand, "the intimacy of silence". Then gradually she became able to endure, and eventually to enjoy, more and more prolonged periods of mutual silence in the sessions. In one particular session, for instance, my words were limited to (a) an initial, "Want to go outside?" (we often spent the sessions sitting on adjoining benches on the hospital grounds) to which she replied, "Yes," the only word she spoke during the interview; (b) an unpressured and unpressuring question, "What's the matter?", about two-thirds of the way through the hour, when she had winced, to which she made no reply; and (c) a parting, "See you in the morning." Throughout the course of this hour, we exchanged innumerable glances, reflective, as I experienced them, of fondness, pleasure, comfort, perplexity, at times a bit of tension, and so on—with, throughout, a feeling of communion on my part with her, and with her facial expressions clearly appearing to reflect such communion on her part. There had been many such predominantly silent hours, by now, in my work with her; but for the first time I experienced a deep conviction that such nonverbal communication is genuine, valid, and to be relied upon. I had little doubt that if she had said much or if I had said much, our words would not have expressed at all accurately or adequately what was being expressed nonverbally; but I realized that *even this* would not negate the validity of the nonverbal.

I was reminded, during the above therapeutic session, of a memorable passage in the writings of the contemporary philosopher, Martin Buber, in which there is conveyed with rare eloquence the author's daring to rely upon, and to experience deep meaning in, purely nonverbal communion with a fellow human being. In this passage, Buber describes the communication which can flow between two men, only recently met, who are sitting silently beside one another. One of these is psychologically there, whereas

> . . . The other, whose attitude does not betray him, is a man who holds himself in reserve, withholds himself. But if we know about him we know that a childhood's spell is laid on him, that his withholding of himself is something other than an attitude, behind all attitude is entrenched the impenetrable inability to communicate himself. And now—let us imagine that this is one of the hours which succeed in bursting asunder the seven iron bands about our heart—imperceptibly the spell is lifted. But even now the man does not speak a word, does not stir a finger. Yet he does something. The lifting of the spell has happened to him—no matter from where—without his doing. But this is what he does now: he releases in himself a reserve over which only he himself has power. Unreservedly

254

communication streams from him, and the silence bears it to his neighbor. Indeed it was intended for him, and he receives it unreservedly as he receives all genuine destiny that meets him. He will be able to tell no one, not even himself, what he has experienced. What does he now 'know' of the other? No more knowing is needed. For where unreserve has ruled, even wordlessly, between men, the word of dialogue has happened sacramentally.[3a]

To be sure, this hypothetical incident which Buber describes only in part approximates that which transpired between the paranoid woman and me, for neither of us had become, as yet, as unanxiously receptive to nonverbal communication as is one of the men—undoubtedly the philosopher himself—in Buber's portrayal. I had every impression that we were moving *mutually* toward an acceptance of the validity which inheres in deep and nonverbal communion. Moreover, recurrently there appears in Buber's writings a note of mysticism—for example, "Speech can renounce all the media of sense, and it is still speech"[3b] which I cannot accept. But we psychiatrists have been trained for so many years to revere *words* as the prime carriers of meaning that, confronted now with the discovery that the schizophrenic patient can become well only if we can make contact with the meaning implicit in the neglected and unfamiliar realm of nonverbal communication, we can be grateful for the rare illumination which Buber throws upon this terrain.

My few remaining points concerning technique have to do with various aspects of patients' verbal communications.

I have learned slowly and painfully, at great cost to myself and even greater cost to my patients, that when one is working with a deeply-fragmented patient who vocalizes only isolated words or phrases, each of which one senses to possess multiple possible references, it is well to wait until the fragments coalesce more fully, and the referents become thereby more clearly focussed and sure to one, before responding with any great frequency. The coalescence to which I refer is, of course, gradual and may require a considerable number of months; but for the therapist to respond earlier, very abundantly, to these isolated words and phrases only serves to inundate the confused patient with the therapist's own free associations to these verbal fragments. In line with the already-mentioned point that the deeply confused patient assumes the therapist to be omniscient, the former immediately assumes now that the latter is trying to tell him something, and is further distressed at being unable to find meaning in the therapist's associations, whereas these had been intended to encourage the patient to further verbalize *his* initial, fragmentary communication.

There thus develops, within a matter of seconds, a state of affairs in which *each* person is confused—or, at best, puzzled—and is mistakenly assuming that the other person is trying to tell him something. It is good, of course, for the therapist's free-associational processes to be as unconstricted as possible; but the integration of the patient's fragmentary subjective experience, and of his communications, will proceed relatively unimpededly if the therapist at this stage of the work will keep his free associations, his "hunches", largely *to himself*, storing them up until these have become better integrated within him, and until the patient has developed a sufficiently integrated ego—primarily, I believe, through nonverbal therapeutic interaction—to be able to make use of more liberal verbal responses from his therapist.

I have learned, too, that in the instance of the patient who is better integrated and more verbal, but whose experience involves a high degree of projection, introjection, or displacement, it is well to accept his verbal communications in the frame of reference in which he couches them—that is, in their projected or introjected or displaced form—rather than trying for example to bring the projection home to him where it belongs. A premature effort to cut through the particular defense will quite regularly terminate the state of communicativeness between oneself and the patient, whereas one's accepting his vantage-point will facilitate his elaborating his views more fully, and a progressively elaborated projection, for example, may come gradually to develop a sufficient number of ego-syntonic elements so that the patient can begin to accept the projection as a part of himself.

There are two situations in which I have found that a certain rather specific response facilitates the differentiation of the patient's ego:

In one of these situations, the therapist senses that what the patient is saying comes not from his own ego but from an introject; one detects this from a cliché quality in the content of his words or, more often, from a shift in his vocal tone such that he sounds as though he were parroting some one else, rather than expressing him*self*. Here I have found it useful to reply, "Who used to say that?" At first he will probably be disconcerted by this, and may angrily assert, "Nobody. *I'm* saying it!" But this kind of response, persisted in over the months, helps greatly in his coming to locate, gradually, the parental figures from whom a very high proportion of "his own"—actually introjected—views have come; and, by the same token, this facilitates his getting his parents out of himself so that he can now better experience, and explore, his *feelings toward* them—feelings which had been repressed, partially through the unconscious use of such introjects, since his childhood years.

In the second of these situations, the patient has developed as yet very little of any "observing ego"; he is so inundated by his feelings that, when these well up in him during the therapeutic session for example, he is swept up in their outpouring toward the therapist. The therapist, feeling the full and unrestrained impact of these, and finding the patient so unable to keep an open mind to the possible transference-origin of any of these feelings, is himself caught up, many a time, in a comparably thoughtless feeling-response to the patient's words. For example, it is very difficult to retain much of one's own observing ego when a hebephrenic man glares at one and says, in a deeply insulting tone, "Go to hell, you slimy son of a bitch!" A no-holds-barred retort in kind has often seemed mandatory. And comparably with a paranoid woman's argumentativeness, her power to arouse dissent in me was so great that, for months on end, I could not achieve any appreciable psychological distance from the arguments which would engage us. But in my work with each of these two patients, I have learned eventually to respond to such statements as constituting the patient's effort to *report* his thoughts and feelings to me—an effort in line with my many-times-repeated suggestion made during silent intervals in the sessions. No doubt my eventually "learning" to respond in this new manner was, in each of these instances, in part a function of the patient's advancing ego-differentiation as the therapy progressed.[17,18] It seems at first more than a little incongruous, of course, to reply, in the brief pause after a schizophrenic patient's full throated torrent of abuse, with "Let's see what comes to mind next." But I have found these patients readier than I had imagined to accept such a view of their own verbal productions. With such reinforcement from their therapist, they are helped in developing a growingly consistent observing ego, and one learns that a surprisingly large number of their outpourings of their "own" feelings consist in the patient's serving as the communicational vehicle for the introjects—

consist in his instantaneous and unthinking quotation to the therapist of what the "voices" are saying to him.

Eight years ago in a research seminar led by Frieda Fromm-Reichmann the question early arose, concerning schizophrenic patients' distorted verbal communications, whether such communications are to be regarded as only a manner of speaking, or whether these are to be heard as reasonably accurate representations of a subjective experience which is actually distorted to such a degree. All of us, in discussing this point, found that we were in agreement that one reason why the therapy of schizophrenia is so complex is that, in the instance of any one patient, as I mentioned early in this paper, his communications are at one moment toward one end of a scale in this regard, and at another moment, toward the other end. In the course of my own work during the intervening years, I have seldom found that a communication initially hard to locate on such a scale proved eventually to have been only a manner of *speaking;* recurrently, instead, I have discovered with awe that the patient's subjective experience is, in a high proportion of instances, as genuinely and terribly distorted—as chaotically fragmented, or rudimentarily differentiated, or bleak, or whatnot—as his words suggest. For example, I now have no doubt that a hebephrenic woman struggling against repressed jealousy really did see "triangular pupils" in her rival's eyes; or that a paranoid woman during a phase of depression really did see things in her environment as colored blue; or that a hebephrenic man thought, when I left his room for only a moment, that I had been away for a whole week-end; or that various of these and other patients have perceived me, and themselves, as multiple and often non-human beings.[19] Becoming able to deal skillfully with schizophrenic communication requires, more than anything else, that one become able to endure seeing, and at least momentarily sharing at a feeling level, the world in which the schizophrenic individual exists.

REFERENCES

1. ARIETI, S: *Interpretation of Schizophrenia.* New York: Robert Brunner, 1955. (a) pp. 186-219. (b) p. 451.
2. BERMAN, L.: Countertransferences and attitudes of the analyst in the therapeutic process. *Psychiatry,* Vol. 12, 1949. pp. 159-166. Quote is from p. 165.
3. BUBER, M.: *Between Man and Man.* Boston: Beacon Press, 1955 (originally published in England, 1947; first American publisher, Macmillan Co.). (a) pp. 3-4. (b) p. 3.
4. BURNHAM, D. L.: Some problems in communication with schizophrenic patients. *Journal of American Psychoanalytic Association,* Vol. 3, 1955. pp. 67-81. (a) p. 70. (b) pp. 68-69.

5. EISSLER, K. R.: Remarks on the psycho-analysis of schizophrenia. *International Journal of Psychoanalysis,* Vol. 32, 1951. pp. 139-156.
6. FERENCZI, s: Stages in the development of the sense of reality (1913). In *Sex in Psychoanalysis.* New York: Robert Brunner, 1950. Quote is from pp. 227-228.
7. FREEMAN, T., J. L. CAMERON and A. MCGHIE: *Chronic Schizophrenia.* New York: International Universities Press, 1958. Quote is from p. 75.
8. FROMM-REICHMANN, F.: Transference problems in schizophrenics. *Psychoanalytic Quarterly,* Vol. 8, 1939. pp. 412-426. (Reprinted on pp. 117-128 in *Psychoanalysis and Psychotherapy—Selected Papers of Frieda Fromm-Reichmann,* edited by D. M. Bullard; Chicago: University of Chicago Press, 1959)
9. ————: Notes on the development of treatment of schizophrenics by psychoanalytic psychotherapy. *Psychiatry,* Vol. 11, 1948. pp. 263-273. (Reprinted on pp. 160-175 in *Psychoanalysis and Psychotherapy—Selected Papers of Frieda Fromm-Reichmann,* edited by D. M. Bullard; Chicago: University of Chicago Press, 1959)
10. HILL, L. B.: *Psychotherapeutic Intervention in Schizophrenia.* Chicago: University of Chicago Press, 1955. Quote is from pp. 30-31.
11. LIDZ, R. W. and LIDZ, T.: Therapeutic considerations arising from the intense symbiotic needs of schizophrenic patients. In *Psychotherapy with Schizophrenics,* edited by E. B. Brody and F. C. Redlich. New York: International Universities Press, 1952. (a) p. 175. (b) p. 173.
12. RUESCH, J.: Nonverbal language and therapy. *Psychiatry,* Vol. 18, 1955. pp. 323-330. (a) p. 323. (b) p. 327. (c) p. 326. (d) p. 329.
13. SEARLES, H. F.: Dependency processes in the psychotherapy of schizophrenia. *Journal of American Psychoanalytic Association,* Vol. 3, 1955, pp. 19-66. (Reprinted under the title, "Verlaufsformen der Abhängigkeit in der Psychotherapie von Schizophrenen," in the German psychoanalytic journal *Psyche,* 10:448-481, 1956)
14. ————: The schizophrenic's vulnerability to the therapist's unconscious processes. *Journal of Nervous & Mental Diseases,* Vol. 127, 1958. pp. 247-262. (Reprinted under the title, "Die Empfänglichkeit des Schizophrenen für Unbewüsste Prozesse im Psychotherapeuten," in *Psyche,* 12:323-343, 1958)
15. ————: Positive feelings in the relationship between the schizophrenic and his mother. *International Journal of Psychoanalysis,* Vol. 39, 1958. pp. 569-586. (Reprinted under the title, "Positive Gefühle in der Beziehung zwischen dem Schizophrenen und seiner Mutter," in *Psyche* 14:165-203, 1960)
16. ————: The effort to drive the other person crazy—an element in the aetiology and psychotherapy of schizophrenia. *British Journal of Medical Psychology,* Vol. 32, 1959. pp. 1-18.
17. ————: Integration and differentiation in schizophrenia. *Journal of Nervous & Mental Diseases,* Vol. 129, 1959. pp. 542-550.
18. ————: Integration and differentiation in schizophrenia—an over-all view. *British Journal of Medical Psychology,* Vol. 32, 1959. pp. 261-281.
19. ————: *The Nonhuman Environment in Normal Development and in Schizophrenia.* New York: International Universities Press, 1960.
20. ————: The differentiation between concrete and metaphorical thinking in the recovering schizophrenic patient. To appear in *Journal of American Psychoanalytic Association* and, subsequently, in *Psyche.*
21. ————: Anxiety concerning change, as seen in the psychotherapy of schizophrenic patients—with particular reference to the sense of personal identity. Presented at the meeting of The American Psychoanalytic Association in New York, December 5, 1959. To appear in *International Journal of Psychoanalysis* in 1961.

CHARACTER AND NEUROSIS REVISITED—THE CASE OF MISS K

LYNNETTE BEALL

In deciding treatment plans for clients, clinicians frequently attempt to determine whether the person's difficulties are the result of a character disorder or a neurotic conflict. Although theoretical conceptualizations that differentiate character disorders from neurotic conflicts imply ideal types and all-or-none distinctions, rarely, if ever, in clinical practice do clinicians actually find pure character disorders or pure neurotics. Instead, clients' problems can be characterized as more characterological or more neurotic (with these two ideal types representing anchorage points on a continuum).

Miss K's problems involve an interesting interaction between typically characterological solutions and neurotic conflicts. Before examining her problems, however, it is useful as background to the case discussion to describe briefly the ways in which the "ideal" types—character problems and neurotic difficulties—have been differentiated.

Sometimes the distinction is based on the degree of self-acceptance of the symptom. Character problems are more "ego-syntonic" while neurotic problems are more "ego-dystonic." This is essentially the difference between the obsessional character who prides himself on the fact that he never neglects a single detail and the obsessional neurotic who is worried because his perfectionistic tendencies often cause him to "miss the forest for the trees."

Sometimes the difference is phrased in terms of when and where the anxiety appears. Does the individual experience anxiety about having to cope as the character problem does or about failing to cope as the neurotic does? If someone is angry about the necessity of moving out of a dependent relationship when it is time to go to college, we tend to think in terms of a character problem, but if he is anxious about his inability to leave home, we tend to think in terms of neurosis instead.

The difference can also be phrased in terms of the response to gratification. The character problem is the one who tends to fuss because some older form of gratification is no longer available; the neurotic, on the other hand, is disturbed because there really is no gratification where he expects to find it—only neurotic substitute gratification.

Sometimes the difference is phrased in terms of the way the problem is experienced. The person suffering from a character disorder speaks of a vague discomfort with "the way things are" (little suspecting that it is his character style that is the problem because it is no longer working at the new stage of development or in the new environment). The neurotic is more dissatisfied with himself than with the way things are in the world and more often speaks of specific conflicts instead of vague discomforts.

Basically, the difference comes down to the juxtaposition of impulse and defense and the relative difficulty with the environment or

JOURNAL OF CONSULTING AND CLINICAL PSYCHOLOGY, 1968, 32, pp. 348-354.

the self. In character problems the defense is a prelude or an excuse for impulse expression, whereas in the neurotic the defense blocks expression or substitutes partial disguised gratification. It is the difference between apology before and apology after—the "I'm sorry" that provides an excuse for the cutting remark, or the "I'm sorry" that silently prevents its utterance. The crucial difference is seen in the attitude toward the impulse and the relative use of the environment (the extent to which the environment is brought into the defense). The narcissistic character, for instance, views the world in a way that justifies his life style. The neurotic, on the other hand, tries to disown the impulse and brings the world less into the squabble. More specifically, it is the distinction between the oral character who thinks the world owes him a living and provokes others to meet his demands with helplessness or deliberate guilt-induction and the oral-dependent neurotic who curses his own dependency in others and tries to deny his own needs in a counter-dependent style. Helpful here is the old distinction between the alloplastic character solution, where others are provoked to act out the other half of the ambivalence, and the auto-plastic neurotic solution, where the self is manipulated to solve the conflict. Phrased still another way, it is the difference between an external defense where the choice of an inhibited object is used to deny one's own inhibitions and an internal defense (an admitted neurotic inhibition) where the other person is not used as a defense.

These are the major distinctions usually made between character problems and neurotic disorders. While they represent valid theoretical distinctions, one usually finds that there are characterological features and neurotic constructions in every client—only more or less of one or the other kind of solution. These distinctions can be misleading instead of clarifying to the extent that ideal types predispose one to think in terms of all-or-none distinctions and to consider character problems as preventing neurotic difficulties. Character problems can function as an attempt to escape severe neurotic difficulties, that is, character problems rather than minimizing neurotic conflicts can maximize them

while disguising them at the same time. This is particularly true in acting-out impulse disorder problems where the impulsive behavior is an attempt to escape a neurotic conflict. Miss K is an example of such a case.

THE BACKGROUND OF THE CASE

Miss K is a flamboyant Catholic girl of 21 who was studying to be an elementary school teacher. She came for help at the beginning of her junior year, puzzled as to why she was so "screwed up," considering all her parents had done for her. She defined her problems as having three parts: "school—little incentive and much apathy; parents—guilt complex; men—putting pleasure before business." She worried that her parents were disappointed in her because of her poor school performance and the fact that she was dating a married man.

She had flunked out of two schools and was on probation for a semester at a third. In between schools she held several office jobs where she dated a number of married men. Because she made so many mistakes typing their work herself, the men at the office did it for her. While they were typing, she was playing cards, seeing movies, and generally having a good time. At one point she adopted an alias to avoid paying agency fees if she did not like the job they found, but also to prevent married men from harrassing her if she was not interested after the first date. At the age of 21 she was worried that she was too old and might end up an "old maid," never able to love or trust anyone who was suitable and available. Part of her worry stemmed from what she called her "weakness for married men." She did not get the same "kicks" dating single men. Although she had gone out with a number of married men, she prided herself on being a "technical virgin" in spite of skiing weekends and nights in motels with her married boyfriend, Willie. Although she felt it was immoral, she and Willie spent the night of their first date in a motel because she had left her house key at home and did not want to disturb her sleeping sister. Although Willie was ready to divorce his wife, Miss K could not commit herself because, as she saw it, if Willie cheated on his wife with her, he would be just as likely to do the same thing to her later on, even if they were married. In addition, although she objected to church rituals, she felt she could not marry a divorced man because it would hurt her parents, particularly her mother. She also hesitated because she was afraid she would become bored with one person after a long period of time.

Once she was supposed to meet an old boyfriend but stood him up when a more interesting offer came along from another boy. Somehow Miss K and the new boyfriend showed up at the parking lot where the old boyfriend was waiting for her. Later, when she heard that the old boyfriend, who had gone to jail, had committed suicide, she wondered ingenuously if he could have possibly killed himself over anything she had done.

Miss K's apathy toward school was another disturbing problem. She found herself bored with courses as well as men. In high school she used to think that "booking it" was "square" and that it was "cool" to get away with as much as possible. In college she felt "gypped" rather than bored because her impossibly slow reading speed prevented her from getting as much as the faster readers. It also bothered her that while she was "messing around" in school, others were getting more valuable job experience in the outside world. She had trouble working in school until the pressure was on and then it would be too late to get everything done. Her characteristic pattern involved last-minute anxiety, late papers, and missed exams. She thought it was "nervy" of a professor not to allow her a make-up examination just because she had missed the final exam and had neglected to call and explain for 3 days due to her upset condition. She felt funny being on time and spoke contemptuously of her roommate, who childishly complied with every deadline and every assignment, failing to realize that "authorities didn't always have the right answers." Miss K often refused to read an assignment if she could not see what the book would do for her personally. Her difficulty in school, not surprisingly, carried over to her practice teaching. She tried not to be an arbitrary authority, worried that she was too indulgent or too harsh, but sympathized with the children who could not see why they should learn and tried to get away with as little effort as possible. Occasionally she succeeded in providing a stimulating experience for her pupils, but even then she would be upset because "nobody was making school interesting" for her.

Although school seemed like a farce most of the time, even when she tried she felt a helpless futility about her efforts. She complained most about her slow reading speed, her inability to concentrate, and the difficulty she had in remembering what she read. She had still another complaint about school. In the midst of indignant objections about a young Teaching Fellow who insisted that she hand a paper in on time for once, she admitted that she was pleased that someone finally made her "toe the line." She hastened to add that if only others had insisted all along, she would never have flunked out of school.

The guilt complex she talked about in connection with her parents referred to her fear of hurting them by her "sinful" behavior with Willie and her fear of disappointing them by flunking out of school again. More than anything, it was her apathetic attitude that bothered her. She did not care about failing as much as she should or as much as her parents thought she should. She complained that she was unable to accept responsibility and unable to commit herself to anything with enthusiasm. She felt without values and worried that somehow she was defeating herself.

Miss K was the oldest of three—with a sister age 18, and brother age 10. As she looked back at her early years, she described herself as a "good child," in fact, a model student who did well in school and always listened to her teachers. Suddenly, with the onset of adolescence in junior high school (at about the time her brother was born), things changed drastically. While she had thought it important to be "good" in order to be liked, she suddenly felt that to be "cool" and "in" with the popular teenagers she had to be "fast," as they were. While her parents were vacationing in the Virgin Islands she attended a number of wild parties, participating in much drinking, fast driving, and heavy petting.

Whether or not she was in real trouble, she managed to produce some trouble by writing to a boy she had dated telling him she was pregnant. She was not and knew she was not, but thought it was "cool" at the time. The boy wrote to another girl to ask about Miss K's situation and when this girl later told Miss K, as Miss K later reported, her parents were "worried as they should have been." Her parents, bewildered that she could trouble them so, called in a priest who lectured her on her lack of virtue and general badness. Miss K listened politely, but distantly, feeling that her parents were exaggerating things and making too much commotion over nothing.

She remembered a few mild disappointments in her parents. Once she had come home from church feeling especially bad about her "sinful" ways, particularly because she was then in a "state of grace." When she began to cry and at her parents urging tried to tell them how worried she was about seeing a married man, to Miss K's horror, her mother, instead of taking her seriously and being upset, merely amused and laughed about "what a pickle she was in." She was somewhat disturbed at their lack of disappointment. She was also hurt when her mother phoned on one occasion, asked her if she was still seeing Willie, and then hung up when Miss K admitted that she was. She was somewhat confused, too, when her mother sent her literature reminding her that non-Catholics could not go to Heaven. She knew her mother was hoping to discourage her from marrying Willie, who was non-Catholic, but she wondered if she was not forgetting about her own husband, who was also a non-Catholic! She also complained about her father's arbitrary rules, particularly because she always wanted to know his reasons for making the rules and he insisted that she do things just because he said so. In spite of these mild disappointments, she felt that her parents were completely good and she was completely wrong. She denied any resentment, feeling only guilt because she had been such a disappointment to them.

IMPRESSIONS AND ASSESSMENTS

Miss K is a very pretty girl, but her smiling face had a blank look and her exuberance an affected quality that gave the impression of eager wide-eyed innocence. She presented herself as both candidly sexual and ingenuously innocent, helplessly confounded by her "problems." When she referred to her problems one could almost see them in quotes, like a cloak of helplessness she wore to manipulate others to her ends and avoid blame for her actions. She generally placed responsibility for her behavior on a third party or avoided it altogether by her helplessness.

Both her apathy in school and the guilt complex about her parents seemed related to the covert resentment she felt toward her parents' arbitrary authority. Her attitude toward the school as an authority was an exact repetition of her reaction to her father's rule. At home she had always wanted to know why she had to do things and objected when her father told her to forget the "why" and just do as he said; in school she could write papers only after the deadline was over and read books only if they were not required. She was constantly concerned because she did not see why she should study.

Aside from the defiant aspect of her difficulty in school, one also sees evidence of a demanding rage that constantly interfered with her studying. The envy she felt for those who read faster and for her students, who got more from their teachers than she got from hers, as well as her feeling of being gypped because she got less for her efforts, had the quality of an accusing, demanding rage that could be expressed in no other way. Her helplessness, too, served as both a demand and an accusation aimed at depriving adults. Similarly, her procrastination and attempts to get away with things, like her more desperate provocations in early adolescence, demanded that the authorities demonstrate their concern by "shaping her up," as he frequently phrased it.

What Miss K seemed to mean in describing her problem with men as "putting pleasure before business" was putting an antisocial intrigue or the exciting pleasure of the forbidden ahead of the usual business of love and marriage with a nice Catholic boy in a church wedding, in short, all the expectations her parents had for her. While she recognized that there was something pleasurable in dating married men, she was concerned about the "immorality" of her actions. She initially indicated that she got "kicks" only in dating

married men, although she felt this was a weakness. In the course of the therapy it became apparent that Willie, her married boy friend, was not just an outlet for covert rebellion or more exciting because he represented forbidden territory. He was also safer, surprisingly enough, because he did not force himself on her sexually. With other men she felt forced to play a "cat and mouse" game to avoid sexual advances or else worried that she was "on the prowl." In spite of her candidly sexual front, she admitted that she was afraid of sex, disgusted by the "animalistic loss of control," and "turned off" by caresses as soon as she sensed the man's arousal or her own. She experienced her wild adolescence and her parents' indulgence as frightening license, and was relieved when they insisted on a curfew. Thus, while she claimed to enjoy the forbidden kicks and tried to get away with as much as possible, she worried that she might "go too far" and always seemed anxious for someone to "shape her up." Much of her behavior, in fact, seemed an attempt to provoke moral indignation and stern authority so she would not get away with anything.

While both parents initially appeared to be overly indulgent, on closer examination they seemed to be involved in a compliant way in Miss K's acting-out. Gaining some vicarious enjoyment from her exploits, they indulged her for awhile and then countered with a guilt-driven punishment, letting someone else take the responsibility for final decisions. The vicarious enjoyment, subtle provocation, and inconsistent outrage seemed more characteristic of the mother. She seemed involved not just in some peculiar enjoyment of her daughter's sexual adventures but also in seeing Miss K hurt either herself or someone else. The mother's concern about numerous speeding tickets which Miss K had accumulated was not for her daughter's safety but for fear that others might be maimed. Here, as in her laughter at Miss K's predicament with Willie, she practically invited her daughter to hurt someone else. She seemed, from the client's reports, to be the kind of mother who offers her daughter candy, but admonishes her against eating it.

Now we can return to the problem posed at the beginning, that of the complicated interaction between characterological solutions and neurotic conflicts, and examine Miss K's unusual mixture of solutions in that context. She presents a real diagnostic dilemma if looked at from the standpoint of character or neurosis. One might ask whether her problem is basically a neurotic one associated with unresolved Oedipal problems, infantile dependency needs, and underlying depression, or whether she might be best described as a narcissistic character disorder. One could probably make a good case for describing her as an hysteric or a narcissistic character disorder, but at the expense of excluding contradictory data.

If one were to see her as a narcissistic character disorder, one would emphasize the unconcerned insistence on gratification regardless of others' interests, the pride in her sexual escapades, the anxiety about having to cope with the unentertaining and frustrating banalities of school, and the ease with which she acted on impulse once blame had been externalized. But Miss K's candidly sexual behavior was hardly ego-syntonic, nor was her apparent self-indulgence really providing gratification. Miss K's candid sexual front, in her initial self-presentation, looked like the ultimate in guilt-free self-seeking gratification, but appeared after a more detailed examination to be an attempted denial of sexual inhibition. What originally looked like a self-indulgent character problem began to sound like a cover for neurotic inhibition and fear of gratification. Willie was not just illicit "kicks," as she tried to pretend, but a safe escape from the "cat and mouse" game. Likewise, her difficulties in school initially looked like a defiant anticonvention refusal. But she chose an independent topic for papers not just as an expression of rebellious independence or personal gratification, but because she thus avoided the danger of competing and failing. She was not simply angry about having to cope with the dull school projects, but anxious that she might fail. What she, herself, labeled as self-defeating behavior could also be seen as an attempt to bring about the failure she

might otherwise have to fear as beyond her control. Her apathetic attitude about failure covered a depressing fear of failure just as her exaggerated sexuality disguised an admitted fear of sexuality.

Attempts to describe Miss K's problems as more characterological or more neurotic in nature were only misleading and confusing, conveying only half-truths. By taking a slightly new perspective we can reach a better understanding of her peculiar mixture of traits and symptoms. One encounters in clinical work one paradox after another—the wish that always hides behind the fear, the purpose in the seemingly accidental, the compulsion behind apparent freedom and the similarity uniting apparent opposites. If paradox is the very stuff of clinical material, Miss K is an excellent example—of apparent characterological "excess" that masks neurotic "inhibition," of the "strong" superego that only looks "weak," and of the depression behind apparently impulsive behavior.

Miss K's behavior, in some ways, is similar to the psychopathic "crime out of a sense of guilt" in which antisocial attitudes hide underlying guilt. Such criminals are thought to be without a superego, or, in the usual jargon, to have a weak superego. In fact they have a "corrupt" superego—one that works only part-time, but viciously when on duty. If one looks closely at the checkerboard careers of such criminals, one finds that they are model prisoners in jail and frequently merit early probation. Jail, strangely enough, is a comfort in that the punishment relieves a profound sense of guilt. Freedom is much more frightening. The bitter archaic superego can not tolerate comfort and forces the criminal to commit a crime in order to be jailed again. It is not an absence of superego pressure that causes such behavior, but the presence of an archaic superego that abhors comfort and demands punishment (Douvan & Adelson, 1966).

Miss K's apparently blatant sexuality was not genuine self-indulgence but a parade of sexual transgressions, demanding jailing (at least a lecture from the priest or a protective curfew from the parents).

The paradoxically close relationship between the "inhibition" of depression and the "freedom" of impulsive action is also evident in Miss K's behavior. The kind of criminal behavior described above is not as impulsive as it sounds at first; it is often a deliberate impulsive action—an action pushed by the superego. Such deliberate, apparently impulsive crimes are used to fend off a vindictive superego and avoid the harshness of a depression (Douvan & Adelson, 1966). Miss K unfailingly managed to invite the world to punish her for what appeared to be wantonly impulsive behavior. After the slightest bit of sexual indulgence, she would deliberately fail (for example, miss an exam) in order to invite some authority's wrath. The proof came when she was disappointed if she was indulged and relieved if punished and made to pay for her "crime." The guilt payment, however, was not for the academic failure but for the brief foray into sexuality.

The primary paradox that concerns us in Miss K's case, however, is the paradox of apparent characterological problems that mask neurotic conflicts while maximizing them at the same time. This paradox becomes more understandable when we examine the major differences in defensive patterns between the basically neurotic solution, the characterological solution, and the combination of characterological expression and neurotic inhibition that characterizes Miss K's behavior.

In the neurotic solution there is a denial of the impulse ("I'm not dependent, I'm independent"). Both sides of the ambivalent conflict are expressed, if alternately, so that one sees first the wish for dependency and then the counterdependent stance as the defense against the wish or the denial of its presence.

In the character solution there is no need for denial of the impulse because blame is disowned or externalized. The expression of impulse or the demand for gratification is justified by the world view or the other person's actions ("I'm dependent because the world owes me a living" or "I'm dependent because you keep me that way").

In the more complicated interaction between characterological and neurotic solutions, as in Miss K's case, one sees a pseudoexpression that functions as the denial, hiding the underlying neurotic difficulty. Miss K acts like the seductress, but while she claims to enjoy the excitement of dating married men, it is really the absence of sexual pressure that she finds safer. She flaunts her sexuality, fearing frigidity at the same time, but priding herself, nevertheless, on her technical virginity. The neurotic fear, in other words, is sandwiched in between pseudoexpression and a phony pride over what is really an inhibition.

Although Miss K's solution is undoubtedly over-determined, one can speculate about the origins on the basis of some reported interaction.

The peculiar combination Miss K shows, of characterological denial via pseudoexpression, may come from a parent-child interaction where the child's impulse is both encouraged and punished by the parent—encouraged unconsciously and punished consciously, as where Miss K's mother seems to say invitingly, "you aren't seeing Willie are you?" or with anticipatory excitement in her voice, "wouldn't it be awful if you hurt someone in an accident?"

This kind of interaction is particularly difficult because the child receives two conflicting messages, in Miss K's case approval for dating Willie (or at least lack of disappointment) and condemnation. Trying to act on both messages, Miss K managed, not in the typical neurotic fashion by doing and then undoing or even in the typical characterological style of doing because someone else makes it necessary, but by doing and undoing at the same time. She would go through the motions without meaning, acting helpless and indifferent, or would manage to place responsibility for her actions elsewhere.

The combination of parental invitation to impulse and condemnation of its expression helps to explain why Miss K felt so "screwed up." It also helps to account for the unusual combination of neurotic fears and characterological solutions. No wonder she glibly said she couldn't accept responsibility and felt without values; her parents gave her an incongruent set of values, "go head, but don't you dare!" The fact that she felt peculiar being on time or doing things right, like any nice conventional girl would, is not so surprising either; acting with her parents' covert encouragement, she would feel peculiar not being "bad." She seemed without real guilt in spite of her mention of guilt complexes and the stern superego that often looked so "soft"; and in a very real sense she was without guilt because she was only doing what she was being told, unconsciously at least, by her parents. The fact that she maintained so insistently that her parents were all right and she all wrong was an indication of the extent to which she participated in her parents' system. It also helps to explain the underlying negative identity that seemed so apparent beneath her efforts at omnipotence. In this light it is not so surprising that her wild acting-out came after the birth of her brother when her "perfect mother paraded the proof of her own "sinful" behind-the-scenes sexuality with her pregnancy. The fact that Miss K was so frantically inviting someone to "shape her up" also makes more sense in this context. Her parents could not do so legitimately, given their implicit collaboration. Even the peculiar pride she took in her technical virginity and the insight into her self-defeating behavior is more understandable. The fact that she labeled this implicit collaboration as self-defeating seems to suggest her partial awareness that she was doing this for someone else. Perhaps, at this point, the fact that she maintained at least a technical virginity can be seen as a peculiar kind of integrity.

To summarize briefly, Miss K presented an unusual mixture of traits and symptoms. She was both candidly sexual and ingenuously innocent. She seems to flaunt her sexual escapades, but feared frigidity and at the same time prided herself on being a technical virgin. Her particular pattern of traits and symptoms presented a diagnostic dilemma, if looked at from the standpoint of character or neurosis. The usual distinctions made between character problems and neurotic conflicts were not helpful, but misleading, in attempting to understand her behavior. Her problems seem best understood as a complicated interaction between characterological and neurotic solutions, where apparent characterological self-indulgence serves to mask hidden neurotic inhibition.

REFERENCE

DOUVAN, E., & ADELSON, J. *The adolescent experience.* New York: Wiley, 1966.

Loneliness†

Frieda Fromm-Reichmann

I AM NOT SURE what inner forces have made me, during the last years, ponder about and struggle with the psychiatric problems of loneliness. I have found a strange fascination in thinking about it—and subsequently in attempting to break through the aloneness of thinking about loneliness by trying to communicate what I believe I have learned.

Perhaps my interest began with the young catatonic woman who broke through a period of completely blocked communication and obvious anxiety by responding when I asked her a question about her feeling miserable: She raised her hand with her thumb lifted, the other four fingers bent toward her palm, so that I could see only the thumb, isolated from the four hidden fingers. I interpreted the signal with, "That lonely?," in a sympathetic tone of voice. At this, her facial expression loosened up as though in great relief and gratitude, and her fingers opened. Then she began to tell me about herself by means of her fingers, and she asked me by gestures to respond in kind. We continued with this finger conversation for one or two weeks, and as we did so, her anxious tension began to decrease and she began to break through her noncommunicative isolation; and subsequently she emerged altogether from her loneliness.

I have had somewhat similar experiences with other patients; and so I have finally been prompted to write down what I have learned about loneliness from my work with these patients and from other experiences of my own.

The writer who wishes to elaborate on the problems of loneliness is faced with a serious terminological handicap. Loneliness seems to be such a painful, frightening experience that people will do practically everything to avoid it. This avoidance seems to include a strange reluctance on the part of psychiatrists to seek scientific clarification of the subject. Thus it comes about that loneliness is one of the least satisfactorily conceptualized psychological phenomena, not even mentioned in most psychiatric textbooks. Very little is known among scientists about its genetics and psychodynamics, and various different experiences which are descriptively and dynamically as different from one another as culturally determined loneliness, self-imposed aloneness, compulsory solitude, isolation, and real loneliness are all thrown into the one terminological basket of "loneliness."

† Editor's note: This paper was left in draft form by Dr. Fromm-Reichmann. Preliminary work on it was done by Mrs. Virginia Gunst, and further editing and bibliographical work was done by the staff of PSYCHIATRY.

PSYCHIATRY, 1959, 22, pp. 1-15.

Before entering into a discussion of the psychiatric aspects of what I call real loneliness, I will briefly mention the types of loneliness which are *not* the subject of this paper. The writings of modern sociologists and social psychologists are widely concerned with culturally determined loneliness, the "cut-offness and solitariness of civilized men"—the "shut-up-ness," in Kierkegaard's phrase [1] which they describe as characteristic of this culture. While this is a very distressing and painful experience, it is by definition the common fate of many people of this culture. Unverbalized as it may remain, it is nevertheless potentially a communicable experience, one which can be shared. Hence it does not carry the deep threat of the uncommunicable, private emotional experience of severe loneliness, with which this paper will be concerned.

I am not here concerned with the sense of solitude which some people have, when, all by themselves, they experience the infinity of nature as presented by the mountains, the desert, or the ocean—the experience which has been described with the expression, "oceanic feelings." [2] These oceanic feelings may well be an expression of a creative loneliness, if one defines creativity, with Paul Tillich, in the wider sense of the term, as "living spontaneously, in action and reaction, with the contents of one's cultural life." [3]

I am also not concerned in this paper with the seclusion which yields creative artistic or scientific products. In contrast to the disintegrative loneliness of the mental patient, these are states of constructive loneliness, and they are often temporary and self-induced, and may be voluntarily and alternately sought out and rejected. Nearly all works of creative originality are conceived in such states of constructive aloneness; and, in fact, only the creative person who is not afraid of this constructive aloneness will have free command over his creativity. Some of these people, schizoid, artistic personalities in Karl Menninger's nomenclature, submit to the world, as a product of their detachment from normal life, "fragments of their own world—bits of dreams and visions and songs that we—out here—don't hear except as they translate them." [4] It should be added that an original, creative person may not only be lonely for the time of his involvement in creative processes, but subsequently *because* of them, since the appearance of new creations of genuine originality often antedates the ability of the creator's contemporaries to understand, or to accept them.

I am not talking here about the temporary aloneness of, for instance, a person who has to stay in bed with a cold on a pleasant Sunday afternoon while the rest of the family are enjoying the outdoors. He may complain about loneliness and feel sorry for himself, for to the "other-directed" types of the culture, "loneliness is such an omnipotent and painful threat . . . that they have little conception of the positive values of solitude, and even at times are very frightened at the prospect of being alone." [5] But however much this man with a cold may complain about loneliness, he is, needless to say, not lonely in the sense I am talking about; he is just temporarily alone.

Here I should also like to mention the sense of isolation or temporary loneliness which a person may feel who is in a situation of pseudo-companionship with others, with whom an experience cannot be shared, or who actively interfere with his enjoyment of an experience. To convey more clearly what I have in mind, I quote Rupert Brooke's poem, "The Voice":

Safe in the magic of my woods
I lay, and watched the dying light.
Faint in the pale high solitudes,
   And washed with rain and veiled by
      night,

[1] Søren Kierkegaard, *The Concept of Dread*, translated by Walter Lowrie; Princeton, N. J., Princeton Univ. Press, 1944; p. 110. See also Erich Fromm, *Escape from Freedom;* New York, Rinehart, 1941.
[2] Sigmund Freud, *Civilization and its Discontents;* London, Hogarth, 1939; see, for instance, p. 8.
[3] Paul Tillich, *The Courage to Be;* New Haven, Yale Univ. Press, 1952; p. 46.

[4] Karl Menninger, *The Human Mind;* New York, Knopf, 1930; p. 79.
[5] Rollo May, *Man's Search for Himself;* New York, Norton, 1953; p. 26. See also David Riesman, *The Lonely Crowd;* New Haven, Yale Univ. Press, 1950.

Silver and blue and green were showing.
And the dark woods grew darker still;
And birds were hushed; and peace was
 growing;
And quietness crept up the hill;

And no wind was blowing

And I knew
That this was the hour of knowing,
And the night and the woods and you
Were one together, and I should find
Soon in the silence the hidden key
Of all that had hurt and puzzled me—
Why you were you, and the night was
 kind,
And the woods were part of the heart
 of me.

And there I waited breathlessly,
Alone; and slowly the holy three,
The three that I loved, together grew
One, in the hour of knowing,
Night, and the woods, and you——
And suddenly
There was an uproar in my woods,

The noise of a fool in mock distress,
Crashing and laughing and blindly going,
Of ignorant feet and a swishing dress,
And a Voice profaning the solitudes.

The spell was broken, the key denied me
And at length your flat clear voice beside
 me
Mouthed cheerful clear flat platitudes.

You came and quacked beside me in the
 wood.
You said, "The view from here is very
 good!"
You said, "It's nice to be alone a bit!"
And, "How the days are drawing out!"
 you said.
You said. "The sunset's pretty, isn't it?"

* * * * * * *

By God! I wish—I wish that you were
dead! [6]

While the loneliness of the person who
suffers the sense of loss and of being alone
following the death of someone close to
him is on another level, it too does not concern me here. Freud and Abraham have
described the dynamics by which the
mourner counteracts this aloneness by in-
corporation and identification; this can
often be descriptively verified by the way
in which the mourner comes to develop a
likeness in looks, personality, and activities to the lost beloved one.[7] By such in-
corporation and identification the human
mind has the power of fighting the aloneness after the loss of a beloved person.
Somewhat similar is the sense of lone-
someness which lovers may suffer after a
broken-off love affair. Daydreams, fantasies, and the love songs of others—or
sometimes original compositions—help
the unhappy lover to overcome his temporary solitude: "Out of my great worry
I emerge with my little songs," as the
German poet Adelbert von Chamisso put
it.

The kind of loneliness I am discussing
is nonconstructive if not disintegrative,
and it shows in, or leads ultimately to,
the development of psychotic states. It
renders people who suffer it emotionally
paralyzed and helpless. In Sullivan's
words, it is "the exceedingly unpleasant
and driving experience connected with an
inadequate discharge of the need for human intimacy, for interpersonal intimacy." [8] The longing for interpersonal
intimacy stays with every human being
from infancy throughout life; and there is
no human being who is not threatened by
its loss.

I have implied, in what I have just said,
that the human being is born with the
need for contact and tenderness. I should
now like to review briefly how this need
is fulfilled in the various phases of childhood development—if things go right—in
order to provide a basis for asking and
answering the question, What has gone
wrong in the history of the lonely ones?
That is, what has gone wrong in the history of those people who suffer from their
failure to obtain satisfaction of the universal human need for intimacy?

The infant thrives in a relationship of
intimate and tender closeness with the
person who tends him and mothers him.

[6] Reprinted by permission of Dodd, Mead & Co.
from The Collected Poems of Rupert Brooke, copyright 1915 by Dodd, Mead & Co., Inc. Copyright 1943
by Edward Marsh.

[7] Sigmund Freud, The Ego and the Id; London,
Hogarth, 1935; pp. 36-37. Freud, "Mourning and
Melancholia," in Collected Papers 4:152-170; London,
Hogarth, 1934; see especially p. 160. Karl Abraham,
"Notes on the Psycho-Analytical Investigation and
Treatment of Manic-Depressive Insanity and Allied
Conditions," Ch. 6; in Selected Papers on Psycho-
Analysis, London, Hogarth, 1927.
[8] Harry Stack Sullivan, The Interpersonal Theory
of Psychiatry; New York, Norton, 1953; p. 290.

In childhood, the healthy youngster's longing for intimacy is, according to Sullivan, fulfilled by his participation in activities with adults, in the juvenile era by finding compeers and acceptance, and in preadolescence by finding a "chum." In adolescence and in the years of growth and development which should follow it, man feels the need for friendship and intimacy jointly with or independently of his sexual drive.[9]

A number of writers have investigated what may happen, at various stages of development, if the need for intimacy goes unsatisfied. For example, René Spitz demonstrated the fatal influence of lack of love and of loneliness on infants, in what he called their "anaclytic depression."[10] An interesting sidelight on this is provided by experiments in isolation with very young animals, in which the effect of isolation can be an almost completely irreversible lack of development of whole systems, such as those necessary for the use of vision in accomplishing tasks put to the animal.[11] Sullivan and Suttie have noted the unfortunate effects on future development if a person's early need for tenderness remains unsatisfied, and Anna Freud, in her lecture at the 1953 International Psychoanalytic meetings in London, described sensations of essential loneliness in children under the heading of "Losing and Being Lost."[12]

Both Sullivan and Suttie have particularly called attention to the fact that the lonely child may resort to substitute satisfactions in fantasy, which he cannot share with others. Thus his primary sense of isolation may subsequently be reinforced if, despite the pressures of socialization and acculturation, he does not sufficiently learn to discriminate between realistic phenomena and the products of his own lively fantasy. In order to escape being laughed at or being punished for replacing reports of real events by fictitious narratives, he may further withdraw, and may continue, in his social isolation, to hold on to the uncorrected substitutive preoccupation. An impressive example of the results of such a faulty development has been presented by Robert Lindner, in his treatment history of Kirk Allen, the hero of the "true psychoanalytic tale," "The Jet-Propelled Couch."[13]

Incidentally, I think that the substitutive enjoyment which the neglected child may find for himself in his fantasy life makes him especially lonely in the present age of overemphasis on the conceptual differentiation between subjective and objective reality. One of the outcomes of this scientific attitude is that all too frequently even healthy children are trained to give up prematurely the subjective inner reality of their normal fantasy life and, instead, to accept the objective reality of the outward world.

The process by which the child withdraws into social isolation and into his substitutive fantasies may occur if the mothering one weans him from her caressing tenderness before he is ready to try for the satisfactions of the modified needs for intimacy characteristic of his ensuing developmental phase. As Suttie has put it, separation from the direct tenderness and nurtural love relationship with the mother may outrun the child's ability for making substitutions.[14] This is a rather serious threat to an infant and child in a world where a taboo exists on tenderness among adults. When such a premature weaning from mothering tenderness occurs, the roots for permanent aloneness and isolation, for "love-shyness," as Suttie has called it, for fear of intimacy and ten-

[9] See footnote 8; especially pp. 261-262.

[10] René Spitz and Katherine M. Wolf, "Anaclytic Depression," pp. 313-342; in *Psychoanalytic Study of the Child*, Vol. 2; New York, International Univ. Press, 1946.

[11] John C. Lilly has referred to these experiments in "Mental Effects of Reduction of Ordinary Levels of Physical Stimuli on Intact, Healthy Persons," *Psychiatric Research Reports*, No. 5; American Psychiatric Association, June, 1956.

[12] Sullivan, footnote 8. Ian D. Suttie, *The Origins of Love and Hate*; New York, Julian Press, 1952. Anna Freud, *Internat. J. Psycho-Anal.* (1953) 34:288; (1954) 35:283.
An interesting description by a layman of the impact of loneliness in childhood is given by Lucy Sprague Mitchell in her *Two Lives: The Story of Wesley Clair Mitchell and Myself* (New York, Simon and Schuster, 1953). In this book she vividly contrasts her own childhood loneliness with the affection, approval, and security her husband had as a child.

[13] Robert Lindner, *The Fifty-Minute Hour: A Collection of True Psychoanalytic Tales*; New York, Rinehart, 1955; pp. 221-293.

[14] Suttie, footnote 12; pp. 87-88.

derness, are planted in the child's mind; and the defensive counterreactions against this eventuality may lead to psychopathological developments.

Zilboorg, on the other hand, has warned against psychological dangers which may arise from other types of failure in handling children—failures in adequate guidance in reality testing. If the omnipotent baby learns the joy of being admired and loved but learns nothing about the outside world, he may develop a conviction of his greatness and all-importance which will lead to a narcissistic orientation to life— a conviction that life is nothing but being loved and admired. This narcissistic-megalomanic attitude will not be acceptable to the environment, which will respond with hostility and isolation of the narcissistic person. The deeply seated triad of narcissism, megalomania, and hostility will be established, which is, according to Zilboorg, at the root of the affliction of loneliness.[15]

The concepts of Sullivan, Suttie, and Zilboorg are all based on the insight that the person who is isolated and lonely in his present environment has anachronistically held on to early narcissistic need fulfillments or fantasied substitutive satisfactions. According to Sullivan and Suttie, it may be the fulfillment of his early needs which has been critical; or, according to Zilboorg, the failure may have been in meeting his needs later on for adequate guidance in reality testing.

Karl Menninger has described the milder states of loneliness which result from these failures in handling infants and children in his "isolation types of personality"—that is, lonely and schizoid personalities.[16] The more severe developments of loneliness appear in the unconstructive, desolate phases of isolation and real loneliness which are beyond the state of feeling sorry for oneself—the states of mind in which the fact that there were people in one's past life is more or less forgotten, and the possibility that there may be interpersonal relationships in one's future

life is out of the realm of expectation or imagination. This loneliness, in its quintessential form, is of such a nature that it is incommunicable by one who suffers it. Unlike other noncommunicable emotional experiences, it cannot even be shared empathically, perhaps because the other person's empathic abilities are obstructed by the anxiety-arousing quality of the mere emanations of this profound loneliness.[17]

I wonder whether this explains the fact that this real loneliness defies description, even by the pen of a master of conceptualization such as Sullivan. As a matter of fact, the extremely uncanny experience of real loneliness has much in common with some other quite serious mental states, such as panic. People cannot endure such states for any length of time without becoming psychotic—although the sequence of events is often reversed, and the loneliness or panic is concomitant with or the outcome of a psychotic disturbance. Subject to further dynamic investigation, I offer the suggestion that the experiences in adults usually described as a loss of reality or as a sense of world catastrophe can also be understood as expressions of profound loneliness.

On the other hand, while some psychiatrists seem to think of severe psychotic loneliness as part of, or as identical with, other emotional phenomena, such as psychotic withdrawal, depression, and anxiety, I do not agree with this viewpoint, in general. I shall elaborate on the interrelationship between loneliness and anxiety later. So far as psychotic withdrawal is concerned, it constitutes only seemingly a factual isolation from others; the relationship of the withdrawn person to his interpersonal environment, and even his interest in it, is by no means extinguished in the way that is true of the lonely person. So far as depressed patients are concerned, every psychiatrist knows that they

[15] Gregory Zilboorg, "Loneliness," *The Atlantic Monthly*, January, 1938.
[16] See footnote 4.

[17] Some attention has been given to this interference of anxiety with the freedom of utilizing intuitive abilities by a seminar in which I participated, dealing specifically with intuitive processes in the psychiatrist who works with schizophrenics. See "The 'Intuitive Process' and Its Relation to Work with Schizophrenics," introduced by Frieda Fromm-Reichmann and reported by Alberta Szalita-Pemow; *J. Amer. Psychoanal. Assn.* (1955) 3:7-18.

complain about loneliness; but let me suggest that the preoccupation with their relationships with others, and the pleas for fulfillment of their interpersonal dependency-needs—which even withdrawn depressives show—are proof that their loneliness is not of the same order as the state of real detachment I am trying to depict.

The characteristic feature of loneliness, on which I shall elaborate later, is this: It can arouse anxiety and fear of contamination which may induce people—among them the psychiatrists who deal with it in their patients—to refer to it euphemistically as "depression." One can understand the emotional motivation for this definition, but that does not make it conceptually correct.

People who are in the grip of severe degrees of loneliness cannot talk about it; and people who have at some time in the past had such an experience can seldom do so either, for it is so frightening and uncanny in character that they try to dissociate the memory of what it was like, and even the fear of it. This frightened secretiveness and lack of communication about loneliness seems to increase its threat for the lonely ones, even in retrospect; it produces the sad conviction that nobody else has experienced or ever will sense what they are experiencing or have experienced.

Even mild borderline states of loneliness do not seem to be easy to talk about. Most people who are alone try to keep the mere fact of their aloneness a secret from others, and even try to keep its conscious realization hidden from themselves. I think that this may be in part determined by the fact that loneliness is a most unpopular phenomenon in this group-conscious culture. Perhaps only children have the independence and courage to identify their own loneliness as such—or perhaps they do it simply out of a lack of imagination or an inability to conceal it. One youngster asked another, in the comic strip "Peanuts," "Do you know what you're going to be when you grow up?" "Lonesome," was the unequivocal reply of the other.

Incidentally, one element in the isolation of some lonely psychotics may be the fact that, perhaps because of their interpersonal detachment, some of them are more keen, sensitive, and fearless observers of the people in their environment than the average nonlonely, mentally healthy person is. They may observe and feel free to express themselves about many painful truths which go unobserved or are suppressed by their healthy and gregarious fellowmen. But unlike the court jester, who was granted a fool's paradise where he could voice his unwelcome truths with impunity, the lonely person may be displeasing if not frightening to his hearers, who may erect a psychological wall of ostracism and isolation about him as a means of protecting themselves. Cervantes, in his story, "Man of Glass," has depicted a psychotic man who observes his fellowmen keenly and offers them uncensored truths about themselves. As long as they look upon him as sufficiently isolated by his "craziness," they are able to laugh off the narcissistic hurts to which he exposes them.[18]

I would now like to digress for a moment from the subject of real, psychotogenic loneliness to consider for a moment the fact that while all adults seem to be afraid of real loneliness, they vary a great deal in their tolerance of aloneness. I have, for example, seen some people who felt deeply frightened at facing the infinity of the desert, with its connotations of loneliness, and others who felt singularly peaceful, serene, and pregnant with creative ideas. Why are some people able to meet aloneness with fearless enjoyment, while others are made anxious even by temporary aloneness—or even by silence, which may or may not connote potential aloneness? The fear of these latter people is such that they make every possible effort to avoid it—by playing bridge, by looking for hours at television, by listening to the radio, by going compulsively to dances, parties, the movies. As Kierkegaard has put it, ". . . one does everything possible by way of diversions and the Janizary

18 Cervantes Saavedra, "Man of Glass," pp. 760-796; in The Portable Cervantes, translated and edited by Samuel Putnam; New York, Viking Press, 1951.

music of loud-voiced enterprises to keep lonely thoughts away. . . ."[19]

Perhaps the explanation for the fear of aloneness lies in the fact that, in this culture, people can come to a valid self-orientation, or even awareness of themselves, only in terms of their actual overt relationships with others. "Every human being gets much of his sense of his own reality out of what others say to him and think about him," as Rollo May puts it.[20] While alone and isolated from others, people feel threatened by the potential loss of their boundaries, of the ability to discriminate between the subjective self and the objective world around them. But valid as this general explanation for the fear of loneliness may be, it leaves unanswered the question of why this fear is not ubiquitous.

Generally speaking, I believe that the answer lies in the *degree* of a person's dependence on others for his self-orientation, and that this depends in turn on the particular vicissitudes of the developmental history. Here, you may recall, I am talking about aloneness, and not what I term real loneliness; and whether the same holds true for loneliness, I do not know. Only an intensive scrutiny of the developmental history of the really lonely ones might give the answer; and the nature of real loneliness is such that one cannot communicate with people who are in the grip of it. Once they emerge from it, they do not wish—or they are unable—to talk about their loneliness or about any topic which is psychologically connected with it, as I suggested earlier.

Descriptively speaking, however, one can understand why people are terrified of the "naked horror"—in Binswanger's term—of real loneliness. Anyone who has encountered persons who were under the influence of real loneliness understands why people are more frightened of being lonely than of being hungry, or being deprived of sleep, or of having their sexual needs unfulfilled—the three other basic needs which Sullivan assigns to the same

group as the avoidance of loneliness. As Sullivan points out, people will even resort to anxiety-arousing experiences in an effort to escape from loneliness, even though anxiety itself is an emotional experience against which people fight, as a rule, with every defense at their disposal.[21] Needless to say, however, the person who is able to do this is not fully in the grip of true, severe loneliness, with its specific character of paralyzing hopelessness and unutterable futility. This "naked horror" is beyond anxiety and tension; defense and remedy seem out of reach. Only as its all-engulfing intensity decreases can the person utilize anxiety-provoking defenses against it. One of my patients, after she emerged from the depths of loneliness, tried unconsciously to prevent its recurrence, by pushing herself, as it were, into a pseudo-manic state of talkativeness, which was colored by all signs of anxiety.

Another drastic defensive maneuver which should be mentioned is compulsive eating. As Hilde Bruch's research on obesity has shown, the attempt to counteract loneliness by overeating serves at the same time as a means of getting even with the significant people in the environment, whom the threatened person holds responsible for his loneliness.[22] The patient I have just mentioned, who resorted to pseudo-manic talkativeness as a defense against loneliness, told me that her happiest childhood memory was of sitting in the darkened living room of her home, secretly eating stolen sweets. In her first therapeutic interview, she said to me, "You will take away my gut pains [from overeating], my trance states [her delusional states of retreat], and my food; and where will I be then?" That is, if she gave up her defenses against her loneliness, where would she be then?

Sullivan, it should be added, thought that loneliness—beyond his description of it in terms of the driving force to satisfy the universal human need for intimacy— is such an intense and incommunicable

---

[19] Kierkegaard, footnote 1; p. 107.
[20] Rollo May, *Man's Search for Himself;* New York, Norton, 1953; p. 32.

[21] See footnote 8; p. 262.
[22] Hilde Bruch, *The Importance of Overweight;* New York, Norton, 1957; "Developmental Obesity and Schizophrenia," PSYCHIATRY (1958) 21:65-70.

experience that psychiatrists must resign themselves to describing it in terms of people's defenses against it. Freud's thinking about it seems to point in the same direction, in his references to loneliness and defenses against it in *Civilization and its Discontents*.[23]

SOME DESCRIPTIONS OF LONELINESS BY POETS AND PHILOSOPHERS

I think that many poets and philosophers have come closer to putting into words what loneliness is than we psychiatrists have. Loneliness is a theme on which many poets have written—for instance, Friedrich Hölderlin, Nikolaus Lenau, and Joseph von Eichendorf among the German romanticists, T. S. Eliot in England, and Walt Whitman and Thomas Wolfe in this country. Let me remind you, for instance, of Walt Whitman's poem, "I Saw in Louisiana a Live-Oak Growing," which, although it is not a song of real loneliness, depicts beautifully the experience of the alone person:

I saw in Louisiana a live-oak growing,
All alone stood it, and the moss hung down from the branches;
Without any companion it grew there, uttering joyous leaves of dark green,
And its look, rude, unbending, lusty, made me think of myself;
But I wonder'd how it could utter joyous leaves, standing alone there, without its friend, its lover near—for I knew I could not. . . .[24]

More recently, Thomas Wolfe has written of the development from Judaism to Christianity as the development from loneliness to love. To him, the books of the Old Testament—particularly the Book of Job and the sermon of Ecclesiastes—provide the most final and profound literature of human loneliness that the world has known. Wolfe, in contrast to all of the dramatists and most of the poets, sees the essence of human tragedy in loneliness, not in conflict. But he senses a solution of the tragedy of loneliness in the fact that the lonely man is invariably the man who loves life dearly. His hymn to loneliness must be understood in this spirit:

Now, Loneliness forever and the earth again! Dark brother and stern friend, immortal face of darkness and of night, with whom the half part of my life was spent, and with whom I shall abide now till my death forever, what is there for me to fear as long as you are with me? Heroic friend, blood-brother of Proud Death, dark face, have we not gone together down a million streets, have we not coursed together the great and furious avenues of night, have we not crossed the stormy seas alone, and known strange lands, and come again to walk the continent of night and listen to the silence of the earth? Have we not been brave and glorious when we were together, friend, have we not known triumph, joy and glory on this earth—and will it not be again with me as it was then, if you come back to me? Come to me, brother, in the watches of the night, come to me in the secret and most silent heart of darkness, come to me as you always came, bringing to me once more the old invincible strength, the deathless hope, the triumphant joy and confidence that will storm the ramparts of the earth again.[25]

Incidentally, Wolfe's polar concept of loneliness as such and yet also as an expression of great potentiality for love is reflected in the psychiatric hypothesis about the childhood experience of the lonely schizophrenic. Many psychiatrists now believe that the lack of real attention and acceptance by the significant adults of his infancy and early childhood hits him especially hard because of his innate, specific potentialities for sensitive responsiveness to love and intimacy. This situation forms the cradle of his later loneliness and simultaneous yearning for, yet fear of, interpersonal closeness. The lonely schizophrenic's capacity for love is the reason why he is able sometimes to develop intense experiences of transference in his relationship with the psychotherapist —something with which psychiatrists are now familiar, although they used to be misled by his simultaneous fear of closeness into doubting the possibility of establishing workable therapeutic relationships. I think that Thomas Wolfe's concept of loneliness is useful to the psy-

---

[23] See footnote 2.
[24] Walt Whitman, *Leaves of Grass*; New York, Harper, 1950; pp. 273-274.

[25] Reprinted from "Death the Proud Brother," by Thomas Wolfe (copyright 1933, Charles Scribner's Sons) with the permission of the publishers. See Thomas Wolfe, *The Face of a Nation*; New York; Scribners, 1957; pp. 179-180.

chiatrist in attempting to understand this bipolarity of schizophrenic dynamics.

Among philosophers, I think that Binswanger has come nearest to a philosophical and psychiatric definition of loneliness when he speaks of it as "naked existence," "mere existence," and "naked horror," and when he characterizes lonely people as being "devoid of any interest in any goal."[26] Tillich describes, by implication, the people whom I would call lonely as those in whom the essentially united experiences of the courage to be as oneself and the courage to be as a part are split, so that both "disintegrate in their isolation."[27] Kierkegaard,[28] Nietzsche, Buber, and others are also able to say more about loneliness than we psychiatrists have said so far. Buber, in particular, has presented psychiatrists with the understanding of an important link between loneliness, schizophrenic states, and psychotherapy.[29] He states that isolated and lonely people can communicate and be communicated with only in the most concrete terms; one cannot break through their isolation with abstractions. Buber's remarks add an emotional basis for understanding the concreteness of schizophrenic communication and thinking, which psychiatrists and psychologists have so far primarily studied from the viewpoint of the theory of thought processes.

PATIENTS' DESCRIPTIONS OF LONELINESS

One of our patients at Chestnut Lodge, as she emerged from a severe state of schizophrenic depression, asked to see me because she wished to tell me about the deep state of hopeless loneliness and subjective isolation which she had undergone during her psychotic episodes. But even though she was now in fine command of the language, and even though she came with the intention of talking, she was just as little able to tell me about her loneliness in so many words as are most people who are engulfed in or have gone through a period of real psychotic loneliness. After several futile attempts, she finally burst out, "I don't know why people think of hell as a place where there is heat and where fires are burning. That is not hell. Hell is if you are frozen in isolation into a block of ice. That is where I have been."

I don't know whether this patient was familiar with Dante's description of the ninth and last, or frozen circle of the Inferno. It is in essence quite similar to the patient's conception of hell—the "lowest part of the Universe, and farthest remote from the Source of all light and heat,"—reserved for the gravest sinners, namely those "who have done violence to their own kindred (like Cain who slew Abel), and those who committed treachery against their native land." Among others, Dante met there "two sinners that are frozen close together in the same hole."[30]

Despite the difficulty of communicating about loneliness, every now and then a creative patient succeeds in conveying his experience of essential loneliness artistically after having emerged from it. Mary Jane Ward succeeded in doing so in her novel, *The Snake Pit*.[31]

The most impressive poetic document of loneliness from a mental patient of which I know has been written by Eithne Tabor, a schizophrenic patient at St. Elizabeths Hospital:

PANIC

And is there anyone at all?
And is
There anyone at all?
I am knocking at the oaken door . . .
And will it open
Never now no more?
I am calling, calling to you—
Don't you hear?
And is there anyone
Near?
And does this empty silence have to be?

[26] Ludwig Binswanger, *Grundformen und Erkenntnis Menschlichen Daseins*; Zurich, Niehans, 1942; pp. 130, 177-178.
[27] See footnote 3; p. 90.
[28] Søren Kierkegaard, *Fear and Trembling*; New York, Doubleday, 1954. *The Sickness Unto Death*; Princeton, Princeton Univ. Press, 1945; see especially pp. 102-103.
[29] Martin Buber, *Dialogisches Leben: Gesammelte philosophische und pädagogische Schrifte*; Zurich, Gregor Muller Verlag, 1947; pp. 135, 397.

[30] *The Divine Comedy of Dante Alighieri: The Carlyle Wiksteed Translation*; New York, Modern Library, 1932; p. 169.
[31] Mary Jane Ward, *The Snake Pit*; New York, Random House, 1946.

And is there no-one there at all
To answer me?

I do not know the road—
I fear to fall.
And is there anyone
At all? [32]

Another patient, after her recovery, wrote the following poem, "The Disenchanted," which she dedicated to me:

The demented hold love
In the palm of the hand,
And let it fall
And grind it in the sand.
They return by darkest night
To bury it again,
And hide it forever
From the sight of men.[33]

In another poem, "Empty Lot," also written after her recovery, she depicted symbolically what loneliness feels like:

No one comes near here
Morning or night.
The desolate grasses
Grow out of sight.
Only a wild hare
Strays, then is gone.
The landlord is silence.
The tenant is dawn.[34]

All these poems have—only seemingly coincidentally—a common feature: They are not entitled "Loneliness," but "Panic," "The Disenchanted," and "Empty Lot." Is this because of the general inclination of the word-conscious and word-suspicious schizophrenic to replace direct communications and definitions by allusions, symbols, circumlocutions, and so on? Or is it an unconscious expression of the fear of loneliness—a fear so great that even naming it is frightening? If one remembers that fear of loneliness is the common fate of the people of this Western culture, be they mentally healthy or disturbed, it seems that the choice of the titles of these poems is determined by this fear.

ENFORCED AND EXPERIMENTAL ISOLATION

There are two sources of verification for the assumption that severe loneliness cannot ordinarily be endured more than tem-porarily without leading to psychotic developments—if it does not, in fact, occur as an inherent part of mental illness. One source of verification is found in the psychoses which develop in people undergoing an experience of enforced isolation, the other in the psychosis-like states ensuing from experimentally induced states of loneliness.

Three types of nonexperimental isolation may be differentiated. The first is the voluntary isolation which comes about in the course of polar expeditions, or in the lives of rangers at solitary outposts. Such isolation may be tolerated without serious emotional disturbances. Courtauld's "Living Alone Under Polar Conditions" may be mentioned as representative to some degree.[35] Courtauld, who was isolated on the Greenland icecap in a weather station, writes that there is no objection, in his judgment, to a solitary voluntary mission if one is certain of adequate measures for one's safety and of ultimate relief. He recommends, however, that only persons with active, imaginative minds, who do not suffer from a nervous disposition and are not given to brooding, and who can occupy themselves by such means as reading, should go on polar expeditions.

The second type of isolation is represented by solitary seafarers, who seem to be in a considerably more complex situation than the polar isolates or solitary rangers. Most of the solitary sailors seem to suffer from symptoms of mental illness. Slocum, for instance, developed hallucinations of a savior who appeared in times of particular stress—a reflection, probably, of his inner conviction that he would survive.[36]

The third group consists of those who are subjected to solitary confinement in prisons and concentration camps. They are, of course, seriously threatened by psychotic developments, and they do frequently become victims of mental illness.

Christopher Burney has written a report about his survival, without mental

[32] Eithne Tabor, *The Cliff's Edge: Songs of a Psychotic;* New York, Sheed and Ward, 1950; p. 36. Reprinted by permission of the author.
[33] By permission of the author.
[34] By permission of the author.

[35] A. Courtauld, "Living Alone Under Polar Conditions," *The Polar Record,* No. 4, July, 1932; Cambridge, The University Press.
[36] Joshua Slocum, *Sailing Alone Around the World;* London, Rupert-Hart-Davis, 1948.

illness, of eighteen months of solitary confinement by the Germans during World War II.[37] His isolation was made worse by cold, physical and emotional humiliation, and a near-starvation diet. On the few occasions when he had an opportunity for communication, ". . . I found that the muscles of my mouth had become stiff and unwilling and that the thoughts and questions I had wanted to express became ridiculous when I turned them into words."[38] "Solitude," he says, "had so far weaned me from the habit of intercourse, even the thin intercourse of speculation, that I could no longer see any relationship with another person unless it were introduced gradually by a long overture of common trivialities."[39]

Burney describes the systematic devices he developed to counteract the danger of becoming mad; he forced himself to divide his lonely days into fixed periods, with a daily routine made up of such items as manicuring his fingernails with a splinter of wood he had managed to peel from his stool, doing physical exercises, pacing up and down his cell, counting the rounds he made, and whistling a musical program made up of every tune he could remember. He forced himself to divide the eating of his one meager meal per day between noon and evening, despite the craving of his hungry stomach. On one of the rare occasions when he was allowed to go outside for exercise, he brought back with him to his cell a snail; "It was company of a sort, and as it were an emissary from the world of real life. . . ."[40] He disciplined his mind to work on intellectual and spiritual problems, whose starting point had frequently to come from the torn and ancient sheets of newspaper, or sometimes pages of books, given him for toilet paper.

Secretly routinizing his life proved to be an important safeguard for his mental equilibrium. The importance of this device can be measured by the degree to which Burney felt threatened by even small changes, such as a change in the sequence of receiving first soup and then bread, to receiving first bread and then soup. He also felt being moved from one cell to another as a threat to his equilibrium, even though the new cell, as such, was obviously preferable to the old one.

While Burney survived his ordeal without mental illness, he was aware, toward the end of the eighteen months of solitary confinement, that isolation was threatening his mental health. "As long as my brain worked," he says, "solitude served a purpose, but I could see that it was slowly exhausting the fuel with which it had started, and if it stopped from inanition I would have nothing left but cold and hunger, which would make short work of me. Metaphysics were not enough: they are an exercise, weakening rather than nourishing; and the brain requires food of real substance."[41] The intensity of the effort it had taken to stay adjusted to his solitary life may be measured by the fact that, at the first opportunity to communicate, he did not dare to talk, "because I thought it quite probable that if I opened my mouth I should show myself to be mad."[42] "I tried to talk . . . and succeeded a little, but constantly had to check my tongue for fear of uttering some impossibility."[43]

The reports of Ellam and Mudie, and Bernicot include statements similar to these last remarks of Burney's.[44] As Lilly says, in discussing these accounts, "The inner life becomes so vivid and intense that it takes time to readjust to the life among other persons and to reestablish one's inner criteria of sanity."[45]

One more remark about Burney's experience: I believe that his unquestioning, matter-of-fact belief in the spiritual validity of the political convictions which were the cause of his imprisonment may have been an additional factor which helped him to survive his ordeal without

---

[37] Christopher Burney, *Solitary Confinement;* New York, Clerke and Cockeran, 1952.
[38] See footnote 37; p. 86.
[39] See footnote 37; p. 105.
[40] See footnote 37; p. 109.

[41] See footnote 37; p. 150.
[42] See footnote 37; p. 151.
[43] See footnote 37; p. 152.
[44] Patrick Ellam and Colin Mudie, *Sopranino;* New York, Norton, 1953. Louis Bernicot, *The Voyage of the Anahita;* London, Rupert-Hart-Davis, 1953.
[45] See footnote 11; p. 4.

becoming mentally ill. In this sense, his confinement was more of a piece with the voluntary isolation of the polar explorers than, for example, with the imprisonment of a delinquent. The delinquent prisoner is not likely to have the determination and devotion to a cause which helped Burney to stay mentally sound, even though he was deprived of the opportunity to work or to receive stimulation through reading —which for many others seem to have been the two most effective antidotes or remedies for the humiliation of confinement and the rise of disintegrating loneliness.

My suggestion that Burney's conviction and determination were factors in his remaining mentally healthy raises a question about the inner emotional factors which determine whether a person can tolerate isolation or will be particularly vulnerable to its dangers. So far, I have not succeeded in finding specific psychodynamic or descriptive data which could be helpful in differentiating between people who react to solitude with or without succumbing to psychotic loneliness. However, it should be possible to learn more by interrogating persons who have exposed themselves voluntarily to a life of solitude and isolation.

The last important source of insight into the psychodynamics of loneliness is the significant experimental work of Donald Hebb and his group at McGill University [46] and of John C. Lilly at the National Institute of Mental Health,[47] who have exposed their subjects to experimentally created states of physical and emotional isolation. Both investigators have brought about marked temporary impairments of people's emotional reactions, mental activities, and mental health by cutting down the scope of their physical contact with the outside world through experimental limitations of their sensory perception and decreased variation in their sensory environment. In the Canadian experiments the aim has been to reduce the *patterning* of stimuli to the lowest level; while the National Institute of Mental Health experiments have endeavored to reduce the *absolute intensity* of all physical stimuli to the lowest possible level.

The subjects of the McGill experiments spent twenty-four hours a day, with time out for eating and elimination, on a comfortable bed with a foam rubber pillow. Although communication was kept to a minimum, an amplifier connected with earphones was provided, through which an observer could test the subject verbally. Other noises were masked by fans and the humming of air-conditioners. The subjects wore translucent goggles which transmitted diffused light but prevented patterned vision, and gloves and cardboard cuffs reaching from below the elbow to beyond the fingertips. The most striking result of these experiments was the occurrence of primarily visual, but also auditory, kinesthetic, and somesthetic hallucinatory experiences. The subjects, even though they had insight into the objective unreality of these experiences, found them extremely vivid.

In Lilly's experiments at the National Institute of Mental Health, the subject was immersed, except for his head, in a tank of water at such temperature that he felt neither hot nor cold. In fact, he tactually could feel the supports which held him, and a blacked-out mask over his whole head, but not much else. The sound level was also low, and the total environment was an even and monotonous one. Lilly has reported the various stages of experience through which subjects go, with, eventually, the projection of visual imagery.

[46] W. H. Bexton, Woodburn Heron, and T. H. Scott, "Effects of Decreased Variation in the Sensory Environment," *Canadian J. Psychol.* (1954) 8:70-76; Woodburn Heron, "The Pathology of Boredom," *Scientific American* (1957) 196:52-56. Woodburn Heron, W. H. Bexton, and Donald O. Hebb, "Cognitive Effects of a Decreased Variation in the Sensory Environment," *Amer. Psychologist* (1953) 8:366 (abstract).
[47] See footnote 11.

LONELINESS AND ANXIETY

My impression is that loneliness and the fear of loneliness, on the one hand, and anxiety, on the other, are sometimes used interchangeably in our psychiatric thinking and in our clinical terminology. For instance, it is probably true that what psychiatrists describe as separation-anxiety can also be described as fear of loneliness. Furthermore, most authors agree, explicitly or implicitly, with the definition of anxiety as a response to the anticipated loss of love and approval by significant people in one's environment. Tillich expresses a similar idea when he postulates the ability to accept acceptance in spite of the anxiety of guilt as the basis for the courage of confidence.[48] Does that not imply that man with his imperfections is threatened by loneliness if his anxiety prevents him from accepting acceptance? And does this in turn not mean that anxiety is closely related to the fear of isolation or loneliness? Or, when Tillich says that "the anxiety of meaninglessness is anxiety about the loss of an ultimate concern," is that not synonymous with Binswanger's depiction of loneliness as a state of need in which people are bare of any interest in any goal?[49]

Yet I suspect that if we psychiatrists can learn to separate the two dynamisms more sharply from one another, we will come to see that loneliness in its own right plays a much more significant role in the dynamics of mental disturbance than we have so far been ready to acknowledge. I find good reason for this hypothesis in my own experience with my patients and on the basis of the many reports about other patients which I have heard from my colleagues.

This, in turn, makes me wonder about the origin of this conceptual merger between anxiety and loneliness. I have already suggested that this may have been brought about originally by the fear of loneliness, which the psychiatrist, of course, shares with his nonprofessional fellowmen. But perhaps this is an oversimplification. Perhaps a contributing factor is the ever-increasing insight of psychiatrists into the enormous psychodynamic significance of anxiety for the understanding of human psychology and psychopathology, which has brought about such a degree of preoccupation with

this universal emotional experience that it has limited our ability to study other ubiquitous emotional experiences adequately. For instance, the neglect accorded loneliness has also existed, to a lesser degree, for grief, which has, by and large, been mentioned only as a part of mourning, depression, and melancholia; as far as I know, nowhere, except in Sullivan's writings, has its significance as an independent emotional experience in its own right been recognized.[50] Hope, as an outcome of memories of previous satisfaction, as a stimulus for efforts focused upon positive goals, and as a means of relieving tension, has only recently been introduced as an important concept by Thomas French.[51] The psychodynamics of realistic worry in its own right have been recently investigated for the first time by Judd Marmor.[52] Very little is known about the psychodynamics of pain. Envy is a universal human experience whose significance as an independent emotional experience has again been noted only by Sullivan, as far as I know.[53] And above all, real loneliness has only quite rarely been mentioned, in so many words, in the psychiatric literature. Thus I believe that the suggestion is justified that the interrelation of loneliness and anxiety be thoroughly scrutinized, with the goal of accomplishing a new and more precise differentiation between the two dynamisms.

PHYSICAL LONELINESS

I would like to add to this discussion of emotional loneliness a word about physical loneliness. The need, or at least the wish, to have, at times, physical contact with another is a universal human phenomenon, innate and constant, from the time when the human infant leaves the womb and is physically separated from his

---

[48] See footnote 3; p. 164.
[49] See footnote 3; p. 47. See also footnote 26.

[50] Harry Stack Sullivan, *Clinical Studies in Psychiatry;* New York, Norton, 1956; pp. 105-112.
[51] Thomas French, *The Integration of Behavior.* Vol. I: *Basic Postulates;* Chicago, Univ. of Chicago Press, 1952.
[52] Judd Marmor, "The Psychodynamics of Realistic Worry," pp. 155-263; in *Psychoanalysis and the Social Sciences,* Vol. 5; New York, International Univ. Press, 1958.
[53] See footnote 50; pp. 128-138.

mother. Physical and emotional disturbances in infants due to consistent lack of physical contact have been repeatedly described, and such a wise and experienced psychotherapist as Georg Groddeck has repeatedly elaborated on the topic of loneliness for nonsexual physical contact in adults.

In the middle and upper social strata of Western culture, physical loneliness has become a specific problem, since this culture is characterized by so many obsessional taboos with regard to people's touching each other, or having their physical privacy threatened in other ways. I agree with Gorer's suggestion that American drinking habits can be understood as a means of counteracting the threats of physical loneliness.[54]

People who give massages or osteopathic treatment are quite aware of the fact that their treatment, irrespective of the specific physical ailment for which it is primarily applied, often helps their patients emotionally by relieving their physical loneliness. Pointing in the same direction is the pacifying influence which an alcohol back rub often has on mental patients, and the eagerness with which many of them ask for it.

PSYCHOTHERAPY WITH THE LONELY

Now I would like to make some observations drawn from my experience in psychotherapy with lonely patients. I have said that most patients keep their loneliness hidden as a secret from others, often even from themselves. In Otto A. Will's recorded interview in psychotherapy, the doctor and Miss A, the patient, talk about an internist whose patients go to see him allegedly for physical treatment, but actually because they are lonely. And while Miss A herself "may talk of many things . . . one of her most essential problems is that of loneliness." [55]

I think that this great difficulty of patients in accepting the awareness of being lonely, and their even greater difficulty in admitting it to the therapist in so many words, explains the relief with which some lonely mental patients respond if the psychiatrist takes the initiative and opens the discussion about it—for example, by offering a sober statement to the effect that he knows about the patient's loneliness. Of course, I do not mean to say that such a statement can be offered to patients before they have overcome at least some fraction of their isolation. This can be accomplished by the doctor's mere presence, without therapeutic pressure; that is, the doctor should offer his presence to the lonely patient first in the spirit of expecting nothing but to be tolerated, then to be accepted simply as a person who is there. The possibility that psychotherapy may be able to do something about the patient's loneliness should, of course, not be verbalized at this point. To offer any such suggestion in the beginning of one's contact with an essentially lonely patient could lend itself only to one of two interpretations in the patient's mind: Either the psychotherapist does not know anything about the inexplicable, uncanny quality of the patient's loneliness, or the psychotherapist himself is afraid of it. The mere statements, however, that "I know," and "I am here," put in at the right time, by implication or in so many words, may be accepted and may replace the patient's desolate experience of "nobody knows except me." I have tried this device with several patients and have been gratified by its results. It has helped patients to make an initial dent in their inner loneliness and isolation, and has thus become a beneficial turning point in the course of their treatment.

The psychiatrist's specific personal problem in treating lonely patients seems to be that he has to be alert for and recognize traces of his own loneliness or fear of loneliness, lest it interfere with his fearless acceptance of manifestations of the patient's loneliness. This holds true, for example, when the psychiatrist, hard as he may try, cannot understand the meaning of a psychotic communication. He may then feel excluded from a 'we-experi-

[54] Geoffrey Gorer, *The American People;* New York, Norton, 1948; p. 130.

[55] Otto A. Will and Robert A. Cohen, "A Report of a Recorded Interview in the Course of Psychotherapy," PSYCHIATRY (1953) 16:263-282; p. 278.

ence' with his patient; and this exclusion may evoke a sense of loneliness or fear of loneliness in the doctor, which makes him anxious.

I have made an attempt in this paper to invite the interest of psychiatrists to the investigation of the psychodynamics of loneliness, as a significant, universal emotional experience with far-reaching psychopathological ramifications. Such investigation may identify certain trends in the developmental history as specific for persons suffering from real loneliness.

I have postulated a significant interrelatedness between loneliness and anxiety, and suggested the need for further conceptual and clinical examination of loneliness in its own right and in its relation to anxiety. I expect that, as a result of such scrutiny, it will be found that real loneliness plays an essential role in the genesis of mental disorder. Thus I suggest that an understanding of loneliness is important for the understanding of mental disorder.

ADOLESCENCE

Adolescence has been viewed as a normal period of crises and turmoil by some writers. The introspectiveness of the adolescent and his assertiveness, if not rebelliousness, against parental authority have always been noted as part of this developmental stage. The conflict between the adolescent and his parents often brings him into conflict with other symbols of authority such as teachers, standards of society which are psychodynamically linked to his inner life. Therefore, an adolescent having difficulty with a particular teacher may not only be responding to the reality of this this teacher (some teachers may be authoritarian like some parents are), but also to the meaning attributed to this teacher by his unconscious processes. In non-conflictual behavior there is also an interaction between the inner feeling and the external reality, which includes society. Therefore, rather than use the term 'intrapsychic' and/or 'interpersonal', we prefer the term 'psychosocial' in general and in particular for the adolescent period. Hirsch and Keniston, in "Psychosocial Issues in Talented College Dropouts", demonstrate the link between familial conflicts and social behavior.

While the adolescent period has always been viewed as having certain characteristics which are independent of the era in which the adolescent period is experienced, each era does affect and define the particular characteristics that will be observed. Josselyn clearly delineates three types of adolescent syndromes currently observable.

The adolescent is also at the stage of development which requires him to make certain commitments to life choices. The prolongation of the period during which these alternatives are experienced have lengthened in recent decades. This prolongation attests to the difficulty inherent in the task to resolve inner feelings and desires with the opportunities available within a particular society. A society provides many defined roles with varying degrees of acceptable and unacceptable attributes. Writers have often referred to the concept of identity to describe the process whereby an individual integrates inner desires with a socially acceptable role. We have included an article by Schachtel because he penetratingly discusses the ways a society may interfere, limit or distort a true sense of self by offering identities which are socially acceptable but not reflective of a person's inner feeling. Schechter, in his discussion of Schachtel's thesis, adds useful insights into this process.

Wachtel's article stands by itself in terms of the issues that he discusses. Its place in this section reflects the editors' belief that these issues are important in their own right and that a discussion of them would be a fitting way to conclude the book. In addition, it was their judgment that adolescent people are often concerned with the question of 'freedom'; and while what they often mean by this term is at variance with the definition offered by Wachtel, a disciplined discussion is invaluable.

Psychosocial Issues in Talented College Dropouts[†]

Steven J. Hirsch and Kenneth Keniston

OF ALL FRESHMEN who enter four-year colleges in America, considerably less than half graduate from the same colleges four years later.[1] If the term "dropout" is defined as any student who interrupts or discontinues his education, there are far more dropouts than nondropouts, although the reverse is usually cited as the "typical" condition. Even at colleges with highly selective admissions policies, approximately 20 percent of all entering freshmen do not graduate with their class. The issue of educational discontinuity has obvious importance for understanding American students and American higher education. The present study is an effort to develop hypotheses about psychosocial issues involved in the decision to withdraw from college.

An extensive but unfocused literature has attempted to define factors associated with withdrawal from college. As Summerskill has noted in his review of dropout research, most studies are limited by focusing on a small number of easily defined demographic variables, by failing to distinguish between different kinds of dropouts, by calling dropouts "academic casualties" or "mortalities," by neglecting the role of institutional factors in dropping out, or by failing to consider dropping out in the light of the student's overall development.

Recently, a number of studies have begun to ask more sophisticated questions about dropouts. Trent and Medsker, in a four-year study of more than 10,000 high school graduates, showed that persistence in college is related to a variety of factors, including intellectual ability, personal motivation, family background, and academic (nonvocational) orientation. They conclude that "the indications are strong that the academic orientation necessary for successful completion of college is extensively derived from very early family environment and beginning school ex-

† The data reported here were gathered in cooperation with Robert Nemiroff, MD, and many of the observations and conclusions herein are based on his comments. Robert L. Arnstein, MD, Chief Psychiatrist, and other members of the staff of the Department of University Health, Yale University, contributed generously of their time and understanding.
1 The exact proportion of "dropouts" obviously depends on the definition of this term. See Eckland and Smith, Thistlethwaite, and Summerskill for varying estimates. Trent and Medsker found that only 28% of all students who entered any college as freshmen in 1959 had received BA's four years later. Of those who entered four-year colleges in 1959, approximately 35 percent had graduated from any college in 1963, while 40 percent of those who entered universities had graduated. Trent and Medsker do not count transfers as dropouts. Although many students eventually graduate later from some college, it is clear that the pattern of four uninterrupted years is anything but typical.

PSYCHIATRY, 1970, 33, pp. 1-20.

periences." Pervin, Reik, and Dalrymple provide an overview on the issue of withdrawal from college, and also point to the role of psychological factors in withdrawal from college. Suczek and Alfert differentiated between students who dropped out of two California colleges for academic and nonacademic reasons, and found that students who left college in good academic standing were more intellectual, innovative, autonomous, and tolerant of ambiguity than those who persisted for four years in college. In general, then, there is some consensus that "psychological" factors play an important role, along with social and demographic factors, in leading some students to withdraw from college.

There is less consensus, however, on precisely what these factors are (Trent and Medsker). Studies of psychological factors in withdrawal from college have concentrated on single institutions, and are therefore difficult to generalize to other colleges. Most thoroughly studied have been dropouts from "elite" (highly selective and academically challenging) institutions. Nicholi, in a study of Harvard College dropouts, emphasizes that dropouts have consulted the University Psychiatric Service more often than have nondropouts. Wertenbaker, in an anecdotal account, stresses issues of identity diffusion in Harvard dropouts. Pervin, in a recent clinical paper (1966), has emphasized problems of "counter-identification" in dropouts seen in psychotherapy at Princeton. Levenson and his associates, in a series of papers,[2] have emphasized among other things the "unauthenticity" of the parents of dropouts seen in individual and group therapy. Many dropouts, they find, appear to be reenacting a parental pattern of dropping out, in response to covert parental instigation. Wright, in

two comprehensive studies of Harvard College dropouts, finds that a major determinant of withdrawal from Harvard is lack of integration with the college community coupled with high subjective stress.

Still another approach to the study of college dropouts is the "transactional" orientation advocated by Pervin (Pervin, 1966; Pervin and Rubin, 1965). This approach sees the probability of dropping out as a function of the lack of congruence or "fit" between the student and his college. Stern, for example, found that authoritarian students tended to withdraw from the University of Chicago, a nonauthoritarian institution. And Pervin and Rubin report that the discrepancy between self-image and image of the college predicts intention to drop out. This approach to the study of dropouts focuses not on the personality characteristics of the students *in vacuo*, but on these characteristics as related to the characteristics of the college environment. It thus helps explain why findings on the psychological characteristics of students who withdraw from college have differed so much from one college to another.

In seeking to develop further hypotheses in this area of investigation, we used a study sample consisting of a group of academically talented, psychologically intact, male college undergraduates who withdrew from college for "personal" reasons. Taking the point of view of the clinician rather than the demographer, we will emphasize: first, the characteristic feelings, attitudes, and fantasies of students in our study sample considering withdrawal from college; second, the most salient psychosocial issues observed in dropouts; and finally, our general hypotheses concerning the "transaction" between the timing of individual psychological development

---

[2] Levenson, 1964, 1968; Levenson and Kohn, 1965; Levenson, Stockhamer, and Feiner, 1967.

and the timetable of college life.

SUBJECTS AND METHODS

Forty Yale College undergraduates were studied as they decided whether or not to withdraw from college. Of these, 31 actually did drop out, almost all for "personal" reasons. We interviewed 25 of the 40 students personally. Of these, approximately 15 were seen for from three to twenty interviews, while 10 were interviewed only once or twice. Case reports and records of the remaining students in the sample were made available by colleagues in the University Health Service.

Subjects were recruited by asking all residential college deans to refer to us students who consulted them about withdrawal from college for nonacademic reasons. Since our study was conducted during 1965-1966, when growing selective service pressures led to an unusually low voluntary dropout rate, only 11 students were directly referred to us.[3] The remaining 29 students in our sample were self-referred. Of these, two-thirds came to the University Psychiatric Service for consultation about their decision to withdraw from college, while the remainder were seeking psychotherapy, in the course of which, dropping out of college became the central issue.[4]

Within the study sample, then, students came to us for three reasons: (1) one group of students agreed to be interviewed primarily to assist our research study; (2) another group of students sought to clarify their own decision whether to withdraw from college; (3) another group of students sought psychotherapy for personal problems focused on dropping out. The lines between these groups were shifting and blurred, and since we noted no important differences in other areas between these three groups, they are treated as one group in the following discussion.

None of the students in our sample who withdrew from college was required to do so for academic, disciplinary, or medical reasons. Administratively, their withdrawals were classified as "withdrew for personal reasons." All left college in good academic standing, and none had compelling financial reasons for dropping out. Almost all of these students viewed dropping out as a *temporary* interruption of their college careers. Furthermore, these students, like their classmates at Yale as a group, had the social, attitudinal, and demographic characteristics that have been shown in other studies to be associated with persistence in college—for example, extremely high aptitudes, parental support for continuing higher education, high socioeco-

---

[3] During the four years preceding 1965-1966 an average of between 200 and 250 students withdrew from Yale College each year, while approximately 150 returned. Thus, the cumulative dropout rate (which does not consider the returnees) over a four-year period is approximately 20-25% of each class of 1000 men. Of those who leave college, a majority do so during the summer, not during the college term itself. And approximately 65% of those dropping out do so for nonmedical, nonacademic reasons. They are classified, like the subjects studied, as "withdrew for personal reasons," or "leave of absence." During the year of our study, the proportions of students returning and leaving were reversed, with 150 leaving and 250 returning, as a result of selective service pressures. On medical leaves and returnees at Yale, see Peszke and Arnstein.

[4] We also interviewed a small number of students with acute psychiatric disturbances who were given medical leaves of absence because of incapacitating symptoms. Since dropping out was not "voluntary" for these students, we have not included them in this discussion. The number

of students who referred themselves to the psychiatric service for the prime purpose of discussing their decision about dropping out leads us to question whether high rates of use of the college counseling facilities by dropouts necessarily reflect higher rates of actual psychopathology. First, there is surprisingly little evidence that students who consult college psychiatric services are significantly more disturbed than those who do not. Second, at least some students consult counseling facilities *because* they are dropping out and not necessarily because of other psychological problems. A better test of the psychopathology hypothesis involves a comparison of dropouts and non-dropouts on the basis of data gathered at the beginning of freshman year. See Suczek and Alfert. Third, use of the college psychiatric service to discuss dropping out depends on the local view of that service as an appropriate or inappropriate place to discuss such a problem.

nomic status, a nonvocational orientation to college, early decision to attend college. We did not find in the group studied an unusual incidence of drug use, sociopolitical activism, or disturbances in sexual functioning or orientation, or any specific character structure. The study sample, then, is an elite male group whose withdrawal from college cannot readily be explained on social, economic, financial, or medical grounds.

Several informal comparison groups were also available to us. One of the authors (KK) had previously interviewed 10 returnees (voluntary nonacademic dropouts) about their reasons for leaving college and their experiences while away; 12 students in an experimental program involving a year of work in a developing nation between sophomore and junior years were being studied concurrently; and the regular non-dropout patient load of one of the authors (SH) made possible comparisons between dropouts and psychiatric patients who were continuing as undergraduates.

Our interviews were unstructured and nondirective, aimed primarily at assisting each student to explore and clarify the factors that had made him question continuation at college. In addition, we sought to explore the individual's perception of the college environment, and his fantasies and plans about dropping out and the years to come. We did not attempt to influence the individual's decision, but tried to help him understand better the factors that lay behind it.

THE DROPOUT CRISIS

The decision to leave college was in none of our subjects conflict-free, lighthearted, or hedonistic. On the contrary, deciding whether to leave college was, for all of the students we interviewed, a *crisis* in every sense of the word—a moment of intensified anxiety and stress, a turning point, and the culmination of a long process of reflection and growing dissatisfaction. Although our subjects reported a great variety of conscious reasons for leaving college, we came to recognize a characteristic set of feelings in the students we interviewed.

(1) *Withdrawal from academic work — work paralysis.* — For most of our subjects, dropping out was the culmination of a longer, more gradual process of withdrawal from academic work. Some students reported growing problems of concentration, while others, who had kept abreast of their assignments, reported little interest, enthusiasm, or zest in their work. Still others found it increasingly difficult to attend classes, do assigned reading, or complete required papers. Pre-dropouts commonly reported feeling that they were "just going through the motions" or "wasting my own time and my parents' money." Renewed efforts to apply themselves academically by the use of "will power" generally proved futile and led instead to growing feelings of despair. Although none of the students we interviewed failed out, confronting the decision of whether to withdraw from college was usually the cognitive reflection of a *prior* loss of interest in academic work.

(2) *Collapse of time perspective.*— Concern over time, particularly a marked collapse of future orientation, was prominent among all our subjects. On the one hand, they reported not having enough time to study, enjoy themselves, or read, but on the other hand, they often felt that they were wasting time. To some, it seemed as if they were living in a grey and featureless present, and that their college lives lacked connection both to their future goals and to their past endeavors. For many, previously cherished plans had now lost much of their relevance—in particular, our subjects reported having abandoned earlier vocational commitments.

(3) *Sense of urgency.*—The feeling of stagnating in an empty present often led to a great sense of urgency, occasionally bordering on panic, about leaving college. For a few students, to remain in college one day longer or to reflect upon their motives for leaving or their plans on withdrawal seemed extremely difficult. Many potential dropouts felt that they had "no time" to reflect, but must act immediately and even impulsively in order to break out of an increasingly impossible situation.

(4) *Feelings of meaninglessness.*— Some of the urgency felt by dropouts was related to feelings of hollowness, emptiness, and meaninglessness of the present. In a few instances, these feelings involved mild states of depersonalization and estrangement from others. More often, students reported a loss of interest in their immediate surroundings and an incapacity to relate themselves to their activities, both academic and nonacademic. Relationships with friends and roommates, girl friends, and extracurricular activities had also lost their savor; life seemed profitless, stale, and tasteless. For most, the entire college environment became tainted with "nonreality": our subjects habitually contrasted their current lives with "really" living in the "real" world. "Really living" usually involved the fantasy of some manual, practical, nonintellectual activity requiring simple motor skills and leading to a useful and visible finished product, often in a faraway place.

(5) *Self-reproach — altered self-conception.*—Feelings of inadequacy and changed self-conception were frequent among potential dropouts. In only a few students did these feelings reach severe despondency and depression; but in almost all others, we observed milder feelings of self-blame and worthlessness, and a heightened sense of inadequacy. Although some students were critical of the college, in none did criticism of the college outweigh self-criticism. In particular, growing loss of interest in academic work, frequently accompanied by inability to concentrate, had led many potential dropouts to question their academic and intellectual competence, and in some cases, their basic worth as human beings. Thus, the students often thought that their consideration of the possibility of dropping out of college was a symptom of intellectual and/or psychological inadequacy, and a few students wondered aloud whether dropping out was a sign of clinical mental illness. Although many articulate critics of Yale College exist among Yale undergraduates, they were not overrepresented in our dropout sample.

(6) *Evocation of earlier problems.*— Students considering dropping out discussed their pasts, and particularly their relationships with their parents, with an immediacy, a concreteness, and an abundance of feeling that are uncommon even among students consulting a college psychiatric service. Partly, no doubt, this can be explained by the intense contact with parents (telephone calls, consultations, parental visits) that often ensued when the student announced that he was considering leaving college. But in addition, the reactivation of the past seemed a part of a more general intensification of conscious concern about ambivalent and in some cases mutually incompatible feelings about others, and especially parents. Problems, conflicts, and troubled relationships which had been covered over and "forgotten" before the dropout crisis were reactivated during this period and brought into consciousness. Our subjects experienced former crises and present conflicts with an intensity that surprised and sometimes frightened them.

(7) *Eagerness to talk—need for contact.*—Regardless of their reasons for seeing us and despite their urgent need to act, potential dropouts were as a group very willing to explore their mo-

289

tives and eager to maintain contact with us as researcher-therapists. Part of this eagerness for contact reflects the fact that dropping out was experienced by all students as a major conscious crisis in their lives, which evoked painful personal feelings regarding unresolved conflicts. Thus, many students sought support, clarification, and reassurance in their interviews—support for a prior decision to drop out, clarification of the motives that had brought them to this decision, reassurance about their own psychological intactness. But in addition, the eagerness with which students who had "definitely" decided to drop out sought appointments with us, like the faithfulness with which they kept these appointments, seemed to express one side of their ambivalence about dropping out. Not only did we offer an opportunity for students to clarify their feelings, motivations, and plans, but our interviews also allowed many students to express indirectly their desire for continuing contact with the institution they were planning to leave. It was not unusual for students who had their suitcases packed to delay their departure for days and even weeks in order to participate in our study.

(8) *Search for a new self.*—We have so far emphasized our subjects' desire to withdraw from a situation that was becoming increasingly meaningless or unpleasant to them. For most potential dropouts, however, leaving college was not merely an "escape" but an attempt at solution. To be sure, the sense of urgency felt by many dropouts often prevented their formulating coherent and specific plans for their extraacademic experience. But in the course of our interviews, it became clear that many students who are anticipating leaving college have similar fantasies about their goals. The prototypical fantasy involved the hope that after a period of rest and recoupment of strength, the dropout would obtain a

job, would travel, and so forth, and eventually would return to college to complete his formal education.

Some students emphasized a wish to regain lost self-confidence and to try to understand what had "gone wrong"— in short, a desire to reconstitute a self that had become undermined during the dropout crisis. Others spoke of more affirmative developmental goals— becoming more independent, learning to live on their own, becoming less affected by public opinion and social pressures, articulating more positive commitments, and gaining self-understanding, perspective, and maturity. The precise goals of the student naturally varied with his formulation of his major difficulties; but to a greater or lesser extent for all our subjects, dropping out was viewed not only as an escape, but as a step *toward* the formulation of a more competent, integrated, directed, and adequate self. As one student put it, dropping out for him represented the possible fulfillment of a desire for a more "vibrant, exciting and alive experience" than he had found in college.

Insofar as our sample was representative, then, we concluded that the undergraduate myth of the carefree, happy, hedonistic, and unconcerned dropout is largely fictitious. For our subjects, at least, conscious thoughts of dropping out came at the end of a painful period of growing aimlessness, sense of disconnection, and intensification of personal conflicts. To most students, dropping out seemed a possible way to resolve this personal crisis, rather than its *prima facie* cause.

In general, the feelings we observed in dropouts have much in common with Erikson's descriptions of the phenomenology of intense identity diffusion (1960, 1968). Thus, work paralysis, diffusion of time perspective, a search for a "rock bottom," and role diffusion are characteristic of both syndromes. We do not believe that "identity diff-fusion" alone is specific enough to explain college dropouts, but it is noteworthy that these students manifest many of the characteristics of this condition.

In more conventional psychiatric diagnostic terms, the feelings of potential dropouts are similar to the symptoms of an agitated depression. Feelings of meaninglessness, hollowness, unconnectedness to previously enjoyed activities and relationships, barrenness of the present, and loss of future goals and values were frequent. Sleep, appetite, and concentration problems were also common. The response to these feelings was agitation, a sense of urgency, a need to act, a feeling that the present situation was completely unendurable, and the search for an alternative. The depressive affect found in our subjects may be partly explained by the impending loss of their relationship with the college. But in most students, depression had preceded and to a certain extent determined the decision to withdraw from college, so that the impending loss of a connection with the college does not adequately explain their depression.

The feelings of dropouts are of course not specific to students who withdraw from college: similar feelings can be observed in many undergraduates who do not drop out. To begin to understand why some students withdraw from college while others with similar feelings remain, it is necessary to examine some of the more specific themes of family relationship, adaptive style, and perception of the college found in our subjects.

CHARACTERISTIC PSYCHOSOCIAL ISSUES AMONG DROPOUTS

Before undertaking our study, we had hoped that it would prove possible to define a set of psychological and sociological factors that would sharply distinguish dropouts from non-dropouts. We were encouraged in this hope by the work of other investigators, who have related dropping out to such factors as parental inauthenticity (Levenson, Stockhamer, and Feiner, 1967), identity crises (Wertenbaker), problems of identification and counter-identification (Pervin, 1966), and reenactment of parental "dropouts" (Levenson, 1966).

Our interviews, however, soon led us to conclude that no single factor or set of factors could enable us to "explain" dropping out in all of our subjects. The students in our sample were extremely diverse and we were unable to define clear psychological or sociological "types." Issues that appeared central in understanding one student's decision were peripheral in other students. Thus, while we found other studies helpful in explaining the motives of *some* of our subjects, none of these studies provided a framework adequate for explaining *all* of our sample. As our study progressed, we came to doubt that it is possible to provide a unitary explanation for dropping out.

We were, however, impressed by the frequency and urgency with which three issues were discussed in our interviews. A preliminary formulation of these issues midway through our study found confirmation from subjects interviewed subsequently. The importance and salience of each issue varied from student to student; furthermore, *each* of these issues is often raised by students who are *not* considering dropping out. But the themes we describe below were raised with particular insistence by dropouts, and after comparing our research group to "normal" and patient populations, we have hypothesized that the three issues below are more salient in the dropout group than in otherwise similar college populations.

(1) Family Relationships: Problems of Identifying with the Father

The issue most frequently discussed by potential dropouts was their ambivalent relationship with their fathers.[5] Our subjects characteristically made conflicting and contradictory statements about their fathers, damning with faint praise, alternating between praise and criticism, or recounting a history of growing disillusionment, disenchantment, and disappointment with a father toward whom they had once felt very close. Most commonly, dropouts were struggling to come to terms with a father whom they had recently learned to view as inadequate, weak, or for some other reason impossible to accept as a model.

For some potential dropouts, problems of relationship with the father had been intensified by some recent specific event. Several students, for example, reported that their fathers had contracted incurable or terminal illnesses within the past year. Other students had become conscious, during the preceding months, of a crisis in their father's life, often involving depression and dissatisfaction with his life work. In such cases, the son's previous image of his father as adequate, healthy, and competent and as an exemplar for the son had been challenged and perhaps undermined by critical events in the father's own life. These students, further, acted as if they had lost not only their unqualifiedly positive conscious image of their fathers, but an important part of themselves as well.

In another group of subjects illustrating this same theme, we found no specific event in the father's life that had precipitated the son's crisis. Rather, the son had gradually become aware of inadequacies or deficiencies in his father to which he had previously been blind. This revised perception of the father was often precipitated by new developmental demands upon the son, and seemed to involve increased awareness of previously repressed, disassociated, or denied feelings that had existed long before the son's disillusionment became conscious. The need to choose a field of college concentration or a career, for example, sometimes served to make the son realize that he did not wish to emulate his father's life. In other cases, the father's insistence that the son prepare himself to enter the father's profession had forced the son to confront his ambivalent image of his father.

In some of our subjects, the father-son relationship seemed characterized by a particular "stickiness." A number of these fathers had shown for years a special intrusiveness into their sons' lives—for example, by seeking confidences or sharing intimate feelings in a way that is generally considered inappropriate for parents of college-age sons. Other fathers in this group seemed unusually oversolicitous and apprehensive about their son's welfare, sometimes to a degree that suggested anxious or hostile dependency on the son rather than genuine paternal concern. Several of these fathers had direct contact with us in the course of our study. They sometimes wrote us long, introspective letters about themselves, their sons, and the father-son relationship; they requested interviews with members of our research group; they voiced the fear that their sons were becoming all too like themselves. In such fathers, it was clear that the father's own ambivalence about himself extended to his image of the son, and had affected the son's image both of his father and of himself.[6] The following example illustrates some of these elements:

[5] Our emphasis on problems of identification with the father is a reflection of the material as it was presented to us in relatively unstructured interviewing. The relative absence of discussion of the mother in these interviews obviously does not indicate that she played an unimportant role in the son's development or in his decision to drop out. It does, however, point to the prominence in the conscious and preconscious thinking of future dropouts of their relationships with their fathers. More intensive interviewing would have undoubtedly revealed a more complex picture of family dynamics.

[6] A similar pattern has been observed by Levenson, Stockhamer, and Feiner.

One freshman, whose father is a college history teacher, began to question his own choice of history as a field of early concentration. This field was not as attractive to him as he had thought it would be: "I feel that my interest in history was inspired by my father, not me." He added that before coming to college, he had been dealing with "big ideas," and that having to get down to the actual business of "routine scholarly research" had made him fear he was not really motivated for history. He considered dropping out "to see whether I can reorient myself better by getting out of the educational world and focusing on day-to-day life, and trying to fill in some of the void in my own life."

Further consultation revealed that this student's repudiation of history represented not a simple rebellion against his father, but rather a preconscious awareness of his father's inadequacy as a model. The father himself requested an interview with us, in which he discussed his disappointment and disillusionment after having assumed what had promised to be a challenging new position in the past year. This disillusionment had represented a massive blow to the father's self-esteem, and he expressed a desire to enter psychotherapy. Although the father had never discussed his unhappiness or his need for therapy with his son, we inferred that the son's unexpressed awareness of his father's growing dissatisfaction with his life work had helped to undermine the son's perception of the father as an adequate, competent model, and to create the "void in my own life."

In the course of his interviews with us, the son began to become more conscious of his previously unexpressed reservations about his father's life. As he expressed these reservations, he seemed to be mourning the loss of an important component of his own developing identity, namely, those commitments which had been based upon identification with a strong and admirable father. As he put it, "I guess, before I can distinguish myself *at* Yale, I'll have to try to distinguish myself *from* Yale, and from those things at Yale that are allied with my father and his interests. I've got to find my *own* real interests." He dropped out.

In still another group of our subjects, the problem of relationship with the father was primarily complicated by parental strife, discord, divorce, or separation. These parents had told their son of their discontent with their marriage, and implicitly (or sometimes explicitly) each parent had warned the potential dropout not to emulate the spouse, threatening rejection and withdrawal of love should the son "take after" him or her. Often, too, each parent had used the son as the primary means of communicating with the other, and the parental struggle had been translated into an indirect attempt to gain the son's exclusive affection and loyalty.

Students with such backgrounds had understandable difficulties in making life commitments and vocational choices. To emulate the father by choice of vocation, graduate school, field of concentration, or even the topic of a term paper reactivated the student's conflictual relationships with his parents. To choose any option that might be approved of by the father inevitably meant running the risk of displeasing the mother, and vice versa. Conscious (and unconscious) efforts at synthesis of conflicting parental pressures were made difficult by the adamant hostility of each parent to the other, which was translated into internal conflict in our subjects. It was as if, for these students, any choice, commitment, or decision was sure to displease one of the internalized parents; no major decision could be made without intense conflict and ambivalence. For example:

Such a student was a 21-year-old senior who had recently learned of a serious rift between his parents. At the time he was seen by us, he was in the throes of trying to choose between what he perceived to be two conflicting directions for his future life. Significantly, he verbalized a feeling of "being torn apart" and "less than whole"— very probably a reflection of his internalization of the interpersonal struggle between his parents. For this student, the family disruption was effectively blocking identity synthesis.

In attempting to understand the subjects' characteristic problems in relationship with the father (and sometimes with the mother as well), we were impressed with the students' unsuccessful struggle to reconcile sharply contrasting identifications derived from a split in the conscious and unconscious image of the father. On the one hand, the father (especially in the past) appeared strong, competent, capable, caring, and emulable; on the other hand, the father appeared weak, impotent, ineffectual, dependent, and bad. The resolution of this conflictual identification was usually impeded by the fact that the student's ambivalence was not fully conscious and sometimes emerged only indirectly in the brief course of our interviews. And in some instances, the son clearly felt guilty over abandoning his identification with his father, partly because of his genuine affection for him and partly because of his awareness of his father's dependency.

Furthermore, for many subjects, to become fully conscious either of the father's own defects or of the extent of filial ambivalence entailed a major sense of loss, sometimes intensified during our brief contact with these subjects. The comfort and direction that had been given by an unambivalently positive view of the father was now lost and this loss was often accompanied by a devaluation of an important part of the student's own personality.

Our clinical observation agrees in substance with Pervin's (1966) discussion of identification and "counteridentification" (i.e., the effort to resist identification with the father) among dropouts.[7] It is also consistent with many of the issues of family dynamics discussed by Levenson and his colleagues. Our students had reached, we believe, a developmental impasse, such that further growth was temporarily blocked by an inability to resolve or synthesize an ambivalent

---

[7] See also Greenson.

identification with the parents, particularly the father. Their depression seems related to the "spoiling" of their positive identification with their fathers, and to their preconscious sense of having lost an important and valued component of themselves. And their sense of stagnation and emptiness may reflect in part a preconscious recognition of the blocking of development. The feeling that continuing attendance at college was undesirable or impossible reflected a covert acknowledgment of submerged difficulties, of vague dissatisfactions and yearnings, and of unresolved problems of identification that impeded the individual's further psychological growth within the college environment. One major issue in the dropouts we studied was thus an inability to accomplish one of the major developmental tasks of adolescence— the need to free one's self from childhood identifications and the fantasies connected with them in order to make room for new objects, relationships, and commitments. As far as their strongest feelings were concerned, the students we interviewed seemed bound to their parents.

As we noted earlier, we do not believe that the concept of "identity crisis" is sufficiently specific to account for the particular psychodynamic issues we encountered in our subjects. Rather, for the potential dropout, identity formation itself had been truncated. Our students seemed to be grappling with earlier issues of identification—to be unable thus far to move beyond identifying. Having been unable to achieve differentiation from their parents, they had not yet been able to gain that critical distance which makes possible the selection, rejection, and modification of earlier identifications, and their subsequent synthesis into a unique identity. Bound by their earlier identifications, our students were not yet able to become "circumscribed individual[s] in relation to a predictable universe which transcends the circumstances of childhood" (Erikson, 1960, p. 90). For students for whom role experimentation has been seriously inhibited from within and without, the decision to leave college may represent, for virtually the first time, an exercise of individual choice and the first step toward the development of an autonomous personality.

The issue of paternal identification is obviously not unique to potential dropouts. But this issue arose with particular intensity among the students we studied. While the problem of reconciling conflicting and ambivalent identifications to the parent of the same sex is a normative problem during adolescence, and adult identity normally develops from the resolution of this problem, we would speculate that most college students confront and begin to resolve this problem before they arrive at college. The discovery that one's parents have "feet of clay" commonly occurs among talented middle-class American adolescents during the high school years. Thus, we might think of potential dropouts as lagging behind their classmates in terms of their psychosocial development. At the same time, there are many college students who manifest a similar "developmental lag," but do *not* seriously consider dropping out of college. Thus, we must examine other issues in our subjects in order to attempt to explain why they decided to leave college.

(2) Adaptation: Disengagement in Response to Conflict

Given our finding that the active confrontation of the possibility of dropping out was almost always preceded by a prolonged period of intensifying crisis, it is tautological to describe dropping out as a manifestation of leaving the field in response to conflict. But several observations led us to conclude that many or most drop-outs, long before ever considering dropping out, exhibited a pattern of disengagement, active withdrawal, avoidance, and "leaving the field" as a characteristic response to stress, crisis, and conflict. We have already noted that the voluntary decision to drop out was almost always preceded by a longer period during which the student *involuntarily* lost interest and connection with his academic work, his extracurricular activities, his college friends, his teachers and advisors, and his previous commitments to the future. Upon inquiry, it further emerged that many of our subjects had also exhibited a similar pattern of disengagement when confronted with earlier conflicts. In some instances, this pattern was apparent in relationships with girls; in a few other cases, the student had previously dropped out of secondary school or even college. In still other instances, the student had avoided difficult confrontations with parents and others by "taking off," going away, seeking a new environment, and so on. Thus, on a variety of levels, we observed a tendency to turn away from difficult or conflict-arousing situations.

In some students, the origins of this pattern of avoidance could be discerned. In a few cases, we encountered the syndrome described by Levenson (1966) wherein the son vengefully identifies with and reenacts a pattern of parental dropping out. Specifically, some of our subjects had fathers (or, more rarely, mothers) who had themselves dropped out of college. This "acting out" of parental history often had an ambivalent and even hostile quality: the parents of such students seemed exceptionally distressed by their son's decision to drop out, perhaps because his decision repeated a pattern the parents deplored in themselves. Since, however, college "dropouts" have for many decades been more numerous than students who completed their B.A.'s without interruption (Summerskill;

Eckland and Smith), by chance alone we would expect over 75 percent of all students whose parents both began college to have a "dropout" father, mother, or both.

In other cases, avoidance seemed to have been learned in childhood as a means of coping with conflicting demands within the student's family. For example:

One student, after attempting to act as a mediator and go-between for his warring parents, finally informed both parents that he no longer wished to discuss their relationship with them, and insisted on avoiding their quarrels, often by leaving home during parental fights. Now, confronted with a college that, in his view, was full of internal contradictions, he again contemplated absenting himself from the scene of perceived conflict.

Other students seemed to have been confronted by family situations best described as "double binds" (Bateson et al.). For example, a number of fathers had pushed their sons to enter their own fields, but at the same time indicated their profound dissatisfaction with their own lives. Repeatedly confronted with such conflicting messages from the father, some students had long ago concluded that their best hope was to "leave the field" altogether. When these students were faced, during college, with a reintensification of earlier problems in a new setting, they seem to have fallen back on an adaptation that had served them well in the past.

Theoretically, adaptations to stress and conflict can be classified into three types: *autoplastic* adaptations, which involve transforming the self so as to cope with conflict; *alloplastic* adaptations, which involve efforts to transform the environment so as to make it less stressful; and *avoidant* adaptations, which seek to increase the distance between the individual and the source of stress (Hartmann). At Yale, most students confronted with acute developmental crises choose either au-

toplastic or alloplastic adaptations, rather than avoidance. For example, one response to stress around academic work is alloplastic: a determined effort to modify academic programs, change courses, or even join one of several student groups concerned with promoting educational reform in the college. Another common reaction to stress is to seek to change one's self: by seeking psychotherapy in order to overcome "study problems"; by programs of self-reform, hard work, or "self-analysis"; or by the use of drugs that alter consciousness. Our dropout sample chose neither of these two general options. Their disengagement from academic life seemed far too profound to be remedied by changes of courses or even of majors. Nor were these students especially vociferous critics of the college, much less educational reformers. Similarly, most of those in our sample who sought therapy did so not in order to overcome the difficulties that led them to consider dropping out, but to understand better why they were dropping out.

By emphasizing the importance to these students of disengagement as a response to conflict we do not mean to suggest that dropping out is necessarily an "escape" or a maladaptive choice. For many of the students we interviewed, the decision to resign from college was part of a preconscious effort to master, actively and effectively, the conflicts which led up to the crisis. The decision to leave college transformed a prior involuntary and conflict-laden work paralysis into an act for which the student accepted full personal responsibility. In principle, many dropouts might have been capable of a solution chosen by some of their classmates as a reaction to personal crisis during college—namely, to continue "going through the motions" of academic work in order to secure passing grades, while turning their major energies toward some noncurricular activity such as dating, bridge-playing, or immersion in sociopolitical activism. As compared with the latter solutions, leaving college seemed an equally "active" and direct confrontation of the students' difficulties. Nor was it self-evident to us that students' problems were such that psychotherapy, with the student remaining in college, clearly constituted the best way of resolving them.

Thus, although our observations led us to hypothesize that disengagement is a preferred adaptation to stress among college dropouts, we would not conclude that dropping out is for that reason always a maladaptive decision. On the contrary, our impression is that for many or most of our subjects, the decision was probably justified, although rarely fully thought through. It would be a mistake to lionize the college dropout, seeing him as a creative dissenter against an oppressive educational machine. But for at least some of the students we studied, dropping out clearly did represent an exercise in courage. For them, the road to graduation might have been smoother had they been content to slide by with passing grades, seeking a psychosocial moratorium within the college rather than outside its walls. But remaining in an unrewarding academic environment is not necessarily the road to intellectual and emotional maturity, much less to the development of creative potential. In more clinical terms, there may be value in allowing the student who is struggling with the idea of dropping out to use this tentative mode of conflict resolution, recognizing that its neurotic aspects may perhaps best be seen as developmental steps toward healthier patterns of adaptation.

(3) Social: Transference to the Institution

Dropping out of college is obviously a transaction between an individual and an institution, and to consider only the familial and adaptive factors of this act is to study but part of the picture. It is beyond the scope of our study to try to characterize the curriculum and climate of Yale College; in any case, an earlier study (Keniston and Helmreich) suggested that Yale students actively considering dropping out of college were not characterized by any distinctive view of or complaint about the college. Our interviews in general confirmed this finding.

We were, however, impressed with the way in which our subjects' idiosyncratic images of the college paralleled their equally idiosyncratic descriptions of their parents and family life. More than most students, they seemed to have a family transference to the institution, involving a selective and even projective perception of those aspects of the college environment that corresponded to characteristics of their early family situation. Although such institutional transferences were rarely evident to our subjects themselves, the parallels between their descriptions of their families and of the college were impressive to us. For example:

One sophomore's idiosyncratic view of the college as being harsh and repressive, yet devoid of real strength and moral purpose, found a striking parallel in his description of his own family. His father's surface violence and brutality served to veil an underlying passivity and dependency that was betrayed by chronic alcoholism. This student's reasons for dropping out were complex, but his dissatisfaction with the college's lack of underlying purpose and strength was important among them.

In promoting such transferences, the attitude of the student's family toward the college is important. For example, among our subjects there were some whose fathers (and sometimes grandfathers and great-grandfathers) had attended Yale College. A family tradition that is a source of ambivalent pride and respect to the son can foster a strong positive transference to the institution which may in turn motivate him to stay in college regardless of his discontents. Such positive transferences were evident even in our dropout sample among those whose initial decision to attend Yale College had been premised on the assumption that it was in some sense a reflection of a valued part of their family tradition. But when these students began to question their families' values and heritage or to feel oppressed by their families' traditions, they also began to see dropping out as a means of repudiating the families' values. Once again, we are dealing with genuine ambivalence rather than simple hostility: attending Yale in the first place was an expression of the student's positive feelings about his father and his family tradition; withdrawing from Yale was an expression of the negative side of his ambivalence.

Similar family pressures affected students whose fathers were not graduates of Yale College. Some parents had strongly urged their sons to apply to Yale because of its academic and social prestige. For these parents, having a son admitted to Yale was the fulfillment of a long-standing dream in which they vicariously expressed their own strivings for intellectual and social status. And in other cases, attending Yale was an expression by the son of parental and suburban ideals that value (and overvalue) an Ivy League education. For such students, dropping out of Yale was, among other things, a way of repudiating not only parental identifications and values but a suburban, middle-class way of life.

In marked contrast to these students are other undergraduates, not in our dropout sample, whose view of the college is more unambivalently positive. They, too, relate to the institution as if it were a family. And for them, as well as for dropouts, the internalized representation of the college is complex, overdetermined, and an important determinant of their behavior vis-à-vis

the institution.[8] But for many students, the college is like a *new* family that provides a chance to learn, explore, and develop in a way that was not possible within the confines of their original families. And for still others, the college is valued because it is *like* certain positive aspects of the family: for example, it encourages independence, learning, curiosity, and autonomy.

Our interviews with dropouts have impressed us with the importance of the intrapsychic meaning of institutions to individuals. In some of our subjects, we would have found it almost impossible to understand the students' motives for leaving college without considering this factor. In many cases, college stood psychologically *in loco parentis*—despite its determined institutional effort to avoid a parental role. To be sure, positive transferences to the institution undoubtedly make dropping out less likely. Furthermore, there are students who do *not* appear to identify the college with their families. But for those who do, and who perceive their families as constricting, destructive, or subversive of further personal development, the probability that they will drop out is increased. It may be that in colleges that deliberately assume a parental role, institutional transferences are even more frequent.

TOWARD A DEVELOPMENTAL
TRANSACTIONALISM

Our observations all focus on one overriding theme: the way in which differential rates of psychological development mesh with or fail to mesh with the changing opportunities and

[8] This internalized representation of the college constitutes, we believe, the intrapsychic structure upon which the deep and often nonrational feeling of college graduates for their alma mater is based. Our observations here agree with those of Reider on transferences to institutions. See also Keniston. The psychic power of images of institutions and symbolic entities (college, nation, business, society, etc.) deserves more exploration than it has so far received.

298

procedures that impinge upon the student within the college context. To put this another way, the act of dropping out seems basically related to the incongruence between the student's own developmental timetable and the normative timetable of demands and opportunities of the college setting at each point in the student's college career.

Many investigators of student development have insisted that institutional characteristics must be considered along with psychological variables in understanding student phenomena. Dropping out is, as we have noted, a "transaction" between the individual and his college: in principle, an ideal institution for one student may be abhorrent to another, who may be impelled to leave college partly because of his distaste for that particular college. Despite the obviousness of these propositions, studies that relate dropping out to explicit discontent with the college experience or to a characteristic perception of the college (e.g., as impersonal, authoritarian, excessively demanding, or too frivolous) have been relatively few. Only Pervin and Rubin, using a variation of the semantic differential test, have reported significant relationships between perceived discrepancy between self and college and stated willingness to drop out. Our own research suggests the fruitfulness of this approach, which focuses on the lack of congruence of college and student rather than upon independent characteristics of either. Dropouts, as we have studied them, appear to have few shared personal characteristics or complaints about the college; what they do share is a sense that whatever their own developmental needs and goals, these cannot be fulfilled within the college context.

But in interpreting our findings, it is crucial to recall that students are not homogeneous and static bundles of traits who interact with a simple and unchanging environment. Any approach that merely "matches" self-characterizations with college characteristics at one point in time is at best a first approximation to the extremely complex and changing transactions between student and college. With regard to the student, naive transactionalism overlooks two crucial student characteristics: first, students change in the course of their college careers; second, students have inner tensions, ambivalences, alternations in behavior and mood, and unconscious mental processes that cannot be adequately summarized in their conscious self-conceptions. The psychological assets and qualities of students change in complex ways at many levels as students pass through a "typical" college education. These changes, for example, are reflected in the problems students present to their counselors. In a university psychiatric service, freshmen present a disproportionate number of problems concerning separation from parents and first adaptations to the college environment. Once an initial adaptation to college has been more or less achieved, a new set of problems assumes prominence. These "crises" of the middle college years, often summarized as "sophomore slump," characteristically revolve around problems of commitment and choice of a philosophy of life; of a field of concentration; of friends, roommates, and girls; of a congenial subculture and life style. Finally, during the last years in college, the focus of student concern is on the "unfinished business" of a college career that has not always yielded what the student had hoped for, and on "the next phase"—hopes, expectations, and plans for the future. And in all of these problems, the student brings to his development not only the pressures and psychological tasks of the college years themselves, but the conscious and unconscious legacy of his past.

On the other side of the equation, the

college is also a dynamic and often contradictory culture, not easily summarized in a brief set of questionnaire responses. Educational institutions are no less complex and changing than individuals: furthermore, they invariably have their own timetables of demands, challenges, and opportunities they place before the student as he passes through college. For example, freshmen are not thought ready to make a choice of majors, but sophomores are. Sophomores are not usually expected to do independent work, but seniors sometimes are. Colleges, then, make implicit assumptions about the timing of the intellectual and psychological development of their students, and these assumptions are embodied in the class-graded demands of the curriculum and the college's informal culture. "The college" that confronts a senior is often extremely different in its psychological meanings and demands from "the college" that confronts a freshman in the same institution at the same time. And students who respond successfully to one set of class-graded college demands may not be as successful with later college pressures.

Finally, not only is "the college" a dynamic culture which the student encounters variously in the course of his career, but at each stage of his college life, the student may experience a "college" very different from that experienced by his classmates. Academic demands on the student in history may differ vastly from those in physics or sociology. Even more important, the freshman whose assigned roommate is a dedicated football aspirant has a different experience than his classmate with a hippie, bridge-player, socialite, radical, or intellectual for a roommate.

The basic hypothesis we derive from our study, then, is that dropping out of college is indeed a transaction between the student and his institution, but it is a transaction that cannot be adequately understood without considering the constantly changing relationship between the developmental schedule of the student and the college's timetable of demands on him as he passes through it. Our observations are confined to one highly selective liberal arts college. At other colleges, the nature and phasing of institutional demands and opportunities at each stage of a college career will often be different. But all institutions of higher education presuppose the attainment of a certain level of psychological development if the student is to thrive at any given point in college. For example, to enter a residential college, a freshman must have sufficiently separated himself from his parents so as to be able to live without their physical presence. Survival of the first year at many competitive colleges presupposes a capacity to endure the almost universal blows to self-esteem that accompany freshman grades. At academically demanding colleges, the relatively conflict-free use of highly developed ego functions is clearly a prerequisite for continuing successful academic performance. In some colleges, the steady increase in freedom of choice given students as they progress through the four years of college requires, at the psychological level, an increase in the capacity to make vital choices and commitments without undue ambivalence and internal conflict. Finally, the ability to "allow" one's self to graduate may presuppose that the individual feels ready to make further commitments after graduation. In each case, the changing demands of the college environment must be matched by new developmental accomplishments in the student. For example:

One student whose own unfinished developmental business interfered with his readiness to "commence" on his own was a 21-year-old senior for whom the idea of becoming a Yale graduate was terrifying: graduating represented the expectation that he would "go on to bigger and better things," a commitment to himself and to the world which he did not yet feel ready to unlike. This student's relationship with his family had always been a tenuous one, marked by lengthy physical as well as psychological separations because of his father's missionary profession. These separations and discontinuities had interfered with the student's achievement of differentiation from his parents and had prevented the consolidation of identity fragments into a new organization. It was his preconscious awareness of this unfinished developmental business which he seemed to be attempting to convey by his felt need "to go back before I can move forward," to "try to find my real self, my capacities and goals," before once and for all committing himself to the status of graduate.

We would hypothesize that other students who are equally "behind schedule" as compared to the timetable of college life are also subjected to great psychological stress. Similarly, students who are developmentally "ahead of schedule" may be subjected to equal stress in colleges that do not permit them to "accelerate" or that persist in treating them as psychologically less adult than they are.[9] According to this hypothesis, given a psychologically heterogeneous student body whose members are developing at different rates, the best way to produce dropouts is to create a curriculum and an informal culture that make inflexible demands upon the student. Indeed, the concept of a regular and uninterrupted four-year progression from freshman year to the B.A. bears little relationship to what we know about the extreme variability in the rates of individual psychological development during late adolescence and early adulthood.

While our study strongly supports an emphasis upon the interaction between the student and the college as an important determinant of persistence or withdrawal from college, we have concluded that, to be useful, a transactional approach must be both *developmental* and *dynamic*. Changes in the student's psychological assets, accomplishments, vulnerabilities, and conflicts as he progresses through college must be taken into account, along with the role in current behavior of often unconscious themes and conflicts whose origins lie in earlier life. Similarly, educational institutions invariably make class-graded demands on students and provide changing opportunities as they progress through college. Our study confirms that students drop out of college for many different conscious reasons, but in our sample, the outcome of the dropout crisis depended not only on the student's psychosocial capacities but on the ability of the college environment to provide him with the resources and support he needed to continue his personal growth.

CONCLUSIONS

There are many kinds of "dropouts," and this study is focused on only one kind: the talented male undergraduate who withdraws in good academic standing and without incapacitating psychiatric symptoms from a residential liberal arts college. Even within this narrowly defined sample, we found great diversity. So it is only by way of oversimplified hypothesis that we can discuss the "typical" student we interviewed. It was nonetheless impressive to us that the talented college dropouts we studied tended to have intense conflicts centering around ambivalent or spoiled identifications with their fathers, and that many had had a longstanding pattern of disengagement as a response to conflict. Our students generally had a "negative transference" to the college, which they saw as possessing many of the bad features of their families and therefore as a place where their own further development was impossible. Finally, the issues around

---

[9] We have observed this phenomenon in some students who have returned to college after a prolonged leave of absence during which they have more than "caught up" with their classmates. To such students, accustomed to and ready for a high degree of self-determination, freedom, and responsibility, the regulations, constraints, and life style of a residential liberal arts college may seem "childish" and restrictive.

which students tended to drop out seemed closely related to the implicit developmental timetable of the college itself—dropping out was most likely at times when the college demanded of the student a level of psychological development he had not attained.

Many of the problems we observed in college dropouts seemed to us more characteristic of early and middle adolescence than of late adolescence. Thus, the intensified problems of identification we found in dropouts are probably very common in students in high school, but less common in college students. Similarly, the students' inability to differentiate the psychosocial aura of the college from that of their families also might be interpreted as a sign of developmental lag. Because dropouts seemed developmentally out of phase with the demands of the college, the actual decision to drop out often seemed, from our perspective, a sound one.

Our study convinces us that most views of college dropouts advanced in the literature err on the side of excessive simplification. Although we interviewed very few parents, it does not seem sufficient to say that dropouts are uniformly "acting out" a covert parental wish or reenacting some characteristic of the father's life. Nor do those formulations that link dropping out with "identity diffusion" seem adequately explanatory to us. We found problems of identification more central than issues of identity in our subjects: indeed, autonomous identity development often seemed blocked in most students by their inability to synthesize ambivalent identifications.

Despite our emphasis on the problems of dropouts, we do not believe that dropping out is always most usefully viewed in the context of psychiatric disorder. Whatever the personal discomfort and sense of crisis experienced by our students, we came to believe

that most of them, with minimal help and average good luck, would eventually be able to resolve their psychological conflicts, thus "catching up" with those of their classmates whose progression through college was continuous. Although our interviews with returnees were few in number, they supported this impression. Returnees, although seldom able to explain fully what had happened psychologically during their time away from college, generally believed that their dropout experience had been personally useful. The sense of urgency and depression with which they had left college had abated; their "hang-ups" either had been satisfactorily resolved or seemed not to matter so much. For many of these students the mere act of withdrawing from college has been itself an important accomplishment. At the time they left, their expressed desire for a sense of autonomy and control, coupled with an inner need to see their behavior as defiant and rebellious, had made it difficult for them to perceive even supportive authorities as potentially helpful. Upon their return, they were much more able to view their college experience as an instrument in their *own* personal and intellectual growth. The returnees we interviewed were not, in general, eager to "rake up the past"; they preferred to discuss their present activities and future goals rather than their past difficulties and conflicts, many of which they had now "forgotten." This attitude, coupled with greater tranquility and with generally improved academic performance, suggests that for these students, dropping out of college had been an adaptive step, allowing them to escape the pressures of academic routine long enough to connect their education to their lives.

Finally, given the increase in the diversity of social and cultural backgrounds from which college students are drawn, we believe that the relationnhip ol the changing demands and rewards of college curricula and college life with the student's developmental needs, schedules, and accomplishments must be examined more closely. Colleges that systematically seek heterogeneous student bodies must increasingly plan systematically for students who arrive at college with a wide variety of developmental timetables. Dropping out of college may be, in part, one way in which students with "atypical" developmental schedules and problems can cope with the pressures of a college geared to the "typical" student. The high proportion of college students who discontinue or interrupt their education may in part reflect the fact that most college students are, in terms of their colleges, "atypical."

REFERENCES

BATESON, GREGORY, et al. "Toward a Theory of Schizophrenia," *Behavioral Science* (1956) 1:251-264.

ECKLAND, B. K., and SMITH, ANITA C. *A Follow-up Survey of Male Members of the Freshman Class of the University of Illinois in September, 1952*, Office of Instructional Research, Report No. 105; Univ. of Ill., 1963.

ERIKSON, ERIK H. *Insight and Responsibility;* Norton, 1960.

ERIKSON, ERIK H. *Identity: Youth and Crisis;* Norton, 1968.

GREENSON, R. R. "The Struggle Against Identification," *J. Amer. Psychoanal. Assn.* (1954) 2:200-217.

HARTMANN, HEINZ. *Ego Psychology and the Problem of Adaptation;* Internat. Univ. Press, 1958.

KENISTON, KENNETH. "College Students and Children in Developmental Institutions," *Children* (1967) 14:2-7.

KENISTON, KENNETH, and HELMREICH, R. "An Exploratory Study of Discontent and Dropouts at Yale," Dept. of Psychiatry, Yale Univ., 1965; mimeographed.

LEVENSON, EDGAR A. "The College Drop-out: A Manifestation of Family Homeostasis," paper presented at Amer. Orthopsychiatric Assn., March, 1964.

LEVENSON, EDGAR A. "Why Do They Drop Out?" *Teaching & Learning* (1965) 25-32.

LEVENSON, EDGAR A. "Some Socio-Cultural Issues in the Etiology and Treatment of College Dropouts," in Pervin, Reik, and Dalrymple.

LEVENSON, EDGAR A. "Counseling the College Drop-out," *J. Assn. College Admissions Counselors* (1968) 12:6-9.

LEVENSON, EDGAR A., and KOHN, MARTIN. "A Demonstration Clinic for College Drop-outs," *College Health* (1964) 12:382-391.

LEVENSON, EDGAR A., and KOHN, MARTIN. "A Treatment Facility for College Drop-outs," *Mental Hygiene* (1965) 49:413-424.

LEVENSON, EDGAR A., STOCKHAMER, NATHAN, and FEINER, ARTHUR H. "Family Transaction in the Etiology of Dropping Out of College," *Contemporary Psychoanal.* (1967) 3: 134-157.

NICHOLI, ARMAND M. "Harvard Dropouts: Some Psychiatric Findings," *Amer. J. Psychiatry* (1967) 124:651-658.

PERVIN, LAWRENCE A. "Identification, Identity and the College Drop-out," *J. Amer. College Health Assn.* (1966) 14:158-164.

PERVIN, LAWRENCE A. "Performance and Satisfaction as a Function of Individual-Environmental Fit," *Psychol. Bull.* (1968) 69: 56-68.

PERVIN, LAWRENCE A., REIK, LOUIS, and DALRYMPLE, WILLARD (Eds.). *The College Dropout and the Utilization of Talent;* Princeton Univ. Press, 1966.

PERVIN, LAWRENCE A., and RUBIN, DONALD B. "The College Drop-out: A Transactional Approach," Dept. of Psychology, Princeton Univ., 1965; mimeographed.

PESZKE, M. A., and ARNSTEIN, ROBERT L. "Readmission to College After Psychiatric Medical Leave," in Pervin, Reik, and Dalrymple.

REIDER, NORMAN, "A Type of Transference to Institutions," *Bull. Menninger Clinic* (1953) 17:58-63.

STERN, GEORGE. "Environments for Learning," in N. Sanford (Ed.), *The American College;* Wiley, 1962.

SUCZEK, ROBERT F., and ALFERT, ELIZABETH A. "Personality Characteristics of College Dropouts," Cooperative Research Project No. 5-8232; Berkeley, Univ. of Calif., 1966.

SUMMERSKILL, J. "Drop-outs from College," in N. Sanford (Ed.). *The American College;* Wiley, 1962.

THISTLETHWAITE, D. *Recruitment and Retention of Talented College Students;* Washington, D.C., Office of Education, 1966.

TRENT, JAMES W., and MEDSKER, LELAND. *Beyond High School: A Psychological Study of 10,000 High School Graduates;* Jossey-Bass, 1968.

WERTENBAKER, WILLIAM. "A Problem of Identity," *New Yorker,* Dec. 1, 1962.

WRIGHT, ERIK OLIN. "Student Leaves of Absence from Harvard College: A Personality and Social Systems Approach," unpublished paper, Harvard Univ., 1966.

WRIGHT, ERIK OLIN. "A Psycho-Social Study of Student Leaves of Absence from Harvard," unpublished BA thesis, Harvard Univ., 1968.

ETIOLOGY OF THREE

CURRENT ADOLESCENT SYNDROMES:

A HYPOTHESIS

IRENE M. JOSSELYN

Certain adolescents have, as we know, always been a disturbing part of a culture, unless the culture has imposed such rigid rules of conduct and/or provided structured outlets for the young individual so that the adolescent phase is masked. I will not bore you with the many quotations from history that confirm this, but adolescents have always, in most cultures, been a problem to their parents and a threat to those members of a stable society who fear change. With the exception of a few individuals in the past, it has only been during this century that adults have realized that adolescents are not only a problem to others but that they may also be a problem to themselves and that, with cause, their parents and the social structure are equally problems to them.

Students of human psychological maturation—Erikson (1968), Deutsch (1967), and Blos (1962) to mention a few—have given us insight into the significance of the maturational [1] phase of adolescence. Paralleling the gradual clarification of this phase has been a rapidly enriched knowledge of the psychological steps from birth on. It is possible that our knowledge of the steps of childhood have advanced more rapidly than our guidelines for fostering optimum development of the personality.

Observation of child behavior and a study of adult psychopathology give clues as to what has influenced the gradual maturation of the indi-

This chapter was presented as the 1970 Distinguished Service Award address, annual meeting of the American Society for Adolescent Psychiatry, May 10, 1970, San Francisco, Cal.

ADOLESCENT PSYCHIATRY, 1971, 1, pp. 125-138.

vidual. I would suggest, however, that the most productive phase to study is adolescence. The adolescent's format is fluid, blending the various psychological streams of childhood. Its resolution is the attainment of adulthood, at which time the final psychological structure has become relatively crystallized. It is during adolescence that we can most clearly understand the impact of childhood experiences and can observe the gradual formation of the adult defenses against and adaptation to those early experiences and the reality of living. For this reason I have chosen to present a question: "Do we see in some of the adolescents of today a behavioral Gestalt that, on the basis of our knowledge of adolescents, should be offered as a challenge to present theories of child-rearing?"

There are at least three different groups of adolescents whose behavior, though not necessarily reflecting their childhood experiences, may do so. If it does in a sufficient number of cases it would raise serious questions concerning the current concepts of child care, as well as offer an important therapeutic challenge to those of us working with the adolescent. I have chosen these three groups because certain members of them present a constellation of behavioral and attitudinal characteristics that I did not see, except in seriously disturbed young people, prior to about fifteen years ago.

There is a group of adolescents who show a marked level of self-centeredness. It is axiomatic that the adolescent is primarily interested in himself and that much of his interest in others is because of projection of his own needs and/or wishes. However, I have at times felt that the degree of self-centeredness I now observe I did not see fifteen years ago unless the individual's psychological state was seriously pathological. An example will perhaps clarify what I have in mind.

Tom, a seventeen-year-old boy, was very strongly antiwar and had made elaborate plans for avoiding the draft. The argument he gave was an ideological one: He did not believe in killing people; war, therefore, was never justified. If his country were attacked he would not defend it because that, he stated, would be a violation of his ideals. When I asked what if the attack on his country might possibly involve his own destruction his answer was, "At that time I will no longer be in this country so they won't have a chance to kill me." This discussion went on at a time when it looked as if the administration would use as a justification for continuance of the war in Vietnam the fear of a widespread massacre of South Vietnamese should the United States suddenly withdraw all troops. I suggested to him that we consider a hypothetical condition. Suppose it were true that the South Vietnamese would be massacred in toto were we suddenly to withdraw. If he would consider this hypothesis, though he might think it an absurd fantasy, would he feel that under such conditions the United States should withdraw? His answer was, "Yes, I don't want to be killed to save the life of a South Vietnamese." I cited an example of people having stood by watching a woman murdered in an attempted rape, the observers making no move to save the victim. I asked him what he would have done had he been in the crowd. He said, "I would have done as the rest of the crowd. Why should I run a risk of being hurt, or maybe killed, in order to save somebody else's life?"

Time does not permit me to give all the details about this boy. I had known him for many years; in my judgment, in any situation except where his own life, or some other severe disadvantage to him, were concerned, he gave the impression of being a generous, idealistic, thoughtful boy; his statements would seem superficially to be incompatible with his personality. They were not give for the sake of arguing; the same self-preservation theme came out in a variety of contexts.

In the past an adolescent boy with the same instinctual self-preservation impulse would more typically have kept the mask of his idealism intact. His ideal for himself would have been a fantasy of noble martyrdom, his dying for his belief that one does not kill even to save one's country or oneself, and expressing the conviction that a saint-like approach to the rapist would have stopped him. Tom's idealism, at times unrealistic perhaps, but admirable, was his philosophy of life, except when it, even in fantasy, inconvenienced him.

The second group that has interested me comprises those adolescents who long for closeness and readily verbalize that they have never really felt close to anyone. Adolescents characteristically seek closeness with others, particularly with special peer group members and with nonparental adults who, they feel, understand them. They have always, in phases, denied closeness to their parents. But typically a tone of nostalgia crept in, a recall that at one time parents and child were close. They also, in spite of their attempt to emancipate themselves, had turned to parents for emotional support when they felt too overwhelmed. (Now they turn to them for financial support.) As members of this group verbalize their wish for closeness there is a chronic, frantic quality or a chronic, deep, depressive tone. Again I was aware of these reactions in the past, primarily in those who were extremely deprived in their childhood and/or had alienated themselves from peers and adults because of their atypical behavior.

During the love-in festivals and devotion of flower children the young people put adults to shame; the young people impressively expound the value of "love" as a basis for interpersonal relationships. They extoll Judeo-Christian philosophy as if it had suddenly come into style. I asked one boy, who had an excellent sense of humor, that if one should love everyone, why not his parents whom he violently disliked; he did many acts primarily to make them miserable. His answer, with a smile, was immediate. "They," he said, "are subhuman. I don't go for this stuff of loving spiders and worms."

The group whose members extoll love accept, excluding the Establishment, the behavior of everyone as long as the behavior is the Thing of the other person and does not hurt anyone else (except the Establishment). Such seeming tolerance may be in reality interpersonal indifference; it is scarcely a pathway to closeness; closeness implies a mutuality of either identical or complementary nature. Is it really love of another person that prompts them to say that if their friend wants to blow his mind with Speed it is his mind, his Thing, and therefore his right? What seems clear from my experience with certain participants in the group's love philosophy is that, as many other students of this age currently have said, these particular members of the group love everyone, but no one individual.

A patient of mine spent a summer away from her family. Her time during that vacation was chiefly devoted to a group of young people who lived, took care of, and protected one another with a verbal conviction that their mutual intimacy and closeness made others unnecessary to them. After her return to the parental nest her description of her experience was enviable. Love had encompassed the group like a benign, billowing cloud. When she paused for breath I asked her if she planned to return to that area the following summer. She said that she did not know where they would be then. One boy had been particularly meaningful to her. She and he had found real closeness. When I asked if she planned to keep in touch with him by correspondence during the winter she indicated she could not because they had never exchanged last names or addresses. Is this true closeness?

In contrast to the members of this group who seek but never find real closeness are those who do find closeness in sexual behavior that involves a meaningful relationship with the person with whom they share the experience. Though in some ways this would seem to indicate sexual maturity, what is absent is the realness of true heterosexuality. The girls in this group find it unimportant whether they have an orgasm. This, of course, is not so true with the boys because of the fear of manifesting a masculine inadequacy either to others or to themselves. However, both the boy and the girl stress not the sexual gratification per se, but rather the feeling of deep closeness, experienced through the sexual act, and the happiness this brings.

A very interesting example of the use of sex as a way to experience closeness was manifested by a young couple, the boy a patient of mine. He repeatedly stressed the value of their mutual sexuality, emphasizing the sense of closeness it provided for both of them. They finally decided to marry. With this decision they also decided they would have no further sexual experiences until marriage. Their primary gratification from that time on was in mutually planning for the present, their marriage, and the future. The boy reported a discussion that he and his fiancee had the night prior to a therapy hour. They had both agreed that they had never felt as close as they had since the day they decided to marry. Neither of them had had any impulse to have intercourse; there were too many other things with which they were mutually occupied. What this attitude foreshadowed for their sexual adjustment after marriage was, of course, problematical. I did receive one letter from him after they had settled down to married life in a new community. He indicated he hoped it was just a passing phase, but in spite of their happiness together they were not often sexually interested in each other. The aspect that I wish to stress is that the primary goal for both these young people prior to marriage was to be close to someone; they had never experienced that before. Yet from the family history it would appear that both these young people had had a relatively normal childhood, with both of them reared by parents who did care about their children.

The members of the third group are those adolescents who wish to escape. Instead of feeling challenged by the possibility of utilizing their adolescent understanding to modify the world, they have no confidence that they can do so. It is possible to identify with them and say, "Well, who thinks it can be changed?" But why are adolescents oriented this way? The adolescent in the past typically felt that he knew the answers and in the future would make those answers effective. Then the relatively healthy adolescent faced with dissatisfactions in the current situation, particularly if the dissatisfaction was in the broad abstractions of the social world, believed that adults had been stupid and that he and his friends alone had the solutions that, once they had an opportunity, they would put into effect.

Currently, certain members of this third group do not accept that challenge, or else do not believe in their ability to meet such a challenge. Instead they escape from the real world into a world that does not challenge them but rather offers gratification without effort. Many of them have superior intelligence, are creative, sensitive, and within the limitations of their experience capable of formulating new solutions to old problems. They abandon educational goals because the institution does not teach them the way they want to be taught; to learn beyond what is taught they consider requires too much effort. There is a tragic validity to their castigation of the educational system, but if the system will not modify, their retribution is not to be educated. They drop out of the social world, a world that certainly has real disadvantages but also positive values. They see no hope, or experience no wish to remove the disadvantages or enrich the positive aspects. Instead they live on the desert or in a cave either within a big city or in the mountains, often with their materialistically oriented and therefore subhuman parents providing the funds that prevent starvation. They may or may not use drugs.

Others of the group, even though they remain physically a part of their home and school, use drugs. They become dependent on drugs not through addiction or even habituation, but rather with a specific goal in mind—that of escaping into a fantasy world rather than living within the limitations of the real world. They avoid what is faced by other adolescents who, while protesting, endure reality because of the anticipation that eventually the world will change, an event that will occur when adolescent dreams of today become the reality of life tomorrow. Certain users of drugs accept the philosophy that parents or the Establishment are to blame. Because parents are biological necessities, and the Establishment controls today, there is nothing to do but drop out of the current world and live in the artificially induced state drugs provide.

Parenthetically it is interesting to speculate whether the Establishment has not become the symbol of the omnipotent father who, according to Freud, in the past became God as the child recognized the clay feet of his real father. It is difficult to carry on the child-father battle with a God; he is feared but loved. The Establishment furnishes a father figure who is unlovable and hostile or crippling. It is easier to fight an omnipotent, omnipresent father symbol whose clay feet are always visible and toward whom one can avoid the ambivalence that cannot be avoided toward the real father, or God. The longing to be loved by the father is not consciously experienced in the relationship with the Establishment.

Is it possible that certain members of these three groups of adolescents are manifesting an understandable response to their childhood past? Their rearing was dictated by a misconception of the implications of the insight that has been gained into psychological disturbances, be they the psychosis, the neurosis, personality or character disorders, or the autism and symbiotic psychosis of childhood. In broad terms, it has been assumed that such conditions are primarily the fault of neurotic parents utilizing the child as a tool of their neurosis, with an additional factor increasingly being introduced related to the inherent ego potential of the child. There has been a response to the knowledge of the etiological factors of such conditions, which would have a parallel if, when the cause of the symptoms of diabetes was recognized and insulin given to alleviate those symptoms, it had been advised that *all* children be given insulin. Not all children have diabetes, nor are all parents neurotic!

For some time our culture has been proud that our children are reared in a child-centered world. The behavior of many parents, in large part because of advice they have been given, has implied that the only reason for adults existing is to make sure that children have a truly child-centered world. Though there is a sound basis for flexibility in the feeding schedule for the small infant the implication of demand feeding, a current popular concept, is that what the infant wants must be immediately gratified, an attitude that remains one of the major pillars of child-rearing long after physiological idiosyncrasies are no longer dominant. There is minimal recognition that the child grows through wise frustration as well as the avoidance of arbitrary frustration.

There are apparently sound reasons for providing a child-centered milieu for a child who as a result of inability to handle certain deprivations manifests signs of psychological disturbance, sound reasons until the symptoms disappear. Is it valid however to assume that, because the damaged child requires such a corrective experience, all individuals through their entire childhood should find that they need not explore to find happiness, but rather that it will be served to them on a silver platter by a slavish waiter-parent who anxiously seeks assurance that his services are satisfactory to the child? Are we now, perhaps, in some situations, facing the consequences of the failure to understand the real needs of a child, which if met will help him mature to a true adulthood?

Initially I became aware of these questions not through work with adolescents, but rather with adults who were either contemplating divorce, were already divorced, or had been divorced and were planning a new marriage. By no means do I wish to imply that I have found the univer-

311

sal cause for divorces. But there is an aspect to divorce at the present time that, though it was present in some instances in the past, has become much more frequent. The explanation for the divorce, succinctly stated, is "My marital partner does not make me happy." This does not mean that the marital partner is an alcoholic, is unfaithful, is promiscuous, fails (if a man) to fulfill his basic responsibilities of supporting the family or (if a woman) to maintain the home and take care of the children. It is much less limited than that. The one definitive statement that people involved make is that they are (or were) not happy. They want (or wanted) to get out of the marriage, with no implication that either one wants (or wanted) to work at the marriage to see whether they could find mutual enjoyment in it.

One woman's chief complaint about her husband was that he did not pick up his clothes and put them in the dirty clothes chute. When I asked her if that was really so catastrophic, would it really be too much work to pick them up herself, her answer was, "Why should I live the rest of my life with a man who won't pick up his own clothes?" I will grant that this women was an unusually rabid battle-ax; I felt that if her husband could not even revolt against her by not picking up his clothes he was well out of the marriage. But this example is a caricature of the type of complaints that I hear repeatedly from those seeking divorce, or from those who are already divorced, with little or no evidence that they have tried, before seeking the divorce route, to share the responsibility of preserving the marriage. In some instances they have sought marriage counseling, but soon abandoned that approach because it did not result in the other partner changing. They act like the small child living in a child-centered world in which the entire implication is that it is the responsibility of others to make him happy.

In a child-centered world the assumption by adults is that the child will be damaged psychologically if he is not provided a world in which he is happy. The child's needs are paramount and must be met by others, not by his own initiative, let alone his own creative imagination. If he is bored, activities must be provided to alleviate his boredom. If he does not like the food offered at the family meal and must be coaxed to eat it, other food that he does like should be provided. It is the child's right to be happy, and the parents obligation to provide a ready means for that happiness.

The historically typical self-centeredness of the adolescent is now flavored by the expectation that his child-centered world of yesterday should continue as his right. If he does not like the peas and carrots served as part of his current psychological dinner he wants to pull the tablecloth off and destroy the entire dinner, rather than enjoy what he does like about the meal, while loudly protesting and expounding that when he can plan his own meals he will not serve peas and carrots, but lima beans. The implication in much of the anger of this group is that they have been promised they can always have what they want and now they are refused.

Fred's was a typical response. He had reached driving age. He refused the second-hand car that his parents offered to him, demanding a new sports car. His father had suffered financial reverses and realistically could not afford to purchase the car his son wanted. When I discussed the reality with Fred his comment was, "Dad's financial difficulties are his problem. He promised me a sports car when I was sixteen. He *owes* the car to me." Fred has been reared in a child-centered world.

The child-centered world has resulted possibly in another fallacy. One of the most essential components of a happy childhood is the child's confidence that he is loved. The biological need for care during the neonatal period is the anlage of the psychological need to feel loved. It has been assumed that from this need to be loved develops later a capacity to love others. Is this necessarily the pathway toward a mature capacity to fuse the desire to be loved and to love in return? In a previous work (Josselyn, 1968) I have suggested that not only is there the biological anlage of a psychological need to be loved, but there is also a biological response of turning outward for need gratification which is the anlage of a later response of a need to love. Is it possible that in our present theory of child-rearing the child's longing to love is not given sufficient nutriment to develop into a need to find a real area of gratification?

To document this would obviously require an intensive study of very subtle manifestations, but there is a suggestion in an example which may seem too superficial. The present-day parent freely gives toys. The affluence of the society is blamed for this; the parent believes that giving a toy to the child is indicative of his love for the child. It often is; but it is not always a compensatory means of handling the guilt over not loving the child sufficiently. If the toy is broken, the toy is replaced. The child is not encouraged to love the toy, let alone the giver of the toy. The toy, to the child, is his right; its ready replacement encourages the child not to love the toy. Parents say to the child crying over a broken toy, "Don't cry. We'll get you another one." The child is deprived of the experience of mourning for something lovable.

Not only is the child not encouraged to love, but the parents, possibly

313

by their eagerness to show love for the child without anticipating any reciprocal response, do not foster any inherent potential of the child to love. They, to cite a familiar example, often say to the misbehaving child, "I love you; I just don't like the act." Actually this is usually an insincere statement; the parent does not love the part of the child that misbehaved. If parents repeatedly separate the act and the child in their response, is it surprising that the more sophisticated adolescent says that his associate is doing his Thing and has a right to do so, even if the Thing is using heroin, without recognizing that to be loved one must be lovable, and love for another is expressed in part by concern for the latter's welfare?

There is another aspect of the concept of the value of mutual love that is possibly important; it involves a peculiar contradiction in the current theory of optimum child development. Whatever the source of a capacity to love may be, the critical time for its development is probably during the developmental phase when the child is becoming aware of his own individuality and the symbiotic tie, as formulated by Mahler (1965) and others, is beginning to disintegrate. It would seem justified to postulate that during this period the child gradually experiences being loved as an individual and also being aware of love for someone separate from himself. How quickly this interrelatedness becomes established is speculative.

In the current culture there is an urgency to physically separate the mother and the child. Day care centers for the lower economic group and nursery schools for the more affluent society are encouraged. Two contradictory messages are promulgated by the same school of thought. The primary relationship, the beginning of all meaningful relationships, is hypothesized as having roots in the child-mother relationship, with expansion to others of the family group. On the other hand, it is strongly urged that as soon as the child is toilet trained the child should be separated from the mother and find substitutes. Is it not possible that this fosters the establishment of secondary, transient relationships before the primary and in-depth relationships are well crystallized? At present the primary relationship is treated as a dangerous form of medication; it is necessary during the acute infection of infancy, but once the disease shows signs of lessening its effect, it is essential that the drug be stopped.

The wish for closeness in the adolescent implies something quite different from what is offered in a pure and simple child-centered world. I suspect that many adolescents of today have never really experienced closeness to their parents. Closeness is the result of a mutual interchange in which the gratification from loving is equal to the gratification of being loved. The longing for closeness in some may indicate that a frustration of a basic need to love has led to a hunger, the relief of which is sought by trying nonnutritional sawdust, or trying substitutes that are inadequately nutritional, chosen because of lack of knowledge based on early experiences. They use drugs to artificially create closeness because they do not know how to find it in reality; they use sexuality as a means of regressing to the infantile experience of closeness through bodily contact.

The third group of adolescents, those wanting to escape, are possibly also responding to a childhood experienced in a child-centered world. The current attitude is that the child's needs must be met by avoiding a challenging situation for him. If he does not like his teacher he is changed to another classroom. If he is afraid at night someone sleeps with him. If he has difficulty learning to read a tutor is provided whose responsibility is to teach him to read. I would put in the same category the pattern of our educational system at present. When the child begins to study history, for example, he is not challenged to understand history, he is drilled in remembering the details of history. A person who is an enthusiast for, and supposedly a specialist in, sex education told me with a great deal of pride that the program he has organized starts now in kindergarten, and he hopes to get it into the nursery schools. He wishes the child to be given sexual information that is just a step beyond where one would expect the child's curiosity to be. In other words, one should not wait for a child to ask a question; one should know at what age it is anticipated he will ask the question and be sure that prior to that age he is already being given the answer.

Examples I have given in the last paragraph are obviously not valid as generalizations. There are some children who should have their classrooms changed; there are those who, because of night terrors, should have someone sleep with them. Certainly the child with a reading disability needs the help of a tutor who knows special techniques for overcoming reading handicaps. Certainly children who fear their sexual curiosity should be given knowledge they have not sought. Too often, when any of these steps is taken it is taken with the philosophical approach that the child should not be asked to take part in the necessary adaptation; the immediate situation must be remedied so that he will not have to face any challenge in it. This same attitude is observable in some of our adolescents who are using drugs. They either insist they should not be expected to make an effort, or else their self-concept includes the conviction that they are incapable of succeeding if they did make an effort to find in reality what they are seeking in their use of drugs.

A semihumorous, if not so tragic, example is the very artistically talented girl who was describing to me the glorious pictures she saw during a psychedelic trip, pictures that were primarily a vivid blending of colors. We were standing where we could see a rather unusually brilliant sunset and I commented that it seemed to me she was describing what we could see then in the west. Her answer was,

I get your point, but you know usually I'd have to make some effort to find things that are beautiful. I might have to drive out to the desert, for instance, to see a sunset. Why bother when LSD will give it to me whenever I want it without waiting until the sun sets and without having to go to look for it? After all, I've never had a bad trip with LSD, but imagine going out to the desert and seeing nothing but a big yellow ball going down over the horizon.

I commented that the desert is surrounded by colorful mountains; even if the sun is just a round yellow ball, the shadows on the mountains offer a kaleidoscopic panorama. Her answer was, "Yes, but you can't lie down and have that panorama before you; you have to look around. You don't have to move with LSD."

Another adolescent, very talented in music, justified his former use of LSD on the basis that he had never appreciated Bach until he took LSD; now Bach was one of his favorite composers. When I questioned whether he had ever had a teacher who helped him to see the beauty of Bach's music, his answer was, "No, my teacher always praised me for how well I played. He never shared with me his enjoyment of music."

The patient who did not want to make the effort to see a sunset felt all life's pleasures should be provided to her on a silver platter that someone else would hold. The one who learned to love Bach under LSD had had an unstimulating childhood, also served on a silver platter.

Not all individual adolescents who are found in one of these groups, or a combination of the three groups, had a childhood that was provided by well-intentioned parents striving to make their child's life easy by creating a child-centered world. Many of the members of these groups did. Also, many from such a milieu have handled the crisis of adolescence without manifest difficulty, not because their childhood was so ideal, but possibly because they have been able to overcome the handicap created by those years. Many adolescents of today appear to be ill equipped emotionally to relate to a world other than that of which they are the center; they are hungry for closeness and yet have difficulty in finding it; they are frightened about the world they are in because they do not believe they can meet, without chaos, the challenges it presents.

I am confident that a large majority of today's adolescents will weather the turmoil and contribute to the evolution of a better world than the one they entered. I have not discussed, but I realize that today's real world is confusing and disturbing to adults; little wonder it is to adolescents. Is it possible, however, that the tasks the adolescents face are more difficult for them than would be inevitable, more difficult because they were reared in a child-centered world rather than in a world dedicated to the proposition that the validity of childhood is as preparation for a rich adulthood?

Those of us who strive to understand the adolescent, where he has been and where he is going, have a contribution to make to the understanding of the effect of child-rearing practices on the modes of seeking and on the final configuration of adulthood. As therapists it is important that we not only recognize the reality, both internal and external, in which the adolescent is struggling to find himself and striving to change so it will comply more with his idealism; it is equally important to recognize that he is also, in some instances, seeking to find fulfillment of basic needs and inherent potentials that were not fulfilled in childhood.

We adults should listen to the adolescent's current ideas and strivings. By so listening we can learn about the individual adolescent's struggles to find an answer to the multiple problems pressing on him. As he reveals these problems and the tentative solutions he envisions, we will be protected from becoming static in our thinking!

We, with our expertise, should be acutely attuned to the individual adolescent's past milieu, not just share with him our negativism toward the adult world. Our ultimate goals and his may appear identical; our empathic response should not indiscriminately encompass his current or projected method of attaining those goals. The method he advocates may not be determined so much by his drive to attain the goal because it is a response to earlier emotional deprivation. If we, as we empathize with the adolescent, lose sight of our responsibility as therapists and instead accept uncritically his strategy for reaching his goal, we may strengthen destructive impulses and encourage him to strive for a goal that, masked by idealistic formulations, is in actuality that of correcting egocentrically the defects of his childhood maturational steps. The further evolution of our society will not come through adults who as adolescents failed to gain a perspective beyond that offered by their own idiosyncratic needs; as therapists and as interpreters of adolescence we can encourage either maturation beyond or fixation at the egocentric level.

Our country as never before in its history is caught in a vicious circle. The responses of the adolescent group have created extreme anxiety among many adults, resulting in hysterical deafness and emotionally charged attempts to stifle the younger group. The latter response has created a degree of frustration in the young, which has stimulated emotional striking out against a basic philosophy as it is imperfectly expressed in the social structure. The consequences will be that the vicious circle either will be chained down to a static state or will explode into anarchistic lack of any structure. We therapists, of all people, should as students of the adolescent age be able to find the means and urge approaches by which to reconvert the vicious circle back to its former spiral path of which the apex is progressive growth from its base.

NOTE

1. The term "maturation" in this context connotes the attainment of a "ripe" stage, the origin of the word according to Webster's (1969). Development manifests the maturational process but is affected by external circumstances that may result in deformity or optimum fulfillment of the inherent maturational potential. Child-rearing practices, social structures, and events beyond control affect the way in which the inherent maturational process develops to be "ripened" into adulthood.

REFERENCES

Blos, P. (1962). On adolescence: A psychoanalytic interpretation. New York: The Free Press.

Erikson, E. H. (1968). Identity: Youth and crisis. New York: Norton.

Deutsch, H. (1967). Selected problems of adolescence. New York: International Universities Press.

Josselyn, I. M. (1968). How many basic drives? Smith College Studies in Social Work, 39:1–19.

Mahler, M. (1965). On the significance of the normal separation-individuation phase: With reference to research in symbiotic child psychosis. In M. Schur, ed., Drives, Affects, Behavior. New York: International Universities Press. 2:161–169.

Webster's Third New International Dictionary. (1969). Springfield, Mass.: Merriam.

ON ALIENATED CONCEPTS
OF IDENTITY

ERNEST G. SCHACHTEL

IN DAILY LIFE the question of identity arises when we want to claim something from the post office, or when we want to pay by check in a store where we are not known, or in crossing a border. On such occasions we are asked: "Who are you, so that I can know for sure it is you and nobody else?" And we establish our identity by showing a driver's license or a passport or some similar document which tells our name, our address, the date of our birth, and perhaps some physical characteristics. Together, these will tell us apart from anybody else and will also establish that we are the same person that was born on such and such a date. We have *papers* to establish our identity, and this paper-identity is something fixed and definite. This is also the meaning of the word "identity," as applied to people, for the average person.

Such paper-identity seems far removed, at first glance, from the current concern of psychoanalysts, philosophers, and other students of the contemporary scene, with man's search for and doubt in his identity. But actually it is quite central to it. It is a telling symbol of alienated identity. It is a kind of identity which is the product of bureaucratic needs of commerce or administration. Its most gruesome and tragic manifestations occurred in our time when men's identities were reduced to numbers in concentration and extermination camps, and when countless people fleeing from the terror of the totalitarian states were shunted from country to country because they did not have the right paper-identities.

In the case of paper-identities, the person who demands and examines one's papers is the one who, in his role as an official, is alienated from the other person as a human being. Similarly, the guards in the concentration camps were alienated from their victims. However, many of these victims, systematically robbed of any meaningful purpose and dignity in their lives, succumbed to their tormentors and lost their sense of identity long before they lost their lives.

In our own and many other societies the loss of identity takes place without the terror of the concentration camps, in more insidious ways. I have described elsewhere how many people in our time tend to think of their lives as though they were answering the kind of questionnaire that one has to fill out when, for example, applying for a passport.[1] They tend to accept the paper-identity as their real identity. It is tempting to do so because it is something fixed and definite and does not require that the person be really in touch with himself. The paper-identity corresponds to the

AMERICAN JOURNAL OF PSYCHOANALYSIS, 1961, 21, pp. 120-127.

logical propositions concerning identity: A = A, and A is not non-A.

But man is not a logical proposition and the paper-identity does not answer the question who this person, identified by some scrap of paper, is as a person. This question is not simple to answer. It has haunted many people increasingly in the last hundred years. They no longer feel certain who they are because in modern industrial society, as Hegel and Marx first showed, they are alienated from nature, alienated from their fellow men, alienated from the work of their hands and minds, and alienated from themselves. I can only state here my belief that self-alienation, the doubt about and search for identity, always goes together with alienation from others and from the world around us.

The problem of identity and alienation from the self came to the attention of psychoanalysts in the last thirty years when they observed its role in an increasing number of patients. Karen Horney formulated it as the problem of the real self, as distinguished from the idealized self-image;[2] Fromm as the problem of the original, real self as distinguished from the conventional or pseudo-self*;[3, 4] Erikson, who has made the most detailed study in the development of the sense of identity, as the problem of ego-identity.[5]

Many patients who come to us suffer in one form or another from the lack of a sense of identity. This may take the form of feeling like imposters—in their work, or in relation to their background, their past, or to some part of themselves that they repress or consciously want to hide because they feel

---

* In his latest book he seems to see the real self in what he calls "universal man" and considers the conscious self, especially the social self, as alienated from this universal man who, in turn, is repressed.

ashamed or guilty. Or else they feel that they *ought* to *have* something they lack or imagine they lack, such as material possessions, prestige, or certain personal qualities or traits; or they feel that a different husband or wife, or friends different from those they have, would give them the status they want and thereby, miraculously, transform them into full-blown persons. When the lack of a sense of identity becomes conscious, it is often experienced—probably always—as a feeling that compared with others one is not fully a person.

Among adults one can observe two frequent reactions to the conscious or unconscious feeling of not being fully a person, of not having found an identity acceptable to oneself. One is an anxious retreat or depressive resignation, or a mixture of these. The other is a more or less conscious effort at disguise, at playing a role, at presenting an artificial façade to the world. These reactions are not mutually exclusive. They usually occur together, one of them being more emphasized or closer to consciousness than the other. The fear of exposure is present in both, but especially strong in people who rely on a façade. They tend to feel that they travel with a forged passport, under an assumed identity. When their disguise and the reasons for it have been analyzed, the sense of a lack of identity often comes to the fore as strongly as in those who, to begin with, have been aware of and suffered from the feeling of not really or fully being a person with a meaningful place in life. Both tend to feel that they do not really know who they are, what they want, or how they feel about other people.

When these people consult an analyst, they often expect, implicitly or explicitly, that he will tell them who they are or who they should be. Their wish and search is for a *definite, fixed iden-*

ity. They want to be a *personality*. Often these are people who suffer from over-adaptation to whatever situation they are in, and to whomever they are dealing with at the moment. They have been described pointedly in several plays and stories by Pirandello. They long for a definite, fixed, circumscribed personality. "Having" such a personality, as one has a possession, they hope will solve their dilemma. Having such a personality, they feel, is good; not having it, bad. Their wish to "possess" a definite identity does not and cannot solve the problem of their alienation from themselves, because it actually is the continuation of alienation. They want to substitute a fixed, reified personality for the on-going process of living, feeling, acting, and thinking in which alone they could find themselves. They search for a definite, stable shell called "personality" to which they want to cling. Their quest is self-defeating, because what they search for is an alienated concept of a thing, rather than a living, developing person. Their wish is a symptom, not a cure. In this symptom, however, both the malady of alienation and the longing for a more meaningful life find expression, even though in a way which perpetuates the ill from which they seek to escape. The self-conscious preoccupation with this wished-for magic object called "personality" interferes with the actual experience of living.

In calling the object of these people's search an alienated "concept" of identity, I do not mean a scientific or even an explicit concept. I am describing an implicit concept, which becomes apparent only in the analysis of the underlying, often not conscious, assumptions that direct this kind of search. This applies equally to the following examples of alienated concepts of identity.

There is one psychoanalytic term that has gained wide popularity and in popular use has changed its meaning. Such popular use always indicates a significant fact about a society and therefore deserves our attention. I refer to the term "ego." People say that something is good or bad for their "ego." They mean by this that their self-feeling—in the sense of the status which they accord to themselves—rises when something is good and falls when something is bad for their ego. In this usage ego is only part of the person.* My "ego" is not identical with "I" or "self." It is not identical with the I who is well or ill, who sees and hears and touches and tastes and smells, who acts, walks, sits, stands, lies, who is moved by others, by what is seen and experienced. Moreover, what is "good" or "bad" for my ego is not at all necessarily good or bad for me, although I may be inclined to think so. The popular "ego" gains from success, winning in competition, status, being admired, flattered, loved; it does not gain from facing the truth, from loving somebody else, from humility. It behaves like a stock or a piece of merchandise endowed with self-awareness: if it is much in demand it rises, is blown up, feels important; if not, it falls, shrinks, feels it is nothing.† Thus, it is an *alienated* part of the self. But while it is only part of the self, it has the tendency to become the *focal point* of the feeling of identity and to dominate the

---

* The psychoanalytic concept of ego also is not identical with the whole person, but its relation to the total personality is radically different from the relation of the popular ego to the total personality, and most of the ego-processes, in the psychoanalytic meaning of the term, are not part of the popular "ego."

† Some psychologists who speak of "ego involvement" adopt in this phrase the described popular meaning of "ego." The term usually means that a person's ambition is involved in wanting to be successful in some task or situation.

whole life of the people who are involved with their "ego" to a significant degree. Their mood fluctuates with their "ego." They are haunted by their "ego" and preoccupied with its enhancement or its downfall. They no longer seem to feel that they have a life apart from their "ego," but they stand or fall with it. The "ego" has become their identity and at the same time the main object of their worry, ambition, and preoccupation, crowding out any real concern with themselves and with others. The popular ego can serve as the most important model of an alienated concept of identity, even though it may be surpassed in rigidity and fixedness by some other examples of such concepts, to which I shall turn now.

In her thoughtful book, *On Shame and the Search for Identity,* Helen Lynd quotes Dostoevsky's Mitya Karamazov who, on trial for the murder of his father, suffers his worst misery when the prosecutor asks him to take off his socks. "They were very dirty . . . and now everyone could see it. All his life he had thought both his big toes hideous. He particularly loathed the coarse, flat, crooked nail on the right one and now they would all see it. Feeling intolerably ashamed. . . ."[6] The accidental, unchangeable appearance of his feet, of the nail of his right big toe, here becomes the focal point of his identity. It is on this that he feels the peasants who stand around him and look at him will judge him and that he judges himself. Very often real or imagined physical attributes, parts of the body image or the entire body image, become focal points of identity. Many people build around such a negative identity the feeling that this particular feature unalterably determines the course of their lives, and that they are thereby doomed to unhappiness. Usually, in these cases, qualities such as attractiveness and beauty are no longer felt to be based on the alive expression and flux of human feelings, but have become fixed and dead features, or a series of poses, as in so many Hollywood stars or fashion models. These features are cut off from the center of the person and worn like a mask. Unattractiveness is experienced as not possessing this mask.

In the same way, other real or imagined attributes, or the lack of them, become focal points for a reified, alienated, negative identity. For example: feeling not sufficiently masculine or feminine, being born on the wrong side of the tracks, being a member of a minority group against which racial or religious prejudices are directed, and, in the most general form, feeling intrinsically inadequate or "bad." I do not imply, of course, that in our society the accidental circumstance of being born as the member of one social, national, or religious group or class rather than another does not result in very real, objective difficulties, disadvantages or privileges. I am concerned here only with the *attitude* which the person takes toward such handicaps or advantages, which is important for his ability to deal with them. In this attitude the structure of the sense of identity and the way in which such factors as the social background and innate advantages or handicaps are incorporated in the sense of identity play a decisive role.

What are the dynamics of such alienated concepts of identity? Sometimes they crystallize around repeated parental remarks which, rather than referring to a particular act of the child, say or imply that the child *is* or *lacks,* by its very nature, such and such; that Tom is a lazy good-for-nothing or that he is "just like Uncle Harry," who happens to be the black sheep in the family. Frequently they develop from an ego-ideal that is alien to the child's own personality, but about which he has come to feel that, unless he is such and such, he is nothing.* Whatever their genetic origin, I shall consider here mainly the phenomenological structure of alienated identity concepts and the dynamics of this structure which tend to perpetuate self-alienation.

By making some quality or circumstance, real or exaggerated or imagined, the focal point of a reified identity, I look upon myself as though I were a thing (res) and the quality or circumstance were a fixed attribute of this thing or object.† But the "I" that feels that I am this or that, in doing so, distances itself from the very same reified object attribute which it experiences as determining its identity and very often as a bane on its life. In feeling that I am such and such, I distinguish between the unfortunate I and the presumably unalterable quality or lack which, for all time, condemns me to have this negative identity. I do not feel that *I* am *doing* this or that or failing to do it, but that there *is* a something in me or about me, or that I lack something and that this, once and for all, *makes* me this or that, fixes my identity.

---

* I cannot discuss here the genetic individual and social causes of self-alienation and of the formation of alienated identity concepts. Regarding the social roots of alienation, compare Erich Fromm, The Sane Society, Rinehart & Company, New York, 1955. Regarding the individual vicissitudes of the development of the sense of identity, compare Erik II. Erikson, Identity and the Life Cycle, International Universities Press, New York, 1959 (Monograph 1, Psychological Issues); Edith Jacobson, The Self and the Object World, The Psychoanalytic Study of the Child, 1954, Vol. IX, 75-127. Compare also the sections on perception and on memory in Ernest Schachtel, op. cit.

† The significance of such fixation has been emphasized by D. J. van Lennep, The Four-Picture Test, in: Harold H. and Gladys L. Anderson, eds., An Introduction to Projective Techniques, Prentice-Hall, Inc., New York, 1951, 153-4.

The person who has this attitude toward himself usually is unaware of its being a particular attitude with concrete and far-reaching implications. He takes his attitude for granted as a natural, inevitable one and is aware only of the painful self-consciousness and self-preoccupation it involves. He cannot imagine how anyone with his "fate" could have any other attitude.

The two most significant implications of this attitude to oneself are 1) the severance from the living I of the reified attribute which is experienced as a fixed, unchangeable quality, and 2) the severance of this reified attribute from its dynamic and structural connection with other qualities, needs, acts, and experiences of the person. In other words, the reified attribute is cut off from the living, developing, fluctuating I in *time*, since it is experienced as immutable. But it is also cut off from being experienced as an *integral* part of the living personality, connected with the totality of the person's strivings, attitudes, perceptions, feelings, with his acting and failing to act.

In reality, of course, we can observe that certain actions, moods, and experiences cause changes in the role of the negative identity in the conscious feelings and thoughts of the person. However, he usually does not experience the reified attribute which forms the core of his negative self-feeling as something connected with, and due to, his own actions and attitudes, but as something fixed on which he has no influence. Furthermore, just as the person's feeling about himself may fluctuate with the ups and downs of his "ego," * so it also varies with the intensity of the negative self-feeling based on some reified attribute which, at times, may disappear altogether from the conscious

---

* See above, page 122.

thoughts of the person. However, when it reappears it is "recognized" as the same unfortunate quality that throughout the past has tainted—and will forever taint—the person's life. Thus, in spite of such fluctuations, the alienated attribute is experienced as a "something" that basically does not and cannot change.

To be saddled with a reified, negative identity seems, on the face of it, nothing but a painful burden. Yet one often can see people cling to such negative self-images with a great deal of stubbornness and in the face of contradictory evidence. In psychoanalytic therapy, it is often seen that the patient who comes for help tries to convince the therapist that nothing can be done for him, since he is born with such and such a handicap or without such and such an advantage. On closer scrutiny, one may find that such insistence by the patient on the hopelessness of the situation has a way of occurring at a point when the patient is afraid to face an issue, or when he wants to be pitied rather than helped. Thus, the reified identity concept often provides a protection against an anxiety-arousing challenge, a way out of a feared situation, and thereby a certain relief.

This relief is dynamically similar to the relief observable in certain hypochondriacal and paranoid patients. It sounds paradoxical to speak of relief in the case of patients who are so obviously beset by worry, suffering, and fear as the hypochondriac and the paranoid. However, as Sullivan has pointed out, the hypochondriacal patient who is preoccupied with imagined, anticipated, or real ailments sees himself as the "customarily handicapped" one and thereby avoids the anxiety-provoking prospect of facing and dealing with his real problems. His hypochondriacal preoccupation gets the patient, in Sullivan's

words, "off the spot with himself"— namely, off the spot where he would have to deal with his realistic personality problems.*

The person living with an alienated and reified, negative identity concept of himself closely resembles the hypochondriacal patient, except that his unhappy preoccupation concerns not a physical ailment but a reified physical or psychic quality that has become the focal point of his self-image. The relief he gains from his burdensome preoccupation is due to the fact that the reified "bad" quality no longer is viewed as part of the on-going process of living and of goal-directed thought and action. It has been severed from the "I" that acts with foresight and responsibility and is looked upon as an inherent, unalterable, unfortunate something, an ossified part of oneself that no longer participates in the flux, growth, and development of life. It is experienced as an unchangeable fate whose bearer is doomed to live and die with it. The relief this brings is that the person no longer feels *responsible* for the supposed consequences of this fixed attribute; he is not *doing* anything for which he can be blamed, even though he may feel ashamed and unacceptable for *being* such and such. The preoccupation with the reified identity directs attention away from what he *does* to what he supposedly *is*. Furthermore, he now no longer has to do anything about it because, obviously, he can't do anything about it. Thus, the anxiety, fear, and effort that would be connected with facing and acting upon the real problem is avoided by putting up with the

---

* For this analysis of the dynamics of hypochondria and for the close relation between hypochondria and paranoia see Harry Stack Sullivan, The Interpersonal Theory of Psychiatry, W. W. Norton, New York, 1953, 355-358, 362-363.

324

negative, fixed identity which, in addition, may be used to indulge self-pity and to enlist the sympathy of others.

The similarity in the dynamics of hypochondria and paranoia, on the one hand, and the alienated, reified self-concept, on the other, lies in this *shift of responsibility and of focus* from my own actions and conduct of life to something else over which I have no control. In the alienated self-concept this something else is a reified quality, or the lack of such a quality; in hypochondria an ailment, real or imagined; in paranoia the delusional persecutors. The difference between paranoia and the alienated self-concept lies in the fact that in paranoia the shift in responsibility is brought about by delusions distorting reality, while in the alienated, negative identity concept it is brought about by an attitude which excludes part of oneself from the process of living and freezes it into a cancer-like, uncontrollable, and unalterable thing. This "thing" very often also becomes the focus, in the paranoid neuroses, of the imagined judgments, observation, and talk of other people about the patient. He believes that, just as his own thoughts tend to revolve around some reified and alienated quality, other people will be similarly preoccupied with this quality in him.

So far I have discussed mainly negative self-images. However, alienated identity concepts may be positive as well as negative. Alienated identity of the positive variety occurs in vanity, conceit and—in its more pathological form—in delusions of grandeur, just as in its negative counterpart the "I" of the vain person is severed from a fixed attribute on which the vanity is based. The person feels that he *possesses* this quality. It becomes the focal point of his identity and serves at its prop. Beauty, masculinity or femininity, being born on the right side of the tracks, success, money, prestige, or "being good" may serve as such a prop. While in the negative identity feeling a reified attribute haunts the person, such an attribute serves the positive self-image as a support. Yet it is equally alienated from the living person. This is expressed nicely in the phrase "a stuffed shirt." It is not the person in the shirt but some dead matter, some stuffing that is used to bolster and aggrandize the self-feeling. It often becomes apparent in the behavior of the person that he *leans* on this real or imagined attribute, just as it often is apparent that a person feels pulled down by the weight of some alienated negative attribute.

The reliance on an identity, on a self-image based on the prop of some reified attribute remains precarious even where it seems to work, after a fashion, as it does in the self-satisfaction of the vain. This precariousness is inevitable, since the positive self-evaluation of such a person does not rest on a feeling of wholeness and meaningfulness in life, in thought, feeling, and deed. He is always threatened with the danger of losing this "thing," this possession, on which his self-esteem is based. This is the theme of Oscar Wilde's novel, *The Picture of Dorian Gray*. Dorian Gray exchanges his identity with the portrait of his youthful charm. He becomes the picture of himself as the beautiful youth, alienated from his actual life, which affects the portrait he has hidden in the attic, marking it over the years with his cruelty, selfishness, and greed, and with his advancing age. The portrait is the skeleton in the closet, the secret threat that hangs over the unchanging mask. Today, especially in this country where youth has become a public fetish, many thousands try to preserve its alienated mask while terrified by the prospect of suddenly growing old, when the mask can no longer be worn or will become grotesque.

I believe that in every case of alienated identity concepts there is a secret counterimage. In Dorian Gray, this is the actual, living person, transplanted to the portrait. Very often such a hidden self announces itself merely in a vague background feeling that the person would be lost, would be nothing if it were not for the alienated, reified quality on which the feeling of being something, somebody, or the feeling of vanity, is based. In this feeling both a truth and an irrational anxiety find expression. The truth is that no man who looks upon himself as a thing and bases his existence on the support of some reified attribute of this thing has found himself and his place in life. The irrational anxiety is the feeling that without the prop of such an attribute he could not live.

Similarly, in the negative alienated identity concepts there usually is a positive counterimage. It may take a generalized, vague form: If it were not for such and such (the reified attribute forming the focus of the negative identity), I would be all right, successful, wonderful, etc. Or it may take the more concrete form of some grandiose, exaggerated fantasy about one's positive qualities. These positive counterimages, too, express both an irrational hope and a truth. The irrational hope is that one may have some magical quality which will transport him into a state of security, or even superiority, because then he will possess that attribute which, instead of haunting him, will save him. But actually it is nothing but the equally reified counterpart of what at present drags him down. The truth is that man has potentialities for overcoming his alienation from himself and for living without the burden and the artificial props of alienated, reified identity concepts.

Goethe, in an interpretation of the Delphic word, "Know thyself," distinguishes between helpful self-awareness and futile and self-tormenting rumination. He opposes the "ascetic" interpretation he finds among "our modern hypochondrists" and those who turn their vengeance against themselves. Instead, he sees the real meaning of self-knowledge in taking notice of oneself and becoming aware of one's relation to other people and to the world.[7] The pseudo-self-knowledge against which he speaks foreshadows the widespread present-day self-preoccupation which is concerned, fruitlessly, with an alienated, negative sense of identity. In contrast to this, Goethe counsels a productive self-knowledge: to pay attention to what one is actually doing in his relation to others, to the world and—we might add —to himself.

REFERENCES

1. Schachtel, E.: Metamorphosis: On the Development of Affect Perception, Attention and Memory, Basic Books, New York, 1959, 287-8.
2. Horney, Karen: Neurosis and Human Growth, W. W. Norton, New York, 1950.
3. Fromm, Erich: Escape from Freedom, Farrar & Rinehart, New York, 1941, 195-206.
4. Fromm, Erich: Psychoanalysis and Zen Buddhism, in: D. T. Suzuki, Erich Fromm and Richard De Martino, Zen Buddhism and Psychoanalysis, Harper, New York, 1960, 106-109.
5. Erikson, Erik H.: Identity and the Life Cycle, International University Press, New York, 1959.
6. Dostoevski, Fyodor: The Brothers Karamazov, Modern Library, New York, 1950, 587.
7. Goethe, J. W.: Maximen und Reflexionen, in Sämmtliche Werke, I. G. Cotta'scher Verlag, Stuttgart and Tübingen, 1853, Vol. 3, 225-6.

DAVID E. SCHECTER, M.D., New York: On the day preceding the symposium on which this volume is based I received a gift of a book called, *Zen Flesh, Zen Bones*.[1] When I opened the book the first story my eyes fell upon, the "Calling Card," seemed to capture exquisitely the spirit of Schachtel's "alienated concept of identity":

> *Keichu, the great Zen teacher of the Meiji era, was the head of Tofuku, a cathedral in Kyoto. One day the governor of Kyoto called upon him for the first time.*
>
> *His attendant presented the card of the governor, which read: Kitagaki, Governor of Kyoto.*
>
> *"I have no business with such a fellow," said Keichu to his attendant. "Tell him to get out of here."*
>
> *The attendant carried the card back with apologies. "That was my error," said the governor, and with a pencil he scratched out the words Governor of Kyoto. "Ask your teacher again."*
>
> *"Oh, is that Kitagaki?" exclaimed the teacher when he saw the card. "I want to see that fellow."*

Schachtel's lucid description of alienated concepts of identity poses a real challenge to the understanding of these phenomena in the light of psychoanalytic theory. We have witnessed in recent years a theoretical expansion of Freud's basic framework in order to account for the very phenomena which Schachtel graphically brings to our attention.

Much of what Schachtel refers to as "the structure of the sense of identity" may be subsumed in the psychoanalytic concepts of "identification" and "ego identity."[2] The ego identity is seen as a structure that has both integrated and transcended earlier childhood identifications. Identification and identity-formation are the conceptual links between the individual and his culture and provide us with keys to understanding how certain aspects of the personality remain alien and unintegrated while others are ex-perienced as belonging to the self. Identification is seen as a process by which the psychic structure of an individual is altered in the direction of similarity to that of a person significant to his existence.[*] Identification is central to the process of separation and individuation from the original symbiotic child-parent unit. The study of the development of such identifications and their integrations would illuminate the structure of the identity including its alienated aspects.

If the identification process arises under conditions of stress, such as fear, or loss of the love object, we note that the ensuing identification with that object is characterized by a defensive, rigid, compelling quality. By means of substitutive internalization the identification serves as a defense against the anxiety of separation or of loss of dependent relationship. We might say the individual tries to build intrapsychic structure where interpersonal structure is breaking down. A somewhat similar process occurs in normal development. However, under conditions of traumatic loss, excessive anxiety, or premature weaning from an appropriately dependent relationship, the defense identification becomes exaggerated, urgent, and stands apart, uninte-grated with the rest of the personality. The self feels driven and whipped by the striv-ings and images associated with these patho-logical identifications. The very meaning of the self, as Schachtel has described, becomes attached to the attainment of these alien-ated images and strivings.

---

[*] By contrast, there is another mode of re-latedness that characterizes interpersonal rela-tions: the mode of object attachment or need-oriented relatedness (the anaclitic mode). The transactional relations between the identifica-tory and anaclitic modes, i.e., between identifi-cation and need-attchament, are considered in a paper delivered before the William Alanson White Psychoanalytic Society, Febru-ary 14, 1961, (Schecter, David): "Psychoanalytic Conceptions of the Identification Process."

AMERICAN JOURNAL OF PSYCHOANALYSIS, 1961, 21, pp. 128-131.

The above description may be especially true for identifications that are part of the ego ideal—that part of the personality that largely defines what we "ought to be." Many of the phenomena Schachtel describes are related to the discrepancy between aspects of the ego ideal ("what I ought to be"), and the self-image ("how I see myself"). The greater this discrepancy the more the ego relies upon fantasies that are not connected with the real capacities of the self. With this alienation of ego ideal from self-image we find an urgent attempt to reunite the two by achieving the aims of the ego ideal at all costs. Schachtel describes how the individual will search for a fixed identity as a "possession," how he will "cling" to it, how he "leans on" the reified attribute of the alienated identity. I believe these expressions I have quoted from Schachtel describe the attempt at union with the alienated ego ideal which is largely, but not simply, representative of his dependent relationships to his idealized parents. The child who does not receive validation and acceptance desperately tries to obtain them by incorporating ersatz symbolic substitutes of status, popularity, power. His life career is then motivated largely by the attempt to approximate these substitutive symbols. We note how frequently, upon the achievement of such alienated goals, there is often severe depression and, in rare cases, suicide. The depression occurs upon the conscious or preconscious insight of the falsely substitutive quality of such symbols. The patient speaks of feeling "cheated" or "deserted" by his hope upon the very achievement of his success. This phenomenon frequently represents, symbolically, a repetition of the original sense of disappointment or disillusion in his parents.

The conditions for healthy identification, by contrast, are characterized by a continuity of trust in the relationship to the object of identification, and an opportunity for a degree of fluidity between the anaclitic and identificatory modes. That is to say, after ventures into more active, individuated roles, representing underlying identifications, the child (and even the adult) may need to feel free and sufficiently unashamed to gratify more dependent needs at an appropriate level of interpersonal mutuality. Trust is the nutriment for healthy identification, and its lack results in a defensive warping or actual breakdown in the identification process. The ultimate of the "alienated identity concept" is seen in the schizophrenic patient and the "as-if" personality described by Helene Deutsch,[3] where a desperate attempt to maintain a dissolving sense of identity is made by the mimicry of gestures, speech, and manners of other persons.

The new focal points of an alienated identity (whether the "good boy," "the powerful one," or "the masculine one") are characterized by their dependency on outside judgment and evaluation, and are lacking in inner conviction that they are related to the subject "I." The individual with such identifications will feel observed and judged, will feel himself as object rather than subject, will feel attached to and dependent on his judge or his admirer. As Fromm[4] points out, for the phenomenon of idolatry the real powers of the self are projected and bestowed upon the alienated image of what we should become. The ego ideal here is experienced as ego-alien, and the ego as passive and submissive to the ideal. The ego often will attempt to assert its autonomy by "passive resistance" and by forms of "sit-down strike" and "guerrilla warfare," as we see in the phenomena of work inhibition, procrastination, and immature rebelliousness.

Schachtel notes the striking clinical fact that people cling to their negative self-attributes and seem to derive the gratification of self-pity and evasion of responsibility in so doing. However, in analyzing the structure of such defenses we often see that the pity the patient seeks is unconsciously related to the burden of his guilt-born identifications. He attempts to convert the necessity of passive guilty suffering into the virtue of "pseudo-active" martyrdom. He tends to convert unconscious self-blame into blame of others. He tries to evade a primitive overweaning conscience by shifting the responsibility to others, to his "failing body," or to a reified self-attribute, as Schachtel points out.

In the notion of the "counterimage" to the alienated identity concept, we see the depth of significance to a defensive structure in which can be found hidden the "longing for a more meaningful life," in Schachtel's words. It is especially for this reason that the defense structure of a patient in psychoanalysis must be treated with utmost respect. A moralistic confrontation of this structure may lead to panic or to a thicker defensive façade, in the forms of compliant submission, self-flagellation, increased helpless dependence on the analyst, as well as to a serious fall in self-esteem. As I see it, one of the ways psychoanalysis pays its respect to the defensive system and hence to the patient is by investigating the conditions of its origins, the crossroads at which defenses were erected and decisions were made, impulsively or compulsively, without a sense of choice. A dynamic approach always implies the genetic dimension. The defense was born out of a conflict of forces and, in a sense, the defense represents these forces, those of "authentic" as well as "alienated" development, as Schachtel demonstrates in his notion of the "counterimage."

Man has to actively overcome his existentially given propensity to alienation which is based on his capacity to experience himself in the dual modes of subject and object. He cannot erase his dualistic nature by denying either mode, as the ultra-scientist or ultra-mystic attempts to do. At best, he can try to achieve a sense of harmony in his split which is engendered by his dual modes of experience and exacerbated by a lingering sense of separateness, his heritage of his early individuation from the symbiotic matrix. Man has also to actively overcome the alienation which is fostered in him by mass culture, where human feelings and aspirations are becoming homogenized into standard expectations and forms. Authentic self-identity is thus rarely, if ever, given by simple privilege or grace. It is achieved rather by the transcendence of alienated experience through a series of developmental crises and tasks.

REFERENCES

1. Reps, P.: Zen Flesh, Zen Bones, Rutland (Vermont), Charles E. Tuttle Company, 1957, 49.
2. Erikson, E. H.: Ego Development and Historical Change, The Psychoanalytic Study of the Child, International University Press, New York, Vol. 2, 1946.
3. Deutsch, H.: Some Forms of Emotional Disturbances and Their Relationship to Schizophrenia, Psychoanalytic Quarterly, Vol. 11, 1942.
4. Fromm, E.: The Sane Society, Rinehart, New York, 1955, 121-124.

BERNARD ZUGER, M.D., New York:* Dr.
Schachtel has shown how prevalent is the search for an alienated identity. It extends from what can be considered normal for our culture to that which is frankly pathological. But what makes it alienated is that it is predetermined, and as such it can be nothing but an illusion. It precludes organic development, and when attained it leaves the individual still a stranger to himself.

For in the search for a personality that already has bounds, the individual has immediately performed a separation between himself and what he seeks. He has jeopardized his development as a whole person. In many areas the individual remains the same, no matter how intricate the structure he builds for himself and no matter how authentic it appears on the surface. And when attained, it becomes a great burden. Thence the cry so often heard from our patients: "If only I weren't so self-conscious . . . if only I could forget myself for a little while. . . ."

All areas of the personality suffer. Work, for instance, is not motivated by immediate satisfaction, as much as that can be attained in our society, but by how it sets up the individual in comparison with others. There are always others to compare oneself with, and there is no rest. The individual cannot entrust himself to the world. Activity, other people are seen only as they allow aggrandizement of a positive image of himself, or bring into awareness a negative image (the "popular ego"). Accomplishment, approbation are not simply the by-products of life lived as an organic whole, but become objectives themselves, with the result that attainment is overvalued and failure becomes catastrophic. Envy and vindictiveness of course rear their heads.

Dr. Schachtel has indicated that apparently simple objectifying on body parts as identities may be counterweighted by opposite feelings about oneself. I think that that should be underscored. The counterbalancing may indeed be a fabulous grandiosity, without there being dissociation or psychosis. As an example, I want only to mention a fifteen-year-old girl who was very sensitive about an intermittent darkening of a small area of her face (melasma or chloasma?), not too noticeable at worst. She had difficulty in going to school, reciting in class, making friends, and so on. But actually she was living a fantastically adventurous and heroic life in the person of a companion she had created. She could not remain in school the full day because she had to attend to the needs and activities of this image of hers, which spanned continents and crumpled time. And it was all on a perfectly conscious level.

Dr. Schachtel has mentioned some of the clinical forms these alienated—and alienating—identities may take. I know that later papers will describe others and in great detail. I should like to mention one form of an implicit alien identity, which is less well structured, and perhaps for that reason more difficult to recognize as such. This is the assumption that an individual as he was at any one point in the past could have behaved differently from the way he did behave. This sort of thinking is, of course, very prevalent in depressions, but is a part of every neurosis. It is the "grand delusion" of the neurotic.

The individual will blame others, circumstances, and especially himself, but not accept that whatever may have been the influences operating on him, what he did was the result of what he was at that time. A later insight, resulting from knowledge after-the-fact, or from therapy, will result in severe recrimination at oneself or others. Instead of feeling freed and released by insights, the patient will take them as further indications of how worthless he is.

What is really behind this assumption? It presupposes that the individual was full-grown from the very beginning, was completed and able to deal wisely with all experience. Here again the goal for the individual is not growth through living and experiencing, but something that comes prefabricated and automatic and should have been there all the time.

It becomes, therefore, the task of therapy for the individual to see that only as he genuinely accepts the inevitability of the past—". . . that's who I was and that's what made it possible . . ."—can he free himself from the past, can growth begin, and can real change take place. There is then a shift into the present, the unpredictable, and the living and developing.[1]

REFERENCE

1. Zuger B.: The States of Being and Awareness in Neurosis and Their Redirection in Therapy, Jour. of Nerv. and Ment. Dis., 121, 573, 1955.

PSYCHOLOGY, METAPSYCHOLOGY, AND PSYCHOANALYSIS

PAUL L. WACHTEL [1]

Perhaps the most encouraging trend in psychoanalytic theory since the death of Freud has been the tendency to dismantle the iron curtain surrounding its brilliant insights and enabling fruitful intercourse and integrative merger between the observations and viewpoints of psychoanalysts and those of academic psychologists. Such integrative efforts are essential to counter the narrowed perspective and narrowed definition of problems that result from the limited sources of data upon which theories in psychology are generally built. Thus, the structure of psychoanalytic theory, the nature of its assumptions and emphases, derives not only from the nature of Freud's personality and training (Amacher, 1965; Holt, 1965), but also from the fact that its primary data source is the free associations of neurotic patients. Other theories in psychology place similarly heavy emphasis on the bar pressing of rats, the problem solving of college students, etc., and

such emphasis cannot help but constrict the range of questions asked and models proposed.

In the course of the development of psychoanalytic theory, it became the hope of Freud and his followers that psychoanalytic theory would became a general psychology, that it would account not only for neurotic phenomena but for all phenomena in the realm of psychological science. An almost inevitable result of such efforts will be a change in the structure of psychoanalytic theory. As the data base of the theory expands, as it attempts to encompass new observations, to include, for example, the data of laboratory experiments, the theoretical concepts that tie together the observations will require revision. This has been the case generally in the history of science, and even in the history of psychoanalytic theory itself. Thus, as psychoanalytic observation began to focus upon the mechanisms of defense, the topographic model of the conscious, preconscious, and unconscious systems (Freud, 1959) had to be replaced by the structural model of ego, id, and superego; the former model was adequate to account for the early observations but could not survive new data. One can imagine that efforts to expand the explanatory realm of psychoanalytic theory may one day become so successful that the original theory will disappear of its own success. To the extent that the theory

[1] This article was written while the author was a Fellow in the Program for Postdoctoral Study and Research in Psychology and on the staff of the Research Center for Mental Health. The author wishes to express his gratitude to George S. Klein, J. G. Schimek, Linda H. Schoeman, and Philip Bromberg for their valuable comments on earlier drafts of this paper.

JOURNAL OF ABNORMAL PSYCHOLOGY, 1969, 74, pp. 651-660.

truly becomes a general psychology it will cease to be *psychoanalytic* theory, and will tend to be simply psychological theory. The total disappearance of separate theories in psychology and the emergence of a single psychological theory free of the parochial origins of its parts is of course an asymptote from which we are still quite distant, but it is important to keep the emerging goal in mind, for the goal determines what is the essential product of psychoanalytic research.

Freud was far less reverent toward his theoretical constructions than are many of his followers. He recognized (Freud, 1949) quite clearly that it is the *facts* discovered by psychoanalytic work that will stand as his major achievement, rather than the theories. The latter were merely ingenious working principles to tie together the data that had emerged up until then and to point toward new observations. Freud's discoveries regarding unconscious motivation, the expressive meaning of dreams, and the organization of primitive thought will remain valuable long after the words ego, id, or libido have become obsolete. Concern with the distinction between psychoanalytic data and the theory used to account for it has led to increasing critical discussion of the basic theoretical assumptions of psychoanalytic theory in recent years. That aspect of the theory that Freud called his metapsychology has come under the most critical scrutiny. Some of this criticism has been helpful in clarifying assumptions and opening the way for theoretical formulation more suited to our present level of knowledge, but blanket dismissal of all metapsychological perspectives as "reductionistic" (Loevinger, 1966) may obscure some important issues. In particular, it will be suggested below that the energy constructs of Freudian metapsychology, while clearly in need of drastic revision and perhaps even amputation, have served to direct researchers to an important realm of questions. Without careful consideration of the role of energy constructs and other impersonal process descriptions in the theory, there is a danger that a poor formulation may be replaced not by a more adequate one, but by a reluctance to encompass the observations that led to the formulation in the first place.

MEANING AND METAPSYCHOLOGY

Psychoanalytic theory is characterized by two rather separate theoretical approaches. The clinical theory consists of "inferences of *directional* gradients in behavior, and of the *object-relations* involved in these directions [Klein, 1966, p. 10]"; it represents a search for meaning and purpose in behavior. Psychoanalytic metapsychology, on the other hand, reflects Freud's view that purposive concepts are scientifically unacceptable. It is a mechanical quasi-thermodynamic model in the language of forces and energies. Klein (1966) has called it a theory to explain a theory, and has argued that, unlike the clinical propositions, metapsychological concepts are "impervious to the type of data obtainable from the psychoanalyst's hour [p. 15]."

Tension between a humanistic and a mechanistic view of man, between the sense that man is a choosing responsible moral agent and the idea that human actions are as impersonally determined as the motion of the planets, is woven tightly into the fabric of psychoanalysis. One could not expect such tension to be absent from any meaningful psychology, for the paradox of human choice has been a central problem in the study of man for many centuries. Klein (1966) has noted that the impersonal, metapsychological perspective on human behavior has been fallaciously put forth as more *basic* than the purposive explanations of the clinical theory. To understand a man's strivings and feelings, to know him from the inside, is somehow regarded as inferior to observing him as an object in the most literal sense.

Questions of freedom and determinism in psychoanalysis do not directly parallel the conflict between the clinical and metapsychological perspectives. Much of Freud's argument for a determinist position was in the service of building the *clinical* theory, of demonstrating that seemingly meaningless events such as dreams and slips of the tongue could be given meaning if the determining chain of associations were followed back to its source. Nonetheless, the role of metapsychological theorizing is related to the view of human behavior as ultimately determined by an impersonal "natural" process, even if "meanings" are a convenient description of the intervening events that occur. A brief examination of the psychoanalytic view of determinism and freedom is therefore in order.

FREEDOM AND DETERMINISM

Knight's (1946) discussion of the freedom–determinism issue is probably as close to a standard psychoanalytic position on this issue as one can find. Knight believed that determinism was an essential assumption for a scientific psychology. Yet like many other analysts and therapists (e.g., Mazer, 1960; Wheelis, 1956), Knight recognized that a deterministic viewpoint may be used by patients as resistance to effort at therapeutic change. Many patients claim that they simply cannot help what they are doing, that their behavior is determined and they have no choice or responsibility. Such an attitude may effectively inhibit necessary effort on the part of the patient and may function as a self-fulfilling prophecy that indeed results in the patient remaining the same.

In dealing with this dilemma, Knight emphasized the distinction between determinism as a construct and freedom as a subjective experience. For Knight, freedom is an experience of harmony between one's behavior and one's character, a sense that one is behaving in one's own best interests and is free from compulsion, anxiety, and irrational doubts;

this kind of "freedom" is experienced only by emotionally mature, well-integrated persons, it is the goal sought for one's patients in psychotherapy; and this freedom has nothing whatever to do with free will as a principle governing human behavior, but is a subjective experience *which is itself determined* [italics added, Knight, 1946, p. 372].

Knight claims that such freedom, while subjective, need not be spurious.

The behavior of a well-integrated civilized person can be objectively assessed as "free." Observers see that such a person makes ego-syntonic choices, that his motives are "good," and that he is able to carry out what he wills to do [p. 372].

Nonetheless one is left with the impression from Knight's paper that man's every act and thought is *really* determined, and that freedom, however precious, is finally just an epiphenomenon.

Knight is certainly correct that the term "free will" confuses the issue. One can hardly use the term without calling up visions of medieval theological debate. But simply to define free will as a subjective experience, causally determined in the same way as the experience of pain upon being burned is determined, seems to be begging the question. Such an approach *assumes* determinism without ever questioning it, and deals with the perplexing issue of freedom by redefining it, and thereby essentially dismissing it.

Free will is a frustrating conception because no one is clear what is meant by "free." It is easy to topple the straw man who speaks of freedom as if it were caprice, of freely willed acts as those that are unrelated to a person's history, character, or environment. But the great hold that the concept of freedom has had on men does not stem from the belief that man's actions are random. It stems from the belief that men's choices are meaningful and that the agony of decision is not simply an interesting phenomenon, to be explained by causal laws external to it, but rather the central fact from which to launch an investigation of man.

In this light, it may be seen that the determinism subscribed to by Knight and other analysts and the freedom proclaimed, for example, by the existentialists are two different perspectives on the same set of observations. Both groups of theorists see men walk and talk and make love and war. In order to organize and make sense of these observations, the determinist views the men he observes as he views all other objects in the universe. They are to him (while he is wearing the cap of the determinist) ultimately understood as bits of moving matter whose motions are described in terms similar in principle (though far more complex and perhaps at a different "level") to those describing the motion of any other particles. From this perspective, free will is indeed simply a "subjective experience," to be explained causally like any other phenomenon.

But there is another perspective on human behavior, another way of organizing the data, which all (healthy?) determinists use in much of their personal lives, and which some psychologists (e.g., the phenomenologists) use in their professional lives as well. Starting not with what is similar between man and the rest of the universe, but rather with what seems unique to man, one may view men's actions as through their own eyes, one may attempt to construct their phenomenal world, to understand them as men who act and decide on the basis of what they see and feel. From this second perspective (one may call it a "common sense" perspective, though modern psychoanalytic and phenomenological research have carried it far beyond common sense) determinism is neither right nor wrong—it is simply irrelevant, a different way of looking at things. The terms of discourse for such a perspective are feeling and decision rather than cause and effect.

Both perspectives on the facts of human behavior have their utility. As Klein (1966) seems to suggest in a different context, they are mutually incompatible ways of organizing and comprehending observations of human beings (including oneself). Perhaps (though it is doubtful) some day a synthesizing formulation will be created that resolves the contradiction and shows each perspective to be a special case of some general and consistent view. For the present, however, it seems necessary to recognize the need for both perspectives. No man can get along well with just one, and to reduce "psychological science" to those organizations of observations that employ the determinist perspective is simply to impoverish the realm of psychological inquiry. To completely exclude a determinist viewpoint is of course equally productive of sterility.

CAUSAL AND PURPOSIVE PERSPECTIVES

To the extent that metapsychology is, as Klein (1966) suggests, a theory to explain a theory, it reflects a nonrational, quasi-religious commitment to a determinist position. There is false hope (or fear) in the view that we have not *yet* explained all the nuances of human thought, feeling, and behavior in terms of energies and forces. The present author is in agreement with Klein that there are difficulties *in principle* with automatically "converting the terms of clinical observation to impersonal process terms." Neurophysiological or information-processing models, no less than energy models, represent only one perspective on human affairs, and have no

greater claim to describing an *ultimate* truth than do descriptions of striving and meaning. Both perspectives, if used wisely, can provide useful insights.

Psychoanalytic observation is tuned in on a unique level of coherence (Klein, 1966). The structure of the analytic situation facilitates perception by the analyst of patterns of thought organization in the patient, and enables the analyst to notice characteristics of the patient's thinking and behavior that might otherwise go undetected. Certain seemingly unrelated ideas may be expressed in close contiguity with remarkable frequency. Or free association may lead to the expression of ideas and thoughts that are rarely directly expressed at all in any other context. Who would have expected, on the basis of other models of observation, that free-associating patients would so often express incestuous fantasies? On the other hand, psychoanalytic observations also highlights *gaps* in expression not generally as visible elsewhere. The analyst may notice that every time his patient's thoughts seem to be leading toward criticism of an authority, something happens to halt or deflect the progress of his associations. Or he may notice that certain topics, or certain expected reactions, simply never come up as the patient talks about himself and his life day after day.

Such observations, and the generalizations derived from them, are what give psychoanalytic thinking its special cast. Psychoanalysts are trained to notice when a person says he is trying to do one thing and consistently acts as if he were trying to do quite another (or more frequently some odd combination of both). Greater knowledge of the full range of human strivings and of the manifold fears and compromises that bend, disguise, and complicate those strivings is the special fruit of psychoanalytic research. For knowledge of mechanism, on the other hand, and for the building of models based on physical and biological analogies, the data of psychoanalytic sessions are largely irrelevant.

Klein (1966) is careful to point out that impersonal causal models of behavior are not without a place in psychology; they simply are a poor strategy for dealing with the particular opportunities for observation provided

334

by the psychoanalytic session. Loevinger (1966), however, seems to dismiss metapsychological perspectives more categorically. She is concerned with finding a set of principles that is distinctively psychoanalytic. But what does it mean for a principle to be psychoanalytic? Does it mean that the data upon which it is based came originally from psychoanalytc sessions? Are other sources of data to be dismissed, with psychoanalytic principles remaining "pure" but of little value for answering the more sophisticated questions called for by new observations? Or is a principle psychoanalytic if it is in essence a theoretical statement formulated by Freud or at least an elaboration of such? Then psychoanalytic theory is destined to becoming an interesting historical curio, to be respected for its eminence among early twentieth-century efforts, but of little interest to those concerned with understanding the latest observations of human behavior.

Psychoanalytic insights are far too important to be so embalmed and preserved. The psychoanalytic tradition in psychological thought has been one of the most vital and original. Perhaps the historical accident of its isolation from the academic world and its development into a "movement" contributed to that vitality. But there is now danger that what was once a revolutionary way of thinking is becoming a conservative, consolidated "system," an outcome that is fostered by that same isolation. A psychoanalytic perspective, that is, a view of human behavior based largely on psychoanalytic observations, and emphasizing the role of unconscious motivations, defenses, compromise formations, etc., is still vitally relevant to psychological inquiry. A separate psychoanalytic *theory*, however, at least to the extent that such a theory is not receptive to data from non-psychoanalytic sources, seems increasingly a poor enterprise in which to invest effort. That some metapsychological propositions are "as congenial to many antianalytic psychologies as to psychoanalysis [Loevinger, 1966, p. 433]" is irrelevant. What matters is how congenial they are to the latest data.

Let us consider Loevinger's solution to "one of the most baffling theoretical problems of psychoanalysis [p. 437]," how an impulse contributes to its own control. She claims that notions such as bound cathexis and countercathexis add little to the explanation, and suggests instead that "one is controlled, simultaneously or in turn, by one's impulses and one's parents, and one therefore needs to control something in return, if not one's parents, then one's impulses [Loevinger, 1966, p. 437]." This may perhaps be an adequate account of why the developing personality *wants* to control the impulse, but it says nothing about why he *succeeds*. What is lacking in a psychology solely of meanings, as Loevinger calls for, is adequate consideration of *capacities*. As did early psychoanalytic writings, Loevinger's suggested system implies a kind of motivational omnipotence, whereby it is sufficient to explore the *motives* for behavior without considering the *ability* of the individual to efficiently order and execute all the wishes pressing for fulfillment at a given moment. As an example, if a person gets into an accident, it is certainly not always correct to say that he is expressing a wish to hurt himself. A self-destructive wish would no doubt lower the threshold for such events, but it is clear that such wishes are often kept from direct expression by a strong ego, and phenomena such as "distraction" may often play a more important role in accounting for accidents.

Phenomena such as distraction are at the heart of what is missing in Loevinger's scheme. Korchin (1964), for example, has summarized a great deal of evidence suggesting that anxiety may reduce the capacity to "do two things at once." The perceptual-cognitive effects he describes seem vitally relevant in understanding the kinds of behavior that psychoanalysts observe. Certainly, the exact form that behavior in an anxious state takes, as well as the origin of the anxiety itself, is largely a matter of meanings; but without consideration of the constriction of perspective and general narrowing of cognitive organization characteristic of the anxious individual, our understanding of his experience and behavior is incomplete. Similarly, the accounts of individual differences in the organization of attention attempted by Gardner, Klein, and their colleagues (e.g., Gardner, Holzman, Klein, Linton, & Spence,

1959) represent a psychoanalytically oriented approach to character style complementary to and consistent with Freud's discussions of character in terms of libidinal organization. It is a strength rather than a weakness of such work that it is almost impossible to distinguish that part of the conceptual underpinning that comes from psychoanalytic theory and that which comes from other psychological approaches.

COGNITIVE STYLE AND MEANING

The need-in-perception studies were an effort to counter the overly impersonal view of perception prevalent at the time and to highlight the personal meaning of the stimulus for the perceiver. Many of these studies both explicitly and implicitly borrowed from psychoanalytic discoveries of the role of drive and wish in shaping perceptual and cognitive events. As Klein (1958) has pointed out, however, these corrective efforts themselves tended to be one-sided, erring in the direction of overemphasizing the role of drive and disregarding the structural constraints upon drive influence. More precisely, it was the recruiting or meaning-inducing activity of drives that was overemphasized, to the exclusion of the accommodative structures, for Klein's (1958) conception of drive is a unitary one, which emphasizes the coordination of intentions and the means of carrying them out.

One does not understand an individual very well if one knows only the wishes that dominate the recruitment aspects of his personality structure. One must also understand his modes of accommodation and the hierarchic ordering of his wishes and cognitions. Human perception is only sometimes distorted, but it is always selective, and such selection is always limited even if accurate. Regardless of what wishes are currently active, the field-independent individual (Witkin, Dyk, Faterson, Goodenough, & Karp, 1962) will perceive and experience a different world than the field-dependent, the world of the sharpener will differ from that of the leveler (Gardner et al., 1959), etc. The origin of such differing modes of accommodation may well be largely a matter of the meaning to an individual of certain ways of experiencing the world.[2] Such characteristics of the individual's accommodative efforts, however, also enter into his encounters with the world as a kind of automatic filter that he can no longer readily change. Some aspects of personality often designated as styles may better be thought of as capacities than as stylistic preferences (Wachtel, 1968b).

The need for some impersonal process descriptions in personality theory (even for understanding the events of the psychoanalytic hour) is clearer, however, when one considers the somewhat automatic effects of such variables as anxiety upon cognitive functioning. To be sure, the effects of anxiety also are probably subject to individual differences related to the meaning of the anxiety-provoking stimulus. There are indications, for example, that anxiety due to a threat perceived as possible to avert seems to have different consequences than anxiety due to an inevitable harm (Wachtel, 1968a). Nonetheless, the breadth of the individual's cognitive and attentive field does seem to be usefully regarded as a dependent variable in a functional relationship between anxiety and attention (Easterbrook, 1959; Korchin, 1964; Wachtel, 1968a), and breadth of attention is important to consider in understanding phenomena of the therapy hour.

Consider the following clinical example: A female patient, in her early twenties, has a great stake in perceiving herself as a young child, though such an image is, of course, not experienced without considerable conflict. This image of herself helps to reassure her that she is not like her mother, who she perceives as selfish, nasty, and controlling. She lives in a black and white world, where to be a child is to be innocent, pretty, and acceptable, and to be an adult is to be dirty, voracious, and despised.[3] Without full awareness, she often behaves in childish ways that call forth responses from others appropriate to

[2] Shapiro (1965), for example, has vividly illustrated the personal meaning of individual differences in cognitive style.

[3] For purposes of exposition, the dynamics of the case must here be greatly simplified. There are, for example, many indications that her identification with her mother is also a cherished key to power, and further that her mother in many respects is also viewed as a kind of ideal.

dealing with someone much younger. Though she complains at times about such treatment, it seems to be quite comfortable for her. On several occasions, she has reported situations in which she was treated with greater respect than usual, and compliments, which she found gratifying, were combined with requests for her to assume responsibilities commensurate with her considerable talents. She found her distress on these occasions puzzling, and it was suggested to her that she would have preferred to receive a simple pat on the head that did not imply that she was an adult capable of making an adult's contribution. On each of these occasions, she became quite agitated and complained that her therapist was talking to her as if she were a child. Similar complaints were made at times about her husband, always at times when he asked her to behave like an adult, for example, by keeping track of her checkbook balance.

Her response to her therapist, as to her husband, obviously had great personal meaning. Threatened with the exposure of and threat to her wish to be a child, she shifted her attention from the content of the therapist's comments to their tone; she further gratified her wish right in the hour by experiencing him as talking to her as if she were a child. But how did she manage to see her therapist in such a fashion? It is not sufficient merely to note that her perception was influenced by the pressure of strong wishes, for as we noted earlier there are considerable constraints upon the distorting effect of wishes. We must assume, I believe, that this patient focused upon some actual features of her therapist's behavior. No doubt her generally childlike manner called forth in her therapist some responses that were more appropriate to addressing a child. The rhythm, tone of voice, or style of phrasing must have provided the cues that led to her perception. That these aspects of the interaction, which meshed so well with her needs, should have become the focus of her attention is not surprising. What is worth noting, however, is the degree to which they remained unmodified by other aspects of the situation. Her field of attention was largely limited to these isolated cues. The larger context in which they occurred, including an explicit message directly opposite to her perceived meaning (i.e., you were being treated as an adult—people perceive you as an adult), was hardly noticed. In her state of arousal and anxiety, she experienced a narrower range of her therapist's behavior than she normally does, and this narrowing of her field of attention enabled her to focus exclusively on the infantalizing aspect of his remarks. Clearer understanding of the exact nature of the narrowing of attention occurring in anxious states (Wachtel, 1967) would clarify the structural limits within which her motivational and perceptual efforts were expressed, and would suggest what efforts would be needed to correct and amplify her perception of the interpersonal situation. Understanding of the "meaning" of infantilization to her is necessary but not sufficient to guide the therapist's approach to such behavior.

ROLE OF ENERGY CONSTRUCTS

The aspect of psychoanalytic metapsychology that has come under the most intense and persistent criticism has been the economic viewpoint (Rapaport & Gill, 1959), or energy theory. Holt (1967) has pointed out that despite Freud's explicit commitment to physicalistic mechanistic explanation, his concept of psychic energy "is a vitalistic concept in the sense of being similar to and influenced by vital force, and being to a large extent functionally equivalent to it. They are at the least historically and methodologically homologus—buds from the same branch [pp. 24–25]." Holt has discussed in detail the limitations that are thereby inherent in the traditional psychoanalytic energy concept.

It should be noted, however, that the energy concepts of psychoanalysis have had several different functions in the theory. One main function of the energy concept was to deal with the mind–body problem. Freud referred to instincts as a borderland concept between mind and body; and as Holt (1967) points out, Freud often discussed libidinal energy as if it were not simply an abstract psychological concept but rather a form of physical-neural energy, transformed much as heat may be converted to kinetic energy. It is within this framework that loose metaphorical thinking and anthropomorphism have characterized discussion of psychic energy (libido seen as pushing, pressing for discharge, etc.).

There has been, however, another use of energy concepts by psychoanalytic thinkers that is less subject to the difficulties noted above. The concept of ego energies has been more consistently employed as an abstract nonexistential construct representing the capacity to do (psychological) work, and has thus played a role in theory construction somewhat more akin to the role of energy in physics. As we shall note, this use of an energy concept has its drawbacks too, but examination of the utility of the concept thus far and of the nature of its limitations can pave the way for a better replacement.

Consider the concept of attention cathexis, an aspect of ego energy emphasized by Rapaport (1967). It is based in a general way upon the obvious observation that at any given moment attention to certain aspects of the inner or outer world makes awareness of other aspects less likely. The energy construct is used to coordinate reciprocities among psychological phenomena, relating changes in different parts of the system to each other, much as physical energy is a hypothetical construct simplifying the coordination of reciprocities among physical phenomena. If we divest the concept of the controversial theories of the origins of such energies (cf. Hartmann, Kris, & Loewenstein, 1949; White, 1963), we seem to be left with a useful scheme for relating psychological phenomena, one that may lead to testable hypotheses.

For example, central to the psychoanalytic conception of defense and to the theory of neurosis is the idea that defenses use energy and require a constant effort to prevent the defended-against material from reaching awareness. Rapaport (1951) has described the psychoanalytic conception of consciousness as

a matter of the distribution of attention cathexes, which are available only in a certain quantity. Evidence seems to suggest that these attention-cathexes are identical with those used in countercathecting and where excessive energies are required for the latter it limits those available for the former [p. 699].

Gardner et al. (1959) have used this conception in accounting for the empirical relation between the cognitive style of leveling and repressive defenses, and many neurotic phenomena are also explained psychoanalytically by the impoverishment of the ego, which such diversion of energies implies (Fenichel, 1945). One might expect from this view that if an individual were defending against perceiving an aspect of the stimulus field, his responsiveness to the rest of the field would also be reduced, for part of his capacity to attend is engaged in preventing perception of the offending stimulus.[4]

Some authors, on the other hand (e.g., Kellner, Butters, & Wiener, 1964), have maintained that defenses do not involve a continuing struggle of the sort implied above but rather are a matter merely of the individual's reinforcement history making some responses more likely and others less likely. If this is so, then defending would not consume any of the individual's capacity to attend, and no reduction in overall responsiveness to the field should be evident in those instances of conspicuous inattention to particular features from which defense is inferred. In fact, since some features are avoided, the rest of the field would have less competition for the individual's attention and should be *more* completely perceived. Defense studies that focus not on whether or not a particular brief stimulus is perceived, but rather on the individual's selective attention to a complex field through time, should be able to shed light on the merits of these two competing conceptions, and thereby on the important relation between defense on the one hand and character and neurosis on the other.

It is possible, then, to use energy concepts to guide empirical inquiry. A fair number of studies have originated at least in part from economic concepts (e.g., Lustman, 1957; Schimek & Wachtel, 1968; Schwartz & Schiller, in press; Spence & Greif, 1968; Toman, 1954; Wachtel & Blatt, 1965). The utility of such concepts is considerably limited, however, by the difference in the kinds of quanti-

4 The issue is of course far more complicated than can be described in this brief presentation. To maintain and reinforce the defense, for example, some *particular* aspect of the field might be *more* likely noticed when defending (e.g., loving implications when defending against hostility), but overall awareness of nuances in all aspects of the field might still be reduced.

338

tative statements made by physicists and psychologists. Energy in physics is measured (indirectly, of course, as in psychology) on an interval scale. There are a precisely specifiable number of footpounds of potential energy embodied in an object suspended above the earth. If that body falls, its velocity upon hitting the ground can be exactly predicted by the formula $1/2\ mv^2$ (kinetic energy) $= ghM$ (Potential energy). If these two numbers are not exactly equal, then one knows precisely what portion of the potential energy has been used in moving the resisting air particles, heating the falling object, etc. Since the same "quantity" is presumed to be involved in, for example, mechanical, electrical, and thermal phenomena, a powerful set of equations can be devised to precisely predict changes in seemingly diverse phenomenal realms. There are even "economic" consequences in the more common meaning of the term, for the electric company can bill people for a specific number of kilowatt hours of energy, regardless of whether they heated their house, lit their lamps, cooked a meal, ran electric trains, or brushed their teeth.

The case is quite different in psychology. Here energy is measured on an ordinal scale. One can say only that there is more or less energy used in a given process. To state, for example, the simple functional relationship that the more one exhibits signs of defending against forbidden wishes or ideas, the less one will be attentive to his (internal and external) environment, seems to be exactly equivalent to the proposition that defenses use attentional energy. The formulation in energic terms adds nothing. This is quite different from the situation in physics, where numerical specification of the quantity of energy involved leads to specific determination of other measures and to the possibility of checking whether all the energy in the system is accounted for. Physicists and engineers would not need an energy concept if the most that could be said was: The more water that falls on the generator, the more houses we can light. It is the possibility of measuring the energy on an interval scale that makes the postulation of such a quantity superior to simple functional description of the relationship between two observable variables. If one could actually quantify on an interval scale the amount of defensive activity, the amount of perceptual activity, the amount of organizing and structure formation, etc., and show their sum to be a constant, then psychological energy would be an invaluable construct. The day when such measurement is possible, however, seems at this point a matter for psychological science fiction.

At our present level of knowledge, the use of energy constructs may do more harm than good. That the term is used superfluously does not in itself seem a serious matter; it can still be consistently related to observations, and the imagery evoked by the particular metaphor may inspire original hypotheses in some investigators. (Rapaport, 1967, for example, created a complex set of hypotheses that might not have occurred without an energy notion.) It *is* a serious matter, however, if the illusion of an adequate explanation blinds investigators to the many unanswered questions that remain and delays seeking more precise descriptions of the state of affairs. It is not being unfaithful to an old friend to ask of a theoretical conception: What have you done for me lately? On the contrary, such irreverence is essential for scientific advance. Many concepts are perfectly adequate at an early stage of scientific investigation but may freeze progress if held on to too long. Energy statements have the ring of a finished system, and may perhaps best be held in abeyance until such a system is a more imminent possibility.

If the energy construct is discarded, however, it will be important to bear in mind the reasons for discarding it. In scientific endeavor it is often as important *why* a concept is abandoned as *whether* it is. The difficulties inherent in the use of an energy construct at this stage of theoretical development should not obscure the need for *some* kind of process description and causal analysis in psychological investigation.

The metaphor of a limited quantity of energy that may be deployed in various ways has its problems and limitations, but it does highlight some important issues that it is well to keep in mind. In particular, it is essential to explore the nature of the limits and consequences of human choices, to understand the

339

price that one pays for committing oneself to a course of action, a style of life, or a mode of perception. The economic point of view emphasizes the limits or boundary conditions of human existence, and the importance of its message should not be dismissed because of the crudity of its formulation. Loevinger (1966) is correct that understanding the *meaning* of psychological events is an essential aspect of psychoanalytic research, perhaps the most important contribution that such research can make. But unless such understanding is integrated with a firm knowledge of the fabric of constraints within which meaning is given, the psychoanalytic endeavor is not likely to have much meaning at all.

REFERENCES

AMACHER, M. P. Freud's neurological education and its influence on psychoanalytic theory. *Psychological Issues*, 1964, 4(4), 5–93.

EASTERBROOK, J. A. The effect of emotion on cue utilization and the organization of behavior. *Psychological Review*, 1959, 66, 183–201.

FENICHEL, O. *The psychoanalytic theory of neurosis.* New York: Norton, 1945.

FREUD, S. An outline of psycho-analysis. (Trans. by J. Strachey) New York: Norton, 1949.

FREUD, S. The unconscious. In, *Collected Papers of Sigmund Freud.* (Trans. by J. Riviere) Vol. 4. New York: Basic Books, 1959.

GARDNER, R. W., HOLZMAN, P. S., KLEIN, G. S., LINTON, H. P., & SPENCE, D. P. Cognitive control: A study of individual consistencies in cognitive behavior. *Psychological Issues*, 1959, 1(4), 1–186.

HARTMANN, H., KRIS, E., & LOEWENSTEIN, R. M. Notes on the theory of aggression. *Psychoanalytic Study of the Child*, 1949, 3/4, 9–36.

HOLT, R. R. A review of some of Freud's biological assumptions and their influence on his theories. In N. S. Greenfield & W. C. Lewis (Eds.), *Psychoanalysis & current biological thought.* Madison: University of Wisconsin Press, 1965.

HOLT, R. R. Beyond vitalism and mechanism: Freud's concept of psychic energy. In J. Masserman (Ed.), *Science and psychoanalysis.* Vol. 11. New York: Grune & Stratton, 1967.

KELLNER, H., BUTTERS, N., & WIENER, M. Mechanisms of defense: An alternative response. *Journal of Personality*, 1964, 32, 601–621.

KLEIN, G. S. Cognitive control and motivation. In G. Lindzey (Ed.), *Assessment of human motives.* New York: Rinehart, 1958.

KLEIN, G. S. Two theories or one? Perspectives to change in psychoanalytic theory. Paper presented at conference of Psychoanalysts of the Southwest, Galveston, Texas, March 1966.

KNIGHT, R. Determinism, "freedom," and psychotherapy. *Psychiatry*, 1946, 9, 251–262.

KORCHIN, S. J. Anxiety and cognition. In C. Scheerer (Ed.), *Cognition: Theory, research, promise.* New York: Harper & Row, 1964.

LOEVINGER, J. Three principles for a psychoanalytic psychology. *Journal of Abnormal Psychology*, 1966, 71, 432–443.

LUSTMAN, S. Psychic energy and mechanisms of defense. *Psychoanalytic Study of the Child*, 1957, 12, 151–165.

MAZER, M. The therapeutic function of the belief in will. *Psychiatry*, 1960, 23, 45–52.

RAPAPORT, D. *The organization and pathology of thought.* New York: Columbia University Press, 1951.

RAPAPORT, D. The theory of attention cathexis. In M. M. Gill (Ed.), *The collected papers of David Rapaport.* New York: Basic Books, 1967.

RAPAPORT, D., & GILL, M. M. The points of view and assumptions of metapsychology. *International Journal of Psycho-Analysis*, 1959, 40, 153–162.

SCHIMEK, J. G., & WACHTEL, P. L. Exploration of effects of distraction, competing tasks and cognitive style on attention deployment. *Perceptual and Motor Skills*, 1969, 28, 567–574.

SCHWARTZ, F., & SCHILLER, P. A psychoanalytic model of attention and learning. *Psychological Issues*, in press.

SHAPIRO, D. *Neurotic styles.* New York: Basic Books, 1965.

SPENCE, D. P., & GREIF, B. Randomness of serial letters as a monitor of attention to distracting prose. Unpublished manuscript, Research Center for Mental Health, New York University, 1968.

TOMAN, W. Mental or psychic energy and its relation to learning and retention: An experimental contribution. *Acta Psychologica*, 1954, 10, 317–350.

WACHTEL, P. L. Conceptions of broad and narrow attention. *Psychological Bulletin*, 1967, 68, 417–429.

WACHTEL, P. L. Anxiety, attention, and coping with threat. *Journal of Abnormal Psychology*, 1968, 73, 137–143. (a)

WACHTEL, P. L. Style and capacity in analytic functioning. *Journal of Personality*, 1968, 36, 202–212. (b)

WACHTEL, P. L., & BLATT, S. J. Energy deployment and achievement. *Journal of Consulting Psychology*, 1965, 29, 302–308.

WHEELIS, A. Will and psychoanalysis. *Journal of the American Psychoanalytic Association*, 1956, 4, 285–303.

WHITE, R. W. Ego and reality in psychoanalytic theory. *Psychological Issues*, 1963, 3(11).

WITKIN, H. A., DYK, R., FATERSON, H., GOODENOUGH, D., & KARP, S. *Psychological differentiation.* New York: Wiley, 1962.

DATE DUE

JA 7'91		
OC 30'92		
FE 7'93		
JA 29 '03		